THE
LIVING
ART An Introduction to Theatre and Drama

RINEHART PRESS • San Francisco

THE
LIVING
ART An Introduction to Theatre

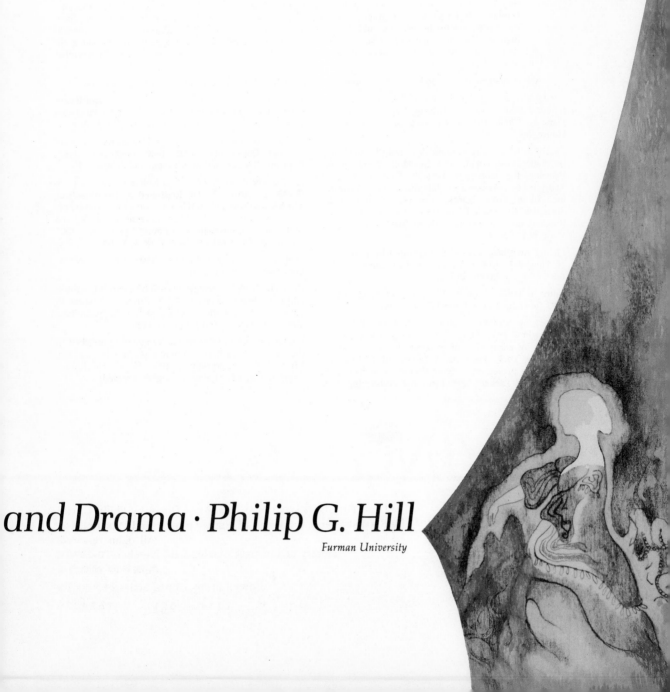

and Drama · *Philip G. Hill*

Furman University

Acknowledgment is made to copyright holders and publishers for permission to reprint the following:

The Little Foxes by Lillian Hellman. Copyright 1939 and renewed 1967 by Lillian Hellman. Reprinted from *Six Plays by Lillian Hellman* by permission of Random House, Inc.

Cyrano de Bergerac by Edmond Rostand, Brian Hooker translation. Copyright 1923 by Holt, Rinehart and Winston, Inc. Copyright 1951 by Doris C. Hooker. Reprinted by permission of Holt, Rinehart and Winston, Inc. All inquiries regarding this play should be addressed to the Trade Permissions Department of Holt, Rinehart and Winston, Inc., 383 Madison Avenue, New York, N.Y. 10017.

J.B. by Archibald MacLeish. Reprinted by permission of Houghton Mifflin Company. Copyright © 1956, 1957, 1958 by Archibald MacLeish.

Notes to *Twelfth Night* by Philip G. Hill. Copyright © 1971 by Holt, Rinehart and Winston, Inc.

Tartuffe by Molière. Translated by Richard Wilbur. Copyright © 1961, 1962, 1963 by Richard Wilbur. Reprinted by permission of Harcourt Brace Jovanovich, Inc., New York, and Faber & Faber, Ltd, London. Inquiries on professional rights should be addressed to Mr. Gilbert Parker, Agency for the Performing Arts,

Inc., 120 West 57 Street, New York, N.Y.; inquiries on translation rights should be addressed to Harcourt Brace Jovanovich, Inc., 757 Third Avenue, New York, N.Y.

Oedipus the King by Sophocles. Translated by John Gassner. Copyright © 1935, 1940, 1950, 1951, 1963. Reprinted by permission of Simon and Schuster, Inc.

A View from the Bridge by Arthur Miller. Copyright 1955, © 1957 by Arthur Miller. Reprinted by permission of The Viking Press, Inc., and International Famous Agency, Inc. Communication should be addressed to the author's representative, International Famous Agency, Inc., 1301 Avenue of the Americas, New York, N.Y. 10019.

"Paper Doll." Copyright Edward Marks Music Corporation. Used by permission.

Galileo by Bertolt Brecht, translated by Charles Laughton and published in *From the Modern Repertoire*, Volume II, edited by Eric Bentley. Copyright © 1952 by Indiana University Press. Used by permission.

Fotodeath by Claes Oldenburg. Originally published in the *Tulane Drama Review*, Volume 10, Number 2 (T30), Winter, 1965. Copyright © 1966 *The Drama Review*. Reprinted by permission. All rights reserved.

The purpose of this book is to provide a foundation in theatre for the beginning student; to enhance his appreciation of its complexities; to give him a broad understanding of the way apparently diverse literary and theatrical elements function together to create a unified work of art; and finally to whet his appetite for more and better theatre, both on the stage and on the printed page. My approach is organic, moving from concepts that are easiest to understand and closest to the student's prior experience, to those which, for many students, may seem at first strange or difficult. Classroom experience with the material contained herein, however, has verified that students are interested and excited by these plays and challenged by the complexities of staging them; and hence these interested beginners may be quickly brought from the naive eagerness which characterizes many neophytes in the field of theatre to a relatively sophisticated appreciation of the importance of theatrical art in their own lives. Students who plan to go on to more advanced work in theatre and drama profit by a comprehensive discussion of the art and by an understanding of the interrelationship of its functions, before undertaking courses in one or more of these functions separately. Students who will decide not to pursue further work in this area profit by a deeper appreciation of the theatre, and, I hope, will be more discriminating spectators.

Although this text offers samples from a variety of styles and periods of drama, I have made no attempt to select plays for their historical significance. Historical notes are provided where they seem essential to an appreciation of the plays, but it is not my purpose to survey the history of drama. The plays have been selected, rather, because each has real appeal as good theatre to beginning students. These plays will provoke argument and discussion; they have both strengths and weaknesses which students will learn to distinguish; and they are so interesting that students find it easy and pleasant to read and re-read the scripts. Of course the instructor will see that each was also very carefully selected to illustrate a series of points about dramatic structure and about the arts and crafts of the theatre.

The essays that accompany the plays integrate the study of dramatic literature with the study of production techniques, showing that acting, scene

Preface

design, even makeup and properties, are not independent, isolated arts or skills but grow meaningfully out of an appreciation and understanding of the script. Few of us can successfully talk about costume design or directing in isolation; we talk about costumes for *Othello* or directing *The Iceman Cometh.* I prefer, then, to think of this textbook not as an anthology of plays with explicatory essays, but as a long essay on the theatre, illustrated with play scripts. Nor have I made an attempt to provide a definitive critical discussion of any play; my emphasis is on exploring the possibilities of the theatre with beginning students, and in order to follow this course of study the students need to have some familiarity with a few scripts. Most teachers are dedicated to the concept that dramatic literature is best taught when it is accompanied by a real understanding of the staging possibilities and difficulties of the script at hand, especially the staging concepts intended by the playwright. Most of us also agree that acting, directing, and the other arts and crafts of the theatre must grow out of careful textual analysis. This text uses these approaches in order to give to the student the best possible introduction to the theatre.

Some readers may find that I am unduly committed to defining terms and es- tablishing categories—even at the risk of appearing simplistic. I offer no apology for this approach, although there is probably some truth in the charge. I am well aware that graduate seminars may be devoted to defining expressionism or tragedy with no discernable success beyond the confusion of all parties involved. Any art, but especially so eclectic an art as the theatre, is almost by definition beyond the power of direct analysis; it is inevitable that the serious student of such a complex art will come to the realization that preconceived standards, preconceived categories, and preconceived principles must often be thrown aside in the face of genuine genius. Such a statement, however, does not imply that there is no longer value in the old standards, categories, and principles as a means of introduction to the theatre. The deeply committed student will soon broaden his horizons as he pursues his interest, and the less deeply committed will profit by having something simple and concrete to which to cling. I have tried to be honest with the student by separating in each case the ideas that are generally accepted by theatrical scholars and practitioners from those that are offered as convenient learning devices.

That I owe a great debt of gratitude to a wide variety of people and works will be altogether too apparent to any theatrical scholar reading these pages. To ac- knowledge all of my sources would not only add unnecessarily to the book's already considerable bulk, but would be rendered virtually impossible by the fact that I am at a loss to say, in many cases, where I first came in contact with certain ideas. Where they may be of significant value to the student, I have tried to identify pre- cise sources; beyond that, I have relied upon the indulgence and discernment of my colleagues. Of course acknowledgment is provided in an appropriate place for all directly quoted material, including the play scripts themselves.

I owe a special expression of appreciation to Furman Univeristy and Dean Francis W. Bonner for providing me with two grants that eased to a considerable extent the financial difficulties of preparing this manuscript. I have also been greatly assisted by my colleagues on the Furman faculty, who have used this material in their classes in mimeographed form and have assisted me in evaluating its effective- ness. Dr. Monroe Lippman and Dr. Clifford Ashby read an early draft and offerred perceptive and detailed comments which have proved very useful. Strangely enough, I owe a debt to some necessary surgery which kept me out of my usual production activities long enough to commit a first draft of this work to paper.

P.G.H.

Greenville, South Carolina
March 1971

Contents

THE
LIVING
ART *An Introduction to Theatre and Drama*

What is a play? Is it a piece of literature which happens to be printed in peculiar fashion, with each speaker of dialogue identified in large capital letters rather than with phrases like "he said" and "she replied"? Is it a short story told largely in dialogue form? Or is a play a work of art in its own right, with principles and practices separate and distinct from those of poetry, music, painting, short-story writing, or any of the other arts? The latter is the case, of course, and, although one can never be completely dogmatic in attempting to characterize an art form, it is nevertheless possible to identify and discuss a number of features which make drama unique, exciting, and interesting in its own right, without regard to the other forms which it may resemble in certain superficial ways.

How, then, may one differentiate drama from some of its sister arts? What are some of the fundamental differences between a play and a short novel? Clearly, the manner in which it is generally printed is purely arbitrary. It would be relatively easy to shift a play around by inserting "he said's" and "she replied's" and recasting the stage directions into more exciting language; thus a play could be disguised by printing it in a form which would look very much like a short novel. Very little would be accomplished by doing this, however. Buried under the confusion, a play would still exist—an essential form quite different from the usual novel or other literary work. A far more fundamental difference would be, however, the original intention of the writer. The novelist, poet, and short story writer communicate directly with the reading public by means of the printed word. There is a direct one-to-one relationship between the writer and his reader. The artist's medium is the written word, but through this medium he makes direct contact with his reader. If, as he hopes, he has many readers, then this one-to-one relationship is re-established with each one who reads. The playwright, on the other hand, has in mind the preparation of a "blueprint," by which a stage production will be put together. His immediate medium, too, is the written word, but his target is the group of actors and technicians who will perform his work, and only through these interpreters can his thoughts eventually reach their ultimate target —the audience in the theatre.

"But," you say, "what of the playwright who has his play printed and obviously intends it for

Introduction

the reading public? Does he not by-pass the trappings of the theatre and enjoy the same direct contact with his reader as does the novelist?" By and large, no, he does not. Plays are printed and sold to the reading public for the same reason that most literary works are: to make money. But the product that the reader of a play buys was never really intended for him in the first place. If the playwright and the publisher can gain an extra income by selling these blueprints for theatrical production to the public, so much the better for them; but unless the playwright takes the trouble to re-do completely his work for the reading public, the latter are only getting an opportunity to peek over the shoulder of the playwright as he tries to communicate with the artists who will present his play in the theatre. Until this reading public learns to read blueprints, it can only be puzzled and confused by this peek; unfortunately, it doesn't even know it is confused, since the "blueprints" appear to be written in language with which all are familiar. "Closet dramas"—plays written solely with the intent that they be read rather than performed—do exist, of course, but this rather unusual literary form has never attained any real prominence. The fact is that every significant playwright has been aiming, first of all, at theatrical production. Aeschylus, Sophocles, Euripides, Shakespeare, Moliere, Lope de Vega, Goethe, Brecht, O'Neill —all were active, practicing men of the theatre, who generally had a specific group of actors and technicians in mind when they wrote their plays, and who intended to communicate with an audience in a theatre using the various theatrical devices at their command.

No one would think of picking up a piece of sheet music, reading it silently to himself, and feeling that, as a result of this experience, he had enjoyed the full range of insight offered by, let us say, a Mozart concerto. Only a limited segment of the population can read music at all, and even among those who read it rather well, there are very few who can "hear" in their minds anything resembling the richness of a concerto properly performed. Because one recognizes the limitations in regard to reading music, there is little chance that one would be foolish enough to think that he can "read" the music with full appreciation. Plays, on the other hand, are written in ordinary English (or English translation), and since the American public has been reading English with reasonable efficiency for some years, it is easily fooled into believing that a play can be understood just because the general concept is intelligible. To read a play and fully appreciate its possibilities as a work of art is a highly complex and difficult task. It is a skill which one can develop (just as one can learn to read the Mozart concerto), but real proficiency comes only with a great deal of study and practice.

Of course, many plays have great literary value. Some scripts are so rich in literary terms that it is difficult to imagine that the writer did not consider his reading public, as well. But much which is termed "literary value" can, in fact, have theatrical importance when the play is well produced; although the richness of literary embellishment may not seem, at first glance, to be communicable in a theatre, it often adds depth to a theatrical performance: it may, in other words, be subliminally sensed even if not directly communicated. Purely literary values in a play script, communicable only to a reader and not really germane to theatrical production, are, in the vast majority of cases, entirely tangential to the script's basic intents. A narrow view, which seeks out only these literary values and attempts to make them the primary focus of the artistic experience, misses the playwright's intent.

The very spelling of the word "playwright" is a clue to an understanding of this point. A "playwrite" would, one supposes, be primarily an author, a literary man, a writer of plays. But a "playwright" is a craftsman, an artisan, one who puts a play together out of many disparate elements. If his first aim, then, is to assemble the parts of a play, it seems only reasonable that those who attempt to understand and interpret his work should think in the terms of this assemblage. To view only the literary elements is to miss a great deal of what the playwright had in mind. People who work in the theatre often emphasize this distinction by differentiating between the "play" and the "script". The script is the series of speeches and stage directions which the playwright records for the actors and technicians; the play, on the other hand, is the fully rehearsed presentation as it is enjoyed by an audience. The "play," in other words, is not complete until the work of the playwright has been interpreted by the director, the actors, and the technicians before an audience; a play is a communal artistic experience shared by a group of artists and an audience. Only the script is available to the reading public; it requires a vivid imagination, together with some rudimentary knowledge of the contributions which the director, actors, technicians, and audience would normally make to the communal experience, for the reader to reconstruct the play in his mind in terms resembling those originally intended by the playwright. The analogy to the Mozart concerto mentioned above is now quite complete: in order to appreciate fully the concerto as Mozart intended it, the conductor, the orchestra, the leading instruments, and the audience must come together under carefully controlled circumstances. So it is in the theatre.

The fact that a play requires a group of interpreters standing between the playwright and his ultimate audience is certainly the primary factor which differentiates it from any other literary form. The implications of this arrangement are incredibly far-reaching and complex for the playwright, for an almost complete objectivity is forced upon him. Whereas the novelist may stop his action and communicate directly with his audience, describing at length the physical environment, detailing the most intimate thoughts of a character, or philosophizing along whatever lines strike his fancy, the playwright has no opportunity for this kind of direct communication. Occasionally, as in Thornton Wilder's *Our Town,* one character may serve as narrator, giving some descriptions and even stating the playwright's philosophical point of view; but even in these instances there is an actor, an interpreter, who stands between the playwright and his audience, and who creates a character separate and distinct from either the playwright or the actor. Objectivity is still enforced upon the playwright. Even in his stage directions, the playwright experiences the same enforced objectivity. If the directions serve their primary purpose, they are notes from the playwright to the performers suggesting how the play is to be performed; if, as in Bernard Shaw's stage directions, they become direct communication with a reading public, the playwright has to some extent partaken of the advantages available to the novelist, but he has often at the same time sacrificed meaningful communication with the performers—many of Shaw's stage directions are of no practical help to actors and technicians performing his play. As a matter of fact, a large share of the stage directions which find their way into printed editions of plays have not been written by the playwright anyway. They are supplied, in the case of the older plays, by editors who may or may not have any real sense of how the scene at hand might best be performed; or in the case of newer plays, by the stage manager of the first complete production the play receives. Sometimes stage directions have to be examined very carefully to be sure they really do reflect accurately the playwright's intentions.

The extended discussion, above, of the way in which a playwright relies upon interpreters to present his ideas to an audience, might tempt one to suspect that a writer with anything worthwhile to say would be well advised to choose another literary form by which to express himself. However, there are significant ways in which a play varies from a short novel, for example, which provide decided advantages to the playwright. Not the least of these is immediacy. Everything in a theatre takes place *here* and *now*. The spectator sees an action being performed before his very eyes, and partakes in it in the present tense. Even if the scene of the action is the court of Denmark or before the palace at Thebes, the spectator sees it happen—for him, while he is in the theatre; the time is the present; the place is right here, and agonies or pleasures are lived out in front of him. The difference between this technique and that of the novel has been compared to the difference between witnessing an automobile accident and simply reading about it in the morning papers. No newspaper description, however vivid, can begin to create the same emotional intensity experienced by the eyewitness who hears the grinding impact, feels the heat of the flames, smells the gasoline spilled on the highway, and sees a broken body removed from the wreckage. Mere literary description is replaced by direct, visual impact: no need to describe the locale when the setting is there before one's eyes; no need to depend upon the mind's eye to sort out color imagery when significant juxtaposition of colors is directly in front of one. This is a tremendous, an incalculable, advantage to the playwright who knows how to employ all of these elements effectively.

Another factor which helps to differentiate the play from the novel is the high degree of compression which the play enjoys. This is a feature shared by the play with many kinds of poetry—indeed, poetry is often employed very effectively in the theatre. The novel tends to expand time, whereas plays almost without exception pack into a relatively short time a series of events which would occur over a far longer period of time in real life. The typical stage meal, for example, which may be a feast of major proportions, is unusually long if it requires more than ten minutes of playing time. Audiences do not complain, however, that this is "unrealistic;" they have been conditioned by the very nature of the theatrical medium to accept time compression along with many other stage conventions. The Japanese Noh drama makes such extensive use of the principle of compression that it may seem quite esoteric to Western sensibilities; a single gesture may represent a whole journey, a single bit of verse may detail a lifetime. Yet this same principle is at work in virtually all drama, and can be a highly effective device for the playwright.

Another characteristic which the play shares with some forms of poetry, but which helps to differentiate it from the novel, is the almost absolute requirement for a tightly organized structure. Some avant garde forms, such as multi-media and improvisational theatre, are attempting to escape from all traditional structural forms, but even in these cases the more successful attempts are deriving new structures every bit as exacting as the traditional ones. Novels, by contrast, tend to be loosely knit in structural terms, able to flow in any direction without upsetting a preconceived pattern. When one refers to the structure of a play, one means the way its various parts are articulated. Of course, one must be able to identify these parts in the first place. This is not easy for a beginner to do, and even the most expert professionals struggle endlessly over many details of structural analysis. The fact remains, however, that great plays are constructed by playwrights of genius who, consciously or not, had some sort of plan or pattern in mind. In the vast majority of cases, this plan or pattern is complex and carefully worked out to the last detail:

the critic who can see through the various parts to the plan which lies behind them has acquired a real depth of insight into the genius of the playwright who constructed it. In the pages ahead, a great deal of attention will be devoted to structural analysis of play scripts.

A play is a markedly different art form from other literary types with which it is often lumped; this principle has been established in some detail above. But how can drama be distinguished from some of the other arts, especially the performing arts? There is no need to be concerned with the obvious differences: no one is likely to confuse a play with a concert or with a painting; although in some modern "happenings" the attempt is being made to break down even these distinctions. More important for consideration here, however, is the frequently voiced misconception that a theatrical performance is some sort of amalgamation of all the arts—a chance to combine the "pure" arts of music, painting, poetry, etc., to create some sort of super art form. Actually, nothing could be further from the truth. The art of the theatre is a "pure" art in and of itself, in which a number of seemingly disparate elements are brought together in a precise and carefully controlled fashion. A work of theatrical art exists only on the night of the performance, when the audience, the last of these disparate elements, is brought into the equation. Prior to the moment when the work of art is finally created, there have, of course, been many weeks of effort, often involving genius, insight, and creativity; but all this effort has been attuned to one goal, the one artistically meaningful moment, which occurs when the play is being performed before the audience. Talented painters may make a real contribution to this moment, but their work in relation to theatre is different from what they would do if they were working in their normal medium. Musicians can lend impact to a play's performance, but only as a part of the whole theatrical production. Their effort is altogether different from what it would be if the end product were the performance of a piece of music. The art of the theatre may be broken down into a number of parts, including acting, directing, scene painting, and so forth; but when all of these elements finally come together, they produce a work of art which is uniquely theatrical, and more than an amalgamation of all its parts.

How, then, is the beginner to learn something about how all these elements are combined in the special art form known as drama? Clearly, he must begin by analyzing the elements separately, for the whole is much too large and complex to assimilate without first considering individual aspects. On the other hand, it is important not to lose sight of the whole while attempting to analyze the parts, lest a failure to understand the complex relationships among them result. The audience has been shown to be a vital element in putting together a theatrical experience, and there is an advantage in preparing the members of the audience for the roles they are to play. The importance of an "educated" audience can be over-estimated, and used as an *ex post facto* excuse for unclear and confusing performances which fail to gain a desired impact; but at the same time, it is clear that going to the live theatre today has become an experience available to such a limited few, that it is easy for one to grow up in America totally unaware of what he should expect to find in a theatre. Some basic instruction on how to enter fully into the theatrical experience, and to understand some rudimentary features of what is going on, would appear to be very much in order.

Almost all phases of theatrical art begin with the script. Directors, actors, scene designers, prop masters, and makeup assistants are all urged to begin their work with a thorough understanding of the script to be performed. It is a fruitful starting point for the spectator as well. The playwright, if he is capable, has provided a blueprint for production which is so complete that a careful study of his work will provide clues for all of the other theatrical artists to follow, and the spectator or the play reader who wishes to create a full-scale production in his mind must always return to this solid starting point. Script analysis, then, will constitute a major share of the study which is to follow. On the other hand, a script cannot be analyzed in a vacuum. It must be analyzed with a full awareness, not only of the literary factors involved, but also of the impact which sets, lights, costumes, and capable acting will have on the script when it is performed before an audience. For this reason, it will be necessary to consider these aspects of play production simultaneously with analysis of the script.

Reading a play is not really such a difficult task as may have been suggested in the preceding pages. The reader who comes to understand the various elements of theatrical production and the fundamentals of script analysis can begin to create a production in his own mind as he reads, which may be far superior to many that he will actually see. Just as the musician can be trained to read music so well that the Mozart concerto can be a real and living experience for him in his mind, so the play reader can be trained to read a script with a vivid and active imagination. Probably no musician will become so competent that he will prefer *not* to hear the music performed, and no play reader should become so confident of his imaginative powers as to scorn a trip to the theatre—something can usually be learned, even from a poor production. The reader, having realized that a play script is very different from other forms of literature, can train himself to read and enjoy play scripts. He will find that he can indeed experience the *play* in a fashion reasonably close to that intended by the playwright.

The Basic Elements of Drama

Lillian Hellman was born in New Orleans, Louisiana, on June 20, 1905. At an early age, however, she moved to New York with her parents. Hence she may be considered a product of a metropolitan environment rather than the rural south. Occasional visits to relatives in the south may have had some influence on her later writing, but the fact that her most famous play is set in the deep south would appear to be coincidental rather than a direct outgrowth of her background. Miss Hellman matriculated at both New York University and Columbia University, but did not complete degree requirements at either school. She holds honorary degrees from several institutions. In 1925 she married Arthur Kober, a playwright and agent, was divorced seven years later, and has not subsequently remarried.

After her college days, Miss Hellman worked as writer and play reader in New York and Hollywood for several years; while employed in this capacity by Herman Shumlin she achieved her first notable success in playwriting, when *The Children's Hour* was produced on Broadway in 1934. It gained immediate notoriety, not only because it was taut and effective theatre, but also because its subject matter (an alleged lesbian relationship) was considered shocking at that time. Her next play, entitled *Days to Come,* although it had some merit, was a financial flop on Broadway in 1936; her greatest success, *The Little Foxes,* followed in 1939.

Miss Hellman took a deep interest in social and political causes during the 1930's, and was especially moved by the plight of the Loyalists whom she visited during the Spanish Civil War. Her strong anti-fascist viewpoint was especially notable in *Watch on the Rhine,* produced in 1941 just before the American entrance into World War II. It was widely acclaimed as the best of the many anti-Nazi plays written during that era, and won the New York Drama Critics' Circle Award for the best play of 1940–41. *The Searching Wind,* an analysis of the U.S. involvement in World War II, was produced in 1944 while the outcome of the war was still uncertain. In 1946, Miss Hellman returned to the characters of *The Little Foxes* to write *Another Part of the Forest,* a play about the Hubbard family during an earlier part of their lives. *The Autumn Garden* was produced in 1951, followed by *Toys in the Attic* in 1960. This last play won its author her second New York Drama Critics' Circle Award, for the best play

The Little Foxes
by Lillian Hellman

of 1959–60. Miss Hellman has also been represented on Broadway by several collaborative efforts and adaptations of foreign works.

When *The Little Foxes* opened at the National Theatre in New York on February 15, 1939, the critical reaction was not unanimously favorable. All agreed that Miss Hellman was an extraordinary craftsman; but some argued that the plot was too contrived, the evil characters too one dimensional, and the thematic viewpoints unclear. However, repeated productions and continued analysis have tended to exonerate the play on all three counts. The plot is so neatly articulated that audiences tend to be unconcerned with the improbabilities; World War II has renewed awareness that there is no apparent limit to man's capacity for evil; and the thematic content of the play, although never profound, is fascinating in its complexity. No critic can deny that the play has a tightly-knit organization and structure; for this reason Miss Hellman and Ibsen have frequently been compared. Miss Hellman has remarked that "the theatre has limitations: it is a tight, unbending, unfluid, meager form in which to write." With the toughness of her task in mind, Miss Hellman has proceeded very carefully to articulate a plot which accounts, in a truly remarkable way, for the motivation and the inciting circumstances of every character and every situation.

The original production was directed by Herman Shumlin, whose ability Miss Hellman respected very highly, and enjoyed the considerable advantage of having Tallulah Bankhead in the leading role. Not every critic who attended opening night gave Miss Bankhead top acting honors, but the role became one of the significant landmarks of her career. Her cold beauty and flexible baritone voice made her characterization so effective that it captivated audiences and held them spellbound. The detailed, realistic set and other aspects of the production evidently worked together to make the play a memorable evening in the theatre. It is now necessary to examine the script in some detail. Read *The Little Foxes* straight through, preferably all at one sitting, in order to experience it as you would in the theatre.

Facing page: Tallulah Bankhead (Regina) and Charles Dingle (Benjamin) in Act I of *The Little Foxes*. National Theatre, New York, 1939. Sets, Howard Bay; costumes, Aline Bernstein. Photograph: Vandamm, Theatre Collection, New York Public Library at Lincoln Center.

Page 13: Act III in the Repertory Theater of Lincoln Center production, 1967, of *The Little Foxes*. George C. Scott (Benjamin), Anne Bancroft (Regina), E. G. Marshall (Oscar); foreground, Richard A. Dysart (Horace), Margaret Leighton (Birdie). Sets and lighting, Howard Bay; Costumes, Patricia Zipprodt. Photograph: Martha Swope. Courtesy The Repertory Theater of Lincoln Center.

The Little Foxes

A play in three acts by
LILLIAN HELLMAN

"Take us the foxes, the little foxes, that spoil the vines; for our vines have tender grapes."

Addie	*Regina Giddens*
Cal	*William Marshall*
Birdie Hubbard	*Benjamin Hubbard*
Oscar Hubbard	*Alexandra Giddens*
Leo Hubbard	*Horace Giddens*

The scene of the play is the living room of the Giddens house, in a small town in the South.

ACT I: The Spring of 1900, evening.
ACT II: A week later, early morning.
ACT III: Two weeks later, late afternoon.

There has been no attempt to write Southern dialect. It is to be understood that the accents are Southern.

ACT I

SCENE: The living room of the Giddens house, in a small town in the deep South, the Spring of 1900. Upstage is a staircase leading to the second story. Upstage, right, are double doors to the dining room. When these doors are open we see a section of the dining room and the furniture. Upstage, left, is an entrance hall with a coat-rack and umbrella stand. There are large lace-curtained windows on the left wall. The room is lit by a center gas chandelier and painted china oil lamps on the tables. Against the wall is a large piano. Downstage, right, are a high couch, a large table, several chairs. Against the left back wall are a table and several chairs. Near the window there are a smaller couch and tables. The room is good-looking, the furniture expensive; but it reflects no particular taste. Everything is of the best and that is all.

AT RISE: **Addie,** a tall, nice-looking Negro woman of about fifty-five, is closing the windows. From behind the closed dining-room

doors there is the sound of voices. After a second, **Cal,** a middle-aged Negro, comes in from the entrance hall carrying a tray with glasses and a bottle of port. **Addie** crosses, takes the tray from him, puts it on table, begins to arrange it.

Addie: [*Pointing to the bottle*] You gone stark out of your head?

Cal: No, smart lady, I ain't. Miss Regina told me to get out that bottle. [*Points to bottle*] That very bottle for the mighty honored guest. When Miss Regina changes orders like that you can bet your dime she got her reason.

Addie: [*Points to dining room*] Go on. You'll be needed.

Cal: Miss Zan she had two helpings frozen fruit cream and she tell that honored guest, she tell him that you make the best frozen fruit cream in all the South.

Addie: [*Smiles, pleased*] Did she? Well, see that Belle saves a little for her. She like it right before she go to bed. Save a few little cakes, too, she like—

[*The dining-room doors are opened and quickly closed again by* **Birdie Hubbard. Birdie** *is a woman of about forty, with a pretty, well-bred, faded face. Her movements are usually nervous and timid, but now, as she comes running into the room, she is gay and excited.* **Cal** *turns to* **Birdie.**]

Birdie: Oh, Cal. [*Closes door*] I want you to get one of the kitchen boys to run home for me. He's to look in my desk drawer and—[*To* **Addie**] My, Addie. What a good supper! Just as good as good can be.

Addie: You look pretty this evening, Miss Birdie, and young.

Birdie: [*Laughing*] Me, young? [*Turns back to* **Cal**] Maybe you better find Simon and tell him to do it himself. He's to look in my desk, the left drawer, and bring my music album right away. Mr. Marshall is very anxious to see it because of his father and the opera in Chicago. [*To* **Addie**] Mr. Marshall is such a polite man with his manners and very educated and cultured and I've told him all about how my mama and papa used to go to Europe for the music—[*Laughs. To* **Addie**] Imagine going all the way to Europe just to listen to music. Wouldn't that be nice, Addie? Just to sit

there and listen and—[*Turns and steps to* **Cal**] Left drawer, Cal. Tell him that twice because he forgets. And tell him not to let any of the things drop out of the album and to bring it right in here when he comes back.

[*The dining-room doors are opened and quickly closed by* **Oscar Hubbard.** *He is a man in his late forties.*]

Cal: Yes'm. But Simon he won't get it right. But I'll tell him.

Birdie: Left drawer, Cal, and tell him to bring the blue book and—

Oscar: [*Sharply*] Birdie.

Birdie: [*Turning nervously*] Oh, Oscar. I was just sending Simon for my music album.

Oscar: [*To* **Cal**] Never mind about the album. Miss Birdie has changed her mind.

Birdie: But, really, Oscar. Really I promised Mr. Marshall. I—

[**Cal** *looks at them, exits.*]

Oscar: Why do you leave the dinner table and go running about like a child?

Birdie: [*Trying to be gay*] But, Oscar, Mr. Marshall said most specially he *wanted* to see my album. I told him about the time Mama met Wagner, and Mrs. Wagner gave her the signed program and the big picture. Mr. Marshall wants to see that. Very, very much. We had such a nice talk and—

Oscar: [*Taking a step to her*] You have been chattering to him like a magpie. You haven't let him be for a second. I can't think he came South to be bored with you.

Birdie: [*Quickly, hurt*] He wasn't bored. I don't believe he was bored. He's a very educated, cultured gentleman. [*Her voice rises*] I just don't believe it. You always talk like that when I'm having a nice time.

Oscar: [*Turning to her, sharply*] You have had too much wine. Get yourself in hand now.

Birdie: [*Drawing back, about to cry, shrilly*] What am I doing? I am not doing anything. What am I doing?

Oscar: [*Taking a step to her, tensely*] I said get yourself in hand. Stop acting like a fool.

Birdie: [*Turns to him, quietly*] I don't believe he was bored. I just don't believe it. Some people like music and like to talk about it. That's all I was doing.

[**Leo Hubbard** *comes hurrying through the dining-room door. He is a young man of twenty, with a weak kind of good looks.*]

Leo: Mama! Papa! They are coming in now.

Oscar: [*Softly*] Sit down, Birdie. Sit down now.

[**Birdie** *sits down, bows her head as if to hide her face.*]

[*The dining-room doors are opened by* **Cal.** *We see people beginning to rise from the table.* **Regina Giddens** *comes in with* **William Marshall.** **Regina** *is a handsome woman of forty.* **Marshall** *is forty-five, pleasant-looking, self-possessed. Behind them comes* **Alexandra Giddens,** *a very pretty, rather delicate-looking girl of seventeen. She is followed by* **Benjamin Hubbard,** *fifty-five, with a large jovial face and the light graceful movements that one often finds in large men.*]

Regina: Mr. Marshall, I think you're trying to console me. Chicago may be the noisiest, dirtiest city in the world but I should still prefer it to the sound of our horses and the smell of our azaleas. I should like crowds of people, and theatres, and lovely women—*Very* lovely women, Mr. Marshall?

Marshall: [*Crossing to sofa*] In Chicago? Oh, I suppose so. But I can tell you this: I've never dined there with three *such* lovely ladies.

[**Addie** *begins to pass the port.*]

Ben: Our Southern women are well favored.

Leo: [*Laughs*] But one must go to Mobile for the ladies, sir. Very elegant worldly ladies, too.

Ben: [*Looks at him very deliberately*] Worldly, eh? *Worldly*, did you say?

Oscar: [*Hastily, to* **Leo**] Your uncle Ben means that worldliness is not a mark of beauty in any woman.

Leo: [*Quickly*] Of course, Uncle Ben. I didn't mean—

Marshall: Your port is excellent, Mrs. Giddens.

Regina: Thank you, Mr. Marshall. We had been saving that bottle, hoping we could open it just for you.

Alexandra: [*As* **Addie** *comes to her with the tray*] Oh. May I *really*, Addie?

Addie: Better ask Mama.

Alexandra: May I, Mama?

Regina: [*Nods, smiles*] In Mr. Marshall's honor.

Alexandra: [*Smiles*] Mr. Marshall, this will be the first taste of port I've ever had.

[**Addie** *serves* **Leo.**]

Marshall: No one ever had their first taste of a better port. [*He lifts his glass in a toast; she lifts hers; they both drink*] Well, I suppose it is all true, Mrs. Giddens.

Regina: What is true?

Marshall: That you Southerners occupy a unique position in America. You live better than the rest of us, you eat better, you drink better. I wonder you find time, or want to find time, to do business.

Ben: A great many Southerners don't.

Marshall: Do all of you live here together?

Regina: Here with me? [*Laughs*] Oh, no. My brother Ben lives next door. My brother Oscar and his family live in the next square.

Ben: But we are a very close family. We've always *wanted* it that way.

Marshall: That is very pleasant. Keeping your family together to share each other's lives. My family moves around too much. My children seem never to come home. Away at school in the winter; in the summer, Europe with their mother—

Regina: [*Eagerly*] Oh, yes. Even down here we read about Mrs. Marshall in the society pages.

Marshall: I dare say. She moves about a great deal. And all of you are part of the same business? Hubbard Sons?

Ben: [*Motions to* **Oscar**] Oscar and me. [*Motions to* **Regina**] My sister's good husband is a banker.

Marshall: [*Looks at* **Regina,** *surprised*] Oh.

Regina: I am so sorry that my husband isn't here to meet you. He's been very ill. He is at Johns Hopkins. But he will be home soon. We think he is getting better now.

Leo: I work for Uncle Horace. [**Regina** *looks at him*] I mean I work for Uncle Horace at his bank. I keep an eye on things while he's away.

Regina: [*Smiles*] Really, Leo?

Ben: [*Looks at* **Leo,** *then to* **Marshall**] Modesty in the young is as excellent as it is rare. [*Looks at* **Leo** *again.*]

Oscar: [*To* **Leo**] Your uncle means that a young man should speak more modestly.

Leo: [*Hastily, taking a step to* **Ben**] Oh, I didn't mean, sir—

Marshall: Oh, Mrs. Hubbard. Where's that Wagner autograph you promised to let me see? My train will be leaving soon and—

Birdie: The autograph? Oh. Well. Really, Mr. Marshall, I didn't mean to chatter so about it. Really I—[*Nervously, looking at* **Oscar**] You must excuse me. I didn't get it because, well, because I had—I—I had a little headache and—

Oscar: My wife is a miserable victim of headaches.

Regina: [*Quickly*] Mr. Marshall said at supper that he would like you to play for him, Alexandra.

Alexandra: [*Who has been looking at* **Birdie**] It's not I who play well, sir. It's my aunt. She plays just wonderfully. She's my teacher. [*Rises. Eagerly*] May we play a duet? May we, Mama?

Birdie: [*Taking* **Alexandra**'s *hand*] Thank you, dear. But I have my headache now. I—

Oscar: [*Sharply*] Don't be stubborn, Birdie. Mr. Marshall wants you to play.

Marshall: Indeed I do. If your headache isn't—

Birdie: [*Hesitates, then gets up pleased*] But I'd like to, sir. Very much. [*She and* **Alexandra** *go to the piano.*]

Marshall: It's very remarkable how you Southern aristocrats have kept together. Kept together and kept what belonged to you.

Ben: You misunderstand, sir. Southern aristocrats have *not* kept together and have *not* kept what belonged to them.

Marshall: [*Laughs, indicates room*] You don't call this keeping what belongs to you?

Ben: But we are not aristocrats. [*Points to* **Birdie** *at the piano*] Our brother's wife is the only one of us who belongs to the Southern aristocracy.

[**Birdie** *looks toward* **Ben**.]

Marshall: [*Smiles*] My information is that you people have been here, and solidly here, for a long time.

Oscar: And so we have. Since our great-grandfather.

Ben: [*Smiles*] Who was *not* an aristocrat, like Birdie's.

Marshall: [*A little sharply*] You make great distinctions.

Ben: Oh, they have been made for us. And maybe they are important distinctions. [*Leans forward, intimately*] Now you take Birdie's family. When my great-grandfather came here they were the highest-tone plantation owners in this state.

Leo: [*Steps to* **Marshall**. *Proudly*] My mother's grandfather was *governor* of the state before the war.

Oscar: They owned the plantation, Lionnet. You may have heard of it, sir?

Marshall: [*Laughs*] No, I've never heard of anything but brick houses on a lake, and cotton mills.

Ben: Lionnet in its day was the best cotton land in the South. It still brings us in a fair crop. [*Sits back*] Ah, they were great days for those people—even when I can remember. They had the best of everything. [**Birdie** *turns to them*] Cloth from Paris, trips to Europe, horses you can't raise any more, niggers to lift their fingers—

Birdie: [*Suddenly*] We were good to our people. Everybody knew that. We were better to them than—

[**Marshall** *looks up at* **Birdie**.]

Regina: Why, Birdie. You aren't playing.

Ben: But when the war comes these fine gentlemen ride off and leave the cotton, *and* the women, to rot.

Birdie: My father was killed in the war. He was a fine soldier, Mr. Marshall. A fine man.

Regina: Oh, certainly, Birdie. A famous soldier.

Ben: [*To* **Birdie**] But that isn't the tale I am telling Mr. Marshall. [*To* **Marshall**] Well, sir, the war ends. [**Birdie** *goes back to piano*] Lionnet is almost ruined, and the sons finish ruining it. And there were thousands like them. Why? [*Leans forward*] Because the Southern aristocrat can adapt himself to nothing. Too high-tone to try.

Marshall: Sometimes it is difficult to learn new ways. [**Birdie** *and* **Alexandra** *begin to play.* **Marshall** *leans forward, listening.*]

Ben: Perhaps, perhaps. [*He sees that* **Marshall** *is listening to the music. Irritated, he turns to* **Birdie** *and* **Alexandra** *at the piano, then back to* **Marshall**] You're right, Mr. Marshall. It is difficult to learn new ways. But maybe that's why it's profitable. *Our* grandfather and *our* father learned the new ways and learned how to make them pay. They work. [*Smiles nastily*] *They are in trade. Hubbard Sons, Merchandise. Others, Birdie's family, for example, look down on them. [*Settles back in chair*] To make a long story short, Lionnet now belongs to us. [*Birdie stops playing*] Twenty years ago we took over their land, their cotton, and their daughter. [*Birdie rises and stands stiffly by the piano. Marshall, who has been watching her, rises.*]

Marshall: May I bring you a glass of port, Mrs. Hubbard?

Birdie: [*Softly*] No, thank you, sir. You are most polite.

Regina: [*Sharply, to* **Ben**] You are boring Mr. Marshall with these ancient family tales.

Ben: I hope not. I hope not. I am trying to make an important point— [*Bows to* **Marshall**] for our future business partner.

Oscar: [*To* **Marshall**] My brother always says that it's folks like us who have struggled and fought to bring to our land some of the prosperity of your land.

Ben: Some people call that patriotism.

Regina: [*Laughs gaily*] I hope you don't find my brothers too obvious, Mr. Marshall. I'm afraid they mean that this is the time for the ladies to leave the gentlemen to talk business.

Marshall: [*Hastily*] Not at all. We settled everything this afternoon. [*Marshall looks at his watch*] I have only a few minutes before I must leave for the train. [*Smiles at her*] And I insist they be spent with you.

Regina: *And* with another glass of port.

Marshall: Thank you.

Ben: [*To* **Regina**] My sister is right. [*To* **Marshall**] I am a plain man and I am trying to say a plain thing. A man ain't only in business for what he can get out of it. It's got to give him something here. [*Puts hand to his breast*] That's every bit as true for the nigger picking cotton for a silver quarter, as it is for you and me. [*Regina gives* **Marshall** *a glass of port*] If it don't give him something here, then he don't pick the cotton right. Money isn't all. Not by three shots.

Marshall: Really? Well, I always thought it was a great deal.

Regina: And so did I, Mr. Marshall.

Marshall: [*Leans forward. Pleasantly, but with mean-*

ing] Now you don't have to convince me that you are the right people for the deal. I wouldn't be here if you hadn't convinced me six months ago. You want the mill here, and I want it here. It isn't my business to find out *why* you want it.

Ben: To bring the machine to the cotton, and not the cotton to the machine.

Marshall: [*Amused*] You have a turn for neat phrases, Hubbard. Well, however grand your reasons are, mine are simple: I want to make money and I believe I'll make it on you. [*As* **Ben** *starts to speak, he smiles*] Mind you, I have no objections to more high-minded reasons. They are mighty valuable in business. It's fine to have partners who so closely follow the teachings of Christ. [*Gets up*] And now I must leave for my train.

Regina: I'm sorry you won't stay over with us, Mr. Marshall, but you'll come again. Any time you like.

Ben: [*Motions to* **Leo,** *indicating the bottle*] Fill them up, boy, fill them up. [**Leo** *moves around filling the glasses as* **Ben** *speaks*] Down here, sir, we have a strange custom. We drink the *last* drink for a toast. That's to prove that the Southerner is always still on his feet for the last drink. [*Picks up his glass*] It was Henry Frick, your Mr. Henry Frick, who said, "Railroads are the Rembrandts of investments." Well, *I* say, "Southern cotton mills *will be* the Rembrandts of investment." So I give you the firm of Hubbard Sons and Marshall, Cotton Mills, and to it a long and prosperous life.

> [*They all pick up their glasses.* **Marshall** *looks at them, amused. Then he, too, lifts his glass, smiles.*]

Oscar: The children will drive you to the depot. Leo! Alexandra! You will drive Mr. Marshall down.

Leo: [*Eagerly, looks at* **Ben** *who nods*] Yes, sir. [*To* **Marshall**] Not often Uncle Ben lets *me* drive the horses. And a beautiful pair they are. [*Starts for hall*] Come on, Zan.

Alexandra: May I drive tonight, Uncle Ben, please? I'd like to and—

Ben: [*Shakes his head, laughs*] In your evening clothes? Oh, no, my dear.

Alexandra: But Leo always—

[*Stops, exits quickly.*]

Regina: I don't like to say good-bye to you, Mr. Marshall.

Marshall: Then we won't say good-bye. You have promised that you would come and let me show you Chicago. Do I have to make you promise again?

Regina: [*Looks at him as he presses her hand*] I promise again.

Marshall: [*Touches her hand again, then moves to* **Birdie**] Good-bye, Mrs. Hubbard.

Birdie: [*Shyly, with sweetness and dignity*] Good-bye, sir.

Marshall: [*As he passes* **Regina**] Remember.

Regina: I will.

Oscar: We'll see you to the carriage.

> [**Marshall** *exits, followed by* **Ben** *and* **Oscar**. *For a second* **Regina** *and* **Birdie** *stand looking after them. Then* **Regina** *throws up her arms, laughs happily.*]

Regina: And there, Birdie, goes the man who has opened the door to our future.

Birdie: [*Surprised at the unaccustomed friendliness*] What?

Regina: [*Turning to her*] *Our* future. Yours and mine, Ben's and Oscar's, the children— [*Looks at* **Birdie**'s *puzzled face, laughs*] Our future! [*Gaily*] You were charming at supper, Birdie. Mr. Marshall certainly thought so.

Birdie: [*Pleased*] Why, Regina! Do you think he did?

Regina: Can't you tell when you're being admired?

Birdie: Oscar said I bored Mr. Marshall. [*Then quietly*] But he admired *you*. He told me so.

Regina: What did he say?

Birdie: He said to me, "I hope your sister-in-law will come to Chicago. Chicago will be at her feet." He said the ladies would bow to your manners and the gentlemen to your looks.

Regina: Did he? He seems a lonely man. Imagine being lonely with all that money. I don't think he likes his wife.

Birdie: Not like his wife? What a thing to say.

Regina: She's away a great deal. He said that several times. And once he made fun of her being so social and high-tone. But that fits in all right. [*Sits back, arms on back of sofa, stretches*]

Her being social, I mean. She can introduce me. It won't take long with an introduction from her.

Birdie: [*Bewildered*] Introduce you? In Chicago? You mean you really might go? Oh, Regina, you can't leave here. What about Horace?

Regina: Don't look so scared about everything, Birdie. I'm going to live in Chicago. I've always wanted to. And now there'll be plenty of money to go with.

Birdie: But Horace won't be able to move around. You know what the doctor wrote.

Regina: There'll be millions, Birdie, millions. You know what I've always said when people told me we were rich? I said I think you should either be a nigger or a millionaire. In between, like us, what for? [*Laughs. Looks at* **Birdie**] But I'm not going away tomorrow, Birdie. There's plenty of time to worry about Horace when he comes home. If he ever decides to come home.

Birdie: Will we be going to Chicago? I mean, Oscar and Leo and me?

Regina: You? I shouldn't think so. [*Laughs*] Well, we must remember tonight. It's a very important night and we mustn't forget it. We shall plan all the things we'd like to have and then we'll really have them. Make a wish, Birdie, any wish. It's bound to come true now.

> [**Ben** *and* **Oscar** *enter.*]

Birdie: [*Laughs*] Well. Well, I don't know. Maybe. [**Regina** *turns to look at* **Ben**] Well, I guess I'd know right off what I wanted.

> [**Oscar** *stands by the upper window, waves to the departing carriage.*]

Regina: [*Looks up at* **Ben**, *smiles. He smiles back at her*] Well, you did it.

Ben: Looks like it might be we did.

Regina: [*Springs up, laughs*] Looks like it! Don't pretend. You're like a cat who's been licking the cream. [*Crosses to wine bottle*] Now we must all have a drink to celebrate.

Oscar: The children, Alexandra and Leo, make a very handsome couple, Regina. Marshall remarked himself what fine young folks they were. How well they looked together!

Regina: [*Sharply*] Yes. You said that before, Oscar.

Ben: Yes, sir. It's beginning to look as if the

deal's all set. I may not be a subtle man—but—[*Turns to them. After a second*] Now somebody ask me how I know the deal is set.

Oscar: What do you mean, Ben?

Ben: You remember I told him that down here we drink the *last* drink for a toast?

Oscar: [*Thoughtfully*] Yes. I never heard that before.

Ben: Nobody's ever heard it before. God forgives those who invent what they need. I already had his signature. But we've all done business with men whose word over a glass is better than a bond. Anyway it don't hurt to have both.

Oscar: [*Turns to* **Regina**] You understand what Ben means?

Regina: [*Smiles*] Yes, Oscar. I understand. I understood immediately.

Ben: [*Looks at her admiringly*] Did you, Regina? Well, when he lifted his glass to drink, I closed my eyes and saw the bricks going into place.

Regina: And *I* saw a lot more than that.

Ben: Slowly, slowly. As yet we have only our hopes.

Regina: Birdie and I have just been planning what we want. I know what I want. What will you want, Ben?

Ben: Caution. Don't count the chickens. [*Leans back, laughs*] Well, God would allow us a little daydreaming. Good for the soul when you've worked hard enough to deserve it. [*Pauses*] I think I'll have a stable. For a long time I've had my good eyes on Carter's in Savannah. A rich man's pleasure, the sport of kings, why not the sport of Hubbards? Why not?

Regina: [*Smiles*] Why not? What will you have, Oscar?

Oscar: I don't know. [*Thoughtfully*] The pleasure of seeing the bricks grow will be enough for me.

Ben: Oh, of course. Our *greatest* pleasure will be to see the bricks grow. But we are all entitled to a little side indulgence.

Oscar: Yes, I suppose so. Well, then, I think we might take a few trips here and there, eh, Birdie?

Birdie: [*Surprised at being consulted*] Yes, Oscar. I'd like that.

Oscar: We might even make a regular trip to Jekyll Island. I've heard the Cornelly place is for sale. We might think about buying it. Make a nice change. Do you good, Birdie, a change of climate. Fine shooting on Jekyll, the best.

Birdie: I'd like—

Oscar: [*Indulgently*] What would you like?

Birdie: *Two* things. Two things I'd like most.

Regina: Two! I should like a thousand. You are modest, Birdie.

Birdie: [*Warmly, delighted with the unexpected interest*] I should like to have Lionnet back. I know you own it now, but I'd like to see it fixed up again, the way Mama and Papa had it. Every year it used to get a nice coat of paint—Papa was very particular about the paint—and the lawn was so smooth all the way down to the river, with the trims of zinnias and red-feather plush. And the figs and blue little plums and the scuppernongs—[*Smiles. Turns to* **Regina**] The organ is still there and it wouldn't cost much to fix. We could have parties for Zan, the way Mama used to have for me.

Ben: That's a pretty picture, Birdie. Might be a most pleasant way to live. [*Dismissing* **Birdie**] What do you want, Regina?

Birdie: [*Very happily, not noticing that they are no longer listening to her*] I could have a cutting garden. Just where Mama's used to be. Oh, I do think we could be happier there. Papa used to say that *nobody* had ever lost their temper at Lionnet, and *nobody* ever would. Papa would never let anybody be nasty-spoken or mean. No, sir. He just didn't like it.

Ben: What do you want, Regina?

Regina: I'm going to Chicago. And when I'm settled there and know the right people and the right things to buy—because I certainly don't now—I shall go to Paris and buy them. (*Laughs*) I'm going to leave you and Oscar to count the bricks.

Birdie: Oscar. Please let me have Lionnet back.

Oscar: [*To* **Regina**] You are serious about moving to Chicago?

Ben: She is going to see the great world and leave us in the little one. Well, we'll come and visit you and meet all the great and be proud to think you are our sister.

Regina: [*Gaily*] Certainly. And you won't even have to learn to be subtle, Ben. Stay as you are. You will be rich and the rich don't have to be subtle.

Oscar: But what about Alexandra? She's seventeen. Old enough to be thinking about marrying.

Birdie: And, Oscar, I have one more wish. Just one more wish.

Oscar: [*Turns*] What is it, Birdie? What are you saying?

Birdie: I want you to stop shooting. I mean, so much. I don't like to see animals and birds killed just for the killing. You only throw them away—

Ben: [*To* **Regina**] It'll take a great deal of money to live as you're planning, Regina.

Regina: Certainly. But there'll be plenty of money. You have estimated the profits very high.

Ben: I have—

Birdie: [**Oscar** *is looking at her furiously*] And you never let anybody else shoot, and the niggers need it so much to keep from starving. It's wicked to shoot food just because you like to shoot, when poor people need it so—

Ben: [*Laughs*] I have estimated the profits very high—for myself.

Regina: What did you say?

Birdie: I've always wanted to speak about it, Oscar.

Oscar: [*Slowly, carefully*] What are you chattering about?

Birdie: [*nervously*] I was talking about Lionnet and—and about your shooting—

Oscar: You are exciting yourself.

Regina: [*To* **Ben**] I didn't hear you. There was so much talking.

Oscar: [*To* **Birdie**] You have been acting very childish, very excited, all evening.

Birdie: Regina asked me what I'd like.

Regina: What did you say, Ben?

Birdie: Now that we'll be so rich everybody was saying what they would like, so *I* said what *I* would like, too.

Ben: I said— [*He is interrupted by* **Oscar**.]

Oscar: [*To* **Birdie**] Very well. We've all heard you. That's enough now.

Ben: I am waiting. [*They stop*] I am waiting for you to finish. You and Birdie. Four conversations are three too many. [**Birdie** *slowly sits down*. **Ben** *smiles, to* **Regina**] I said that I had, and I do, estimate the profits very high—for myself, and Oscar, of course.

Regina: [*Slowly*] And what does that mean?
    [**Ben** *shrugs, looks towards* **Oscar**.]

Oscar: [*Looks at* **Ben**, *clears throat*] Well, Regina, it's like this. For forty-nine per cent Marshall will put up four hundred thousand dollars. For fifty-one per cent— [*Smiles archly*] a controlling interest, mind you, we will put up two hundred and twenty-five thousand dollars besides offering him certain benefits that our [*looks at* **Ben**] local position allows us to manage. Ben means that two hundred and twenty-five thousand dollars is a lot of money.

Regina: I know the terms and I know it's a lot of money.

Ben: [*Nodding*] It is.

Oscar: Ben means that we are ready with our two-thirds of the money. Your third, Horace's I mean, doesn't seem to be ready. [*Raises his hand as* **Regina** *starts to speak*] Ben has written to Horace, I have written, and you have written. He answers. But he never mentions this business. Yet we have explained it to him in great detail, and told him the urgency. Still he never mentions it. Ben has been very patient, Regina. Naturally, you are our sister and we want you to benefit from anything we do.

Regina: And in addition to your concern for me, you do not want control to go out of the family. [*To* **Ben**] That right, Ben?

Ben: That's cynical. [*Smiles*] Cynicism is an unpleasant way of saying the truth.

Oscar: No need to be cynical. We'd have no trouble raising the third share, the share that you want to take.

Regina: I am sure you could get the third share, the share you were saving for me. But that would give you a strange partner. And strange partners sometimes want a great deal. [*Smiles unpleasantly*] But perhaps it would be wise for you to find him.

Oscar: Now, now. Nobody says we *want* to do that. We would like to have you in and you would like to come in.

Regina: Yes. I certainly would.

Ben: [*Laughs, puts up his hand*] But we haven't heard from Horace.

Regina: I've given my word that Horace will put up the money. That should be enough.

Ben: Oh, it was enough. I took your word. But I've got to have more than your word now. The contracts will be signed this week, and Marshall will want to see our money soon after. Regina, Horace has been in Baltimore for five months. I know that you've written him to come home, and that he hasn't come.

Oscar: It's beginning to look as if he doesn't want to come home.

Regina: Of course he wants to come home. You can't move around with heart trouble at any moment you choose. You know what doctors are like once they get their hands on a case like this—

Oscar: They can't very well keep him from answering letters, can they? [**Regina** *turns to* **Ben**] They couldn't keep him from arranging for the money if he wanted to—

Regina: Has it occurred to you that Horace is also a good business man?

Ben: Certainly. He is a shrewd trader. Always has been. The bank is proof of that.

Regina: Then, possibly, he may be keeping silent because he doesn't think he is getting enough for his money. [*Looks at* **Oscar**] Seventy-five thousand he has to put up. That's a lot of money, too.

Oscar: Nonsense. He knows a good thing when he hears it. He knows that we can make *twice* the profit on cotton goods manufactured *here* than can be made in the North.

Ben: That isn't what Regina means. [*Smiles*] May I interpret you, Regina? [*To* **Oscar**] Regina is saying that Horace wants *more* than a third of our share.

Oscar: But he's only putting up a third of the money. You put up a third and you get a third. What else *could* he expect?

Regina: Well, *I* don't know. I don't know about these things. It would seem that if you put up a third you should only get a third. But then again, there's no law about it, is there? I should think that if you knew your money was very badly needed, well, you just might say, I want more, I want a bigger share.

You boys have done that. I've heard you say so.

Ben: [*After a pause, laughs*] So you believe he has deliberately held out? For a larger share? [*Leaning forward*] Well, I *don't* believe it. But I *do* believe that's what *you* want. Am I right, Regina?

Regina: Oh, I shouldn't like to be too definite. But I *could* say that I wouldn't like to persuade Horace unless he did get a larger share. I must look after his interests. It seems only natural—

Oscar: And where would the larger share come from?

Regina: I don't know. That's not my business. [*Giggles*] But perhaps it could come off your share, Oscar.

　　　　[**Regina** *and* **Ben** *laugh.*]

Oscar: [*Rises and wheels furiously on both of them as they laugh*] What kind of talk is this?

Ben: I haven't said a thing.

Oscar: [*To* **Regina**] *You* are talking very big tonight.

Regina: [*Stops laughing*] Am I? Well, you should know me well enough to know that I wouldn't be asking for things I didn't think I could get.

Oscar: Listen. I don't believe you can even get Horace to come home, much less get money from him or talk quite so big about what you want.

Regina: Oh, I can get him home.

Oscar: Then why haven't you?

Regina: I thought I should fight his battles for him, before he came home. Horace is a very sick man. And even if *you* don't care how sick he is, I do.

Ben: Stop this foolish squabbling. How can you get him home?

Regina: I will send Alexandra to Baltimore. She will ask him to come home. She will say that she *wants* him to come home, and that I want him to come home.

Birdie: [*Suddenly*] Well, of course she wants him here, but he's sick and maybe he's happy where he is.

Regina: [*Ignores* **Birdie**, *to* **Ben**] You agree that he will come home if she asks him to, if she says that I miss him and want him—

Ben: [*Looks at her, smiles*] I admire you, Regina. And I agree. That's settled now and— (*Starts to rise.*)

Regina: [*Quickly*] But before she brings him home, I want to know what he's going to get.

Ben: What do you want?

Regina: Twice what you offered.

Ben: Well, you won't get it.

Oscar: [*To* **Regina**] I think you've gone crazy.

Regina: I don't want to fight, Ben—

Ben: I don't either. You won't get it. There isn't any chance of that. [*Roguishly*] You're holding us up, and that's not pretty, Regina, not pretty. [*Holds up his hand as he sees she is about to speak*] But we need you, and I don't want to fight. Here's what I'll do: I'll give Horace forty per cent, instead of the thirty-three and a third he really should get. I'll do that, provided he is home and his money is up within two weeks. How's that?

Regina: All right.

Oscar: I've asked before: where is this extra share coming from?

Ben: [*Pleasantly*] From you. From your share.

Oscar: [*Furiously*] From me, is it? That's just fine and dandy. That's my reward. For thirty-five years I've worked my hands to the bone for you. For thirty-five years I've done all the things you didn't want to do. And this is what I—

Ben: [*Turns slowly to look at* **Oscar. Oscar** *breaks off*] My, my. I am being attacked tonight on all sides. First by my sister, then by my brother. And I ain't a man who likes being attacked. I can't believe that God wants the strong to parade their strength, but I don't mind doing it if it's got to be done. [*Leans back in his chair*] You ought to take these things better, Oscar. I've made you money in the past. I'm going to make you more money now. You'll be a very rich man. What's the difference to any of us if a little more goes here, a little less goes there—it's all in the family. And it will stay in the family. I'll never marry. [**Addie** *enters, begins to gather the glasses from the table.* **Oscar** *turns to* **Ben**] So my money will go to Alexandra and Leo. They may even marry some day and— [**Addie** *looks at* **Ben.**]

Birdie: [*Rising*] Marry—Zan and Leo—

Oscar: [*Carefully*] That would make a great difference in my feelings. If they married.

Ben: Yes, that's what I mean. Of course it would make a difference.

Oscar: [*Carefully*] Is that what *you* mean, Regina?

Regina: Oh, it's too far away. We'll talk about it in a few years.

Oscar: I want to talk about it now.

Ben: [*Nods*] Naturally.

Regina: There's a lot of things to consider. They are first cousins, and—

Oscar: That isn't unusual. Our grandmother and grandfather were first cousins.

Regina: [*Giggles*] And look at us.
        [**Ben** *giggles.*]

Oscar: [*Angrily*] You're both being very gay with my money.

Ben: [*Sighs*] These quarrels. I dislike them so. [*Leans forward to* **Regina**] A marriage might be a very wise arrangement, for several reasons. And then, Oscar has given up something for you. You should try to manage something for him.

Regina: I haven't said I was opposed to it. But Leo is a wild boy. There were those times when he took a little money from the bank and—

Oscar: That's all past history—

Regina: Oh, I know. And I know all young men are wild. I'm only mentioning it to show you that there are considerations—

Ben: [*Irritated because she does not understand that he is trying to keep* **Oscar** *quiet*] All right, so there are. But please assure Oscar that you will think about it very seriously.

Regina: [*Smiles, nods*] Very well. I assure Oscar that I will think about it seriously.

Oscar: [*Sharply*] That is not an answer.

Regina: [*Rises*] My, you're in a bad humor and you shall put me in one. I have said all that I am willing to say now. After all, Horace has to give his consent, too.

Oscar: Horace will do what you tell him to.

Regina: Yes, I think he will.

Oscar: And I have your word that you will try to—

Regina: [*Patiently*] Yes, Oscar. You have my word that I will think about it. Now do leave me alone.

        [*There is the sound of the front door being closed.*]

Birdie: I—Alexandra is only seventeen. She—

Regina: [*Calling*] Alexandra? Are you back?

Alexandra: Yes, Mama.

Leo: [*Comes into the room*] Mr. Marshall got off safe and sound. Weren't those fine clothes he had? You can always spot clothes made in a good place. Looks like maybe they were done in England. Lots of men in the North send all the way to England for their stuff.

Ben: [*To* **Leo**] Were you careful driving the horses?

Leo: Oh, yes, sir. I was. [**Alexandra** *has come in on* **Ben**'s *question, hears the answer, looks angrily at* **Leo**].

Alexandra: It's a lovely night. You should have come, Aunt Birdie.

Regina: Were you gracious to Mr. Marshall?

Alexandra: I think so, Mama. I liked him.

Regina: Good. And now I have great news for you. You are going to Baltimore in the morning to bring your father home.

Alexandra: [*Gasps, then delighted*] Me? Papa said I should come? That must mean— [*Turns to* **Addie**] Addie, he must be well. Think of it, he'll be back home again. We'll bring him home.

Regina: You are going alone, Alexandra.

Addie: [**Alexandra** *has turned in surprise*] Going alone? Going by herself? A child that age! Mr. Horace ain't going to like Zan traipsing up there by herself.

Regina: [*Sharply*] Go upstairs and lay out Alexandra's things.

Addie: He'd expect me to be along—

Regina: I'll be up in a few minutes to tell you what to pack. [**Addie** *slowly begins to climb the steps. To* **Alexandra**] I should think you'd like going alone. At your age it certainly would have delighted me. You're a strange girl, Alexandra. Addie has babied you so much.

Alexandra: I only thought it would be more fun if Addie and I went together.

Birdie: [*Timidly*] Maybe I could go with her, Regina. I'd really like to.

Regina: She is going alone. She is getting old enough to take some responsibilities.

Oscar: She'd better learn now. She's almost old enough to get married. [*Jovially, to* **Leo**, *slapping him on shoulder*] Eh, son?

Leo: Huh?

Oscar: [*Annoyed with* **Leo** *for not understanding*] Old enough to get married, you're thinking, eh?

Leo: Oh, yes, sir. [*Feebly*] Lots of girls get married at Zan's age. Look at Mary Prester and Johanna and—

Regina: Well, she's not getting married tomorrow. But she is going to Baltimore tomorrow, so let's talk about that. [*To* **Alexandra**] You'll be glad to have Papa home again.

Alexandra: I wanted to go before, Mama. You remember that. But you said *you* couldn't go, and that *I* couldn't go alone.

Regina: I've changed my mind. [*Too casually*] You're to tell Papa how much you missed him, and that he must come home now—for your sake. Tell him that you *need* him home.

Alexandra: Need him home? I don't understand.

Regina: There is nothing for you to understand. You are simply to say what I have told you.

Birdie: [*Rises*]— He may be too sick. She couldn't do that—

Alexandra: Yes. He may be too sick to travel. I couldn't make him think he had to come for me, if he is too sick to—

Regina: [*Looks at her, sharply, challengingly*] You *couldn't* do what I tell you to do, Alexandra?

Alexandra: [*Quietly*] No. I couldn't. If I thought it would hurt him.

Regina: [*After a second's silence, smiles pleasantly*] But you are doing this for Papa's own good. [*Takes* **Alexandra**'s *hand*] You must let me be the judge of his condition. It's the best possible cure for him to come home and be taken care of here. He mustn't stay there any longer and listen to those alarmist doctors. You are doing this entirely for his sake. Tell your papa that I want him to come home, that I miss him very much.

Alexandra: [*Slowly*] Yes, Mama.

Regina: [*To the others. Rises*] I must go and start getting Alexandra ready now. Why don't you all go home?

Ben: [*Rises*] I'll attend to the railroad ticket. One of the boys will bring it over. Good night, everybody. Have a nice trip, Alexandra. The food on the train is very good. The celery is so crisp. Have a good time and act like a little lady. [*Exits*]

Regina: Good night, Ben. Good night, Oscar— [*Playfully*] Don't be so glum, Oscar. It makes you look as if you had chronic indigestion.

Birdie: Good night, Regina.

Regina: Good night, Birdie. [*Exits upstairs.*]

Oscar: [*Starts for hall*] Come along.

Leo: [*To* **Alexandra**] Imagine your not wanting to go! What a little fool you are. Wish it were me. What I could do in a place like Baltimore!

Alexandra: [*Angrily, looking away from him*] Mind your business. I can guess the kind of things *you* could do.

Leo: [*Laughs*] Oh, no, you couldn't. [*He exits.*]

Regina: [*Calling from the top of the stairs*] Come on, Alexandra.

Birdie: [*Quickly, softly*] Zan.

Alexandra: I don't understand about my going, Aunt Birdie. [*Shrugs*] But anyway, Papa will be home again. [*Pats* **Birdie**'s *arm*] Don't worry about me. I can take care of myself. Really I can.

Birdie: [*Shakes her head, softly*] That's not what I'm worried about. Zan—

Alexandra: [*Comes close to her*] What's the matter?

Birdie: It's about Leo—

Alexandra: [*Whispering*] He beat the horses. That's why we were late getting back. We had to wait until they cooled off. He always beats the horses as if—

Birdie: [*Whispering frantically, holding* **Alexandra**'s *hands*] He's my son. My own son. But you are more to me—more to me than my own child. I love you more than anybody else—

Alexandra: Don't worry about the horses. I'm sorry I told you.

Birdie: [*Her voice rising*] I am not worrying about the horses. I am worrying about *you*. You are *not* going to marry Leo. I am not going to let them do that to you—

Alexandra: Marry? To Leo? [*Laughs*] I wouldn't marry, Aunt Birdie. I've never even thought about it—

Birdie: But they have thought about it. [*Wildly*] Zan, I couldn't stand to think about such a thing. You and—

[**Oscar** *has come into the doorway on* **Alexandra**'s *speech. He is standing quietly, listening.*]

Alexandra: [*Laughs*] But I'm not going to marry. And I'm certainly not going to marry Leo.

Birdie: Don't you understand? They'll make you. They'll make you—

Alexandra: [*Takes* **Birdie**'s *hands, quietly, firmly*] That's foolish, Aunt Birdie. I'm grown now. Nobody can make me do anything.

Birdie: I just couldn't stand—

Oscar: [*Sharply*] Birdie. [**Birdie** *looks up, draws quickly away from* **Alexandra**. *She stands rigid, frightened. Quietly*] Birdie, get your hat and coat.

Addie: [*Calls from upstairs*] Come on, baby. Your mama's waiting for you, and she ain't nobody to keep waiting.

Alexandra: All right. [*Then softly, embracing* **Birdie**] Good night, Aunt Birdie. [*As she passes* **Oscar**] Good night, Uncle Oscar. [**Birdie** *begins to move slowly towards the door as* **Alexandra** *climbs the stairs.* **Alexandra** *is almost out of view when* **Birdie** *reaches* **Oscar** *in the doorway. As* **Birdie** *quickly attempts to pass him, he slaps her hard, across the face.* **Birdie** *cries out, puts her hand to her face. On the cry,* **Alexandra** *turns, begins to run down the stairs*] Aunt Birdie! What happened? What happened? I—

Birdie: [*Softly, without turning*] Nothing, darling. Nothing happened. [*Quickly, as if anxious to keep* **Alexandra** *from coming close*] Now go to bed. [**Oscar** *exits*] Nothing happened. [*Turns to* **Alexandra** *who is holding her hand*] I only—I only twisted my ankle. [*She goes out.* **Alexandra** *stands on the stairs looking after her as if she were puzzled and frightened.*]

CURTAIN

ACT II

SCENE: Same as Act I. A week later, morning.

AT RISE: The light comes from the open shutter of the right window; the other shutters are tightly closed. **Addie** is standing at the window, looking out. Near the dining-room doors are brooms, mops, rags, etc. After a second, **Oscar** comes into the entrance hall, looks in the room, shivers, decides not to take his hat and coat off, comes into the room. At the sound of the door, **Addie** turns to see who has come in.

Addie: [*Without interest*] Oh, it's you, Mr. Oscar.

Oscar: What is this? It's not night. What's the matter here? [*Shivers*] Fine thing at this time of the morning. Blinds all closed. [**Addie** *begins to open shutters.*] Where's Miss Regina? It's cold in here.

Addie: Miss Regina ain't down yet.

Oscar: She had any word?

Addie: [*Wearily*] No, sir.

Oscar: Wouldn't you think a girl that age could get on a train at one place and have sense enough to get off at another?

Addie: Something must have happened. If Zan say she was coming last night, she's coming last night. Unless something happened. Sure fire disgrace to let a baby like that go all that way alone to bring home a sick man with-out—

Oscar: You do a lot of judging around here, Addie, eh? Judging of your white folks, I mean.

Addie: [*Looks at him, sighs*] I'm tired. I been up all night watching for them.

Regina: [*Speaking from the upstairs hall*] Who's downstairs, Addie? [*She appears in a dressing gown, peers down from the landing.* **Addie** *picks up broom, dustpan and brush and exits*] Oh, it's you, Oscar. What are you doing here so early? I haven't been down yet. I'm not finished dressing.

Oscar: [*Speaking up to her*] You had any word from them?

Regina: No.

Oscar: Then something certainly has happened. People don't just say they are arriving on Thursday night, and they haven't come by Friday morning.

Regina: Oh, nothing has happened. Alexandra just hasn't got sense enough to send a message.

Oscar: If nothing's happened, then why aren't they here?

Regina: You asked me that ten times last night. My, you do fret so, Oscar. Anything might have happened. They may have missed connections in Atlanta, the train may have been delayed—oh, a hundred things could have kept them.

Oscar: Where's Ben?

Regina: [*As she disappears upstairs*] Where should he be? At home, probably. Really, Oscar, I don't tuck him in his bed and I don't take him out of it. Have some coffee and don't worry so much.

Oscar: Have some coffee? There isn't any cof-fee. [*Looks at his watch, shakes his head. After a second*

Cal *enters with a large silver tray, coffee urn, small cups, newspaper*] Oh, there you are. Is everything in this fancy house always late?

Cal: [*Looks at him surprised*] You ain't out shooting this morning, Mr. Oscar?

Oscar: First day I missed since I had my head cold. First day I missed in eight years.

Cal: Yes, sir. I bet you. Simon he say you had a mighty good day yesterday morning. That's what Simon say. [*Brings* **Oscar** *coffee and newspaper*]

Oscar: Pretty good, pretty good.

Cal: [*Laughs, slyly*] Bet you got enough bobwhite and squirrel to give every nigger in town a Jesus-party. Most of 'em ain't had no meat since the cotton picking was over. Bet they'd give anything for a little piece of that meat—

Oscar: [*Turns his head to look at* **Cal**] Cal, if I catch a nigger in this town going shooting, you know what's going to happen.

          [**Leo** *enters.*]

Cal: [*Hastily*] Yes, sir, Mr. Oscar. I didn't say nothing about nothing. It was Simon who told me and— Morning, Mr. Leo. You gentlemen having your breakfast with us here?

Leo: The boys in the bank don't know a thing. They haven't had any message.

          [**Cal** *waits for an answer, gets none, shrugs, moves to door, exits.*]

Oscar: [*Peers at* **Leo**] What you doing here, son?

Leo: You told me to find out if the boys at the bank had any message from Uncle Horace or Zan—

Oscar: I told you if they had a message to bring it here. I told you that if they didn't have a message to stay at the bank and do your work.

Leo: Oh, I guess I misunderstood.

Oscar: You didn't misunderstand. You just were looking for any excuse to take an hour off. [**Leo** *pours a cup of coffee*] You got to stop that kind of thing. You got to start settling down. You going to be a married man one of these days.

Leo: Yes, sir.

Oscar: You also got to stop with that woman in Mobile. [*As* **Leo** *is about to speak*] You're young and I haven't got no objections to outside women. That is, I haven't got no objections so long as they don't interfere with serious things. Outside women are all right in their place, but *now* isn't their place. You got to realize that.

Leo: [*Nods*] Yes, sir. I'll tell her. She'll act all right about it.

Oscar: Also, you got to start working harder at the bank. You got to convince your Uncle Horace you going to make a fit husband for Alexandra.

Leo: What do you think has happened to them? Supposed to be here last night—[*Laughs*] Bet you Uncle Ben's mighty worried. Seventy-five thousand dollars worried.

Oscar: [*Smiles happily*] Ought to be worried. Damn well ought to be. First he don't answer the letters, then he don't come home— [*Giggles.*]

Leo: What will happen if Uncle Horace don't come home or don't—

Oscar: Or don't put up the money? Oh, we'll get it from outside. Easy enough.

Leo: [*Surprised*] But *you* don't want outsiders.

Oscar: What do I care who gets my share? I been shaved already. Serve Ben right if he had to give away some of his.

Leo: Damn shame what they did to you.

Oscar: [*Looking up the stairs*] Don't talk so loud. Don't you worry. When I die, you'll have as much as the rest. You might have yours *and* Alexandra's. I'm not so easily licked.

Leo: I wasn't thinking of myself, Papa—

Oscar: Well, you should be, you should be. It's every man's duty to think of himself.

Leo: You think Uncle Horace don't want to go in on this?

Oscar: [*Giggles*] That's my hunch. He hasn't showed any signs of loving it yet.

Leo: [*Laughs*] But he hasn't listened to Aunt Regina yet, either. Oh, he'll go along. It's too good a thing. Why wouldn't he want to? He's got plenty and plenty to invest with. He don't even have to sell anything. Eighty-eight thousand worth of Union Pacific bonds sitting right in his safe deposit box. All he's got to do is open the box.

Oscar: [*After a pause. Looks at his watch*] Mighty late breakfast in this fancy house. Yes, he's

had those bonds for fifteen years. Bought them when they were low and just locked them up.

Leo: Yeah. Just has to open the box and take them out. That's all. Easy as easy can be. [*Laughs*] The things in that box! There's all those bonds, looking mighty fine. [**Oscar** *slowly puts down his newspaper and turns to* **Leo**] Then right next to them is a baby shoe of Zan's and a cheap old cameo on a string, and, *and*—nobody'd believe this—a piece of an old violin. Not even a whole violin. Just a piece of an old thing, a piece of a violin.

Oscar: [*Very softly, as if he were trying to control his voice*] A piece of a violin! What do you think of that!

Leo: Yes, sirree. A lot of other crazy things, too. A poem, I guess it is, signed with his mother's name, and two old schoolbooks with notes and— [**Leo** *catches* **Oscar**'*s look. His voice trails off. He turns his head away.*]

Oscar: [*Very softly*] How do you know what's in the box, son?

Leo: [*Stops, draws back, frightened, realizing what he has said*] Oh, well. Well, er. Well, one of the boys, sir. It was one of the boys at the bank. He took old Manders' keys. It was Joe Horns. He just up and took Manders' keys and, and—well, took the box out. [*Quickly*] Then they all asked me if I wanted to see, too. So I looked a little, I guess, but then I made them close up the box quick and I told them never—

Oscar: [*Looks at him*] Joe Horns, you say? He opened it?

Leo: Yes, sir, yes, he did. My word of honor. [*Very nervously looking away*] I suppose that don't excuse *me* for looking— [*Looking at* **Oscar**] but I did make him close it up and put the keys back in Manders' drawer—

Oscar: [*Leans forward, very softly*] Tell me the truth, Leo. I am not going to be angry with you. Did you open the box yourself?

Leo: *No, sir, I didn't.* I told you I didn't. No, I—

Oscar: [*Irritated, patient*] I am *not* going to be angry with you. [*Watching* **Leo** *carefully*] Sometimes a young fellow deserves credit for looking round him to see what's going on. Sometimes that's a good sign in a fellow your age.

[**Oscar** rises] Many great men have made their fortune with their eyes. Did you open the box?

Leo: [Very puzzled] No. I—

Oscar: [Moves to **Leo**] Did you open the box? It may have been—well, it may have been a good thing if you had.

Leo: [After a long pause] I opened it.

Oscar: [Quickly] Is that the truth? [**Leo** nods] Does anybody else know that you opened it? Come, Leo, don't be afraid of speaking the truth to me.

Leo: No. Nobody knew. Nobody was in the bank when I did it. But—

Oscar: Did your Uncle Horace ever know you opened it?

Leo: [Shakes his head] He only looks in it once every six months when he cuts the coupons, and sometimes Manders even does that for him. Uncle Horace don't even have the keys. Manders keeps them for him. Imagine not looking at all that. You can bet if I had the bonds, I'd watch 'em like—

Oscar: If you had them. [**Leo** watches him] If you had them. Then you could have a share in the mill, you and me. A fine, big share, too. [Pauses, shrugs] Well, a man can't be shot for wanting to see his son get on in the world, can he, boy?

Leo: [Looks up, begins to understand] No, he can't. Natural enough. [Laughs] But I haven't got the bonds and Uncle Horace has. And now he can just sit back and wait to be a millionaire.

Oscar: [Innocently] You think your Uncle Horace likes you well enough to lend you the bonds if he decides not to use them himself?

Leo: Papa, it must be that you haven't had your breakfast! [Laughs loudly] Lend me the bonds! My God—

Oscar: [Disappointed] No, I suppose not. Just a fancy of mine. A loan for three months, maybe four, easy enough for us to pay it back then. Anyway, this is only April— [Slowly counting the months on his fingers] and if he doesn't look at them until Fall, he wouldn't even miss them out of the box.

Leo: That's it. He wouldn't even miss them. Ah, well—

Oscar: No, sir. Wouldn't even miss them. How could he miss them if he never looks at them? [Sighs as **Leo** stares at him] Well, here we are sitting around waiting for him to come home and invest his money in something he hasn't lifted his hand to get. But I can't help thinking he's acting strange. You laugh when I say he could lend you the bonds if he's not going to use them himself. But would it hurt him?

Leo: [Slowly looking at **Oscar**] No. No, it wouldn't.

Oscar: People ought to help other people. But that's not always the way it happens. [**Ben** enters, hangs his coat and hat in hall. Very carefully] And so sometimes you got to think of yourself. [As **Leo** stares at him, **Ben** appears in the doorway] Morning, Ben.

Ben: [Coming in, carrying his newspaper] Fine sunny morning. Any news from the runaways?

Regina: [On the staircase] There's no news or you would have heard it. Quite a convention so early in the morning, aren't you all? [Goes to coffee urn.]

Oscar: You rising mighty late these days. Is that the way they do things in Chicago society?

Ben: [Looking at his paper] Old Carter died up in Senateville. Eighty-one is a good time for us all, eh? What do you think has really happened to Horace, Regina?

Regina: Nothing.

Ben: [Too casually] You don't think maybe he never started from Baltimore and never intends to start?

Regina: [Irritated] Of course they've started. Didn't I have a letter from Alexandra? What is so strange about people arriving late? He has that cousin in Savannah he's so fond of. He may have stopped to see him. They'll be along today some time, very flattered that you and Oscar are so worried about them.

Ben: I'm a natural worrier. Especially when I am getting ready to close a business deal and one of my partners remains silent and invisible.

Regina: [Laughs] Oh, is that it? I thought you were worried about Horace's health.

Oscar: Oh, that too. Who could help but

worry? I'm worried. This is the first day I haven't shot since my head cold.

Regina: [*Starts towards dining room*] Then you haven't had your breakfast. Come along. [**Oscar** and **Leo** *follow her.*]

Ben: Regina. [*She turns at dining-room door*] That cousin of Horace's has been dead for years and, in any case, the train does not go through Savannah.

Regina: [*Laughs, continues into dining room, seats herself*] Did he die? You're always remembering about people dying. [**Ben** *rises*] Now I intend to eat my breakfast in peace, and read my newspaper.

Ben: [*Goes towards dining room as he talks*] This is second breakfast for me. My first was bad. Celia ain't the cook she used to be. Too old to have taste any more. If she hadn't belonged to Mama, I'd send her off to the country.

[**Oscar** and **Leo** *start to eat.* **Ben** *seats himself.*]

Leo: Uncle Horace will have some tales to tell, I bet. Baltimore is a lively town.

Regina [*To* **Cal**] The grits isn't hot enough. Take it back.

Cal: Oh, yes'm. [*Calling into kitchen as he exits*] Grits didn't hold the heat. Grits didn't hold the heat.

Leo: When I was at school three of the boys and myself took a train once and went over to Baltimore. It was so big we thought we were in Europe. I was just a kid then—

Regina: I find it very pleasant [**Addie** *enters*] to have breakfast alone. I hate chattering before I've had something hot. [**Cal** *closes the dining-room doors*] Do be still, Leo.

[**Addie** *comes into the room, begins gathering up the cups, carries them to the large tray. Outside there are the sounds of voices. Quickly* **Addie** *runs into the hall. A few seconds later she appears again in the doorway, her arm around the shoulders of* **Horace Giddens,** *supporting him.* **Horace** *is a tall man of about forty-five. He has been good looking, but now his face is tired and ill. He walks stiffly, as if it were an enormous effort, and carefully, as if he were unsure of his balance.* **Addie** *takes off his overcoat and hangs it on the hall tree. She then helps him to a chair.*]

Horace: How are you, Addie? How have you been?

Addie: I'm all right, Mr. Horace. I've just been worried about you.

[**Alexandra** *enters. She is flushed and excited, her hat awry, her face dirty. Her arms are full of packages, but she comes quickly to* **Addie.**]

Alexandra: Now don't tell me how worried you were. We couldn't help it and there was no way to send a message.

Addie: [*Begins to take packages from* **Alexandra**] Yes, sir, I was mighty worried.

Alexandra: We had to stop in Mobile over night. Papa— [*Looks at him*] Papa didn't feel well. The trip was too much for him, and I made him stop and rest— [*As* **Addie** *takes the last package*] No, don't take that. That's father's medicine. I'll hold it. It mustn't break. Now, about the stuff outside. Papa must have his wheel chair. I'll get that and the valises—

Addie: [*Very happy, holding* **Alexandra**'*s arms*] Since when you got to carry your own valises? Since when I ain't old enough to hold a bottle of medicine? [**Horace** *coughs*] You feel all right, Mr. Horace?

Horace: [*Nods*] Glad to be sitting down.

Alexandra: [*Opening package of medicine*] He doesn't feel all right. [**Addie** *looks at her, then at* **Horace**] He just says that. The trip was very hard on him, and now he must go right to bed.

Addie:]*Looking at him carefully*] Them fancy doctors, they give you help?

Horace: They did their best.

Alexandra: [*Has become conscious of the voices in the dining room*] I bet Mama was worried. I better tell her we're here now. [*She starts for door.*]

Horace: Zan. [*She stops*] Not for a minute, dear.

Alexandra: Oh, Papa, you feel bad again. I knew you did. Do you want your medicine?

Horace: No, I don't feel that way. I'm just tired, darling. Let me rest a little.

Alexandra: Yes, Mama will be mad if I don't tell her we're here.

Addie: They're all in there eating breakfast.

Alexandra: Oh, are they all here? Why do they *always* have to be here? I was hoping Papa wouldn't have to see anybody, that it would be nice for him and quiet.

Addie: Then let your papa rest for a minute.

Horace: Addie, I bet your coffee's as good as ever. They don't have such good coffee up

North. [*Looks at the urn*] Is it as good, Addie? [**Addie** *starts for coffee urn.*]

Alexandra: No. Dr. Reeves said not much coffee. Just now and then. I'm the nurse now, Addie.

Addie: You'd be a better one if you didn't look so dirty. Now go and take a bath, Miss Grown-up. Change your linens, get out a fresh dress and give your hair a good brushing—go on—

Alexandra: Will you be all right, Papa?

Addie: Go on.

Alexandra: [*On stairs, talks as she goes up*] The pills Papa must take once every four hours. And the bottle only when—only if he feels very bad. Now don't move until I come back and don't talk much and remember about his medicine, Addie—

Addie: Ring for Belle and have her help you and then I'll make you a fresh breakfast.

Alexandra: [*As she disappears*] How's Aunt Birdie? Is she here?

Addie: It ain't right for you to have coffee? It will hurt you?

Horace: [*Slowly*] Nothing can make much difference now. Get me a cup, Addie. [*She looks at him, crosses to urn, pours a cup*] Funny. They can't make coffee up North. [**Addie** *brings him a cup*] They don't like red pepper, either. [*He takes the cup and gulps it greedily*] God, that's good. You remember how I used to drink it? Ten, twelve cups a day. So strong it had to stain the cup. [*Then slowly*] Addie, before I see anybody else, I want to know why Zan came to fetch me home. She's tried to tell me, but she doesn't seem to know herself.

Addie: [*Turns away*] I don't know. All I know is big things are going on. Everybody going to be high-tone rich. Big rich. You too. All because smoke's going to start out of a building that ain't even up yet.

Horace: I've heard about it.

Addie: And, er— [*Hesitates—steps to him*] And— well, Zan, she going to marry Mr. Leo in a little while.

Horace: [*Looks at her, then very slowly*] What are you talking about?

Addie: That's right. That's the talk, God help us.

Horace: [*Angrily*] What's the talk?

Addie: I'm telling you. There's going to be a wedding— [*Angrily turns away*] Over my dead body there is.

Horace: [*After a second, quietly*] Go and tell them I'm home.

Addie: [*Hesitates*]— Now you ain't to get excited. You're to be in your bed—

Horace: Go on, Addie. Go and say I'm back. [**Addie** *opens dining-room doors. He rises with difficulty, stands stiff, as if he were in pain, facing the dining room.*]

Addie: Miss Regina. They're home. They got here—

Regina: Horace! [**Regina** *quickly rises, runs into the room. Warmly*] Horace! You've finally arrived. [*As she kisses him, the others come forward, all talking together.*]

Ben: [*In doorway, carrying a napkin*] Well, sir, you had us all mighty worried. [*He steps forward. They shake hands.* **Addie** *exits.*]

Oscar: You're a sight for sore eyes.

Horace: Hello, Ben.

[**Leo** *enters, eating a biscuit.*]

Oscar: And how you feel? Tip-top, I bet, because that's the way you're looking.

Horace: [*Coldly, irritated with* **Oscar**'s *lie*] Hello, Oscar. Hello, Leo, how are you?

Leo: [*Shaking hands*] I'm fine, sir. But a lot better now that you're back.

Regina: Now sit down. What did happen to you and where's Alexandra? I am so excited about seeing you that I almost forgot about her.

Horace: I didn't feel good, a little weak, I guess, and we stopped over night to rest. Zan's upstairs washing off the train dirt.

Regina: Oh, I am so sorry the trip was hard on you. I didn't think that—

Horace: Well, it's just as if I had never been away. All of you here—

Ben: Waiting to welcome you home. [**Birdie** *bursts in. She is wearing a flannel kimono and her face is flushed and excited.*]

Birdie: [*Runs to him, kisses him*] Horace!

Horace: [*Warmly pressing her arm*] I was just wondering where you were, Birdie.

Birdie: [*Excited*] Oh, I would have been here. I didn't know you were back until Simon said he saw the buggy. [*She draws back to look at him.*

Her face sobers] Oh, you don't look well, Horace. No, you don't.

Regina: [*Laughs*] Birdie, what a thing to say—

Horace: [*Looking at* **Oscar**] Oscar thinks I look very well.

Oscar: [*Annoyed. Turns on* **Leo**] Don't stand there holding that biscuit in your hand.

Leo: Oh, well. I'll just finish my breakfast, Uncle Horace, and then I'll give you all the news about the bank— [*He exits into the dining room.*]

Oscar: And what is that costume you have on?

Birdie: [*Looking at* **Horace**] Now that you're home, you'll feel better. Plenty of good rest and we'll take such fine care of you. [*Stops*] But where is Zan? I missed her so much.

Oscar: I asked you what is that strange costume you're parading around in?

Birdie: [*Nervously, backing towards stairs*] Me? Oh! It's my wrapper. I was so excited about Horace I just rushed out of the house—

Oscar: Did you come across the square dressed that way? My dear Birdie, I—

Horace: [*To* **Regina,** *wearily*] Yes, it's just like old times.

Regina: [*Quickly to* **Oscar**] Now, no fights. This is a holiday.

Birdie: [*Runs quickly up the stairs*] Zan! Zannie!

Oscar: Birdie! [*She stops.*]

Birdie: Oh. Tell Zan I'll be back in a little while. [*Whispers*] Sorry, Oscar. [*Exits.*]

Regina: [*To* **Oscar** *and* **Ben**] Why don't you go finish your breakfast and let Horace rest for a minute?

Ben: [*Crossing to dining room with* **Oscar**] Never leave a meal unfinished. There are too many poor people who need the food. Mighty glad to see you home, Horace. Fine to have you back. Fine to have you back.

Oscar: [*To* **Leo** *as* **Ben** *closes dining-room doors*] Your mother has gone crazy. Running around the streets like a woman—

[*The moment* **Regina** *and* **Horace** *are alone, they become awkward and self-conscious.*]

Regina: [*Laughs awkwardly*] Well. Here we are. It's been a long time. [**Horace** *smiles*] Five months. You know, Horace, I wanted to come and be with you in the hospital, but I didn't know where my duty was. Here, or with you.

But you know how much I *wanted* to come.

Horace: That's kind of you, Regina. There was no need to come.

Regina: Oh, but there was. Five months lying there all by yourself, no kinfolks, no friends. Don't try to tell me you didn't have a bad time of it.

Horace: I didn't have a bad time. [*As she shakes her head, he becomes insistent*] No, I didn't, Regina. Oh, at first when I—when I heard the news about myself—but after I got used to that, I liked it there.

Regina: You *liked* it? [*Coldly*] Isn't that strange. You liked it so well you didn't want to come home?

Horace: That's not the way to put it. [*Then, kindly, as he sees her turn her head away*] But there I was and I got kind of used to it, kind of to like lying there and thinking. [*Smiles*] I never had much time to think before. And time's become valuable to me.

Regina: It sounds almost like a holiday.

Horace: [*Laughs*] It was, sort of. The first holiday I've had since I was a little kid.

Regina: And here I was thinking you were in pain and—

Horace: [*Quietly*] I was in pain.

Regina: And instead you were having a holiday! A holiday of thinking. Couldn't you have done that here?

Horace: I wanted to do it before I came here. I was thinking about us.

Regina: About us? About you and me? Thinking about you and me after all these years. [*Unpleasantly*] You shall tell me everything you thought—some day.

Horace: [*There is silence for a minute*] Regina. [*She turns to him*] Why did you send Zan to Baltimore?

Regina: Why? Because I wanted you home. You can't make anything suspicious out of that, can you?

Horace: I didn't mean to make anything suspicious about it. [*Hesitantly, taking her hand*] Zan said you wanted me to come home. I was so pleased at that and touched, it made me feel good.

Regina: [*Taking away her hand, turns*] Touched that I should want you home?

Horace: [*Sighs*] I'm saying all the wrong things as usual. Let's try to get along better. There isn't so much more time. Regina, what's all this crazy talk I've been hearing about Zan and Leo? Zan and Leo marrying?

Regina: [*Turning to him, sharply*] Who gossips so much around here?

Horace: [*Shocked*] Regina!

Regina: [*Annoyed, anxious to quiet him*] It's some foolishness that Oscar thought up. I'll explain later. I have no intention of allowing any such arrangement. It was simply a way of keeping Oscar quiet in all this business I've been writing you about—

Horace: [*Carefully*] What has Zan to do with any business of Oscar's? Whatever it is, you had better put it out of Oscar's head immediately. You know what I think of Leo.

Regina: But there's no need to talk about it now.

Horace: There is no need to talk about it ever. Not as long as I live. [**Horace** *stops, slowly turns to look at her*] As long as I live. I've been in a hospital for five months. Yet since I've been here you have not once asked me about—about my health. [*Then gently*] Well, I suppose they've written you. I can't live very long.

Regina: [*Coldly*] I've never understood why people have to talk about this kind of thing.

Horace: [*There is a silence. Then he looks up at her, his face cold*] You misunderstand. I don't intend to gossip about my sickness. I thought it was only fair to tell you. I was not asking for your sympathy.

Regina: [*Sharply, turns to him*] What do the doctors think caused your bad heart?

Horace: What do you mean?

Regina: They didn't think it possible, did they, that your fancy women may have—

Horace: [*Smiles unpleasantly*] Caused my heart to be bad? I don't think that's the best scientific theory. You don't catch heart trouble in bed.

Regina: [*Angrily*] I didn't think you did. I only thought you might catch a bad conscience—in bed, as you say.

Horace: I didn't tell them about my bad conscience. Or about my fancy women. Nor did I tell them that my wife has not wanted me in bed with her for— [*Sharply*] How long is it, Regina? [**Regina** *turns to him*] Ten years? Did you bring me home for this, to make me feel guilty again? That means you want something. But you'll not make me feel guilty any more. My "thinking" has made a difference.

Regina: I see that it has. [*She looks towards dining-room door. Then comes to him, her manner warm and friendly*] It's foolish for us to fight this way. I didn't mean to be unpleasant. I was stupid.

Horace: [*Wearily*] God knows I didn't either. I came home wanting so much not to fight, and then all of a sudden there we were. I got hurt and—

Regina: [*Hastily*] It's all my fault. I didn't ask about—about your illness because I didn't want to remind you of it. Anyway I never believe doctors when they talk about— [*Brightly*] when they talk like that.

Horace: [*Not looking at her*] Well, we'll try our best with each other. [*He rises.*]

Regina: [*Quickly*] I'll try. Honestly, I will. Horace, Horace, I know you're tired but, but—couldn't you stay down here a few minutes longer? I want Ben to tell you something.

Horace: Tomorrow.

Regina: I'd like to now. It's very important to me. It's very important to all of us. [*Gaily, as she moves toward dining room*] Important to your beloved daughter. She'll be a very great heiress—

Horace: Will she? That's nice.

Regina: [*Opens doors*] Ben, are you finished breakfast?

Horace: Is this the mill business I've had so many letters about?

Regina: [*To* **Ben**] Horace would like to talk to you now.

Horace: Horace would not like to talk to you now. I am very tired, Regina—

Regina: [*Comes to him*] Please. You've said we'll try our best with each other. I'll try. Really, I will. Please do this for me now. You will see what I've done while you've been away. How I watched your interests. [*Laughs gaily*] And I've done very well too. But things can't be delayed any longer. Everything must be settled this week— [**Horace** *sits down.* **Ben** *enters.* **Oscar** *has stayed in the dining room, his head turned to watch them.* **Leo** *is pretending to read the newspaper*] Now you must tell Horace all about it. Only be quick because he is very tired and must go to bed. [**Horace** *is looking up at her. His face hardens as she speaks*] But I think your news will be better for him than all the medicine in the world.

Ben: [*Looking at* **Horace**] It could wait. Horace may not feel like talking today.

Regina: What an old faker you are! You know it can't wait. You know it must be finished this week. You've been just as anxious for Horace to get here as I've been.

Ben: [*Very jovial*] I suppose I have been. And why not? Horace has done Hubbard Sons many a good turn. Why shouldn't I be anxious to help him now?

Regina: [*Laughs*] Help him! Help him when you need him, that's what you mean.

Ben: What a woman you married, Horace. [*Laughs awkwardly when* **Horace** *does not answer*] Well, then I'll make it quick. You know what I've been telling you for years. How I've always said that every one of us little Southern business men had great things— [*Extends his arm*]—right beyond our finger tips. It's been my dream: my dream to make those fingers grow longer. I'm a lucky man, Horace, a lucky man. To dream and to live to get what you've dreamed of. That's *my* idea of a lucky man. [*Looks at his fingers as his arm drops slowly*] For thirty years I've cried bring the cotton mills to the cotton. [**Horace** *opens medicine bottle*] Well, finally I got up nerve to go to Marshall Company in Chicago.

Horace: I know all this. [*He takes the medicine.* **Regina** *rises, steps to him.*]

Ben: Can I get you something?

Horace: Some water please.

Regina: [*Turns quickly*] Oh, I'm sorry. Let me. [*Brings him a glass of water. He drinks as they wait in silence*] You feel all right now?

Horace: Yes. You wrote me. I know all that.

[**Oscar** *enters from dining room.*]

Regina: [*Triumphantly*] But you don't know that in the last few days Ben has agreed to give us—you, I mean—a much larger share.

Horace: Really? That's very generous of him.

Ben: [*Laughs*] It wasn't so generous of me. It was smart of Regina.

Regina: [*As if she were signaling* **Horace**] I ex-plained to Ben that perhaps you hadn't answered his letters because you didn't think he was offering you enough, and that the time was getting short and you could guess how much he needed you—

Horace: [*Smiles at her, nods*] And I could guess that he wants to keep control in the family?

Regina: [*To* **Ben,** *triumphantly*] Exactly. [*To* **Horace**] So I did a little bargaining for you and convinced my brothers they weren't the only Hubbards who had a business sense.

Horace: Did you have to convince them of that? How little people know about each other! [*Laughs*] But you'll know better about Regina next time, eh, Ben? [**Ben, Regina, Horace** *laugh together.* **Oscar**'s *face is angry*] Now let's see. We're getting a bigger share. [*Looking at* **Oscar**] Who's getting less?

Ben: Oscar.

Horace: Well, Oscar, you've grown very unselfish. What's happened to you?

[**Leo** *enters from dining room.*]

Ben: [*Quickly, before* **Oscar** *can answer*] Oscar doesn't mind. Not worth fighting about now, eh, Oscar?

Oscar: [*Angrily*] I'll get mine in the end. You can be sure of that. I've got my son's future to think about.

Horace: [*Sharply*] Leo? Oh, I see. [*Puts his head back, laughs.* **Regina** *looks at him nervously*] I am beginning to see. Everybody will get theirs.

Ben: I knew you'd see it. Seventy-five thousand, and that seventy-five thousand will make you a million.

Regina: [*Steps to table, leaning forward*] It will, Horace, it will.

Horace: I believe you. [*After a second*] Now I can understand Oscar's self-sacrifice, but what did you have to promise Marshall Company besides the money you're putting up?

Ben: They wouldn't take promises. They wanted guarantees.

Horace: Of what?

Ben: [*Nods*] Water power. Free and plenty of it.

Horace: You got them that, of course.

Ben: Cheap. You'd think the Governor of a great state would make his price a little higher. From pride, you know. [**Horace** *smiles.*

Ben *smiles*] Cheap wages. "What do you mean by cheap wages?" I say to Marshall. "Less than Massachusetts," he says to me, "and that averages eight a week." "Eight a week! By God," I tell him, "I'd work for eight a week myself." Why, there ain't a mountain white or a town nigger but wouldn't give his right arm for three silver dollars every week, eh, Horace?

Horace: Sure. And they'll take less than that when you get around to playing them off against each other. You can save a little money that way, Ben. [*Angrily*] And make them hate each other just a little more than they do now.

Regina: What's all this about?

Ben: [*Laughs*] There'll be no trouble from anybody, white or black. Marshall said that to me. "What about strikes? That's all we've had in Massachusetts for the last three years." I say to him, "What's a strike? I never heard of one. Come South, Marshall. We got good folks and we don't stand for any fancy fooling."

Horace: You're right. [*Slowly*] Well, it looks like you made a good deal for yourselves, and for Marshall, too. [*To* **Ben**] Your father used to say he made the thousands and you boys would make the millions. I think he was right. [*Rises.*]

Regina: [*They are all looking at* **Horace.** *She laughs nervously*] Millions for *us*, too.

Horace: Us? You and me? I don't think so. We've got enough money, Regina. We'll just sit by and watch the boys grow rich. [*They watch* **Horace** *tensely as he begins to move towards the staircase. He passes* **Leo,** *looks at him for a second*] How's everything at the bank, Leo?

Leo: Fine, sir. Everything is fine.

Horace: How are all the ladies in Mobile? [**Horace** *turns to* **Regina,** *sharply*] Whatever made you think I'd let Zan marry—

Regina: Do you mean that you are turning this down? Is it possible that's what you mean?

Ben: No, that's not what he means. Turning down a fortune. Horace is tired. He'd rather talk about it tomorrow—

Regina: We can't keep putting it off this way. Oscar must be in Chicago by the end of the week with the money and contracts.

Oscar: [*Giggles, pleased*] Yes, sir. Got to be there end of the week. No sense going without the money.

Regina: [*Tensely*] I've waited long enough for your answer. I'm not going to wait any longer.

Horace: [*Very deliberately*] I'm very tired now, Regina.

Ben: [*Hastily*] Now, Horace probably has his reasons. Things he'd like explained. Tomorrow will do. I can—

Regina: [*Turns to* **Ben,** *sharply*] I want to know his reasons now! [*Turns back to* **Horace.**]

Horace: [*As he climbs the steps*] I don't know them all myself. Let's leave it at that.

Regina: We shall not leave it at that! We have waited for you here like children. Waited for you to come home.

Horace: So that you could invest my money. So this is why you wanted me home? Well, I had hoped— [*Quietly*] If you are disappointed, Regina, I'm sorry. But I must do what I think best. We'll talk about it another day.

Regina: We'll talk about it now. Just you and me.

Horace: [*Looks down at her. His voice is tense*] Please, Regina. It's been a hard trip. I don't feel well. Please leave me alone now.

Regina: [*Quietly*] I want to talk to you, Horace. I'm coming up. [*He looks at her for a minute, then moves on again out of sight. She begins to climb the stairs.*]

Ben: [*Softly.* **Regina** *turns to him as he speaks*] Sometimes it is better to wait for the sun to rise again. [*She does not answer*] And sometimes, as our mother used to tell you, [**Regina** *starts up stairs*] it's unwise for a good-looking woman to frown. [**Ben** *rises, moves towards stairs*] Softness and a smile do more to the heart of men— [*She disappears.* **Ben** *stands looking up the stairs. There is a long silence. Then, suddenly,* **Oscar** *giggles.*]

Oscar: Let us hope she'll change his mind. Let us hope. [*After a second* **Ben** *crosses to table, picks up his newspaper.* **Oscar** *looks at* **Ben.** *The silence makes* **Leo** *uncomfortable.*]

Leo: The paper says twenty-seven cases of yellow fever in New Orleans. Guess the flood-waters caused it. [*Nobody pays attention*] Thought they were building the levees high enough. Like the niggers always say: a man born of woman can't build nothing high enough for the Mississippi. [*Gets no answer. Gives an embarrassed laugh.*]

> [*Upstairs there is the sound of voices. The voices are not loud, but* **Ben, Oscar, Leo** *become conscious of them.* **Leo** *crosses to landing, looks up, listens.*]

Oscar: [*Pointing up*] Now just suppose she don't change his mind? Just suppose he keeps on refusing?

Ben: [*Without conviction*] He's tired. It was a mistake to talk to him today. He's a sick man, but he isn't a crazy one.

Oscar: [*Giggles*] But just suppose he is crazy. What then?

Ben: [*Puts down his paper, peers at* **Oscar**] Then we'll go outside for the money. There's plenty who would give it.

Oscar: And plenty who will want a lot for what they give. The ones who are rich enough to give will be smart enough to want. That means we'd be working for them, don't it, Ben?

Ben: You don't have to tell me the things I told you six months ago.

Oscar: Oh, you're right not to worry, She'll change his mind. She always has. [*There is a silence. Suddenly* **Regina**'s *voice becomes louder and sharper. All of them begin to listen now. Slowly* **Ben** *rises, goes to listen by the staircase.* **Oscar**, *watching him, smiles. As they listen* **Regina**'s *voice becomes very loud.* **Horace**'s *voice is no longer heard*] Maybe. But I don't believe it. I never did believe he was going in with us.

Ben: [*Turning on him*] What the hell do you expect me to do?

Oscar: [*Mildly*] Nothing. You done your almighty best. Nobody could blame you if the whole thing just dripped away right through our fingers. You can't do a thing. But there may be something I could do for us. [**Oscar** *rises*] Or, I might better say, Leo could do for us. [**Ben** *stops, turns, looks at* **Oscar**. **Leo** *is staring at* **Oscar**] Ain't that true, son? Ain't it true you might be able to help your own kinfolks?

Leo   [*Nervously taking a step to him*] Papa, I—

Ben: [*Slowly*] How would he help us, Oscar?

Oscar: Leo's got a friend. Leo's friend owns eighty-eight thousand dollars in Union Pacific bonds. [**Ben** *turns to look at* **Leo**] Leo's friend don't look at the bonds much—not for five or six months at a time.

Ben: [*After a pause*] Union Pacific. Uh, huh. Let me understand. Leo's friend would—would lend him these bonds and he—

Oscar: [*Nods*] Would be kind enough to lend them to us.

Ben: Leo.

Leo: [*Excited, comes to him*] Yes, sir?

Ben: When would your friend be wanting the bonds back?

Leo: [*Very nervous*] I don't know. I—well, I—

Oscar: [*Sharply. Steps to him*] You told me he won't look at them until Fall—

Leo: Oh, that's right. But I—not till Fall. Uncle Horace never—

Ben: [*Sharply*] Be still.

Oscar: [*Smiles at* **Leo**] Your uncle doesn't wish to know your friend's name.

Leo: [*Starts to laugh*] That's a good one. Not know his name—

Oscar: Shut up, Leo! [**Leo** *turns away slowly, moves to table.* **Ben** *turns to* **Oscar**] He won't look at them again until September. That gives us five months. Leo will return the bonds in three months. And we'll have no trouble raising the money once the mills are going up. Will Marshall accept bonds?

> [**Ben** *stops to listen to sudden sharp voices from above. The voices are now very angry and very loud.*]

Ben: [*Smiling*] Why not? Why not? [*Laughs*] Good. We are lucky. We'll take the loan from Leo's friend—I think he will make a safer partner than our sister. [*Nods towards stairs. Turns to* **Leo**] How soon can you get them?

Leo: Today. Right now. They're in the safe-deposit box and—

Ben: [*Sharply*] I don't want to know where they are.

Oscar: [*Laughs*] We will keep it secret from you. [*Pats* **Ben**'s *arm.*]

Ben: [*Smiles*] Good. Draw a check for our part. You can take the night train for Chicago. Well, Oscar [*holds out his hand*], good luck to us.

Oscar: Leo will be taken care of?

Leo: I'm entitled to Uncle Horace's share. I'd enjoy being a partner—

Ben: [*Turns to stare at him*] You would? You can go to hell, you little— [*Starts towards* **Leo.**]

Oscar: [*Nervously*] Now, now. He didn't mean that. I only want to be sure he'll get something out of all this.

Ben: Of course. We'll take care of him. We won't have any trouble about that. I'll see you at the store.

Oscar: [*Nods*] That's settled then. Come on, son. [*Starts for door.*]

Leo: [*Puts out his hand*] I didn't mean just that. I was only going to say what a great day this was for me and— [**Ben** *ignores his hand.*]

Ben: Go on.

[**Leo** *looks at him, turns, follows* **Oscar** *out.* **Ben** *stands where he is, thinking. Again the voices upstairs can be heard.* **Regina**'s *voice is high and furious.* **Ben** *looks up, smiles, winces at the noise.*]

Alexandra: [*Upstairs*] Mama—Mama—don't . . . [*The noise of running footsteps is heard and* **Alexandra** *comes running down the steps, speaking as she comes*] Uncle Ben! Uncle Ben! Please go up. Please make Mama stop. Uncle Ben, he's sick, he's so sick. How can Mama talk to him like that—please, make her stop. She'll—

Ben: Alexandra, you have a tender heart.

Alexandra: [*Crying*] Go on up, Uncle Ben, please—

[*Suddenly the voices stop. A second later there is the sound of a door being slammed.*]

Ben: Now you see. Everything is over. Don't worry. [*He starts for the door.*] Alexandra, I want you to tell your mother how sorry I am that I had to leave. And don't worry so, my dear. Married folk frequently raise their voices, unfortunately. [*He starts to put on his hat and coat as* **Regina** *appears on the stairs.*]

Alexandra: [*Furiously*] How can you treat Papa like this? He's sick. He's very sick. Don't you know that? I won't let you.

Regina: Mind your business, Alexandra. [*To* **Ben.** *Her voice is cold and calm*] How much longer can you wait for the money?

Ben: [*Putting on his coat*] He has refused? My, that's too bad.

Regina: He will change his mind. I'll find a way to make him. What's the longest you can wait now?

Ben: I could wait until next week. But I can't wait until next week. [*He giggles, pleased at the joke*] I could but I can't. Could and can't. Well, I must go now. I'm very late—

Regina: [*Coming downstairs towards him*] You're not going. I want to talk to you.

Ben: I was about to give Alexandra a message for you. I wanted to tell you that Oscar is going to Chicago tonight, so we can't be here for our usual Friday supper.

Regina: [*Tensely*] Oscar is going to Chi— [*Softly*] What do you mean?

Ben: Just that. Everything is settled. He's going on to deliver to Marshall—

Regina: [*Taking a step to him*] I demand to know what— You are lying. You are trying to scare me. *You haven't got the money. How could you have it? You can't have—* [**Ben** *laughs*] You will wait until I—

[**Horace** *comes into view on the landing.*]

Ben: You are getting out of hand. Since when do I take orders from you?

Regina: Wait, you— [**Ben** *stops*] How *can* he go to Chicago? Did a ghost arrive with the money? [**Ben** *starts for the hall*] I don't believe you. Come back here. [**Regina** *starts after him*] Come back here, you— [*The door slams. She stops in the doorway, staring, her fists clenched. After a pause she turns slowly.*]

Horace: [*Very quietly*] It's a great day when you and Ben cross swords. I've been waiting for it for years.

Alexandra: Papa, Papa, please go back! You will—

Horace: And so they don't need you, and so you will not have your millions, after all.

Regina: [*Turns slowly*] You hate to see anybody live now, don't you? You hate to think that I'm going to be alive and have what I want.

Horace: I should have known you'd think that was the reason.

Regina: Because you're going to die and you know you're going to die.

Alexandra: [*Shrilly*] Mama! Don't—Don't listen, Papa. Just don't listen. Go away—

Horace: Not to keep you from getting what you want. Not even partly that. [*Holding to the* rail] I'm sick of you, sick of this house, sick of my life here. I'm sick of your brothers and their dirty tricks to make a dime. There must be better ways of getting rich than cheating niggers on a pound of bacon. Why should I give you the money? [*Very angrily*] To pound the bones of this town to make dividends for you to spend? You wreck the town, you and your brothers, *you* wreck the town and live on it. Not me. Maybe it's easy for the dying to be honest. But it's not my fault I'm dying. [**Addie** *enters, stands at door quietly*] I'll do no more harm now. I've done enough. I'll die my own way. And I'll do it without making the world any worse. I leave that to you.

Regina: [*Looks up at him slowly, calmly*] I hope you die. I hope you die soon. [*Smiles*] I'll be waiting for you to die.

Alexandra: [*Shrieking*] Papa! Don't— Don't listen— Don't—

Addie: Come here, Zan. Come out of this room.

[**Alexandra** *runs quickly to* **Addie,** *who holds her.* **Horace** *turns slowly and starts upstairs.*]

CURTAIN

ACT III

SCENE: Same as Act I. Two weeks later. It is late afternoon and it is raining.

AT RISE: **Horace** is sitting near the window in a wheel chair. On the table next to him is a safe-deposit box, and a small bottle of medicine. **Birdie** and **Alexandra** are playing the piano. On a chair is a large sewing basket.

Birdie: [*Counting for* **Alexandra**] One and two and three and four. One and two and three and four. [*Nods—turns to* **Horace**] We once played together, Horace. Remember?

Horace: [*Has been looking out of the window*] What, Birdie?

Birdie: We played together. You and me.

Alexandra: *Papa* used to play?

Birdie: Indeed he did. [**Addie** *appears at the door in a large kitchen apron. She is wiping her hands on a towel*] He played the fiddle and very well, too.

Alexandra: [*Turns to smile at* **Horace**] I never knew—

Addie: Where's your mama?

Alexandra: Gone to Miss Safronia's to fit her dresses. [**Addie** *nods, starts to exit.*]

Horace: Addie.

Addie: Yes, Mr. Horace.

Horace: [*Speaks as if he had made a sudden decision*] Tell Cal to get on his things. I want him to go an errand.

[**Addie** *nods, exits.* **Horace** *moves nervously in his chair, looks out of the window.*]

Alexandra: [*Who has been watching him*] It's too bad it's been raining all day, Papa. But you can go out in the yard tomorrow. Don't be restless.

Horace: I'm not restless, darling.

Birdie: I remember so well the time we played together, your papa and me. It was the first time Oscar brought me here to supper. I had never seen all the Hubbards together before, and you know what a ninny I am and how shy. [*Turns to look at* **Horace**] You said you could play the fiddle and you'd be much obliged if I'd play with you. *I* was obliged to *you,* all right, all right. [*Laughs when he does not answer her*] Horace, you haven't heard a word I've said.

Horace: Birdie, when did Oscar get back from Chicago?

Birdie: Yesterday. Hasn't he been here yet?

Alexandra: [*Stops playing*] No. Neither has Uncle Ben since—since that day.

Birdie: Oh, I didn't know it was *that* bad. Oscar never tells me anything—

Horace: [*Smiles, nods*] The Hubbards have had their great quarrel. I knew it would come some day. [*Laughs*] It came.

Alexandra: It came. It certainly came all right.

Birdie: [*Amazed*] But Oscar was in such a good humor when he got home, I didn't—

Horace: Yes, I can understand that.

[**Addie** *enters carrying a large tray with glasses, a carafe of elderberry wine and a plate of cookies, which she puts on the table.*]

Alexandra: Addie! A party! What for?

Addie: Nothing for. I had the fresh butter, so I made the cakes, and a little elderberry does the stomach good in the rain.

Birdie: Isn't this nice! A party just for us. Let's play party music, Zan.

[**Alexandra** *begins to play a gay piece.*]

Addie: [*To* **Horace,** *wheeling his chair to center*]

Come over here, Mr. Horace, and don't be thinking so much. A glass of elderberry will do more good.

[**Alexandra** *reaches for a cake.* **Birdie** *pours herself a glass of wine.*]

Alexandra:　Good cakes, Addie. It's nice here. Just us. Be nice if it could always be this way.

Birdie:　[*Nods happily*] Quiet and restful.

Addie:　Well, it won't be that way long. Little while now, even sitting here, you'll hear the red bricks going into place. The next day the smoke'll be pushing out the chimneys and by church time that Sunday every human born of woman will be living on chicken. That's how Mr. Ben's been telling the story.

Horace:　[*Looks at her*] They believe it that way?

Addie:　Believe it? They use to believing what Mr. Ben orders. There ain't been so much talk around here since Sherman's army didn't come near.

Horace:　[*Softly*] They are fools.

Addie:　[*Nods, sits down with the sewing basket*] You ain't born in the South unless you're a fool.

Birdie:　[*Has drunk another glass of wine*] But we didn't play together after that night. Oscar said he didn't like me to play on the piano. [*Turns to* **Alexandra**] You know what he said that night?

Alexandra:　Who?

Birdie:　Oscar. He said that music made him nervous. He said he just sat and waited for the next note. [**Alexandra** *laughs*] He wasn't poking fun. He meant it. Ah, well— [*She finishes her glass, shakes her head.* **Horace** *looks at her, smiles*] Your papa don't like to admit it, but he's been mighty kind to me all these years. [*Running the back of her hand along his sleeve*] Often he'd step in when somebody said something and once— [*She stops, turns away, her face still*] Once he stopped Oscar from— [*She stops, turns. Quickly*] I'm sorry I said that. Why, here I am so happy and yet I think about bad things. [*Laughs nervously*] That's not right, now, is it? [*She pours a drink.* **Cal** *appears in the door. He has on an old coat and is carrying a torn umbrella.*]

Alexandra:　Have a cake, Cal.

Cal:　[*Comes in, takes a cake*] Yes'm. You want me, Mr. Horace?

Horace:　What time is it, Cal?

Cal:　'Bout ten minutes before it's five.

Horace:　All right. Now you walk yourself down to the bank.

Cal:　It'll be closed. Nobody'll be there but Mr. Manders, Mr. Joe Horns, Mr. Leo—

Horace:　Go in the back way. They'll be at the table, going over the day's business. [*Points to the deposit box*] See that box?

Cal:　[*Nods*] Yes, sir.

Horace:　You tell Mr. Manders that Mr. Horace says he's much obliged to him for bringing the box, it arrived all right.

Cal:　[*Bewildered*] He know you got the box. He bring it himself Wednesday. I opened the door to him and he say, "Hello, Cal, coming on to summer weather."

Horace:　You say just what I tell you. Understand?

[**Birdie** *pours another drink, stands at table.*]

Cal:　No, sir. I ain't going to say I understand. I'm going down and tell a man he give you something he already know he give you, and you say "understand."

Horace:　Now, Cal.

Cal:　Yes, sir. I just going to say you obliged for the box coming all right. I ain't going to understand it, but I'm going to say it.

Horace:　And tell him I want him to come over here after supper and to bring Mr. Sol Fowler with him.

Cal:　[*Nods*] He's to come after supper and bring Mr. Sol Fowler, your attorney-*at*-law, with him.

Horace:　[*Smiles*] That's right. Just walk right in the back room and say your piece. [*Slowly*] In front of everybody.

Cal:　Yes, sir. [*Mumbles to himself as he exits.*]

Alexandra:　[*Who has been watching* **Horace**] Is anything the matter, Papa?

Horace:　Oh, no. Nothing.

Addie:　Miss Birdie, that elderberry going to give you a headache spell.

Birdie:　[*Beginning to be drunk. Gaily*] Oh, I don't think so. I don't think it will.

Alexandra:　[*As* **Horace** *puts his hand to his throat*] Do you want your medicine, Papa?

Horace:　No, no. I'm all right, darling.

Birdie:　Mama used to give me elderberry wine when I was a little girl. For hiccoughs. [*Laughs*]

You know, I don't think people get hiccoughs any more. Isn't that funny? [**Birdie** *laughs.* **Horace** *and* **Alexandra** *laugh*] I used to get hiccoughs just when I shouldn't have.

Addie: [*Nods*] And nobody gets growing pains no more. That is funny. Just as if there was some style in what you get. One year an ailment's stylish and the next year it ain't.

Birdie: [*Turns*] I remember. It was my first big party, at Lionnet I mean, and I was so excited, and there I was with hiccoughs and Mama laughing. [*Softly. Looking at carafe*] Mama always laughed. [*Picks up carafe*] A big party, a lovely dress from Mr. Worth in Paris, France, and hiccoughs. [*Pours drink*] My brother pounding me on the back and Mama with the elderberry bottle, laughing at me. Everybody was on their way to come, and I was such a ninny, hiccoughing away. [*Drinks*] You know, that was the first day I ever saw Oscar Hubbard. The Ballongs were selling their horses and he was going there to buy. He passed and lifted his hat—we could see him from the window—and my brother, to tease Mama, said maybe we should have invited the Hubbards to the party. He said Mama didn't like them because they kept a store, and he said that was old-fashioned of her. [*Her face lights up*] And then, and *then*, I saw Mama angry for the first time in my life. She said that wasn't the reason. She said she was old-fashioned, but not that way. She said she was old-fashioned enough not to like people who killed animals they couldn't use, and who made their money charging awful interest to poor, ignorant niggers and cheating them on what they bought. She was very angry, Mama was. I had never seen her face like that. And then suddenly she laughed and said, "Look, I've frightened Birdie out of the hiccoughs." [*Her head drops. Then softly*] And so she had. They were all gone. [*Moves to sofa, sits.*]

Addie: Yeah, they got mighty well off cheating niggers. Well, there are people who eat the earth and eat all the people on it like in the Bible with the locusts. Then there are people who stand around and watch them eat it.

[*Softly*] Sometimes I think it ain't right to stand and watch them do it.

Birdie: [*Thoughtfully*] Like I say, if we could only go back to Lionnet. Everybody'd be better there. They'd be good and kind. I like people to be kind. [*Pours drink*] Don't you, Horace; don't you like people to be kind?

Horace: Yes, Birdie.

Birdie: [*Very drunk now*] Yes, that was the first day I ever saw Oscar. Who would have thought— [*Quickly*] You all want to know something? Well, I don't like Leo. My very own son, and I don't like him. [*Laughs, gaily*] My, I guess I even like Oscar more.

Alexandra: Why did you marry Uncle Oscar?

Addie: [*Sharply*] That's no question for you to be asking.

Horace: [*Sharply*] Why not? She's heard enough around here to ask anything.

Alexandra: Aunt Birdie, why did you marry Uncle Oscar?

Birdie: I don't know. I thought I liked him. He was kind to me and I thought it was because he liked me too. But that wasn't the reason— [*Wheels on* **Alexandra**] Ask why *he* married *me.* I can tell you that: He's told it to me often enough.

Addie: [*Leaning forward*] Miss Birdie, don't—

Birdie: [*Speaking very rapidly, tensely*] My family was good and the cotton on Lionnet's fields was better. Ben Hubbard wanted the cotton and [*Rises*] Oscar Hubbard married it for him. He was kind to me, then. He used to smile at me. He hasn't smiled at me since. Everybody knew that's what he married me for. [**Addie** *rises*] Everybody but me. Stupid, stupid me.

Alexandra: [*To* **Horace,** *holding his hand, softly*] I see. [*Hesitates*] Papa, I mean—when you feel better couldn't we go away? I mean, by ourselves. Couldn't we find a way to go—

Horace: Yes, I know what you mean. We'll try to find a way. I promise you, darling.

Addie: [*Moves to* **Birdie**] Rest a bit, Miss Birdie. You get talking like this you'll get a headache and—

Birdie: [*Sharply, turning to her*] I've never had a headache in my life. [*Begins to cry hysterically*] You know it as well as I do. [*Turns to* **Alexandra**]

I never had a headache, Zan. That's a lie they tell for me. I drink. All by myself, in my own room, by myself, I drink. Then, when they want to hide it, they say, "Birdie's got a headache again"—

Alexandra: [*Comes to her quickly*] Aunt Birdie.

Birdie: [*Turning away*] Even you won't like me now. You won't like me any more.

Alexandra: I love you. I'll always love you.

Birdie: [*Furiously*] Well, don't. Don't love me. Because in twenty years you'll just be like me. They'll do all the same things to you. [*Begins to laugh hysterically*] You know what? In twenty-two years I haven't had a whole day of happiness. Oh, a little, like today with you all. But never a single, whole day. I say to myself, if only I had one more *whole* day, then— [*The laugh stops*] And that's the way you'll be. And you'll trail after them, just like me, hoping they won't be so mean that day or say something to make you feel so bad— only you'll be worse off because you haven't got my Mama to remember— [*Turns away, her head drops. She stands quietly, swaying a little, holding onto the sofa.* **Alexandra** *leans down, puts her cheek on* **Birdie**'s *arm.*]

Alexandra: [*To* **Birdie**] I guess we were all trying to make a happy day. You know, we sit around and try to pretend nothing's happened. We try to pretend we are not here. We make believe we are just by ourselves, some place else, and it doesn't seem to work. [*Kisses* **Birdie**'s *hand*] Come now, Aunt Birdie, I'll walk you home. You and me. [*She takes* **Birdie**'s *arm. They move slowly out.*]

Birdie: [*Softly as they exit*] You and me.

Addie: [*After a minute*] Well. First time I ever heard Miss Birdie say a word. [**Horace** *looks at her*] Maybe it's good for her. I'm just sorry Zan had to hear it. [**Horace** *moves his head as if he were uncomfortable*] You feel bad, don't you? [*He shrugs.*]

Horace: So you didn't want Zan to hear? It would be nice to let her stay innocent, like Birdie at her age. Let her listen now. Let her see everything. How else is she going to know that she's got to get away? I'm trying to show her that. I'm trying, but I've only got a little

time left. She can even hate me when I'm dead, if she'll only learn to hate and fear this.

Addie: Mr. Horace—

Horace: Pretty soon there'll be nobody to help her but you.

Addie: [*Crossing to him*] What can I do?

Horace: Take her away.

Addie: How can I do that? Do you think they'd let me just go away with her?

Horace: I'll fix it so they can't stop you when you're ready to go. You'll go, Addie?

Addie: [*After a second, softly*] Yes, sir. I promise. [*He touches her arm, nods.*]

Horace: [*Quietly*] I'm going to have Sol Fowler make me a new will. They'll make trouble, but you make Zan stand firm and Fowler'll do the rest. Addie, I'd like to leave you something for yourself. I always wanted to.

Addie: [*Laughs*] Don't you do that, Mr. Horace. A nigger woman in a white man's will! I'd never get it nohow.

Horace: I know. But upstairs in the armoire drawer there's seventeen hundred dollar bills. It's money left from my trip. It's in an envelope with your name. It's for you.

Addie: Seventeen hundred dollar bills! My God, Mr. Horace, I won't know how to count up that high. [*Shyly*] It's mighty kind and good of you. I don't know what to say for thanks—

Cal: [*Appears in doorway*] I'm back. [*No answer*] I'm back.

Addie: So we see.

Horace: Well?

Cal: Nothing. I just went down and spoke my piece. Just like you told me. I say, "Mr. Horace he thank you mightily for the safe box arriving in good shape and he say you come right after supper to his house and bring Mr. Attorney-at-law Sol Fowler with you." Then I wipe my hands on my coat. Every time I ever told a lie in my whole life, I wipe my hands right after. Can't help doing it. Well, while I'm wiping my hands, Mr. Leo jump up and say to me, "What box? What you talking about?"

Horace: [*Smiles*] Did he?

Cal: And Mr. Leo say he got to leave a little early cause he got something to do. And then

Mr. Manders say Mr. Leo should sit right down and finish up his work and stop acting like somebody made him Mr. President. So he sit down. Now, just like I told you, Mr. Manders was mighty surprised with the message because he knows right well he brought the box— [*Points to box, sighs*] But he took it all right. Some men take everything easy and some do not.

Horace: [*Puts his head back, laughs*] Mr. Leo was telling the truth; he *has* got something to do. I hope Manders don't keep him too long. [*Outside there is the sound of voices.* **Cal** *exits.* **Addie** *crosses quickly to* **Horace,** *puts basket on table, begins to wheel his chair towards the stairs. Sharply*] No. Leave me where I am.

Addie: But that's Miss Regina coming back.

Horace: [*Nods, looking at door*] Go away, Addie.

Addie: [*Hesitates*] Mr. Horace. Don't talk no more today. You don't feel well and it won't do no good—

Horace: [*As he hears footsteps in the hall*] Go on. [*She looks at him for a second, then picks up her sewing from table and exits as* **Regina** *comes in from hall.* **Horace's** *chair is now so placed that he is in front of the table with the medicine.* **Regina** *stands in the hall, shakes umbrella, stands it in the corner, takes off her cloak and throws it over the banister. She stares at* **Horace.**]

Regina: [*As she takes off her gloves*] We had agreed that you were to stay in your part of this house and I in mine. This room is *my* part of the house. Please don't come down here again.

Horace: I won't.

Regina: [*Crosses towards bell-cord*] I'll get Cal to take you upstairs.

Horace: [*Smiles*] Before you do I want to tell you that after all, we have invested our money in Hubbard Sons and Marshall, Cotton Manufacturers.

Regina: [*Stops, turns, stares at him*] What are you talking about? You haven't seen Ben—When did you change your mind?

Horace: I didn't change my mind. *I* didn't invest the money. [*Smiles*] It was invested for me.

Regina: [*Angrily*] What—?

Horace: I had eighty-eight thousand dollars' worth of Union Pacific bonds in that safe-deposit box. They are not there now. Go and look. [*As she stares at him, he points to the box*] Go

and look, Regina. [*She crosses quickly to the box, opens it*] Those bonds are as negotiable as money.

Regina: [*Turns back to him*] What kind of joke are you playing now? Is this for my benefit?

Horace: I don't look in that box very often, but three days ago, on Wednesday it was, because I had made a decision—

Regina: I want to know what you are talking about.

Horace: [*Sharply*] Don't interrupt me again. Because I had made a decision, I sent for the box. The bonds were gone. Eighty-eight thousand dollars gone. [*He smiles at her.*]

Regina: [*After a moment's silence, quietly*] Do you think I'm crazy enough to believe what you're saying?

Horace: [*Shrugs*] Believe anything you like.

Regina: [*Stares at him, slowly*] Where did they go to?

Horace: They are in Chicago. With Mr. Marshall, I should guess.

Regina: What did they do? Walk to Chicago? Have you really gone crazy?

Horace: Leo took the bonds.

Regina: [*Turns sharply then speaks softly, without conviction*] I don't believe it.

Horace: [*Leans forward*] I wasn't there but I can guess what happened. This fine gentleman, to whom you were willing to marry your daughter, took the keys and opened the box. You remember that the day of the fight Oscar went to Chicago? Well, he went with my bonds that his son Leo had stolen for him. [*Pleasantly*] And for Ben, of course, too.

Regina: [*Slowly, nods*] When did you find out the bonds were gone?

Horace: Wednesday night.

Regina: I thought that's what you said. Why have you waited three days to do anything? [*Suddenly laughs*] This *will* make a fine story.

Horace: [*Nods*] Couldn't it?

Regina: [*Still laughing*] A fine story to hold over their heads. How could they be such fools? [*Turns to him.*]

Horace: But I'm not going to hold it over their heads.

Regina: [*The laugh stops*] What?

Horace: [*Turns his chair to face her*] I'm going to

let them keep the bonds—as a loan from you. An eighty-eight-thousand-dollar loan; they should be grateful to you. They will be, I think.

Regina: [*Slowly, smiles*] I see. You are punishing me. But I won't let you punish me. If you won't do anything, I will. Now. [*She starts for door.*]

Horace: You won't do anything. Because you can't. [**Regina** *stops*] It won't do you any good to make trouble because I shall simply say that I lent them the bonds.

Regina: [*Slowly*] You would do that?

Horace: Yes. For once in your life I am tying your hands. There is nothing for you to do. [*There is silence. Then she sits down.*]

Regina: I see. You are going to lend them the bonds and let them keep all the profit they make on them, and there is nothing I can do about it. Is that right?

Horace: Yes.

Regina: [*Softly*] Why did you say that I was making this gift?

Horace: I was coming to that. I am going to make a new will, Regina, leaving you eighty-eight thousand dollars in Union Pacific bonds. The rest will go to Zan. It's true that your brothers have borrowed your share for a little while. After my death I advise you to talk to Ben and Oscar. They won't admit anything and Ben, I think, will be smart enough to see that he's safe. Because I knew about the theft and said nothing. Nor will I say anything as long as I live. Is that clear to you?

Regina: [*Nods, softly, without looking at him*] You will not say anything as long as you live.

Horace: That's right. And by that time they will probably have replaced your bonds, and then they'll belong to you and nobody but us will ever know what happened. [*Stops, smiles*] They'll be around any minute to see what I am going to do. I took good care to see that word reached Leo. They'll be mighty relieved to know I'm going to do nothing and Ben will think it all a capital joke on you. And that will be the end of that. There's nothing you can do to them, nothing you can do to me.

Regina: You hate me very much.

Horace: No.

Regina: Oh, I think you do. [*Puts her head back, sighs*] Well, we haven't been very good together. Anyway, I don't hate you either. I have only contempt for you. I've always had.

Horace: From the very first?

Regina: I think so.

Horace: I was in love with *you*. But why did *you* marry *me*?

Regina: I was lonely when I was young.

Horace: *You* were lonely?

Regina: Not the way people usually mean. Lonely for all the things I wasn't going to get. Everybody in this house was so busy and there was so little place for what I wanted. I wanted the world. Then, and then— [*Smiles*] Papa died and left the money to Ben and Oscar.

Horace: And you married me?

Regina: Yes, I thought— But I was wrong. You were a small-town clerk then. You haven't changed.

Horace: [*Nods, smiles*] And that wasn't what you wanted.

Regina: No. No, it wasn't what I wanted. [*Pauses, leans back, pleasantly*] It took me a little while to find out I had made a mistake. As for you—I don't know. It was almost as if I couldn't stand the kind of man you were— [*Smiles, softly*] I used to lie there at night, praying you wouldn't come near—

Horace: Really? It was as bad as that?

Regina: [*Nods*] Remember when I went to Doctor Sloan and I told you he said there was something the matter with me and that you shouldn't touch me any more?

Horace: I remember.

Regina: But you believed it. I couldn't understand that. I couldn't understand that anybody could be such a soft fool. That was when I began to despise you.

Horace: [*Puts his hand to his throat, looks at the bottle of medicine on table*] Why didn't you leave me?

Regina: I told you I married you for something. It turned out it was only for this. [*Carefully*] This wasn't what I wanted, but it was something. I never thought about it much but if I had [**Horace** *puts his hand to his throat*] I'd have known that you would die before I would. But I couldn't have known that you would get heart trouble so early and so bad. I'm lucky, Horace. I've always been lucky. [**Horace** *turns slowly to the medicine*] I'll be lucky again. [**Horace** *looks at her. Then he puts his hand to his throat. Because he cannot reach the bottle he moves the chair closer. He reaches for the medicine, takes out the cork, picks up the spoon. The bottle slips and smashes on the table. He draws in his breath, gasps.*]

Horace: Please. Tell Addie— The other bottle is upstairs. [**Regina** *has not moved. She does not move now. He stares at her. Then, suddenly as if he understood, he raises his voice. It is a panic-stricken whisper, too small to be heard outside the room*] Addie! Addie! Come— [*Stops as he hears the softness of his voice. He makes a sudden, furious spring from the chair to the stairs, taking the first few steps as if he were a desperate runner. On the fourth step he slips, gasps, grasps the rail, makes a great effort to reach the landing. When he reaches the landing, he is on his knees. His knees give way, he falls on the landing, out of view.* **Regina** *has not turned during his climb up the stairs. Now she waits a second. Then she goes below the landing, speaks up*]

Regina: Horace. Horace. [*When there is no answer, she turns, calls*] Addie! Cal! Come in here. [*She starts up the steps.* **Addie** *and* **Cal** *appear. Both run towards the stairs*] He's had an attack. Come up here. [*They run up the steps quickly.*]

Cal: My God. Mr. Horace—
[*They cannot be seen now.*]

Regina: [*Her voice comes from the head of the stairs*] Be still, Cal. Bring him in here.
[*Before the footsteps and the voices have completely died away,* **Alexandra** *appears in the hall door, in her raincloak and hood. She comes into the room, begins to unfasten the cloak, suddenly looks around, sees the empty wheel chair, stares, begins to move swiftly as if to look in the dining room. At the same moment* **Addie** *runs down the stairs.* **Alexandra** *turns and stares up at* **Addie.**]

Alexandra: Addie! What?

Addie: [*Takes* **Alexandra** *by the shoulders*] I'm going for the doctor. Go upstairs. [**Alexandra** *looks at her, then quickly breaks away and runs up the steps.* **Addie** *exits. The stage is empty for a minute. Then the front door bell begins to ring. When there is no answer, it rings again. A second later* **Leo** *appears in the hall, talking as he comes in.*]

Leo: [*Very nervous*] Hello. [*Irritably*] Never saw any use ringing a bell when a door was open. If you are going to ring a bell, then somebody should answer it. [*Gets in the room, looks around, puzzled, listens, hears no sound*] Aunt Regina. [*He moves around restlessly*] Addie. [*Waits*] Where the hell— [*Crosses to the bell cord, rings it impatiently, waits, gets no answer, calls*] Cal! Cal! [**Cal** *appears on the stair landing.*]

Cal: [*His voice is soft, shaken*] Mr. Leo. Miss Regina says you stop that screaming noise.

Leo: [*Angrily*] Where is everybody?

Cal: Mr. Horace he got an attack. He's bad. Miss Regina says you stop that noise.

Leo: Uncle Horace— What— What happened? [**Cal** *starts down the stairs, shakes his head, begins to move swiftly off.* **Leo** *looks around wildly*] But when— You seen Mr. Oscar or Mr. Ben? [**Cal** *shakes his head. Moves on.* **Leo** *grabs him by the arm*] Answer me, will you?

Cal: No, I ain't seen 'em. I ain't got time to answer you. I got to get things. [**Cal** *runs off.*]

Leo: But what's the matter with him? When did this happen— [*Calling after* **Cal**] You'd think Papa'd be some place where you could find him. I been chasing him all afternoon.
[**Oscar** *and* **Ben** *come into the room, talking excitedly.*]

Oscar: I hope it's not a bad attack.

Ben: It's the first one he's had since he came home.

Leo: Papa, I've been looking all over town for you and Uncle Ben—

Ben: Where is he?

Oscar: Addie said it was sudden.

Ben: [*To* **Leo**] Where is he? When did it happen?

Leo: Upstairs. Will you listen to me, please? I been looking for you for—

Oscar: [*To* **Ben**] You think we should go up? [**Ben,** *looking up the steps, shakes his head.*]

Ben: I don't know. I don't know.

Oscar: [*Shakes his head*] But he was all right—

Leo: [*Yelling*] Will you listen to me?

Oscar: [*Sharply*] What is the matter with you?

Leo: I been trying to tell you. I been trying to find you for an hour—

Oscar: Tell me what?

Leo: Uncle Horace knows about the bonds. He

knows about them. He's had the box since Wednesday—

Ben: [*Sharply*] Stop shouting! What the hell are you talking about?

Leo: [*Furiously*] I'm telling you he knows about the bonds. Ain't that clear enough—

Oscar: [*Grabbing Leo's arm*] You God-damn fool! Stop screaming!

Ben: Now what happened? Talk quietly.

Leo: You heard me. Uncle Horace knows about the bonds. He's known since Wednesday.

Ben: [*After a second*] How do you know that?

Leo: Because Cal comes down to Manders and says the box came O.K. and—

Oscar: [*Trembling*] That might not mean a thing—

Leo: [*Angrily*] No? It might not, huh? Then he says Manders should come here tonight and bring Sol Fowler with him. I guess that don't mean a thing either.

Oscar: [*To* **Ben**] Ben— What— Do you think he's seen the—

Ben: [*Motions to the box*] There's the box. [*Both* **Oscar** *and* **Leo** *turn sharply.* **Leo** *makes a leap to the box*] You ass. Put it down. What are you going to do with it, eat it?

Leo: I'm going to— [*Starts.*]

Ben: [*Furiously*] Put it down. Don't touch it again. Now sit down and shut up for a minute.

Oscar: Since Wednesday. [*To* **Leo**] You said he had it since Wednesday. Why didn't he say something— [*To* **Ben**] I don't understand—

Leo: [*Taking a step*] I can put it back. I can put it back before anybody knows.

Ben: [*Who is standing at the table, softly*] He's had it since Wednesday. Yet he hasn't said a word to us.

Oscar: Why? Why?

Leo: What's the difference why? He was getting ready to say plenty. He was going to say it to Fowler tonight—

Oscar: [*Angrily*] Be still. [*Turns to* **Ben**, *looks at him, waits.*]

Ben: [*After a minute*] I don't believe that.

Leo: [*Wildly*] *You* don't believe it? What do I care what *you* believe? I do the dirty work and then—

Ben: [*Turning his head sharply to* **Leo**] I'm remem-

bering that. I'm remembering that, Leo.

Oscar: What do you mean?

Leo: You—

Ben: [*To* **Oscar**] If you don't shut that little fool up, I'll show you what I mean. For some reason he knows, but he says a word.

Oscar: Maybe he didn't know that *we*—

Ben: [*Quickly*] That *Leo*— He's no fool. Does Manders know the bonds are missing?

Leo: How could I tell? I was half crazy. I don't think so. Because Manders seemed kind of puzzled and—

Oscar: But we got to find out— [*He breaks off as* **Cal** *comes into the room carrying a kettle of hot water.*]

Ben: How is he, Cal?

Cal: I don't know, Mr. Ben. He was bad. [*Going towards stairs.*]

Oscar: But when did it happen?

Cal: [*Shrugs*] He wasn't feeling bad early. [**Addie** *comes in quickly from the hall*] Then there he is next thing on the landing, fallen over, his eyes tight—

Addie: [*To* **Cal**] Dr. Sloan's over at the Ballongs. Hitch the buggy and go get him. [*She takes the kettle and cloths from him, pushes him, runs up the stairs*] Go on. [*She disappears.* **Cal** *exits.*]

Ben: Never seen Sloan anywhere when you need him.

Oscar: [*Softly*] Sounds bad.

Leo: He would have told *her* about it. Aunt Regina. He would have told his own wife—

Ben: [*Turning to* **Leo**] Yes, he might have told her. But they weren't on such pretty terms and maybe he didn't. Maybe he didn't. [*Goes quickly to* **Leo**] Now, listen to me. If she doesn't know, it may work out all right. If she does know, you're to say he lent you the bonds.

Leo: Lent them to me! Who's going to believe that?

Ben: Nobody.

Oscar: [*To* **Leo**] Don't you understand? It can't do no harm to say it—

Leo: Why should I say he lent them to me? Why not to you? [*Carefully*] Why not to Uncle Ben?

Ben: [*Smiles*] Just because he didn't lend them to me. Remember that.

Leo: But all he has to do is say he didn't lend them to me—

Ben: [*Furiously*] But for some reason, he doesn't seem to be talking, does he?

>   [*There are footsteps above. They all stand looking at the stairs.* **Regina** *begins to come slowly down.*]

Ben: What happened?

Regina: He's had a bad attack.

Oscar: Too bad. I'm so sorry we weren't here when—when Horace needed us.

Ben: When *you* needed us.

Regina: [*Looks at him*] Yes.

Ben: How is he? Can we—can we go up?

Regina: [*Shakes her head*] He's not conscious.

Oscar: [*Pacing around*] It's that—it's that bad? Wouldn't you think Sloan could be found quickly, just once, just once?

Regina: I don't think there is much for him to do.

Ben: Oh, don't talk like that. He's come through attacks before. He will now.

>   [**Regina** *sits down. After a second she speaks softly.*]

Regina: Well. We haven't seen each other since the day of our fight.

Ben: [*Tenderly*] That was nothing. Why, you and Oscar and I used to fight when we were kids.

Oscar: [*Hurriedly*] Don't you think we should go up? Is there anything we can do for Horace—

Ben: You don't feel well. Ah—

Regina: [*Without looking at them*] No, I don't. [*Slight pause*] Horace told me about the bonds this afternoon.

>   [*There is an immediate shocked silence.*]

Leo: The bonds. What do you mean? What bonds? What—

Ben: [*Looks at him furiously. Then to* **Regina**] The Union Pacific bonds? *Horace's* Union Pacific bonds?

Regina: Yes.

Oscar: [*Steps to her, very nervously*] Well. Well what—what about them? What—what could he say?

Regina: He said that Leo had stolen the bonds and given them to you.

Oscar: [*Aghast, very loudly*] That's ridiculous, Regina, absolutely—

Leo: I don't know what you're talking about. What would I— Why—

Regina: [*Wearily to* **Ben**] Isn't it enough that he stole them from me? Do I have to listen to this in the bargain?

Oscar: You are talking—

Leo: I didn't steal anything. I don't know why—

Regina: [*To* **Ben**] Would you ask them to stop that, please? [*There is silence for a minute.* **Ben** *glowers at* **Oscar** *and* **Leo.**]

Ben: Aren't we starting at the wrong end, Regina? What did Horace tell you?

Regina: [*Smiles at him*] He told me that Leo had stolen the bonds.

Leo: I didn't steal—

Regina: Please. Let me finish. Then he told me that he was going to pretend that he had lent them to you [**Leo** *turns sharply to* **Regina**, *then looks at* **Oscar**, *then looks back at* **Regina**] as a present from me—to my brothers. He said there was nothing I could do about it. He said the rest of his money would go to Alexandra. That is all. [*There is a silence.* **Oscar** *coughs,* **Leo** *smiles slyly.*]

Leo: [*Taking a step to her*] I told you he had lent them— I could have told you—

Regina: [*Ignores him, smiles sadly at* **Ben**] So I'm very badly off, you see. [*Carefully*] But Horace said there was nothing I could do about it as long as he was alive to say he had lent you the bonds.

Ben: You shouldn't feel that way. It can all be explained, all be adjusted. It isn't as bad—

Regina: So you, at least, are willing to admit that the bonds were stolen?

Ben: [**Oscar** *laughs nervously*] I admit no such thing. It's possible that Horace made up that part of the story to tease you— [*Looks at her*] Or perhaps to punish you. Punish you.

Regina: [*Sadly*] It's not a pleasant story. I feel bad, Ben, naturally. I hadn't thought—

Ben: Now you shall have the bonds safely back. That was the understanding, wasn't it, Oscar?

Oscar: Yes.

Regina: I'm glad to know that. [*Smiles*] Ah, I had greater hopes—

Ben: Don't talk that way. That's foolish. [*Looks at his watch*] I think we ought to drive out for

Sloan ourselves. If we can't find him we'll go over to Senateville for Doctor Morris. And don't think I'm dismissing this other business. I'm not. We'll have it all out on a more appropriate day.

Regina: [*Looks up, quietly*] I don't think you had better go yet. I think you had better stay and sit down.

Ben: We'll be back with Sloan.

Regina: Cal has gone for him. I don't want you to go.

Ben: Now don't worry and—

Regina: You will come back in this room and sit down. I have something more to say.

Ben: [*Turns, comes towards her*] Since when do I take orders from you?

Regina: [*Smiles*] You don't—yet. [*Sharply*] Come back, Oscar. You too, Leo.

Oscar: [*Sure of himself, laughs*] My dear Regina—

Ben: [*Softly, pats her hand*] Horace has already clipped your wings and very wittily. Do I have to clip them, too? [*Smiles at her*] You'd get farther with a smile, Regina. I'm a soft man for a woman's smile.

Regina: I'm smiling, Ben. I'm smiling because you are quite safe while Horace lives. But I don't think Horace will live. And if he doesn't live I shall want seventy-five per cent in exchange for the bonds.

Ben: [*Steps back, whistles, laughs*] Greedy! What a greedy girl you are! You want so much of everything.

Regina: Yes. And if I don't get what I want I am going to put all three of you in jail.

Oscar: [*Furiously*] You're mighty crazy. Having just admitted—

Ben: And on what evidence would you put Oscar and Leo in jail?

Regina: [*Laughs, gaily*] Oscar, listen to him. He's getting ready to swear that it was you and Leo! What do you say to that? [*Oscar turns furiously towards* **Ben**] Oh, don't be angry, Oscar. I'm going to see that he goes in with you.

Ben: Try anything you like, Regina. [*Sharply*] And now we can stop all this and say good-bye to you. [**Alexandra** *comes slowly down the steps*] It's his money and he's obviously willing to let us borrow it. [*More pleasantly*] Learn to make threats when you can carry them through.

For how many years have I told you a good-looking woman gets more by being soft and appealing? Mama used to tell you that. [*Looks at his watch*] Where the hell is Sloan? [*To* **Oscar**] Take the buggy and— [*As* **Ben** *turns to* **Oscar**, *he sees* **Alexandra**. *She walks stiffly. She goes slowly to the lower window, her head bent. They all turn to look at her.*]

Oscar: [*After a second, moving toward her*] What? Alexandra— [*She does not answer. After a second,* **Addie** *comes slowly down the stairs, moving as if she were very tired. At foot of steps, she looks at* **Alexandra**, *then turns and slowly crosses to door and exits.* **Regina** *rises.* **Ben** *looks nervously at* **Alexandra**, *at* **Regina**.]

Oscar: [*As* **Addie** *passes him, irritably to* **Alexandra**] Well, what is— [*Turns into room—sees* **Addie** *at foot of steps*] —what's? [**Ben** *puts up a hand, shakes his head*] My God, I didn't know—who *could* have known—I didn't know he was that sick. Well, well—I— [**Regina** *stands quietly, her back to them.*]

Ben: [*Softly, sincerely*] Seems like yesterday when he first came here.

Oscar: [*Sincerely, nervously*] Yes, that's true. [*Turns to* **Ben**] The whole town loved him and respected him.

Alexandra: [*Turns*] Did you love him, Uncle Oscar?

Oscar: Certainly, I— What a strange thing to ask! I—

Alexandra: Did you love him, Uncle Ben?

Ben: [*Simply*] He had—

Alexandra: [*Suddenly starts to laugh very loudly*] And you, Mama, did you love him, too?

Regina: I know what you feel, Alexandra, but please try to control yourself.

Alexandra: [*Still laughing*] I'm trying, Mama. I'm trying very hard.

Ben: Grief makes some people laugh and some people cry. It's better to cry, Alexandra.

Alexandra: [*The laugh has stopped. Tensely moves toward* **Regina**] What was Papa doing on the staircase?

[**Ben** *turns to look at* **Alexandra**.]

Regina: Please go and lie down, my dear. We all need time to get over shocks like this. [**Alexandra** *does not move.* **Regina's** *voice becomes softer, more insistent*] Please go, Alexandra.

Alexandra: No, Mama. I'll wait. I've got to talk to you.

Regina: Later. Go and rest now.

Alexandra: [*Quietly*] I'll wait, Mama. I've plenty of time.

Regina: [*Hesitates, stares, makes a half shrug, turns back to* **Ben**] As I was saying. Tomorrow morning I am going up to Judge Simmes. I shall tell him about Leo.

Ben: [*Motioning toward* **Alexandra**] Not in front of the child, Regina. I—

Regina: [*Turns to him. Sharply*] I didn't ask her to stay. Tomorrow morning I go to Judge Simmes—

Oscar: And what proof? What proof of all this—

Regina: [*Turns sharply*] None. I won't need any. The bonds are missing and they are with Marshall. That will be enough. If it isn't, I'll add what's necessary.

Ben: I'm sure of that.

Regina: [*Turns to* **Ben**] You can be quite sure.

Oscar: We'll deny—

Regina: Deny your heads off. You couldn't find a jury that wouldn't weep for a woman whose brothers steal from her. And you couldn't find twelve men in this state you haven't cheated and hate you for it.

Oscar: What kind of talk is this? You couldn't do anything like that! We're your own brothers. [*Points upstairs*] How can you talk that way when upstairs not five minutes ago—

Regina: [*Slowly*] There are people who can never go back, who must finish what they start. I am one of those people, Oscar. [*After a slight pause*] Where was I? [*Smiles at* **Ben**] Well, they'll convict you. But I won't care much if they don't. [*Leans forward, pleasantly*] Because by that time you'll be ruined. I shall also tell my story to Mr. Marshall, who likes me, I think, and who will not want to be involved in your scandal. A respectable firm like Marshall and Company. The deal would be off in an hour. [*Turns to them angrily*] And you know it. Now I don't want to hear any more from any of you. *You'll do no more bargaining in this house.* I'll take my seventy-five per cent and we'll forget the story forever. That's one way of doing it, and the way I prefer. You know me well enough to know that I don't mind taking the other way.

Ben: [*After a second, slowly*] None of us have ever known you well enough, Regina.

Regina: You're getting old, Ben. Your tricks aren't as smart as they used to be. [*There is no answer. She waits, then smiles*] All right. I take it that's settled and I get what I asked for.

Oscar: [*Furiously to* **Ben**] Are you going to let her do this—

Ben: [*Turns to look at him, slowly*] You have a suggestion?

Regina: [*Puts her arms above her head, stretches, laughs*] No, he hasn't. All right. Now, Leo, I have forgotten that you ever saw the bonds. [*Archly, to* **Ben** *and* **Oscar**] And as long as you boys both behave yourselves, I've forgotten that we ever talked about them. You can draw up the necessary papers tomorrow. [**Ben** *laughs.* **Leo** *stares at him, starts for door. Exits.* **Oscar** *moves towards door angrily.* **Regina** *looks at* **Ben,** *nods, laughs with him. For a second,* **Oscar** *stands in the door, looking back at them. Then he exits.*]

Regina: You're a good loser, Ben. I like that.

Ben: [*He picks up his coat, then turns to her*] Well, I say to myself, what's the good? You and I aren't like Oscar. We're not sour people. I think that comes from a good digestion. Then, too, one loses today and wins tomorrow. I say to myself, years of planning and I get what I want. Then I don't get it. But I'm not discouraged. The century's turning, the world is open. Open for people like you and me. Ready for us, waiting for us. After all this is just the beginning. There are hundreds of Hubbards sitting in rooms like this throughout the country. All their names aren't Hubbard, but they are all Hubbards and they will own this country some day. We'll get along.

Regina: [*Smiles*] I think so.

Ben: Then, too, I say to myself, things may change. [*Looks at* **Alexandra**] I agree with Alexandra. What is a man in a wheel chair doing on a staircase? I ask myself that.

Regina: [*Looks up at him*] And what do you answer?

Ben: I have no answer. But maybe some day I will.   Maybe never, but maybe some day. [*Smiles. Pats her arm*] When I do, I'll let you know. [*Goes towards hall.*]

Regina: When you do, write me. I will be in Chicago. [*Gaily*] Ah, Ben, if Papa had only left me his money.

Ben: I'll see you tomorrow.

Regina: Oh, yes. Certainly. You'll be sort of working for me now.

Ben: [*As he passes* **Alexandra**, *smiles*] Alexandra, you're turning out to be a right interesting girl. [*Looks at* **Regina**] Well, good night all. [*He exits.*]

Regina: [*Sits quietly for a second, stretches, turns to look at* **Alexandra**] What do you want to talk to me about, Alexandra?

Alexandra: [*Slowly*] I've changed my mind. I don't want to talk. There's nothing to talk about now.

Regina: You're acting very strange. Not like yourself. You've had a bad shock today. I know that. And you loved Papa, but you must have expected this to come some day. You knew how sick he was.

Alexandra: I knew. We all knew.

Regina: It will be good for you to get away from here. Good for me, too. Time heals most wounds, Alexandra. You're young, you shall have all the things I wanted. I'll make the world for you the way I wanted it to be for me. [*Uncomfortably*] Don't sit there staring. You've been around Birdie so much you're getting just like her.

Alexandra: [*Nods*] Funny. That's what Aunt Birdie said today.

Regina: [*Nods*] Be good for you to get away from all this.

[**Addie** *enters*]

Addie: Cal is back, Miss Regina. He says Dr. Sloan will be coming in a few minutes.

Regina: We'll go in a few weeks. A few weeks! That means two or three Saturdays, two or three Sundays. [*Sighs*] Well, I'm very tired. I shall go to bed. I don't want any supper. Put the lights out and lock up. [**Addie** *moves to the piano lamp, turns it out*] You go to your room, Alexandra. Addie will bring you something hot. You look very tired. [*Rises. To* **Addie**] Call me when Dr. Sloan gets here. I don't want to see anybody else. I don't want any condolence calls tonight. The whole town will be over.

Alexandra: Mama, I'm not coming with you. I'm not going to Chicago.

Regina: [*Turns to her*] You're very upset, Alexandra.

Alexandra: [*Quietly*] I mean what I say. With all my heart.

Regina: We'll talk about it tomorrow. The morning will make a difference.

Alexandra: It won't make any difference. And there isn't anything to talk about. I am going away from you. Because I want to. Because I know Papa would want me to.

Regina: [*Puzzled, careful, polite*] You *know* your papa wanted you to go away from me?

Alexandra: Yes.

Regina: [*Softly*] And if I say no?

Alexandra: [*Looks at her*] Say it, Mama, say it. And see what happens.

Regina: [*Softly, after a pause*] And if I make you stay?

Alexandra: That would be foolish. It wouldn't work in the end.

Regina: You're very serious about it, aren't you? [*Crosses to stairs*] Well, you'll change your mind in a few days.

Alexandra: You only change your mind when you want to. And I won't want to.

Regina: [*Going up the steps*] Alexandra, I've come to the end of my rope. Somewhere there has to be what I want, too. Life goes too fast. Do what you want; think what you want; go where you want. I'd like to keep you with me, but I won't make you stay. Too many people used to make me do too many things. No, I won't make you stay.

Alexandra: You couldn't, Mama, because I want to leave here. As I've never wanted anything in my life before. Because now I understand what Papa was trying to tell me. [*Pause*] All in one day: Addie said there were people who ate the earth and other people who stood around and watched them do it. And just now Uncle Ben said the same thing. Really, he said the same thing. [*Tensely*] Well, tell him for me, Mama, I'm not going to stand around and watch you do it. Tell him I'll be fighting as hard as he'll be fighting [*Rises*] some place where people don't just stand around and watch.

Regina: Well, you have spirit, after all. I used to think you were all sugar water. We don't have to be bad friends. I don't want us to be bad friends, Alexandra. [*Starts, stops, turns to* **Alexandra**] Would you like to come and talk to me, Alexandra? Would you—would you like to sleep in my room tonight?

Alexandra: [*Takes a step towards her*] Are you afraid, Mama? [**Regina** *does not answer. She moves slowly out of sight.* **Addie** *comes to* **Alexandra,** *presses her arm.*]

THE CURTAIN FALLS

Examine in some detail exactly what the playwright is trying to do in *The Little Foxes*, and—what is perhaps even more to the point—what she is *not* trying to do. As you read through this play, what is the over-riding feature that interests you, that makes you want to continue from scene to scene until you reach the end of the play? Is it the thought content, the important fundamental issues of life with which the playwright grapples? Apparently not. Some important issues are raised by the playwright here, and there are some lessons to be learned by an audience in a theatre viewing this play. The audience is shown in graphic terms that greed is an evil thing, that the meek, in order to inherit the earth, must exert a little strength to resist the forces of evil. The title of the play and the Bible verse from which it comes (Solomon 2:15) were not casually selected by the playwright. The Hubbards are, indeed, "little foxes" who are spoiling the vines, and the wider thematic implications of the Hubbards' behavior are rather too obviously pointed out on page 46 when Ben says, "This is just the beginning. There are hundreds of Hubbards sitting in rooms like this throughout the country. All their names aren't Hubbard, but they are all Hubbards and they will own this country someday. We'll get along." The playwright seems to be saying that the world is full of Hubbards, and it is the duty of the "good" people to resist their greedy exploitation of others and to prevent their taking over our society. As Addie points out on page 38 it is also wrong for good people to stand around and watch the greedy ones eat the earth. Evil must be resisted actively, or one is, by default, guilty of abetting it.

These issues are important and clearly meaningful in the context of the play. An audience would be expected to leave the theatre following a good production of this play pondering some of these ideas. However, it is clear that it is not the ideas that keep the play moving forward. Although the interweaving of important ideas is the central concern in some plays, the primary focus of *The Little Foxes* lies elsewhere. Might it not be in character development? Certainly the development of strong, vital, living characterizations is a matter of major concern to the playwright. Regina, particularly, is a role that most actresses would like to "get their teeth into." Sufficient clues are given in the text to reveal something of Regina's early child-

A Discussion of the Script

hood, her upbringing, the importance of being disinherited by her father, and her dissatisfaction with her marriage—motivated less by any love for Horace than by her belief that he would rise financially in the world. These and a variety of other factors in the play build a complete picture of Regina, a sort of psychological case study that an actress can mull over, build upon, and finally make her own; they help her bring to her portrayal a depth of insight that allows the audience to believe that this is a real human being and that they really understand her reasons for proceeding as she does throughout the play. Regina is clearly an evil person, and actors as well as audiences seem to take particular pleasure in plumbing the depths of such evil, trying to understand the factors which motivate it. Ben, Oscar, and Leo are also evil, each in his own way, and again the playwright has so carefully put together a web of "facts" about each character that a capable actor can grasp the essence of his character and can portray it convincingly for an audience. The "good" people in the play, like Horace, Birdie and Alexandra, are also clearly characterized by the playwright; they are developed with sympathy and understanding so that an audience can understand what motivates each one. Even a relatively minor character, such as Addie, is more than just the "typical servant," for she is given certain key thematic lines and is portrayed as one of the stronger forces in the Hubbard household, resisting their greed when weaker members of the family have given up. All of this is no mean accomplishment for a playwright. Anyone who has ever tried to write a play can testify that creating even one character who seems to live and breathe, to be a real person reacting in a real situation, is a difficult undertaking indeed. There are many plays which have attained considerable success without extending reality of characterization to virtually the entire cast. In *The Little Foxes*, it is fair to say that only Cal and Mr. Marshall offer the actor very little with which to work, and the audience very little with which to identify. This is a very good average for any playwright.

But is character development the *central* concern of *The Little Foxes?* In some plays, complete understanding of one or more characters seems to be the central factor that controls the playwright's thinking. When this happens the audience learns more about the characters than their motivations for the action within the play. Indeed, in real life, the most interesting people are usually the unpredictable ones whose motivating forces are difficult to understand, about whom one is forever discovering new facets and new depths of understanding and insight. And so it is in drama. In fact, on second thought, it seems a little too neat, a little too pat, that one understands so completely what makes each of the characters in *The Little Foxes* tick. "Penny-in-the-slot heroes," Bernard Shaw has called such neatly developed characters, "who only work when you drop a motive into them." Such characters, he adds, are "oppressively automatic and uninteresting." Well, perhaps not totally uninteresting, but it is true that they seem quite automatic, and that human nature is in fact far more complex than this. Some few playwrights have had a great deal of success in developing characters who are so wonderously complex, so unpredictable and yet so true to human nature that, like the most interesting people one knows in real life, they are forever revealing new facets, new depths. The characters in *The Little Foxes* hardly qualify for this kind of praise. Two or three well-chosen adjectives virtually sum up all there is to know about most of the characters (Oscar, for example, is greedy, small-minded, and cruel). Thus, their reactions in any given situation can be predicted with considerable accuracy.

This observation does not necessarily indicate a serious fault in the play, for it may not have been the playwright's intention, after all, to put her primary focus on character development. In order to discover the true focus of the play one must note that the motivations and psychological background of each character are only explained sufficiently to make clear to the audience why the character *acts* as he does. His acts are truly important; the reasons for these actions are important only insofar as they are necessary to make the audience accept the actions. Indeed, the overriding feature that holds interest in *The Little Foxes* appears to be what the characters do, their actions, and hence, the plot. Despite the fact that the lessons taught by the play and the characters developed therein are of considerable interest, one's overriding interest, what keeps one turning page after page or returning to one's seat after each intermission, is what happens next. What happens next? Every television crime story or adventure movie that plays the local cinema relies on this device to maintain interest. The effectiveness of a strong plot can hardly be disputed when one sees how audiences clamor for more of the same. No less an authority than Aristotle, the Greek philosopher and the first great drama critic, has insisted that a good plot is the soul of all successful drama, and, although some critics have disputed this contention in the intervening ages, it is still a principle that is widely accepted. A good plot is not easy to put together, but it is a sure-fire device for bringing the audience back into the theatre again and again to find out what happens next.

Miss Hellman has done a masterful job of putting together such a plot in *The Little Foxes.* Beginning with the opening scenes, in which one wonders mildly why Mr. Marshall is in Regina's home and what his presence means for the Hubbards, interest is drawn steadily inward into the machinations of the evil Hubbard family, as each struggles for the upper hand and financial advantage over the other. Will Regina succeed in getting the $75,000 from her husband? Can she persuade Alexandra to bring her father home? What will Horace say when he gets there? Can Ben and Oscar cut Regina out of the money altogether? Will Leo get away with stealing Horace's bonds? Can Horace get to his medicine supply in time? Can Regina finally control her brothers by threatening to reveal their theft? These and other questions occupy attention throughout the play, and as each question is answered, another, even more pressing, is skillfully moved in to take its place. In *The Little Foxes* the art of plot-making attains a high level of accomplishment indeed, as anyone who has seen this play competently produced on the stage can readily testify. Plot construction is the playwright's primary concern, and thus the play should be judged on the success of its plot. A play in which the plot is the primary element, in which "what happens next?" is the principal force that holds interest from scene to scene, is termed a *melodrama.*

Somehow the word "melodrama" has come to have unpleasant connotations in recent years. Perhaps this unpleasantness arises from the large number of melodramas written in America during the nineteenth century which were appallingly bad—so bad that now, if they are revived at all, they are revived only as objects of ridicule. Surely, however, once melodrama is defined as it is above, there exists the possibility of both good and bad melodrama. "Good" melodrama, presumably, would be that which succeeds in building interest by means of plot. The attention of the audience is captivated by "what happens next?" "Bad" melodrama attempts to hold interest by the same means, but fails, or holds interest only to the extent that the audience laughs at its poor construction. There are many perfectly commendable plays (including *The Little Foxes*) that rely primarily on plot and thus may be termed melodrama. Melodramas have often been described as having a series of plot incidents that are "improbable," of relying too heavily on the sensational, or of using character development that is oversimplified, that reduces every character to a "good guy" or a "bad guy." These are all, no doubt, possible characteristics of melodrama, but surely each melodrama should be considered in the light of each of the above qualities. One must judge whether, in the context of that play, the incidents are improbable or sensational, or the characterizations oversimplified. If these qualities are apparent one is probably dealing with "bad" melodrama. Melodrama has a long and honorable tradition, beginning at least as early as some of the works of Euripides, and to classify *The Little Foxes* as melodrama is simply to classify it and not to damn it.

Not every play which has a strong plot is a melodrama, of course. Many fine plays have strong plots and, in addition, other factors which make them different from melodrama. A melodrama, however, is a play which relies on strong plot to the exclusion of other factors, and which enjoys interesting themes, well-developed characterizations, effective language, and so forth only insofar as these elements are necessary to sustain the plot. In some cases these elements may be developed somewhat without interfering with the plot. As soon as these other elements assume equal importance with plot, one has a more complex dramatic form than melodrama. Many, many plays, of course, do not yield to easy categorization of any sort. Some of the well-known categories, such as melodrama, tragedy, farce, and comedy, have from time to time been stretched in an effort to include many plays that do not really fit into them. However, it seems more honest in the long run to admit that, although many plays can conveniently be labeled, many others cannot. Further, some critics attempt to rank these forms, as though melodrama were inferior while tragedy might be ranked as the "highest" genre. Little evidence can be advanced to support such claims. Again, it is probably far more honest simply to admit that the various dramatic types are different, without attempting to say that one is better than the other. Tragedy is generally a good deal more complex than melodrama, but this only makes it different, not better. Tragedy, farce, and comedy will be defined more completely later on.

There are, of course, many ways to put the plot of a play together, and probably no such thing as a "right" way or a "wrong" way exists. On the other hand, in the course of the development of western drama from the Greeks to the present day, perhaps half a dozen fairly standard plot structures have evolved. It would be unreasonable, having defined these structures, to proclaim any play unsatisfactory simply because it fails to measure up to one of them, since many playwrights have experimented, often successfully, with new and different structures that do not appear to conform to any recognizable pattern. On the other hand, an even larger number of playwrights have set out to follow one of the standard patterns and have demonstrably fallen short. Close structural analysis can help one to see these faults. Several of the plays later in this volume do not seem to adhere to any of the readily recognizable structural patterns. *The Little Foxes,* however, can be analyzed quite neatly in terms of the standard form known as the "well-made play." This name, sometimes used derogatorily, developed out of the practice of the nineteenth century French playwright, Eugene Scribe, who was the first to describe in concrete terms this way in which a plot might be put together for sure-fire commercial success. Scribe was essentially a hack commercial playwright with little genius beyond the development of this plot formula. It became fashionable later in the century to sneer at Scribe's work, and such playwrights as Shaw and Ibsen considered themselves above such crassly commercial practice. The fact is, however, that Scribe's structural pattern, the "well-made play," had become so widely accepted in the meantime that Ibsen and Shaw also followed it in its essentials. However, Ibsen and Shaw brought true genius to the *content* of their plays, and thus elevated to true art the *form* that Scribe had synthesized. Because of the commercialism that Scribe had attached to the form, some derogatory connotations have accrued to it, but in fact a great many plays of real merit, as well as an even larger number of no merit, have been structured along the lines of the well-made play; the form can be highly effective when properly used, and it is the dominant form in much of the commercial theatre of today. The typical, mindless Broadway comedy is a well-made play; much of the more serious work on Broadway, particularly during the nineteen thirties and forties, also took the form of the well-made play; and most television situation comedies and dramas, although modified to allow for commercials at regular intervals, still use the form.

In order to follow the structure of the well-made play, one must first understand an even more fundamental concept that originates with Aristotle. A well-plotted play, said Aristotle, must have *unity of action,* and critics have been arguing ever since as to exactly what he meant. Aristotle defined a play as "an imitation of an action." Putting aside the finer points of the controversy regarding the exact meaning of these terms, the *central action,* the "action" which is being "imitated," may be understood as the one central objective that stands behind the plot; one main purpose which one or more of the characters in the play may be trying to accomplish. When this purpose is undertaken, the plot of the play is really underway; when either the purpose has been accomplished or final defeat has been faced, the plot of the play is completed. Usually this purpose, this central action, can be expressed in terms of an infinitive phrase; this phrase tells nothing about the thematic impact the play may have, the characters it may develop, or anything else of a more profound nature—it is simply a statement of that one central concept around which the plot is built. In *Oedipus the King,* a play included later in this text but with which most students are no doubt already familiar, the central action may be stated thus: "to find the killer of Laius." Note that, as the play opens, the audience is first informed of certain essential background information (in well-made play terms, this is called "exposition"). As soon as this information is presented, Oedipus resolves to find the killer of Laius, and the real action of the play begins. When he has found him (the killer, of course, turns out to be Oedipus himself), the play is over. From a description of this sort, one learns nothing whatsoever of the play's values; such a central action might serve just as well for the latest detective story on television. What it does do, however, is provide a useful starting point for the study of the play's plot structure. A play has "unity of action" when it possesses one clear central action and all incidents in the plot are clearly designed to further this central action. A play which is tightly structured and employs this concept would eliminate any and all incidents that did not directly contribute to moving this central action toward its conclusion. Of course, not all plays were intended to have unity of action; certain Renaissance plays, for example, were deliberately structured with two or more plots and thus two or more actions, whereas a number of modern, "plotless" plays appear to have no central action whatsoever. A very large number of good plays do seem to share unity of action, and a great number of weaker plays could demonstrably be improved had the playwright adhered more closely to this principle. Stanislavski, the great Russian acting teacher of the early part of this century, was apparently talking about precisely the same concept when he advised actors always to keep in mind the play's "super-objective." The concept of central action is not a "dry" one reserved for the study—it is an active means of getting at the fundamental elements in a play, and must be understood by those who propose to produce one.

The term "well made" refers to the way the parts of the plot fit together to form or to support the central action. Thus, the first question the critic asks himself, in an attempt to analyze such a play, is "what is the central action?" Usually this is not difficult to perceive if he simply "backs off" from the play and tries to observe what action the central character or characters undertake at the beginning of the play and complete by its end. In the case of *The Little Foxes*, the student might first be inclined to say that the central action is "to gain money," but this would be far too general. The Hubbards have all been trying to gain money for decades, and will no doubt continue to try to gain it long after the play ends. Certainly greed is central to their characters, but this is not the one "action" that the play "imitates." Another student might suggest that the central action is "to get Horace's $75,000," but this, in turn, is too limited a view. Certainly several characters find this a very important objective for a significant portion of the play, but note that, by the end of Act II, it has been accomplished. If one were to agree that this were the central action, he would be forced to the conclusion that the play's third act is extraneous—a conclusion that is quite justified in the case of some poorly constructed plays, but would certainly be inaccurate in the case of *The Little Foxes*. A far more useful working hypothesis for this play's central action might be: "to gain a controlling interest in the mill." This, it would appear, is what the play is about. After a suitable bit of exposition in which the audience is informed of such background data as is necessary, the Hubbards begin to wrangle among themselves with this specific objective in view. The action becomes more and more complicated and intensifies interest until it reaches a point near the end of the third act when the question is finally resolved: Regina will have the controlling interest. Once this is settled, the play is, for all practical purposes, over. Of course, Ben hints that he may re-open the struggle at some future date, but for the time being, at least, it appears that Regina's victory is complete and that the play has reached a clear-cut conclusion. It is only fair to note, however, that this statement of the central action is termed a "working hypothesis." Rarely in dramatic criticism is it possible to prove a point of view indisputably. Even the playwright himself, who might be assumed to be the final authority on such matters, often has worked more from inspired creativity than any coldly rational plan, and cold rationality applied *ex post facto* can hardly be expected to define the product of artistic genius. It is also possible that the playwright genuinely does not know what he has done. Nevertheless, critics who wish to apply rational analysis to a play script must return constantly to the text, and keep in mind that, with any very complex work of art, more than one point of view is usually both admissable and defensible.

"To gain a controlling interest in the mill" may be accepted, then, as a statement of the central action of *The Little Foxes*. With this central action in mind, begin a close, careful re-reading of the script, keeping in mind the necessity to locate its principal structural features and to describe how they fit together to advance this central action. Only after such a careful analysis can one offer some value judgments about the success that the playwright has achieved in the plotting of her play. Please re-read Act I of *The Little Foxes* before continuing with the material below.

Examine what has happened in the first act of this play. It opens with a conversation between the two Negro servants, Addie and Cal. Opening with two servants who tell each other all about what the family is doing (which both would surely have known anyway) has become a tired old cliché of well-made play construction. Thus the audience is made aware of important basic information before the central action can get under way. For a few moments, it might appear that Miss Hellman is going to resort to this cliché to get *The Little Foxes* underway. However, Birdie enters, followed shortly by Oscar, Leo, and finally Regina with Marshall, Ben, and Alexandra, and thus the stage is quickly filled with most of the principal personages of the play. Indeed, within two pages all of the characters except Horace have been introduced. A conversation between two people on stage is difficult enough, but eight at the same time is very, very challenging indeed. The playwright must keep all of them active in some way, which generally means that all must participate in the one central conversation; two or more conversations going on simultaneously (although some playwrights have tried it) are very difficult for an audience to follow. Note how successfully Miss Hellman manages the eight characters in this scene: they have plenty to do and all are involved in the central conversation. The dialogue appears to be natural enough, and at the same time the exposition is proceeding—the audience is learning what it needs to know about the situation which exists at the opening of the play. Thus Miss Hellman is able to begin immediately the complex matter of showing the audience something about the characters on stage. Birdie's giddiness, Oscar's cruelty to her, Leo's adolescent foolishness, and Regina's dominance are established within the first few pages, and hardly a line is spoken which does not give some further insight into the character of the person who speaks or the person spoken about—or both.

As the first act of a well-made play proceeds, one may next expect to find a specific incident which gets the plot under way. Strictly speaking, it should come when all of the necessary exposition has been completed; however, more subtle playwrights have discovered that it can be more interesting to give only the most essential exposition at first, reserving the rest to be slipped in throughout the play as it is needed. Miss Hellman follows the latter technique. The incident which gets the plot under way is known as the "inciting incident." It may be something as direct as a murder in a detective story or Oedipus' resolution to find the killer of Laius. However, in *The Little Foxes*, what specific incident causes the Hubbards to begin to fight each other for control of the mill? Their battle has been going on for years to some extent, as they have apparently always been avaricious and spiteful in their treatment of each other. The specific infighting for control of the mill, however, cannot really break out among the Hubbards until the mill is a definite prospect. Indeed, it is evident that, for a variety of selfish motives, they have cooperated quite effectively up to the point of striking a firm bargain with Marshall. Since the contract with Marshall was signed in the afternoon preceding the dinner party, one might be tempted to say that the signing was the inciting incident; however, that poses the problem of proposing as the inciting incident something that took place before the play even opens. Ben makes it quite clear, however, that he does not consider the contract really firm until they have drunk a toast to it—an idea which is a bit strained, perhaps, but which is introduced to serve precisely this function: to provide a starting point from which the principal action of the play may proceed. It would have been time-consuming and rather out of place at a fashionable dinner party to stage the actual signing of a contract. The substitution of the toast does the job quite effectively, and in retrospect, it is quite clear that this is the moment the jockeying begins in the Hubbard family. As soon as Marshall's 49 per cent of the mill is definitely arranged, he has served his function in the play and can be dismissed from the scene; the precise division of the remaining 51 per cent is now at issue.

After the inciting incident, there begins what is known as the "rising action." During the rising action, additional complications are introduced as the struggle implied by the central action begins to get under way. Many critics have pointed out that *conflict* is at the heart of the drama; certainly, conflict between opposing forces is central to the well-made play structure, and during the rising action this conflict becomes more and more intense. It is an over simplification, but indeed indicative of fundamental truth, to say that exposition sets the scene, the inciting incident identifies what the conflict will be, and the rising action shows this conflict in process. More and more complications are introduced at this point by the playwright. New facets of the problem are suddenly revealed, new characters (who complicate the problem) are often introduced, the combatants (whoever they may be) draw out such weapons as they possess in an effort to win the struggle. In *The Little Foxes*, Ben and Oscar demand that Regina get her share of the necessary capital from Horace without further delay and suggest that they might proceed without her; Regina counters by pointing out that they do not want to involve people outside the family. Regina presses her advantage by demanding a larger share of the profits; Ben agrees (taking her larger portion out of Oscar's share), but sets a two-week time limit. Oscar objects to losing some of his share, but is placated by a half-promise that Leo can marry Alexandra. Alexandra is talked into going to Baltimore to bring her father home, but Birdie warns her of the plot to marry her to Leo. All these factors complicate the struggle among the principal parties, and, at that particular moment, do not point to any specific solution of the problems involved. The various ramifications of the central action are merely explored, increasing both the interest and the complication as the play moves toward the first act curtain.

Two other technical devices used by the playwright should be pointed out here. One is called "foreshadowing." Note that on page 000 the point is made that Leo has previously stolen money from the bank in which he works. The introduction of this idea at this point helps to characterize Leo, of course, and to show why he would be a most unsuitable mate for Alexandra. Indeed, if mention of the theft did not fit so naturally into the conversation, it would serve very poorly its other, and more important function, which is to pave the way for the crucial business of stealing Horace's bonds from his safe-deposit box. If a device such as this is so obvious that the attention of each member of the audience is forcibly directed to it, thinking, "Ah, that must be important for some future action," then it is poorly used indeed. Foreshadowing skillfully used, as it is here, simply allows the viewer to realize later that the foreshadowed action, important as it is, seems logical and credible—indeed, sometimes ironic—in view of what has been established earlier in the play. He may or may not remember specific lines (such as the one referred to here), but Leo's character and the actions of which he is capable have been clearly fixed in his mind.

The second technical device is the use of sufficiently strong material to end the act. Since rising action is in progress, the less skillful playwright might be tempted simply to cut the act off after a sufficient number of complications had been introduced and send the audience out for intermission. What Miss Hellman has done, however, is far more effective. In the process of building these complications, she has managed to find one that has especially strong emotional impact and to use it to bring the curtain down with unusual force. She brings in Oscar in time to overhear Birdie telling Alexandra of the plan to marry her to Leo, and has Oscar slap her face by way of rebuke. The effect is heightened even further by the use of *dramatic irony* (the device by which the audience knows something that some of the characters on stage do not), for Oscar stands there listening long before Birdie knows of his presence, and tension is built up in the audience as they wait to see how he will react to Birdie's betrayal of his plans. The effect of this provides an emotional climax just before the curtain—a device which repeats in miniature within the act itself the over-all pattern of the well-made play. If the audience members are not brought to the edges of their seats just before the intermission, it is assumed, some may simply leave instead of returning for the second act. Whatever validity this theory may have, the technique is skillfully applied here in a scene that is bound to evoke strong empathic response from an audience.

At this point, return to the script and read Act II, then continue with the material below.

The second act of a well-made play is, in many ways, the most difficult to write. In the first act, the novelty of meeting new characters and the interest of seeing a new situation developing will often be sufficient to maintain the interest of an audience, and in the third act, the climax, the workingout of the central action, and the conclusion of the play will almost surely be of interest to an audience that has remained through two acts. The second act, however, calls for all the inventive powers that the playwright can muster to recapture the attention of an audience after an intermission; raise their interest level back to the pitch of the first act curtain; and then sustain this interest through the ever-increasing series of complications that constitute the continuing action of the play. Again, the playwright will probably repeat in miniature within the act something of the over-all pattern of the play. If any length of time is understood to have elapsed since the conclusion of the first act (one week has elapsed in *The Little Foxes*), the second act must begin with exposition, telling the audience what has happened in the interim. Then there must be an "inciting incident" of sorts to get the action of the act under way, building finally to another climax and a strong curtain. *The Little Foxes* follows this pattern.

As the act opens Oscar enters to find Addie already in the room. Their conversation begins to establish the amount of time that has passed and the concern of Oscar and the other Hubbards over the fact that Horace, although expected no later than the night before, still has not returned. The playwright is faced with the problem of getting the principal characters into Regina's living room to face Horace, for it would be awkward and difficult to have them all burst in after his arrival. She can perform the necessary task of exposition and also assemble them in a natural manner by bringing them in first, out of concern to see whether he has arrived yet. However, rather than simply bringing them in one after another, the playwright has skillfully introduced another extremely important complicating feature in the rising action: Leo enters shortly after his father and reveals how easily he has access to Horace's safe-deposit box. Perhaps this revelation is a bit contrived, but it is so completely in accord with the Leo's bumbling nature, as it has been established, that a moderately skilled actor can bring it off without making the audience feel it is unnatural. With this information established, Ben and Regina can make their entrance; all the Hubbards go in to breakfast, and the stage is set for the incident that really gets the action of this act underway—the arrival of Horace.

With Horace in the house, it is clear that the plot is going to escalate in another series of complications that will move it toward a final solution. Before these complications begin, however, the playwright has several key things to accomplish. Note how she accomplishes this. On page 000 there is another extremely important bit of foreshadowing. Before Horace has had a chance to say anything more than, "How are you, Addie? How have you been?", Alexandra establishes the importance of the bottle of medicine that will figure so strongly in the next act. "No, don't take that. That's father's medicine. I'll hold it. It mustn't break." The medicine is mentioned three more times in the next several lines concluding with "Remember about his medicine, Addie." If anyone in the audience has failed to note the significance of the medicine by this time, he must surely be asleep. It must also be clearly established right away that Horace is a dying man, and this, too, is accomplished by a series of devices throughout the early part of the scene. One appearance of so significant a device is rarely enough; the playwright knows that it is necessary to mention the really important plot ideas several times in order to plant them firmly in the audience's minds. That Horace knows about the proposed mill has already been established, but it is also necessary to show that he understands the danger to his daughter if he were to participate in the deal. This, too, is accomplished by having Addie tell him outright before the others come in. Thus, in one short, quick scene, the playwright has been able to establish all the necessary details and prepare the audience fully for the impending confrontation between Horace and the Hubbards.

The increasing complications of the rising action which fill out the bulk of the second act can really be reduced to three principal scenes. The first is the confrontation between Horace and Regina. (The entrance of the Hubbard family to greet Horace is merely preliminary—it allows the audience to get an even clearer picture of Horace's relationship to each of them—but the really important business of the scene occurs when the other Hubbards retire and Regina is left alone with Horace.) Very skillfully the playwright allows us to see Regina probing Horace's armor, trying to learn exactly where she stands with him after their long separation. The frustrations of each as they sense that the relationship will not be an easy one are clearly depicted, and finally Regina forces a confrontation between Ben and Horace that will clearly be a key one in the struggle for control of the mill. This confrontation is the second of the three scenes referred to above, and of course, the outcome is Horace's refusal to invest the $75,000 for which he has been asked. As Horace retires upstairs and Regina follows him to continue their fight, the third principal complicating scene takes place: Oscar and Leo broach the plan to steal Horace's bonds from his safe-deposit box.

Toward the end of the second act of a well-made play, one can expect to find a key structural feature known as the *turning point*. The turning point is defined as the one incident which turns the course of events in the central action and determines the final outcome of the play. In a detective story, the turning point might be the discovery of that one clue which, the detective later points out, revealed to him once and for all who the murderer was. This illustration shows that the audience does not necessarily realize at the time the incident occurs that it is the turning point; it is only necessary that in retrospect, one be able to determine that this was the one point which made the outcome of the central action inevitable. Obviously, then, the incident in question must be given sufficient prominence by the playwright and by the actors to insure that the audience will not miss it altogether, although, as has been suggested, they need not recognize at the time its full significance. In *The Little Foxes*, the central action is "to gain control of the mill," and Regina is the character who eventually gains this control. Therefore, the turning point may be located by asking which single incident finally tips the balance in her favor and leads inevitably to her victory. One might be tempted to say that the death of Horace is such an incident, but this occurs too late in the play. By this time, events are already running in Regina's favor, although perhaps she does not recognize the fact. Had Horace lived, Regina's triumph would no doubt have been delayed, but it would not have been averted. Ben and Oscar were entirely at Horace's mercy, and surely it is reasonable to say that it would only be a question of time before Regina could exploit this situation to her advantage. No, a far more reasonable identification of the turning point is the moment when Ben agrees to the stealing of Horace's bonds. This is true, not only because it occurs near the end of the second act, where one expects to find the turning point in the typical well-made play, but also because, in retrospect, it is clear that at this moment the tide turns and begins to run against Ben, Oscar, and Leo. Until this moment, it has been a fairly equal battle, with perhaps a slight advantage on Ben's side. Certainly it has not been clear who would win control of the mill, and the victory could have gone either way. But when Ben agrees to the stealing of the bonds, he sets in motion a series of consequences over which he has no further control and which lead inevitably to his downfall—the action is "out of human control," so to speak, and begins to move under its own power toward a solution of the problem implicit in the central action. These are the qualities which characterize the turning point.

The turning point is also of interest because it signals the end of the rising action and the beginning of what is known as the *falling action*. The falling action is a series of incidents, too, just as is the rising action, but it is "falling" only in the sense outlined above—events moving "out of human control," under their own power and without the introduction of further complications by the playwright, as they rush inevitably toward the play's climax. Of course this in no sense implies a falling off of the audience's interest. If the playwright does his job well, interest will continue to increase, the sense of "what happens next" will continue to rise, throughout the falling action. The turning point does represent a significant change in the *nature* of the events that occur as the central action moves forward, however, and thus it is useful to use separate names to distinguish clearly beween the rising action and the falling action. The falling action of *The Little Foxes* begins immediately after the turning point; as Oscar is dispatched to Chicago, Ben tells Regina that she has lost her chance to invest in the mill, and Regina and Horace have their final, powerful quarrel. However, there is time for very little falling action in the few remaining pages of Act II. In general, the falling action is reserved for the third act of the typical well-made play. Again, note how skillfully the playwright has met her need for an emotionally powerful moment with which to end the act. She contrives to get Horace and Regina together on the stage once again, and Regina, speaking out of bitterness and frustration at apparently having lost all she had hoped to gain, openly attacks Horace with, "I hope you die. I hope you die soon. I'll be waiting for you to die." When performed by a competent actress, this is indeed a powerful and gripping moment in the theatre.

Now re-read the third act, and then continue with the material on the next page.

It is typical of the structure of the well-made play that the turning point should appear to leave the protagonist at the lowest point of his fortunes, doomed to certain defeat, when in fact his ultimate success has been assured. This, of course, is exactly what occurs in *The Little Foxes.* When Ben, Oscar, and Leo decide to steal the bonds, it appears that Regina has been cut out of the mill venture once and for all, when in fact it is this very act which finally hands her complete control. It is the business of the falling action in the third act to show this ironic solution. The act begins rather slowly, for the playwright has exposition to take care of. She decides to combine the exposition with a relatively lengthy scene in which Birdie's character is more fully explored and the thematic implications of the central action are more directly stated than anywhere else in the play. Because this scene does not advance the central action, the forward movement of the play seems to come to a halt; this produces an unfortunate effect at a critical moment. The playwright does several specific things to minimize this negative effect, however. In the first place, she has made Birdie's character so touchingly pathetic that one tends to overlook the structural problem created. Secondly, by directing attention to the thematic significance of the action, she takes attention away from the action itself. But, perhaps most significantly in structural terms, the scene is interrupted by a specific bit of forward-moving action: Cal is sent to the bank to reveal to Leo that Horace has opened the safe-deposit box. The box has been in full view of the audience since the scene opened, but it is doubtful that the audience will realize its full significence until Horace draws attention to it on page 37. This simple device, then, is most skillfully used to reveal to the audience the key fact that Horace knows his bonds are gone, to break up the rather static scene at the opening of the act, and to get the falling action under way again. As the audience waits for the explosive results of this message, the playwright can provide the further exposition necessary—and Birdie's "drunk scene" is a touching one indeed when performed by a competent actress. Also, Horace plans to make a new will, Alexandra is removed from the Hubbard's reach and Cal returns from the bank: all these necessary bits of plot, are quickly disposed of before Regina's entrance.

The significant falling action of the play gets under way in earnest in the first of three key scenes: the final confrontation between Regina and Horace. Horace tells Regina about the bonus and how he proposes to prevent her from profiting from her brothers' mistake. Regina, however, seeing at once that there is one way she can interfere with Horace's plan and at the same time regain control of the mill, withholds Horace's medicine, and, in effect, murders him. As Horace is moved upstairs and the room cleared, Leo, Ben, and Oscar enter and immediately the second major scene of the falling action takes place. Leo reveals to the brothers that the safe-deposit box has been opened. Finally, in the third major scene, Regina re-enters and, step by step, proceeds to clinch her victory, taking control of the mill. First, she reveals that she knows about the bonds and threatens to put her brothers in jail; Horace dies, giving her the power to carry out her threat, so finally she is able to proclaim her triumph once and for all. The brothers concede her victory.

At this point the play reaches another very important feature of well-made play construction, its *climax:* The play's climax is the moment at which the objective or central action, is finally accomplished—or denied. If the central action is "to find the killer of Laius," then the climax is the moment at which the killer is revealed. If the central action is "to gain a controlling interest in the mill," then the climax is the moment at which Regina attains this objective: it occurs on page 46 immediately following Horace's death, when Regina announces that she has triumphed and the brothers concede her victory. The word "climax" is often popularly used to denote the moment of highest *interest* in a piece of literature; usually this does coincide with the moment when the central action is finally resolved. Indeed, if interest has been held throughout the play by the question of who will gain control of the mill it seems reasonable that the highest point of interest should occur when that question is finally answered. In the case of *The Little Foxes*, however, it has been argued that Horace's collapse on the stairs is so emotionally powerful that it is the point of highest interest in the play. It is clearly not the climax in structural terms, however, since the question of who is to control the mill has not yet been resolved. Furthermore, if the play's climax did come at that point, a serious problem would arise in the several scenes that occur after it: they would be, literally, anticlimactic. Fortunately, however, a director and his actors who understand the problem can help the playwright if there is a structural weakness in the script. Skillful playing of the succeeding scenes can continue to raise the interest level and hold the audience's attention to the key question, "who will gain control of the mill." If there is any doubt where the true climax of the play lies, an effective performance can resolve this issue so that the point of highest interest coincides with the point at which the central problem is resolved.

All which follows the climax of a well-made play is known as the *denouement*. The word comes from a French word meaning to untie, and the denouement is that portion of the play in which any remaining complications are untied and any unresolved questions are settled. Often, in a comedy, this involves a pairing off of lovers; in a detective story, the scene in which the detective explains how he discovered the killer. In *The Little Foxes* most of the business has been settled. Ben makes it clear that he will continue to look for an opportunity to re-open the struggle; Alexandra establishes once and for all her independence and suggests that she will escape her mother's influence as Horace wished her to. The denouement gives the playwright the important opportunity to state once again any thematic insights that may be derived from the action just concluded. A playwright may stop a play exactly at the climax—if there are no remaining knots to be untied, he may simply omit the denouement altogether. But playwrights who have thematic statements to make usually value this last opportunity to state them strongly; a play that ends exactly on the climax is usually a bit too much of a jolt for an audience anyway. Miss Hellman makes excellent use of her denouement to let the audience know that Regina's victory has been a hollow one indeed; that if the good were not so meek, the greedy could not inherit the earth. Again making use of an emotion-packed curtain line, she reaffirms that the kind of victory Regina has gained can lead only to loneliness and fear.

The Little Foxes, then, is a play in which the plot is the dominant feature. Characterization, theme, and language are important and make their contribution to the play's success; but the ultimate effectiveness of the play as performed must rest upon the plot. Miss Hellman has constructed her plot along the familiar lines of the well-made play; although this is not the only effective play structure, it is a significant one, the influence of which is widely felt in the modern theatre. The typical well-made play includes the features outlined above. It opens with exposition, the imparting of basic information necessary to an audience's understanding of the play. Then, there is an inciting incident, a single occurrence that gets the central action under way by motivating the central character or characters to perform a specific task. As this central action moves from its inciting incident to its turning point, there is the rising action, a series of complications introduced by the playwright to develop fully the complexities inherent in the central action. At the turning point, one specific incident takes place which determines once and for all the outcome of the central action; from this point on there is no necessity for the playwright to introduce new complications. The action is borne by its own momentum, so to speak, through the falling action, which is a series of incidents working out the central action in the inevitable fashion already determined by the turning point. The falling action reaches its culmination at the climax, the single point at which the central action is finally resolved. Following the climax, there is a short denouement in which any unresolved questions are settled and any remaining knots untied. Most significantly however, a well-made play (and many other plays, for that matter) has a clear, definable central action, which has a beginning, a middle, and an end within the play, as illustrated by *The Little Foxes.* It is the one "action" of which the play is an "imitation." The form of this central action as it progresses through the well-made play structure may be diagrammed as follows:

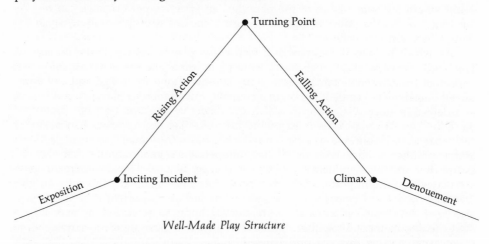

Well-Made Play Structure

Perhaps the diagram will help to give a clearer understanding of the meaning of the various terms discussed earlier. The diagram, however, should be recognized as representing the *central action* of the play. The audience' *interest level*, if it were to be diagrammed, might look something like this:

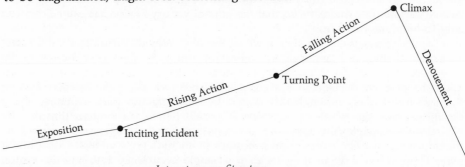

Interest versus Structure

It is important not to confuse the two concepts.

The term *central action* is by no means unique to the study of the well-made play. It has been applied to various other forms since its basic concept was first delineated in Aristotle's *Poetics.* The other terms used earlier, such as exposition, inciting incident, rising action, turning point, falling action, climax, and denouement, *are* closely associated with the well-made play; however, some of them are often used in describing features of other types of plays. Most plays open with some sort of device to let the audience know certain basic information which it will need, and whatever this device may be, it is usually referred to as exposition. Virtually any play with a central action has that central action finally resolved in some way; the point at which this occurs is called the climax. However, not every play described in these terms is a well-made play. Only a play that exhibits all these features, and in the order described, may be properly termed thus. In their enthusiasm over the apparent effectiveness of the well-made play structure, some critics have tried to force *all* plays into this one Procrustean form, and to condemn any play that does not conform. To do so, however, is to deny the artist his creative freedom and to debilitate the form itself. The well-made play structure must be stretched beyond all recognition to accommodate such recognized standards of excellence as *Oedipus the King* and *Hamlet.* The well-made play is not the *only* structural pattern, but it is a highly effective form and a useful beginning point for a study of drama.

The Little Foxes, with its relatively uncomplicated and straightforward content, may be used to illustrate one more concept which is all too often clouded with mysticism—the concept of symbolism. A symbol is simply something which, by common agreement within a group of people, is allowed to represent something else. These marks on the paper before you, called letters and words, are simply a series of symbols for certain sounds which people make with their vocal mechanisms. These sounds, in turn, are symbols for certain things which exist in nature (at least in the case of nouns). A red light hanging at a traffic intersection is a symbol which nearly everyone knows how to interpret. In the theatre, a great many symbols are employed for the purpose of *compression,* an essential ingredient of drama. What a symbol can convey need not be explained in complex dialogue, and concepts of enormous complexity can be put before an audience without wasting time. Consider Birdie in *The Little Foxes.* She serves a function just as she is, and the playwright need not have employed her further. By the addition of some very simple lines here and there, however, Miss Hellman makes Birdie a *symbol* of the southern aristocracy of by-gone days. Birdie's pitiful inadequacy in the face of abuse symbolizes the inadequacy of a whole segment of the southern people to face the rise of a new, industrial era. If anyone fails to see this connection between Birdie and the larger concept she symbolizes, he has certainly not lost the main threads of the play; but if he does perceive the relationship, the play suddenly takes on wider thematic implications. The playwright, with very little effort, makes her audience aware of the Hubbards as a microcosm of a whole society. Some playwrights, of course, are not attempting to make their audience think; they are satisfied if an audience simply enjoys itself. Others, however, like to raise philosophical issues of major proportions, and the use of symbols is an effective, shorthand way to accomplish this. The "foxes" of the play's title are, of course, another important symbol. By suggesting that the Hubbards are like the Biblical foxes that spoil the vines, the playwright can, in one stroke, say more about the Hubbards and their effect on society than she might otherwise say in ten pages of dialogue. The foxes, of course, are only a verbal symbol in this play; no real foxes are ever seen on stage. Birdie, on the other hand, is really there; a stage metaphor is always far, far more effective when it is actually present.

Many plays make use of a stage property, a piece of scenery, a light, or some other device as a real, tangible symbol for a more abstract concept. If this is well done, and the audience really comprehends its significance, the device can be devastatingly effective. *The Little Foxes* is not a play rich in symbols, but a few provide a useful opportunity to understand the use of symbolism at its simplest level. Some plays have such a complex structure of interweaving symbols that understanding them on the written page is extremely difficult. Needless to say, it is an even greater accomplishment to convey their significence to a theatre audience.

Acting is the fundamental art of the theatre. Good theatre can exist without settings, special lighting effects, makeup, properties, or other physical appurtenances. Good theatre can even exist without a script, witness the improvised Commedia dell' Arte of the Renaissance. But the very nature of theatre dictates that an actor shall perform before an audience; attention must now be directed to this basic art of performing before an audience. Because acting is an art rather than a craft, it is difficult to define exactly what the actor does, what the primary differences between good acting and bad acting are, or even what acting is. Like most arts, acting involves certain mechanical crafts that can be identified, classified, and studied, but acting differs from painting and piccolo playing in that the actor's instrument is himself: even the mechanical crafts relate to the control of his own body and mind, perhaps as difficult a challenge as a human being can face. It will not be possible in this short space to do more than introduce certain facets of acting which an observant audience might notice. The concepts presented here do not claim to be a complete theory of acting; they introduce, rather, certain aspects of the art with which the interested observer will want to be concerned.

In the first place, perhaps it is necessary to point out one or two things that acting is not. Good acting is not necessarily acting totally different from the actor's own personality. Who can say that the acting of John Wayne, for example, who has played essentially the same character in dozens of movies throughout his lifetime (a character which is popularly assumed to be his own personality), is either better or worse than the acting of Alec Guiness, who is able to change his mannerisms from one role to the next so totally that he is barely recognizable? It would be fair to say that Guiness demonstrates a versatility that Wayne does not, but insofar as Wayne plays his one role well, he is a "good actor." Furthermore, good acting does not necessarily make one totally forget the actor. Few would deny the talent and skill of Bob Hope or Jack Benny, and yet it is clear that when either one of these entertainers plays a role that presumably represents another person, the audience never actually forgets whom they are watching. The fact is, of course, that aside from certain technical attributes such as a voice that can be

Acting

Greek Tragedian

heard and a body which is controlled and expressive, the actor must possess the intangible quality which allows him to project a personality to an audience. In some circumstances, it is his own personality which is appropriate, and in other circumstances, he must assume the personality of someone else, but in either case the personality used must be projected so that an audience can relate to it. Perhaps the ability to project a personality, more than any other quality is what is meant by "talent." In some people it appears to be inborn, in others apparently it can be developed, but this intangible quality called talent is a fundamental feature of good acting.

The actor who can project his own personality well is in a class by himself, and need not be of further concern here. Many of the world's truly outstanding plays call for actors who can bring their own personalities to bear, "commenting on" a role at the same time they are interpreting it for an audience. However, this discussion will begin with the type of acting in which the actor must, to a large extent, lay aside his own personality and create another in its place. Never, even in the most intensely emotional scene, may the actor totally forget his own identity; he still retains his obligation as an actor to speak loudly and clearly enough that everyone may hear, to move in such a manner that everyone may see and interpret his more meaningful gestures, and to confine himself almost entirely to the exact patterns that have been rehearsed so that his fellow actors will not become confused. In short, even in the most "realistic" of stage situations, in which the viewer may totally forget himself, a good actor must retain control. He is bound by what has been called the "dual function of the actor;" in other words he must adopt the personality of the character he is playing to whatever degree is appropriate to the script and the production, retaining his own identity sufficiently to carry out the mechanical obligations mentioned above. The balance between these two concepts will vary from one play to another and even from one scene to another within a play, but the actor who ignores the balance altogether and goes to either extreme is guilty of bad acting. At least three errors can upset this balance: the actor might enter too completely into the character and forget to project it to his audience; this is relatively rare, but when it occurs it is certainly undesirable. The actor might strike a reasonable balance between the two concepts, but it might be the wrong balance for the stylistic requirements of the play; this mistake is a good deal more common, and is a basis for reasonable criticism and discussion. The actor might fail to enter completely enough into the personality of the character he is playing, and thus appear stiff and awkward to an audience. This is the most common difficulty, especially in amateur productions, and because of this danger most discussions of acting are largely devoted to the problem of entering fully into a character.

Because the actor's own body is his instrument, he must gain complete control of it. Most plays have a strongly verbal orientation; therefore, one thinks first of the voice and what it must be able to do: the actor must be heard, which is not so much a matter of speaking loudly as it is *projection*—the actor learns to "speak to the back row" without undue strain on his vocal mechanism. Not only must he be heard, but he must also be understood, which means that an actor must develop good, clear diction. Relatively few actors have problems with not being loud enough; their trouble is more likely to be either in projection or diction. These skills are fundamental, but a good actor must also develop vocal variety so that he may delib-

The illustrations in this chapter depict some major acting styles.

erately choose a pitch and a quality suitable for any role he may be playing. The actor must develop his body in other ways as well. He must have grace and physical control: an actor's training may include tumbling, fencing, dancing, and other activities designed to develop grace, strength, and coordination—not so much to perform unusual or difficult feats when they are needed, but rather to enable him to move about the stage, sitting, standing, walking, and climbing stairs in an easy and graceful manner. People who perform these simple acts every day without difficulty may become impossibly awkward when asked to do them on stage unless they have had some training. Finally, the novice actor learns a number of mechanical "tricks of the trade" regarding physical movement, which he is expected to apply in any proscenium stage situation where there is not a definite reason for doing otherwise. These include making turns downstage (toward the audience) in order not to turn one's back on the audience, standing with the upstage foot ahead of the downstage, sitting by feeling for the edge of the chair with the calf of the upstage leg, and a number of other such details. It is most revealing to watch how two experienced actors play a scene together. If they are equally important within the scene, they will usually be expected to "share" the scene—that is, to stand facing each other on a line parallel to the curtain line, each with his upstage ahead of his downstage foot. In certain situations, the director may instruct one actor to "give" the scene to the other by turning slightly upstage, while the other actor moves a little upstage and then turns to face downstage. In other situations, however, an actor may actually try to "steal" a scene by deliberately "upstaging" the other actor, that is, maneuvering himself into a position which forces the other actor to give him the scene. Somehow, inexperienced amateurs seem invariably to work themselves into such awkward positions. Ask one of them to approach another actor on stage, and he will usually upstage him. These examples are typical of the many mechanical matters with which the actor must concern himself, yet they still do not get to the heart of the problem facing the actor.

Around the turn of the century, a Russian director and teacher of acting, Konstantin Stanislavski, became internationally famous for the system which he had developed for training actors. Without ignoring the mechanical matters mentioned above, Stanislavski reduced to comprehensible units the formidable matter of preparing the inner self to assume the personality of another. Translated, Americanized, and overpublicized, this approach has become "The Method", about which there has been a great deal of talk in recent years. Since it neither promises nor delivers any miracles, this aspect of the Stanislavski system may best be described as an approach by which the painstaking actor may develop his inner resources. It emphasizes such concepts as development of the imagination, concentration of attention on stage, relaxation of the muscles, emotional memory, tempo, rhythm, and others too complex for consideration here. Perhaps the distinguishing feature of the Stanislavski method, from the actor's point of view, is its emphasis on the inner approach to a role as opposed to an exterior approach. An actor using an exterior approach (and good actors are almost equally divided about which approach they use) would first select and adopt the physical mannerisms of the character he was playing. A special walk, characteristic arm movements, use of props such as glasses or a cane, special vocal patterns—all these decisions become important in creating the character as the actor might see him in his mind's eye. Assuming these physical characteristics one by one, the actor expects the emotional to develop out of the physical qualities. If all outward details are right, he assumes the inner feeling will follow. If, indeed,

Roman Comedian

all the outward details are right, he has achieved a perfect imitation of the correct emotion and his internal state is immaterial. The actor using the inner approach, on the other hand, studies the life and background of the character, his motivations and psychology, and real life situations which may be similar to the character's. His objective is understanding, as completely as possible, what it actually feels like to be the character. With the aid of his own trained imagination and emotions he tries to feel just as the character might feel in any given situation throughout the play; he assumes, within reasonable limits, that the appropriate physical characteristics will naturally follow. For instance, the actor assumes, if he feels real anger, as a corporate executive might feel it, the action of crashing his fist down on the desk (or a similar appropriate action) might naturally follow. The difference between these two approaches is not as simple as it may have been made to appear here, and most actors would admit to using at least some elements of both; however, the basic distinction is an important one.

Itinerant actors of the Middle Ages. From Dr. Essenwein: *Mittelalterliches Hausbuch,* 1908.

Whether he uses an inner or an outer approach to his role, the actor is obligated to begin with the script. He must study the character he is playing and the play as a whole in order to understand every detail of the character's life, background, and motivations and their relationship to the whole play. What is referred to here as the central action, Stanislavski called the play's "super-objective," and added that it is the business of the actor to relate everything he does to this super-objective. Furthermore, Stanislavski recommended breaking down each character's role into units and determining an objective for each, so that each time the actor goes on stage he knows exactly what objective he is trying to attain within that particular unit, as well as its relationship to the super-objective of the entire play. In addition to that, Stanislavski said, it is necessary for each actor to plot out the "unbroken line of his role," so that as he moves from unit to unit he keeps in mind what relates one unit to the next. He must also be cognizant of what has happened to the character in the interim, if he was off stage between units. If this analysis is not performed in Stanislavski's terms, the actor must find another method. The actor who wishes to be effective must understand intimately the character he is playing, and if the play does not provide all the information he needs, he must dig it up elsewhere. Good plays by good playwrights provide a wealth of detail about each of the characters, and there is almost no limit to the new things an actor may learn by studying his own lines, what other characters say about him, and so forth. Even the best actors report again and again that, after playing a role for performance after performance, they suddenly gain a new insight from the script which alters their playing in some way. The actor may often go outside the script to observe people in real life who seem to have personality traits similar to those of the character he is playing, do research into the lives of historical figures, or study certain types of neuroses. The actor fills in from his own repertoire the details unobtainable elsewhere, by using his imagination and his intelligence. No fictional character, however well developed, is ever 100 per cent complete, and the actor's own mind and body must fill in whatever is left. No details are ever omitted on the stage; they are all there, whether right or wrong for the role.

Of course it is possible to clutter up a play or a single role with useless details. The actor strives for more than mere imitation: the actor is an artist, and, consistent

Punchinello, a commedia dell'arte character. From *Philobiblon.*
Vienna: Herbert Reichner, 1938.

with the other arts, he strives for simplicity and a seeming effortlessness that conveys all he wishes to convey with all the power and economy that he can muster. Art which is apparently "artless" is often the best. In conjunction with simplicity, the actor must create what has been called the "illusion of the first time," which means simply that, despite the weeks of rehearsal during which every detail of a performance has been worked out, the audience must be able to believe that the character is facing his situation for the first time—that Alexandra, for example, has never before seen her mother in the awful light that she does by the end of Act III. Of course, no sane member of the audience *really* believes that the events are occurring for the first time, any more than he believes that he is really seeing Regina and Horace up there on the stage; however, the illusion must be strong enough so that the audience can believe what is happening. Audience members come to the theatre ready to suspend their disbelief willingly; they want to enter into the theatrical experience, and given half a chance, they will. It is important, however, in any play which operates on the principle of suspended disbelief, that the actor do nothing to break the illusion.

The principal force working for the actor in creating the illusion of reality is called "empathy." Empathy is a not-fully-understood psychological phenomenon by which the spectator actually enters imaginatively into the being of the character on the stage; he lives and suffers with him and feels afterward as though he has personally lived through what the character on stage has experienced. Empathy involves more than a merely emotional association; a spectator who has entered fully into a character on the stage will actually react physically (but in miniature) as the character is reacting. If the character is fencing, the spectator's arm muscles will contract; if Horace strains to get up those stairs to his medicine, the spectator's whole body will strain in that direction as well. An analogous situation occurs in the football stadium when the home team, behind by one point, has the ball, fourth down and goal to go, in the last three minutes of the game. The spectators enter into the game physically as well as emotionally even though, presumably, they remain in the grandstands. They are on their feet, pushing toward the goal line along with the ball carrier. Occasionally, in the theatre as in the ballpark, a spectator will actually lose control of himself sufficiently to leave his seat and enter into the action; empathy has made him lose control. The actor who plays his role well in a realistic context can count on empathy to be a powerful force, creating a bond between himself (or rather, his character) and the audience. In certain types of nonrealistic plays, however, illusion is not desired and empathy is deliberately negated. Such situations are discussed later in this text.

For the purpose of illustrating some of the principles outlined above, assume that you are the actor who is going to play Horace in a production of *The Little Foxes*.

A French actor. From an engraving in the Picture Collection of the New York Public Library.

You know the super-objective of the play (the central action) is "to gain a controlling interest in the mill," but you also know that this is not *your* objective at all. You are the principal force preventing Regina's gaining that controlling interest, and your objective, during at least a part of the play, is to stop her from doing so. But do you do this because you hate her? No, you say very plainly on page 41 that this is not your reason, and there is no basis for believing that you are lying at this point. Your exact relationship with your wife is a matter of great importance, however, and it will be necessary to trace in detail how you met her, how you felt when you married her, how that emotion has changed over the years, and how you feel toward her today. Her coldness may have contributed to your poor relationship now, but it is also true that you have been unfaithful to her, openly carrying on affairs with "fancy women," as Regina calls them. Your exact relationship with the other members of Regina's family is also of great importance and must be worked out in detail. This leads you to consider your business affairs, the manner in which you run your bank, the business relationship you have established with other leading citizens in the town, and so forth. All of this information is either present or hinted at in the script itself. What is not actually stated will have to be worked out in a logical way in your imagination, for you are more than just "a sick husband" when you finally enter early in Act II. You are a living human being with an entire lifetime behind you who now knows that he has only a little time to live, and all of your past must be a part of you when you finally enter. Some actors like to actually write out a full biography of the character they play, setting down in detail everything significant that he has been and done. Others may work this out only in their minds, but any good actor using the principles illustrated here could discuss with you in great detail the life of his character beyond what he actually portrays in the play.

Assuming, then, that you have carefully considered all of the biographical details that make up your background, you can now turn your attention to how you are going to create your character on the stage. If you are an actor who takes the "inner approach," you will want to think in terms of how Horace feels and what he wants during the time he is on the stage. When you first enter near the beginning of Act II, you are glad to be home. You are tired from the long journey and eager to rest, but it is also a pleasure (albeit a mixed one) to find yourself in familiar surroundings again. You are not eager to see your wife, however, and ask Alexandra not to tell Regina you are home until you can gain a little strength for the meeting. When Alexandra leaves, a new unit begins for you in which your objective is to learn from Addie as much of the background of the current situation as possible. Having learned what you can from her, your objective changes, and you decide to learn the rest of the story directly from Regina and her brothers. A new unit begins as they enter. You are diverted temporarily by the entrance of Birdie, whom you genuinely like, but after she and the men leave, you and your wife are left alone to have a direct confrontation. Her objective is to wheedle the money out of you, and yours is to learn the full truth about why she wants it. You are further motivated by the fact that you resolved, before coming home, that you would try to get along better with Regina during the short time left to you. Regina rejects your advances along this line, however, and throughout the scene your attitude gradually hardens toward her. Finally, Regina insists that you talk to Ben immediately, and with his entrance a new unit begins for you. You still do not see the exact connection between the mill business and the idea that Alexandra marry Leo, but you are determined to put a stop to all such plans. Thus, you are curious to learn the rest of the details. How-

Actors in a Goldoni play. From a 1760 Venetian edition of Goldoni comedies. Bertoldo Wiese: *Storia della litteratura italiana. . . .* Turin: Unione Tipografico, 1904.

ever, you begin the unit already predisposed against whatever suggestion Ben may propose. As the interview begins, you suddenly feel heart pains, and you take some medicine for them. (Here is a simple example of the importance of establishing motivation. An inexperienced actor might simply reach for the medicine when his cue comes; the more experienced actor would see the need for beginning to "feel pain" at a much earlier cue in order to motivate reaching for the medicine at the proper moment.) As the scene progresses, you come to understand fully the connection between the money and Alexandra's marriage. It is important, of course, that you work out, step by step, exactly how much you understand at each successive point throughout this scene. You also begin to see how the whole community will be affected by the proposed mill, and your benevolent attitude, based on years of living and working in the community, becomes important. You definitely do not intend to invest in such a venture, but you try to end the interview without further argument by simply stating your point of view and starting for your bedroom to rest. You try to prevent Regina's coming with you because you do not wish to fight with her, but finally, knowing it is hopeless, you go on upstairs.

During the time that you are offstage, you have a violent quarrel with Regina. In this particular case, the audience is supposed to hear voices from offstage, so the director will make specific arrangements for the cues when your voice is to be heard, and you will be expected to work out specific lines to speak. Actually, this will make it easier for you at your next entrance, since you will have actually experienced at least a portion of what is presumed to have happened offstage. The playwright has not provided you with any specific motivation for your next entrance (on page 35). You might have overheard the loud voices, but it is more logical to assume that you would stay in your room in that case to avoid further painful arguments. You will have to make up a logical motivation. Assume that the argument has been a tremendous strain on you, that you begin to feel heart pains. You left your medicine downstairs on the table, so it is necessary to go down to get it. This gives you a specific and reasonable objective when you enter. Of course, once you enter you overhear the quarrel between Ben and Regina and you take some cruel pleasure in it. Your argument with your wife has removed any hope of getting along better with her, and thus your attitude toward her now is hard and triumphant. You flare up angrily at the suggestion that this is your primary motivation for withholding the money (perhaps because you feel guilty that the charge contains an element of truth), and suffer real pain when Regina replies with the cruelest hope she can express—that you will die soon. You are still reacting to this as the curtain falls.

You are onstage when the next act begins. Two weeks have passed, and a great deal has happened. Your quarrel with Regina has led to a partitioning of the house, with the understanding that neither party may enter the other's portion. You are now in Regina's portion, however, deliberately awaiting her return. You have discovered the loss of your bonds, realized the significance of the loss, and laid your plans accordingly. Your objective throughout the first part of the act is to carry out these plans, and the scene between Alexandra and Birdie would be little more than a distraction to you if you were not tender-hearted enough to allow yourself to be caught by their plight. Still, your primary objective must be kept in mind as you send Addie for Cal, then send Cal to the bank, and await the return of both Cal and Regina. Your exact attitude must be traced from line to line as your thoughts focus on an objective and listen at the same time to what is going on around you. When you are left alone with Addie, you take advantage of the opportunity to explain to her the part she is to play in your plans, so this short scene with Addie may be treated as a separate unit with its own objective. Finally Regina arrives, and you focus upon your principal objective of explaining to her the nature of your new plans. You know that she will learn about the bonds soon enough anyway, and you want to make it clear to her that her hands are tied. You fail, at first, to understand why she deliberately begins to pick a quarrel with you, bringing up the subject of your rocky marital relationship which is always so painful to you. As you become emotionally involved in that, you begin to feel your heart giving you trouble again and reach for your medicine. When you drop it, and suddenly realize what she is doing to you, your objective changes to the very simple one of getting to that other bottle of medicine. In your weakened condition, you cannot make it up the stairs, you collapse, and are carried off. For you, the play is over.

This has, necessarily, been a greatly abridged version of the sort of analysis

David Garrick as Abel Drugger. An engraving, from a painting, in the catalogue of Libbie & Co., Boston, 1901.

Sarah Bernhardt as Mrs. Clarkson in *The Stranger*. From Paul Howard: *Stage and Its Stars Past and Present*. Philadelphia: Gebbie & Co., 1887.

that you would perform on your scenes if you were playing the role of Horace. If you take the internal approach to your role, you will do all of this analysis beforehand and will have done some rehearsing before you give much thought to what your physical interpretation will be. You assume that if you understand the character and all his relationships thoroughly and can begin to feel as he would feel, the appropriate movements will come to you. If you take the exterior approach, however, you will consider that he is a sick man, that his heart condition gives him a great deal of pain, that he can only walk with difficulty and so forth. Under the supervision of the director, you will plan out what you are to do at each moment of the play (where is the medicine bottle to be placed? Which hand shall I pick it up with? On which step should I collapse? and so on), and you will count on the necessary emotional quality arising from these details. Actually, most actors will work from a combination of these two approaches, especially in view of the fact that this is a realistic play (Stanislavski's inner approach is especially well adapted to realism); however, physical details are unusually important in Horace's death scene. It will not be necessary to go through all of these to illustrate how the actor works with them; the implications are clear from the sample that has been outlined above.

Whatever approach is used in the preparation of a role, all details need to be worked out eventually within the context of the production as a whole. A thorough discussion of fitting all the parts together will be found in the unit on directing where such a discussion is more appropriate. It must be understood, however, that the responsibility of each actor is to be sure that what he is doing fits well into the larger context. He must make sure that all his lines are spoken loudly enough so that the entire audience can hear, even though his "feeling" about Horace being a sick man may suggest very quiet tones. He must, in cooperation with the director, set a definite pattern for his physical movements, whether he does this early, or toward the end of the rehearsal period. He must learn his lines exactly as they are written to avoid confusing his fellow actors, even if his inner feelings may sometimes

Konstantin Stanislavski as Satine in *The Lower Depths*, Moscow Art Theatre, 1902. From M. Gorki: *Five Plays*, Moscow, Foreign Languages Publishing House.

suggest that a line should be phrased otherwise. (If the playwright is competent, this usually means that the actor has made some mistake in his emotional preparation and is feeling the wrong thing. Such a misunderstanding needs to be worked out.) Finally, he must set his lines, his physical movements, even his emotional builds into a definite pattern that can be repeated night after night with only minor variations (preventing variation altogether is out of the question). Thus the work of all the artists and technicians involved in the production may be brought together into a satisfactory whole. When the play is finally put before an audience, the actor knows that he has another variable to deal with, for no two audiences are alike and no two performances proceed in exactly the same fashion. The actor must adjust what he does in minor ways which are appropriate to the audience response. When laughter is provoked, he must learn to hold his next line and then "top" the laugh, cutting if off at the right moment. When empathy is building, he must learn to feel this response and encourage the build where it is desirable and choke it off where it is not. (*The Little Foxes*, of course, is an emotional melodrama, and most of the time, the highest possible degree of empathy is desirable.) Any actor knows that a play is not really a play until it has been put before an audience. The audience is the final, indispensable ingredient, without which even the most brilliant performance is not a true work of art, but merely a technical triumph. The audience is not a passive fact but an active force in creating the theatrical experience; and the actor learns finally to work with this variable, too, to create a polished performance.

A contemporary experimental production, the Living Theatre's *Mysteries and Smaller Pieces*. Photograph © 1968 by Fred W. Mc-Darrah.

Edmond Rostand was born in Marseilles, in the south of France, on April 1, 1868, the son of educated and refined parents. He studied law at the Collège Stanislas in Paris, but was already actively interested in literary pursuits and published his first book of poems in 1890. He was married that same year to Rosemonde Gerard, also a writer and poet, and settled in Paris to pursue an already promising career as poet and playwright. He formed close friendships with Sarah Bernhardt and Constant Coquelin, two leading actors of the age, and relied heavily upon their advice and support in the writing and production of his plays.

Rostand's first play to be produced was *The Romancers* (1894) which, in its musical adaptation *The Fantasticks,* is now widely known to American audiences. The play is lightly romantic in tone, set "wherever you please, provided the costumes are pretty," and depends entirely upon the nostalgic willingness of an audience to enter into the spirit of the love story. *The Romantics* was followed by *The Faraway Princess* in 1895 and *The Woman of Samaria* in 1897; both are notable for lovely poetry but neither has achieved great success on the stage. His next play, *Cyrano de Bergerac,* opened a long and successful run late in 1897, and secured its author's position as one of the leading playwrights of his day. Rostand was admitted to the French Academy on May 30, 1901, the youngest person ever to receive this honor.

The Eaglet (1900), although it starred Sarah Bernhardt in the pathetic role of Napoleon's son, was less than a complete success, and *Chantecler* (1910) was widely hailed by the critics for its philosophical profundity but has never seemed to work really effectively in the theatre—perhaps in part because its characters are animals. Rostand's last play, *The Last Night of Don Juan,* was not entirely completed at the time of his death, which occurred after several years of poor health in 1918. In a sense, Rostand was a playwright born out of his time, for the romantic poetic drama to which he was devoted had been out of fashion for half a century. Nevertheless, Rostand almost single-handedly restored it to wide-spread, if temporary, popularity, echoing once again the brilliance of the alexandrine verse form which was scorned by the realistic writers of the day. Rostand's public must have been tired of naturalism, symbolism, the well-made play, and the social problem play, for

Cyrano de Bergerac
by
Edmond Rostand
Translated by
Brian Hooker

Savinien de Cyrano de Bergerac, 1619–1655, from an
etching in Joseph Bédier and
Paul Hazard: *Histoire de la lit-
térature française illustré*, Paris:
Larousse, c. 1923.

audiences responded enthusiastically to the escape that his poetic dramas offered.

Cyrano de Bergerac was written specifically for and in close consultation with Coquelin. Rostand dedicated the play to him with the note: "[Cyrano's] soul has been reborn in you." When the play opened at the Théâtre de la Porte Saint-Martin in Paris on December 28, 1897, Coquelin's performance in the title role is reported to have been masterful. The play was soon translated into many languages and was widely produced and acclaimed; however, early English translations failed to capture much of the spirit and beauty of the French original. Despite this limitation the play was a notable success in America with Richard Mansfield in the role of Cyrano until, in 1902, an extraordinary action was brought in the courts of Illinois charging that Rostand had plagiarized the play from a work entitled *The Merchant Prince of Cornville* by Samuel E. Gross, an eccentric millionaire and sometime author. Rostand denied the charges, but the American producers named in the suit chose not to contest it in order to avoid court expenses, and hence the Supreme Court of Illinois found for the plaintiff. Only in 1920 was this action reversed by the U.S. District Court of the Southern District of New York, which determined that, although Rostand may have seen a script of the American play (it was never produced), he was not guilty of plagiarism. Soon thereafter (October 1923), Walter Hampden opened in New York in the new Brian Hooker translation of the play and scored an overwhelming success. Hampden found perhaps the best role of his career in Cyrano, and the Hooker translation at last did what so few theatrical translations can ever do—measured up in effectiveness and beauty to the original. Cyrano was also a tour de force for José Ferrer in the late 1940s, and has been revived countless times by amateur and professional groups around the world.

The real, historical Cyrano de Bergerac was born in Paris in 1619. He enjoyed some small success as an author and playwright, and was, indeed, a formidable swordsman. He became a cadet in the company of Carbon de Castel-Jaloux, was involved in several major battles, on one occasion drove the actor Montfleury from the stage, defended a poet friend from attack by a large gang of thugs, and died in 1655 in Paris after a lingering illness resulting from a blow on the head from a dropped block of wood. During his last years, he was close to the widow of a friend who had died in battle, although probably this relationship had nothing to do with any love affair. He did in fact write a book in 1649 entitled *Voyage to the Moon,* in which he mentioned several possible ways of getting to the moon; reference to them is made in the latter part of Act III of Rostand's play. Cyrano de Bergerac was the first writer to suggest rocket propulsion as a means of space travel. Obviously, Rostand made great use of these and other historical facts in the delineation of his central figure, but he did not allow himself to be bound by historical accuracy. A few pedantic critics have argued that the historical inaccuracies weaken the play, but several generations of audiences have found that the excitement, romance, and beauty of the play are the only things that matter in the theatre.

Page 76: The dueling scene from *Cyrano de Bergerac,* Act I, Robert Symonds as Cyrano in the Repertory Theater of Lincoln Center's 1968 production. Sets, David Hays; costumes, James Hart Stearns. Photograph: Martha Swope.

Page 81: The balcony scene from *Cyrano de Bergerac,* Act III, of the same production. Robert Symonds (Cyrano), Suzanne Grossmann (Roxane), Dennis Cooney (Christian). Courtesy of the Repertory Theater of Lincoln Center; photograph: Martha Swope.

Cyrano de Bergerac

An Heroic Comedy in Five Acts by
EDMOND ROSTAND

A New Version in English Verse
by BRIAN HOOKER

It was to the soul of CYRANO *that I
intended to dedicate this poem.
But since that soul has been reborn in you,*
COQUELIN, *it is to you that I dedicate it.*

E. R.

Cyrano de Bergerac	The Porter
Christian de Neuvillette	A Citizen
Comte de Guiche	His Son
Ragueneau	A Cut-Purse
Le Bret	A Spectator
Carbon de Castel-Jaloux	A Sentry
The Cadets	Bertrandou the Fifer
Lignière	A Capuchin
Vicomte de Valvert	Two Musicians
A Marquis	The Poets
Second Marquis	The Pastry cooks
Third Marquis	The Pages
Montfleury	Roxane
Bellerose	Her Duenna
Jodelet	Lise
Cuigy	The Orange Girl
Brissaille	Mother Marguerite de Jesus
A Meddler	Sister Marthe
A Musketeer	Sister Claire
Another Musketeer	An Actress
A Spanish Officer	A Soubrette
A Cavalier	The Flower Girl

The Crowd, Citizens, Marquis, Musketeers, Thieves, Pastrycooks, Poets, Cadets of Gascoyne, Actors, Violins, Pages, Children, Spanish Soldiers, Spectators, Intellectuals, Academicians, Nuns, etc.

(The first four Acts in 1640; the fifth in 1655.)

ACT I: A Performance at the Hotel de Bourgogne.
ACT II: The Bakery of the Poets.
ACT III: Roxane's Kiss.
ACT IV: The Cadets of Gascoyne.
ACT V: Cyrano's Gazette.

ACT I

A Performance at the Hôtel de Bourgogne

THE HALL OF THE HÔTEL DE BOURGOGNE IN 1640. A sort of Tennis Court, arranged and decorated for Theatrical productions.

The Hall is a long rectangle; we see it diagonally, in such a way that one side of it forms the back scene, which begins at the First Entrance on the Right and runs up to the Last Entrance on the Left, where it makes a right angle with the Stage which is seen obliquely.

This Stage is provided on either hand with benches placed along the wings. The curtain is formed by two lengths of Tapestry which can be drawn apart. Above a Harlequin cloak, the Royal Arms. Broad steps lead from the Stage down to the floor of the Hall. On either side of these steps, a place for the Musicians. A row of candles serving as footlights. Two tiers of Galleries along the side of the Hall; the upper one divided into boxes.

There are no seats upon the Floor, which is the actual stage of our theatre; but toward the back of the Hall, on the right, a few benches are arranged; and underneath a stairway on the extreme right, which leads up to the galleries, and of which only the lower portion is visible, there is a sort of Sideboard, decorated with little tapers, vases of flowers, bottles and glasses, plates of cake, et cetera.

Farther along, toward the centre of our stage is the Entrance to the Hall; a great double door which opens slightly to admit the Audience. On one of the panels of this door, as also in other places about the Hall, and in particular just over the Sideboard, are Playbills in red, upon which we may read the title LA CLORISE.

As THE CURTAIN RISES, the Hall is dimly lighted and still empty. The Chandeliers are lowered to the floor, in the middle of the Hall, ready for lighting.

> [*Sound of voices outside the door. Then a* **Cavalier** *enters abruptly.*]

The Porter: [*Follows him*]
Halloa there!—Fifteen sols!

The Cavalier:
                                   I enter free.

The Porter:
Why?

The Cavalier:
Soldier of the Household of the King!

The Porter: [*Turns to another* **Cavalier** *who has just entered*]
You?

Second Cavalier:
   I pay nothing.

The Porter:
                              Why not?

Second Cavalier:
                              Musketeer!

First Cavalier: [*To the Second*]
The play begins at two. Plenty of time—
And here's the whole floor empty. Shall we try
Our exercise?
   [*They fence with the foils which they have brought.*]

A Lackey: [*Enters*]
   —Pst! . . . Flanquin! . . .

Another: [*Already on stage*]
                              What, Champagne?

First Lackey: [*Showing games which he takes out of his doublet*]
Cards. Dice. Come on.
   [*Sits on the floor.*]

Second Lackey: [*Same action*]
                              Come on, old cock!

First Lackey: [*Takes from his pocket a bit of candle, lights it, sets it on the floor*]
                              I have stolen
A little of my master's fire.

A Guardsman: [*To a* **Flower Girl** *who comes forward*]
                              How sweet
Of you, to come before they light the hall!
   [*Puts his arm around her.*]

First Cavalier: [*Receives a thrust of the foil*]
    A hit!
Second Lackey:
         A club!
The Guardsman: [*Pursuing the girl*]
         A kiss!
The Flower Girl: [*Pushing away from him*]
         They'll see us!—
The Guardsman: [*Draws her into a dark corner*]
         No danger!
A Man: [*Sits on the floor, together with several others
who have brought packages of food*]
    When we come early, we have time to eat.
A Citizen: [*Escorting* **his son,** *a boy of sixteen*]
    Sit here, my son.
First Lackey:
         Mark the Ace!
Another Man: [*Draws a bottle from under his cloak
and sits down with the others*]
              Here's the spot
    For a jolly old sot to suck his Burgundy—
         [*Drinks*]
    Here—in the house of the Burgundians!
The Citizen: [*To* **his son**]
    Would you not think you were in some den
         of vice?
         [*Points with his cane at the drunkard*]
    Drunkards—
         [*In stepping back, one of the* **cavaliers** *trips him
         up.*]
    Bullies!—
         [*He falls between the lackeys*]
         Gamblers!—
The Guardsman: [*Behind him as he rises, still strug-
gling with the* **Flower Girl**]
              One kiss—
The Citizen:
              Good God!—
         [*Draws* **his son** *quickly away.*]
    Here!—And to think, my son, that in this hall
    They play Rotrou!
The Boy:
         Yes father—and Corneille!
The Pages: [*Dance in, holding hands and singing:*]
    Tra-la-la-la-la-la-la-la-la-lère . . .
The Porter:
    You pages there—no nonsense!
First Page: [*With wounded dignity*]
         Oh, monsieur!

Really! How could you?
         [*To the* **Second,** *the moment the* **Porter** *turns his
         back.*]
              Pst!—a bit of string?
Second Page: [*Shows fishline with hook*]
    Yes—and a hook.
First Page:
         Up in the gallery,
    And fish for wigs!
A Cut-Purse: [*Gathers around him several evil-look-
ing young fellows*]
         Now then, you picaroons,
    Perk up, and hear me mutter. Here's your
         bout—
    Bustle around some cull, and bite his bung . . .
Second Page: [*Calls to other pages already in the gal-
lery*]
    Hey! Brought your pea-shooters?
Third Page: [*From above*]
              And our peas, too!
         [*Blows, and showers them with peas.*]
The Boy:
    What is the play this afternoon?
The Citizen:
              "Clorise."
The Boy:
    Who wrote that?
The Citizen:
              Balthasar Baro. What a play! . . .
         [*He takes the* **Boy**'s *arm and leads him upstage.*]
The Cut-Purse: [*To his pupils*]
    Lace now, on those long sleeves, you cut it
         off—
         [*Gesture with thumb and finger, as if using scis-
         sors.*]
A Spectator: [*To another, pointing upward toward the
gallery*]
    Ah, *Le Cid!*—Yes, the first night, I sat there—
The Cut-Purse:
    Watches—
         [*Gesture as of picking a pocket.*]
The Citizen: [*Coming down with* **his son**]
    Great actors we shall see to-day—
The Cut-Purse:
    Handkerchiefs—
         [*Gesture of holding the pocket with left hand, and
         drawing out handkerchief with right.*]
The Citizen:
              Montfleury—

A Voice: [*In the gallery.*]
                                Lights! Light the lights!
The Citizen:
Bellerose, l'Epy, Beaupré, Jodelet—
A Page: [*On the floor*]
Here comes the orange girl.
The Orange Girl:
                                Oranges, milk,
Raspberry syrup, lemonade—
        [*Noise at the door.*]
A Falsetto Voice: [*Outside*]
                                Make way,
Brutes!
First Lackey:
                What, the Marquis—on the floor?
        [*The Marquis enter in a little group.*]
Second Lackey:
                                Not long—
Only a few moments; they'll go and sit
On the stage presently.
First Marquis: [*Seeing the hall half empty*]
                                How now! We enter
Like tradespeople—no crowding, no distur-
    bance!—
No treading on the toes of citizens?
Oh fie! Oh fie!
        [*He encounters two gentlemen who have already
        arrived*]
                Cuigy! Brissaille!
        [*Great embracings*]
Cuigy:
                                The faithful!
        [*Looks around him.*]
We are here before the candles.
First Marquis:
                                Ah, be still!
You put me in a temper.
Second Marquis:
                                Console yourself,
Marquis—The lamplighter!
The Crowd: [*Applauding the appearance of the lamp-
        lighter*]
                                Ah! . . .
        [*A group gathers around the chandelier while he
        lights it. A few people have already taken their
        place in the gallery.* **Ligniére** *enters the hall,
        arm in arm with* **Christian de Neuvillette.**
        Ligniére *is a slightly disheveled figure, dissipated
        and yet distinguished looking.* **Christian,** *ele-*

*gantly but rather unfashionably dressed, appears
preoccupied and keeps looking up at the boxes.*]
Cuigy:
                                Ligniére!—
Brissaille: [*Laughing*]
Still sober—at this hour?
Ligniére: [*To* **Christian**]
                                May I present you?
        [**Christian** *assents.*]
Baron Christian de Neuvillette.
        [*They salute.*]
The Crowd: [*Applauding as the lighted chandelier is
    hoisted into place*]
                                Ah!—
Cuigy: [*Aside to* **Brissaille,** *looking at* **Christian**]
                                Rather
A fine head, is it not? The profile . . .
First Marquis: [*Who has overheard*]
                                Peuh!
Ligniére: [*Presenting them to* **Christian**]
Messieurs de Cuigy . . . de Brissaille . . .
Christian: [*Bows*]
                                Enchanted!
First Marquis: [*To the second*]
He is not ill-looking; possibly a shade
Behind the fashion.
Ligniére: [*To* **Cuigy**]
                                Monsieur is recently
From the Touraine.
Christian:
                                Yes, I have been in Paris
Two or three weeks only. I join the Guards
To-morrow.
First Marquis: [*Watching the people who come into the
        boxes*]
                Look—Madame la Présidente
Aubry!
The Orange Girl:
                                Oranges, milk—
The Violins: [*Tuning up*]
                                La . . . la . . .
Cuigy: [*To* **Christian,** *calling his attention to the in-
    creasing crowd*]
                                We have
An audience to-day!
Christian:
                                A brilliant one.
First Marquis:
Oh yes, all our own people—the gay world!

[*They name the ladies who enter the boxes elaborately dressed. Bows and smiles are exchanged.*]

Second Marquis:
Madame de Guémené . . .

Cuigy:
De Bois-Dauphin . . .

First Marquis:
Whom we adore—

Brissaille:
Madame de Chavigny . . .

Second Marquis:
Who plays with all our hearts—

Lignière:
Why, there's Corneille
Returned from Rouen!

The Boy:　[*To his father*]
Are the Academy
All here?

The Citizen:
I see some of them . . . there's Boudu—
Boissat—Cureau—Porchères—Colomby—
Bourzeys—Bourdon—Arbaut—
Ah, those great names,
Never to be forgotten!

First Marquis:
Look—at last!
Our Intellectuals! Barthénoide,
Urimédonte, Félixérie . . .

Second Marquis:　[*Languishing*]
Sweet heaven!
How exquisite their surnames are! Marquis,
You know them all?

First Marquis:
I know them all, Marquis!

Lignière:　[*Draws* **Christian** *aside*]
My dear boy, I came here to serve you— Well,
But where's the lady? I'll be going.

Christian:
Not yet—
A little longer! She is always here.
Please! I must find some way of meeting her.
I am dying of love! And you—you know
Everyone, the whole court and the whole
town,
And put them all into your songs—at least
You can tell me her name!

The First Violin:　[*Raps on his desk with his bow*]
Pst— Gentlemen!

[*Raises his bow*]

The Orange Girl:
Macaroons, lemonade—

Christian:
Then she may be
One of those aesthetes . . . Intellectuals,
You call them— How can I talk to a woman
In that style? I have no wit. This fine manner
Of speaking and of writing nowadays—
Not for me! I am a soldier—and afraid.
That's her box, on the right—the empty one.

Lignière:　[*Starts for the door*]
I am going.

Christian:　[*Restrains him*]
No—wait!

Lignière:
Not I. There's a tavern
Not far away—and I am dying of thirst.

The Orange Girl:　[*Passes with her tray*]
Orange juice?

Lignière:
No!

The Orange Girl:
Milk?

Lignière:
Pouah!

The Orange Girl:
Muscatel?

Lignière:
Here! Stop!
[*To* **Christian**]
I'll stay a little.
[*To the* **Girl**]
Let me see
Your Muscatel.
[*He sits down by the sideboard.* **The Girl** *pours out wine for him.*]

Voices:
[*In the crowd about the door, upon the entrance of a spruce little man, rather fat, with a beaming smile*]
Ragueneau!

Lignière:　[*To* **Christian**]
Ragueneau,
Poet and pastry-cook—a character!

Ragueneau:　[*Dressed like a confectioner in his Sunday clothes, advances quickly to* **Lignière**]
Sir, have you seen Monsieur de Cyrano?

Lignière:　[*Presents him to* **Christian**]
Permit me . . . Ragueneau, confectioner,

The chief support of modern poetry.
Ragueneau: [*Bridling*]
Oh—too much honor!
Lignière:
            Patron of the Arts—
Mæcenas! Yes, you are—
Ragueneau:
               Undoubtedly,
The poets gather around my hearth.
Lignière:
                 On credit—
Himself a poet—
Ragueneau:
        So they say—
Lignière:
              Maintains
The Muses.
Ragueneau:
        It is true that for an ode—
Lignière:
You give a tart—
Ragueneau:
      A tartlet—
Lignière:
           Modesty!
And for a triolet you give—
Ragueneau:
          Plain bread.
Lignière: [*Severely*]
Bread and milk! And you love the theatre?
Ragueneau:
I adore it!
Lignière:
       Well, pastry pays for all.
Your place to-day now— Come, between ourselves,
What did it cost you?
Ragueneau:
      Four pies; fourteen cakes.
    [*Looking about*]
But— Cyrano not here? Astonishing!
Lignière:
Why so?
Ragueneau:
      Why— Montfleury plays!
Lignière:
            Yes, I hear
That hippopotamus assumes the rôle
Of Phédon. What is that to Cyrano?

Ragueneau:
Have you not heard? Monsieur de Bergerac
So hates Montfleury, he has forbidden him
For three weeks to appear upon the stage.
Lignière: [*Who is, by this time, at his fourth glass*]
Well?
Ragueneau:
      Montfleury plays!—
Cuigy: [*Strolls over to them*]
          Yes—what then?
Ragueneau:
             Ah! That
Is what I came to see.
First Marquis:
        This Cyrano—
Who is he?
Cuigy:
    Oh, he is the lad with the long sword.
Second Marquis:
Noble?
Cuigy:
    Sufficiently; he is in the Guards.
    [*Points to a gentleman who comes and goes about
    the hall as though seeking for someone*]
His friend Le Bret can tell you more.
    [*Calls to him*]
            Le Bret!
    [**Le Bret** *comes down to them*]
Looking for Bergerac?
Le Bret:
          Yes. And for trouble.
Cuigy:
Is he not an extraordinary man?
Le Bret:
The best friend and the bravest soul alive!
Ragueneau:
Poet—
Cuigy:
     Swordsman—
Le Bret:
       Musician—
Brissaille:
         Philosopher—
Lignière:
Such a remarkable appearance, too!
Ragueneau:
Truly, I should not look to find his portrait
By the grave hand of Philippe de Champagne.
He might have been a model for Callot—

One of those wild swashbucklers in a
    masque—
Hat with three plumes, and doublet with six
    points—
His cloak behind him over his long sword
Cocked, like the tail of strutting Chanticleer—
Prouder than all the swaggering Tam-
    burlaines
Hatched out of Gascony. And to complete
This Punchinello figure—such a nose!—
My lords, there is no such nose as that nose—
You cannot look upon it without crying: "Oh,
    no,
Impossible! Exaggerated!" Then
You smile, and say: "Of course—I might have
    known;
Presently he will take it off." But that
Monsieur de Bergerac will never do.

Lignière: [*Grimly*]
He keeps it—and God help the man who
    smiles!

Ragueneau:
His sword is one half of the shears of Fate!

First Marquis: [*Shrugs*]
He will not come.

Ragueneau:
                        Will he not? Sir, I'll lay you
A pullet à la Ragueneau!

First Marquis: [*Laughing*]
                        Done!
[*Murmurs of admiration;* **Roxane** *has just appeared in her box. She sits at the front of the box,
and her* **Duenna** *takes a seat toward the rear.*
Christian, *busy paying the Orange Girl, does
not see her at first.*]

Second Marquis: [*With little excited cries*]
                        Ah!
Oh! Oh! Sweet sirs, look yonder! Is she not
Frightfully ravishing?

First Marquis:
                        Bloom of the peach—
Blush of the strawberry—

Second Marquis: So fresh—so cool,
That our hearts, grown all warm with loving
    her,
May catch their death of cold!

Christian: [*Looks up, sees* **Roxane,** *and seizes* **Lignière** *by the arm*]
                        There! Quick—up there—

In the box! Look!—

Lignière: [*Coolly*]
                        Herself?

Christian:
                        Quickly—Her name?

Lignière: [*Sipping his wine, and speaking between sips*]
Madeleine Robin, called Roxane . . . re-
    fined . . .
Intellectual . . .

Christian:
                        Ah!—

Lignière:
                        Unmarried . . .

Christian:
                        Oh!—

Lignière:
No title . . . rich enough . . . an orphan . . .
    cousin
To Cyrano . . . of whom we spoke just
    now . . .
[*At this point, a very distinguished looking gentleman, the Cordon Bleu around his neck, enters
the box, and stands a moment talking with* **Roxane.**]

Christian: [*Starts*]
And the man? . . .

Lignière: [*Beginning to feel his wine a little; cocks his
eye at them*]
    Oho! That man . . . Comte de Guiche . . .
In love with her . . . married himself, however,
To the niece of the Cardinal—Richelieu . . .
Wishes Roxane, therefore, to marry one
Monsieur de Valvert . . . Vicomte . . . friend of
    his . . .
A somewhat melancholy gentleman . . .
But . . . well, accommodating! . . . She says
    No . . .
Nevertheless, de Guiche is powerful . . .
Not above persecuting . . .
            [*He rises, swaying a little, and very happy*]
                        I have written
A little song about his little game . . .
Good little song, too . . . Here, I'll sing it for
    you . . .
Make de Guiche furious . . . naughty little
    song . . .
Not so bad, either— Listen! . . .
            [*He stands with his glass held aloft, ready to
sing.*]

Christian:

No. Adieu.

Lignière:

Whither away?

Christian:

To Monsieur de Valvert!

Lignière:

Careful! The man's a swordsman . . .

[*Nods toward* **Roxane**, *who is watching* **Christian**]

Wait! Someone

Looking at you—

Christian:

Roxane! . . .

[*He forgets everything, and stands spellbound, gazing toward* **Roxane**. *The Cut-Purse and his crew, observing him transfixed, his eyes raised and his mouth half open, begins edging in his direction.*]

Lignière:

Oh! Very well,

Then I'll be leaving you . . . Good day . . .
Good day! . . .

[**Christian** *remains motionless.*]

Everywhere else, they like to hear me sing!—
Also, I am thirsty.

[*He goes out, navigating carefully.* **Le Bret**, *having made the circuit of the hall, returns to* **Ragueneau**, *somewhat reassured.*]

Le Bret:

No sign anywhere

Of Cyrano!

Ragueneau: [*Incredulous*]

Wait and see!

Le Bret:

Humph! I hope

He has not seen the bill.

The Crowd:

The play!—The play!—

First Marquis: [*Observing* **de Guiche**, *as he descends from* **Roxane**'s *box and crosses the floor, followed by a knot of obsequious gentlemen, the* **Vicomte de Valvert** *among them*]

This man de Guiche—what ostentation!

Second Marquis:

Bah!—

Another Gascon!

First Marquis:

Gascon, yes—but cold

And calcuulating—certain to succeed—
My word for it. Come, shall we make our
bow?
We shall be none the worse, I promise
you . . .

[*They go toward* **de Guiche**.]

Second Marquis:

Beautiful ribbons, Count! That color, now,
What is it—"Kiss-me-Dear" or "Startled-
Fawn"?

De Guiche:

I call that shade "The Dying Spaniard."

First Marquis:

Ha!

And no false colors either—thanks to you
And your brave troops, in Flanders before
long
The Spaniard will die daily.

De Guiche:

Shall we go

And sit upon the stage? Come, Valvert.

Christian: [*Starts at the name*]   Valvert!—

The Vicomte— Ah, that scoundrel! Quick—my
glove—
I'll throw it in his face—

[*Reaching into his pocket for his glove, he catches the hand of the Cut-Purse.*]

The Cut-Purse:

Oh!—

Christian: [*Holding fast to the man's wrist*]

Who are you?

I was looking for a glove—

The Cut-Purse: [*Cringing*]

You found a hand.

[*Hurriedly*]

Let me go— I can tell you something—

Christian: [*Still holding him*]

Well?

The Cut-Purse:

Lignière—that friend of yours—

Christian: [*Same business*]

Well?

The Cut-Purse:

Good as dead—

Understand? Ambuscaded. Wrote a song
About—no matter. There's a hundred men
Waiting for him to-night—I'm one of them.

Christian:

A hundred? Who arranged this?

The Cut-Purse:

            Secret.

Christian:

                Oh!

The Cut-Purse: [*With dignity*]
Professional secret.

Christian:

        Where are they to be?

The Cut-Purse:
Porte de Nesle. On his way home. Tell him
so.
Save his life.

Christian: [*Releases the man*]
      Yes, but where am I to find him?

The Cut-Purse:
Go round the taverns. There's the Golden
  Grape,
The Pineapple, the Bursting Belt, the Two
Torches, the Three Funnels—in every one
You leave a line of writing—understand?
To warn him.

Christian: [*Starts for the door*]
      I'll go! God, what swine—a hundred
Against one man! . . .
    [*Stops and looks longingly at* **Roxane**]
              Leave *her* here!—
    [*Savagely, turning toward* **Valvert**]
               And leave *him!*—
    [*Decidedly*]
I must save Lignière!
    [*Exit.*]
    [**De Guiche, Valvert,** *and all the Marquis
have disappeared through the curtains, to take
their seats upon the stage. The floor is entirely
filled; not a vacant seat remains in the gallery
or in the boxes.*]

The Crowd:

          The play! The play!
Begin the play!

A Citizen: [*As his wig is hoisted into the air on the
end of a fishline, in the hands of a page in the gallery*]
          My wig!!

Cries of Joy:

           He's bald! Bravo,
You pages! Ha ha ha!

The Citizen: [*Furious, shakes his fist at the boy*]
          Here, you young villain!

Cries of Laughter: [*Beginning very loud, then suddenly repressed*]

HA HA! Ha Ha! ha ha . . .
    [*Complete silence.*]

Le Bret: [*Surprised*]
             That sudden hush? . . .
    [*A Spectator whispers in his ear*]
Yes?

The Spectator:
  I was told on good authority . . .

Murmurs: [*Here and there*]
What? . . . Here? . . . No . . . Yes . . . Look—in
  the latticed box—
The Cardinal! . . . The Cardinal! . . .

A Page:

             The Devil!—
Now we shall all have to behave ourselves!
    [*Three raps on the stage. The audience becomes
motionless. Silence.*]

The Voice of a Marquis: [*From the stage, behind
the curtains*]
Snuff that candle!

Another Marquis: [*Puts his head out through the
curtains*]
          A chair! . . .
    [*A chair is passed from hand to hand over the
heads of the crowd. He takes it, and disappears
behind the curtains, not without having blown a
few kisses to the occupants of the boxes.*]

A Spectator:

           Silence!

Voices:

          Hssh! . . . Hssh! . . .
    [*Again the three raps on the stage. The curtains
part. Tableau. The Marquis seated on their
chairs to right and left of the stage, insolently
posed. Back drop representing a pastoral scene,
bluish in tone. Four little crystal chandeliers light
up the stage. The violins play softly.*]

Le Bret: [*In a low tone, to* **Ragueneau**]
Montfleury enters now?

Ragueneau: [*Nods*]
          Opens the play.

Le Bret: [*Much relieved*]
Then Cyrano is not here!

Ragueneau:

           I lose . . .

Le Bret:

             Humph!—
So much the better!
    [*The melody of a Musette is heard.* **Montfleury**
appears upon the scene, a ponderous figure in the

costume of a rustic shepherd, a hat garlanded with roses tilted over one ear, playing upon a beribboned pastoral pipe.]

The Crowd: [*Applauds*]
  Montfleury! . . . Bravo! . . .

Montfleury: [*After bowing to the applause, begins the rôle of Phédon*]
  "Thrice happy he who hides from pomp and power
  In sylvan shade or solitary bower;
  Where balmy zephyrs fan his burning cheeks—"

A Voice: [*From the midst of the hall*]
  Wretch. Have I not forbade you these three weeks?

  [*Sensation. Everyone turns to look. Murmurs.*]

Several Voices:
  What? . . . Where? . . . Who is it? . . .

Cuigy:
  Cyrano!

Le Bret: [*In alarm*]
  Himself!

The Voice:
  King of clowns! Leave the stage—*at once!*

The Crowd:
  Oh!—

Montfleury:
  Now,
  Now, now—

The Voice:
  You disobey me?

Several Voices: [*From the floor, from the boxes*]
  Hsh! Go on—
  Quiet!—Go on, Montfleury!—Who's afraid?—

Montfleury: [*In a voice of no great assurance*]
  "Thrice happy he who hides from . . ."

The Voice: [*More menacingly*]
  Well? Well? Well? . . .
  Monarch of mountebanks! Must I come and plant
  A forest on your shoulders?

  [*A cane at the end of a long arm shakes above the heads of the crowd.*]

Montfleury: [*In a voice increasingly feeble*]
  "Thrice hap—"

  [*The cane is violently agitated.*]

The Voice:
  GO!!!

The Crowd:
  Ah . . .

Cyrano: [*Arises in the centre of the floor, erect upon a chair, his arms folded, his hat cocked ferociously, his moustache bristling, his nose terrible*]
  Presently I shall grow angry!
  [*Sensation at his appearance.*]

Montfleury: [*To the Marquis*]
  Messieurs,
  If you protect me—

A Marquis: [*Nonchantly*]
  Well—proceed!

Cyrano:
  Fat swine!
  If you dare breathe one balmy zephyr more,
  I'll fan your cheeks for you!

The Marquis:
  Quiet down there!

Cyrano:
  Unless these gentlemen retain their seats,
  My cane may bite their ribbons!

All the Marquis: [*On their feet*]
  That will do!—
  Montfleury—

Cyrano:
  Fly, goose! Shoo! Take to your wings,
  Before I pluck your plumes, and draw your gorge!

A Voice:
  See here—

Cyrano:
  Off stage!!

Another Voice:
  One moment—

Cyrano:
  What—still there?
  [*Turns back his cuffs deliberately.*]
  Very good—then I enter—*Left—with knife—*
  To carve this large Italian sausage.

Montfleury: [*Desperately attempting dignity*]
  Sir,
  When you insult me, you insult the Muse!

Cyrano: [*With great politeness*]
  Sir, if the Muse, who never knew your name,
  Had the honor to meet you—then be sure
  That after one glance at that face of yours,
  That figure of a mortuary urn—
  She would apply her buskin—toward the rear!

The Crowd:

Montfleury! . . . Montfleury! . . . The play! The
Play!

Cyrano: [*To those who are shouting and crowding about
him*]

Pray you, be gentle with my scabbard here—
She'll put her tongue out at you presently!—

[*The circle enlarges.*]

The Crowd: [*Recoiling*]

Keep back—

Cyrano: [*To* **Montfleury**]

Begone!

The Crowd: [*Pushing in closer, and growling*]

Ahr! . . . ahr! . . .

Cyrano: [*Turns upon them*]

Did someone speak?

[*They recoil again.*]

A Voice: [*In the back of the hall, sings*]

Monsieur de Cyrano.
Must be another Caesar—
Let Brutus lay him low,
And play us "La Clorise"!

All the Crowd: [*Singing*]

"La Clorise!" "La Clorise!"

Cyrano:

Let me hear one more word of that same song,
And I destroy you all!

A Citizen:

Who might you be?

Samson?—

Cyrano:

Precisely. Would you kindly lend me
Your jawbone?

A Lady: [*In one of the boxes*]

What an outrage!

A Noble:

Scandalous!

A Citizen:

Annoying!

A Page:

What a game!

The Crowd:

Kss! Montfleury!

Cyrano!

Cyrano:

Silence!

The Crowd: [*Delirious*]

Woof! Woof! Baaa! Cockadoo!

Cyrano:

I—

A Page:

Meow!

Cyrano: I say be silent!—

[*His voice dominates the uproar. Momentary
hush.*]

And I offer
One universal challenge to you all!
Approach, young heroes—I will take your
names.
Each in his turn—no crowding! One, two,
three—
Come, get your numbers—who will head the
list—
You sir? No— You? Ah, no. To the first man
Who falls I'll build a monument! . . . Not one?
Will all who wish to die, please raise their
hands? . . .
I see. You are so modest, you might blush
Before a sword naked. Sweet innocence! . . .
Not one name? Not one finger? . . . Very well,
Then I go on:

[*Turning back towards the stage, where* **Montfleury** *waits in despair*]

I'd have our theatre cured
Of this carbuncle. Or if not, why then—

[*His hand on his sword hilt*]

The lancet!

Montfleury:

I—

Cyrano: [*Descends from his chair, seats himself comfortably in the centre of the circle which has formed
around him, and makes himself quite at home*]

Attend to me—full moon!
I clap my hands, three times—thus. At the
third
You will eclipse yourself.

The Crowd: [*Amused*]

Ah!

Cyrano:

Ready? One!

Montfleury:

I—

A Voice: [*From the boxes*]

No!

The Crowd:

He'll go— He'll stay—

Montfleury:

I really think,
Gentlemen—

Cyrano:

Two!

Montfleury:

Perhaps I had better—

Cyrano:

Three!

[**Montfleury** *disappears, as if through a trap-door. Tempest of laughter, hoots and hisses.*]

The Crowd:

Yah!—Coward— Come back—

Cyrano: [*Beaming, drops back in his chair and crosses his legs*]

Let him—if he dare!

A Citizen:

The Manager! Speech! Speech!

[**Bellerose** *advances and bows.*]

The Boxes:

Ah! Bellerose!

Bellerose: [*With elegance*]

Most noble—most fair—

The Crowd:

No! The Comedian—
Jodelet!—

Jodelet: [*Advances, and speaks through his nose*]

Lewd fellows of the baser sort—

The Crowd:

Ha! Ha! Not bad! Bravo!

Jodelet:

No Bravos here!
Our heavy tragedian with the voluptuous bust
Was taken suddenly—

The Crowd:

Yah! Coward!

Jodelet:

I mean . . .
He had to be excused—

The Crowd:

Call him back— No!—
Yes!—

The Boy: [*To* **Cyrano**]

After all, Monsieur, what reason have you
To hate this Montfleury?

Cyrano: [*Graciously, still seated*]

My dear young man,
I have two reasons, either one alone

Conclusive. *Primo:* A lamentable actor,
Who mouths his verse and moans his tragedy,
And heaves up— Ugh!—like a hod-carrier, lines
That ought to soar on their own wings.
Secundo:—
Well—that's my secret.

The Old Citizen: [*Behind him*]

But you close the play—
"La Clorise"—by Baro! Are we to miss
Our entertainment, merely—

Cyrano: [*Respectfully, turns his chair toward the old man*]

My dear old boy,
The poetry of Baro being worth
Zero, or less, I feel that I have done
Poetic justice!

The Intellectuals: [*In the boxes*]

Really!—our Baro!—
My dear!—Who ever?—Ah, dieu! The idea!—

Cyrano: [*Gallantly, turns his chair toward the boxes*]

Fair ladies—shine upon us like the sun,
Blossom like the flowers around us—be our songs,
Heard in a dream— Make sweet the hour of death,
Smiling upon us as you close our eyes—
Inspire, but do not try to criticise!

Bellerose:

Quite so!—and the mere money—possibly
You would like that returned— Yes?

Cyrano:

Bellerose,
You speak the first word of intelligence!
I will not wound the mantle of the Muse—
Here, catch!—
[*Throws him a purse*]
And hold your tongue.

The Crowd: [*Astonished*]

Ah! Ah!

Jodelet: [*Deftly catches the purse, weighs it in his hand*]

Monsieur,
You are hereby authorized to close our play
Every night, on the same terms.

The Crowd:

Boo!

Jodelet:

And welcome!

Let us be booed together, you and I!
Bellerose:
Kindly pass out quietly . . .
Jodelet: [*Burlesquing* **Bellerose**]
                              Quietly . . .
[*They begin to go out, while* **Cyrano** *looks about
him with satisfaction. But the exodus ceases pre-
sently during the ensuing scene. The ladies in the
boxes who have already risen and put on their
wraps, stop to listen, and finally sit down again.*]
Le Bret: [*To* **Cyrano**]
                              Idiot!
A Meddler: [*Hurries up to* **Cyrano**]
      But what a scandal! Montfleury—
      The great Montfleury! Did you know the Duc
      de Candale was
      his patron? Who is yours?
Cyrano:
      No one.
The Meddler:
                  No one—no patron?
Cyrano:
                              I said no.
The Meddler:
      What, no great lord, to cover with his name—
Cyrano: [*With visible annoyance*]
      No, I have told you twice. Must I repeat?
      No sir, no patron—
            [*His hand on his sword*]
                  But a patroness!
The Meddler:
      And when do you leave Paris?
Cyrano:
                              That's as may be.
The Meddler:
      The Duc de Candale has a long arm.
Cyrano:
                                          Mine
      Is longer,
            [*Drawing his sword*]
                  by three feet of steel.
The Meddler:
                              Yes, yes,
      But do you dream of daring—
Cyrano:
                              I do dream
      Of daring . . .
The Meddler: But—

Cyrano:
                  You may go now.
The Meddler:
                              But—
Cyrano:
                              You may go—
      Or tell me why are you staring at my nose!
The Meddler: [*In confusion*]
      No—I—
Cyrano: [*Stepping up to him*]
            Does it astonish you?
The Meddler: [*Drawing back*]
                              Your grace
      Misunderstands my—
Cyrano:
                  Is it long and soft
      And dangling, like a trunk?
The Meddler: [*Same business*]
                              I never said—
Cyrano:
      Or crooked, like an owl's beak?
The Meddler:
                                          I—
Cyrano:
                              Perhaps
      A pimple ornaments the end of it?
The Meddler:
      No—
Cyrano:
            Or a fly parading up and down?
      What is this portent?
The Meddler:
                  Oh!—
Cyrano:
                  This phenomenon?
The Meddler:
      But I have been careful not to look—
Cyrano:
                              And why
      Not, if you please?
The Meddler:
                  Why—
Cyrano:
                  It disgusts you, then?
The Meddler:
      My dear sir—
Cyrano: Does its color appear to you
      Unwholesome?

The Meddler:

> Oh, by no means!

Cyrano:

> Or its form

Obscene?

The Meddler:

> Not in the least—

Cyrano:

> Then why assume

This deprecating manner? Possibly
You find it just a trifle large?

The Meddler: [*Babbling*]

> Oh no!—

Small, very small, infinitesimal—

Cyrano: [*Roars*]   What?
How? You accuse me of absurdity?
Small—*my nose?* Why—

The Meddler: [*Breathless*]

> My God!—

Cyrano:

> Magnificent,

My nose! ... You pug, you knob, you
> button-head,
Know that I glory in this nose of mine,
For a great nose indicates a great man—
Genial, courteous, intellectual,
Virile, courageous—as I am—and such
As you—poor wretch—will never dare to be
Even in imagination. For that face—
That blank, inglorious concavity
Which my right hand finds—

> [*He strikes him.*]

The Meddler:

> Ow!

Cyrano:

> —on top of you,

Is as devoid of pride, of poetry,
Of soul, of picturesqueness, of contour,
Of character, of NOSE in short—as that
> [*Takes him by the shoulders and turns him
> around, suiting the action to the word*]
Which at the end of that limp spine of yours
My left foot—

The Meddler: [*Escaping*]

> Help! The Guard!

Cyrano:

> Take notice, all

Who find this feature of my countenance
A theme for comedy! When the humorist
Is noble, then my custom is to show

Appreciation proper to his rank—
More heartfelt ... and more pointed ...

De Guiche: [*Who has come down from the stage, surrounded by the Marquis*]

> Presently

This fellow will grow tiresome.

Valvert: [*Shrugs*]

> Oh, he blows

His trumpet!

De Guiche:

> Well—will no one interfere?

Valvert:

No one?
> [*Looks around*]
> Observe. I myself will proceed
To put him in his place.
> [*He walks up to* **Cyrano,** *who has been watching
> him, and stands there, looking him over with an
> affected air.*]
> Ah ... your nose ... hem! ...
Your nose is ... rather large!

Cyrano: [*Gravely*]

> Rather.

Valvert: [*Simpering*]

> Oh well—

Cyrano: [*Coolly*]

Is that all?

Valvert: [*Turns away with a shrug*]

> Well, of course—

Cyrano:

> Ah, no, young sir!

You are too simple. Why, you might have
> said—
Oh, a great many things! Mon dieu, why
> waste
Your opportunity? For example, thus:—
AGGRESSIVE: I, sir, if that nose were mine,
I'd have it amputated—on the spot!
FRIENDLY: How do you drink with such a nose?
You ought to have a cup made specially.
DESCRIPTIVE: 'Tis a rock—a crag—a cape—
A cape? say rather, a peninsula!
INQUISITIVE: What is that receptacle—
A razor-case or a portfolio?
KINDLY: Ah, do you love the little birds
So much that when they come and sing to
> you,
You give them this to perch on? INSOLENT:
Sir, when you smoke, the neighbors must
> suppose

Your chimney is one fire. CAUTIOUS: Take
    care—
A weight like that might make you topheavy.
THOUGHTFUL: Somebody fetch my parasol—
Those delicate colors fade so in the sun!
PEDANTIC: Does not Aristophanes
Mention a mythologic monster called
Hippocampelephantocamelos?
Surely we have here the original!
FAMILIAR: Well, old torchlight! Hang your hat
Over that chandelier—it hurts my eyes.
ELOQUENT: When it blows, the typhoon howls,
And the clouds darken. DRAMATIC: When it
    bleeds—
The Red Sea! ENTERPRISING: What a sign
For some perfumer! LYRIC: Hark—the horn
Of Roland calls to summon Charlemagne!—
SIMPLE: When do they unveil the monument?
RESPECTFUL: Sir, I recognize in you
A man of parts, a man of prominence—
RUSTIC: Hey? What? Call that a nose? Na na—
I be no fool like what you think I be—
That there's a blue cucumber! MILITARY:
Point against cavalry! PRACTICAL: Why not
A lottery with this for the grand prize?
Or—parodying Faustus in the play—
‹"Was this the nose that launched a thousand
    ships
And burned the topless towers of Ilium?"
These, my dear sir, are things you might have
    said
Had you some tinge of letters, or of wit
To color your discourse. But wit,—not so,
You never had an atom—and of letters,
You need but three to write you down—an
    Ass.
Moreover,—if you had the invention, here
Before these folks to make a jest of me—
Be sure you would not then articulate
The twentieth part of half a syllable
Of the beginning! For I say these things
Lightly enough myself, about myself,
But I allow none else to utter them.

De Guiche: [*Tries to lead away the amazed* **Valvert.**]
Vicomte—come.

Valvert: [*Choking*]
          Oh— These arrogant grand airs!—
A clown who—look at him—not even gloves!
No ribbons—no lace—no buckles on his
    shoes—

Cyrano:
I carry my adornments on my soul.
I do not dress up like a popinjay;
But inwardly, I keep my daintiness.
I do not bear with me, by any chance,
An insult not yet washed away—a conscience
Yellow with unpurged bile—an honor frayed
To rags, a set of scruples badly worn.
I go caparisoned in gems unseen,
Trailing white plumes of freedom, garlanded
With my good name—no figure of a man,
But a soul clothed in shining armor, hung
With deeds for decorations, twirling—thus—
A bristling wit, and swinging at my side
Courage, and on the stones of this old town
Making the sharp truth ring, like golden
    spurs!

Valvert:
But—

Cyrano:
         But I have no gloves! A pity too!
I had one—the last one of an old pair—
And lost that. Very careless of me. Some
Gentleman offered me an impertinence.
I left it—in his face.

Valvert:
             Dolt, bumpkin, fool,
Insolent puppy, jobbernowl!

Cyrano: [*Removes his hat and bows*]
            Ah, yes?
And I—Cyrano-Savinien-Hercule
De Bergerac!

Valvert: [*Turns away.*]
           Buffoon!

Cyrano: [*Cries out as if suddenly taken with a cramp*]
            Oh!

Valvert: [*Turns back*]
           Well, what now?

Cyrano: [*With grimaces of anguish*]
I must do something to relieve these cramps—
This is what comes of lack of exercise—
Ah!—

Valvert:
           What is all this?

Cyrano:
           My sword has gone to sleep?

Valvert: [*Draws*]
         So be it!

Cyrano:
You shall die exquisitely.

Valvert: [*Contemptuously*]
Poet!
Cyrano:

        Why yes, a poet, if you will;
So while we fence, I'll make you a Ballade
Extempore.
Valvert:

        A Ballade?
Cyrano:

                Yes. You know
What that is?
Valvert:

                I—
Cyrano:

        The Ballade, sir, is formed
Of three stanzas of eight lines each—
Valvert:

                Oh, come!
Cyrano:
And a refrain of four.
Valvert:

                You—
Cyrano:

                I'll compose
One, while I fight with you; and at the end
Of the last line—thrust home!
Valvert:

                Will you?
Cyrano:

                I will.
        [*Declaims*]
    Ballade of the duel at the Hôtel de
    Bourgogne
    Between de Bergerac and a Boeotian."
Valvert: [*Sneering*]
What do you mean by that?
Cyrano:

                Oh, that? The title.
The Crowd: [*Excited*]
Come on—
        A circle—
                Quiet—
                Down in front!
[TABLEAU. *A ring of interested spectators in the
centre of the floor, the Marquis and the Officers
mingling with the citizens and common folk. Pages
swarming up on men's shoulders to see better; the
Ladies in the boxes standing and leaning over.*

To the right, **De Guiche** *and his following; to
the left,* **Le Bret, Cuigy, Ragueneau,** *and
others of* **Cyrano**'s *friends.*]
Cyrano: [*Closes his eyes for an instant*]
Stop . . . Let me choose my rimes. . . . Now!
        Here we go—
        [*He suits the action to the word, throughout the
        following:*]
Lightly I toss my hat away,
        Languidly over my arm let fall
The cloak that covers my bright array—
        Then out swords, and to work withal!
        A Launcelot, in his Lady's hall . . .
        A Spartacus, at the Hippodrome! . . .
        I dally awhile with you, dear jackal,
Then, as I end the refrain, thrust home!
        [*The swords cross—the fight is on.*]
Where shall I skewer my peacock? . . . Nay,
        Better for you to have shunned this brawl!—
Here, in the heart, thro' your ribbons gay?
        —In the belly, under your silken shawl?
        Hark, how the steel rings musical!
Mark how my point floats, light as the foam,
        Ready to drive you back to the wall,
Then, as I end the refrain, thrust home!

Ho, for a rime! . . . You are white as whey—
        You break, you cower, you cringe, you . . .
        crawl!
Tac!—and I parry your last essay:
        So may the turn of a hand forestall
Life with its honey, death with its gall;
        So may the turn of my fancy roam
Free, for a time, till the rimes recall,
Then, as I end the refrain, thrust home!
        [*He announces solemnly.*]
Refrain:
        Prince! Pray God, that is Lord of all,
Pardon your soul, for your time has come!
        Beat—pass—fling you aslant, asprawl—
Then, as I end the refrain . . .
        [*He lunges;* **Valvert** *staggers back and falls into
        the arms of his friends.* **Cyrano** *recovers, and
        salutes.*]

                —Thrust home!
[*Shouts. Applause from the boxes. Flowers and
handkerchiefs come fluttering down. The Officers
surround* **Cyrano** *and congratulate him.* **Ra-**

gueneau *dances for joy.* **Le Bret** *is unable to conceal his enthusiasm. The friends of* **Valvert** *hold him up and help him away.*]

The Crowd: [*In one long cry*]
Ah-h!
A Cavalier:
                    Superb!
A Woman:
                         Simply sweet!
Ragueneau:
                              Magnelephant!
A Marquis:
A novelty!
Le Bret:
                    Bah!
The Crowd: [*Thronging around* **Cyrano**]
                         Compliments—regards—
Bravo!—
A Woman's Voice:
Why, he's a hero!
A Musketeer: [*Advances quickly to* **Cyrano,** *with outstretched hands*]
                              Monsieur, will you
Permit me?—It was altogether fine!
I think I may appreciate these things—
Moreover, I have been stamping for pure joy!
     [*He retires quickly.*]
Cyrano: [*To* **Cuigy**]
What was that gentleman's name?
Cuigy:
                         Oh . . . D'Artagnan.
Le Bret: [*Takes* **Cyrano**'s *arm*]
Come here and tell me—
Cyrano:
                         Let this crowd go first—
     [*To* **Bellerose**]
May we stay?
Bellerose: [*With great respect*]
                    Certainly!
     [*Cries and cat-calls off stage.*]
Jodelet: [*Comes down from the door where he has been looking out.*]
                         Hark!— Montfleury—
They are hooting him.
Bellerose: [*Solemnly*]
                    "Sic transit gloria!"
     [*Changes his tone and shouts to the* **Porter** *and the* **Lamplighter.**]

—Strike! . . . Close the house! . . . Leave the
lights—
     We rehearse
The new farce after dinner.
     [**Jodelet** *and* **Bellerose** *go out after elaborately saluting* **Cyrano.**]
The Porter: [*To* **Cyrano**]
                              You do not dine?
Cyrano:
I?— No!
     [**The Porter** *turns away.*]
Le Bret:
                    Why not?
Cyrano: [*Haughtily*]
                         Because—
     [*Changing his tone when he sees* **the Porter** *has gone.*]
                              Because I have
No money.
Le Bret: [*Gesture of tossing*]
                    But—the purse of gold?
Cyrano:
                                   Farewell,
Paternal pension!
Le Bret:
                    So you have, until
The first of next month—?
Cyrano:
                         Nothing.
Le Bret:
                              What a fool!—
Cyrano:
But—what a gesture!
The Orange Girl: [*Behind her little counter; coughs*]
                         Hem!
     [**Cyrano** *and* **Le Bret** *look around; she advances timidly.*]
                              Pardon, monsieur . . .
A man ought never to go hungry . . .
     [*Indicating the sideboard*]
                                   See,
I have everything here . . .
     [*Eagerly*]
                              Please!—
Cyrano: [*Uncovers*]
                              My dear child,
I cannot bend this Gascon pride of mine
To accept such a kindness— Yet, for fear

That I may give you pain if I refuse,
I will take . . .
[*He goes to the sideboard and makes his selection*]
Oh, not very much! A grape . . .
[*She gives him the bunch; he removes a single grape.*]
One only! And a glass of water . . .
[*She starts to pour wine into it; he stops her.*]
Clear!
And . . . half a macaroon!
[*He gravely returns the other half.*]

Le Bret:
Old idiot!

The Orange Girl:
Please!— Nothing more?

Cyrano:
Why yes— Your hand to kiss.
[*He kisses the hand which she holds out, as he would the hand of a princess.*]

The Orange Girl:
Thank you, sir.
[*She curtseys.*]
Good-night.
[*She goes out.*]

Cyrano:
Now, I am listening.
[*Plants himself before the sideboard and arranges thereon—*]
Dinner!—
[*—the macaroon*]
Drink!—
[*—the glass of water*]
Dessert!—
[*—the grape*]
There—now I'll sit down.
[*Seats himself*]
Lord, I was hungry! Abominably!
[*Eating*]
Well?

Le Bret:
These fatheads with the bellicose grand airs
Will have you ruined if you listen to them;
Talk to a man of sense and hear how all
Your swagger impresses him.

Cyrano: [*Finishes his macaroon*]
Enormously.

Le Bret:
The Cardinal—

Cyrano: [*Beaming*]
Was he there?

Le Bret:
He must have thought you—

Cyrano:
Original.

Le Bret:
Well, but—

Cyrano:
He is himself
A playwright. He will not be too displeased
That I have closed another author's play.

Le Bret:
But look at all the enemies you have made!

Cyrano: [*Begins on the grape*]
How many—do you think?

Le Bret:
Just forty-eight
Without the women.

Cyrano:
Count them.

Le Bret:
Montfleury,
Baro, de Guiche, the Vicomte, the Old Man,
All the Academy—

Cyrano:
Enough! You make me
Happy!

Le Bret:
But where is all this leading you?
What is your plan?

Cyrano:
I have been wandering—
Wasting my force upon too many plans.
Now I have chosen one.

Le Bret:
What one?

Cyrano:
The simplest—
To make myself in all things admirable!

Le Bret:
Hmph!— Well, then, the real reason why you hate
Montfleury—Come, the truth, now!

Cyrano: [*Rises*]
That Silenus,
Who cannot hold his belly in his arms,
Still dreams of being sweetly dangerous
Among the women—sighs and languishes,
Making sheeps' eyes out of his great frog's face—
I hate him ever since one day he dared

Smile upon—
                    Oh, my friend, I seemed to see
Over some flower a great snail crawling!
Le Bret: [*Amazed*]
                                              How,
What? Is it possible?—
Cyrano: [*With a bitter smile*]
                              For me to love? . . .
[*Changing his tone; seriously*]
I love.
Le Bret:
                    May I know? You have never said—
Cyrano:
Whom I love? Think a moment. Think of
    me—
Me, whom the plainest woman would
    despise—
Me, with this nose of mine that marches on
Before me by a quarter of an hour!
Whom should I love? Why—of course—it
    must be
The woman in the world most beautiful.
Le Bret:
Most beautiful?
Cyrano:
                    In all this world—most sweet:
Also most wise; most witty; and most fair!
Le Bret:
Who and what is this woman?
Cyrano:
                                        Dangerous
Mortally, without meaning; exquisite
Without imagining. Nature's own snare
To allure manhood. A white rose wherein
Love lies in ambush for his natural prey.
Who knows her smile has known a perfect
    thing.
She creates grace in her own image, brings
Heaven to earth in one movement of her
    hand—
Nor thou, O Venus! balancing thy shell
Over the Mediterranean blue, nor thou,
Diana! marching through broad, blossoming
    woods,
Art so divine as when she mounts her chair,
And goes abroad through Paris!
Le Bret:
                              Oh, well—of course,
That makes everything clear!
Cyrano: Transparently.

Le Bret:
Madeleine Robin—your cousin?
Cyrano:
                                        Yes; Roxane.
Le Bret:
And why not? If you love her, tell her so!
You have covered yourself with glory in her
    eyes
This very day.
Cyrano:
                    My old friend—look at me,
And tell me how much hope remains for me
With this protuberance! Oh I have no more
Illusions! Now and then—bah! I may grow
Tender, walking alone in the blue cool
Of evening, through some garden fresh with
    flowers
After the benediction of the rain;
My poor big devil of a nose inhales
April . . . and so I follow with my eyes
Where some boy, with a girl upon his arm,
Passes a patch of silver . . . and I feel
Somehow, I wish I had a woman too,
Walking with little steps under the moon,
And holding my arm so, and smiling. Then
I dream—and I forget. . . .
                              And then I see
The shadow of my profile on the wall!
Le Bret:
My friend! . . .
Cyrano:
                    My friend, I have my bitter days,
Knowing myself so ugly, so alone.
Sometimes—
Le Bret:
                              You weep?
Cyrano: [*Quickly*]
                              Oh, not that ever! No,
That would be too grotesque—tears trickling
    down
All the long way along this nose of mine?
I will not so profane the dignity
Of sorrow. Never any tears for me!
Why, there is nothing more sublime than
    tears,
Nothing!—Shall I make them ridiculous
In my poor person?
Le Bret:
                    Love's no more than chance!
Cyrano: [*Shakes his head*]

No. I love Cleopatra; do I appear
Cæsar? I adore Beatrice; have I
The look of Dante?

Le Bret:
                    But your wit—your courage—
Why, that poor child who offered you just
    now
Your dinner! She—you saw with your own
    eyes,
Her eyes did not avoid you.

Cyrano: [*Thoughtful*]
                    That is true . . .

Le Bret:
Well then! Roxane herself, watching your
    duel,
Paler than—

Cyrano:
            Pale?—

Le Bret:
                Her lips parted, her hand
Thus, at her breast—I saw it! Speak to her
Speak, man!

Cyrano:
    Through my nose? She might laugh at me;
That is the one thing in this world I fear!

The Porter: [*Followed by the Duenna, approaches*
Cyrano *respectfully*]
A lady asking for Monsieur.

Cyrano:
                    Mon dieu . . .
Her Duenna!—

The Duenna: [*A sweeping curtsey*]
                Monsieur . . .
                    A message for you:
From our good cousin we desire to know
When and where we may see him privately.

Cyrano: [*Amazed*]
To see me?

The Duenna: [*An elaborate reverence*]
                To see you. We have certain things
To tell you.

Cyrano:
            Certain—

The Duenna:
                Things.

Cyrano: [*Trembling*]
                Mon dieu! . . .

The Duenna:
                        We go

To-morrow, at the first flush of the dawn,
To hear Mass at St. Roch. Then afterwards,
Where can we meet and talk a little?

Cyrano: [*Catching* **Le Bret***'s arm*]
                        Where?—
I—Ah, mon dieu! . . . mon dieu! . . .

The Duenna:
                    Well?

Cyrano:
                I am thinking . . .

The Duenna:
And you think?

Cyrano:
            I . . . The shop of Ragueneau . . .
Ragueneau—pastrycook . . .

The Duenna:
                Who dwells?—

Cyrano:
                    Mon dieu! . . .
Oh, yes . . . Ah, mon dieu! . . . Rue St.-Honoré.

The Duenna:
We are agreed. Remember—seven o'clock.
    [*Reverence*]
Until then—

Cyrano:
            I'll be there.
    [*The Duenna goes out.*]

Cyrano: [*Falls into the arms of* **Le Bret**]
                Me . . . to see me! . . .

Le Bret:
You are not quite so gloomy.

Cyrano:
                After all,
She knows that I exist—no matter why!

Le Bret:
So now, you are going to be happy.

Cyrano:
                    Now! . . .
    [*Beside himself*]
I—I am going to be a storm—a flame—
I need to fight whole armies all alone;
I have ten hearts; I have a hundred arms; I
    feel
Too strong to war with mortals—
    [*He shouts at the top of his voice*]
                BRING ME GIANTS!
    [*A moment since, the shadows of the comedians
    have been visible moving and posturing upon the
    stage. The violins have taken their places.*]

A Voice: [*From the stage*]
Hey—pst—less noise! We are rehearsing here!

Cyrano: [*Laughs*]
We are going.

    [*He turns up stage. Through the street door enter* **Cuigy, Brissaille,** *and a number of officers, supporting* **Lignière,** *who is now thoroughly drunk.*]

Cuigy:
          Cyrano!

Cyrano:
            What is it?

Cuigy:
                    Here—
Here's your stray lamb!

Cyrano: [*Recognizes* **Lignière**]
        Lignière—What's wrong with him?

Cuigy:
He wants you.

Brissaille:
        He's afraid to go home.

Cyrano:
                 Why?

Lignière: [*Showing a crumpled scrap of paper and speaking with the elaborate logic of profound intoxication*]
This letter—hundred against one—that's me—
I'm the one—all because of little song—
Good song— Hundred men, waiting,
    understand?
Porte de Nesle—way home— Might be
    dangerous—
Would you permit me spend the night with
    you?

Cyrano:
A hundred—is that all? You are going home!

Lignière: [*Astonished*]
Why—

Cyrano: [*In a voice of thunder, indicating the lighted lantern which the* **Porter** *holds up curiously as he regards the scene*]
        Take that lantern!
    [**Lignière** *precipitately seizes the lantern.*]
              Forward march! I say
I'll be the man to-night that sees you home.
    [*To the officers*]
You others follow—I want an audience!

Cuigy:
A hundred against one—

Cyrano: Those are the odds

To-night!

    [**The Comedians** *in their costumes are descending from the stage and joining the group.*]

Le Bret:
But why help this—

Cyrano:
                There goes Le Bret
Growling!

Le Bret:
      —This drunkard here?

Cyrano: [*His hand on* **Le Bret**'s *shoulder*]
            Because this drunkard—
This tun of sack, this butt of Burgundy—
Once in his life has done one lovely thing:
After the Mass, according to the form,
He saw, one day, the lady of his heart
Take holy water for a blessing. So
This one, who shudders at a drop of rain,
This fellow here—runs headlong to the font
Bends down and drinks it dry!

A Soubrette:
                I say that was
A pretty thought!

Cyrano:
          Ah, was it not?

The Soubrette: [*To the others*]
                  But why
Against one poor poet, a hundred men?

Cyrano:
March!
    [*To the officers*]
    And you gentlemen, remember now,
No rescue— Let me fight alone.

A Comedienne: [*Jumps down from the stage*]
                Come on!
I'm going to watch—

Cyrano:
          Come along!

Another Comedienne: [*Jumps down, speaks to a Comedian costumed as an old man*]
              You, Cassandre?

Cyrano:
Come all of you—the Doctor, Isabelle,
Léandre—the whole company—a swarm
Of murmuring, golden bees—we'll parody
Italian farce and Tragedy-of-Blood;
Ribbons for banner, masks for blazonry,
And tambourines to be our rolling drums!

All the Women: [*Jumping for joy*]

Bravo!—My hood— My cloak— Hurry!
Jodelet: [*Mock heroic*]

Lead on!—

Cyrano: [*To the violins*]
You violins—play us an overture—
[*The violins join the procession which is forming.
The lighted candles are snatched from the stage
and distributed; it becomes a torchlight proces-
sion.*]
Bravo!—Officers— Ladies in costume—
And twenty paces in advance . . .
[*He takes his station as he speaks.*]

Myself,
Alone, with glory fluttering over me,
Alone as Lucifer at war with heaven!
Remember—no one lifts a hand to help—
Ready there? One . . . two . . . three! Porter,
the doors! . . .
[*The Porter flings wide the great doors. We see
in the dim moonlight a corner of old Paris, purple
and picturesque.*]
Look—Paris dreams—nocturnal, nebulous,
Under blue moonbeams hung from wall to
wall—
Nature's own setting for the scene we play!—
Yonder, behind her veil of mist, the Seine,
Like a mysterious and magic mirror
Trembles—

And you shall see what you shall
see!
All:
To the Porte de Nesle!
Cyrano: [*Erect upon the threshold*]
To the Porte de Nesle!
[*He turns back for a moment to the* **Soubrette**]
Did you not ask, my dear, why against one
Singer they send a hundred swords?
[*Quietly, drawing his own sword*]

Because
They know this one man for a friend of mine!
[*He goes out. The procession follows:* **Lignière**
*zigzagging at its head, then the Comediennes on
the arms of the Officers, then the Comedians,
leaping and dancing as they go. It vanishes into
the night to the music of the violins, illuminated
by the flickering glimmer of the candles.*]

Curtain

ACT II

The Bakery of The Poets

The Shop of Ragueneau, Baker and Pastrycook:
a spacious affair at the corner of the Rue St.-
Honoré and the Rue de l'Arbre Sec. The street,
seen vaguely through the glass panes in the door
at the back, is gray in the first light of dawn.

In the foreground, at the Left, a Counter is
surmounted by a Canopy of wrought iron from
which are hanging ducks, geese, and white peacocks. Great crockery jars hold bouquets of
common flowers, yellow sunflowers in particular. On the same side farther back, a huge fireplace; in front of it, between great andirons, of
which each one supports a little saucepan, roast
fowls revolve and weep into their drippingpans.
To the Right at the First Entrance, a door.
Beyond it, Second Entrance, a staircase leads up
to a little dining-room under the eaves, its interior visible through open shutters. A table is set
there and a tiny Flemish candlestick is lighted;
there one may retire to eat and drink in private.
A wooden gallery, extending from the head of
the stairway, seems to lead to other little din-
ing-rooms.

In the centre of the shop, an iron ring hangs
by a rope over a pulley so that it can be raised
or lowered; adorned with game of various kinds
hung from it by hooks, it has the appearance
of a sort of gastronomic chandelier.

In the shadow under the staircase, ovens are
glowing. The spits revolve; the copper pots and
pans gleam ruddily. Pastries in pyramids. Hams
hanging from the rafters. The morning baking
is in progress: a bustle of tall cooks and timid
scullions and scurrying apprentices; a blossoming of white caps adorned with cock's feathers
or the wings of guinea fowl. On wicker trays
or on great metal platters they bring in rows of
pastries and fancy dishes of various kinds.

Tables are covered with trays of cakes and
rolls; others with chairs placed about them are
set for guests.

One little table in a corner disappears under
a heap of papers. At the Curtain Rise Ragueneau is seated there. He is writing poetry.

A Pastrycook: [*Brings in a dish*]
  Fruits en gelée!
Second Pastrycook: [*Brings dish*]
          Custard!
Third Pastrycook: [*Brings roast peacock ornamented with feathers*]
          Peacock rôti!
Fourth Pastrycook: [*Brings tray of cakes*]
  Cakes and confections!
Fifth Pastrycook: [*Brings earthen dish*]
          Beef en casserole!
Ragueneau: [*Raises his head; returns to mere earth*]
  Over the coppers of my kitchen flows
  The frosted-silver dawn. Silence awhile
  The god who sings within thee, Ragueneau!
  Lay down the lute—the oven calls for thee!
          [*Rises; goes to one of the cooks.*]
  Here's a hiatus in your sauce; fill up
  The measure.
The Cook:
          How much?
Ragueneau: [*Measures on his finger*]
          One more dactyl.
The Cook:
                Huh? . . .
First Pastrycook:
  Rolls!
Second Pastrycook:
          Roulades!
Ragueneau: [*Before the fireplace*]
          Veil, O Muse, thy virgin eyes
  From the lewd gleam of these terrestrial fires!
          [*To **First Pastrycook***]
  Your rolls lack balance. Here's the proper
          form—
  An equal hemistich on either side,
  And the caesura in between.
          [*To another, pointing out an unfinished pie*]
                Your house
  Of crust should have a roof upon it.
          [*To another, who is seated on the hearth, placing poultry on a spit*]
                And you—
  Along the interminable spit, arrange
  The modest pullet and the lordly Turk
  Alternately, my son—as great Malherbe
  Alternates male and female rimes. Remember,
  A couplet, or a roast, should be well turned.

An Apprentice: [*Advances with a dish covered by a napkin*]
  Master, I thought of you when I designed
  This, hoping it might please you.
Ragueneau:
                Ah! A lyre—
The Apprentice:
  In puff-paste—
Ragueneau:
          And the jewels—candied fruit!
The Apprentice:
  And the strings, barley-sugar!
Ragueneau: [*Gives him money*]
                Go and drink
  My health.
          [**Lise** *enters*]
                St!—My wife— Circulate, and hide
  That money!
          [*Shows the lyre to **Lise**, with a languid air.*]
          Graceful—yes?
Lise:
                Ridiculous!
          [*She places on the counter a pile of paper bags.*]
Ragueneau:
  Paper bags? Thank you . . .
          [*He looks at them*]
                Ciel! My manuscripts!
  The sacred verses of my poets—rent
  Asunder, limb from limb—butchered to make
  Base packages of pastry! Ah, you are one
  Of those insane Bacchantes who destroyed
  Orpheus!
Lise:
  Your dirty poets left them here
  To pay for eating half our stock-in-trade:
  We ought to make some profit out of them!
Ragueneau:
  Ant! Would you blame the locust for his
          song?
Lise:
  I blame the locust for his appetite!
  There used to be a time—before you had
  Your hungry friends—you never called me
          Ants—
  No, nor Bacchantes!
Ragueneau:
                What a way to use
  Poetry!

Lise:

Well, what is the use of it?

Ragueneau:

But, my dear girl, what would you do with prose?

[**Two children** *enter*]

Well, dears?

A Child:

Three little patties.

Ragueneau: [*Serves them*]

There we are!

All hot and brown.

The Child:

Would you mind wrapping them?

Ragueneau:

One of my paper bags! . . .

Oh, certainly.

[*Reads from the bag, as he is about to wrap the patties in it.*]

"Ulysses, when he left Penelope"—

Not that one!

[*Takes another bag; reads*]

"Phoebus, golden-crowned"—

Not that one.

Lise:

Well? They are waiting!

Ragueneau:

Very well, very well!—

The Sonnet to Phyllis . . .

Yet—it does seem hard . . .

Lise:

Made up your mind—at last! Mph!—Jack-o'-Dreams!

Ragueneau: [*As her back is turned, calls back the children, who are already at the door*]

Pst!—Children— Give me back the bag. Instead

Of three patties, you shall have six of them!

[*Makes the exchange. The children go out. He reads from the bag, as he smooths it out tenderly.*]

"Phyllis"—

A spot of butter on her name!—

"Phyllis"—

Cyrano: [*Enters hurriedly*]

What is the time?

Ragueneau:

Six o'clock.

Cyrano:

One

Hour more . . .

Ragueneau:

Felicitations!

Cyrano:

And for what?

Ragueneau:

Your victory! I saw it all—

Cyrano:

Which one?

Ragueneau:

At the Hôtel de Bourgogne.

Cyrano:

Oh—the duel!

Ragueneau:

The duel in Rime!

Lise:

He talks of nothing else.

Cyrano:

Nonsense!

Ragueneau:

[*Fencing and foining with a spit, which he snatches up from the hearth*]

"Then, as I end the refrain, thrust home!"

"Then, as I end the refrain"—

Gods! What a line!

"Then, as I end"—

Cyrano:

What time now, Ragueneau?

Ragueneau: [*Petrified at the full extent of a lunge, while he looks at the clock*]

Five after six—

[*Recovers*]

"—thrust home!"

A Ballade, too!

Lise: [*To* **Cyrano,** *who in passing has mechanically shaken hands with her*]

Your hand—what have you done?

Cyrano:

Oh, my hand?—Nothing.

Ragueneau:

What danger now—

Cyrano:

No danger.

Lise:

I believe

He is lying.

Cyrano:

Why? Was I looking down my nose?

That must have been a devil of a lie!

[*Changing his tone; to* **Ragueneau**]

I expect someone. Leave us here alone,

When the times comes.

Ragueneau:

How can I? In a moment,
My poets will be here.

Lise:

To break their ... fast!

Cyrano:

Take them away, then, when I give the sign.
—What time?

Ragueneau:

Ten minutes after.

Cyrano:

Have you a pen?

Ragueneau: [*Offers him a pen*]

An eagle's feather!

A Musketeer: [*Enters, and speaks to* **Lise** *in a stentorian voice*]

Greeting!

Cyrano: [*To* **Ragueneau**]

Who is this?

Ragueneau:

My wife's friend. A terrific warrior,
So he says.

Cyrano:

Ah— I see.
[*Takes up the pen; waves* **Ragueneau** *away.*]
Only to write—
To fold— To give it to her—and to go ...
[*Throws down the pen.*]
Coward! And yet—the Devil take my soul
If I dare speak one word to her ...
[*To* **Ragueneau**]
What time now?

Ragueneau:

A quarter after six.

Cyrano: [*Striking his breast*]

—One little word
Of all the many thousand I have here!
Whereas in writing ...
[*Takes up the pen*]
Come, I'll write to her
That letter I have written on my heart,
Torn up, and written over many times—
So many times ... that all I have to do
Is to remember, and to write it down.
[*He writes. Through the glass of the door appear vague and hesitating shadows.* **The Poets** *enter, clothed in rusty black and spotted with mud.*]

Lise: [*To* **Ragueneau**]

Here come your scarecrows!

First Poet:

Comrade!

Second Poet: [*Takes both* **Ragueneau**'*s hands*]

My dear brother!

Third Poet: [*Sniffing*]

O Lord of Roasts, how sweet thy dwellings
are!

Fourth Poet:

Phoebus Apollo of the Silver Spoon!

Fifth Poet:

Cupid of Cookery!

Ragueneau: [*Surrounded, embraced, beaten on the back*]

These geniuses,
They put one at one's ease!

First Poet:

We were delayed
By the crowd at the Porte de Nesle.

Second Poet:

Dead men
All scarred and gory, scattered on the stones,
Villainous-looking scoundrels—eight of them.

Cyrano: [*Looks up an instant*]

Eight? I thought only seven—

Ragueneau:

Do you know
The hero of this hecatomb?

Cyrano:

I? ... No.

Lise: [*To the* **Musketeer**]

Do you?

The Musketeer:

Hmm—perhaps!

First Poet: They say one man alone
Put to flight all this crowd.

Second Poet:

Everywhere lay
Swords, daggers, pikes, bludgeons—

Cyrano: [*Writing*]

"Your eyes ..."

Third Poet:

As far
As the Quai des Orfevres, hats and cloaks—

First Poet:

Why, that man must have been the devil!

Cyrano:

"Your lips ..."

First Poet:

Some savage monster might have done this
thing!

Cyrano:
"Looking upon you, I grow faint with fear . . ."
Second Poet:
What have you written lately, Ragueneau?
Cyrano:
            "Your Friend— Who loves you . . ."
                    So. No signature;
I'll give it to her myself.
Ragueneau:
                    A Recipe
In Rime.
Third Poet:
                    Read us your rimes!
Fourth Poet:
                            Here's a brioche
Cocking its hat at me.
                [He bites off the top of it]
First Poet:
                    Look how those buns
Follow the hungry poet with their eyes—
Those almond eyes!
Second Poet:
                    We are listening—
Third Poet:
                        See this cream-puff—
Fat little baby, drooling while it smiles!
Second Poet: *[Nibbling at the pastry lyre]*
For the first time, the lyre is my support.
Ragueneau: *[Coughs, adjusts his cap, strikes an attitude]*
A Recipe in Rime—
Second Poet: *[Gives **First Poet** a dig with his elbow]*
            Your breakfast?
First Poet:
                            Dinner!
Ragueneau: *[Declaims]*
A Recipe for Making Almond Tarts

Beat your eggs, the yolk and white,
            Very light;
        Mingle with their creamy fluff
            Drops of lime-juice, cool and
green;
                Then pour in
        Milk of Almonds, just enough.
    Dainty patty-pans, embraced
        In puff-paste—
    Have these ready within reach;
        With your thumb and finger, pinch

            Half an inch
    Up around the edge of each—

    Into these, a score or more,
            Slowly pour
    All your store of custard; so
            Take them, bake them
golden-brown—
            Now sit down! . . .
        Almond tartlets, Ragueneau!
The Poets:
Delicious! Melting!
A Poet: *[Chokes]*
                    Humph!
Cyrano: *[To **Ragueneau**]*
                    Do you not see
Those fellows fattening themselves?—
Ragueneau:
                            I know.
I would not look—it might embarrass them—
You see, I love a friendly audience.
Besides—another vanity—I am pleased
When they enjoy my cooking.
Cyrano: *[Slaps him on the back]*
                        Be off with you!
    *[**Ragueneau** goes upstage.]*
Good little soul!
    *[Calls to **Lise**]*
            Madame!—
    *[She leaves the **Musketeer** and comes down to him]*
                        This musketeer—
He is making love to you?
Lise: *[Haughtily]*
                    If any man
Offends my virtue—all I have to do
Is look at him—once!
Cyrano: *[Looks at her gravely; she drops her eyes]*
                    I do not find
Those eyes of yours unconquerable.
Lise: *[Panting]*
                            —Ah!
Cyrano: *[Raising his voice a little]*
Now listen— I am fond of Ragueneau;
I allow no one—do you understand?—
To . . . take his name in vain!
Lise:
                        You think—
Cyrano: *[Ironic emphasis]*
                            I think

I interrupt you.

[*He salutes the* **Musketeer,** *who has heard without daring to resent the warning.* **Lise** *goes to the* **Musketeer** *as he returns* **Cyrano**'s *salute.*]

Lise:

You—you swallow that?—
You ought to have pulled his nose!

The Muskeeteer:

His nose?—His nose! . . .

[*He goes out hurriedly.* **Roxane** *and the* **Duenna** *appear outside the door.*]

Cyrano: [*Nods to* **Ragueneau**]
Pst!—

Ragueneau: [*To the* **Poets**]
Come inside—

Cyrano: [*Impatient*]

Pst! . . . Pst! . . .

Ragueneau: We shall be more
Comfortable . . .

[*He leads the* **Poets** *into inner room.*]

First Poet:
The cakes!

Second Poet:
Bring them along!

[*They go out.*]

Cyrano:
If I can see the faintest spark of hope,
Then—

[*Throws door open—bows*]
Welcome!

[**Roxane** *enters, followed by the* **Duenna,** *whom* **Cyrano** *detains*]
Pardon me—one word—

The Duenna:

Take two.

Cyrano:
Have you a good digestion?

The Duenna:

Wonderful!

Cyrano:
Good. Here are two sonnets, by Benserade—

The Duenna:
Euh?

Cyrano:

Which I fill for you with éclairs.

The Duenna:

Ooo!

Cyrano:
Do you like cream-puffs?

The Duenna:

Only with whipped cream.

Cyrano:
Here are three . . . six—embosomed in a poem
By Saint-Amant. This ode of Chapelin
Looks deep enough to hold—a jelly roll.
—Do you love Nature?

The Duenna:

Mad about it.

Cyrano:

Then
Go out and eat these in the street. Do not
Return—

The Duenna:
Oh, but—

Cyrano:

Until you finish them.

[*Down to* **Roxane**]
Blessed above all others be the hour
When you remembered to remember me,
And came to tell me . . . what?

Roxane: [*Takes off her mask*]
First let me thank you
Because . . . That man . . . that creature, whom your sword
Made sport of yesterday— His patron, one—

Cyrano:
De Guiche?—

Roxane:
—who thinks himself in love with me
Would have forced that man upon me for—
a husband—

Cyrano:
I understand—so much the better then!
I fought, not for my nose, but your bright eyes.

Roxane:
And then, to tell you—but before I can
Tell you—Are you, I wonder, still the same
Big brother—almost—that you used to be
When we were children, playing by the pond
In the old garden down there—

Cyrano: I remember—
Every summer you came to Bergerac! . . .

Roxane:
You used to make swords out of bulrushes—

Cyrano:
Your dandelion-dolls with golden hair—

Roxane:
And those green plums—

Cyrano:

     And those black mulberries—

Roxane:

In those days, you did everything I wished!

Cyrano:

Roxane, in short skirts, was called Madeleine.

Roxane:

Was I pretty?

Cyrano:

    Oh—not too plain!

Roxane:

       Sometimes

When you had hurt your hand you used to
 come

Running to me—and I would be your mother,

And say— Oh, in a very grown-up voice:

  [She takes his hand]

"Now, what have you been doing to yourself?
Let me see—"

  [She sees the hand—starts]

    Oh!—

    Wait— I said, "Let me see!"

Still—at your age! How did you do that?

Cyrano:

       Playing

With the big boys, down by the Porte de
 Nesle.

Roxane: *[Sits at a table and wets her handkerchief in
a glass of water]*

Come here to me.

Cyrano:

   —Such a wise little mother!

Roxane:

And tell me, while I wash this blood away,

How many you—played with?

Cyrano:

     Oh, about a hundred.

Roxane:

Tell me.

Cyrano:

No. Let me go. Tell me what you

Were going to tell me—if you dared?

Roxane: *[Still holding his hand]*

       I think

I do dare—now. It seems like long ago

When I could tell you things. Yes—I dare . . .

  Listen:

I . . . love someone.

Cyrano: Ah! . . .

Roxane:

     Someone who does not know.

Cyrano:

Ah! . . .

Roxane:

    At least—not yet.

Cyrano:

       Ah! . . .

Roxane:

      But he will know

Some day.

Cyrano:

    Ah! . . .

Roxane:

    A big boy who loves me too,

And is afraid of me, and keeps away,

And never says one word.

Cyrano:

     Ah! . . .

Roxane:

      Let me have

Your hand a moment—why how hot it is!—

I know. I see him trying . . .

Cyrano:

     Ah! . . .

Roxane:

      There now!

Is that better?—

  *[She finishes bandaging the hand with her hand-
kerchief]*

   Besides—only to think—

(This is a secret.) He is a soldier too,

In your own regiment—

Cyrano:

    Ah! . . .

Roxane:

     Yes, in the Guards,

Your company too.

Cyrano:

    Ah! . . .

Roxane:

     And such a man!—

He is proud—noble—young—brave—beautiful—

Cyrano: *[Turns pale; rises]*

Beautiful!—

Roxane:

    What's the matter?

Cyrano: *[Smiling]*

      Nothing—this—

My sore hand!

Roxane:

Well, I love him. That is all.
Oh—and I never saw him anywhere
Except the *Comedie.*

Cyrano:

You have never spoken?—

Roxane:

Only our eyes ...

Cyrano:

Why, then— How do you know?—

Roxane:

People talk about people; and I hear
Things ... and I know.

Cyrano:

You say he is in the Guards:
His name?

Roxane:

Baron Christian de Neuvillette.

Cyrano:

He is not in the Guards.

Roxane:

Yes. Since this morning.
Captain Carbon de Castel-Jaloux.

Cyrano:

So soon! ...

So soon we lose our hearts!—
But, my dear child,—

The Duenna: [*Opens the door*]

I have eaten the cakes, Monsieur de Bergerac!

Cyrano:

Good! Now go out and read the poetry!
[*The* **Duenna** *disappears*]
—But, my dear child! You, who love only
words,
Wit, the grand manner— Why, for all you
know,
The man may be a savage, or a fool.

Roxane:

His curls are like a hero from D'Urfé.

Cyrano:

His mind may be as curly as his hair.

Roxane:

Not with such eyes. I read his soul in them.

Cyrano:

Yes, all our souls are written in our eyes!
But—if he be a bungler?

Roxane: Then I shall die—
There!

Cyrano: [*After a pause*]

And you brought me here to tell me this?
I do not yet quite understand, Madame,
The reason for your confidence.

Roxane:

They say
That in your company— It frightens me—
You are all Gascons ...

Cyrano:

And we pick a quarrel
With any flat-foot who intrudes himself.
Whose blood is not pure Gascon like our
own?
Is this what you have heard?

Roxane:

I am so afraid
For him!

Cyrano: [*Between his teeth*]

Not without reason!—

Roxane:

And I thought
You ... You were so brave, so invincible
Yesterday, against all of those brutes!—If you,
Whom they all fear—

Cyrano:

Oh well— I will defend
Your little Baron.

Roxane:

Will you? Just for me?
Because I have always been—your friend!

Cyrano:

Of course ...

Roxane:

Will you be *his* friend?

Cyrano:

I will be his friend.

Roxane:

And never let him fight a duel?

Cyrano:

No—never.

Roxane:

Oh, but you are a darling!—I must go—
You never told me about last night— Why,
You must have been a hero! Have him write
And tell me all about it—will you?

Cyrano:

Of course ...

Roxane: [*Kisses her hand*]

I always did love you!—A hundred men

Against one— Well.... Adieu. We are great
   friends,
Are we not?

Cyrano:

   Of course ...

Roxane:

   He *must* write to me—
A hundred— You shall tell me the whole story
Some day, when I have time. A hundred
   men—
What courage—

Cyrano: [*Salutes as she goes out*]
   Oh ... I have done better since!
[*The door closes after her.* **Cyrano** *remains motionless, his eyes on the ground. Pause. The other door opens;* **Ragueneau** *puts in his head.*]

Ragueneau:
   May I come in?

Cyrano: [*Without moving*]
   Yes ...
[**Ragueneau** *and his friends re-enter. At the same time,* **Carbon de Castel-Jalous** *appears at the street door in uniform as Captain of the Guards; recognizes* **Cyrano** *with a sweeping gesture.*]

Carbon:
   Here he is!—Our hero!

Cyrano: [*Raises his head and salutes*]
   Our Captain!

Carbon:
   We know! All our company
Are here—

Cyrano: [*Recoils*]
   No—

Carbon:
   Come! They are waiting for you.

Cyrano:

   No!

Carbon: [*Tries to lead him out*]
Only across the street— Come!

Cyrano:

   Please—

Carbon: [*Goes to the door and shouts in a voice of thunder*]
   Our champion
Refuses! He is not feeling well to-day!

A Voice Outside:
Ah! Sandious!
   [*Noise outside of swords and trampling feet approaching.*]

Carbon:
   Here they come now!

The Cadets: [*Entering the shop*]
   Mille dious!—
Mordious!—Capdedious!—Pocapdedious!

Ragueneau: [*In astonishment*]
   Gentlemen—
You are all Gascons?

The Cadets:
   All!

First Cadet: [*To* **Cyrano**]
   Bravo!

Cyrano:
   Baron!

Another Cadet: [*Takes both his hands*]
   Vivat!

Cyrano:
   Baron!

Third Cadet:
   Come to my arms!

Cyrano:
   Baron!

Others:
To mine!—To mine!—

Cyrano:
   Baron ... Baron ... Have mercy—

Ragueneau:
You are all Barons too?

The Cadets:
   Are we?

Ragueneau:
   Are they? ...

First Cadet:
Our coronets would star the midnight sky!

Le Bret: [*Enters: Hurries to* **Cyrano**]
The whole town's looking for you! Raving
   mad—
A triumph! Those who saw the fight—

Cyrano:
   I hope!
You have not told them where I—

Le Bret: [*Rubbing his hands*]
   Certainly
I told them!

Citizen: [*Enters, followed by a group*]
   Listen! Shut the door!—Here comes
All Paris!
   [*The street outside fills with a shouting crowd. Chairs and carriages stop at the door.*]

Le Bret: [*Aside to* **Cyrano**, *smiling*]

And Roxane?

Cyrano: [*Quickly*]
                    Hush!

The Crowd Outside:
                              Cyrano!

[*A mob bursts into the shop. Shouts, acclamations, general disturbance.*]

Ragueneau: [*Standing on a table*]
My shop invaded— They'll break everything—
Glorious!

Several Men: [*Crowding about* **Cyrano**]
                    My friend! . . . My friend! . . .

Cyrano: Why, yesterday
I did not have so many friends!

Le Bret: Success

At last!

A Marquis: [*Runs to* **Cyrano**, *with outstretched hands*]
                    My dear—really!—

Cyrano: [*Coldly*]
                         So? And how long
Have I been dear to you?

Another Marquis:
                              One moment—pray!
I have two ladies in my carriage here;
Let me present you—

Cyrano:
                         Certainly! And first,
Who will present you, sir—to me?

Le Bret: [*Astounded*]
                              Why, what

The devil?—

Cyrano:
                    Hush!

A Man of Letters: [*With a portfolio*]
                    May I have the details? . . .

Cyrano:
You may not.

Le Bret: [*Plucking* **Cyrano**'s *sleeve*]
                    Theophraste Renaudot!—Editor
Of the *Gazette*—your reputation! . . .

Cyrano:
                              No!

A Poet: [*Advances*]
Monsieur—

Cyrano:
                    Well?

The Poet:
                    Your full name? I will compose
A pentacrostic—

Another:
                    Monsieur—

Cyrano:
                    That will do!
[*Movement. The crowd arranges itself.* **De Guiche** *appears, escorted by* **Cuigy, Brissaille**, *and the other officers who were with* **Cyrano** *at the close of the First Act.*]

Cuigy: [*Goes to* **Cyrano**]
Monsieur de Guiche!—
                    [*Murmur. Everyone moves*]
                              A message from the Marshal
De Gassion—

De Guiche: [*Saluting* **Cyrano**]
                    Who wishes to express
Through me his admiration. He has heard
Of your affair—

The Crowd: Bravo!

Cyrano: [*Bowing*]
                              The Marshal speaks
As an authority.

De Guiche:
                    He said just now
The story would have been incredible
Were it not for the witness—

Cuigy: Of our eyes!

Le Bret: [*Aside to* **Cyrano**]
What is it?

Cyrano:
                    Hush!—

Le Bret:
                    Something is wrong with you;
Are you in pain?

Cyrano: [*Recovering himself*]
                    In pain? Before this crowd?
[*His moustache bristles. He throws out his chest.*]
I? In pain? You shall see!

De Guiche: [*To whom* **Cuigy** *has been whispering*]
                    Your name is known
Already as a soldier. You are one
Of those wild Gascons, are you not?

Cyrano:
                              The Guards,
Yes. A Cadet.

A Cadet: [*In a voice of thunder*]
                    One of ourselves!

De Guiche:
                         Ah! So—
Then all these gentlemen with the haughty
    air,

These are the famous—
Carbon:

Cyrano!
Cyrano:

Captain?
Carbon:
Our troop being all present, be so kind
As to present them to the Comte de Guiche!
Cyrano: [*With a gesture presenting the* **Cadets** *to* **De Guiche,** *declaims:*]
The Cadets of Gascoyne—the defenders
    of Carbon de Castel-Jaloux:
Free fighters, free lovers, free spenders—
The Cadets of Gascoyne—the defenders
Of old homes, old names, and old splendors—
    A proud and a pestilent crew!
The Cadets of Gascoyne, the defenders
    Of Carbon de Castel-Jaloux.

Hawk-eyed, they stare down all contenders—
    The wolf bares his fangs as they do—
Make way there, you fat money-lenders!
    (Hawk-eyed, they stare down all con-
    tenders)
Old boots that have been to the menders,
    Old cloaks that are worn through and
    through—
Hawk-eyed, they stare down all contenders—
    The wolf bares his fangs as they do!

Skull-breakers they are, and sword-benders;
    Red blood is their favorite brew;
Hot haters and loyal befrienders,
Skull-breakers they are, and sword-benders.
Wherever a quarrel engenders,
    They're ready and waiting for you!
Skull-breakers they are, and sword-benders;
    Red blood is their favorite brew!

Behold them, our Gascon defenders
    Who win every woman they woo!
There's never a dame but surrenders—
Behold them, our Gascon defenders!
Young wives who are clever pretenders—
    Old husbands who house the cuckoo—
Behold them—our Gascon defenders
    Who win every woman they woo!
De Guiche: [*Languidly, sitting in a chair*]
Poets are fashionable nowadays

To have about one. Would you care to join
My following?
Cyrano:

No, sir. I do not follow.
De Guiche:
Your duel yesterday amused my uncle
The Cardinal. I might help you there.
Le Bret:

Grand Dieu!
De Guiche:
I suppose you have written a tragedy—
They all have.
Le Bret: [*Aside to* **Cyrano**]
Now at last you'll have it played—
Your "Agrippine!"
De Guiche:

Why not? Take it to him.
Cyrano: [*Tempted*]
Really—
De Guiche:

He is himself a dramatist;
Let him rewrite a few lines here and there,
And he'll approve the rest.
Cyrano: [*His face falls again*]
Impossible.
My blood curdles to think of altering
One comma.
De Guiche:

Ah, but when he likes a thing
He pays well.
Cyrano:

Yes—but not so well as I—
When I have made a line that sings itself
So that I love the sound of it—I pay
Myself a hundred times.
De Guiche:

You are proud, my friend.
Cyrano:
You have observed that?
A Cadet:

[*Enters with a drawn sword, along the whole
blade of which is transfixed a collection of disrep-
utable hats, their plumes draggled, their crowns
cut and torn.*]
Cyrano! See here—
Look what we found this morning in the
    street—
The plumes dropped in their flight by those
    fine birds

Who showed the white feather!

Carbon:

Spoils of the hunt—

Well mounted!

The Crowd:

Ha-ha-ha!

Cuigy:

Whoever hired

Those rascals, he must be an angry man

To-day!

Brissaille:

Who was it? Do you know?

De Guiche: Myself!—

[*The laughter ceases*]

I hired them to do the sort of work

We do not soil our hands with—punishing

A drunken poet. . . .

[*Uncomfortable silence*]

The Cadet: [*To* **Cyrano**]

What shall we do with them?

They ought to be preserved before they

spoil—

Cyrano: [*Takes the sword, and in the gesture of saluting*

De Guiche *with it, makes all the hats slide off at his*

feet]

Sir, will you not return these to your friends?

De Guiche:

My chair—my porters here—immediately!

[*To* **Cyrano** *violently*]

—As for you, sir!—

A Voice: [*In the street*]

The chair of Monseigneur

Le Comte de Guiche!—

De Guiche: [*Who has recovered his self-control; smil-*

ing]

Have you read *Don Quixote?*

Cyrano:

I have—and found myself the hero.

A Porter: [*Appears at the door*]

Chair

Ready!

De Guiche:

Be so good as to read once more

The chapter of the windmills.

Cyrano: [*Gravely*]

Chapter Thirteen.

De Guiche:

Windmills, remember, if you fight with

them—

Cyrano:

My enemies change, then, with every wind?

De Guiche:

—May swing round their huge arms and cast

you down

Into the mire.

Cyrano:

Or up—among the stars!

[**De Guiche** *goes out. We see him get into the*

chair. The Officers follow murmuring among

themselves. **Le Bret** *goes up with them. The crowd*

goes out.]

Cyrano: [*Saluting with burlesque politeness, those who*

go out without daring to take leave of him]

Gentlemen. . . . Gentlemen. . . .

Le Bret: [*As the door closes, comes down, shaking his*

clenched hands to heaven]

You have done it now—

You have made your fortune!

Cyrano:

There you go again,

Growling!—

Le Bret:

At least this latest pose of yours—

Ruining every chance that comes your way—

Becomes exaggerated—

Cyrano:

Very well,

Then I exaggerate!

Le Bret: [*Triumphantly*]

Oh, you do!

Cyrano:

Yes;

On principle. There are things in this world

A man does well to carry to extremes.

Le Bret:

Stop trying to be Three Musketeers in one!

Fortune and glory—

Cyrano:

What would you have me do?

Seek for the patronage of some great man,

And like a creeping vine on a tall tree

Crawl upward, where I cannot stand alone?

No thank you! Dedicate, as others do,

Poems to pawnbrokers? Be a buffoon

In the vile hope of teasing out a smile

On some cold face? No thank you! Eat a toad

For breakfast every morning? Make my knees

Callous, and cultivate a supple spine,—

Wear out my belly groveling in the dust?
No thank you! Scratch the back of any swine
That roots up gold for me? Tickle the horns
Of Mammon with my left hand, while my
    right
Too proud to know his partner's business,
Takes in the fee? No thank you! Use the fire
God gave me to burn incense all day long
Under the nose of wood and stone? No thank
    you!
Shall I go leaping into ladies' laps
And licking fingers?—or—to change the
    form—
Navigating with madrigals for oars,
My sails full of the sighs of dowagers?
No thank you! Publish verses at my own
Expense? No thank you! Be the patron saint
Of a small group of literary souls
Who dine together every Tuesday? No
I thank you! shall I labor night and day
To build a reputation on one song,
And never write another? Shall I find
True genius only among Geniuses,
Palpitate over little paragraphs,
And struggle to insinuate my name
In the columns of the *Mercury?*
No thank you! Calculate, scheme, be afraid,
Love more to make a visit than a poem,
Seek introductions, favors, influences?—
No thank you! No, I thank you! And again
I thank you!—But . . .
                    To sing, to laugh, to dream,
To walk in my own way and be alone,
Free, with an eye to see things as they are,
A voice that means manhood—to cock my hat
Where I choose— At a word, a *Yes,* a *No,*
To fight—or write. To travel any road
Under the sun, under the stars, nor doubt
If fame or fortune lie beyond the bourne—
Never to make a line I have not heard
In my own heart; yet, with all modesty
To say: "My soul, be satisfied with flowers,
With fruit, with weeds even; but gather them
In the one garden you may call your own."
So, when I win some triumph, by some
    chance,
Render no share to Caesar—in a word,
I am too proud to be a parasite,
And if my nature wants the germ that grows

Towering to heaven like the mountain pine,
Or like the oak, sheltering multitudes—
I stand, not high it may be—but alone!

Le Bret:
Alone, yes!—But why stand against the world?
What devil has possessed you now, to go
Everywhere making yourself enemies?

Cyrano:
Watching you other people making friends
Everywhere—as a dog makes friends! I mark
The manner of these canine courtesies
And think: "My friends are of a cleaner breed;
Here comes—thank God!—another enemy!"

Le Bret:
But this is madness!

Cyrano:
                    Method, let us say.
It is my pleasure to displease. I love
Hatred. Imagine how it feels to face
The volley of a thousand angry eyes—
The bile of envy and the froth of fear
Spattering little drops about me— You—
Good nature all around you, soft and warm—
You are like those Italians, in great cowls
Comfortable and loose— Your chin sinks
    down
Into the folds, your shoulders droop. But I—
The Spanish ruff I wear around my throat
Is like a ring of enemies; hard, proud,
Each point another pride, another thorn—
So that I hold myself erect perforce
Wearing the hatred of the common herd
Haughtily, the harsh collar of Old Spain,
At once a fetter and—a halo!

Le Bret: Yes . . .
    [*After a silence, draws* **Cyrano**'*s arm through
    his own*]
Tell this to all the world— And then to me
Say very softly that . . . She loves you not.

Cyrano: [*Quickly*]
Hush!
    [*A moment since,* **Christian** *has entered and
    mingled with the* **Cadets,** *who do not offer to
    speak to him. Finally, he sits down alone at a
    small table, where he is served by* **Lise.**]

A Cadet: [*Rises from a table up stage, his glass in his
hand*]

                    Cyrano!—Your story!

Cyrano: Presently . . .

> [*He goes up, on the arm of* **Le Bret,** *talking to him.* **The Cadet** *comes down stage.*]

The Cadet:

The story of the combat! An example
For—

> [*He stops by the table where* **Christian** *is sitting*]

—this young tadpole here.

Christian: [*Looks up*]

Tadpole?

Another Cadet:

Yes, you!—
You narrow-gutted Northerner!

Christian:

Sir?

First Cadet:

Hark ye,
Monsieur de Neuvillette: You are to know
There is a certain subject—I would say,
A certain object—never to be named
Among us: utterly unmentionable!

Christian:

And that is?

Third Cadet: [*In an awful voice*]

Look at me! . . .

> [*He strikes his nose three times with his finger, mysteriously.*]

You understand?

Christian:

Why, yes; the—

Fourth Cadet:

Sh! . . . We never speak that word—

> [*Indicating* **Cyrano** *by a gesture*]

To breathe it is to have to do with HIM!

Fifth Cadet: [*Speaks through his nose*]

He has exterminated several
Whose tone of voice suggested . . .

Sixth Cadet: [*In a hollow tone; rising from under the table on all fours*]

Would you die
Before your time? Just mention anything
Convex . . . or cartilaginous . . .

Seventh Cadet: [*His hand on* **Christian**'s *shoulder*]

One word—
One syllable—one gesture—nay, one sneeze—
Your handkerchief becomes your winding-
sheet!

> [*Silence. In a circle around* **Christian,** *arms crossed, they regard him expectantly.*]

Christian: [*Rises and goes to* **Carbon,** *who is conversing with an officer, and pretending not to see what is taking place*]

Captain!

Carbon: [*Turns, and looks him over*]

Sir?

Christian:

What is the proper thing to do
When Gascons grow too boastful?

Carbon:

Prove to them
That one may be a Norman, and have
courage.

> [*Turns his back*]

Christian:

I thank you.

First Cadet: [*To* **Cyrano**]

Come—the story!

All:

The story!

Cyrano: [*Come down*]

Oh,
My story? Well . . .

> [*They all draw up their stools and group themselves around him, eagerly.* **Christian** *places himself astride of a chair, his arms on the back of it.*]

I marched on, all alone
To meet those devils. Overhead, the moon
Hung like a gold watch at the fob of heaven,
Till suddenly some Angel rubbed a cloud,
As it might be his handkerchief, across
The shining crystal, and—the night came
down.
No lamps in those back streets— It was so
dark—
Mordious! You could not see beyond—

Christian:

Your nose.

> [*Silence. Every man slowly rises to his feet. They look at* **Cyrano** *almost with terror. He has stopped short, utterly astonished. Pause.*]

Cyrano:

Who is that man there?

A Cadet: [*In a low voice*]

A recruit—arrived
This morning.

Cyrano: [*Takes a step toward* **Christian**]

A recruit—

Carbon: [In a low voice]

His name is Christian

De Neuvil—

Cyrano: [Suddenly motionless]

Oh . . .

[He turns pale, flushes, makes a movement as if to throw himself upon **Christian**]

I—

[Controls himself, and goes on in a choking voice]

I see. Very well,

As I was saying—

[With a sudden burst of rage]

Mordious! . . .

[He goes on in a natural tone]

It grew dark,

You could not see your hand before your eyes.

I marched on, thinking how, all for the sake

Of one old souse

[They slowly sit down, watching him.]

who wrote a bawdy song

Whenever he took—

Christian:

A noseful—

[Everyone rises. **Christian** balances himself on two legs of his chair.]

Cyrano: [Half strangled]

—Took a notion.

Whenever he took a notion— For his sake,

I might antagonize some dangerous man,

One powerful enough to make me pay—

Christian:

Through the nose—

Cyrano: [Wipes the sweat from his forehead]

—Pay the Piper. After all,

I thought, why am I putting in my—

Christian:

Nose—

Cyrano:

—My oar . . . Why am I putting in my oar?

The quarrel's none of mine. However—now

I am here, I may as well go through with it.

Come Gascon—do your duty!—Suddenly

A sword flashed in the dark. I caught it fair—

Christian:

On the nose—

Cyrano:

On my blade. Before I knew it,

There I was—

Christian:

Rubbing noses—

Cyrano: [Pale and smiling]

Crossing swords

With half a score at once. I handed one—

Christian:

A nosegay—

Cyrano: [Leaping at him]

Ventre-Saint-Gris! . . .

[The Gascons tumble over each other to get a good view. Arrived in front of **Christian,** who has not moved an inch, **Cyrano** masters himself again, and continues.]

He went down;

The rest gave way; I charged—

Christian:

Nose in the air—

Cyrano:

I skewered two of them—disarmed a third—

Another lunged— Paf! And I countered—

Christian:

Pif!

Cyrano: [Bellowing]

TONNERRE! Out of here!—All of you!

[All the **Cadets** rush for the door]

First Cadet:

At last—

The old lion wakes!

Cyrano:

All of you! Leave me here

Alone with that man!

[The lines following are heard brokenly in the confusion of getting through the door.]

Second Cadet:

Bigre! He'll have the fellow

Chopped into sausage—

Ragueneau:

Sausage?—

Third Cadet:

Mince-meat, then—

One of your pies!—

Ragueneau:

Am I pale? You look white

As a fresh napkin—

Carbon: [At the door]

Come!

Fourth Cadet:

He'll never leave

Enough of him to—

Fifth Cadet: Why, it frightens ME
To think of what will—
Sixth Cadet: [*Closing the door*]
                    Something horrible
Beyond imagination . . .

[*They are all gone: some through the street door,
some by the inner doors to right and left. A few
disappear up the staircase.* **Cyrano** *and* **Christian** *stand face to face a moment, and look at
each other.*]

Cyrano:
                    To my arms!

Christian:
Sir?

Cyrano:
         You have courage!

Christian:
                    Oh, that! . . .

Cyrano:
                         You are brave—
That pleases me.

Christian:
              You mean? . . .

Cyrano:
                    Do you not know
I am her brother? Come!

Christian:
                         Whose?

Cyrano:
                         Hers—Roxane!

Christian:
Her . . . brother? You? [*Hurries to him*]

Cyrano:
                    Her cousin. Much the same.

Christian:
And has she told you? . . .

Cyrano:
                    Everything.

Christian:
                         She loves me?

Cyrano:
Perhaps.

Christian: [*Takes both his hands*]
    My dear sir—more than I can say,
I am honored—

Cyrano:
         This is rather sudden.

Christian: Please
    Forgive me—

Cyrano: [*Holds him at arm's length, looking at him*]
    Why, he is a handsome devil.
This fellow!

Christian:
              On my honor—if you knew
How much I have admired—

Cyrano:
                    Yes, yes—and all
Those Noses which—

Christian:
                    Please! I apologize.

Cyrano: [*Change of tone*]
Roxane expects a letter—

Christian:
                    Not from me?—

Cyrano:
Yes. Why not?

Christian:
              Once I write, that ruins all!

Cyrano:
And why?

Christian:
              Because . . . because I am a fool!
Stupid enough to hang myself!

Cyrano:
                    But no—
You are no fool; you call yourself a fool,
There's proof enough in that. Besides, you did
    not
Attack me like a fool.

Christian:
                    Bah! Any one
Can pick a quarrel. Yes, I have a sort
Of rough and ready soldier's tongue. I know
That. But with any woman—paralyzed,
Speechless, dumb. I can only look at them.
Yet sometimes, when I go away, their eyes . . .

Cyrano:
Why not their hearts, if you should wait and
    see?

Christian:
No. I am one of those— I know—those men
Who never can make love.

Cyrano:
                    Strange. . . . Now it seems
I, if I gave my mind to it, I might
Perhaps make love well.

Christian: Oh, if I had words
    To say what I have here!

Cyrano:
> If I could be
> A handsome little Musketeer with eyes!—

Christian:
> Besides—you know Roxane—how sensitive—
> One rough word, and the sweet illusion—
>   gone!

Cyrano:
> I wish you might be my interpreter.

Christian:
> I wish I had your wit—

Cyrano:
> Borrow it, then!—
> Your beautiful young manhood—lend me
>   that,
> And we two make one hero of romance!

Christian:
> What?

Cyrano:
> Would you dare repeat to her the words
> I gave you, day by day?

Christian:
> You mean?

Cyrano:
> I mean
> Roxane shall have no disillusionment!
> Come, shall we win her both together Take
> The soul within this learthern jack of mine,
> And breathe it into you?
>   [*Touches him on the breast*]
> So—there's my heart
> Under your velvet, now!

Christian:
> But— Cyrano!—

Cyrano:
> But— Christian, why not?

Christian:
> I am afraid—

Cyrano:
> I know—
> Afraid that when you have her all alone,
> You lose all. Have no fear. It is yourself
> She loves—give her yourself put into words—
> My words, upon your lips!

Christian:
> But ... but your eyes! ...
> They burn like—

Cyrano:
> Will you? ... Will you?

Christian:
> Does it mean
> So much to you?

Cyrano: [*Beside himself*]
> It means—
> [*Recovers, changes tone*]
> A Comedy,
> A situation for a poet! Come.
> Shall we collaborate? I'll be your cloak
> Of darkness, your enchanted sword, your ring
> To charm the fairy Princess!

Christian:
> But the letter—
> I cannot write—

Cyrano:
> Oh yes, the letter.
> [*He takes from his pocket the letter which he has written.*]
> Here.

Christian:
> What is this?

Cyrano:
> All there; all but the address.

Christian:
> I—

Cyrano:
> Oh, you may send it. It will serve.

Christian:
> But why
> Have you done this?

Cyrano:
> I have amused myself
> As we all do, we poets—writing vows
> To Chloris, Phyllis—any pretty name—
> You might have had a pocketful of them!
> Take it, and turn to facts my fantasies—
> I loosed these loves like doves into the air;
> Give them a habitation and a home.
> Here, take it— You will find me all the more
> Eloquent, being insincere! Come!

Christian:
> First,
> There must be a few changes here and there—
> Written at random, can it fit Roxane?

Cyrano:
> Like her own glove.

Christian:
> No, but—

Cyrano:
> My son, have faith—

Faith in the love of women for themselves—
Roxane will know this letter for her own!

Christian: [*Throws himself into the arms of* **Cyrano.**
They stand embraced.]

My friend!

[*The door up stage opens a little. A* **Cadet** *steals
in.*]

The Cadet:

      Nothing. A silence like the tomb . . .
I hardly dare look— [*He sees the two*]
          Wha-at?

[*The other* **Cadets** *crowd in behind him and see.*]

The Cadets: No!—No!

Second Cadet:

             Mon dieu!

The Musketeer: [*Slaps his knee*]

Well, well, well!

Carbon:

      Here's our devil . . . Christianized!
Offend one nostril, and he turns the other.

The Musketeer:

Now we are allowed to talk about his nose!
[*Calls*]
Hey, Lise! Come here— [*Affectedly*]
          Snf! What a horrid smell!
What is it? . . .

[*Plants himself in front of* **Cyrano,** *and looks at
his nose in an impolite manner*]

You ought to know about such things;
What seems to have died around here?

Cyrano: [*Knocks him backward over a bench*]

           Cabbage-heads!

[*Joy. The Cadets have found their old* **Cyrano**
again. General disturbance.]

CURTAIN

ACT III

Roxane's Kiss

A little square in the old Marais: old houses, and
a glimpse of narrow streets. On the Right, THE
HOUSE OF ROXANE and her garden wall, overhung
with tall shrubbery. Over the door of the house
a balcony and a tall window; to one side of the
door, a bench.

Ivy clings to the wall; jasmine embraces the
balcony, trembles, and falls away.

By the bench and the jutting stonework of the
wall one might easily climb up to the balcony.

Opposite, an ancient house of the like character, brick and stone, whose front door forms an
Entrance. The knocker on this door is tied up
in linen like an injured thumb.

At the CURTAIN RISE the **Duenna** is seated on
the bench beside the door. The window is wide
open on **Roxane's** balcony; a light within suggests that it is early evening. By the **Duenna**
stands **Ragueneau** dressed in what might be the
livery of one attached to the household. He is
by way of telling her something, and wiping his
eyes meanwhile.

Ragueneau:

—And so she ran off with a Musketeer!
I was ruined—I was alone— Remained
Nothing for me to do but hang myself,
So I did that. Presently along comes
Monsieur de Bergerac, and cuts me down,
And makes me steward to his cousin.

The Duenna:

             Ruined?—
I thought your pastry was a great success!

Ragueneau: [*Shakes his head*]

Lise loved the soldiers, and I loved the poets—
Mars ate up all the cakes Apollo left;
It did not take long. . . .

The Duenna: [*Calls up to window*]

         Roxane! Are you ready?
We are late!

Voice of Roxane: [*Within*]

         Putting on my cape—

The Duenna: [*To* **Ragueneau,** *indicating the house
opposite*]

             Clomire
Across the way receives on Thursday nights—
We are to have a psycho-colloquy
Upon the Tender Passion.

Ragueneau:

           Ah—the Tender . . .

The Duenna: [*Sighs*]

—Passion! . . .

[*Calls up to window*]
      Roxane!—Hurry, dear—we shall miss
The Tender Passion!

Roxane:

           Coming!—

[*Music of stringed instruments off-stage approaching.*]

The Voice of Cyrano: [*Singing*]

La, la, la!—

The Duenna:

A serenade?—How pleasant—

Cyrano

No, no, no!—
F natural, you natural born fool!

[*Enters, followed by two pages, carrying theorbos.*]

First Page: [*Ironically*]

No doubt your honor knows F natural
When he hears—

Cyrano:

I am a musician, infant!—
A pupil of Gassendi.

The Page: [*Plays and sings*]

La, la,—

Cyrano:

Here—
Give me that—

[*He snatches the instrument from the Page and continues the tune.*]

La, la, la, la—

Roxane: [*Appears on the balcony*]

Is that you,
Cyrano?

Cyrano: [*Singing*]

I, who praise your lilies fair,
But long to love your ro . . . ses!

Roxane:

I'll be down—
Wait—

[*Goes in through window.*]

The Duenna:

Did you train these virtuosi?

Cyrano:

No—
I won them on a bet from D'Assoucy.
We were debating a fine point of grammar
When, pointing out these two young nightingales
Dressed up like peacocks, with their instruments,
He cries: "No, but I KNOW! I'll wager you
A day of music." Well, of course he lost;
And so until to-morrow they are mine,
My private orchestra. Pleasant at first,
But they become a trifle—

[*To* **The Pages**]

Here! Go play
A minuet to Montfleury—and tell him
I sent you!

[**The Pages** *go up to the exit. Cyrano turns to the* **Duenna**]

I came here as usual
To inquire after our friend—

[*To* **Pages**]

Play out of tune.
And keep on playing!

[**The Pages** *go out. He turns to the* **Duenna**]

Our friend with the great soul.

Roxane: [*Enters in time to hear the last words*]

He is beautiful and brilliant—and I love him!

Cyrano:

Do you find Christian . . . intellectual?

Roxane:

More so than you, even.

Cyrano:

I am glad.

Roxane:

No man
Ever so beautifully said those things—
Those pretty nothings that are everything.
Sometimes he falls into a reverie;
His inspiration fails—then all at once,
He will say something absolutely . . . Oh! . . .

Cyrano:

Really!

Roxane:

How like a man! You think a man
Who has a handsome face must be a fool.

Cyrano:

He talks well about . . . matters of the heart?

Roxane:

He does not *talk*; he rhapsodizes . . . dreams
. . .

Cyrano: [*Twisting his moustache*]

He . . . writes well?

Roxane:

Wonderfully. Listen now:

[*Reciting as from memory.*]

"Take my heart; I shall have it all the more;
Plucking the flowers, we keep the plant in
bloom—"
Well?

Cyrano:

Pooh!

Roxane: And this:
                 "Knowing you have in store
More heart to give than I to find heart-
    room—"
Cyrano:
First he has too much, then too little; just
How much heart does he need?
Roxane: [*Tapping her foot*]
                           You are teasing me!
You are jealous!
Cyrano: [*Startled*]
                 Jealous?
Roxane:
                      Of his poetry—
You poets are like that . . .
                      And these last lines
Are they not the last word in tenderness?—
"There is no more to say: only believe
That unto you my whole heart gives one cry,
And writing, writes down more than you
    receive;
Sending you kisses through my finger-tips—
Lady, O read my letter with your lips!"
Cyrano:
H'm, yes— those last lines . . . but he
    overwrites!
Roxane:
Listen to this—
Cyrano:
            You know them all by heart?
Roxane:
Every one!
Cyrano: [*Twisting his moustache*]
        I may call that flattering . . .
Roxane:
He is a master!
Cyrano:
                 Oh—come!
Roxane:
                      Yes—a master!
Cyrano: [*Bowing*]
A master—if you will!
The Duenna: [*Comes down stage quickly*]
                 Monsieur de Guiche!—
        [*To* **Cyrano,** *pushing him toward the house*]
Go inside— If he does not find you here,
It may be just as well. He may suspect—
Roxane:
—My secret! Yes; he is in love with me

And he is powerful. Let him not know—
One look would frost my roses before bloom.
Cyrano: [*Going into house*]
Very well, very well!
Roxane: [*To De Guiche, as he enters*]
                 We were just going—
De Guiche:
I came only to say farewell.
Roxane:
                                   You leave
    Paris?
De Guiche:
                 Yes—for the front.
Roxane:
                                   Ah!
De Guiche:
                      And to-night!
Roxane:
Ah!
De Guiche:
    We have orders to besiege Arras.
Roxane:
Arras?
De Guiche:
        Yes. My departure leaves you . . . cold?
Roxane: [*Politely*]
Oh! Not that.
De Guiche:
                      It has left me desolate—
When shall I see you? Ever? Did you know
I was made Colonel?
Roxane: [*Indifferent*]
Bravo.
De Guiche:
                           Regiment
    Of the Guards.
Roxane: [*Catching her breath*]
            Of the Guards?—
De Guiche:
                                His regiment
Your cousin, the mighty man of words!—
    [*Grimly*]
                                Down there
We may have an accounting!
Roxane: [*Suffocating*]
                      Are you sure
    The Guards are ordered?
De Guiche:
                 Under my command!

Roxane: [*Sinks down, breathless, on the bench; aside*]
Christian!—

De Guiche:
                    What is it?

Roxane: [*Losing control of herself*]
                              To the war—perhaps
Never again to— When a woman cares,
Is that nothing?

De Guiche: [*Surprised and delighted*]
                    You say this now—to me—
Now, at the very moment?—

Roxane: [*Recovers—changes her tone*]
                              Tell me something:
My cousin— You say you mean to be
revenged
On him. Do you mean that?

De Guiche: [*Smiles*]
                    Why? Would you care?

Roxane:
Not for him.

De Guiche:
                    Do you see him?

Roxane:
                                        Now and then.

De Guiche:
He goes about everywhere nowadays
With one of the Cadets—de Neuve—Neu-
ville—
Neuvillers—

Roxane: [*Coolly*]
                    A tall man?—

De Guiche:
                              Blond—

Roxane:
                                        Rosy cheeks?—

De Guiche:
Handsome!—

Roxane:
                    Pooh!—

De Guiche:
                              And a fool.

Roxane: [*Languidly*]
                              So he appears ...
          [*Animated*]
But Cyrano? What will you do to him?
Order him into danger? He loves that!
I know what *I* should do.

De Guiche:
                    What?

Roxane:
                                        Leave him here
With his Cadets, while all the regiment
Goes on to glory! That would torture him—
To sit all through the war with folded arms—
I know his nature. If you hate that man,
Strike at his self-esteem.

De Guiche:
                    Oh woman—woman!
Who but a woman would have thought of
this?

Roxane:
He'll eat his heart out, while his Gascon
friends
Bite their nails all day long in Paris here.
And you will be avenged!

De Guiche:
                    You love me then,
A little? ...
          [*She smiles.*]
          Making my enemies your own,
Hating them—I should like to see in that
A sign of love, Roxane.

Roxane:
                              Perhaps it is one ...

De Guiche: [*Shows a number of folded despatches*]
Here are the orders—for each company—
Ready to send ...
          [*Selects one*]
                    So— This is for the Guards—
I'll keep that. Aha, Cyrano!
          [*To* **Roxane**]
                              You too,
You play your little games, do you?

Roxane: [*Watching him*]
                              Sometimes ...

De Guiche: [*Close to her, speaking hurriedly*]
And you!—Oh, I am mad over you!—
                              Listen—
I leave to-night—but—let you through my
hands
Now, when I feel you trembling?—Listen—
Close by,
In the Rue d'Orléans, the Capuchins
Have their new convent. By their law, no
layman
May pass inside those walls. I'll see to that—
Their sleeves are wide enough to cover me—
The servants of my Uncle-Cardinal

Will fear his nephew. So—I'll come to you
Masked, after everyone knows I have gone—
Oh, let me wait one day!—

Roxane:
If this be known,
Your honor—

De Guiche:
Bah!

Roxane:
The war—your duty—

De Guiche: [*Blows away an imaginary feather*]
Phoo!—
Only say yes!

Roxane:
No!

De Guiche:
Whisper ...

Roxane: [*Tenderly*]
I ought not
To let you ...

De Guiche:
Ah! ...

Roxane: [*Pretends to break down*]
Ah, go!
[*Aside*]
—Christian remains—
[*Aloud—heroically*]
I must have you a hero—Antoine ...

De Guiche:
Heaven! ...
So you can love—

Roxane:
One for whose sake I fear.

De Guiche: [*Triumphant*]
I go!
Will that content you?
[*Kisses her hand.*]

Roxane:
Yes—my friend!
[*He goes out.*]

The Duenna: [*As* **De Guiche** *disappears, making
a deep curtsey behind his back, and imitating* **Roxane**'s
intense tone]
Yes—my friend!

Roxane: [*Quickly, close to her*]
Not a word to Cyrano—
He would never forgive me if he knew
I stole his war!
[*She calls toward the house*]

Cousin!
[**Cyrano** *comes out of the house; she turns to
him indicating the house opposite*]
We are going over—
Alcandre speaks to-night—and Lysimon.

The Duenna: [*Puts finger in her ear*]
My little finger says we shall not hear
Everything.

Cyrano:
Never mind me—

The Duenna: [*Across the street*]
Look— Oh, look!
The knocker tied up in a napkin— Yes,
They muzzled you because you bark too loud
And interrupt the lecture—little beast!

Roxane: [*As the door opens*]
Enter ...
[*To* **Cyrano**]
If Christian comes, tell him to wait.

Cyrano: Oh—
[**Roxane** *returns.*]
When he comes, what will you talk about?
You always know beforehand.

Roxane:
About ...

Cyrano:
Well?

Roxane:
You will not tell him, will you?

Cyrano:
I am dumb.

Roxane:
About nothing! Or about everything—
I shall say: "Speak of love in your own
    words—
Improvise! Rhapsodize! Be eloquent!"

Cyrano: [*Smiling*]
Good!

Roxane:
Sh!—

Cyrano:
Sh!—

Roxane:
Not a word!
[*She goes in; the door closes.*]

Cyrano: [*Bowing*]
Thank you so much—

Roxane: [*Opens door and puts out her head*]
He must be unprepared—

Cyrano:

Of course!

Roxane:

Sh!—

[*Goes in again.*]

Cyrano: [*Calls*]

Christian!

[**Christian** *enters.*]

I have your theme—bring on your memory!—
Here is your chance now to surpass yourself,
No time to lose— Come! Look intelligent—
Come home and learn your lines.

Christian:

No.

Cyrano:

What?

Christian:

I'll wait
Here for Roxane.

Cyrano:

What lunacy is this?
Come quickly!

Christian:

No, I say! I have had enough—
Taking my words, my letters, all from you—
Making our love a little comedy!
It was a game at first; but now—she cares . . .
Thanks to you. I am not afraid. I'll speak
For myself now.

Cyrano:

Undoubtedly!

Christian:

I will!
Why not? I am no such fool—you shall see!
Besides—my dear friend—you have taught me
    much.
I ought to know something . . . By God, I
    know
Enough to take a woman in my arms!
        [**Roxane** *appears in the doorway, opposite*]
There she is now . . . Cyrano, wait! Stay here!

Cyrano:

[*Bows*]

Speak for yourself, my friend!

[*He goes out.*]

Roxane: [*Taking leave of the company*]

—Barthénoide!
Alcandre! . . . Grémione! . . .

The Duenna: I told you so—
We missed the Tender Passion!

[*She goes into* **Roxane***'s house.*]

Roxane:

Urimédonte!—
Adieu!

[*As the guests disappear down the street, she turns
    to* **Christian**.]

Is that you, Christian? Let us stay
Here, in the twilight. They are gone. The air
Is fragrant. We shall be alone. Sit down
There—so . . .

[*They sit on the bench*]

Now tell me things.

Christian: [*After a silence*]

I love you.

Roxane: [*Closes her eyes*]

Yes,
Speak to me about love . . .

Christian:

I love you.

Roxane:

Now
Be eloquent! . . .

Christian:

I love—

Roxane: [*Opens her eyes*]

You have your theme—
Improvise! Rhapsodize!

Christian:

I love you so!

Roxane:

Of course. And then? . . .

Christian:

And then . . . Oh, I should be
So happy if you loved me too! Roxane,
Say that you love me too!

Roxane: [*Making a face*]

I ask for cream
You give me milk and water. Tell me first
A little, how you love me.

Christian:

Very much.

Roxane:

Oh—tell me how you *feel!*

Christian: [*Coming nearer, and devouring her with his
    eyes*]

Your throat . . . If only
I might . . . kiss it—

Roxane:

Christian!

Christian: I love you so!

Roxane:　[*Makes as if to rise*]
　　Again?
Christian:　[*Desperately, restraining her*]
　　　　No, not again— I do not love you—
Roxane:　[*Settles·back*]
　　That is better . . .
Christian:
　　　　　　I adore you!
Roxane:
　　　　　　　　　Oh!—
　　[*Rises and moves away.*]
Christian:
　　　　　　　　　　I know;
　　I grow absurd.
Roxane:　[*Coldly*]
　　　　And that displeases me
　　As much as if you had grown ugly.
Christian:
　　　　　　　　　　I—
Roxane:
　　Gather your dreams together into words!
Christian:
　　I love—
Roxane:
　　　　I know; you love me. Adieu.
　　[*She goes to the house.*]
Christian:
　　　　　　　　　　　No,
　　But wait—please—let me— I was going to say—
Roxane:　[*Pushes the door open*]
　　That you adore me. Yes; I know that too.
　　No! . . . Go away! . . .
　　[*She goes in and shuts the door in his face.*]
Christian:
　　　　　　　　I . . . I . . .
Cyrano:　[*Enters*]
　　　　　　　　　A great success!
Christian:
　　Help me!
Cyrano:
　　　　Not I.
Christian:
　　　　I cannot live unless
　　She loves me–now, this moment!
Cyrano:
　　　　　　　　How the devil
　　Am I to teach you now—this moment?
Christian:　[*Catches him by the arm*]
　　　　　　　　　—Wait!—
　　Look! Up there!—Quick—

[*The light shows in **Roxane**'s window.*]
Cyrano:
　　　　　　Her window—
Christian:　[*Wailing*]
　　　　　　　　I shall die!—
Cyrano:
　　Less noise!
Christian:
　　　　Oh, I—
Cyrano:
　　　　It does seem fairly dark—
Christian:　[*Excitedly*]
　　Well?—Well?—Well?—
Cyrano:
　　　　　　Let us try what can be done;
　　It is more than you deserve—stand over there,
　　Idiot—there!—before the balcony—
　　Let me stand underneath. I'll whisper you
　　What to say.
Christian:
　　　　She may hear—she may—
Cyrano:
　　　　　　　　　　Less noise!
　　[*The **Pages** appear up stage.*]
First Page:
　　Hep!—
Cyrano:　[*finger to lips*]
　　　Sh!—
First Page:　[*Low voice*]
　　　　We serenaded Montfleury!—
　　What next?
Cyrano:
　　　　　Down to the corner of the street—
　　One this way—and the other over there—
　　If anybody passes, play a tune!
Page:
　　What tune, O musical Philosopher?
Cyrano:
　　Sad for a man, or merry for a woman—
　　Now go!
　　[*The **Pages** disappear, one toward each corner
　　of the street.*]
Cyrano:　[*To **Christian***]
　　　　Call her!
Christian:
　　　　Roxane!
Cyrano:
　　　　Wait . . .
　　[*Gathers up a handful of pebbles.*]
　　　　　　　　Gravel . . .

[*Throws it at the window*]

There!—

Roxane: [*Opens the window*]
Who is calling?

Christian:

I—

Roxane:

Who?

Christian:

Christian.

Roxane:

You again?

Christian:
I had to tell you—

Cyrano: [*Under the balcony*]
Good— Keep your voice down.

Roxane:
No. Go away. You tell me nothing.

Christian:

Please!—

Roxane:
You do not love me any more—

Christian: [*To whom* **Cyrano** *whispers his words*]
No—no—

Not any more— I love you . . . evermore . . .
And ever . . . more and more!

Roxane: [*About to close the window—pauses*]
A little better . . .

Christian: [*Same business*]
Love grows and struggles like . . . an angry
child . . .
Breaking my heart . . . his cradle . . .

Roxane: [*Coming out on the balcony*]
Better still—
But . . . such a babe is dangerous; why not
Have smothered it new-born?

Christian: [*Same business*]
And so I do . . .
And yet he lives . . . I found . . . as you shall
find . . .
This new-born babe . . . an infant . . .
Hercules!

Roxane: [*Further forward*]
Good!—

Christian: [*Same business*]
Strong enough . . . at birth . . . to strangle those
Two serpents—Doubt and . . . Pride.

Roxane: [*Leans over balcony*]
Why, very well!

Tell me now why you speak so haltingly—
Has your imagination gone lame?

Cyrano: [*Thrusts* **Christian** *under the balcony, and
stands in his place*]
Here—
This grows too difficult!

Roxane:
Your words to-night
Hesitate. Why?

Cyrano: [*In a low tone, imitating* **Christian**]
Through the warm summer gloom
They grope in darkness toward the light of
you.

Roxane:
My words, well aimed, find you more readily.

Cyrano:
My heart is open wide and waits for them—
Too large a mark to miss! My words fly home,
Heavy with honey like returning bees,
To your small secret ear. Moreover—yours
Fall to me swiftly. Mine more slowly rise.

Roxane:
Yet not so slowly as they did at first.

Cyrano:
They have learned the way, and you have
welcomed them.

Roxane: [*Softly*]
Am I so far above you now?

Cyrano:
So far—
If you let fall upon me one hard word,
Out of that height—you crush me!

Roxane: [*Turns*]
I'll come down—

Cyrano: [*Quickly*]
No!

Roxane: [*Points out the bench under the balcony*]
Stand you on the bench. Come nearer!

Cyrano: [*Recoils into the shadow*]
No!—

Roxane:
And why—so great a *No?*

Cyrano: [*More and more overcome by emotion*]
Let me enjoy
The one moment I ever—my one chance
To speak to you . . . unseen!

Roxane:
Unseen?—

Cyrano:

Yes!—yes . . .

Night, making all things dimly beautiful,
One veil over us both— You only see
The darkness of a long cloak in the gloom,
And I the whiteness of a summer gown—
You are all light— I am all shadow! . . . How
Can you know what this moment means to
   me?
If I was ever eloquent—

Roxane:
                  You were
Eloquent—

Cyrano:
   —You have never heard till now
My own heart speaking!

Roxane:
                Why not?

Cyrano:
                   Until now,
I spoke through . . .

Roxane:
             Yes?—

Cyrano:
         —through that sweet drunkenness
You pour into the world out of your eyes!
But to-night . . . but to-night, I indeed speak
For the first time!

Roxane:
        For the first time— Your voice,
Even, is not the same.

Cyrano: [*Passionately; moves nearer*]
           How should it be?
I have another voice—my own,
Myself, daring—
   [*He stops, confused; then tries to recover himself.*]
       Where was I? . . . I forget! . . .
Forgive me. This is all sweet like a dream . . .
Strange—like a dream . . .

Roxane:
       How, strange?

Cyrano:
               Is it not so
To be myself to you, and have no fear
Of moving you to laughter?

Roxane:
          Laughter—why?

Cyrano: [*Struggling for an explanation*]
Because . . . What am I . . . What is any man,
That he dare ask for you? Therefore my heart
Hides behind phrases. There's a modesty

In these things too— I come here to pluck
   down
Out of the sky the evening star—then smile,
And stoop to gather little flowers.

Roxane:
                Are they
Not sweet, those little flowers?

Cyrano:
             Not enough sweet
For you and me, to-night!

Roxane: [*Breathless*]
           You never spoke
To me like this . . .

Cyrano:
         Little things, pretty things—
Arrows and hearts and torches—roses red,
And violets blue—are these all? Come away,
And breathe fresh air! Must we keep on and
   on
Sipping stale honey out of tiny cups
Decorated with golden tracery,
Drop by drop, all day long? We are alive;
We thirst— Come away, plunge, and drink,
   and drown
In the great river flowing to the sea!

Roxane:
But . . . Poetry?

Cyrano:
       I have made rimes for you—
Not now— Shall we insult Nature, this night,
These flowers, this moment—shall we set all
   these
To phrases from a letter by Voiture?
Look once at the high stars that shine in
   heaven,
And put off artificiality!
Have you not seen great gaudy hothouse
   flowers,
Barren, without fragrance?—Souls are like
   that:
Forced to show all, they soon become all
   show—
The means to Nature's end ends meaningless!

Roxane:
But . . . Poetry?

Cyrano: Love hates that game of words!
It is a crime to fence with life— I tell you,
There comes one moment, once—and God
   help those

Who pass that moment by!—when Beauty
    stands
Looking into the soul with grave, sweet eyes
That sicken at pretty words!

Roxane:
                    If that be true—
And when that moment comes to you and
    me—
What words will you? ...

Cyrano:
                    All those, all those, all those
That blossom in my heart, I'll fling to you—
Armfuls of loose bloom! Love, I love beyond
Breath, beyond reason, beyond love's own
    power
Of loving! Your name is like a golden bell
Hung in my heart; and when I think of you,
I tremble, and the bell swings and rings—
                                "Roxane!" ...
"Roxane!" ... along my veins, "Roxane! ...
                                I know
And small forgotten things that once meant
    You—
I remember last year, the First of May,
A little before noon, you had your hair
Drawn low, that one time only. Is that
    strange?
You know how, after looking at the sun,
One sees red suns everywhere—so, for hours
After the flood of sunshine that you are,
My eyes are blinded by your burning hair!

Roxane: [*Very low*]
Yes ... that is ... Love—

Cyrano:
                    Yes, that is Love—that wind
Of terrible and jealous beauty, blowing
Over me—that dark fire, that music ...
                                Yet
Love seeketh not his own! Dear, you may take
My happiness to make you happier,
Even though you never know I gave it you—
Only let me hear sometimes, all alone,
The distant laughter of your joy! ...
                                I never
Look at you, but there's some new virtue born
In me, some new courage. Do you begin
To understand, a little? Can you feel
My soul, there in the darkness, breathe on
    you?

—Oh, but to-night, now, I dare say these
    things—
I ... to you ... and you hear them! ... It
    is too much!
In my most sweet unreasonable dreams,
I have not hoped for this! Now let me die,
Having lived. It is my voice, mine, my own,
That makes you tremble there in the green
    gloom
Above me—for you do tremble, as a blossom
Among the leaves— You tremble, and I can
    feel,
All the way down along these jasmine
    branches,
Whether you will or no, the passion of you
Trembling ...
    [*He kisses wildly the end of a drooping spray
    of jasmine.*]

Roxane: Yes, I do tremble ... and I weep ...
And I love you ... and I am yours ... and
    you
Have made me thus!

Cyrano: [*After a pause; quietly*]
                    What is death like, I wonder?
I know everything else now ...
                                I have done
This, to you—I, myself ...
                                Only let me
Ask one thing more—

Christian: [*Under the balcony*]
                    One kiss!

Roxane:]*Startled*]
                                One?—

Cyrano: [*To* **Christian**]
                                You! ...

Roxane:
                                You ask me
    For—

Cyrano:
            I ... Yes, but—I mean—
    [*To* **Christian**]
                                You go too far!

Christian:
She is willing!— Why not make the most of
    it?

Cyrano: [*To* **Roxane**]
I did ask ... but I know I ask too much ...

Roxane:
Only one— Is that all?

Cyrano:

All!—How much more
Than all!—I know—I frighten you—I ask . . .
I ask you to refuse—

Christian: [*To* **Cyrano**]

But why? Why? Why?

Cyrano:

Christian, be quiet!

Roxane: [*Leaning over*]

What is that you say
To yourself?

Cyrano:

I am angry with myself
Because I go too far, and so I say
To myself: "Christian, be quiet!"—

[*The theorbos begin to play.*]

Hark—someone
Is coming—

[**Roxane** *closes her window.* **Cyrano** *listens to
the theorbos, one of which plays a gay melody,
the other a mournful one.*]

A sad tune, a merry tune—
Man, woman—what do they mean?—

[*A* **Capuchin** *enters; he carries a lantern, and
goes from house to house, looking at the doors.*]

Aha!—a priest!

[*To* **The Capuchin**]

What is this new game of Diogenes?

The Capuchin:

I am looking for the house of Madame—

Christian: [*Impatient*]

Bah!—

The Capuchin:

Madeleine Robin—

Christian:

What does he want?

Cyrano: [*To* **The Capuchin;** *points out a street*]

This way—

To the right—keep to the right—

The Capuchin:

I thank you, sir!—
I'll say my beads for you to the last grain.

Cyrano:

Good fortune, father, and my service to you!

[**The Capuchin** *goes out.*]

Christian:

Win me that kiss!

Cyrano:

No.

Christian:

Sooner or later—

Cyrano:

True . . .
That is true . . . Soon or late, it will be so
Because you are young and she is beautiful—

[*To himself*]

Since it must be, I had rather be myself

[*The window re-opens.* **Christian** *hides under
the balcony.*]

The cause of . . . what must be.

Roxane: [*Out on the balcony*]

Are you still there?

We were speaking of—

Cyrano: A kiss. The word is sweet—
What will the deed be? Are your lips afraid
Even of its burning name? Not much afraid—
Not too much! Have you not unwittingly
Laid aside laughter, slipping beyond speech
Insensibly, already, without fear,
From words to smiles . . . from smiles to sighs
    . . . from sighing,
Even to tears? One step more—only one—
From a tear to a kiss—one step, one thrill!

Roxane:

Hush—

Cyrano:

And what is a kiss, when all is done?
A promise given under seal—a vow
Taken before the shrine of memory—
A signature acknowledged—a rosy dot
Over the i of Loving—a secret whispered
To listening lips apart—a moment made
Immortal, with a rush of wings unseen—
A sacrament of blossoms, a new song
Sung by two hearts to an old simple tune—
The ring of one horizon around two souls
Together, all alone!

Roxane:

Hush! . . .

Cyrano:

Why, what shame?—
There was a Queen of France, not long ago,
And a great lord of England—a queen's gift,
A crown jewel!

Roxane:

Indeed!

Cyrano:

Indeed, like him,

I have my sorrows and my silences;
Like her, you are the queen I dare adore;
Like him I am faithful and forlorn—

Roxane:

                           Like him,
Beautiful—

Cyrano: [*Aside*]

      So I am—I forgot that!

Roxane:

Then— Come; . . . Gather your sacred blossom
. . .

Cyrano: [*To* **Christian**]

                      Go!—

Roxane:

Your crown jewel . . .

Cyrano:

         Go on!—

Roxane:

             Your old new song . . .

Cyrano:

Climb!

Christian: [*Hesitates*]

No— Would you?—not yet—

Roxane:

             Your moment made
Immortal . . .

Cyrano: [*Pushing him*]

      Climb up, animal!

[**Christian** *springs on the bench, and climbs by the pillars, the branches, the vines, until he bestrides the balcony railing.*]

Christian:

             Roxane! . . .

[*He takes her in his arms and bends over her*]

Cyrano: [*Very low*]

Ah! . . . Roxane! . . .

      I have won what I have won—
The feast of love—and I am Lazarus!
Yet . . . I have something here that is mine
now
And was not mine before I spoke the words
That won her—not for me! . . . Kissing my
words
My words, upon your lips!

[*The theorbos begin to play.*]

      A merry tune—
A sad tune— So! The Capuchin!

[*He pretends to be running, as if he had arrived from a distance; then calls up to the balcony.*]

      Hola!

Roxane:

Who is it?

Cyrano:

      I. Is Christian there with you?

Christian: [*Astonished*]

Cyrano!

Roxane:

      Good morrow, Cousin!

Cyrano:

            Cousin, . . . good morrow!

Roxane:

I am coming down.

[*She disappears into the house.* **The Capuchin** *enters up stage.*]

Christian: [*Sees him*]

           Oh—again!

The Capuchin: [*To* **Cyrano**]

               She lives *here*,
Madeleine Robin!

Cyrano:

         You said Ro-lin.

The Capuchin:

               No—
R-o-b-i-n

Roxane: [*Appears on the threshold of the house, followed by* **Ragueneau** *with a lantern, and by* **Christian**]

      What is it?

The Capuchin:

      A letter.

Christian:

            Oh! . . .

The Capuchin: [*To* **Roxane**]

Some matter profitable to the soul—
A very noble lord gave it to me!

Roxane: [*To* **Christian**]

De Guiche!

Christian:

      He dares?—

Roxane:

           It will not be for long;
When he learns that I love you . . .

[*By the light of the latern which* **Ragueneau** *holds, she reads the letter in a low tone, as if to herself.*]

           "Mademoiselle
The drums are beating, and the regiment
Arms for the march. Secretly I remain
Here, in the Convent. I have disobeyed;
I shall be with you soon. I send this first
By an old monk, as simple as a sheep,

Who understands nothing of this. Your smile
Is more than I can bear, and seek no more.
Be alone to-night, waiting for one who dares
To hope you will forgive ... —" etcetera—
　　　[*To* **The Capuchin**]
Father, this letter concerns you ...
　　　[*To* **Christian**]
　　　　　　　　　　　　—and you.
Listen:
　　　[*The others gather around her. She pretends to
　　　read from the letter, aloud.*]
　　　"Mademoiselle:
　　　　　　　　　The Cardinal
Will have his way, although against your will;
That is why I am sending this to you
By a most holy man, intelligent,
Discreet. You will communicate to him
Our order to perform, here and at once
The rite of ...
　　　[*Turns the page*]
　　　　　　　—Holy Matrimony. You
And Christian will be married privately
In your house. I have sent him to you. I know
You hesitate. Be resigned, nevertheless,
To the Cardinal's command, who sends
　　herewith
His blessing. Be assured also of my own
Respect and high consideration—*signed*,
Your very humble and—etcetera—"
The Capuchin:
A noble lord! I said so—never fear—
A worthy lord!—a very worthy lord!—
Roxane:　　[*To* **Christian**]
Am I a good reader of letters?
Christian:　　[*Motions toward* **The Capuchin**]
　　　　　　　　　　　Careful!—
Roxane:　　[*In a tragic tone*]
Oh, this is terrible!
The Capuchin:　　[*Turns the light of his lantern on*
Cyrano]
　　　　　　　You are to be—
Christian:
I am the bridegroom!
The Capuchin:　　[*Turns his lantern upon* **Christian**;
*then, as if some suspicion crossed his mind, upon seeing
the young man so handsome*]
　　　　　Oh—why, *you* ...
Roxane:　　[*Quickly*]　　　　Look here—
"Postscript: Give to the Convent in my name
One hundred and twenty pistoles"—

The Capuchin:
　　　　　　　　　　Think of it!
A worthy lord—a worthy lord! ...
　　　[*To* **Roxane,** *solemnly*]
Daughter, resign yourself!
Roxane:　　[*With an air of martyrdom*]
　　　　　　　　I am resigned ...
　　　[*While* **Ragueneau** *opens the door for the Ca-
　　　puchin and* **Christian** *invites him to enter, she
　　　turns to* **Cyrano.**]
De Guiche may come. Keep him out here
　　with you
Do not let him—
Cyrano:
　　　　　　　I understand!
　　　[*To* **The Capuchin**]
　　　　　　　　　　　　How long
Will you be?—
The Capuchin:
　　　　　　Oh, a quarter of an hour.
Cyrano:
　　　[*Hurrying them into the house*]
Hurry—I'll wait here—
Roxane:　　[*To* **Christian**]
　　　　　　　Come!
　　　[*They go into the house.*]
Cyrano:
　　　　　　　　　Now then, to make
His Grace delay that quarter of an hour ...
I have it!—up here—
　　　[*He steps on the bench, and climbs up the wall
　　　toward the balcony. The theorbos begin to play
　　　a mournful melody.*]
　　　　　　　Sad music— Ah, a man! ...
　　　[*The music pauses on a sinister tremolo.*]
Oh—very much a man!
　　　[*He sits astride of the railing and, drawing
　　　toward him a long branch of one of the trees
　　　which border the garden wall, he grasps it with
　　　both hands, ready to swing himself down.*]
　　　　　　　So—not too high—
　　　[*He peers down at the ground*]
I must float gently through the atmosphere—
De Guiche:　　[*Enters, masked, groping in the dark to-
ward the house*]
Where is that cursed, bleating Capuchin?
Cyrano:
What　if　he　knows　my　voice?—the
　　devil!—Tic-tac,
Bergerac—we unlock our Gascon tongue;

A good strong accent—

De Guiche:

Here is the house—all dark—
Damn this mask!—

[*As he is about to enter the house,* **Cyrano** *leaps from the balcony, still holding fast to the branch, which bends and swings him between* **De Guiche** *and the door; then he releases the branch and pretends to fall heavily as though from a height. He lands flatly on the ground, where he lies motionless, as if stunned.* **De Guiche** *leaps back.*]

What is that?

[*When he lifts his eyes, the branch has sprung back into place. He can see nothing but the sky; he does not understand.*]

Why . . . where did this man
Fall from?

Cyrano: [*Sits up, and speaks with a strong accent*]
—The moon!

De Guiche:

You—

Cyrano:

From the moon, the moon!
I fell out of the moon!

De Guiche:

The fellow is mad—

Cyrano: [*Dreamily*]
Where am I?

De Guiche:

Why—

Cyrano:

What time is it? What place
Is this? What day? What season?

De Guiche:

You—

Cyrano:

I am stunned!

De Guiche:

My dear sir—

Cyrano:

Like a bomb—a bomb—I fell
From the moon!

De Guiche:

Now, see here—

Cyrano: [*Rising to his feet, and speaking in a terrible voice*]

I say, the moon!

De Guiche: [*Recoils*]
Very well—if you say so—

[*Aside*]

Raving mad!—

Cyrano: [*Advancing upon him*]
I am not speaking metaphorically!

De Guiche:
Pardon.

Cyrano:

A hundred years—an hour ago—
I really cannot say how long I fell—
I was in yonder shining sphere—

De Guiche: [*Shrugs*]

Quite so.

Please let me pass.

Cyrano: [*Interposes himself*]

Where am I? Tell the truth—
I can bear it. In what quarter of the globe
Have I descended like a meteorite?

De Guiche:
Morbleu!

Cyrano:

I could not choose my place to fall—
The earth spun round so fast— Was it the Earth,
I wonder?—Or is this another world?
Another moon? Whither have I been drawn
By the dead weight of my posterior?

De Guiche:
Sir, I repeat—

Cyrano: [*With a sudden cry, which causes* **De Guiche** *to recoil again*]

His face! My God—black!

De Guiche: [*Carries his hand to his mask*]

Oh!—

Cyrano: [*Terrified*]
Are you a native? Is this Africa?

De Guiche:
—This mask!

Cyrano: [*Somewhat reassured*]

Are we in Venice? Genoa?

De Guiche: [*Tries to pass him*]
A lady is waiting for me.

Cyrano: [*Quite happy again*]

So this is Paris!

De Guiche: [*Smiling in spite of himself*]
This fool becomes amusing

Cyrano:

Ah! You smile?

De Guiche:
I do. Kindly permit me—

Cyrano: [*Delighted*]

Dear old Paris—

Well, well!—

[*Wholly at his ease, smiles, bows, arranges his dress.*]

Excuse my appearance. I arrive
By the last thunderbolt—a trifle singed
As I came through the ether. These long
    journeys—
You know! There are so few conveniences!
My eyes are full of star-dust. On my spurs,
Some sort of fur . . . Planet's apparently . . .

[*Plucks something from his sleeve*]

Look—on my doublet— That's a Comet's hair!

[*He blows something from the back of his hand.*]

Phoo!

De Guiche: [*Grows angry*]

Monsieur—

Cyrano: [*As **De Guiche** is about to push past, thrusts his leg in the way*]

Here's a tooth, stuck in my boot,
From the Great Bear. Trying to get away,
I tripped over the Scorpion and came down
Slap, into one scale of the Balances—
The pointer marks my weight this mo-
    ment . . .

[*Pointing upward*]

See?

[**De Guiche** *makes a sudden movement.* **Cyrano** *catches his arm.*]

Be careful! If you struck me on the nose,
It would drip milk!

De Guiche:

Milk?

Cyrano:

From the Milky Way!

De Guiche:

Hell!

Cyrano:

No, no—Heaven.

[*Crossing his arms.*]

Curious place up there—
Did you know Sirius wore a nightcap? True!

[*Confidentially*]

The Little Bear is still too young to bite.

[*Laughing*]

My foot caught in the Lyre, and broke a string.

[*Proudly*]

Well—when I write my book, and tell the tale

Of my adventures—all these little stars
That shake out of my cloak—I must save those
To use for asterisks!

De Guiche:

That will do now—

I wish—

Cyrano:

Yes, yes—I know—

De Guiche:

Sir—

Cyrano:

You desire
To learn from my own lips the character
Of the moon's surface—its inhabitants
If any—

De Guiche: [*Loses patience and shouts*]

I desire no such thing! I—

Cyrano: [*Rapidly*]

You wish to know by what mysterious means
I reached the moon?—well—confidentially—
It was a new invention of my own.

De Guiche: [*Discouraged*]

Drunk too—as well as mad!

Cyrano: I scorned the eagle
Of Regiomontanus, and the dove
Of Archytas!

De Guiche:

A learned lunatic!—

Cyrano:

I imitated no one. I myself
Discovered not one scheme merely, but six—
Six ways to violate the virgin sky!

[**De Guiche** *has succeeded in passing him, and moves toward the door of* **Roxane**'s *house.* **Cyrano** *follows, ready to use violence if necessary.*]

De Guiche: [*Looks around*]

Six?

Cyrano: [*With increasing volubility*]

As for instance—Having stripped
    myself
Bare as a wax candle, adorn my form
With crystal vials filled with morning dew,
And so be drawn aloft, as the sun rises
Drinking the mist of dawn!

De Guiche: [*Takes a step toward* **Cyrano**]

Yes—that makes one.

Cyrano: [*Draws back to lead him away from the door; speaks faster and faster*]

Or, sealing up the air in a cedar chest,
Rarefy it by means of mirrors, placed
In an icosahedron.
De Guiche: [*Takes another step.*]
                    Two.
Cyrano: [*Still retreating*]
                         Again,
I might construct a rocket, in the form
Of a huge locust, driven by impulses
Of villainous saltpetre from the rear,
Upward, by leaps and bounds.
De Guiche: [*Interested in spite of himself, and counting on his fingers*]
                         Three.
Cyrano: [*Same business*]
                         Or again,
Smoke having a natural tendency to rise,
Blow in a globe enough to raise me.
De Guiche: [*Same business, more and more astonished*]
                         Four!
Cyrano:
Or since Diana, as old fables tell,
Draws forth to fill her crescent horn, the marrow
Of bulls and goats—to anoint myself therewith.
De Guiche: [*Hypnotized*]
Five!—
Cyrano: [*Has by this time led him all the way across the street, close to a bench*]
                    Finally—seated on an iron plate,
To hurl a magnet in the air—the iron
Follows—I catch the magnet—throw again—
And so proceed indefinitely.
De Guiche:
                    Six!—
All excellent,—and which did you adopt?
Cyrano: [*Coolly*]
Why, none of them.... A seventh.
De Guiche:
                         Which was?—
Cyrano:
                              Guess!—
De Guiche:
An interesting idiot, this!
Cyrano: [*Imitates the sound of waves with his voice, and their movement by large, vague gestures*]
                         Hoo! ... Hoo! ...
De Guiche:
Well?

Cyrano:
Have you guessed it yet?
De Guiche:
                         Why, no.
Cyrano: [*Grandiloquent*]
                         The ocean! ...
What hour its rising tide seeks the full moon,
I laid me on the strand, fresh from the spray,
My head fronting the moonbeams, since the hair
Retains moisture—and so I slowly rose
As upon angels' wings, effortlessly,
Upward—then suddenly I felt a shock!— And then ...
De Guiche: [*Overcome by curiosity, sits down on the bench*]
                    And then?
Cyrano:
                         And then—
[*Changes abruptly to his natural voice*]
                         The time is up!—
Fifteen minutes, your Grace!—You are now free;
And—they are bound—in wedlock.
De Guiche: [*Leaping up*]
                         Am *I* drunk?
That voice ...
[*The door of* **Roxane***'s house opens; lackeys appear, bearing lighted candles. Lights up.* **Cyrano** *removes his hat*]
                    And that nose!—Cyrano!
Cyrano: [*Saluting*]
                              Cyrano! ...
This very moment, they have exchanged rings.
De Guiche:
Who?
[*He turns up stage.* **Tableau:** *between the lackeys,* **Roxane** *and* **Christian** *appear, hand in hand.* **The Capuchin** *follows them, smiling.* **Ragueneau** *holds aloft a torch.* **The Duenna** *brings up the rear, in a negligée, and a pleasant flutter of emotion*]
                    Zounds!
[*To* **Roxane**]
                         You?—
[*Recognizes* **Christian**]
                         He?—
[*Saluting* **Roxane**]
                    My sincere compliments!

[*To* **Cyrano**]
You also, my inventor of machines!
Your rigmarole would have detained a saint
Entering Paradise—decidedly
You must not fail to write that book some
   day!
Cyrano: [*Bowing*]
Sir, I engage myself to do so.
   [*Leads the bridal pair down to* **De Guiche** *and
   strokes with great satisfaction his long white
   beard*]
                              My lord,
The handsome couple you—and God—have
   joined
Together!
De Guiche: [*Regarding him with a frosty eye*]
                  Quite so.
   [*Turns to* **Roxane**]
                  Madame, kindly bid
Your . . . husband farewell.
Roxane:
                              Oh!—
De Guiche: [*To* **Christian**]
                              Your regiment
Leaves to-night, sir. Report at once!
Roxane:
                              You mean
For the front? The war?
De Guiche:
                  Certainly!
Roxane:
                              I thought
The Cadets were not going—
De Guiche:
                  Oh yes, they are!
   [*Taking out the despatch from his pocket.*]
Here is the order—
   [*To* **Christian**]
                  Baron! Deliver this.
Roxane:
   [*Throws herself into* **Christian**'s *arms*]
   Christian!
De Guiche: [*To* **Cyrano,** *sneering*]
   The bridal night is not so near!
Cyrano: [*Aside*]
   Somehow that news fails to disquiet me.
Christian: [*To* **Roxane**]
   Your lips again . . .
Cyrano:
                  There . . . That will do now—Come!

Christian: [*Still holding* **Roxane**]
   You do not know how hard it is—
Cyrano: [*Tries to drag him away*]
                              I know!
   [*The beating of drums is heard in the distance.*]
De Guiche: [*Up stage*]
   The regiment—on the march!
Roxane: [*As* **Cyrano** *tries to lead* **Christian** *away,
   follows, and detains them*]
                              Take care of him
For me— [*Appealingly*]
      Promise me never to let him do
Anything dangerous!
Cyrano:
                  I'll do my best—
   I cannot promise—
Roxane: [*Same business*]
                  Make him be careful!
Cyrano:
                                    Yes—
   I'll try—
Roxane: [*Same business*]
   Be sure to keep him dry and warm!
Cyrano:
   Yes, yes—if possible—
Roxane: [*Same business; confidentially, in his ear*]
                  See that he remains
   Faithful!—
Cyrano:
         Of course! If—
Roxane: [*Same business*]
                  And have him write to me
   Every single day!
Cyrano: [*Stops*]
               That, I promise you!

CURTAIN

ACT IV

The Cadets of Gascoyne

THE POST occupied by the Company of CARBON
DE CASTEL-JALOUX at THE SIEGE OF ARRAS.

   In the background, a Rampart traversing the
entire scene; beyond this, and apparently below,
a Plain stretches away to the horizon. The
country is cut up with earthworks and other
suggestions of the siege. In the distance, against
the sky-line, the houses and the walls of Arras.

Tents; scattered Weapons; Drums, et cetera. It is near daybreak, and the East is yellow with approaching dawn. Sentries at intervals. Camp-fires.

CURTAIN RISE discovers the Cadets asleep, rolled in their cloaks. **Carbon De Castel-Jaloux** and **Le Bret** keep watch. They are both very thin and pale. **Christian** is asleep among the others, wrapped in his cloak, in the foreground, his face lighted by the flickering fire. Silence.

Le Bret:
    Horrible!
Carbon:
                Why, yes. All of that.
Le Bret:
                        Mordious!
Carbon: [Gesture toward the sleeping Cadets]
    Swear gently— You might wake them.
        [To Cadets]
                            Go to sleep—
    Hush!
        [To **Le Bret**]
            Who sleeps dines.
Le Bret:
                    I have insomnia.
    God! What a famine.
        [Firing off stage]
Carbon:
                    Curse that musketry!
    They'll wake my babies.
        [To the men]
                        Go to sleep!—
A Cadet: [Rouses]
                            Diantre!
    Again?
Carbon:
            No—only Cyrano coming home.
    [The heads which have been raised sink back again.]
A Sentry: [Off stage]
    Halt! Who goes there?
Voice of Cyrano
                        Bergerac!
The Sentry on the Parapet:
                        Halt! Who goes?—
Cyrano:
        [Appears on the parapet.]
    Bergerac, idiot!

Le Bret: [Goes to meet him]
                Thank God again!
Cyrano:
        [Signs to him not to wake anyone.]
    Hush!
Le Bret:
                    Wounded?—
Cyrano:
                No— They always miss me—quite
    A habit by this time!
Le Bret:
                        Yes— Go right on—
    Risk your life every morning before breakfast
    To send a letter!
Cyrano: [Stops near **Christian**]
                I promised he should write
    Every single day . . .
        [Looks down at him]
                        Hm— The boy looks pale
    When he is asleep—thin too—starving to death—
    If that poor child knew! Handsome, none the less . . .
Le Bret:
    Go and get some sleep!
Cyrano: [Affectionately]
                    Now, now—you old bear,
    No growling!—I am careful—you know I am—
    Every night, when I cross the Spanish lines
    I wait till they are all drunk.
Le Bret:
                        You might bring
    Something with you.
Cyrano:
                    I have to travel light
    To pass through— By the way, there will be news
    For you to-day: the French will eat or die,
    If what I saw means anything.
Le Bret:
                        Tell us!
Cyrano:
                                No—
    I am not sure—we shall see!
Carbon:
                    What a war,
    When the besieger starves to death!
Le Bret:
                                Fine war—

Fine situation! We besiege Arras—
The Cardinal Prince of Spain besieges us—
And—here we are!

Cyrano:
                    Someone might besiege *him.*

Carbon:
A hungry joke!

Cyrano:
            Ho, ho!

Le Bret:
                        Yes, you can laugh—
Risking a life like yours to carry letters—
Where are you going now?

Cyrano: [*At the tent door*]
                    To write another.

[*Goes into tent.*]
[*A little more daylight. The clouds redden. The
towns of Arras shows on the horizon. A cannon
shot is heard, followed immediately by a roll of
drums, far away to the left. Other drums beat
a little nearer. The drums go on answering each
other here and there, approach, beat loudly almost
on the stage, and die away toward the right,
across the camp. The camp awakes. Voices of
officers in the distance.*]

Carbon: [*Sighs*]
Those drums! another good nourishing sleep
Gone to the devil.
            [*The Cadets rouse themselves*]
                    Now then!—

First Cadet: [*Sits up, yawns*]
                        God! I'm hungry!

Second Cadet:
Starving!

All: [*Groan*]
        Aoh!

Carbon:
                Up with you!

Third Cadet:
                        Not another step!

Fourth Cadet:
Not another movement!

First Cadet: Look at my tongue—
I said this air was indigestible!

Fifth Cadet:
My coronet for half a pound of cheese!

Sixth Cadet:
I have no stomach for this war—I'll stay
In my tent—like Achilles.

Another: Yes—no bread,
No fighting—

Carbon:
        Cyrano!

Others:
                    May as well die—

Carbon:
Come out here!—You know how to talk to
    them.
Get them laughing—

Second Cadet: [*Rushes up to* **First Cadet** *who is
eating something*]
                    What are you gnawing there?

First Cadet:
Gun wads and axle-grease. Fat country this
Around Arras.

Another: [*Enters*]
                I have been out hunting!

Another: [*Enters*]
Went fishing, in the Scarpe!

All: [*Leaping up and surrounding the newcomers*]
                        Find anything?
Any fish? Any game? Perch? Partridges?
Let me look!

The Fisherman:
                Yes—one gudgeon.
    [*Shows it*]

The Hunter:
                        One fat ... sparrow.
    [*Shows it*]

All:
Ah!—See here, this—mutiny!—

Carbon:
                        Cyrano!
Come and help!

Cyrano: [*Enters from tent*]
                    Well?
    [*Silence. To the* **First Cadet** *who is walking
    away, with his chin on his chest.*]
                    You there, with the long face?

First Cadet:
I have something on my mind that troubles
    me.

Cyrano:
What is that?

First Cadet:
                My stomach.

Cyrano:
                So have I.

First Cadet:

No doubt
You enjoy this!
Cyrano: [*Tightens his belt*]
It keeps me looking young.
Second Cadet:
My teeth are growing rusty.
Cyrano:

Sharpen them!
Third Cadet:
My belly sounds as hollow as a drum.
Cyrano:
Beat the long roll on it!
Fourth Cadet:

My ears are ringing.
Cyrano:
Liar! A hungry belly has no ears.
Fifth Cadet:
Oh for a barrel of good wine!
Cyrano: [*Offers him his own helmet*]

Your casque.
Sixth Cadet:
I'll swallow anything!
Cyrano: [*Throws him the book which he has in his hand*]

Try the "Iliad."
Seventh Cadet:
The Cardinal, he has four meals a day—
What does he care!
Cyrano:

Ask him; he really ought
To send you . . . a spring lamb out of his flock,
Roasted whole—
The Cadet:

Yes, and a bottle—
Cyrano: [*Exaggerates the manner of one speaking to a servant*]

If you please,
Richelieu—a little more of the Red Seal . . .
Ah, thank you!
The Cadet:

And the salad—
Cyrano:

Of course—Romaine!
Another Cadet: [*Shivering*]
I am as hungry as a wolf.
Cyrano: [*Tosses him a cloak*]

Put on
Your sheep's clothing.

First Cadet: [*With a shrug*]
Always the clever answer!
Cyrano:
Always the answer—yes! Let me die so—
Under some rosy-golden sunset, saying
A good thing, for a good cause! By the sword,
The point of honor—by the hand of one
Worthy to be my foeman, let me fall—
Steel in my heart, and laughter on my lips!
Voices Here and There:
All very well— We are hungry!
Cyrano: Bah! You think
Of nothing but yourselves.
[*His eye singles out the old fifer in the background.*]

Here, Bertrandou,
You were a shepherd once— Your pipe now!
Come,
Breathe, blow,— Play to these belly-wor-
shippers
The old airs of the South—
"Airs with a smile in them,
Airs with a sigh in them, airs with the breeze
And the blue of the sky in them—"
Small, demure tunes
Whose every note is like a little sister—
Songs heard only in some long silent voice
Not quite forgotten— Mountain melodies
Like thin smoke rising from brown cottages
In the still noon, slowly— Quaint lullabies,
Whose very music has a Southern tongue—
[*The old man sits down and prepares his fife.*]
Now let the fife, that dry old warrior,
Dream, while over the stops your fingers
dance
A minuet of little birds—let him
Dream beyond ebony and ivory;
Let him remember he was once a reed
Out of the river, and recall the spirit
Of innocent, untroubled country days . . .
[**The fifer** *begins to play a Provençal melody.*]
Listen, you Gascons! Now it is no more
The shrill fife— It is the flute, through
woodlands
far
Away, calling—no longer the hot battle-cry,
But the cool, quiet pipe our goatherds play!
Listen—the forest glens . . . the hills . . . the
downs . . .

The green sweetness of night on the
   Dordogne . . .
Listen, you Gascons! It is all Gascoyne! . . .
   *[Every head is bowed; every eye cast down. Here
   and there a tear is furtively brushed away with
   the back of a hand, the corner of a cloak.]*

Carbon: *[Softly to* **Cyrano**]
You make them weep—

Cyrano:
                For homesickness—a hunger
More noble than that hunger of the flesh;
It is their hearts now that are starving.

Carbon:
                        Yes,
But you melt down their manhood.

Cyrano: *[Motions the drummer to approach]*
                     You think so?
Let them be. There is iron in their blood
Not easily dissolved in tears. You need
Only—
   [He makes a gesture; the drum beats.]

All: *[Spring up and rush toward their weapons]*
   What's that? Where is it?—What?—

Cyrano: *[Smiles]*
                     You see—
Let Mars snore in his sleep once—and farewell
Venus—sweet dreams—regrets—dear thoughts
   of home—
All the fife lulls to rest wakes at the drums!

A Cadet: *[Looks up stage]*
Aha— Monsieur de Guiche!

The Cadets: *[Mutter among themselves]*
                    Ugh! . . .

Cyrano: *[Smiles]*
                    Flattering
Murmur!

A Cadet:
   He makes me weary!

Another:
                With his collar
Of lace over his corselet—

Another:
             Like a ribbon
Tied round a sword!

Another:
          Bandages for a boil
On the back of his neck—

Second Cadet:
          A courtier always!

Another:
The Cardinal's nephew!

Carbon:
         None the less—a Gascon.

First Cadet:
A counterfeit! Never you trust that man—
Because we Gascons, look you, are all mad—
This fellow is reasonable—nothing more
Dangerous than a reasonable Gascon!

Le Bret:
He looks pale.

Another:
        Oh, he can be hungry too,
Like any other poor devil—but he wears
So many jewels on that belt of his
That his cramps glitter in the sun!

Cyrano: *[Quickly]*
                  Is he
To see us looking miserable? Quick—
Pipes!—Cards!—Dice!—
   *[They all hurriedly begin to play, on their stools,
   on the drums, or on their cloaks spread on the
   ground, lighting their long pipes meanwhile.]*
        As for me, I read Descartes.
   *[He walks up and down, reading a small book
   which he takes from his pocket.* TABLEAU: **De
   Guiche** *enters, looking pale and haggard. All are
   absorbed in their games. General air of content-
   ment. De Guiche goes to* **Carbon.** *They look at
   each other askance, each observing with satisfaction the condition of the other.]*

De Guiche:
Good morning!
   [Aside]
          He looks yellow.

Carbon: *[Same business]*
                He is all eyes.

De Guiche: *[Looks at the Cadets]*
What have we here? Black looks? Yes,
   gentlemen—
I am informed I am not popular;
The hill-nobility, barons of Béarn,
The pomp and pride of Périgord—I learn
They disapprove their colonel; call him
   courtier,
Politician—they take it ill that I
Cover my steel with lace of Genoa.
It is a great offense to be a Gascon
And not to be a beggar!

[*Silence. They smoke. They play.*]

                    Well—Shall I have
Your captain punish you? ... No.

Carbon:

                              As to that,
It would be impossible.

De Guiche:

                    Oh?

Carbon:

                              I am free;
I pay my company; it is my own;
I obey military orders.

De Guiche:

                    Oh!
That will be quite enough.

          [*To* **The Cadets**]

                    I can afford
Your little hates. My conduct under fire
Is well known. It was only yesterday
I drove the Count de Bucquoi from Bapaume,
Pouring my men down like an avalanche,
I myself led the charge—

Cyrano: [*Without looking up from his book*]

                    And your white scarf?

De Guiche: [*Surprised and gratified*]
You heard that episode? Yes—rallying
My men for the third time, I found myself
Carried among a crowd of fugitives
Into the enemy's lines. I was in danger
Of being shot or captured: but I thought
Quickly—took off and flung away the scarf
That marked my military rank—and so
Being inconspicuous, escaped among
My own force, rallied them, returned again
And won the day! ...

          [*The Cadets* do not appear to be listening, but
          here and there the cards and the dice boxes remain
          motionless, the smoke is retained in their cheeks.]

                    What do you say to that?
Presence of mind—yes?

Cyrano:

                    Henry of Navarre
Being outnumbered, never flung away
His white plume.

          [*Silent enjoyment. The cards flutter, the dice roll,
          the smoke puffs out.*]

De Guiche:

                    My device was a success,
However!

[*Same attentive pause, interrupting the games and
the smoking.*]

Cyrano:

                    Possibly ... An officer
Does not lightly resign the privilege
Of being a target.

          [*Cards, dice, and smoke fall, roll, and float away
          with increasing satisfaction.*]

                    Now, if I had been there—
Your courage and my own differ in this—
When your scarf fell, I should have put it on.

De Guiche:
Boasting again!

Cyrano:

                    Boasting? Lend it to me
To-night; I'll lead the first charge, with your
          scarf
Over my shoulder!

De Guiche:

                    Gasconnade once more!
You are safe making that offer, and you know
          it—
My scarf lies on the river bank between
The lines, a spot swept by artillery
Impossible to reach alive!

Cyrano: [*Produces the scarf from his pocket*]

                    Yes. Here ...

          [*Silence.* **The Cadets** *stifle their laughter behind
          their cards and their dice boxes.* **De Guiche**
          *turns to look at them. Immediately they resume
          their gravity and their game. One of them whistles
          carelessly the mountain air which the fifer was
          playing.*]

De Guiche: [*Takes the scarf*]
Thank you! That bit of white is what I need
To make a signal. I was hesitating—
You have decided me.

          [*He goes up to the parapet, climbs upon it, and
          waves the scarf at arm's length several times.*]

All:

                    What is he doing?—
What?—

The Sentry on the Parapet:
There's a man down there running away!

De Guiche: [*Descending*]
A Spaniard. Very useful as a spy
To both sides. He informs the enemy
As I instruct him. By his influence
I can arrange their dispositions.

Cyrano:
                                         Traitor!
De Guiche: [*Folding the scarf*]
A traitor, yes; but useful . . .
                                 We were saying?
Oh, yes— Here is a bit of news for you:
Last night we had hopes of reprovisioning
The army. Under cover of the dark,
The Marshall moved to Dourlens. Our
   supplies
Are there. He may reach them. But to return
Safely, he needs a large force—at least half
Our entire strength. At present, we have here
Merely a skeleton.
Carbon:
                                 Fortunately,
The Spaniards do not know that.
De Guiche:
                                 Oh, yes; they know
They will attack.
Carbon:
                     Ah!
De Guiche:
                             From that spy of mine
I learned of their intention. His report
Will determine the point of their advance.
The fellow asked me what to say! I told him:
"Go out between the lines; watch for my
   signal;
Where you see that, let them attack there."
Carbon: [*To the cadets*]
                                         Well.
Gentlemen!
         [*All rise. Noise of sword belts and breastplates
         being buckled on.*]
De Guiche:
You may have perhaps an hour.
First Cadet:
Oh— An hour!
         [*They all sit down and resume their games once
         more.*]
De Guiche: [*To* **Carbon**]
                     The great thing is to gain time.
Any moment the Marshal may return.
Carbon:
And to gain time?
De Guiche:
                         You will all be so kind
As to lay down your lives!

Cyrano:
                                 Ah! Your revenge?
De Guiche:
I make no great pretence of loving you!
But—since you gentlemen esteem yourselves
Invincible, the bravest of the brave,
And at that—why need we be personal?
I serve the king in choosing . . . as I choose!
Cyrano: [*Salutes*]
Sir, permit me to offer—all our thanks.
De Guiche: [*Returns the salute*]
You love to fight a hundred against one;
Here is your opportunity!
         [*He goes up stage with* **Carbon.**]
Cyrano: [*To* **The Cadets**]
                                         My friends,
We shall add now to our old Gascon arms
With their six chevrons, blue and gold, a
   seventh—
Blood-red!
         [**De Guiche** *talks in a low tone to* **Carbon**
         *up stage. Orders are given. The defense is ar-
         ranged.* **Cyrano** *goes to* **Christian** *who has
         remained motionless with folded arms.*]
                     Christian?
         [*Lays a hand on his shoulder.*]
Christian: [*Shakes his head*]
                     Roxane . . .
Cyrano:
                                         Yes.
Christian:
                                 I should like
To say farewell to her, with my whole heart
Written for her to keep.
Cyrano:
                                 I thought of that—
         [*Takes a letter from his doublet.*]
I have written your farewell.
Christian:
                             Show me!
Cyrano:
                                 You wish
   To read it?
Christian:
                 Of course!
         [*He takes the letter; begins to read, looks up
         suddenly.*]
                             What?—
Cyrano: What is it?

Christian:
                                    Look—
This little circle—

Cyrano: [*Takes back the letter quickly, and looks innocent*]
                    Circle?—

Christian:
                        Yes—a tear!

Cyrano:
So it is! ... Well—a poet while he writes
Is like a lover in his lady's arms,
Believing his imagination—all
Seems true—you understand? There's half the
    charm
Of writing— Now, this letter as you see
I have made so pathetic that I wept
While I was writing it!

Christian:
                    You—wept?

Cyrano:
                            Why, yes—
Because ... it is a little thing to die,
But—not to see her ... that is terrible!
And I shall never—
            [**Christian** *looks at him.*]
                    We shall never—
            [*Quickly*]
                                You
Will never—

Christian: [*Snatches the letter*]
        Give me that!
        [*Noise in the distance on the outskirts of the camp*]

Voice of a Sentry:
                    Halt—who goes there?
        [*Shots, shouting, jingle of harness*]

Carbon:
What is it?

The Sentry on the Parapet:
            Why, a coach.
            [*They rush to look*]

Confused Voices:
                        What? In the Camp?
A coach? Coming this way— It must have
    driven
Through the Spanish lines—what the devil—
Fire!—
No— Hark! The driver shouting—what does
    he say?
Wait— He said: "On the service of the King!"

[*They are all on the parapet looking over. The
jingling comes nearer.*]

De Guiche:
    Of the King?
        [*They come down and fall into line.*]

Carbon:
                    Hats off, all!

De Guiche: [*Speaks off stage*]
                        The King! Fall, in,
    Rascals!—
        [*The coach enters at full trot. It is covered with
        mud and dust. The curtains are drawn. Two
        foot-men are seated behind. It stops suddenly.*]

Carbon: [*Shouts*]
                Beat the assembly—
        [*Roll of drums. All the Cadets uncover.*]

De Guiche:
                            Two of you,
    Lower the steps—open the door—
        [*Two men rush to the coach. The door opens.*]

Roxane: [*Comes out of the coach*]
                        Good Morning!
        [*At the sound of a woman's voice, every head is
        raised. Sensation.*]

De Guiche:
    On the King's service— You?

Roxane:
                        Yes—my own king—
    Love!

Cyrano: [*Aside*]
            God is merciful ...

Christian: [*Hastens to her*]
                    You! Why have you—

Roxane:
    Your war lasted so long!

Christian:
                        But why?—

Roxane:
                        Not now—

Cyrano: [*Aside*]
    I wonder if I dare to look at her ...

De Guiche:
    You cannot remain here!

Roxane:
                        Why, certainly!
    Roll that drum here, somebody ...
        [*She sits on the drum, which is brought to her.*]
                        Thank you— There!

        [*She laughs*]

Would you believe—they fired upon us?
                                        —My coach
Looks like the pumpkin in the fairy tale,
Does it not? And my footmen—
[*She throws a kiss to* **Christian**]
                                How do you do?
[*She looks about.*]
How serious you all are! Do you know,
It is a long drive here—from Arras?
[*Sees* **Cyrano**.]
                                        Cousin,
I am glad to see you!
Cyrano: [*Advances*]
                        Oh— How did you come?
Roxane:
How did I find you? Very easily—
I followed where the country was laid waste
—Oh, but I saw such things! I had to see
To believe. Gentlemen, is that the service
Of your King? I prefer my own!
Cyrano:
                                But how
Did you come through?
Roxane:
                        Why, through the Spanish lines
Of course!
First Cadet:
                        They let you pass?—
De Guiche:
                                What did you say?
How did you manage?
Le Bret:
                        Yes, that must have been
Difficult!
Roxane:
                No— I simply drove along.
Now and then some hidalgo scowled at me
And I smiled back—my best smile; where-
        upon,
The Spaniards being (without prejudice
To the French) the most polished gentlemen
In the world—I passed!
Carbon:
                        Certainly that smile
Should be a passport! Did they never ask
Your errand or your destination?
Roxane:
                                Oh,
Frequently! Then I dropped my eyes and said:

"I have a lover . . ." Whereupon, the Spaniard
With an air of ferocious dignity
Would close the carriage door—with such a
        gesture
As any king might envy, wave aside
The muskets that were levelled at my breast,
Fall back three paces, equally superb
In grace and gloom, draw himself up, thrust
        forth
A spur under his cloak, sweeping the air
With his long plumes, bow very low, and
        say:
"Pass, Señorita!"
Christian:
                        But Roxane—
Roxane:
                                        I know—
I said "a lover"—but you understand—
Forgive me!—If I said "I am going to meet
My husband," no one would believe me!
Christian:
                                        Yes,
But—
Roxane:
    What then?
De Guiche:
                You must leave this place.
Cyrano:
                                At once.
Roxane:
I?
Le Bret:
Yes—immediately.
Roxane:
                        And why?
Christian: [*Embarrassed*]
                                Because . . .
Cyrano: [*Same*]
In half an hour . . .
De Guiche: [*Same*]
                        Or these quarters . . .
Carbon: [*Same*]
                                        Perhaps
It might be better . . .
Le Bret:
                        If you . . .
Roxane:
                                        Oh— I see!
You are going to fight. I remain here.

All:

                                No—no!

Roxane:

He is my husband—

[*Throws herself in* **Christian***'s arms*]

                I will die with you!

Christian:

Your eyes! . . . Why do you?—

Roxane:

                            You know why . . .

De Guiche: [*Desperate*]

                            This post

Is dangerous—

Roxane: [*Turns*]

                How—dangerous

Cyrano: The proof

Is, we are ordered—

Roxane: [*To* **De Guiche**]

                Oh—you wish to make

A widow of me?

De Guiche:

                On my word of honor—

Roxane:

No matter. I am just a little mad—

I will stay. It may be amusing.

Cyrano:

                                What,

A heroine—our intellectual?

Roxane:

Monsieur de Bergerac, I am your cousin!

A Cadet:

We'll fight now! Hurrah!

Roxane: [*More and more excited*]

                I am safe with you—my friends!

Another: [*Carried away*]

The whole camp breathes of lilies!—

Roxane:

                            And I think,

This hat would look well on the
    battlefield! . . .

But perhaps—

        [*Looks at* **De Guiche.**]

The Count ought to leave us. Any moment
Now, there may be danger.

De Guiche:

                    This is too much!

I must inspect my guns. I shall return—
You may change your mind— There will yet
be time—

Roxane:

Never!

        [**De Guiche** *goes out.*]

Christian: [*Imploring*]

                    Roxane! . . .

Roxane:

                    No!

First Cadet: [*To the rest*]

                    She stays here!

All: [*Rushing about, elbowing each other, brushing off their clothes*]

                                A comb!—

Soap!—Here's a hole in my— A needle!—Who
Has a ribbon?—Your mirror, quick!—My
    cuffs—
A razor—

Roxane: [*To* **Cyrano,** *who is still urging her*]

            No! I shall not stir one step!

Carbon: [*Having, like the others, tightened his belt, dusted himself, brushed off his hat, smoothed out his plume and put on his lace cuffs, advances to* **Roxane** *ceremoniously*]

In that case, may I not present to you
Some of these gentlemen who are to have
The honor of dying in your presence?

Roxane: [*Bows*]

                                Please!—

[*She waits, standing, on the arm of* **Christian,** *while*

Carbon: —*presents*]

Baron de Peyrescous de Colignac!

The Cadet: [*Salutes*]

Madame . . .

Roxane:

            Monsieur . . .

Carbon: [*Continues*]

                    Baron de Casterac

De Cahuzac—Vidame de Malgouyre
Estressac Lésbas d'Escarabiot—

The Vidame:

Madame . . .

Carbon:

            Chevalier d'Antignac-Juzet—
Baron Hillot de Blagnac-Saléchan
De Castel-Crabioules—

The Baron:

                    Madame . . .

Roxane:

                                How many

Names you all have!
The Baron:
                    Hundreds!
Carbon: [*To* **Roxane**]
                              Open the hand
That holds your handerchief.
Roxane: [*Opens her hand; the handkerchief falls*]
                              Why?
[*The whole company makes a movement toward it.*]
Carbon: [*Picks it up quickly*]
                              My company
Was in want of a banner. We have now
The fairest in the army!
Roxane: [*Smiling*]
                              Rather small—
Carbon: [*Fastens the handerchief to his lance*]
Lace—and embroidered!
A Cadet: [*To the others*]
                    With her smiling on me,
I could die happy, if I only had
Something in my—
Carbon: [*Turns upon him*]
                    Shame on you! Feast your eyes
And forget your—
Roxane: [*Quickly*]
                    It must be this fresh air—
I am starving! Let me see . . .
                              Cold partridges,
Pastry, a little white wine—that would do.
Will some one bring that to me?
A Cadet: [*Aside*]
                              Will some one!—
Another:
Where the devil are we to find—
Roxane: [*Overhears; sweetly*]
                              Why, there—
In my carriage.
All:
                    Wha-at?
Roxane:
                              All you have to do
Is to unpack, and carve, and serve things.
                                        Oh,
Notice my coachman; you may recognize
An old friend
The Cadets: [*Rush to the coach*]
                    Ragueneau!
Roxane: [*Follows them with her eyes.*]

                              Poor fellows . . .
The Cadets: [*Acclamations*]
                                        Ah!
Ah!
Cyrano: [*Kisses her hand*]
                    Our good fairy!
Ragueneau: [*Standing on his box, like a mountebank before a crowd*]
                              Gentlemen!—
[*Enthusiasm*]
The Cadets:
                                        Bravo!
Bravo!
Ragueneau:
    The Spaniards, basking in our smiles,
Smiled on our baskets!
            [*Applause*]
Cyrano: [*Aside, to* **Christian**]
                              Christian!—
Ragueneau:
                              They adored
The Fair, and missed—
[*He takes from under the seat a dish, which he holds aloft.*]
the Fowl!
[*Applause. The dish is passed from hand to hand.*]
Cyrano: [*As before, to* **Christian**]
                              One moment—
Ragueneau:
                              Venus
Charmed their eyes, while Adonis quietly
            [*Brandishing a ham.*]
Brought home the Boar!
[*Applause; the ham is seized by a score of hands outstretched.*]
Cyrano: [*As before*]
                    Pst— Let me speak to you—
Roxane: [*As* **The Cadets** *return, their arms full of provisions*]
Spread them out on the ground.
            [*Calls*]
                              Christian! Come here;
Make yourself useful.
[**Christian** *turns to her, at the moment when* **Cyrano** *was leading him aside. She arranges the food, with his aid and that of the two imperturbable footmen.*]
Raguenau:
                    Peacock, aux truffes!

First Cadet: [*Comes down, cutting a huge slice of the ham*]

Tonnere!

We are not going to die without a gorge—
[*Sees* **Roxane;** *corrects himself hastily*]
Pardon—a banquet!

Ragueneau: [*Tossing out the cushions of the carriage*]
Open these—they are full
Of ortolans!
[*Tumult; laughter; the cushions are eviscerated.*]

Third Cadet:

Lucullus!

Ragueneau: [*Throws out bottles of red wine*]
Flasks of ruby—
[*And of white*]
Flasks of topaz—

Roxane: [*Throws a tablecloth at the head of* **Cyrano**]
Come back out of your dreams!
Unfold this cloth—

Ragueneau: [*Takes off one of the lanterns of the carriage, and flourishes it*]
Our lamps are bonbonniéres!

Cyrano: [*To* **Christian**]
I must see you before you speak with her—

Ragueneau: [*More and more lyrical*]
My whip-handle is one long sausage!

Roxane: [*Pouring wine; passing the food*]

We
Being about to die, first let us dine!
Never mind the others—all for Gascoyne!
And if De Guiche comes, he is not invited!
[*Going from one to another.*]
Plenty of time—you need not eat so fast—
Hold your cup—
[*To another*]
What's the matter?

The Cadet: [*Sobbing*]   You are so good
To us . . .

Roxane:

There, there! Red or white wine?
—Some bread
For Monsieur de Carbon!—Napkins— A
knife—
Pass your plate— Some of the crust? A little
more—
Light or dark?—Burgundy?—

Cyrano: [*Follows her with an armful of dishes, helping to serve*]

Adorable!

Roxane: [*Goes to* **Christian**]
What would you like?

Christian:

Nothing.

Roxane:

Oh, but you must!—
A little wine? A biscuit?

Christian:

Tell me first
Why you came—

Roxane:

By and by. I must take care
Of these poor boys—

Le Bret: [*Who has gone up stage to pass up food to the sentry on the parapet, on the end of a lance*]
De Guiche!—

Cyrano:

Hide everything
Quick!—Dishes, bottles, tablecloth—
Now look
Hungry again—
[*To* **Ragueneau**]
You there! Up on your box—
—Everything out of sight?
[*In a twinkling, everything has been pushed inside the tents, hidden in their hats or under their cloaks.* **De Guiche** *enters quickly, then stops, sniffing the air. Silence.*]

De Guiche:

It smells good here.

A Cadet: [*Humming with an air of great unconcern*]
Sing ha-ha-ha and ho-ho-ho—

De Guiche: [*Stares at him; he grows embarrassed*]
You there—
What are you blushing for?

The Cadet:

Nothing—my blood
Stirs at the thought of battle.

Another:

Pom . . . pom . . . pom! . . .

De Guiche: [*Turns upon him*]
What is that?

The Cadet: [*Slightly stimulated*]
Only song—only little song—

De Guiche:
You appear happy!

The Cadet:

Oh yes—always happy
Before a fight—

De Guiche: [*Calls to* **Carbon,** *for the purpose of giving him an order*]
     Captain! I—
[*Stops and looks at him.*]
        What the devil—
You are looking happy too!—

Carbon:
[*Pulls a long face and hides a bottle behind his back.*]
       No!

De Guiche:
        Here—I had
One gun remaining. I have had it placed
[*He points off stage.*]
There—in that corner—for your men.

A Cadet: [*Simpering*]   So kind!—
Charming attention!

Another: [*Same business; burlesque*]
      Sweet solicitude!—

De Guiche: [*Contemptuous*]
I believe you are both drunk—
[*Coldly*]
        Being unaccustomed
To guns—take care of the recoil!

First Cadet: [*Gesture*]
        Ah-h . . . Pfft!

De Guiche: [*Goes up to him, furious*]
How dare you?

First Cadet:
    A Gascon's gun never recoils!

De Guiche: [*Shakes him by the arm*]
You *are* drunk—

First Cadet: [*Superbly*]
   With the smell of powder!

De Guiche: [*Turns away with a shrug*]
        Bah!

[*To* **Roxane**]
Madame, have you decided?

Roxane:
      I stay here.

De Guiche:
You have time to escape—

Roxane:
    No!

De Guiche:
      Very well—
Someone give me a musket!

Carbon:
     What?

De Guiche:
        I stay
Here also.

Cyrano: [*Formally*]
   Sir, you show courage!

First Cadet:
      A Gascon
In spite of all that lace!

Roxane:
     Why—

De Guiche:
      Must I run
Away, and leave a woman?

Second Cadet: [*To* **First Cadet**]
     We might give him
Something to eat—what do you say?
[*All the food re-appears, as if by magic*]

De Guiche: [*His face lights up*]
       A feast!

Third Cadet:
Here a little, there a little—

De Guiche: [*Recovers his self-control; haughtily*]
     Do you think
I want your leavings?

Cyrano: [*Saluting*]
    Colonel—you improve!

De Guiche:
I can fight as I am!

First Cadet: [*Delighted*]
     Listen to him—
He has an accent!

De Guiche: [*Laughs*]
    Have I so?

First Cadet:
      A Gascon!—
A Gascon after all!
[*They all begin to dance.*]

Carbon: [*Who has disappeared for a moment behind the parapet, reappears on top of it*]
    I have placed my pikemen
Here.
[*Indicates a row of pikes showing above the parapet.*]

De Guiche: [*Bows to* **Roxane**]
We'll review them; will you take my arm?
[*She takes his arm; they go up on the parapet. The rest uncover, and follow them up stage.*]

Christian: [*Goes hurriedly to* **Cyrano**]
Speak quickly!

[*At the moment when* **Roxane** *appears on the parapet the pikes are lowered in salute, and a cheer is heard. She bows.*]

The Pikemen: [*Off stage*]
    Hurrah!
Christian:
               What is it?
Cyrano:
                  If Roxane . . .
Christian:
  Well?
Cyrano:
        Speaks about your letters . . .
Christian:
                  Yes—I know!
Cyrano:
  Do not make the mistake of showing . . .
Christian:
                  What?
Cyrano:
  Showing surprise.
Christian:
          Surprise—why?
Cyrano:
             I must tell you! . . .
It is quite simple—I had forgotten it
Until just now. You have . . .
Christian:
            Speak quickly!—
Cyrano:
                 You
Have written oftener than you think.
Christian:
            Oh—have I!
Cyrano:
  I took upon me to interpret you;
And wrote—sometimes . . . without . . .
Christian:
          My knowing. Well?
Cyrano:
  Perfectly simple!
Christian:
     Oh yes, perfectly!—
For a month, we have been blockaded here!—
How did you send all these letters?
Cyrano:
          Before
Daylight, I managed—

Christian:
      I see. That was also
Perfectly simple!
        —So I wrote to her,
How many times a week? Twice? Three times?
  Four?
Cyrano:
  Oftener.
Christian:
  Every day?
Cyrano:
           Yes—every day . . .
Every single day . . .
Christian: [*Violently*]
        And that wrought you up
Into such a flame that you faced death—
Cyrano: [*Sees* **Roxane** *returning*]
               Hush—
Not before her!
  [*He goes quickly into the tent.* **Roxane** *comes up to* **Christian.**]
Roxane:
        Now—Christian!
Christian: [*Takes her hands*]
             Tell me now
Why you came here—over these ruined
  roads—
Why you made your way among moss-
  troopers
And ruffians—you—to join me here?
Roxane:
             Because—
Your letters . . .
Christian:
      Meaning?
Roxane:
         It was your own fault
If I ran into danger! I went mad—
Mad with you! Think what you have written
  me,
How many times, each one more wonderful
Than the last!
Christian:
     All this for a few absurd
Love-letters—
Roxane:
     Hush—absurd! How can you know?
I thought I loved you, ever since one night

When a voice that I never would have known
Under my window breathed your soul to
  me . . .
But—all this time, your letters—every one
Was like hearing your voice there in the dark,
All around me, like your arms around me . . .

[*More lightly*]
                              At last,
I came. Anyone would! Do you suppose
The prim Penelope had stayed at home
Embroidering,—if Ulysses wrote like you?
She would have fallen like another Helen—
Tucked up those linen petticoats of hers
And followed him to Troy!

Christian:
                    But you—

Roxane:
                    I read them
Over and over. I grew faint reading them.
I belonged to you. Every page of them
Was like a petal fallen from your soul—
Like the light and the fire of a great love,
Sweet and strong and true—

Christian:
          Sweet . . . and strong . . . and true . . .
You felt that, Roxane?—

Roxane:
                    You know how I feel! . . .

Christian:
So—you came . . .

Roxane:
          Oh, my Christian, oh my king,—
Lift me up if I fall upon my knees—
It is the heart of me that kneels to you,
And will remain forever at your feet—
You cannot lift that!—
          I came here to say
'Forgive me'—(It is time to be forgiven
Now, when we may die presently)—forgive
  me
For being light and vain and loving you
Only because you were beautiful.

Christian: [*Astonished*]
                    Roxane! . . .

Roxane:
Afterwards I knew better. Afterwards
(I had to learn to use my wings) I loved you

For yourself too—knowing you more, and
  loving
More of you. And now—

Christian:
                    Now? . . .

Roxane:
                              It is yourself
I love now: your own self.

Christian: [*Taken aback*]
                    Roxane!

Roxane: [*Gravely*]
                              Be happy!—
You must have suffered; for you must have
  seen
How frivolous I was; and to be loved
For the mere costume, the poor casual body
You went about in—to a soul like yours,
That must have been torture! Therefore with
  words
You revealed your heart. Now that image of
  you
Which filled my eyes first—I see better now,
And I see it no more!

Christian:
                    Oh!—

Roxane:
                    You still doubt
Your victory?

Christian: [*Miserably*]
                    Roxane!—

Roxane:
                              I understand:
You cannot perfectly believe in me—
A love like this—

Christian:
                    I want no love like this!
I want love only for—

Roxane:
                    Only for what
Every woman sees in you? I can do
Better than that!

Christian:
                    No—it was best before!

Roxane:
You do not altogether know me . . . Dear,
There is more of me than there was—with
  this,
I can love more of you—more of what makes

You your own self—Truly! ... If you were less
Lovable—
Christian:
No!
Roxane:
—Less charming—ugly even—
I should love you still.
Christian:
You mean that?
Roxane:
I do
Mean that!
Christian:
Ugly? ...
Roxane:
Yes. Even then!
Christian: [*Agonized*]
Oh ... God! ...
Roxane:
Now are you happy?
Christian: [*Choking*]
Yes ...
Roxane:
What is it?
Christian: [*Pushes her away gently*]
Only ...
Nothing ... one moment ...
Roxane:
But—
Christian: [*Gesture toward the Cadets*]
I am keeping you
From those poor fellows— Go and smile at them;
They are going to die!
Roxane: [*Softly*]
Dear Christian!
Christian:
Go—
[*She goes up among the Gascons who gather round her respectfully.*]
Cyrano!
Cyrano: [*Comes out of the tent, armed for the battle*]
What is wrong? You look—
Christian:
She does not
Love me any more.
Cyrano: [*Smiles*]
You think not

Christian:
She loves
You.
Cyrano:
No!—
Christian: [*Bitterly*]
She loves only my soul.
Cyrano:
No!
Christian:
Yes—
That means you. And you love her.
Cyrano:
I?
Christian:
I see—
I know!
Cyrano:
That is true ...
Christian:
More than—
Cyrano: [*Quietly*]
More than that.
Christian:
Tell her so!
Cyrano:
No.
Christian:
Why not?
Cyrano:
Why—look at me!
Christian:
She would love me if I were ugly.
Cyrano: [*Startled*]
She—
Said that?
Christian:
Yes. Now then!
Cyrano: [*Half to himself*]
It was good of her
To tell you that ...
[*Change of tone*]
Nonsense! Do you believe
Any such madness—
It was good of her
To tell you. ...
Do not take her at her word!
Go on—you never will be ugly— Go!
She would never forgive me.

Christian:
                    That is what
We shall see.

Cyrano:
          No, no—

Christian:
                    Let her choose between us!—
Tell her everything!

Cyrano:
              No—you torture me—

Christian:
Shall I ruin your happiness, because
I have a cursed pretty face? That seems
Too unfair!

Cyrano:
          And am I to ruin yours
Because I happen to be born with power
To say what you—perhaps—feel?

Christian:
                      Tell her!

Cyrano:
                          Man—
Do not try me too far!

Christian:
              I am tired of being
My own rival!

Cyrano:
          Christian!—

Christian:
                  Our secret marriage—
No witnesses—fraudulent—that can be
Annulled—

Cyrano:
          Do not try me—

Christian: I want her love
For the poor fool I am—or not at all!
Oh, I am going through with this! I'll know,
One way or the other. Now I shall walk down
To the end of the post. Go tell her. Let her
   choose
One of us.

Cyrano:
          It will be you.

Christian:
                  God—I hope so!
          [*He turns and calls*]
   Roxane!

Cyrano:
          No—no—

Roxane: [*Hurries down to him*]
              Yes, Christian?

Christian:
                      Cyrano
Has news for you—important.
          [*She turns to* **Cyrano. Christian** *goes out.*]

Roxane: [*Lightly*]
                  Oh—important?

Cyrano:
He is gone . . .
          [*To* **Roxane**]
                  Nothing—only Christian thinks
You ought to know—

Roxane:
                  I do know. He still doubts
What I told him just now. I saw that.

Cyrano: [*Takes her hand*]
                          Was it
True—what you told him just now?

Roxane:
                      It was true!
I said that I should love him even . . .

Cyrano: [*Smiling sadly*]
                          The word
Comes hard—before me?

Roxane:
                  Even if he were . . .

Cyrano:
                          Say it—
I shall not be hurt!—Ugly?

Roxane:
                  Even then
I should love him.
          [*A few shots, off stage in the direction in which*
          Christian *disappeared*]
                  Hark! The guns—

Cyrano:
                      Hideous?

Roxane:
Hideous.

Cyrano:
              Disfigured?

Roxane:
                  Or disfigured.

Cyrano:
                          Even
   Grotesque?

Roxane:
          How could he ever be grotesque—

Ever—to me!

Cyrano:

But you could love him so,
As much as?—

Roxane:

Yes—and more!

Cyrano: [*Aside, exicitedly*]

It is true!—true!—
Perhaps—God! This is too much happiness . . .
[*To* **Roxane**]
I—Roxane—listen—

Le Bret: [*Enters quickly; calls to* **Cyrano** *in a low tone*]
Cyrano—

Cyrano: [*Turns*]

Yes?

Le Bret:

Hush! . . .
[*Whispers a few words to him*]

Cyrano:

[*Lets fall* **Roxane's** *hand*]
Ah!

Roxane:

What is it?

Cyrano: [*Half stunned, and aside*]

All gone . . .

Roxane:

[*More shots*]

What is it? Oh,
They are fighting!—
[*She goes up to look off stage.*]

Cyrano:

All gone. I cannot ever
Tell her, now . . .ever . . .

Roxane: [*Starts to rush away*]

What has happened?

Cyrano: [*Restrains her*]

Nothing.
[*Several* **Cadets** *enter. They conceal something
which they are carrying, and form a group so
as to prevent* **Roxane** *from seeing their burden.*]

Roxane:

These men—

Cyrano:

Come away . . .
[*He leads her away from the group.*]

Roxane:

You were telling me
Something—

Cyrano:

Oh, that? Nothing. . . . [*Gravely*]

I swear to you
That the spirit of Christian—that his soul
Was—
[*Corrects himself quickly.*]
That his soul is no less great—

Roxane: [*Catches at the word*]

Was?
[*Crying out*]
[*She rushes among the men, and scatters them.*]

Cyrano:

All gone . . .

Roxane: [*Sees* **Christian** *lying upon his cloak*]

Christian!

Le Bret: [*To* **Cyrano**]

At the first volley.
[**Roxane** *throws herself upon the body of* **Chris-
tian**. *Shots; at first scattered, then increasing.
Drums. Voices shouting.*]

Carbon: [*Sword in hand*]

Here
They come!—Ready!—
[*Followed by* **The Cadets,** *he climbs over the
parapet and disappears.*]

Roxane:

Christian!

Carbon: [*Off stage*]

Come on, there, You!

Roxane:

Christian!

Carbon:

Fall in!

Roxane:

Christian!

Carbon:

Measure your fuse!
[**Ragueneau** *hurries up, carrying a helmet full
of water.*]

Christian: [*Faintly*]

Roxane! . . .

Cyrano: [*Low and quick, in* **Christian's** *ear, while*
Roxane *is dipping into the water a strip of linen torn
from her dress*]
I have told her; she loves you.
[**Christian** *closes his eyes.*]

Roxane: [*Turns to* **Christian**]

Yes,

My darling?

Carbon:
                    Draw your ramrods!

Roxane: [*To* **Cyrano**]
                              He is not dead? . . .

Carbon:
Open your charges!

Roxane:
                    I can feel his cheek
Growing cold against mine—

Carbon:
                              Take aim!

Roxane:
                                        A letter—
Over his heart— [*She opens it*]
                    For me.

Cyrano: [*Aside*]
                              My letter . . .

Carbon:
                                        Fire!
    [*Musketry, cries and groans. Din of battle.*]

Cyrano: [*Trying to withdraw his hand, which* **Roxane,**
still upon her knees, is holding]
But Roxane—they are fighting—

Roxane:
                              Wait a little . . .
He is dead. No one else knew him but
    you . . .
    [*She weeps quietly*]
Was he not a great lover, a great man,
A hero?

Cyrano: [*Standing, bareheaded*]
                    Yes, Roxane.

Roxane:
                              A poet, unknown,
Adorable?

Cyrano:
                    Yes, Roxane,

Roxane:
                              A fine mind?

Cyrano:
Yes, Roxane.

Roxane:
                    A heart deeper than we knew—
A soul magnificently tender?

Cyrano: [*Firmly*]
                                        Yes,
    Roxane!

Roxane: [*Sinks down upon the breast of* **Christian**]
He is dead now . . .

Cyrano: [*Aside; draws his sword*]
                              Why, so am I—
For I am dead, and my love mourns for me
And does not know . . .
    [*Trumpets in distance.*]

De Guiche: [*Appears on the parapet, disheveled,
wounded on the forehead, shouting*]
                    The signal—hark—the trumpets!
The army has returned— Hold them
    now!—Hold them!
The army!—

Roxane:
                    On his letter—blood . . . and tears.

A Voice: [*Off stage*]
Surrender!

The Cadets:
                    No!

Ragueneau:
                    This place is dangerous!—

Cyrano: [*To* **De Guiche**]
Take her away—I am going—

Roxane: [*Kisses the letter; faintly*]
                              His blood . . . his tears . . .

Ragueneau: [*Leaps down from the coach and runs to
her*]
She has fainted—

De Guiche: [*On the parapet; savagely, to* **the Cadets**]
                    Hold them!

Voice off Stage:
                              Lay down your arms!

Voices:
                                        No! No!

Cyrano:
        [*To* **De Guiche**]
Sir, you have proved yourself— Take care of
    her.

De Guiche:
        [*Hurries to* **Roxane** *and takes her up in his
    arms.*]
As you will—we can win, if you hold on
A little longer—

Cyrano:
                    Good!
    [*Calls out to* **Roxane,** *as she is carried away,
    fainting, by* **De Guiche** *and* **Ragueneau.**]
                    Adieu, Roxane!

[*Tumult, outcries. Several Cadets come back wounded and fall on the stage.* **Cyrano,** *rushing to the fight, is stopped on the crest of the parapet by* **Carbon,** *covered with blood.*]

Carbon:
We are breaking—I am twice wounded—
Cyrano: [*Shouts to the Gascons*]

Hardi!

Reculez pas, Drollos!
[*To* **Carbon,** *holding him up.*]

So—never fear!

I have two deaths to avenge now—Christian's
And my own!
[*They come down.* **Cyrano** *takes from him the lance with* **Roxane's** *handerchief still fastened to it.*]

Float, little banner, with her name!
[*He plants it on the parapet; then shouts to the Cadets.*]

Toumbé dessus! Escrasas lous!
[*To the fifer*]

Your fife!

Music!
[**Fife** *plays. The wounded drag themselves to their feet. Other* **Cadets** *scramble over the parapet and group themselves around* **Cyrano** *and his tiny flag. The coach is filled and covered with men, bristling with muskets, transformed into a redoubt.*]

A Cadet:
[*Reels backward over the wall, still fighting. Shouts.*]

They are climbing over!—
[*And falls dead.*]

Cyrano:

Very good—

Let them come!—A salute now—
[*The parapet is crowned for an instant with a rank of enemies. The imperial banner of Spain is raised aloft.*]

Fire!

[*General volley*]

Voice:
[*Among the ranks of the enemy*]

Fire!

[*Murderous counter-fire;* **The Cadets** *fall on every side.*]

A Spanish Officer: [*Uncovers*]
Who are these men who are so fond of death?

Cyrano: [*Erect amid the hail of bullets, declaims*]
The Cadets of Gascoyne, the defenders
Of Carbon de Castel-Jalous—
Free fighters, free lovers, free spenders—
[*He rushes forward, followed by a few survivors.*]
The Cadets of Gascoyne . . .
[*The rest is lost in the din of battle.*]

CURTAIN

ACT V

Cyrano's Gazette

Fifteen years later, in 1655: THE PARK OF THE CONVENT occupied by the Ladies of the Cross, at Paris.

Magnificent foliage. To the Left, the House upon a broad Terrace at the head of a flight of steps, with several Doors opening upon the Terrace. In the centre of the scene an enormous Tree alone in the centre of a little open space. Toward the Right, in the foreground, among Boxwood Bushes, a semi-circular Bench of stone.

All the way across the Background of the scene, an Avenue overarched by the chestnut trees, leading to the door of a Chapel on the Right, just visible among the branches of the trees. Beyond the double curtain of the trees, we catch a glimpse of bright lawns and shaded walks, masses of shrubbery; the perspective of the Park; the sky.

A little side door of the Chapel opens upon a Colonnade, garlanded with Autumnal vines, and disappearing on the Right behind the box-trees.

It is late October. Above the still living green of the turf all the foliage is red and yellow and brown. The evergreen masses of Box and Yew stand out darkly against this Autumnal coloring. A heap of dead leaves under every tree. The leaves are falling everywhere. They rustle underfoot along the walks; the Terrace and the Bench are half covered with them.

Before the Bench on the Right, on the side toward the Tree, is placed a tall embroidery frame and beside it a little Chair. Baskets filled with skeins of many-colored silks and balls of wool. Tapestry unfinished on the Frame.

At the CURTAIN RISE the **nuns** are coming and going across the Park; several of them are seated on the Bench around **Mother Marguérite de Jésus.** The leaves are falling.

Sister Marthe: [*To* **Mother Marguérite**]
Sister Claire has been looking in the glass
At her new cap; twice!
Mother Marguérite: [*To* **Sister Claire**]
            It is very plain;
Very.
Sister Claire:
   And Sister Marthe stole a plum
Out of the tart this morning!
Mother Marguérite: [*To* **Sister Marthe**]
              That was wrong;
Very wrong.
Sister Claire:
        Oh, but such a little look!
Sister Marthe:
Such a little plum!
Mother Marguérite: [*Severely*]
          I shall tell Monsieur
De Cyrano, this evening.
Sister Claire:
              No! Oh, no!—
He will make fun of us.
Sister Marthe:
             He will say nuns
Are so gay!
Sister Claire:
       And so greedy!
Mother Marguérite: [*Smiling*]
            And so good . . .
Sister Claire:
It must be ten years, Mother Marguérite,
That he has come here every Saturday,
Is it not?
Mother Marguérite:
       More than ten years; ever since
His cousin came to live among us here—
Her worldly weeds among our linen veils,
Her widowhood and our virginity—
Like a black dove among white doves.
Sister Marthe:
                No one

Else ever turns that happy sorrow of hers
Into a smile.
All the Nuns:
        He is such fun!—He makes us
Almost laugh!—And he teases everyone—
And pleases everyone— And we all love him—
And he likes our cake, too—
Sister Marthe:
              I am afraid
He is not a good Catholic.
Sister Claire:
           Some day
We shall convert him.
The Nuns:
        Yes—yes!
Mother Marguérite:
            Let him be;
I forbid you to worry him. Perhaps
He might stop coming here.
Sister Marthe:
           But . . . God?
Mother Marguérite:
           You need not
Be afraid. God knows all about him.
Sister Marthe:
            Yes . . .
But every Saturday he says to me,
Just as if he were proud of it: "Well, Sister,
I ate meat yesterday!"
Mother Marguérite:
        He tells you so?
The last time he said that, he had not eaten
Anything, for two days.
Sister Marthe:
           Mother!—
Mother Marguérite:
            He is poor;
Very poor.
Sister Marthe:
   Who said so?
Mother Marguérite:
           Monsieur Le Bret.
Sister Marthe:
Why does not someone help him?
Mother Marguérite:
           He would be
Angry; very angry . . .
    [*Between the trees up stage,* **Roxane** *appears, all in black, with a widow's cap and long veils.* **De**

Guiche, *magnificiently grown old, walks beside her. They move slowly.* **Mother Marguérite** *rises.*]

                    Let us go in—
Madame Madeleine has a visitor.
Sister Marthe: [*To* **Sister Claire**]
The Duc de Grammont, is it not? The Marshal?
Sister Claire: [*Looks toward* **De Guiche**]
I think so—yes.
Sister Marthe:
                    He has not been to see her
For months—
The Nuns:
            He is busy—the Court!—the Camp!—
Sister Claire:
                        The world! ...
[*They go out.* **De Guiche** *and* **Roxane** *come down in silence, and stop near the embroidery frame. Pause.*]
De Guiche:
And you remain here, wasting all that gold—
For ever in mourning?
Roxane:
                    For ever.
De Guiche:
                            And still faithful?
Roxane:
And still faithful ...
De Guiche   [*After a pause*]
                    Have you forgiven me?
Roxane: [*Simply, looking up at the cross of the Convent*]
I am here.
            [*Another pause*]
De Guiche:
            Was Christian ... all that?
Roxane:
                        If you knew him.
De Guiche:
Ah? We were not precisely ... intimate ...
And his last letter—always at your heart?
Roxane:
It hangs here, like a holy reliquary.
De Guiche:
Dead—and you love him still!
Roxane:
                        Sometimes I think
He has not altogether died; our hearts
Meet, and his love flows all around me, living.

De Guiche: [*After another pause*]
You see Cyrano often?
Roxane:
                    Every week.
My old friend takes the place of my Gazette,
Brings me all the news. Every Saturday,
Under that tree where you are now, his chair
Stands, if the day be fine. I wait for him,
Embroidering; the hour strikes; then I hear,
(I need not turn to look!) at the last stroke,
His cane tapping the steps. He laughs at me
For my eternal needlework. He tells
The story of the past week—
            [**Le Bret** *appears on the steps.*]
                        There's Le Bret!—
            [**Le Bret** *approaches.*]
How is it with our friend?
Le Bret:
                    Badly.
De Guiche:
                            Indeed?
Roxane: [*To* **De Guiche**]
Oh, he exaggerates!
Le Bret:
                    Just as I said—
Loneliness, misery—I told him so!—
His satires make a host of enemies—
His attacks the false nobles, the false saints,
The false heroes, the false artists—in short,
Everyone!
Roxane:
                But they fear that sword of his
No one dare touch him!
De Guiche: [*With a shrug*]
                        H'm—that may be so.
Le Bret:
It is not violence I fear for him,
But solitude—poverty—old gray December,
Stealing on wolf's feet, with a wolf's green eyes,
Into his darkening room. Those bravoes yet
May strike our Swordsman down! Every day now,
He draws his belt up one hole; his poor nose
Looks like old ivory; he has one coat
Left—his old black serge.
De Guiche:
                    That is nothing strange
In this world! No, you need not pity him

Overmuch.

Le Bret: [*With a bitter smile*]
  My lord Marshal! ...

De Guiche:
  I say, do not
Pity him overmuch. He lives his life,
His own life, his own way—through, word,
  and deed
Free!

Le Bret: [*As before*]
  My lord Duke! ...

De Guiche: [*Haughtily*]
  Yes, I know—I have all;
He has nothing. Nevertheless, to-day
I should be proud to shake his hand ...
  [*Saluting* **Roxane.**]
  Adieu.

Roxane:
I will go with you.
  [**De Guiche** *salutes* **Le Bret,** *and turns with*
  Roxane *toward the steps.*]

De Guiche: [*Pauses on the steps, as she climbs*]
  Yes— I envy him
Now and then ...
  Do you know, when a man wins
Everything in this world, when he succeeds
Too much—he feels, having done nothing
  wrong
Especially, Heaven knows!—he feels somehow
A thousand small displeasures with himself,
Whose whole sum is not quite Remorse, but
  rather
A sort of vague disgust ... The ducal robes
Mounting up, step by step, to pride and
  power,
Somewhere among their folds draw after
  them
A rustle of dry illusions, vain regrets,
As your veil, up the stairs here, draws along
The whisper of dead leaves.

Roxane: [*Ironical*]
  The sentiment
Does you honor.

De Guiche:
  Oh, yes ...
  [*Pausing suddenly.*]
  Monsieur Le Bret!—
  [*To* **Roxane**]
You pardon us?—

  [*He goes to* **Le Bret,** *and speaks in a low tone.*]
  One moment— It is true
That no one dares attack your friend. Some
  people
Dislike him, none the less. The other day
At Court, such a one said to me: "This man
Cyrano may die—accidentally."

Le Bret: [*Coldly*]
Thank you.

De Guiche:
  You may thank me. Keep him at home
All you can. Tell him to be careful.

Le Bret: [*Shaking his hands to heaven*]
  Careful!—
He is coming here. I'll warn him—yes, but! ...

Roxane: [*Still on the steps, to a* **Nun** *who approaches
her*]
  Here
I am—what is it?

The Nun:
  Madame, Ragueneau
Wishes to see you.

Roxane:
  Bring him here.
  [*To* **Le Bret** *and* **De Guiche**]
  He comes
For sympathy—having been first of all
A Poet, he became since then, in turn,
A Singer—

Le Bret:
  Bath-house keeper—

Roxane:
  Sacristan—

Le Bret:
Actor—

Roxane:
  Hairdresser—

Le Bret:
  Music-master—

Roxane:
  Now,
To-day—

Ragueneau: [*Enters hurriedly*]
  Madame!—
  [*He sees* **Le Bret.**]
  Monsieur!—

Roxane: [*Smiling*]
  First tell your troubles
To Le Bret for a moment.

Ragueneau:

But Madame—

[*She goes out, with* **De Guiche,** *not hearing him.* **Ragueneau** *comes to* **Le Bret.**]

After all, I had rather— You are here—
She need not know so soon— I went to see
him
Just now— Our friend— As I came near his
door,
I saw him coming out. I hurried on
To join him. At the corner of the street,
As he passed— Could it be an accident?—
I wonder!—At the window overhead,
A lackey with a heavy log of wood
Let it fall—

Le Bret:

Cyrano!

Ragueneau:

I ran to him—

Le Bret:

God! The cowards!

Ragueneau:

I found him lying there—
A great hole in his head—

Le Bret:

Is he alive?

Ragueneau:

Alive—yes. But . . . I had to carry him
Up to his room—Dieu! Have you seen his
room?—

Le Bret:

Is he suffering?

Ragueneau:

No; unconscious.

Le Bret:

Did you
Call a doctor?

Ragueneau:

One came—for charity.

Le Bret:

Poor Cyrano!—We must not tell Roxane
All at once . . . Did the doctor say?—

Ragueneau:

He said
Fever, and lesions of the— I forget
Those long names— Ah, if you had seen him
there,
His head all white bandages!—Let us go
Quickly—there is no one to care for him—

All alone— If he tries to raise his head,
He may die!

Le Bret: [*Draws him away to the Right*]

This way— It is shorter—through
The Chapel—

Roxane: [*Appears on the stairway, and calls to* **Le Bret** *as he is going out by the colonnade which leads to the small door of the Chapel*]

Monsieur Le Bret!—

[**Le Bret** *and* **Ragueneau** *rush off without hearing.*]

Running away
When I call to him? Poor dear Ragueneau
Must have been very tragic!

[*She comes slowly down the stair, toward the tree.*]

What a day! . . .
Something in these bright Autumn afternoons
Happy and yet regretful—an old sorrow
Smiling . . . as though poor little April dried
Her tears long ago—and remembered . . .

[*She sits down at her work.* **Two Nuns** *come out of the house carrying a great chair and set it under the tree.*]

Ah—
The old chair, for my old friend!—

Sister Marthe:

The best one
In our best parlor!—

Roxane:

Thank you, Sister—
[**The Nuns** *withdraw.*]

There—
[*She begins embroidering. The clock strikes.*]
The hour!—He will be coming now—my
silks—
All done striking? He never was so late
Before! The sister at the door—my thimble . . .
Here it is—she must be exhorting him
To repent all his sins . . .
[*A pause*]

He ought to be
Converted, by this time— Another leaf—
[*A dead leaf falls on her work; she brushes it away.*]
Certainly nothing could—my scissors—ever
Keep him away—

A Nun: [*Appears on the steps*]
Monsieur de Bergerac.

Roxane: [*Without turning*]

What was I saying? . . . Hard, sometimes, to match
These faded colors! . . .

[*While she goes on working,* **Cyrano** *appears at the top of the steps, very pale, his hat drawn over his eyes. The* **Nun** *who has brought him in goes away. He begins to descend the steps leaning on his cane, and holding himself on his feet only by an evident effort.* **Roxane** *turns to him, with a tone of friendly banter*]

                          After fourteen years,
Late—for the first time!

Cyrano: [*Reaches the chair, and sinks into it; his gay tone contrasting with his tortured face*]
                          Yes, yes—maddening!
I was detained by—

Roxane:
                          Well?

Cyrano:
                          A visitor,
Most unexpected.

Roxane: [*Carelessly, still sewing*]
                          Was your visitor
Tiresome?

Cyrano:
                          Why, hardly that inopportune,
Let us say—an old friend of mine—at least
A very old acquaintance.

Roxane:
                          Did you tell him
To go away?

Cyrano:
                          For the time being, yes.
I said: "Excuse me—this is Saturday—
I have a previous engagement, one
I cannot miss, even for you— Come back
An hour from now."

Roxane:
                          Your friend will have to wait;
I shall not let you go till dark.

Cyrano: [*Very gently*]   Perhaps
A little before dark, I must go . . .

[*He leans back in the chair, and closes his eyes.* **Sister Marthe** *crosses above the stairway.* **Roxane** *sees her, motions her to wait, then turns to* **Cyrano.**]

Roxane:
                          Look—
Somebody waiting to be teased.

Cyrano: [*Quickly, opens his eyes*]
                          Of course!
[*In a big, comic voice*]
Sister, approach!
          [**Sister Marthe** *glides toward him.*]
                          Beautiful downcast eyes!—
So shy—

Sister Marthe: [*Looks up, smiling*]
You—[*She sees his face.*]
                          Oh!—

Cyrano: [*Indicates* **Roxane**]
                          Sh!—Careful!
[*Resumes his burlesque tone*]
                          Yesterday,
I ate meat again!

Sister Marthe:
Yes, I know. [*Aside*]
                          That is why
He looks so pale . . .
          [*To him: low and quickly*]
                          In the refectory,
Before you go—go come to me there—
                          I'll make you
A great bowl of hot soup—will you come?

Cyrano: [*Boisterously*]
                          Ah—
Will I come!

Sister Marthe:
                          You are quite reasonable
To-day!

Roxane:
          Has she converted you?

Sister Marthe:
                          Oh, no—
Not for the world!—

Cyrano:
                          Why, now I think of it,
That is so— You, bursting with holiness,
And yet you never preach! Astonishing
I call it . . .
          [*With burlesque ferocity*]
                          Ah—now I'll astonish you—
I am going to—
          [*With the air of seeking for a good joke and finding it*]
                          —let you pray for me
To-night, at vespers!

Roxane:
                          Aha!

Cyrano:

Look at her—
Absolutely struck dumb!

Sister Marthe: [*Gently*]

I did not wait
For you to say I might. [*She goes out.*]

Cyrano: [*Returns to* **Roxane**, *who is bending over her
work*]

Now, may the devil
Admire me, if I ever hope to see
The end of that embroidery!

Roxane   [*Smiling*]

I thought
It was time you said that.
[*A breath of wind causes a few leaves to fall.*]

Cyrano:

The leaves—

Roxane: [*Raises her head and looks away through the
trees*]

What color—
Perfect Venetian red! Look at them fall.

Cyrano:

Yes—they know how to die. A little way
From the branch to the earth, a little fear
Of mingling with the common dust—and yet
They go down gracefully—a fall that seems
Like flying!

Roxane:

Melancholy—you?

Cyrano:

Why, no,
Roxane!

Roxane:

Then let the leaves fall. Tell me now
The Court news—my gazette!

Cyrano:

Let me see—

Roxane:

Ah!

Cyrano: [*More and more pale, struggling against pain*]
Saturday, the nineteenth; the King fell ill,
After eight helpings of grape marmalade.
His malady was brought before the court,
Found guilty of high treason; whereupon
His Majesty revived. The royal pulse
Is now normal. Sunday, the twentieth:
The Queen gave a grand ball, at which they
burned
Seven hundred and sixty-three wax candles.

Note:
They say our troops have been victorious
In Austria. Later: Three sorcerers
Have been hung. Special post: The little dog
Of Madame D'Athis was obliged to take
Four pills before—

Roxane:

Monsieur de Bergerac,
Will you kindly be quiet!

Cyrano:

Monday . . . nothing.
Lygdamire has a new lover.

Roxane:

Oh!

Cyrano: [*His face more and more altered*]

Tuesday,
The Twenty-second: All the court has gone
To Fontainebleau. Wednesday: The Comte de
Fiesque
Spoke to Madame de Montglat: she said No.
Thursday: Mancini was the Queen of France
Or—very nearly! Friday: La Montglat
Said Yes. Saturday, twenty-sixth. . . .
[*His eyes close; his head sinks back; silence.*]

Roxane:

[*Surprised at not hearing any more, turns, looks
at him, and rises, frightened.*]

He has fainted—
[*She runs to him crying out.*]

Cyrano!

Cyrano: [*Opens his eyes*]
What . . . What is it? . . .
[*He sees* **Roxane** *leaning over him, and quickly
pulls his hat down over his head and leans back
away from her in the chair.*]

No—oh no—
It is nothing—truly

Roxane:

But—

Cyrano:

My old wound—
At Arras—sometimes—you know. . . .

Roxane:

My poor friend!

Cyrano:
Oh it is nothing; it will soon be gone. . . .
[*Forcing a smile*]
There! It is gone!

Roxane: [*Standing close to him*]

We all have our old wounds
I have mine—here . . .
[*Her hand at her breast*]
                under this faded scrap
Of writing. . . . It is hard to read now—all
But the blood—and the tears. . . .
[*Twilight begins to fall.*]

Cyrano:
                                His letter! . . . Did you
Not promise me that some day . . . that some
    day. . . .
You would let me read it?

Roxane:
                                His letter?—You . . .
You wish—

Cyrano:
    I do wish it—to-day.

Roxane: [*Gives him the little silken bag from around
her neck*]
                                Here. . . .

Cyrano:
May I . . . open it?

Roxane:
                        Open it, and read.
[*She goes back to her work, folds it again, re-
arranges her silks.*]

Cyrano: [*Unfolds the letter; reads*]
"Farewell Roxane, because to-day I die—"

Roxane: [*Looks up, surprised*]
Aloud?

Cyrano: [*Reads*]
    "I know that it will be to-day,
My own dearly beloved—and my heart
Still so heavy with love I have not told,
And I die without telling you! No more
Shall my eyes drink the sight of you like wine,
Never more, with a look that is a kiss,
Follow the sweet grace of you—"

Roxane:
                                How you read it—
His letter!

Cyrano: [*Continues*]
    "I remember now the way
You have, of pushing back a lock of hair
With one hand, from your forehead—and my
    heart
Cries out—"

Roxane:
                His letter . . . and you read it so . . .

[*The darkness increases imperceptibly*]

Cyrano:
"Cries out and keeps crying: "Farewell, my
    dear,
My dearest—"

Roxane:
                In a voice. . . .

Cyrano:
                                "—My own heart's own,
My own treasure—"

Roxane: [*Dreamily*]
                        In such a voice. . . .

Cyrano:
                                        —"My love—"

Roxane:
—As I remember hearing . . .
[*She trembles*]
                                —long ago. . . .
[*She comes near him, softly, without his seeing
her; passes the chair, leans over silently, looking
at the letter. The darkness increases.*]

Cyrano:
"—I am never away from you. Even now,
I shall not leave you. In another world,
I shall be still that one who loves you, loves
    you
Beyond measure, beyond—"

Roxane:
[*Lays her hand on his shoulder*]
                                How can you read
Now? It is dark. . .
[*He starts, turns, and sees her there close to him.
A little movement of surprise, almost of fear; then
he bows his head.
A long pause; then in the twilight now completely
fallen, she says very softly, clasping her hands*]
                        And all these fourteen years,
He has been the old friend, who came to me
To be amusing.

Cyrano:
                        Roxane!—

Roxane:
                                It was you.

Cyrano:
    No, no, Roxane, no!

Roxane:
                        And I might have known,
Every time that I heard you speak my
    name! . . .

Cyrano:
No— It was not I—
Roxane:
            It was ... you!
Cyrano:
                        I swear—
Roxane:
I understand everything now: The letters—
That was you ...
Cyrano:
            No!
Roxane:
            And the dear, foolish words—
That was you. . . .
Cyrano:
            No!
Roxane:
            And the voice ... in the dark. . . .
That was ... you!
Cyrano:
            On my honor—
Roxane:
                        And ... the Soul!—
That was all you.
Cyrano:
            I never loved you—
Roxane:
                        Yes,
You loved me.
Cyrano: [*Desperately*]
            No— He loved you—
Roxane:
                        Even now,
You love me!
Cyrano: [*His voice weakens*]
            No!
Roxane: [*Smiling*]
            And why ... so great a "No"?
Cyrano:
No, no, my own dear love, I love you not! ...
      [*Pause*]
Roxane:
How many things have died ... and are
    newborn! ...
Why were you silent for so many years,
All the while, every night and every day,
He gave me nothing—you knew that— You
    knew

Here, in this letter lying on my breast,
Your tears— You knew they were your tears—
Cyrano: [*Holds the letter out to her*]
                        The blood
Was his.
Roxane:
Why do you break that silence now,
To-day?
Cyrano:
            Why? Oh, because—
            [**Le Bret** *and* **Ragueneau** *enter, running*]
Le Bret:
                        What recklessness—
I knew it! He is here!
Cyrano: [*Smiling, and trying to rise*]
                        Well? Here I am!
Ragueneau:
He has killed himself, Madame, coming here!
Roxane:
He— Oh, God. . . . And that faintness ... was
    that?—
Cyrano:
                                    No
Nothing! I did not finish my Gazette—
Saturday, twenty-sixth: An hour or so
Before dinner, Monsieur de Bergerac
Died, foully murdered.
            [*He uncovers his head, and shows it swathed
            in bandages.*]
Roxane:
                        Oh, what does he mean?—
Cyrano!— What have they done to you?—
Cyrano:
                        "Struck down
By the sword of a hero, let me fall—
Steel in my heart, and laughter on my lips!"
Yes, I said that once. How Fate loves a jest!—
Behold me ambushed—taken in the rear—
My battlefield a gutter—my noble foe
A lackey, with a log of wood! ...
                        It seems
Too logical— I have missed everything,
Even my death!
Ragueneau: [*Breaks down*]
            Ah, monsieur!—
Cyrano:
                        Ragueneau,
Stop blubbering! [*Takes his hand*]

What are you writing nowadays,
Old poet?

Ragueneau: [*Through his tears*]
          I am not a poet now;
I snuff the—light the candles—for Molière!

Cyrano:
Oh—Molière!

Ragueneau:
          Yes, but I am leaving him
To-morrow. Yesterday they played "Scapin"—
He has stolen your scene—

Le Bret:
          The whole scene—word for word!

Ragueneau:
Yes: "What the devil was he doing there"—
That one!

Le Bret: [*Furious*]
          And Molière stole it all from you—
Bodily!—

Cyrano:
          Bah— He showed good taste....
          [*To* **Ragueneau**]
                              The Scene
Went well? ...

Ragueneau:
          Ah, monsieur, they laughed—and laughed—
How they did laugh!

Cyrano: Yes—that has been my life....
Do you remember that night Christian spoke
Under your window? It was always so!
While I stood in the darkness underneath,
Others climbed up to win the applause—the
   kiss!—
Well—that seems only justice— I still say,
Even now, on the threshold of my tomb—
"Molière has genius—Christian had good
   looks—"
          [*The chapel bell is ringing. Along the avenue of
          trees above the stairway, the* **Nuns** *pass in
          procession to their prayers.*]
They are going to pray now; there is the bell.

Roxane: [*Raises herself and calls to them*]
Sister!—Sister!—

Cyrano: [*Holding on to her hand*]
          No,—do not go away—
I may not still be here when you return....
          [**The Nuns** *have gone into the chapel. The organ
          begins to play.*]

A little harmony is all I need—
Listen. . . .

Roxane:
          You shall not die! I love you!—

Cyrano:
                              No—
That is not in the story! You remember
When Beauty said "I love you" to the Beast
That was a fairy prince, his ugliness
Changed and dissolved, like magic.... But
   you see
I am still the same.

Roxane: And I—I have done
This to you! All my fault—mine!

Cyrano:
                         You? Why no,
On the contrary! I had never known
Womanhood and its sweetness but for you.
My mother did not love to look at me—
I never had a sister— Later on,
I feared the mistress with a mockery
Behind her smile. But you—because of you
I have had one friend not quite all a friend—
Across my life, one whispering silken
   gown! . . .

Le Bret: [*Points to the rising moon which begins to shine
down between the trees*]
Your other friend is looking at you.

Cyrano: [*Smiling at the moon*]
                              I see. . . .

Roxane:
I never loved but one man in my life,
And I have lost him—twice. . . .

Cyrano:
Le Bret—I shall be up there presently
In the moon—without having to invent
Any flying machines!

Roxane:
                  What are you saying? . . .

Cyrano:
The moon—yes, that would be the place for
   me—
My kind of paradise! I shall find there
Those other souls who should be friends of
   mine—
Socrates—Galileo—

Le Bret: [*Revolting*]
                  No! No! No!

It is too idiotic—too unfair—
Such a friend—such a poet—such a man
To die so—to die so!—
Cyrano: [*Affectionately*]
                        There goes Le Bret,
Growling!
Le Bret: [*Breaks down*]
                        My friend!—
Cyrano: [*Half raises himself, his eye wanders*]
                        The Cadets of Gascoyne,
The Defenders.... The elementary mass—
Ah—there's the point! Now, then ...
Le Bret:
                                Delirious—
And all that learning—
Cyrano:
                        On the other hand,
We have Copernicus—
Roxane:
                        Oh!
Cyrano: [*More and more delirious*]
                        "Very well,
But what the devil was he doing there?—
What the devil was he doing there, up
        there?" ...
        [*He declaims*]
        Philosopher and scientist,
        Poet, musician, duellist—
        He flew high, and fell back again!
        A pretty wit—whose like we lack—
        A lover ... not like other men....
        Here lies Hercule-Savinien
        De Cyrano de Bergerac—
        Who was all things—and all in vain!
Well, I must go—pardon— I cannot stay!
My moonbeam comes to carry me away....
        [*He falls back into the chair, half fainting. The
        sobbing of* **Roxane** *recalls him to reality. Gradu-
        ally his mind comes back to him. He looks at
        her, stroking the veil that hides her hair.*]
I would not have you mourn any the less
That good, brave, noble Christian; but
        perhaps—
I ask you only this—when the great cold
Gathers around my bones, that you may give
A double meaning to your widow's weeds
And the tears you let fall for him may be
For a little—my tears....

Roxane: [*Sobbing*]
                        Oh, my love! ...
Cyrano:
        [*Suddenly shaken as with a fever fit, he raises
        himself erect and pushes her away.*]
                                —Not here!—
Not lying down! ...
        [*They spring forward to help him; he motions
        them back.*]
                        Let no one help me—no one!—
Only the tree....
        [*He sets his back against the trunk. Pause.*]
                        It is coming ... I feel
Already shod with marble ... gloved with
lead ...
        [*Joyously*]
Let the old fellow come now! He shall find
me
On my feet—sword in hand—[*Draws his sword*]
Le Bret:
                        Cyrano!—
Roxane: [*Half fainting*]
                                Oh,
Cyrano!
Cyrano:
        I can see him there—he grins—
He is looking at my nose—that skeleton
—What's that you say? Hopeless?—Why, very
well!—
But a man does not fight merely to win!
No—no—better to know one fights in vain! ...
You there— Who are you? A hundred against
        one—
I know them now, my ancient enemies—
        [*He lunges at the empty air.*]
Falsehood! ... There! There! Prejudice—
Compromise—
Cowardice—[*Thrusting*]
                        What's that? No! Surrender? No!
Never—never! ...
        Ah, you too, Vanity!
I knew you would overthrow me in the end—
No! I fight on! I fight on! I fight on!
        [*He swings the blade in great circles, then pauses,
        gasping. When he speaks again, it is in another
        tone.*]
Yes, all my laurels you have riven away
And all my roses; yet in spite of you,

There is one crown I bear away with me,
And to-night, when I enter before God,
My salute shall sweep all the stars away
From the blue threshold! One thing without
  stain,
Unspotted from the world, in spite of doom
Mine own!—

> [*He springs forward, his sword aloft*]
>> And that is . . .

> [*The sword escapes from his hand; he totters,*

and falls into the arms of **Le Bret** *and* **Ragueneau.**]

Roxane:

> [*Bends over him and kisses him on the forehead.*]
>> —That is . . .

Cyrano:

> [*Opens his eyes and smiles up at her.*]
>> My white plume. . . .

CURTAIN

Aristotle asserted that plot is the most important element in a play—that a play must first of all tell a good story before it can accomplish anything else. Plot, however, is not the only thing that a good play has to offer. Certainly *Cyrano de Bergerac* is full of "action" in the usual, everyday sense of the word. Sword fights, battles, love intrigues, and swashbuckling action of every sort fill the pages of the script and sweep the imagination up in a world so colorful, exciting and vivid that it is difficult to imagine any stage production ever capturing all of it within the walls of an ordinary brick-and-mortar theatre. But is it really a sense of "what happens next" that stirs the emotions and holds the audience's attention throughout the play? As far as the story alone is concerned, might it not be entirely possible to stop at the end of any of the five acts? Any play with even a mildly interesting plot will certainly raise some curiosity about what happens next, but compare this play with *The Little Foxes* and it becomes evident that the plot, in isolation, is not so neatly worked out; there are other factors in *Cyrano de Bergerac* that lift it above the ordinary.

What, then, may be said about thematic content? The nobility of Cyrano's spirit is an inspiration in itself. Even when he is involved in the elaborate subterfuge of wooing Roxane in Christian's name, one senses that it is undertaken in a spirit of love and self-sacrifice so noble as to be above reproach. Cyrano's complete honesty in his traffic with the world, his unwillingness to compromise with deceit and disloyalty, accompany him like his white plume to his death. A study of the symbolism in the play (although, again, as in *The Little Foxes*, it is hardly profound) will reveal some very serious ideas being raised by the playwright. Cyrano's white plume may be said to symbolize his honesty and integrity—his soul that may not be compromised—and the use of this symbolism gives the playwright a convenient shorthand for reminding the audience, in the very last words spoken on the stage, of the play's meaning:

"Yes, all my laurels you have riven away
  And all my roses; yet in spite of you,
  There is one crown I bear away with me,
  And to-night, when I enter before God,
  My salute shall sweep all the stars away
  From the blue threshold! One thing without stain,
  Unspotted from the world, in spite of doom
  Mine own!—And that is . . .
  —That is . . .
  My white plume . . ."

A Discussion of the Script

Cyrano's nose is the one blemish on an otherwise virtually perfect and upright man—the one blemish which he allows to become so all-consuming, so dominant in his life, that his happiness is ruined. It is a strange fact of human nature that most people see in themselves one or more blemishes of this kind; no matter who they are or what kind of lives they lead, each sees within himself some kind of terrible shortcoming that prevents him from being the person he would like to be. Rostand in *Cyrano de Bergerac* speaks of such problems in human lives, and of the nobility and beauty that one can also find if he will only look. In a cynical age, sentiments of this kind may be considered mawkish, but in the context of this play which sweeps the audience along in romantic excitement, some fundamental facts of human nature can be revealed. Despite all of this, thematic content is not the primary value of the play. All that is said has often been said before, and in situations where the impact could be far more profound and thought-provoking. Throughout most of the play, thematic content is even less strongly insisted upon than it was in *The Little Foxes.* One must look elsewhere for its principal strength.

The play's language is certainly one of its stronger features. Here one must hesitate, for of course it was orginally written in French, and the translation of drama is one of the most notoriously difficult tasks in literature. To translate so as to capture not only the sense of what the playwright originally intended, but also the rhythm and beauty of spoken dialogue; at the same time to capture the subtle shades, nuances, and multiple connotations of which any major language is capable, and to make the result such that an actor can speak it on the stage, is an undertaking so complex that rarely in the world's history has it been accomplished to anything like the satisfaction of the artists involved. When poetry is involved as well, the problems are multiplied many-fold. Shakespeare, for example, has never been translated into French in such a manner that French theatregoers can fully appreciate him, whereas he has been translated into German so effectively as to make him almost a German playwright. Racine and Corneille, the masters of French tragedy, have never been rendered in English with anything like full satisfaction. In the case of *Cyrano de Bergerac,* however, the Brian Hooker translation of the play captures much of of the beauty and grandeur of the French original. Some of the sections of love poetry, as well as certain of Cyrano's longer speeches, are so magnificient they can enthrall an audience when performed well by the actor. The very sound of some of the lines is so effective as to create in the spectator much of the same excitement that the content of the scene itself is trying to generate. Nevertheless, fine though the language is in many passages, it would hardly be accurate to describe it as the strongest element in the play. The poetry although stirring is hardly the enduring work of art of a Shakespeare. Some of it actually gets rather tedious, and if it were not for the excitement of the action and the colorful characters, the language alone would be hard put to it to sustain an audience's interest.

The outstanding factor that lifts *Cyrano de Bergerac* above other swashbuckling, romantic plays is the characterization of Cyrano himself. Cyrano is an endlessly fascinating individual, who lives on in one's memory long after he has laid down the script or left the theatre. Cyrano has provided an opportunity for several great actors to develop characterizations so multifaceted that they seemed to grow and develop endlessly as the performances continued. Unlike the Hubbards, who, although "real" enough in the imagination, are actually rather two-dimensional and oversimplified, Cyrano becomes, through the course of the play, like a close friend or relative whom one has known and loved for years. (Of course, during a good performance, the relationship is even closer than this, for through empathy one actually enters vicariously into the characterization and himself becomes Cyrano.) One learns to "understand" Cyrano, to love him not in spite of his weaknesses but because of them, to know how he will react in a given situation and then to enjoy watching him react. And yet, like a friend in real life, he never becomes so predictable that he is a "penny-in-the-slot hero": one is continually discovering new facets of his character, finding new unsuspected depths. Just as most people like to develop relationships of this sort in real life, they also like to get to know such well-rounded characters in drama. Good character development is a tremendous challenge to a playwright, and occasionally it is possible for the characterization to be so effective as to carry the weight of the script. So it is with *Cyrâno de Bergerac.*

The playwright has only a limited number of ways to create effective characterization. The novelist, for instance, can simply describe in minute detail the personality of a character, and, if his command of language is adequate to the task, tell everything one needs to know about him; the playwright, however, has available to him only what the character says, what he does, and what other characters say about him. "What other characters say about him" might appear to be the easiest of the three; but since the character who is speaking may be lying, and even if he is honest and upright, he may not be fully perceptive, his judgment may not be accurate. Thus, the playwright has to fall back finally on what the character says and what he does to characterize him, and an audience will judge the character on much the same basis that they use for judging those they meet in real life. Within the plot line that he establishes for his play, the playwright must find things for his characters to say and do that will reveal to an audience, in perhaps two hours, what they might learn over a period of years if they knew the characters in real life. No wonder playwrights find this extremely difficult, and that their general practice, as in *The Little Foxes,* is to develop their characters only so far as may be necessary to make the action clear. However, characterization, when it is brilliantly handled, lifts a play so far above the ordinary that some critics have proclaimed character rather than plot development the most important element in drama.

The playwright has another factor aiding him in the development of his characters—he is not working alone. Whatever he provides in the way of dialogue and action will be greatly augmented by the work of the playwright's colleague, the interpretive artist, the actor. Whereas the novelist is obliged to provide his reader with everything that he is to know about a character, the playwright has only to provide an outline—the actor will fill in the rest and turn that outline into a fully developed three-dimensional human being. Of course, the more the playwright provides, the more the actor has to work with, but the fact remains that the two artists are working in collaboration (along with the director) to see that the character is fully and properly developed within the context of the play. No novelist can afford to stop and describe in minute detail the exact tone and nuance of every line spoken or the precise play of emotions made evident by the reaction of each hearer, but *all* of these factors are available to the audience enjoying a good production. Often the most telling factor in terms of understanding a character is not what the character says but how he reacts to what someone else is saying; this is entirely available to a theatre audience. The opportunity to witness a character in the process of doing things is what makes the theatre uniquely exciting and character development devastatingly effective.

The playwright has another factor working in his favor. In a novel the author *must* provide at least enough characterization to keep the personages of the story straight. In the theatre every role is played by a living, breathing actor, and (assuming that the actors are reasonably competent) the audience has no trouble whatsoever in distinguishing them. Each character has at least a few distinguishing features, and the playwright develops these characteristics as far as he may wish or as his talent may allow. For instance, consider the other characters in *Cyrano de Bergerac*. As you read the play, did you have trouble keeping straight Le Bret, Lignière, Cuigy, Brissaille, and so forth? Their names may seem strange and difficult to those who do not speak French, and there is little in the script to distinguish them, but in a good production this problem would not arise. The skill of the actors plus good costumes and makeup should at the very least distinguish them as individuals to the extent that one would not be confused for another.

To say all of this, however, is still not to explain why the playwright could not have gone further himself and breathed more real life and individuality into these supporting characters. It may be argued that Rostand's play as it stands is moving and impressive, and more elaborate development of the minor characters is not needed. They serve their functions as they are; if they were more complex, they might remove some of the interest from Cyrano himself, and this would defeat the central purpose of the play. By leaving the other characters two-dimensional and undeveloped, Rostand made Cyrano appear even more interesting and exciting by contrast, and the development of Cyrano was his primary aim.

It should be noted, then, that what is called "two-dimensional" character development is not necessarily a fault. When a character is "two-dimensional," he is a cardboard figure, exhibiting two or three principal characteristics which are indispensable to the plot and that is all. Le Bret is simply Cyrano's loyal friend; beyond that, virtually nothing is provided to distinguish him. Contrasting with "two-dimensional" characters are "three-dimensional" or "well-rounded" characters, whose psychology and motivations are deeply explored. Such characters respond to so complex a series of motivations that they continually offer fresh insights and surprising behavior. They are psychologically consistent and yet humanly inconsistent in a manner that repeatedly renews one's understanding of the character in question and of human nature in general. Cyrano, of course, is the outstanding example of the fully three-dimensional character in the two plays read so far. If a playwright decides to make use of a number of two-dimensional characters, he also has at his disposal the use of what are called "stock types." These are the characters who are used so widely in prose fiction that very little development is needed; their characteristics are already widely known, and thus some of the playwright's work is done for him. Good examples of stock types might be the hero in the typical detective story or the "saloon hostess with the heart of gold" in a western movie. One only needs to see these characters to know a great deal about them simply by certain theatrical conventions that audiences have come to accept. Certainly Christian in *Cyrano de Bergerac* belongs to this category, as well, for the playwright supplies few details about him nor does he need to—one knows exactly what to expect. Roxane is a similar case, with perhaps a slight degree of three-dimensional development as she begins to learn that a pretty face and pretty words are less important than the soul behind them. One admires the playwright who goes deeply into the development of his characters but one cannot deny that in such a play as *Cyrano de Bergerac* the two-dimensional approach provides all that is needed to make the play both exciting and effective. Generally, characters in most good plays lie somewhere between the extremes; few are so fully developed as Cyrano but most have some degree of interest and depth. A talented playwright finds that he can, without detracting from his central purpose, breathe life and color into each of his characters by a few master strokes of action or reaction.

Although characterization is the most important element in *Cyrano de Bergerac,* it is still necessary to analyze the plot structure in some detail. This play, as is the case in most plays, depends on a good plot (even if plot is not the *primary* feature), and a careful analysis of the plot can tell a great deal about what the playwright is trying to accomplish. It is a wise procedure in approaching a structural analysis of any play to look first for a central action. One might be tempted to delineate the central action of this play in terms of the *playwright's purpose:* "to develop the character of Cyrano." This would be a mistake, however; the central action is something that one or more characters *within the play* are trying to accomplish. Therefore, the most accurate definition of the central action would be, "to win the love of Roxane." Virtually the whole first act passes before this action gets underway, and the last act verges on the anticlimactic in view of the fact that Christian's death seals forever any possibility of Cyrano declaring his love to Roxane. However, no other phrasing seems to sum up what is happening throughout the play. "To win the love of Roxane," is, indeed, the motivating force of the play, but the playwright has elected to structure loosely the series of events making up this action, fitting them together into more of a montage than a straight line of development. The order of these events could actually be switched around without seriously altering the meanings inherent in the play. In *The Little Foxes,* each event necessarily has to follow the preceding one in a tightly controlled, logical order building to a resolution of the central action; in *Cyrano de Bergerac,* the outcome of the central action is clear from the start—the play would be quite unsatisfactory if, at any point, Cyrano were to win or lose once and for all. Cyrano can never win the love of Roxane in the usual sense of marrying her and living happily ever after; this is clear from the beginning. What does happen, however, is that as Cyrano tries throughout the play to accomplish his central purpose (and one must understand, of course, that when he is trying to win her for Christian he still feels that he is coming as close as he dares to winning her for himself), the playwright is able to examine his central action in a variety of different lights, to explore the true meaning of self-sacrificing love, and to shape the character of Cyrano. One would attempt in vain to find an inciting incident, rising action, turning point, falling action, and climax. Try to do so, and one is left with disjointed incidents, a "climax" which occurs before the last act begins, and many other confusions. Either Rostand structured his plot poorly, or he had no intention of fitting his plot development into this kind of preconceived formula. It may, indeed, have been "preconceived," but it could not be anything resembling the well-made play.

The structural plan that Rostand uses is unusual. It does not follow any formula for playwriting, and thus the various parts have not been named and numbered as they have for the well-made play. Western dramatic literature offers perhaps half a dozen major structural patterns of which the well-made play is one; but it also offers a number of plays which must be accepted on their own terms and not expected to fit any of the major patterns. It would be pointless here to go through the entire play as with *The Little Foxes* discussing how each incident fits into the over-all pattern. Because the plot is loosely structured, and each group of incidents presents a different aspect of the central action rather than advancing it step by step, the student can trace these relationships for himself. The major group of incidents in which Cyrano woos and wins Roxane for Christian stretches from the middle of the second act to the end of the third; Cyrano takes real satisfaction in feeling that he has won Roxane, even if someone else is to enjoy the fruits of his labor. The group of incidents comprising the fourth act shows another aspect of love: Cyrano, having won Roxane, seeks to deepen the love relationship. No doubt he takes satisfaction in this, but it is more an outgrowth of his Gascon pride—having once undertaken a project, he is satisfied with nothing less than the best. It is established in the last act that Cyrano has continued to be close to Roxane throughout the fifteen years following Christian's death. His love expresses itself in self-sacrifice, representing still another aspect of "winning Roxane's love for himself." However, he never intends her to learn that it was he (in the guise of Christian's soul) with whom she fell in love.

The use of long declamatory passages in *Cyrano de Bergerac* demands special mention, not only for their own sake but also because of the discussion thus opened up of similar features in other plays. Such a passage is obviously an opportunity for a pyrotechnic display of verbal skill on the part of the actor playing Cyrano, which does not further the plot at all. In French, such passages are called *tirades*, but the word does not carry the unpleasant connotation it does in English. It simply means a long passage given to an actor in a play; such passages are meant to be enjoyed by an audience much as the work of one leading instrument is intended to be enjoyed in a concerto. The actor does not drop out of character to deliver the speech, of course, but the audience is expected, nevertheless, to enjoy the sheer skill with which it is performed. A tirade gives the playwright the opportunity to stop his play and wax eloquent on any subject he wishes to emphasize. Cyrano's "nose" speech beginning on page 94 is a chance for the actor to give a virtuoso performance and it also gives the playwright an excellent opportunity to present a whole aspect of Cyrano's character, not previously revealed. Cyrano's ringing proclamation of his refusal to compromise his principles, beginning on page 113, also gives the playwright an opportunity to bring out some thematic concepts that are of great importance to the play. Shakespearean drama offers some supreme examples of similar passages known as *soliloquies*. Tirades and soliloquies are both long passages delivered by one actor; and they afford the actor the opportunity for a considerable display of skill; but soliloquies are far more introspective than tirades in nature and are usually delivered when the actor is alone on stage; thus they allow the playwright to reveal the innermost thoughts of the character speaking. It is an oversimplification to call them "thinking aloud," and yet this is certainly an important aspect of their function. Actual "thinking aloud" is represented by *asides*—lines addressed directly to the audience that reveal what a character does not propose to reveal to the other characters onstage. Asides are generally much shorter than soliloquies and do not contain displays of rhetorical skill or afford opportunities for exceptional displays of acting technique. Tirades, soliloquies, and asides, which are not dialogue in the ordinary sense of that word, are available to the playwright who wishes to stop the action and convey something directly to the audience. The presence of one or more of these techniques is a matter of the playwright's taste, the conventions of the theatre for which he is writing, and the style he has chosen for his play.

Cyrano's first entrance warrants some discussion because it represents a masterful solution to a problem that playwrights frequently face. Since the play centers around the character of Cyrano, Rostand cannot afford to have him simply walk in the door. His entrance must be prepared in such a way that when the audience finally sees him, the impact of his appearance will represent a climactic moment in the play. This is called "building" for an entrance, and may consist of no more than one character shouting, "Here he comes! Here he comes!! Here he is!" In the case of *Cyrano de Bergerac*, however, many pages of dialogue are devoted to building for Cyrano's entrance. The first few pages are not, strictly speaking, part of this build. The play commences with a magnificently constructed crowd scene, full of color, sweep, and excitement. A director should make this first scene a beautifully orchestrated introduction to the French theatre of 1640. Each character has a specific task and yet the actions of all fit together brilliantly to form the whole. Beginning on page 85, however, the introduction of Cyrano is specifically begun. The device is simple: there is one person present who does not know him and several who do. In this manner the playwright can present all the necessary information about him and suggest that he will be arriving shortly, and his arrival will be a momentous occasion. This requires a scant thirty-five lines of dialogue; it is another seventy-five lines before Cyrano's first words, and a great deal happens during this interval. However, Rostand finds plenty of opportunities to bring up Cyrano's name again and again, so that the audience is held in constant anticipation of his arrival. Finally, on page 90, Cyrano's first few lines are heard before he is actually seen, thus increasing the sense of excitement and anticipation. It is the duty of the director to be certain that when Cyrano finally enters, his first appearance is as exciting as possible, with the strongest possible movements and with every crowd member focusing his attention upon him. All of these factors working together let the audience know a great deal about the character even before he appears, and make sure that their full attention will be focused upon him when he does. It is the sort of device for which the playwright has frequent use, and Rostand's particular adaptation of it in this play exhibits unusual brilliance.

There is another fundamental difference between *The Little Foxes* and *Cyrano de Bergerac* that has not yet been defined. The plays tell different stories, set in different periods and places, with different characters and themes and using different types of language. These differences are created by the fundamental difference between the *approaches* of the two playwrights involved. This fundamental approach is what is known as the play's *style*. In *The Little Foxes*, the playwright's primary objective seems to be to make the audience accept the Hubbards as real people, in a real situation, really fighting among themselves for control of the mill. The characters are developed in such a way that one can accept them as real people; the details of the plot are worked out plausibly; everything conforms to the period in which the play is set; the dialogue follows the normal speaking patterns of people who find themselves in such situations—indeed, Miss Hellman's ultimate criterion must have been "how would this happen in real life?" This style is called *realism*, and since its development in the nineteenth-century, it has come to dominate much of the modern theatre. Practically every Hollywood movie, every television play and most Broadway plays are realistic in style. European theatre and movies, on the other hand, include a much wider variety of styles. The American theatre is so saturated with realism that many inexperienced playgoers have come to equate "realistic" with "good." Americans often fail to realize that realism is just one of a number of possible theatrical styles. An inexperienced playgoer may confuse realism with the fact that something in a play or an individual performance strikes a responsive chord within him, suggesting a truth or an insight into human nature. A variety of styles may cause such a sympathetic response.

Is *Cyrano de Bergerac* a realistic play? Its plot can hardly be described as realistic. Although the events *could* happen, they are highly unlikely—a hundred swordsmen against one, for example, are ridiculous odds, and surely a whole theatre full of people could prevent one from closing a show. How is it possible that Roxane could know Cyrano all these years and never suspect that his was the "soul" with which she fell in love? And a man who is dying from a fractured skull could not possibly be hopping around a convent garden fencing with shadows, no matter how strongly motivated. The language of the play is hardly realistic; people simply do not speak in iambic pentameter (or in alexandrine couplets, the verse form used in the original French); tirades are exciting in the theatre, but never, never occur in real life (one may blurt out a long speech, but it is never as well organized and presented as a tirade). In short Rostand's ultimate test of effectiveness was *not* "would it happen this way in real life?", but "what can I introduce that will be vigorous, exciting, romantic, and good theatre?" This style is called *romanticism.* Of course it must be *consistent* within its own set of ground rules, but generally romanticism is not fettered by what would happen in real life. An audience comes to a romatic play wanting to believe, and all that is required of the playwright is not to do anything that will jolt them out of this belief. As long as the excitement and the emotionalism can be maintained, almost anything can happen on stage and an audience will laugh with it, cry with it—in short, accept it. Of course they do not *literally* believe it, any more than they do in a realistic play (in both styles, everyone knows that these are really just actors playing parts), but they want to enter into the spirit of it, and so they do. A serious failing too common in the theatre today is forgetting that audiences come to the theatre because they *do* want to believe, and that they will accept almost any set of conventions, however unlikely, if they are honestly and consistently presented. Romanticism used to be very popular in the theatre, and can still be highly effective if well executed; realism is another style, neither superior nor inferior to romanticism. Other styles will be discussed in connection with the later plays in this volume.

Directing

Only in the last hundred years or so has the director attained the prominence he now holds in the theatre. Someone has always had to fulfill certain of the director's functions, and at various times in history the playwright himself has "directed" his own play, or a leading actor has made such decisions as were necessary to prepare a production for an audience. Only in relatively recent times has the idea developed that there should be a "chief interpretative artist" to oversee the production in order to assure its artistic unity as well as its organizational stability. One of the reasons that this has been so is that only in the last hundred years or so have there been important questions of style to be settled in preparing a production for the stage. Prior to that time, actors in any one era played in the same style and for much the same purpose because there was only one style in vogue at the time. Only in the modern era has the need been felt to produce plays in a wide variety of styles, both historical and artistic, with very different ends in view from one production to the next. Accompanying this great variety came the need for someone to make authoritative choices and to oversee the work of artists with backgrounds or experience in many different modes. Today, the work of the director is extremely important in preparing any production for the stage—usually second only to the work of the playwright, and, in some instances, even more crucial.

It is generally accepted that the work of the director, like that of other theatrical artists, must begin with the script; however, this may not always be the case. The director may begin by attempting to find out precisely what the playwright is trying to say and do with his script and then look for the best means to express this on the stage. It is also possible that he may begin with something he wishes to say by means of the stage, and then proceed to find a script which may be warped into saying it. As a variant of this latter possibility, a director may begin with a script and, disregarding the playwright's intentions, may impose upon it a production pattern which expresses his own ideas. In either of these latter cases, the director is setting himself up as a creative rather than an interpretive artist, and the fundamental relationship of the play to all those involved with it (including the audience) is grossly changed. Since there is no final arbiter who can determine that one of these approaches is right and the other wrong, one must assume that both approaches are legitimate; however, the discussion here will be confined to the attitude prevalent in this country, that the "proper" function of the director is to interpret the play as it was conceived by the playwright. This does not imply a slavish adherence to the historical details of the original production or even an adherence to every detail in the stage directions, but it does mean that the director must determine to his own satisfaction what are the essential values inherent in the script and decide how these values may best be realized in a production in his theatre and for his audience.

Assume, for example, that a director has decided to do a production of *Cyrano de Bergerac.* Even in selecting that script in the first place, the director has made an artistic decision, for he has to think in terms of how it will fit into the season of plays he contemplates, how effective a play it is likely to be in the eyes of the audience he expects to reach, whether he has actors and production facilities suitable to the demands of the play, and whether the play will have enough "box office appeal" to draw an audience in the first place. The Broadway theatre is altogether too dependent on immediate box office success to enjoy more than a small measure of artistic independence, but on the other hand, no theatre, however esoteric, or coterie can accomplish anything significant if *some* audience is not attracted to its productions. A beautiful painting can exist in a dark closet until someone finally comes along to admire it; but a production of a play exists for a limited time only and relative to a specific potential audience. If that audience does not materialize, the production might as well not exist. Assuming, however, that the director has decided that a production of *Cyrano de Bergerac* will meet all of the above criteria, he must begin to think in terms of a specific production style and plan. Presumably a production could be created in which Cyrano was a representative of the downtrodden working class, crushed by the forces of bloated capitalism; the play would become an economic and social tract expressive of a theme the director wished to present. Analysis of the script, however, reveals that this would be an absurd distortion of the playwright's intentions; clearly, Rostand wished to concentrate on romantic adventures in which the character of Cyrano has primary importance. It might be possible to update the script, making Cyrano a young officer in the Confederate army and the whole play a nostalgic evocation of the chivalry in the Old South. Such a transformation might relate to a twentieth-century American audience much as the original related to Rostand's French audience. These examples are a bit absurd, as *Cyrano de Bergerac* is an easy enough play to understand in its own idiom without any such translation, but this is the sort of thinking that can be done in very serious fashion about a number of plays. Most directors would probably elect to perform *Cyrano de Bergerac* in the swashbuckling, romantic style for which it was clearly written, and to select costumes, properties, settings, and so on which are appropriate to the middle of the seventeenth century.

The director, then, must make necessary decisions about style and approach to the play. After that, he must take over-all responsibility for seeing that the settings, the lights, the costumes, and all the other technical elements of production are in keeping with his approach, but since most directors will have working with them a staff of individuals to whom will be delegated authority for each of these functions (final artistic decisions remaining in the hands of the director, of course), it is appropriate to deal with each of these areas separately.

Whether the director is in a professional theatre where he employs any actor he can get (or can afford), or in an amateur theatre where he must depend upon volunteers, the director's basic casting problem is to select from among those actors available to him the ones best suited for the roles in the play. The criteria that he will apply vary widely but often have little to do with the physical descriptions of characters offered by playwrights. Ben, in *The Little Foxes,* is described as a large man, but there is no fundamental reason why he could not be played by a small actor if he could capture the right character qualities of Ben better than any other actor available. Cyrano's large nose is, of course, created by makeup, and beyond that the only physical requirement is that the audience believe he is a fighter. Roxane must be beautiful, but costumes and makeup can do a great deal here, and, as long as she is not obviously overweight and over forty, it makes very little difference whether she is tall or short, blonde or brunette, light or dark. What does matter, of course, is the physical appearance of the acting company together: Roxane cannot be five feet, ten inches if Cyrano is five feet, four inches, and Christian must be the handsomest man on the stage. What normally concerns a director far more than the physical appearance of his actors, is their ability to capture the right quality in the roles they seek to play and the right style for the production as a whole. An actor who is slow and stolid might perform brilliantly as Oscar in *The Little Foxes,* but would be wrong as Cyrano unless he could throw off the slowness and stolidness and appear light on his feet, nimble of tongue, and able to capture the gay romanticism that is so important to the play. Mannerisms, physical appearance in its broader sense, voice, intensity, and magnetism are important determinants for a director in casting his play. Beyond that, directors are anxious to know which actors work well together in ensemble efforts, have the most experience, seem to be the most intelligent, and so forth. It would be impossible to list here all of the factors that the director takes into account in casting his play, but many good directors insist that this is the most important function they perform—that the success or failure of the play is often decided at the point of casting.

As the director moves into the rehearsal period with his cast, he enters a time of hard work and frustration. Unlike the pianist, who can expect his piano to play whatever note he strikes, the director is dealing with human beings who may or may not respond in a predictable fashion when their keys are struck. The director must establish a personal relationship with each actor in order to elicit from him the very best of which he is capable, and for most directors this means a different relationship with each actor involved. A few directors achieve notable success by imposing a preconceived pattern on each actor, treating him like an automaton; but most directors find that they must search for the right devices by which to draw out of the actor the best that lies within him, and there is a great deal of trial and error in this process. The actor, who presumably is a conscientious artist in his own right, usually wishes to understand why he is doing something rather than follow orders. A creative artistic partnership in which the actor brings his own talent and insight to bear on his role is advantageous to the director as well.

In addition to all of these variables with which the director must work, he has several fundamental elements that he must keep in some kind of balance as he plans the progress of his show. It is primarily the director's responsibility to see to it that the meanings inherent in single lines, in discrete scenes, and in the play as a whole are effectively translated into visual images. It is not enough, for example, for Cyrano simply to declaim his famous nose speech; he must work out a series of gestures, movements, or use of properties so that each separate insult is vividly pictured for the audience; and make it clear, at the same time, that he is insulting the intelligence

José Quintero in directing a scene aids the actors to bring out of themselves the inner beauty of the lines and situation. Photograph: Martha Swope.

of the Vicomte de Valvert. The language alone, however effective it may be, cannot accomplish this without the aid of visual images, and these are the primary concern of the director. The entire scene at the beginning of *Cyrano de Bergerac* is a build to the entrance of Cyrano. The director must make this clear not only in the lines but also in the stage movement. Since the play centers around Cyrano, the director may translate this directly into stage metaphor by keeping Cyrano literally in the center of the action most of the time.

The second of the fundamental elements with which the director must cope is movement. No better example of this can be offered than the opening scene of *Cyrano de Bergerac* in which the audience swirls into the theatre in constant and colorful movement which can, if well designed and executed, delight the senses and advance the play. The movement of each actor must be virtually choreographed in order to achieve an effective whole.

The third fundamental element is called "composition." The director who works in a proscenium theatre, especially, will be constantly conscious of the stage picture he is creating within the frame of the proscenium arch. Such esthetic concepts as balance, order, proportion, and harmony enter into the composition of this continually changing stage picture, and the alert director will make sure that the picture is always appropriate and often outstanding as key points need reinforcement. Adjustments of the stage picture can change the focus to different points on the stage, reinforce moods, and express metaphorically the progress of a key character. Sometimes deliberate imbalance or disharmony is sought in order to make a necessary point, but some sort of stage picture is necessarily present at all times, and the alert director will use it to advantage.

Finally among the fundamental elements controlled by the director is the ever-changing relationship of rhythm and pace. The pace of a scene is its *apparent* speed, its rush of movement toward a conclusion. This is usually achieved more by the way the actor "picks up his cues," beginning to speak or move precisely on the moment his cue comes, than by any rushing within lines, but there are many apparently minor adjustments that a director can make to give a scene a sense of fast or slow pace. Generally, a lightly comic scene like Ragueneau's distress at finding his poems turned into paper bags will call for a rapid pace, while Cyrano's death scene is usually played at a far slower pace. There are however infinite variations within single scenes, and a headlong pace can often be effectively broken by a dead stop, as when Christian first deliberately insults Cyrano's nose in the bakery scene. Rhythm, as differentiated from pace, is the over-all beat of the show; and, although it is usually irregular, it must be carefully planned in order to achieve the desired effect. The over-all rhythm of *Cyrano de Bergerac* is like that of romantic music: gay, emotional, and quixotic, whereas the rhythm of a tragedy might be slow and steady at the first but build like a pulse-beat to an awesome climax. Rhythm and pace, therefore, are entirely in the hands of the director, who manipulates them as he does all of the theatrical devices at his command in order to achieve the effect he desires.

In the early stages of rehearsal, a director will "block" his play; that is, he will show the actors the broad movement patterns he has in mind: where they enter and exit, where they cross and on what cue. Most directors will allow actors to experiment with various alternatives within this broad pattern at least during the early rehearsal period. In the early stages of rehearsal, the director will be working with actors, individually, and with groups of actors to discuss character development, to settle questions of interpretation of the script, and to determine the best reading of each line. (It is customary in the theatre to speak of the manner in which a line is "read" even though the actor in fact memorizes it and tries to speak it naturally). All of these details are worked out in accordance with the specific approach to the play that the director has chosen, utilizing such combinations of visualization, movement, composition, rhythm, and pace as he may feel are required. If there were only one "right" approach to a play, the actors would have only to learn what that approach was and proceed to make it; the director would have relatively little to do. If, as in *Cyrano de Bergerac*, however, the director wishes to adopt a florid, romantic style, emphasizing certain aspects of Cyrano's character, it will be necessary for him to tell his actors directly what he is attempting, and also make many decisions on his own concerning matters of detail in the course of his several weeks of rehearsal.

As the play moves into the later stages of rehearsal, the director's function changes gradually. During performance, a director is absolutely useless, and many will not even set foot in the theatre except to watch the show as a member of the audience. Looking ahead to opening night, then, the director during the late stages of rehearsal will begin to withdraw himself more and more from direct contact with the performance. He will gradually transfer authority for starting, stopping, and keeping the show moving smoothly to his stage manager, and he will interrupt his actors less and less frequently. The actors must begin to think in larger and larger units, not just concentrating on their next lines, but on the way whole scenes and acts are playing. The director will want to make final adjustments in rhythm and pace, and he can do so only when whole scenes are playing uninterruptedly. Actors cannot really set the pace of a scene when a rehearsal is repeatedly stopped for forgotten lines, changes in business, or other adjustments; so only in later stages of rehearsal can these important matters be worked out. This final process is called "polishing" and many promising productions have been ruined by lack of polish. An experienced director knows that, whether the actors have or have not achieved exactly the approach desired, a time comes in the rehearsal period when whatever is there must be polished. Most theatre managements regard any postponement of opening night as a violation of the unwritten code, "the show must go on," and so the director is faced with the necessity of having his production ready by a certain night, regardless of its condition and whether or not everything he had wanted has been achieved. Some directors, frustrated by this pressure, have worked with their casts on fundamental matters right up to opening night, only to discover to their chagrin that the show is unsatisfactory through lack of polish. On the other hand, many otherwise mediocre shows have turned out quite satisfactorily because of the imposition of a good, swift pace and an artful polishing of details by a wise director during the last days of rehearsal. Especially in amateur theatre, one learns that a heavy dose of youthful energy and enthusiasm can cover a multitude of sins and give an audience a thoroughly enjoyable evening in the theatre.

On opening night, the director finally has the opportunity to sit in the back of the theatre and view what he has wrought. Until an audience is present, he has only his experience and good taste to guide him in his decisions. When the final theatrical ingredient, the audience, is added, the director can begin at last to tell whether his production is successful. Of course, thunderous applause is not the only measure of success; sometimes an audience may be confused and irritated and yet forced to think about certain issues, and this may be precisely the desired result. As has been pointed out earlier, the audience is a vital part of the theatrical experience and has an active role to play. Unless there is, in the last analysis, genuine communication with that audience, the play has in some sense been a failure. Some directors, recognizing this, choose only scripts that are written on the comic-strip level, but others, rising to the challenge, try to work with better plays and make them communicate with the available audience. When they make this contact, a genuine artistic success has been achieved.

In outlining briefly the work of the director, only passing reference has been made to many areas that are, in fact, extremely complex. The director's function as critic, for example, is in many ways the most important; he must study the script in detail, coming to understand the plot structure, characterization, thematic structure, and use of language. He must know so much about the play that he might almost have been looking over the playwright's shoulder as he wrote it. (Indeed, in the case of a previously unproduced play, the director may in fact work closely with the playwright, even suggesting major revisions of the script.) Only after this kind of thorough analysis can the director make intelligent decisions about production style and approach. The director must understand every character with a thoroughness that will allow him to work closely with each actor. The director must work out every technical detail to insure that every light cue, property, and bit of costume fits meaningfully into the over-all framework which he has established for the play. The director must understand all aspects of the theatre, and is totally responsible for all of them in his production.

Archibald MacLeish has made outstanding contributions to American life and letters throughout a long and productive career; probably the chief of these contributions is in the field of poetry. His occasional excursions into playwriting have not, except in the case of *J. B.*, been marked with great distinction, but *J. B.* has engendered reactions ranging from peremptory dismissal to John Ciardi's assertion that "we now have a great American poetic drama." The author whose work has occasioned all this stir was born in Glencoe, Illinois, on May 7, 1892. His father was a partner in a Chicago department store. After beginning his education in the Glencoe public schools, MacLeish was sent to the Hotchkiss School in Connecticut and then to Yale, where he received his B.A. in 1915 and was elected to membership in Phi Beta Kappa. He went on to the Harvard Law School, where he graduated at the top of his class in 1919. His progress toward this degree was interrupted by service in the Army during World War I, where he rose from private to captain before his discharge.

After practicing law in Boston for three years, MacLeish decided to devote his full time to travel and writing; several years of writing ensued, and he published a long poem (*Conquistador*) in 1932 which won him his first Pulitizer Prize. His reputation established, MacLeish continued to publish a variety of material (including, in 1936, an unsuccessful verse play entitled *Panic*) until the years of World War II. He held a variety of government posts during these years. He served as Librarian of Congress from 1939 to 1944 and Assistant Secretary of State from 1944 to 1945. He was active in founding the United Nations Educational, Scientific, and Cultural Organization (UNESCO). He joined the Harvard faculty in 1949, where he remained until his retirement in 1962. His *Collected Poems, 1917–1952*, won him his second Pulitizer Prize, and *J. B.*, published in 1958, won him a third. Another verse play, *Herakles*, published in 1967, has not been notably successful. He married the former Ada Hitchcock in 1916, and they have had four children.

MacLeish first published the Prologue of *J. B.* in the September 1, 1956, issue of *The Saturday Review*. The rest of the play was in progress at that time, and the editors of *The Saturday Review* were already hailing it as "what may well become one of the lasting achievements of art and mind in our

J. B.
by Archibald
MacLeish

time." The full text of the play was published in 1958, and its first production was undertaken at Yale University in the spring of that year. The playwright worked actively with this production, revising his script slightly, and the event attracted widespread attention and discussion. The entire performance was taken to the World's Fair in Brussels that summer. The first full-scale professional production opened on Broadway on December 11, 1958, following out-of-town tryouts. Elia Kazan directed, and he and MacLeish agreed on extensive script revisions prior to this opening. After the play had been running nearly six months on Broadway, MacLeish again revised the last scene; thus a number of different versions of the play have been seen. The plot was little changed by all these revisions, but the thematic emphasis was notably altered, as will be pointed out later.

From its first publication, *J. B.* has attracted a storm of discussion among critics, theologians, and the general public. Some literary critics argue that it is great poetry, others insist that it is flat. Some theatre critics find it moving and important drama, others contend that they were bored. Some theologians find fault with the play for sticking too closely to the *Book of Job*, others for not sticking closely enough. The general public has made the play a hit, both in a highly successful Broadway run and in professional and amateur productions across the country; but a few critics insist that this public reaction was more dilettantism than genuine understanding or appreciation of the play's content. These various reactions can be traced in part to changes in the script, effected during its several revisions; the different emphases given the play by a variety of directors may account for others. No one has denied, however, that MacLeish had great aspirations: at a time when most American theatre was mindless entertainment, MacLeish attempted to write serious, elevated, poetic drama. His success can only be determined, perhaps, by the way the play withstands the test of time.

Opposite: Raymond Massey (Mr. Zuss) and Christopher Plummer (Nickles) prepare to don masks of God and Satan in the Alfred de Liagre, Jr. production of *J.B.* at the ANTA Theatre, New York, 1959. Directed by Elia Kazan; set by Boris Aronson; lighting by Theron Musser, costumes by Lucinda Ballard. Photograph: Friedman-Ables.

Page 185: Pat Hingle as J.B. (kneeling) seeks comfort from his friends Bildad (Bert Conway), Eliphaz (Andreas Vontsinas), and Zophar (Ivor Francis) in the same production of *J.B.* Photograph: Friedman-Ables.

J.B.

J.B.

A Play in Verse by
ARCHIBALD MacLEISH

Zuss	*First Messenger*
Nickles	*Second Messenger*
Distant Voice	*Girl*
Sarah	*Mrs. Adams*
J. B.	*Jolly Adams*
Rebecca	*Mrs. Lesure*
Ruth	*Mrs. Murphy*
David	*Mrs. Botticelli*
Mary	*Bildad*
Jonathan	*Zophar*
2 Maids	*Eliphaz*

The scene throughout is a corner inside an enormous circus tent where a side show of some kind has been set up. There is a rough stage across the corner, on the left of which a wooden platform has been built at a height of six or seven feet. A wooden ladder leans against it. To the right is a deal table with seven straight chairs. There is a door-shaped opening in the canvas to the right rear. Above, a huge, slanted pole thrusts the canvas out and up to make the peak of the corner. Clothes that have the look of vestments of many churches and times have been left about at one side and the other of the stage and the light at the beginning—such light as there is—is provided by bulbs dangling from hanks of wire. The feel is of a public place at late night, the audience gone, no one about but maybe a stagehand somewhere cleaning up, fooling with the lights.

THE PROLOGUE

Mr. Zuss, followed by **Nickles,** enters from the dimness off to the left. They stop at the edge of the side-show stage. Both wear the white caps and jackets of circus vendors. Both are old. **Mr. Zuss,** who has a bunch of balloons hitched to his belt, is large, florid, deep-voiced, dignified, imposing. **Nickles** is gaunt and sardonic; he has a popcorn tray slung from straps across his shoulders. Both betray in carriage and speech

the broken-down actor fallen on evil days but nevertheless and always actor. Throughout the Prologue, from the moment when they mount the side-show stage, they jockey for position, gesture, work themselves up into theatrical flights and rhetorical emotions, play to each other as though they had an actual audience before them in the empty dark.

Mr. Zuss: This is it.

Nickles: This is what?

Mr. Zuss: Where they play the play, Horatio!

Nickles: Bare stage?

Mr. Zuss: Not in the least.
Heaven and earth. That platform's Heaven.
            [*They step up onto the stage together.*]

Nickles: Looks like Heaven!

Mr. Zuss: As you remember it?

Nickles: Somebody's got to. You weren't there.
They never sold balloons in Heaven—
Not in my time.

Mr. Zuss: Only popcorn.
            [**Nickles** *shrugs a shudder of disgust, heaving his tray.*]

Nickles: The two best actors in America
Selling breath in bags . . .

Mr. Zuss: and bags
To butter breath with . . .

Nickles: when they sell.

Mr. Zuss: Merchandise not moving, Nickles?

Nickles: Moves wherever I do—all of it.
No rush to buy your worlds, I notice.

Mr. Zuss: I could sell one to a . . .

Nickles: . . . child!
You told me. Where's the earth?

Mr. Zuss: Earth?
Earth is where that table is:
That's where Job sits—at the table.
God and Satan lean above.
            [**Mr. Zuss** *peers anxiously up into the canvas sky*]
I wonder if we'd better?

Nickles: What?

Mr. Zuss: Play it.

Nickles:
Why not? Who cares? *They* don't.

Mr. Zuss: At least we're actors. They're not actors.

Never acted anything.

Nickles: That's right.
They only own the show.

Mr. Zuss: I wonder . . .

Nickles: They won't care and they won't know.
            [*His eyes follow* **Mr. Zuss's** *up to the dangling bulbs*]
Those stars that stare their stares at me—
Are those the staring stars I see
Or only lights . . .
                  not meant for me?

Mr. Zuss: What's that got to do with anything?

Nickles: Very little. Shall we start?

Mr. Zuss: You think we ought to?

Nickles: They won't care.

Mr. Zuss: Let's start . . .
            What staring stars?

Nickles: They aren't.
They're only lights. Not meant.

Mr. Zuss: Why don't we
Start?

Nickles: You'll play the part of . . .

Mr. Zuss: Naturally!

Nickles: Naturally! And your mask?

Mr. Zuss: Mask!

Nickles: Mask. Naturally. You wouldn't play God in your
Face would you?

Mr. Zuss: What's the matter with it?

Nickles: God the Creator of the Universe?
God who hung the world in time?
You wouldn't hang the world in time
With a two-days' beard on your chin or a pinky!
Lay its measure! Stretch the line on it!
            [**Mr. Zuss** *stares coldly at* **Nickles,** *unhitches his balloon belt with magnificent deliberation, drops it, steps forward to the front of the wooden stage, strikes an attitude.*]

Mr. Zuss: *Whatsoever is under the whole
            Heaven is mine!*

Nickles: That's what I mean.
You need a mask.

Mr. Zuss: [*Heavy irony*]   Perhaps a more
Accomplished actor . . .

Nickles: Kiss your accomplishments!
Nobody doubts your accomplishments—none of them—
The one man for God in the theater!

They'd all say that. Our ablest actor.
Nobody else for the part, they'd say.
Mr. Zuss: You make me humble.
Nickles: No! I'm serious.
The part was written for you.
Mr. Zuss: [*Gesture of protest*]   Oh!
Nickles: But this is God in *Job* you're playing:
God the Maker: God Himself!
Remember what He says?—the hawk
Flies by His wisdom! And the goats—
Remember the goats? He challenges Job with
them:
Dost thou know the time of the wild goats?
What human face knows time like that time?
You'd need a face of fur to know it.
Human faces know too much too little.
Mr. Zuss: [*Suspiciously*]
What kind of mask?
Nickles: You'll find one somewhere.
They never play without the masks.
Mr. Zuss: It's God the Father I play—not
God the boiling point of water!
Nickles: Nevertheless the mask is imperative.
If God should laugh
The mare would calf
The cow would foal:
Diddle my soul . . .
Mr. Zuss: [*Shocked*]
God never laughs! In the whole Bible!
Nickles: That's what I say. *We* do.
Mr. Zuss: I don't.
Nickles: *Job* does. He covers his mouth with
his hand.
Mr. Zuss: Job is abashed.
Nickles: He says he's abashed.
Mr. Zuss: He should be abashed: it's rank ir-
reverence—
Job there on the earth . . .
Nickles: On his dung heap . . .
Mr. Zuss: Challenging God!
Nickles: Crying to God.
Mr. Zuss: Demanding *justice* of *God!*
Nickles: Justice!
No wonder he laughs. It's ridiculous. All of
it.
God has killed his sons, his daughters,
Stolen his camels, oxen, sheep,
Everything he has and left him
Sick and stricken on a dung heap—

Not even the consciousness of crime to
comfort him—
The rags of reasons.
Mr. Zuss: God is reasons.
Nickles: For the hawks, yes. For the goats.
They're grateful.
Take their young away they'll sing
Or purr or moo or splash—whatever.
Not for Job though.
Mr. Zuss: And that's why.
Nickles: Why what?
Mr. Zuss: He suffers.
Nickles: Ah? Because he's . . .
Not a bird you mean?
Mr. Zuss: You're frivolous . . .
Nickles: That's precisely what you do mean!
The one thing God can't stomach is a man,
That scratcher at the cracked creation!
That eyeball squinting through into His Eye,
Blind with the sight of Sight!
[**Nickles** *tugs himself free of his tray*]
                    Blast this . . .
Mr. Zuss: God created the whole world.
Who is Job to . . .
Nickles: Agh! the world!
The dirty whirler! The toy top!
Mr. Zuss: [*Kicking savagely at the popcorn tray and
the balloon belt to shove them under the platform*]
What's so wrong with the world?
Nickles: Wrong with it!
Try to spin one on a dung heap!
[**Mr. Zuss** *does not answer. He goes on kicking
at the tray.* **Nickles** *sits on a rung of the ladder.
After a time he begins to sing to himself in a kind
of tuneless tune.*]
Nickles: I heard upon his dry dung heap
That man cry out who cannot sleep:
"If God is God He is not good,
If God is good He is not God;
Take the even, take the odd,
I would not sleep here if I could
Except for the little green leaves in the wood
And the wind on the water."
[*There is a long silence.*]
Mr. Zuss: You are a bitter man.
Nickles: [*Pompously*]   I taste of the world!
I've licked the stick that beat my brains out:
Stock that broke my father's bones!
Mr. Zuss: Our modern hero! Our Odysseus

Sailing sidewalks toward the turd
Of truth and touching it at last in triumph!
The honest, disillusioned man!
You sicken me.

Nickles: [*Hurt*]   All right, I sicken you.
No need to be offensive, is there?
If you would rather someone else . . .

Mr. Zuss: Did what?

Nickles: Played Job.

Mr. Zuss: What's Job to do with it?

Nickles: Job was honest. He saw God—
Saw him by that icy moonlight,
By that cold disclosing eye
That stares the color out and strews
Our lives . . . with light . . .for nothing.

Mr. Zuss: Job!
I never thought of you for Job.

Nickles: You never thought of me for Job!
What did you think of?

Mr. Zuss: Oh, there's always
Someone playing Job.

Nickles: There must be
Thousands! What's that got to do with it?
Thousands—not with camels either:
Millions and millions of mankind
Burned, crushed, broken, mutilated,
Slaughtered, and for what? For thinking!
For walking round the world in the wrong
Skin, the wrong-shaped noses, eyelids:
Sleeping the wrong night wrong city—
London, Dresden, Hiroshima.
There never could have been so many
Suffered more for less. But where do
I come in?
              [**Mr. Zuss** *shuffles uncomfortably.*]
                  Play the dung heap?

Mr. Zuss: All we have to do is start.
Job will join us. Job will be there.

Nickles: I know. I know. I know. I've seen him.
Job is everywhere we go,
His children dead, his work for nothing,
Counting his losses, scraping his boils,
Discussing himself with his friends and
  physicians,
Questioning everything—the times, the stars,
His own soul, God's providence.
What do *I* do?

Mr. Zuss: What do *you* do?

Nickles: What do I do? You play God.

Mr. Zuss: I play God. I think I mentioned it.

Nickles: You play God and I play . . .
      [*He lets himself down heavily on the rung of the
      ladder.*]
                                                  Ah!

Mr. Zuss: [*Embarrassed*]
I had assumed you knew.
            [**Nickles** *looks up at him, looks away.*]

Mr. Zuss: You see,
I think of you and me as . . . opposites.

Nickles: Nice of you.

Mr. Zuss: I didn't mean to be nasty.

Nickles: Your opposite! A demanding role!

Mr. Zuss: I know.

Nickles: But worthy of me? Worthy of me!

Mr. Zuss: I have offended you. I didn't mean
to.

Nickles: Did I say I was offended?
      [*There is an awkward silence.* **Nickles,** *his face
      in his hands, begins to hum the tune to his little
      song.* **Mr. Zuss** *looks up and around into the
      corners of the sky, his head moving cautiously.
      At length* **Nickles** *begins to sing the words.*]
I heard upon his dry dung heap
That man cry out who cannot sleep:
"If God is God He is not good,
If God is good He is not God;
Take the even, take the odd,
I would not sleep here if I could . . ."
      [*Silence.*]
So I play opposite to God!
      [*Silence.*]
Father of Lies they call me, don't they?
      [**Mr. Zuss** *does not answer. He is still searching
      the dark above. Silence.* **Nickles** *goes back to the
      song.*]
"I would not sleep here if I could
Except for the little green leaves in the wood
And the wind on the water."
      [*Silence. Then suddenly, theatrically,* **Nickles** *is
      on his feet*]
Who knows enough to know they're lies?
Show me the mask!

Mr. Zuss: What mask?

Nickles: [*Attitude*]   My mask!

Mr. Zuss: Are you sure you wear a mask?

Nickles: Meaning only God should wear one?

Mr. Zuss: Meaning are you sure it's there.

Nickles: *They* never play without them.

Mr. Zuss: Yes but
Where?

Nickles: Where? In Heaven probably:
Up on the platform there in Heaven!

Mr. Zuss: Yes . . . You wouldn't care to . . .

Nickles: What?

Mr. Zuss: Find it for yourself?

Nickles: In Heaven?
Heaven is your department, Garrick.

Mr. Zuss: My department! I suppose it is.
Here! Hold this! Hold it! Steady . . .
[**Nickles** *steadies the ladder.* **Mr. Zuss** *climbs
warily, keeping his eye on the canvas darkness;
heaves himself over the rail; rummages around
on the platform; turns, holding out a huge white,
blank, beautiful, expressionless mask with eyes
lidded like the eyes of the mask in Michelangelo's
Night.*]

Nickles: That's not mine—not *his.* It's His.
I've known that face before. I've seen it.
They find it under bark of marble
Deep within the rinds of stone:
God the Creator . . . [*Nastily*] of the ani-
mals!

Mr. Zuss: [*Outraged*]   God of
Everything that is or can!

Nickles: Is or can—but cannot know.

Mr. Zuss: There is nothing those closed eyes
Have not known and seen.

Nickles: Except
To know they see: to know they've seen it.
Lions and dolphins have such eyes.
They know the way the wild geese know—
Those pin-point travelers who go home
To Labradors they never meant to,
Unwinding the will of the world like string.
What would they make of a man, those
eyelids?

Mr. Zuss: Make of him! They *made* him.

Nickles: Made him
Animal like any other
Calculated for the boughs of
Trees and meant to chatter and be grateful!
But womb-worm wonders and grows wings—
[**Nickles** *breaks off, struck by his own words,
goes on*]:
It actually does! The cock-eyed things
Dream themselves into a buzz
And drown on windowpanes. He made them

Wingless but they learn to wish.
That's why He fumbles Job. Job wishes!—
Thinks there should be justice somewhere—
Beats his bones against the glass.
Justice! In this cesspool! Think of it!
Job knows better when it's over.

Mr. Zuss: Job knows justice when it's over.
Justice has a face like this.

Nickles: Like blinded eyes?

Mr. Zuss: Like skies.

Nickles: Of stone.
Show me the other.
[**Mr. Zuss** *ducks away, rummaging in the clutter
on the platform; turns again.*]

Mr. Zuss: You won't find it
Beautiful, you understand.

Nickles: I know that.
Beauty's the Creator's bait,
Not the Uncreator's: his
Is Nothing, the no-face of Nothing
Grinning with its not-there eyes.
Nothing at all! Nothing ever! . . .
Never to have been at all!
[**Mr. Zuss** *turns, lifts the second mask above*
Nickles' *gesturing. This is large as the first
but dark to the other's white, and open-eyed
where the other was lidded. The eyes, though
wrinkled with laughter, seem to stare and the
mouth is drawn down in agonized disgust.*]

Mr. Zuss: Well?
[**Nickles** *is silent.*]

Mr. Zuss: [*Cheerfully*]
                    That's it.
[*Silence.*]
                    You don't care for it?
It's not precisely the expression
Anyone would choose. I know that.
Evil is never very pretty:
Spitefulness either. Nevertheless it's
His—you'll grant that, won't you?—the tra-
ditional
Face we've always found for him anyway.
God knows where we go to find it:
Some subterranean memory probably.
[**Nickles** *has approached the ladder, staring. He
does not reply.*]
Well, if you won't you won't. It's your
Option. I can't say I blame you.
I wouldn't do it. Fit my face to

That! I'd scrub the skin off afterward!
Eyes to those eyes!
Nickles: [*Harshly*]   You needn't worry.
Your beaux yeux would never bear that
Look of . . .
Mr. Zuss: [*Smugly*]   No. I know.
Nickles: . . . of pity!
Let me have it.

[**Nickles** *starts up the ladder, the mask in* **Mr.**
Zuss's *hands above him.*]
                    Evil you call it!
Look at those lips: they've tasted something
Bitter as a broth of blood
And spat the sup out. Was that evil?

[*He climbs another rung.*]
Was it?

[*Another rung.*]
            Spitefulness you say:
You call that grin of anguish spite?

[*He pulls himself over the rail, takes the mask
in his hands.*]
I'd rather wear this look of loathing
Night after night than wear that other
Once—that cold complacence . . .

[**Mr. Zuss** *has picked up the first mask again,
lifts it.*]
Nickles: Horrible!
Horrible as a star above
A burning, murdered, broken city!
I'll play the part! . . .
                    Put your mask on! . . .
Give me the lines! . . .
Mr. Zuss: What lines?
Nickles: His!
Satan's!
Mr. Zuss: They're in the Bible aren't they?
Nickles: We're supposed to speak the Bible?
Mr. Zuss: *They do . . .*

[*The light bulbs fade out, yellow to red to gone.
A slow, strong glow spots the platform throwing
gigantic shadows up across the canvas. Back to
back the shadows of* **Mr. Zuss** *and* **Nickles**
*adjust their masks. The masked shadows turn
to each other and gravely bow. Their gestures
are the stiff formal gestures of pantomine. Their
voices, when they speak, are so magnified and
hollowed by the masks that they scarcely seem
their own.*]
Godmask: *Whence comest thou?*

Satanmask: *From going to and fro in the earth*

[*There is a snicker of suppressed laughter*]
And from walking up and down in it . . .

[*A great guffaw.* **Mr. Zuss** *tears off his mask.*]
Mr. Zuss: [*Shouting*]   Lights!

[*The spotlight fades out. The dangling bulbs come
feebly on.*]
Nobody told you to laugh like that.
What's so funny? It's irreverent. It's im-
pudent.
After all, you are talking to God.
That doesn't happen every Saturday
Even to kitchen kin like you.
Take that face off! It's indecent!
Makes me feel like scratching somewhere!

[**Nickles** *painfully removes his mask.*]
Nickles: Do I look as though I'd laughed?
If you had seen what I have seen
You'd never laugh again! . . .

[*He stares at his mask.*]
                    Weep either . . .
Mr. Zuss: You roared. I heard you.
Nickles: Those eyes *see.*
Mr. Zuss: Of course they see—beneath the
    trousers
Stalking up the pulpit stair:
Under the skirts at tea—wherever
Decent eyes would be ashamed to.
Why should you laugh at that?
Nickles: It isn't
That! It isn't that at all!
They see the *world.* They do. They see it.
From going to and fro in the earth,
From walking up and down, they see it.
I know what Hell is now—to *see.*
Consciousness of consciousness . . .
Mr. Zuss: Now
Listen! This is a simple scene.
I play God. You play Satan.
God is asking where you've been.
All you have to do is tell him:
Simple as that. "In the earth," you answer.
Nickles: [**Satan** *answers.*]
Mr. Zuss: All right—Satan.
What the difference?
Nickles: Satan *sees.*
He sees the parked car by the plane tree.
He sees behind the fusty door,
Beneath the rug, those almost children

Struggling on the awkward seat—
Every impossible delighted dream
She's ever had of loveliness, of wonder,
Spilled with her garters to the filthy floor.
Absurd despair! Ridiculous agony!

[*He looks at the mask in his hands.*]

What has any man to laugh at!
The panting crow by the dry tree
Drags dusty wings. God's mercy brings
The rains—but not to such as he.

Mr. Zuss: You play your part, I'll say that for you.
In it or out of it, you play.

Nickles: You really think I'm playing?

Mr. Zuss: Aren't you?
Somebody is. Satan maybe.
Maybe Satan's playing *you*.
Let's begin from the beginning.
Ready!

[*They take their places back to back.*]
                    Masks!

[*They raise their masks to their faces.*]
                                    Lights!

[*The bulbs go out. Darkness. Silence. In the silence*]:

A Distant Voice: *Whence comest thou?*

Mr. Zuss: That's my line.

Nickles: I didn't speak it.

Mr. Zuss: You did. Stop your mischief, won't you?

Nickles: Stop your own! Laughing. Shouting.

Mr. Zuss: Lights, I said!

[*The spotlight throws the enormous shadows on the canvas sky.*]

Godmask: *Whence comest thou?*

Satanmask: *From going to and fro in the earth . . .*
[*A choked silence*]
        And from walking up and down in it.

Godmask: *Hast thou considered my servant Job*
        That there is none like him on the earth
        A perfect and an upright man, one
        That feareth God and escheweth evil?

[*The platform lights sink, the masked shadows fading with them, as a strong light comes on below isolating the table where* **J.B.** *stands with his wife and children.*]

SCENE I

The Platform is in darkness, the Table in light.
J.B., a big, vigorous man in his middle or late thirties, stands at one end. At the other stands his wife, **Sarah,** a few years younger than her husband, a fine woman with a laughing, pretty face but a firm mouth and careful eyes, all New England. She is looking reprovingly but proudly at her five blond sons and daughters, who shift from foot to foot behind their chairs, laughing and nudging each other: **David,** 13; **Mary,** 12; **Jonathan,** 10; **Ruth,** 8; **Rebecca,** 6. Two buxom middle-aged **maids** in frilly aprons stand behind with their hands folded. The children subside under their mother's eyes.

Sarah: J.B. . . .

[*The heads bow.*]

J.B.:   Our Father which art in Heaven
Give us this day our daily bread.

Rebecca and **Ruth:** [*Pulling their chairs out, clattering into them*]
Amenamen.

The Older Children: [*Less haste but no less eagerness*]
                    Amen!

The Maids: [*Wheeling majestically but urgently to go out*]
                                Amen!

Sarah: [*To* **J.B.** *over the rattle of dishes and the clatter of talk as she sits down*]
That was short and sweet, my darling.

J.B.: [*Sitting down*]
What was?

Sarah: Grace was.

J.B.: [*Cheerfully*]   All the essentials.

Sarah: Give? Eat?

J.B.:   Besides they're hungry.

Sarah: That's what grace is for—the hunger.
Mouth and meat by grace amazed,
God upon my lips is praised.

J.B.: You think they stand in need of it—grace?
Look at them!

Sarah: [*Beaming*]   Yes! Look! Oh look!
[*The* **maids** *parade in with a huge turkey on a silver platter, china serving dishes with domed, blue covers, a gravy boat, a bottle of wine in a napkin.*]

Mary: Papá! Papá! He heard! He heard!

David: Who did?

Ruth: Ourfatherwhichartinheaven.

J.B.:   [*Nudging the bird gently with his finger*]
He did indeed. What a bird He sent us!
Cooked to a turn!

Ruth: He heard! He heard!

Jonathan: He heard! He heard! He sent a bird!

Sarah: That's enough now, children. Quiet!
Your father's counting.

J.B.:   Not today.
Not this gobbler. Feed a regiment.
Know what I was thinking, Sally?

Sarah: What?

J.B.:   How beautiful you are.

Sarah: With your eye on a turkey? I like that!

J.B.:   Why not? It's an eye-filling bird. Just look
at it.

Sarah: Someday you might look at *me*.

J.B.:   I'm always looking at you, Sarah.
[*He rises, knife and steel in hand, clashing them
against each other in a noble rhythm.*]
Everywhere I look I see you.

Sarah: [*Scornfully*]
You never even see my clothes.

J.B.:   [*A shout of laughter*]
It's true. I don't. But I see *you*.

Sarah: [*Mock indignation*]
J! B!

J.B.:   And what's wrong with the turkey?
What's wrong with that bottle of wine,
either—
Montrachet or I'll drink the whole of it!
What's wrong with the bird or the wine or
with anything—
The day either—what's wrong with the day?
[*He begins carving expertly and rapidly.*]
Tell me what day it is.

Jonathan: Turkey Day.

Mary: Cranberry Day.

Ruth: Succotash Day.

David: When we all can have white

Jonathan: And giblets to bite.

Ruth: And two kinds of pie.

Jonathan: And squash in your eye.

Mary: And mashed potatoes with puddles of
butter.

Jonathan: And gravy and such.

Rebecca: ... and ... and ...
[*The **children** are screaming with laughter.*]

Sarah: Children!

Jonathan: [*Gasping*] And all eat too much.

Sarah: Children!
Quiet! Quiet every one of you or
Kate will take it all—everything—
Knives, forks, turkey, glasses ...

J.B.:   Not the wine though.

Sarah: Job, I'm serious.
Answer your father's question, Jonathan.
Tell him what day it is.

Jonathan: [*Hushed*]   Thanksgiving.

Sarah: What day is that?

Jonathan: Thanksgiving Day.

David: The Day we give thanks to God.

Mary: For His goodness.

Sarah: And did you, David? Did you, Mary?
Has any one of you thanked God?
Really thanked Him?
[*There is an awkward silence.*]
                    Thanked Him for everything?
[*The children's heads are down. **J.B.** busies him-
self with his carving.*]

Sarah: [*Gently*] God doesn't give all this for
nothing:
A good home, good food,
Father, mother, brothers, sisters.
We too have our part to play.
If we do our part He does His,
He always has. If we forget Him
He will forget. Forever. In everything.
David!
[**David** *raises his head reluctantly.*]
                    Did you think of God?
[**David** *does not reply.*]
Did you think, when you woke in your beds
this morning,
Any one of you, of Him?
[*Silence.*]

J.B.:   [*Uncomfortable*]
Of course they did. They couldn't have helped
it ...

Bit of the breast for you, Rebecca?

Sarah: Please, Job. I want them to answer me.

J.B.:   How can they answer things like that?

Gravy? That's the girl ...

                    They know though.
Gift of waking, grace of light,
You and the world brought back together,

You from sleep, the world from night,
By God's great goodness and mercy . . .

Wing for Mary? Wing for Mary! . . .

They know all that. It's hard to talk about.
Sarah: [*Flushed, an edge to her voice*]
Even if it's hard we have to.
We can't just take, just eat, just—relish!
Children aren't animals.
J.B.:   [*He goes on with his serving*] Sweet Sal! Sweet
    Sal!
Children know the grace of God
Better than most of us. They see the world
The way the morning brings it back to them,
New and born and fresh and wonderful . . .

Ruth? She's always ravenous . . .

                                    I remember . . .

Jonathan? He never is . . .

                            . . . When I was
Ten I used to stand behind
The window watching when the light began,
Hidden and watching.
                        That's for David—
Dark and thin.
Mary: Why? Why hidden?
J.B.:   Hidden from the trees of course.
I must have thought the trees would see me
Peeking at them and turn back.
Rebecca: Back where?
J.B.:   Back where they came from, baby.
That's for your mother: crisp and gold.
Ruth: Father, you'd be cold. You didn't.
Sarah: [*The edge still there*]
He still does. He lies there watching
Long before I see the light—
Can't bear to miss a minute of it:
Sun at morning, moon at night,
The last red apple, the first peas!
I've never seen the dish he wouldn't
Taste and relish and want more of:
People either!
J.B.:   [*Serving himself with heaping spoons*]
                        Come on, Sal!
Plenty of people I don't like.
        [*He sits down. Pours himself a glass of wine.*]
I like their being people though . . .
        [*Sips his wine.*]
Trying to be.

Sarah: You're hungry for them—
Any kind. People and vegetables:
Any vegetables so long as
Leaves come out on them. He loves leaves!
J.B.:   You love them too. You love them better.
Just because you know their names
You think you choose among your flowers:
Well, you don't. You love the lot of them.
Sarah: I can't take them as a gift though:
I owe for them. We do. We *owe*.
J.B.:   Owe for the greening of the leaves?
Sarah: Please!
Please, Job. I want the children
Somehow to understand this day, this . . .
Feast . . .
        [*Her voice breaks.*]
J.B.:   Forgive me, Sal. I'm sorry—but
    they
Do. They understand. A little.
Look at me, all of you.
                            Ruth, you answer:
Why do we eat all this, these dishes,
All this food?
        [**Ruth** *twists her napkin.*]
            You say, Rebecca.
You're the littlest of us all.
Why?
Rebecca: Because it's good?
Sarah: Baby!
Ah, my poor baby!
J.B.:   Why your poor baby?
She's right, isn't she? It is. It's good.
Sarah: Good—and God has sent it to us!
J.B.:   She knows that.
Sarah: Does she?
        [*She raises her head sharply.*]
                                Job! . . .
                                do *you*?
        [*Their eyes meet; hers drop.*]
Oh, I think you do . . .
                            but sometimes—
Times like this when we're together—
I get frightened, Job . . .
                                we have so
Much!
J.B.:   [*Dead serious*] You ought to think I do.
Even if no one else should, you should.
Never since I learned to tell
My shadow from my shirt, not once,
Not for a watch-tick, have I doubted

God was on my side, was good to me.
Even young and poor I knew it.
People called it luck: it wasn't.
I never thought so from the first
Fine silver dollar to the last
Controlling interest in some company
I couldn't get—and got. It isn't
Luck.

Mary: That's in the story.

Jonathan: Tell the
Story.

Ruth: Tell the lucky story.

Rebecca: Lucky, lucky, tell the lucky.

J.B.:   [*Getting to his feet again to carve*]
Tell the story?
                      Drumstick, David?
Man enough to eat a drumstick?
You too, Jonathan?

Rebecca: Story, story.

J.B.:   Fellow came up to me once in a restaurant:
"J.B.," he says—I knew him . . .

Mary, want the other wing?

"Why do you get the best of the rest of us?"
Fellow named Foley, I think, or Sullivan:
New-come man he was in town.

Mary: Your turn, Mother.

Sarah: Patrick Sullivan.

J.B. and the children: [*Together in a shouted chant*]
Patrick Sullivan, that's the man!

J.B.:   "Why do you get the best of the rest of
us?
I've got as many brains as you.
I work as hard. I keep the lamp lit.
Luck! That's what it is," says Sullivan.
"Look!" I said. "Look out the window!"
"What do you see?" "The street," he tells me.

J.B. and the children: [*As before*]
"The street?" says I. "The street," says he.

J.B.:   "What do you want me to call it?" he
asks me.
"What do I want you to call it?" says I.
"A road," says I. "It's going somewhere."
"Where?" says he. "You say," I said to him.

J.B. and the children:
"God knows!" says Mr. Sullivan.

J.B.:   "He does," says I. "That's where it's
going.

That's where I go too. That's why."
"Why what?" says he. "I get the best of you:
It's God's country, Mr. Sullivan."

J.B. and the children:
"God forbid!" says Mr. Sullivan.

J.B.:   I laughed till I choked. He only looked
at me.
"Lucky so-and-so," he yells.

Sarah: Poor Mr. Sullivan.

J.B.:   [*Soberly*]   He was wrong.
It isn't luck when God is good to you.
It's something more. It's like those dizzy
Daft old lads who dowse for water.
They feel the alder twig twist down
And know they've got it and they have:
They've got it. Blast the ledge and water
Gushes at you. And they knew.
It wasn't luck. They knew. They felt the
Gush go shuddering through their shoulders,
huge
As some mysterious certainty of opulence.
They couldn't hold it. I can't hold it.
              [*He looks at Sarah.*]
I've always known that God was with me.
I've tried to show I knew it—not
Only in words.

Sarah: [*Touched*]   Oh, you have,
I know you have. And it's ridiculous,
Childish, and I shouldn't be afraid . . .
Not even now when suddenly everything
Fills to overflowing in me
Brimming the fulness till I feel
My happiness impending like a danger.
If ever anyone deserved it, you do.

J.B.:   That's not true. I don't deserve it.
It's not a question of deserving.

Sarah: Oh, it is. That's all the question.
However could we sleep at night . . .

J.B.:   Nobody *deserves* it, Sarah:
Not the world that God has given us.
              [*There is a moment's strained silence, then* **J.B.**
              is laughing.]

J.B.:   But I believe in it, Sal. I trust in it.
I trust my luck—my life—our life—
God's goodness to me.

Sarah: [*Trying to control her voice*] Yes! You do!
I know you do! And that's what frightens me!
It's not so simple as all that. It's not.
They mustn't think it is. God punishes.

God rewards and God can punish.
God is just.

J.B.: [*Easy again*]   Of course He's just.
He'll never change. A man can count on Him.
Look at the world, the order of it,
The certainty of day's return
And spring's and summer's: the leaves'
    green—
That never cheated expectation.

Sarah: [*Vehemently*]
God can reward and God can punish.
Us He has rewarded. Wonderfully.
Given us everything. Preserved us.
Kept us from harm, each one—each one.
And why? Because of you . . .

J.B. [*Raises his head sharply.*]

Sarah: No!
Let me say it! Let me say it!
I need to speak the words that say it—
I need to hear them spoken. Nobody,
Nobody knows of it but me.
You never let them know: not anyone—
Even your children. They don't know.
        [**J.B.** *heaves himself out of his chair, swings round*
        the table, leans over **Sarah,** *his arms around*
        her.]

J.B.: Eat your dinner, Sal my darling.
We love our life because it's good:
It isn't good because we love it—
Pay for it—in thanks or prayers. The thanks
    are
Part of love and paid like love:
Free gift or not worth having.
You know that, Sal . . .
        [*He kisses her.*]
                            better than anyone.
Eat your dinner, girl! There's not a
Harpy on the roof for miles.
        [*She reaches up to touch his cheek with her hand.*]

Sarah: Nevertheless it's true, Job. You
Can trust your luck because you've earned
    the
Right to trust it: earned the right
For all of us to trust it.

J.B.: [*Back at his own place, filling his glass again*]
                            Nonsense!
We get the earth for nothing, don't we?
It's given to us, gift on gift:
Sun on the floor, airs in the curtain.

We lie a whole day long and look at it
Crowing or crying in our cribs:
It doesn't matter—crow or cry
The sun shines, the wind blows . . .

        Rebecca! Back for more already?

Rebecca: I want the wishbone please.

J.B.:   Whatever
        For?

Rebecca: To wish.

Sarah: For what, my baby?

Rebecca: For the wishbone.

Sarah: [*Pulling* **Rebecca** *into her lap*]
                    Little pig!
Wishing for wishes!

J.B.: [*Forking the wishbone onto* **Rebecca's** *plate*]
                            That's my girl!

Sarah: She is! The spit and image of you!
Thinking she can eat the world
With luck and wishes and no thanks!

J.B.: That isn't fair. We're thankful, both of
us.

Sarah: [*Cuddling* **Rebecca**]
Both! And both the same! Just look at you!
A child shows gratitude the way a woman
Shows she likes a pretty dress—
Puts it on and takes it off again—
That's the way a child gives thanks:
She tries the world on. So do you.

J.B.: God understands that language, doesn't
He?
He should. He made the colts.

Sarah: But you're not
Colts! You talk. With tongues. Or ought to.

J.B.: And we use them, don't we, baby?
We love Monday, Tuesday, Wednesday . . .

Sarah: [*Rocking* **Rebecca** *on her knees*]
We love Monday, Tuesday, Wednesday.
Where have Monday, Tuesday, gone?
Under the grass tree,
Under the green tree,
One by one.

Jonathan: Say it again, Mother . . . Mother!

Sarah: I never said it before. I don't
Know . . .
                How would you think it would go?
How does it go, Job? You said it.

J.B.: I didn't. I said we loved the world:
Monday, Tuesday, Wednesday, all of it.

Sarah: How would you think it would go, Jonathan?

> [*The words fall into a little tune as she repeats them.*]

I love Monday, Tuesday, Wednesday.
Where have Monday, Tuesday, gone?
Under the grass tree,
Under the green tree,
One by one.

Caught as we are in Heaven's quandary,
Is it they or we are gone
Under the grass tree,
Under the green tree?

I love Monday, Tuesday, Wednesday
One by one.

Rebecca: [*Drowsily*]   Say it again.
Sarah: Say it again?
Jonathan: You say it, Father.
J.B.: To be, become, and end are beautiful.
Rebecca: That's not what she said at all.
J.B.: Isn't it? Isn't it?
Sarah: [*Kissing her*]   Not at all.

> [*The light fades, leaving the two shadows on the canvas sky.*]

SCENE II

The Platform. As the platform light comes on, the figures fade from the canvas sky and **Mr. Zuss** and **Nickles** straighten up, lifting their masks off, stretching, yawning.

Mr. Zuss: Well, that's our pigeon.
Nickles: Lousy actor.
Mr. Zuss: Doesn't really act at all.
Nickles: Just eats.
Mr. Zuss: And talks.
Nickles: The love of life!
Poisoning their little minds
With love of life! At that age!
Mr. Zuss: No!
Some of that, I thought, was beautiful.
Nickles: Best thing you can teach your children
Next to never drawing breath
Is choking on it.
Mr. Zuss: Who said that?

Someone's spoiled philosophy, it sounds like:
Intellectual butter a long war
And too much talking have turned rancid.
I thought he made that small familiar
Feast a true thanksgiving . . . only . . .
Nickles: Only what?
Mr. Zuss: Something went wrong.
Nickles: That's what I've been telling you.
Mr. Zuss: He didn't Act.
Nickles: He can't. He's not an actor.
Mr. Zuss: I wonder if he knows?
Nickles: Knows what?
Mr. Zuss: Knows that he's in it?
Nickles: Is he?
Mr. Zuss: Certainly.
Nickles: How can you tell?
Mr. Zuss: That's him. That's Job.
He has the wealth, the wife, the children,
Position in the world.
Nickles: The piety!
Mr. Zuss: He loves God, if that's what you're saying.
A perfect and an upright man.
Nickles: Piety's hard enough to take
Among the poor who *have* to practice it.
A rich man's piety stinks. It's insufferable.
Mr. Zuss: You're full of fatuous aphorisms, aren't you!
A poor man's piety is hope of having:
A rich man *has* his—and he's grateful.
Nickles: Bought and paid for like a waiter's smirk!
You know what talks when that man's talking?
All that gravy on his plate—
His cash—his pretty wife—his children!
Lift the lot of them, he'd sing
Another canticle to different music.
Mr. Zuss: That's what Satan says—but better.
Nickles: It's obvious. No one needs to say it.
Mr. Zuss: You don't like him.
Nickles: I don't have to.
You're the one who has to like him.
Mr. Zuss: I thought you spoke of Job with sympathy.
Nickles: Job on his dung hill, yes. That's human.
That makes sense. But this world-master,

This pious, flatulent, successful man
Who feasts on turkey and thanks God!—
He sickens me!

Mr. Zuss: Of course he sickens you,
He trusts the will of God and loves—

> [**Mr. Zuss** *is swollen with indignation and rhetoric. He swoops his mask up from the rail with a magnificent gesture, holds it.*]

Loves a woman who must sometime, somewhere,
Later, sooner, leave him; fixes
All his hopes on little children
One night's fever or a running dog
Could kill between the dark and day;
Plants his work, his enterprise, his labor,
Here where every planted thing
Fails in its time but still he plants it . . .

Nickles: [*Nastily*]
God will teach him better won't He?
God will show him what the world is like—
What man's like—the ignoble creature,
Victim of the spinning joke!

Mr. Zuss: Teach him better than he knows!
God will show him God!

Nickles: [*Shrugging*]   It's the same
Thing. It hurts.

Mr. Zuss: [*Gathering momentum*] God will teach
him!
God will show him what God *is*—
Enormous pattern of the steep of stars,
Minute perfection of the frozen crystal,
Inimitable architecture of the slow,
Cold, silent, ignorant sea-snail:
The unimaginable will of stone:
Infinite mind in midge of matter!

Nickles: Infinite mush! Wait till your pigeon
Pecks at the world the way the rest do—
Eager beak to naked bum!

Mr. Zuss: You ought to have your tongue torn
out!

Nickles: All men should: to suffer silently.

Mr. Zuss: Get your mask back on! I tell you
Nothing this good man might suffer,
Nothing at all, would make him yelp
As you do. He'd praise God no matter.

Nickles: [*Whispering*]
Why must he suffer then?

> [*The question catches* **Mr. Zuss** *with his mask halfway to his face. He lowers it slowly, staring*
> *into it as though the answer might be written inside.*]

Mr. Zuss: [*Too loud*]   To praise!

Nickles: [*Softly*]
He praises now. Like a canary.

> [**Mr. Zuss** *lifts his mask again.*]

Mr. Zuss: Well, will you put it on or won't
you?

Nickles: Shall I tell you why?
[*Violently*]   To learn!
Every human creature born
Is born into the bright delusion
Beauty and loving-kindness care for him.
Suffering teaches! Suffering's good for us!
Imagine men and women dying
Still believing that the cuddling arms
Enclosed them! They would find the worms
Peculiar nurses, wouldn't they? Wouldn't
they?

> [*He breaks off; picks his mask up; goes on in a kind of jigging chant half to himself.*]

What once was cuddled must learn to kiss
The cold worm's mouth. That's all the
mystery.
That's the whole muddle. Well, we learn it.
God is merciful and we learn it . . .
We learn to wish we'd never lived!

Mr. Zuss: This man will not.

Nickles: Won't he? Won't he?
Shall I tell you how it ends?
Shall I prophesy? I see our
Smug world-master on his dung heap,
Naked, miserable, and alone,
Pissing the stars. Ridiculous gesture!—
Nevertheless a gesture—meaning
All there is on earth to mean:
Man's last word . . . and worthy of him!

Mr. Zuss: This man will not. He trusts God.
No matter how it ends, he trusts Him.

Nickles: Even when God tests him?—tortures
him?

Mr. Zuss: Would God permit the test unless
He knew the outcome of the testing?

Nickles: Then why test him if God knows?

Mr. Zuss: So Job can see.

Nickles: See what?

Mr. Zuss: See God.

Nickles: A fine sight from an ash heap, certainly!

Mr. Zuss: Isn't there anything you understand?

It's from the ash heap God is seen
Always! Always from the ashes.
Every saint and martyr knew that.

Nickles: And so he suffers to see God:
Sees God because he suffers. Beautiful!

Mr. Zuss: Put on your mask. I'd rather look at . . .

Nickles: I should think you would! A human
Face would shame the mouth that said that!

[*They put their masks on fiercely, standing face to face. The platform light fades out. The spotlight catches them, throwing the two masked shadows out and up. The voices are magnified and hollow, the gestures formal, as at the end of the Prologue.*]

Godmask: *Hast thou considered my servant Job*
That there is none like him on the earth,
A perfect and an upright man, one
That feareth God and escheweth evil?

Satanmask: [*Sardonic*]
Doth Job fear God for naught?

[*The* **God-shadow** *turns away in a gesture of anger.*]

Satanmask: [*Deprecatingly*]
Hast thou not made an hedge about him
And about his house
And about all that he hath on every side?
Thou hast blessed the work of his hands
And his substance is increased.

[*The voice drops.*]

But put forth thine hand now and touch
All that he hath . . .

[*The voice becomes a hissing whisper*]

                    and he will
Curse thee to thy face!

Godmask: [*In a furious, great voice, arm thrown out in a gesture of contemptuous commitment*]
Behold!
All that he hath is in thy power!

[*The* **Satan-shadow** *bows mockingly; raises its two arms, advancing until the shadows become one shadow. The light fades. Suddenly, out of the darkness the* **Distant Voice** *of the Prologue.*]

The Distant Voice:
Only . . .

[*Silence.*]

Godmask: *Only*
Upon himself

Put not forth thy hand!
[*Darkness. The crash of a drum; a single stroke. Silence.*]

Note: The play is conceived and written
without breaks, but if recesses in
the action are desired one might
well be made at this point.

SCENE III

The Table. As the lights come on the two leaning shadows, one thrown upon the other, are visible on the canvas sky. They fade as the scene brightens. The table has been pushed to one side as though against a window in a living room. **Sarah** stands before it arranging flowers in a bowl. **J.B.** is straddling a chair, watching.

Sarah: Look, Job! Look! Across the street.
Two soldiers.

J.B.:   What about them?

Sarah: Only they
Stare so.

J.B.:   Stare at what?

Sarah: The house.
I think they're drunk . . . A little.

[*J.B. rises, stands beside her, his arm around her waist.*]

J.B.:   Plastered!

Sarah: One of them anyway. He wobbles.

J.B.: That's no wobble. That's a waltz step.

Sarah: They're crossing over.

J.B.:   They sure are.

Sarah: What do you think they . . .

J.B.:   Listen!

Sarah: Yes . . .
What do you think they want, two soldiers?

J.B.: No idea. Johnson will tend to them.

Sarah: I've never seen such staring eyes.

J.B.: Glazed. Just glazed.

Sarah: They keep on ringing.
I know what it is, J.B.,
They have some kind of message for us.
David has sent them with a message—
Something about his regiment. They're coming
Every day now, ship by ship.

I hear them in the harbor coming.
He couldn't write and so he sent them.

J.B.:   Pretty drunk for messengers, those soldiers.

Sarah: What does it matter. They're just boys.
They've just got home. It doesn't matter.

J.B.:   Johnson's a judge of drunks. He'll handle
them.

Sarah: He mustn't send them off. Don't let
him!

[*There is a commotion outside the canvas door.
A voice, off.*]

Voice: Two young . . . gentlemen to see you.
Friends, they say, of Mr. David.

Sarah: Oh, I knew! I knew! I knew!

Voice [*off*]:   That's telling him, Puss-foot!

Voice [*off*]:   Puss-face!

[*The two* **Messengers** *enter, dressed as soldiers.
The* **First** *is flushed and loud; the* **Second,** *very
drunk, pale as bone.*]

J.B.:   Come in, gentlemen. Come in. Come in.
David's friends are always welcome.
This is David's mother.

Sarah: Won't you sit
Down?

First Messenger: What did I tell you, Punk!
Any friends of David's.

Second Messenger: Any at
All . . .

First M.:   I told you that boy meant it.
What did I say when I see the joint?
That's the number, Punk, I told you.
Old Ten Twenty: that's the number.

[*He turns to* **Sarah**]

Twenty if you're men, he told us—
Ten for horses' whatses. What the
Hell, he always said: we're friends.

Second M.:   Any at all he always . . .

First M.:   Pardon the
Language, lady.

Second M.:   Any a' . . .

Sarah: There!
Sit down.

First M.:   It's just, we saw the number.

Sarah: And David asked you to drop in.

First M.:   Any friend of his, he told us.
Any time.

Second M.:   And we were cold:
A cold, hard march . . .

First M.:   What the
Hell's the matter with *you!* You drunk?

Sarah: Sit by the fire, both of you. Where was
he?

First M.:   Where was who?

Sarah: David.

First M.:   When?

J.B.:   When he told you.

First M.:   In the mess.
Any friend of his, he told us.
Any time at all. Why?
You think we're lying to you?

J.B.:   Certainly
Not.

First M.:   You think we never knew him?

Sarah: Of course. Of course you do.

First M.:   We knew him.

Second M.:   Fumbling among the faces . . .
knew him . . .
Night . . . our fingers numb . . .

First M.:   Will you shut
Up or will I clout you, Big Mouth!

[*To* **Sarah**]

That's why we come: because we knew him.
To tell you how we knew him.

Sarah: Thank you.

[*Silence.*]

Second M.:   How it was with him . . .

First M.:   Listen, Punk!

Second M.:   How, by night, by chance, dark-
ling . . .
By the dark of chance . . .

First M.:   He's drunk.

Second M.:   How, the war done, the guns
silent . . .
No one knows who gave the order.

First M.:   [*Raising his voice*]
Like I say, because he said to.
Any friend of his he said to.
Just to tell you we knew David:
Maybe drink to David maybe . . .

Sarah: Yes! Oh yes! Let's drink to David!
J.B.!

J.B.:   Bourbon? Scotch?

First M.:   Now you're
Cooking! Take your pants off, Punk:
We're in.

Sarah: That's right. Put your feet up.
Oh, they're not too dirty. David's are

Dirtier. I'm sure of that.

First M.:   David's feet! I'll say they are.
Look! What's going on here! David's
Feet!

Sarah: I meant—with all that marching.

First M.:   I don't get it. Look, it's true
They didn't have the right length lumber:
We did the best we could . . .
[*J.B. Starts to his feet.*]

J.B.:   What in
God's name are you saying, soldier?

Sarah: [*Rising*]
What does he mean, the lumber?
[*Silence.*]

First M.:   You don't
Know? Ain't that the army for you!
[*To the* **Second Messenger.**]
They don't know. They never told them.

Sarah: Told us what?

First M.:   We better go.

Sarah: No! Please! Please! No!

First M.:   Come on, we're getting out, you
lunkhead.

J.B.:   Not until you've told me. Sarah!
Perhaps you'd better, Sarah . . .

Sarah: Please,
I want to hear it.

First M.:   Jesus! . . . Jesus! . . .
[*There is a long silence. The* **Second Messenger** *turns slowly to* **J.B.,** *his face drunken white, his eyes blank.*]

Second M.:   I only am escaped alone to tell
thee . . .
[*The focus of light opens to include the Platform where* **Mr. Zuss** *and* **Nickles** *stand staring down, their masks in their hands.* **Mr. Zuss**'s *face is expressionless.* **Nickles** *wears a twisted grin. The* **Second Messenger**'s *head falls forward onto his knees.*]

Second M.:   . . . My tongue loosened by
drink . . .

My thought
Darkened as by wind the water . . .

That day is lost where it befell. . .

Sarah: [*She is holding herself by the straining of her clenched hands*]
What is it we were never told?

J.B.:   It isn't

True you little drunken liar!
It can't be true! It isn't possible!
[*Silence. The passion ebbs from* **J.B.**'*s voice.*]
We had a letter from him.
[*Silence. Then, uncertainly.*]
After the
End of it we had a letter. . . .
[**Nickles** *jerks a crooked leg over the rail, starts awkwardly down the ladder, watching intently, peering back up at* **Mr. Zuss,** *watching.*]

Second M.:   What shall I say to you . . . ?

What I saw . . . ?

What I believe I saw . . . ?

Or what
I must have seen . . .

and have forgotten?

Sarah: [*A cry*] David is our son, our son, our
son.

Nickles: [*Prompting her from his ladder in a harsh half-whisper*]
That's the tune. He's *ours.* Go on with it:
Can't be happening to *us!* Can't be!
God won't let it happen, not to
Our kind, God won't!
[*He leers up at* **Mr. Zuss.**]

J.B.:   [*Turning* **Sarah** *away from the* **Second Messenger** *into his arms*]   Sarah! Sarah!
David's all right. He has to be. He is.
I know he is. The war is over.
It never could have happened—never—
Never in this world.

Nickles: [*The whisper harsher*]   Couldn't it?
Ask him! Couldn't it? Suppose it did though:
What would the world be made of then?

Second M.:   I only am escaped alone, companions
Fallen, fallen, fallen . . .

the earth
Smell remembers that there was a man.

Sarah: Job! He's dead! God has taken him!
[*The focus of light narrows, is extinguished.*]

SCENE IV

Darkness. Silence. Then the crash of a drum.
Silence again. Then two cigarettes are lighted,

one high above the stage, one lower. Then gradually the lights come on, making four circles
across the front of the stage like the circles of
sidewalk brightness under street lamps. Where
the cigarettes were lighted **Mr. Zuss** *and* **Nickles**
are now visible on the platform rail and the ladder, squatting there like two tramps on the stairs
of a stoop, turning their heads together one way
and then the other, watching, not speaking.
After a time the **First Messenger** comes strolling
in from their right, a news camera slung from
his neck. The **Second** follows with a notebook.
They wear battered felt hats with their khaki
shirts and trousers. They are followed at a little
distance by a stylishly dressed **girl.**

Girl: I don't like it.
First Messenger: You'll do fine.
Girl: I wish I was home in bed with a good
  Boy or something. I don't like it.
First M.:   You'll do fine.
Girl: I won't do fine:
  I'm frightened.
First M.:   All you do, you go up to them.
  Get them talking, keep them looking.
Girl: Go up to them yourselves, why don't
  you?
First M.:   Sure, and get the brush-off. Girl like
  You can keep them talking; keep them
  Looking, that is. Pretty girl.
Girl: I don't like it.
Second M.:   You'll get used to it.
Girl: Not where I work. Not Society.
  Society page they never die.
  Girl gets asked. Girl gets married.
  Girl gets photographed in night club.
  Girl gets older. Girl gets off.
  Never catch them dead on Society.
Second M.:   Like the robins.
First M.:   Yeah, like robins.
Girl: Why the robins?
Second M.:   Never see one
  Dead.
First M.:   Nor sparrows neither.
Second M.:   Either.
First M.:   Never hardly. Must be millions.
Second M.:   Hardly ever see one dead.
Girl: What happens to them?
Second M.:   They get over it.

Girl: Over what?
Second M.:   Over being there.
Girl: All I know is I don't like it.
  Keep them talking till a flash bulb
  Smacks them naked in the face—
  It's horrible!
First M.:   It's genius! Listen, lady!
  How do I get the photograph without?
  Answer me that. How do I get the
  Look a mother's face has maybe
  Once in a lifetime: just before
  Her mouth knows, when her eyes are know-
    ing?
Girl: I can't do it.
First M.:   *She* can't do it!
  All you got to do is walk.
  Wiggle your can. Keep them looking.
  Then he tells them. Then I take them.
  Then you beat it. Then that's that.
  Except the drink we're going to buy you
  Payday evening if you're good—
  And if you're not there's lots of liars.
Second M.:   You don't have to tell them: I do.
Girl: Why do *you?*
Second M.:   Because I have to.
  I'm the one that has to tell them.
Girl: Why?
Second M.:   [*Shrugging*]
                    Oh . . .
Girl: Why?
Second M.:   There's always
  Someone has to tell them, isn't there?
Girl: Someone else can.
Second M.:   No. There's always . . .
    [*He is groping from word to word.*]
  Someone chosen by the chance of seeing,
  By the accident of sight,
  By stumbling on the moment of it,
  Unprepared, unwarned, unready,
  Thinking of nothing, of his drink, his bed,
  His belly, and it happens, and he sees it . . .
    [*He winces his eyes shut.*]
  Caught in that inextricable net
  Of having witnessed, having seen . . .

  He alone!
Girl: [*Gently*]   But you don't have to.
    [*To the* **First Messenger**]
  Why does he have to?

Second M.:   It was I.
I only. I alone. The moment
Closed us together in its gaping grin
Of horrible incredulity. I saw their
Eyes see mine! We *saw* each other!

First M.:   He has to. He was there. He saw it.
Route Two. Under the viaduct.
Traveling seventy—seventy-five—
Kid was driving them was drunk,
Had to be drunk, just drove into it.
He was walking home. He saw it.
Saw it start to, saw it had to,
Saw it. J.B.'s son. His daughter.
Four in all and all just kids.
They shrieked like kids he said.

Second M.:   Then silent.
Blond in all that blood that daughter.

Girl: [*Her voice rising*]
He can't tell them *that*!

First M.:   He has to.
Someone has to. They don't know.
They been out all evening somewhere.

Girl: [*Hysterically*]
They don't have to know!

First M.:   They have to.

[*Nickles and Mr. Zuss on their perches have seen something off to their right. They turn their heads together.*]

Girl: No!

First M.:   [*Looking right, pulling his camera around*]
That's them. They're coming. Quiet!

Girl: I can't do it.

First M.:   [*Brutally*]   You can do it.

[*J.B. and Sarah, arm in arm, walk slowly into the first circle of light. Nickles and Mr. Zuss lean forward, their masks dangling from their hands.*]

Second M.:   [*Under his breath, staring at them as they come*]
I only, I alone, to tell thee . . .
I who have understood nothing, have known
Nothing, have been answered nothing . . .

Girl: [*Crossing to meet them with an affected walk, the **First Messenger** screening himself behind her, the **Second** following*]   Good
Evening! What a pleasant evening!
Back from the theatre so soon?
We're neighbors, don't you know? You've
met my

Miffkin walking me each morning:
You know Muff, my purple poodle . . .

Isn't it a pleasant evening!

Second M.:   I'm from the press. There's been an accident . . .
[*He falters.*]

First M.:   Four kids in a car. They're dead.
Two were yours. Your son. Your daughter.
Cops have got them in a cab.
Any minute now they'll be here.
[*He raises his camera over the girl's shoulder.*]

Girl: [*In her own voice, screaming*]
Don't look! Cover your face!

Sarah: [*With scarcely the breath to say it*]
Mary . . . Jonathan . . .
[*The flash. **J.B.** throws his elbow up as if to ward off a blow. **Sarah** does not move.*]

J.B.:   You bastards!
I'll beat your god damned brains out . . .
[*He lunges after them blinded by the flash as they scatter.*]

                                    Where have you
Gone?
[*Sarah moves like a sleepwalker through the circles of light, one after the other, touches a chair, goes down on her knees beside it, clinging to it.*]

J.B.:   Answer me!
[*Silence.*]

J.B.:   Answer me!
[*Silence*]

Sarah: [*Her voice dead*]   It wasn't
They that did it . . .
[*J.B. comes slowly back out of the darkness, sees her, crosses to her. There is a long silence, J.B. looking right and left along the street.*]

Sarah: Why did He do it to them?
What had they done to Him—those children . . .
What had they done to Him . . .

                                    and we—
What had *we* done? . . .

                                    What had *we* done?

J.B.:   Don't, Sarah. Don't!
[*Nickles lights a cigarette, grins back over his shoulder to **Mr. Zuss** in the handful of yellow glare.*]

J.B.:   It doesn't
Help to think that.

Sarah: Nothing helps! . . .
Nothing can help them now.

J.B.: [*A clumsy gesture*] It . . . happened . . .

Sarah: [*Fiercely*]
Yes, and Who let it happen?

J.B.: [*Awkwardly*] Shall we . . .
Take the good and not the evil?
We have to take the chances, Sarah:
Evil with good.
> [*Then, in a desperate candor*]
It doesn't mean there
Is no good!

Nickles: [*In his cracked whisper*]
Doesn't it? Doesn't it?

Mr. Zuss: [*Silencing* **Nickles** *with his hand, his whisper hardly heard*]
Go on! Go on! That path will lead you.

Sarah: [*Bitterly*]
When you were lucky it was God!

J.B.: Sticks and stones and steel are chances.
There's no will in stone and steel . . .
> [*His voice breaks.*]
It happens to us . . .
> [*He drops on his knees beside her.*]

Sarah: No! . . .
Don't touch me!
[*She clings to the chair, motionless, not weeping.*]
[*The circles of light fade out.*]

SCENE V

The dark diminishes until the white coats of **Mr. Zuss** and **Nickles** are visible on the platform. **Mr. Zuss** lifts a padded drumstick. **Nickles** balances on the rail and starts cautiously down the ladder.

Mr. Zuss: Ready?

Nickles: [*Cheerfully*] Got to be, don't they?

Mr. Zuss: I meant
You.

Nickles: They've got no choice. Disaster—
Death—mankind are always ready—
Ready for anything that hurts.

Mr. Zuss: And you?

Nickles: I too! I too!

Mr. Zuss: Provided
Someone else will bleed the blood
And wipe the blinded eye?

Nickles: I watch
Your world go round!

Mr. Zuss: It must be wearing.

Nickles: Oh, it has its compensations.
Even a perfect and an upright man
Learns if you keep turning long enough.
First he thought it wasn't happening—
Couldn't be happening—not to him—
Not with you in the stratosphere tooting the
Blue trombone for the moon to dance.
Then he thought it chanced by chance!
> [*A dry hiccup of laughter*]
Childish hypothesis of course
But still hypothesis—a start—
A pair of tongs to take the toad by—
Recognition that it *is* a toad:
Not quite comfort but still comfortable,
Eases the hook in the gills a little:
He'll learn.

Mr. Zuss: [*Preoccupied*] Learn what?

Nickles: Your—purpose for him!

Mr. Zuss: Keep your tongue in your teeth, will
you?
> [*He notices* **Nickles**' *descent on the ladder for the first time.*]
Here! Wait a minute! Wait a
Minute! Where are you off to?

Nickles: Bit of a
Walk in the earth for my health—or
somebody's.
> [*Bitterly*]
Up and down in the earth, you know—
Back and forth in it . . .

Mr. Zuss: Leave him alone!

Nickles: He needs a helping hand: you've seen
that—
A nudge from an old professional.

Mr. Zuss: Leave him a'
Lone! He can't act and you know it.

Nickles: He doesn't have to act. He suffers.
It's an old role—played like a mouth-organ.
Any idiot on earth
Given breath enough can breathe it—
Given tears enough can weep.
All he needs is help to see.

Mr. Zuss: See what?

Nickles: That bloody drum-stick striking;
See Who lets it strike the drum!

[**Mr. Zuss,** *whose lifted arm has been slowly falling, raises it abruptly.*]

Mr. Zuss: Wait!

[*He starts to strike the drum, stops the stroke in mid-air*]

Wait for me. I'm coming.

Down!

Wait!

Wait I tell you!

[*The stroke of the drum. The light fades out.*]

[*Out of the dark two circles of light, one on the platform, one on the table. Behind the table are the two* **Messengers.** *The* **First,** *wearing a police sergeant's cap, sits on a chair. The* **Second,** *wearing a patrolman's cap, stands beside him.* **J.B.,** *a raincoat over rumpled clothes, stands facing them. Above, on the platform, as on the landing of a stair,* **Sarah** *stands pulling a dressing gown around her shoulders.* **Nickles** *and* **Mr. Zuss,** *their masks in their hands, straddle a couple of chairs beyond the circle of light which centers on the table.*]

First M.:   Sorry to question you like this. We got to get the story.

J.B.:   [*Impatiently*]   Go on.

First M.:   Turning your house into a . . .

J.B.:   No. Go on. It doesn't matter.

Sarah: [*Toneless*]   Nothing matters but to Know.

First M.:   How many children?

[*Silence.*]

J.B.:   Two.

First M.:   [*Writing*]

Girls?

Sarah: We had two boys.

First M.:   [*Writing*]   Girls. Names?

J.B.:   Ruth. Rebecca.

Sarah: Ruth is the Oldest . . . now.

First M.:   And you last saw her?

J.B.:   Ruth?

Sarah: [*Her voice rising*]

It's Rebecca is missing!

J.B.:   [*Silencing her*]   He Knows!

Sarah: [*Harshly*] No, it's God that knows!

[*There is an awkward silence. When* **Sarah** *speaks again her voice is dead*]

She's the littlest one. She's gone.

First M.:   How long ago?

Sarah: Oh . . . hours!

First M.:   It's three in the morning now.

J.B.:   Since seven.

First M.:   [*Writing*]

And you reported it?

J.B.:   Yes.

First M.:   When?

J.B.:   One o'clock. A quarter after. We looked for her everywhere, of course. Then we thought—I thought—if somebody . . . Maybe the telephone would ring.

First M.:   And you'd do better on your own?

J.B.:   [*Reluctantly*]

Yes.

Sarah: [*With rising violence*]

Yes! Yes! Yes!

We believe in our luck in this house! We've earned the right to! We believe in it . . .

[*Bitterly*]

All but the bad!

Nickles: [*Rocking back on his chair*]

That's playing it!

That's playing it!

[*He begins to sing in his cracked whisper, beating a jazzed rhythm on the back of his mask as though it were a banjo.*]

If God is Will

And Will is well

Then what is ill?

God still?

Dew tell!

[**Mr. Zuss** *does not seem to hear. He is listening intently to the scene at the table.*]

First M.:   And nobody telephoned?

J.B.:   Nobody telephoned.

First M.:   [*Writing*]   Dressed? How was she Dressed?

J.B.:   [*Turning for the first time to look up at* **Sarah**]

White?

Sarah: White! You saw her Glimmering in the twilight.

First M.:   [*Writing*]   White.

Sarah: All but her Shoes.

[*The* **First Messenger** *looks up at the* **Second.**]
First M.:   Her shoes were what?
Sarah: Red.
[*The* **First Messenger** *looks up again. The*
Second *turns his face away.*]
First M.:   Rebecca have a red umbrella?
Sarah: Parasol.
First M.:   Little toy umbrella.
Sarah: [*Startled*]
Parasol. Yes, she might have had one.
First M.:   You mean she owned one?
Sarah: Yes. It belonged to a
Big doll we bought her once.
Scarlet silk. It opens and closes.
She kept it when the doll gave out.
She used to take it to bed with her even—
Open and close it.
[*The* **First Messenger** *looks up for the third time*
at the **Second,** *whose face, still turned away, is*
like stone.]
J.B.:   [*A step forward*] You've found the parasol!
Second M.:   [*Not looking at him; a voice without ex-*
pression or tone]
What will it tell you? Will it tell you why?
J.B.:   [*To* **First M.**]
I asked you: have you found the parasol?
First M.:   He's the one. Ask him. He'll tell you.
Second M.:   [*With difficulty, like a man speaking out*
of physical pain]
Can the tooth among the stones make an-
swer? . . .

Can the seven bones reply? . . .

Out in the desert in the tombs
Are potter's figures: two of warriors,
Two of worthies, two of camels,
Two of monsters, two of horses.
Ask them why. They will not answer you . . .
[*He brushes his hand heavily across his face*]
Death is a bone that stammers . . .
                                        a tooth
Among the flints that has forgotten.
J.B.:   [*Violently*]
Ask him! Has he found the parasol!
First M.:   We don't know. He found an um-
brella—
Doll's umbrella—red.
Sarah: Oh, where?
J.B.:   Nothing else? Just the umbrella?

First M.:   [*To* **Second**]
Tell them, will you!
[*The* **Second Messenger** *does not move or*
speak. The **First** *shrugs, looks down at his pencil,*
rattles it off in a matter-of-fact monotone.]
                                        Just past midnight
Pounding his beat by the back of the lumber-
yard
Somebody runs and he yells and they stum-
ble—
Big kid—nineteen maybe—
Hopped to the eyes and scared—scared
Bloodless he could barely breathe.
Constable yanks him up by the britches:
"All right! Take me to it!"
Just a shot in the dark, he was so
Goddam scared there had to be something . . .

Well . . .

He took him to it . . .
                                        back of the
Lumber trucks beside the track.
J.B.:   Go on.
First M.:   She had a toy umbrella.
That was all she had—but shoes:
Red shoes and a toy umbrella.
It was tight in her fist when he found her
—still.
J.B.:   Let me see it! The umbrella!
First M.:   Constable will show it to you.
[*The* **Second Messenger** *takes something*
wound in newspaper out of his pocket. He does
not look at it or them. The **First Messenger** *half*
opens it, lays it on the table.]
Sarah: Oh, my baby! Oh, my baby!
[*The* **First Messenger** *gets out of his chair,*
stands a moment awkwardly, goes out. The **Sec-**
ond *follows.* **J.B.** *stands motionless over the table.*
Sarah *hugs her dressing gown around her, rock-*
ing herself slowly, her head bowed.]
Nickles: [*Leaning forward toward* **J.B.,** *a wheedling*
whisper]
Now's the time to say it, mister.
Mr. Zuss: Leave him alone!
J.B.:   [*Touching the parasol*] The Lord giveth . . .
[*His voice breaks*]
                                        the
Lord taketh away!

Mr. Zuss: [*Rising, whispering*] Go on!
   Go on! Finish it! Finish it!
Nickles: What should he
   Finish when he's said it all?
Mr. Zuss: Go on!
Nickles: To what? To where? He's got there,
   hasn't he?
   Now he's said it, now he knows.
   He knows Who gives, he knows Who takes
   now.
J.B.: [*Stands silent over the parasol*]
Mr. Zuss: Why won't he play the part he's
   playing?
Nickles: Because he isn't.
Mr. Zuss: Isn't what?
Nickles: Isn't playing. He's not playing.
   He isn't in the play at all.
   He's where we all are—in our suffering.
   Only . . .
            [**Nickles** *turns savagely on* **Mr. Zuss**]
            . . . Now he knows its Name!
            [**Nickles** *points dramatically toward the canvas*
            sky. **Mr. Zuss**'s *head tilts back following the*
            gesture. He freezes into immobility.]
Mr. Zuss: Look! Look up!
Nickles: That's your direction.
Mr. Zuss: Look, I say! The staring stars!
Nickles: Or only lights not meant . . .
            [**Nickles** *twists his crooked neck, looks sidewise*
            upward. The canvas sky has disappeared into a
            profound darkness. There seem to be stars beyond
            it.]
Nickles: You're mad.
   You've lost your mind. You're maunder-
   ing . . .
            [*They rise together, their heads back, peering into*
            the darkness overhead.]
Nickles: . . . maundering.
Mr. Zuss: Let's get back where we belong.
Nickles: Go on!
Mr. Zuss: No; you.
Nickles: All right . . . together.
            [*They take each other's arm as the light fades.*]

SCENE VI

Darkness and silence as before. The drum—a
great crash and a long roll fading out. A gray

light which has no visible source drifts across
the stage where tables and chairs are scattered
and overturned. **Mr. Zuss** and **Nickles** are huddled together on their platform peering down.
J.B., his clothes torn and white with dust, faces
what was once the door. The two **Messengers,**
wearing steel helmets and brassards, stand
there, carrying **Sarah** between them.

First Messenger:
   She said she lived around here somewhere.
   This is all there is.
J.B.:   Sarah!
First M.: Where do you want her?
J.B.:   Sarah! Sarah!
First M.: On the floor? You got a floor.
   You're lucky if you got a floor.
            [*They lay her carefully down.* **J.B.** *takes his torn*
            coat off, rolls it into a pillow, kneels to put it
            under her head.]
J.B.: Where was she?
First M.:   Underneath a wall.
            [*Indicating* **Second Messenger**]
   He heard her underneath a wall
   Calling.
            [*To* **Second Messenger**]
                    Tell him what you heard her . . .
Second M.: [*Imitating*]
   Ruth! . . . Ruth!
First M.:   Nobody answered:
   Nobody could have.
            [**J.B.** *does not look up or speak. The* **First Mess-**
            enger *starts toward the door, kicking a fallen*
            chair out of his way.]
                         You been down there?
   Whole block's gone. Bank block. All of it.
   J.B.'s bank. You know. Just gone.
   Nothing left to show it ever.
   Just the hole.
            [**Sarah** *stirs, opens her eyes.* **J.B.** *leans over her.*
            She turns away.]
                    J.B.'s millions!
   That's a laugh now—J.B.'s millions!
   All he's got is just the hole.
   Plant went too—all of it—everything.
   Ask him! Just the hole. He'll tell you.
Sarah: [*Faintly, her voice following the rhythm of the*
   Second Messenger]
   Ruth! . . . Ruth!

First M.:   He can tell you.
He can tell you what he saw.
Sarah: [*Tonelessly like a voice counting*]
David ... Jonathan ... Mary ... Ruth ...
I cannot say the last.
J.B.: [*His hands on hers*]   Rebecca.
Sarah: David ... Jonathan ... Mary ... Ruth ...
J.B.: [*Looking up over his shoulder to the* **Second Messenger**]
You didn't find ... there wasn't ...
First M.:   Tell him.
Tell him what you heard.
Second M.:   I heard
Two words. I don't know what they mean.
I have brought them to you like a pair of
    pebbles
Picked up in a path or a pair of
Beads that might belong to somebody.
J.B.: There wasn't ... anyone beside?
Second M.: [*Almost a whisper*]
I only am escaped alone to tell thee.
Sarah: David ... Jonathan ... Mary ... Ruth ...
J.B.: Sarah!
        [*Silence.*]
                Listen to me!
        [*Silence.*]
                        Sarah!
Even desperate we can't despair—
Let go each other's fingers—sink
Numb in that dumb silence—drown there
Sole in our cold selves ...

                    We cannot! ...

God is there too, in the desperation.
I do not know why God should strike
But God is what is stricken also:
Life is what despairs in death
And, desperate, is life still ...

                        Sarah!
Do not let my hand go, Sarah!

Say it after me:

            The Lord
Giveth ... Say it.
Sarah: [*Mechanically*]   The Lord giveth.
J.B.: The Lord taketh away ...
Sarah: [*Flinging his hand from hers, shrieking*]
                        Takes!

Kills! Kills! Kills! Kills!

[*Silence.*]
J.B.: Blessed be the name of the Lord.
        [*The light fades.*]

SCENE VII

Darkness. Silence. Then, out of the dark, **Mr. Zuss**'s voice. It has recovered its confidence and timbre.

Mr. Zuss: Well, my friend ...
        [*The platform comes into light,* **Mr. Zuss** *and*
        Nickles *are still where they were, learning over,*
        elbows on the rail. They straighten up, stretching]
                    ... you see the position.
You see how it all comes out in the end.
Your fears were quite unfounded, weren't
    they?
Nickles: [*Sourly*]
My fears for you?
Mr. Zuss: For me? ... For me!
Why should you fear for me?
Nickles: I can't
Think!
Mr. Zuss: No, for him.
Nickles: That ham!
Mr. Zuss: Ham?
Nickles: Ham!
Mr. Zuss: [*Pleasantly*] And you've been telling
    me
Over and over that he isn't in it—
Isn't acting even: only
Living—breathing ...
Nickles: Man can muff his
Life as badly as his lines and louder.
In it or out of it he's ham.
He wouldn't understand if twenty
Thousand suffocating creatures
Shrieked and tore their tongues out at him
Choking in a bombed-out town. He'd be
Thankful!
Mr. Zuss: [*Stiffly*] I think he understands it
    Perfectly! I think that great
Yea-saying to the world was wonderful—
That wounded and deliberate Amen—
That—affirmation!
Nickles: Affirmation!
Ever watch the worms affirming?

Ever hear a hog's Amen
Just when the knife first hurt? Death is
Good for you! It makes you glisten!
Get the large economy container,
Five for the price of one!

                              You think it's
Wonderful . . .
          [*He wheels on* **Mr. Zuss** *in a sudden fury*]
                    I think it stinks!
One daughter raped and murdered by an
     idiot,
Another crushed by stones, a son
Destroyed by some fool officer's stupidity,
Two children smeared across a road
At midnight by a drunken child—
And all with God's consent!—foreknowledge!—
And he blesses God!
          [**Nickles** *points dramatically at the white, calm,
          unconcerned mask in* **Mr. Zuss***'s hands*]
                              It isn't decent!
It isn't moral even! It's disgusting!
His weeping wife in her despair
And he beside her on this trembling ham-
     bones
Praising God! . . . It's nauseating!
Mr. Zuss: You don't lose gracefully, do you?
Nickles: [*Snarling*]   I don't
Lose.
Mr. Zuss: You have.
Nickles: That's not the end of it.
Mr. Zuss: No, but that's the *way* it ends.
Nickles: Could have ended.
Mr. Zuss: What do you mean?
Nickles: Would have, if God had been content
With this poor crawling victory. He isn't.
Still He must pursue, still follow—
Hunt His creature through his branching
     veins
With agony until no peace is left him—
All one blazing day of pain:
Corner him, compel the answer.
He cannot rest until He wrings
The proof of pain, the ultimate certainty.
God always asks the proof of pain.
Mr. Zuss: And Job, in his affliction, gives it.
Nickles: No! God overreaches at the end—
Pursues too far—follows too fearfully.
He seals him in his sack of skin

And scalds his skin to crust to squeeze
The answer out, but Job evades Him.
Mr. Zuss: Who can evade the will of God!
It waits at every door we open.
What does Dante say? His will . . .
Nickles: Don't chant that chill equation at me!
Mr. Zuss: His will: our peace.
Nickles: Will was never peace, no matter
Whose will, whose peace.
Will is rule: surrender is surrender.
You *make* your peace: you don't give in to it.
Job will make his own cold peace
When God pursues him in the web too far—
Implacable, eternal Spider.
A man can always cease: it's something—
A judgment anyway: reject
The whole creation with a stale pink pill.
Mr. Zuss: World is Will. Job can't reject it.
Nickles: God has forgotten what a man can do
Once his body hurts him—once
Pain has penned him in where only
Pain has room to breathe. He learns!
He learns to spit his broken teeth out—
Spit the dirty world out—spit!
Mr. Zuss: And that's the end of everything—to
spit?
Nickles: Better than that other end
Of pain, of physical agony, of suffering
God prepares for all His creatures.
Mr. Zuss: *Is* it better? *Is* it better?
Job has suffered and praised God.
Would Job be better off asleep
Among the clods of earth in ignorance?
Nickles: Yes, when he suffers in his body:
Yes, when his suffering is *him.*
Mr. Zuss: His suffering will praise.
Nickles: It will not.
Mr. Zuss: Well,
We still have time to see.
Nickles: Put on your
Mask! You'll see!
          [*The light has faded but the faces of the actors
          are still visible.*]
Mr. Zuss: [*Raising his mask*]   Put on your own!
          [**Nickles** *leans over to find it, searching the floor
          of the platform with his hands. A long silence.
          From the silence at length*]:
The Distant Voice:
Hast thou considered my servant Job

That there is none like him on the earth,
A perfect and an upright man, one
That feareth God and escheweth evil?

Nickles: Wait a minute! I can't find . . .

The Distant Voice: [*Louder*]
And still he holdeth fast his integrity . . .

Nickles: Wait a minute, can't you? What
the . . .

The Distant Voice: [*Almost a whisper*]
Although thou movedst me against him
To destroy him . . .

[**Nickles** *rises, his mask in his two hands. He*
wheels on **Mr. Zuss** *only to see that* **Mr. Zuss**
also has his mask in his hands and stands staring
up into the canvas sky.]
[*The* **Distant Voice** *is barely audible.*]
                    without cause . . .
[*Silence. The two old actors stand side by side,*
holding their masks, their heads moving slowly
together as they search the dark.]

Nickles: Who said that?
[*Silence.*]

Mr. Zuss: They want us to go on.

Nickles: Why don't you?

Mr. Zuss: He was asking *you.*

Nickles: Who was?

Mr. Zuss: He was.

Nickles: Prompter probably. Prompter somewhere.
Your lines he was reading weren't they?

Mr. Zuss: Yes but . . .

Nickles: [*Shouting*]   Anybody there?
[*Silence.*]

Mr. Zuss: They want us to go on. I told you.

Nickles: Yes. They want us to go on . . .
I don't like it.

Mr. Zuss: We began it.
[*They put their masks on slowly. The lights fade*
out. The huge shadows appear on the canvas sky,
facing each other.]

Godmask: *. . . And still he holdeth fast his integrity*
Although thou movedst me against him
To destroy him . . .
[*His voice breaks.*]
                    without cause.

Satanmask: *Skin for skin, yea, all that a man*
Hath will he give for his life.
But put forth thine hand now and touch
His bone and his flesh

And he will curse thee to thy face.
[*The* **God-shadow** *raises its arm again in the*
formal gesture of contemptuous commitment.]

Godmask: *Behold he is in thine hand . . .*
[*The* **God-shadow** *turns away. Silence.*]
                    but . . .

Save his life!
[*The two shadows lean together over the earth.*]

Note: A second break in the action may
be made here if it is thought desirable.

SCENE VIII

There is no light but the glow on the canvas sky,
which holds the looming, leaning shadows.
They fade as a match is struck. It flares in
Sarah's hand, showing her face, and glimmers
out against the wick of a dirty lantern. As the
light of the lantern rises, **J.B.** is seen lying on the
broken propped-up table, naked but for a few
rags of clothing. **Sarah** looks at him in the new
light, shudders, lets her head drop into her
hands. There is a long silence and then a movement in the darkness of the open door where
four women and a young girl stand, their arms
filled with blankets and newspapers. They come
forward slowly into the light.

Nickles: [*Unseen, his cracked, cackling voice drifting*
down from the darkness of the platform overhead]
Never fails! Never fails!
Count on you to make a mess of it!
Every blessed blundering time
You hit at one man you blast thousands.
Think of that Flood of yours—a massacre!
Now you've fumbled it again:
Tumbled a whole city down
To blister one man's skin with agony.
[**Nickles'** *white coat appears at the foot of the*
ladder. The women, in the circle of the lantern,
are walking slowly around **J.B.** *and* **Sarah,** *star-*
ing at them as though they were figures in a show
window.]

Nickles: Look at your works! Those shivering
women
Sheltering under any crumbling
Heap to keep the sky out! Weeping!

Mrs. Adams: That's him.

Jolly Adams: Who's him?

Mrs. Adams: Grammar, Jolly.

Mrs. Lesure: Who did she say it was?

Mrs. Murphy: Him she said it was.
Poor soul!

Mrs. Lesure: Look at them sores on him!

Mrs. Adams: Don't look, child. You'll remember them.

Jolly Adams: [*Proudly*]
Every sore I seen I remember.

Mrs. Botticelli:
Who did she say she said it was?

Mrs. Murphy: Him.

Mrs. Adams: That's his wife.

Mrs. Lesure: She's pretty.

Mrs. Botticelli: Ain't she.
Looks like somebody we've seen.

Mrs. Adams: [*Snooting her*]
I don't believe you would have seen her:
Picture possibly—her picture
Posed in the penthouse.

Mrs. Botticelli: Puce with pants?

Mrs. Adams: No, the negligee.

Mrs. Botticelli: The net?

Mrs. Adams: The simple silk.

Mrs. Botticelli: Oh la! With sequins?

Mrs. Murphy:
Here's a place to park your poodle—
Nice cool floor.

Mrs. Lesure: Shove over, dearie.
[*The women settle themselves on their newspapers
off at the edge of the circle of light.* **Nickles** *has
perched himself on a chair at the side. Silence.*]

J.B.: [*A whisper*]
          God, let me die!
[**Nickles** *leers up into the dark toward the unseen
platform.*]

Sarah: [*Her voice dead*] You think He'd help you
Even to that?
[*Silence.* **Sarah** *looks up, turning her face away
from* **J.B.** *She speaks without passion, almost
mechanically.*]

Sarah: God is our enemy

J.B.: No . . . No . . . No . . . Don't
Say that Sarah!
[**Sarah's** *head turns toward him slowly as though
dragged against her will. She stares and cannot
look away.*]

God has something
Hidden from our hearts to show.

Nickles: She knows! She's looking at it!

J.B.:   Try to
Sleep.

Sarah: [*Bitterly*] He should have kept it hidden.

J.B.: Sleep now.

Sarah: You don't have to see it:
I do.

J.B.:   Yes, I know.

Nickles: [*A cackle*]   He knows!
He's back behind it and he knows!
If he could see what she can see
There's something else he might be knowing.

J.B.: Once I knew a charm for sleeping—
Not as forgetfulness but gift,
Not as sleep but second sight,
Come and from my eyelids lift
The dead of night.

Sarah: The dead . . .
                    of night . . .
[*She drops her head to her knees, whispering*]
Come and from my eyelids lift
The dead of night.
[*Silence.*]

J.B.:   Out of sleep
Something of our own comes back to us:
A drowned man's garment from the sea.
[**Sarah** *turns the lantern down. Silence. Then the
voices of the women, low.*]

Mrs. Botticelli:
Poor thing!

Mrs. Murphy: Poor thing!
Not a chick nor a child between them.

Mrs. Adams: First their daughters. Then their
sons.

Mrs. Murphy: First son first. Blew him to
pieces.
More mischance it was than war.
Asleep on their feet in the frost they walked
into it.

Mrs. Adams: Two at the viaduct: that makes
three.

Jolly Adams: [*A child's chant*]
Jolly saw the picture! the picture!

Mrs. Adams: Jolly Adams, you keep quiet.

Jolly Adams: Wanna know? The whole of the
viaduct . . .

Mrs. Adams: Never again will you look at them! Never!

Mrs. Lesure: Them magazines! They're awful! Which?

Mrs. Murphy: And after that the little one.

Mrs. Botticelli: Who in the World are they talking about, the little one? What are they talking?

Mrs. Lesure: I don't know. Somebody dogged by death it must be.

Mrs. Botticelli:
Him it must be.

Mrs. Lesure: Who's him?

Mrs. Adams: You know who.

Mrs. Murphy: You remember the . . .

Mrs. Adams: Hush! The child!

Mrs. Murphy: Back of the lumberyard.

Mrs. Lesure: Oh! Him!

Mrs. Murphy: Who did you think it was— Penthouse and negligees, daughters and dying?

Mrs. Botticelli:
Him? That's him? That millionaire?

Mrs. Lesure: Millionaires he buys like cabbages.

Mrs. Murphy: He couldn't buy cabbages now by the look of him:
The rags he's got on.

Mrs. Botticelli: Look at them sores!

Mrs. Murphy: All that's left him now is her.

Mrs. Botticelli:
Still that's something—a good woman.

Mrs. Murphy: What good is a woman to him with that hide on him?—
Or he to her if you think of it.

Mrs. Adams: Don't!

Mrs. Lesure: Can you blame her?

Mrs. Murphy: I don't blame her.
All I say is she's no comfort.
She won't cuddle.

Mrs. Adams: Really, Mrs. . . .

Mrs. Murphy: Murphy call me. What's got into you? . . .
Nothing recently I'd hazard.

Mrs. Adams: You're not so young yourself, my woman.

Mrs. Murphy: Who's your woman? I was Murphy's.

Mrs. Lesure: None of us are maids entirely.

Mrs. Murphy: Maids in mothballs some might be.

Mrs. Adams: Who might?

Mrs. Murphy: You might.

Mrs. Adams: You! you're . . . historical!

Mrs. Murphy: I never slept a night in history!

Mrs. Botticelli:
I have. Oh, my mind goes back.

Mrs. Adams: None of that! We have a child here! [*Silence.*]
How far back?

Mrs. Botticelli: I often wonder.
Farther than the first but . . . where?

Mrs. Murphy: What do you care? It's lovely country.
        [*Silence.*]
Roll a little nearer, dearie,
Me back side's froze.

Mrs. Lesure: You smell of roses.

Mrs. Murphy: Neither do you but you're warm.

Mrs. Botticelli: Well,
Good night, ladies. Good night, ladies.
        [*Silence. Out of the silence, felt rather than heard at first, a sound of sobbing, a muffled, monotonous sound like the heavy beat of a heart.*]

J.B.: If you could only sleep a little
Now they're quiet, now they're still.

Sarah: [*Her voice broken*]
I try. But oh I close my eyes and . . .
Eyes are open there to meet me!
        [*Silence. Then* **Sarah***'s voice in an agony of bitterness*]
My poor babies! Oh, my babies!
        [**J.B.** *pulls himself painfully up, sits huddled on his table in the feeble light of the lamp, his rags about him.*]

J.B.: [*Gently*] Go to sleep.

Sarah: *Go!* Go where?
If there were darkness I'd go there.
If there were night I'd lay me down in it.
God has shut the night against me.
God has set the dark alight
With horror blazing blind as day
When I go toward it . . .
                            close my eyes.

J.B.: I know. I know those waking eyes.
His will is everywhere against us—
Even in our sleep, our dreams . . .

Nickles: [*A snort of laughter up toward the dark of the platform*]
Your will, *his* peace!
Doesn't seem to grasp that, does he?
Give him another needling twinge
Between the withers and the works—
He'll understand you better.
J.B.:   If I
Knew . . . If I knew why!
Nickles: If he knew
Why he wouldn't be there. He'd be
Strangling, drowning, suffocating,
Diving for a sidewalk somewhere . . .
J.B.:   What I *can't* bear is the blindness—
Meaninglessness—the numb blow
Fallen in the stumbling night.
Sarah: [*Starting violently to her feet*]
Has death no meaning? Pain no meaning?
      [*She points at his body*]
Even these suppurating sores—
Have they no meaning for you?
Nickles: Ah!
J.B.:   [*From his heart's pain*]
God will not punish without cause.
            [**Nickles** *doubles up in a spasm of soundless laughter.*]
J.B.:   God is just.
Sarah: [*Hysterically*]   God is just!
If God is just our slaughtered children
Stank with sin, were rotten with it!
            [*She controls herself with difficulty, turns toward him, reaches her arms out, lets them fall*]
Oh, my dear! my dear! my dear!
Does God demand deception of us?—
Purchase His innocence by ours?
Must we be guilty for Him?—bear
The burden of the world's malevolence
For Him who made the world?
J.B.:   He
Knows the guilt is mine. He must know:
Has He not punished it? He knows its
Name, its time, its face, its circumstance,
The figure of its day, the door,
The opening of the door, the room, the moment . . .
Sarah: [*Fiercely*]
And you? Do you? You do not know it.
Your punishment is all you know.
            [*She moves toward the door, stops, turns*]

I will not stay here if you lie—
Connive in your destruction, cringe to it:
Not if you betray my children . . .

I will not stay to listen . . .

                              They are
Dead and they were innocent: I will not
Let you sacrifice their deaths
To make injustice justice and God good!
J.B.:   [*Covering his face with his hands*]
My heart beats. I cannot answer it.
Sarah: If you buy quiet with their innocence—
Theirs or yours . . .
      [*softly*]
                              I will not love you.
J.B.:   I have no choice but to be guilty.
Sarah: [*Her voice rising*]
We have the choice to live or die,
All of us . . .

                  curse God and die . . .
      [*Silence.*]
J.B.:   God is God or we are nothing—
Mayflies that leave their husks behind—
Our tiny lives ridiculous—a suffering
Not even sad that Someone Somewhere
Laughs at as we laugh at apes.
We have no choice but to be guilty.
God is unthinkable if we are innocent.
            [**Sarah** *turns, runs soundlessly out of the circle of light, out of the door. The women stir.* **Mrs. Murphy** *comes up on her elbow.*]
Mrs. Murphy: What did I say? I said she'd walk out on him.
Mrs. Lesure: She did.
Mrs. Botticelli: Did she?
Mrs. Murphy: His hide was too much for her.
Mrs. Botticelli:
His hide or his heart.
Mrs. Murphy: The hide comes between.
Mrs. Botticelli:
The heart is the stranger.
Mrs. Murphy: Oh, strange!
It's always strange the heart is: only
It's the skin we ever know.
J.B.:   [*Raising his head*]
Sarah, why do you not speak to me? . . .
Sarah!
      [*Silence.*]

Mrs. Adams: Now he knows.

Mrs. Murphy: And he's alone now.

[**J.B.**'s *head falls forward onto his knees. Silence. Out of the silence his voice in an agony of prayer.*]

J.B.:   *Show me my guilt, O God!*

Nickles: *His*

Guilt! His! You heard that didn't you?
He wants to feel the feel of guilt—
That putrid poultice of the soul
That draws the poison in, not out—
Inverted catheter! You going to show him?

[*Silence.* **Nickles** *rises, moves toward the ladder*]

Well? You going to show him . . . Jahveh?

[*Silence. He crosses to the ladder's foot*]

Where are those cold comforters of yours
Who justify the ways of God to
Job by making Job responsible?—
Those three upholders of the world—
Defenders of the universe—where are they?

[*Silence. He starts up the ladder. Stops. The jeering tone is gone. His voice is bitter*]

Must be almost time for comfort! . . .

[**Nickles** *vanishes into the darkness above. The light fades.*]

SCENE IX

Darkness.

J.B.'s Voice: *If I had perished from the womb, not having Been . . .*

[*A light without source rises slowly like the light at evening which enlarges everything. The canvas walls dissolve into distance, the canvas sky into endlessness. The platform has been pushed away to the side until only the ladder is visible. The* **women** *and the* **child** *are huddled together like sleeping figures on a vast plain.* **J.B.** *is alone in an enormous loneliness. Out of that seeming distance the* **Three Comforters** *come shuffling forward dressed in worn-out clothing.* **Zophar,** *a fat, red-faced man wears the wreck of a clerical collar.* **Eliphaz,** *lean and dark, wears an intern's jacket which once was white.* **Bildad** *is a squat, thick man in a ragged wind-breaker. The women do not see them, but* **Jolly Adams** *sits suddenly up clapping her hands to her mouth.* **J.B.,** *his head on his arms, sees nothing.*]

J.B.:   Death cannot heal me . . .
                              Death
Will leave my having been behind it
Like a bear's foot festering in a trap . . .

Jolly Adams: [*Her voice rising word by word to a scream*]

Look! Look! Look! Look!
Mother! Mother!

[*The* **women** *pull themselves up. The* **Three Comforters** *shuffle on, squat in the rubbish around* **J.B.:** Zophar *lighting the stub of a fat, ragged cigar;* **Eliphaz** *lighting a broken pipe;* **Bildad** *lighting a crumpled cigarette.*]

Mrs. Murphy: Agh, the scavengers!

Mrs. Botticelli:

Three old pokey crows they look like.

Mrs. Murphy:

They are, too. It's the smell of the suffering.
See that leather-backed old bucket?—
Kind of character you hear from
Sundays in a public park
Pounding the hell out of everything . . . *you*
know.

Mrs. Botticelli:

I know. Wall Street. Bakers. Bankers.

Mrs. Lesure: All the answers in a book.

Mrs. Botticelli:

Russkys got them all—the answers.

Mrs. Murphy:

Characters like that, they smell the
Human smell of heartsick misery
Farther than a kite smells carrion.

Mrs. Lesure: Who's the collar?

Mrs. Murphy: Some spoiled priest.

Mrs. Botticelli:

They can smell it farther even.

Mrs. Lesure: Not as far as dead-beat doctors:
They're the nosies.

Mrs. Murphy: Let them nose!

[*A tremendous yawn*]

Ohhh, I'm halfway over . . .
                              drownding
Down and down . . .
                              I hear the seagulls
Singing soundings in the sea . . .

[*She lets herself fall back on her newspapers. The others follow one by one.*]

Jolly Adams: I don't hear them.

Mrs. Botticelli: Pound your ears.

Mrs. Lesure: Slip your moorings ... Oh, I'm
numb.
Mrs. Murphy: Come alongside, dear.
Mrs. Lesure: I'm coming.
Mrs. Botticelli:
That doctor one, he makes me creep.
Mrs. Murphy: Keep your thumb on your
thoughts or he'll diddle them.
Mrs. Botticelli:
Let him pry: he'll lose an eyeball.
Mrs. Lesure: He's a peeper. Watch your sleep.
Mrs. Murphy: Who was she, all gore, all story,
Dabbled in a deep blood sea,
And what she washed in, that was she?
Mrs. Lesure: [*From her dream*]
Some queen of Scotland ...
Mrs. Murphy: Queen of Scones ...
[*A long silence. The* **Three Comforters** *squat
smoking and waiting. At length* **J.B.** *pulls himself
painfully up to kneel on his table, his face raised.*]
J.B.: [*A whisper*]
God! My God! My God! What have I
Done?
[*Silence.*]
Bildad: [*Removing his cigarette*]
Fair question, Big Boy.
Anyone answer you yet? No answer?
Zophar: [*Removing his cigar*]
That was answered long ago—
Long ago.
Eliphaz: [*Knocking out his pipe*]
In dreams are answers.
How do your dreams go, Big Boy? Tell!
J.B.: [*Peering*]
Is someone there? Where? I cannot
See you in this little light
My eyes too fail me ...
[*Silence.*]
                Who is there?
[*Silence.*]
I know how ludicrous I must look,
Covered with rags, my skin pustulant ...
[*Silence.*]
I know ...
[*Silence.*]
                I know how others see me.
[*A long silence.*]
Why have you come?
Bildad: [*A coarse laugh*] For comfort, Big Boy.

Didn't you ring?
Zophar: [*A fat laugh*] That's it: for comfort!
Eliphaz: [*A thin laugh*]
All the comfort you can find.
Bildad: All the kinds of.
Eliphaz: *All* the comforts.
Zophar: You called us and we came.
J.B.:   I called
God.
Bildad: Didn't you!
Eliphaz: Didn't you just!
Zophar: Why should God reply to *you*
From the blue depths of His Eternity?
Eliphaz: Blind depths of His Unconsciousness?
Bildad: Blank depths of His Necessity?
Zophar: God is far above in Mystery.
Eliphaz: God is far below in Mindlessness.
Bildad: God is far within in History—
Why should God have time for you?
J.B.: The hand of God has touched me. Look
at me!
Every hope I ever had,
Every task I put my mind to,
Every work I've ever done
Annulled as though I had not done it.
My trace extinguished in the land,
My children dead, my father's name
Obliterated in the sunlight everywhere ...

Love too has left me.
Bildad: Love!
[*A great guffaw*]
What's love to Him? One man's misery!
J.B.: [*Hardly daring*]
If I am innocent ...?
Bildad: [*Snort of jeering laughter*] Innocent! Inno-
cent!
Nations shall perish in their innocence.
Classes shall perish in their innocence.
Young men in slaughtered cities
Offering their silly throats
Against the tanks in innocence shall perish.
What's your innocence to theirs?
God is History. If you offend Him
Will not History dispense with you?
History has no time for innocence.
J.B.: God is just. We are not squeezed
Naked through a ridiculous orifice
Like bulls into a blazing ring

To blunder there by blindfold laws
We never learn or can, deceived by
Stratagems and fooled by feints,
For sport, for nothing, till we fall
We're pricked so badly.

Bildad: [*All park-bench orator*]   Screw your justice!

History is justice!—time
Inexorably turned to truth!—
Not for one man. For humanity.
One man's life won't measure on it.
One man's suffering won't count, no matter
What his suffering; but All will.
At the end there will be justice!—
Justice for All! Justice for everyone!
            [*subsiding*]
On the way—it doesn't matter.

J.B.:   Guilt matters. Guilt must always matter.
Unless guilt matters the whole world is
Meaningless. God too is nothing.

Bildad: [*Losing interest*]
You may be guiltier than Hell
As History counts guilt and not
One smudging thumbprint on your conscience.
Guilt is a sociological accident:
Wrong class—wrong century—
You pay for your luck with your licks, that's all.

            [**Eliphaz** *has been fidgeting. Now he breaks in*
            like a professor in a seminar, poking a forefinger
            at the air.]

Eliphaz: Come! Come! Come! Guilt is a
Psychophenomenal situation—
An illusion, a disease, a sickness:
That filthy feeling at the fingers,
Scent of dung beneath the nails . . .

Zophar: [*Outraged, flushed, head thrown back*]
Guilt is illusion? Guilt is reality!—
The one reality there is!
All mankind are guilty always!

Bildad: [*Jeering*]
The Fall of Man it felled us all!

            [**J.B.**'s *voice breaks through the squabbling with*
            something of its old authority.]

J.B.:   *No doubt ye are the people*
And wisdom shall die with you! I am
Bereaved, in pain, desperate, and you mock
me!

There was a time when men found pity
Finding each other in the night:
Misery to walk with misery—
Brother in whose brother-guilt
Guilt could be conceived and recognized.
We have forgotten pity.

Eliphaz: No.
We have surmounted guilt. It's quite,
Quite different, isn't it? You see the difference.
Science knows now that the sentient spirit
Floats like the chambered nautilus on a sea
That drifts it under skies that drive:
Beneath, the sea of the subconscious;
Above, the winds that wind the world.
Caught between that sky, that sea,
Self has no will, cannot be guilty.
The sea drifts. The sky drives.
The tiny, shining bladder of the soul
Washes with wind and wave or shudders
Shattered between them.

Zophar: Blasphemy!
Bildad: Bullshit!
Eliphaz: [*Oblivious*]
There is no guilt, my man. We all are
Victims of our guilt, not guilty.
We kill the king in ignorance: the voice
Reveals: we blind ourselves. At our
Beginning, in the inmost room,
Each one of us, disgusting monster
Changed by the chilling moon to child,
Violates his mother. Are we guilty?
Our guilt is underneath the Sybil's
Stone: not known.

J.B.: [*Violently*]   I'd rather suffer
Every unspeakable suffering God sends,
Knowing it was I that suffered,
I that earned the need to suffer,
I that acted, I that chose,
Than wash my hands with yours in that
Defiling innocence. Can we be men
And make an irresponsible ignorance
Responsible for everything? I will not
Listen to you!

            [**J.B.** *pulls his rags over his head.*]

Eliphaz: [*Shrugging*] But you will. You will.
Zophar: Ah, my son, how well you said that!
How well you said it! Without guilt
What is a man? An animal, isn't he?

A wolf forgiven at his meat,
A beetle innocent in his copulation.
What divides us from the universe
Of blood and seed, conceives the soul in us,
Brings us to God, but guilt? The lion
Dies of death: we die of suffering.
The lion vanishes: our souls accept
Eternities of reparation.
But for our guilt we too would vanish,
Bundles of corrupting bones
Bagged in a hairless hide and rotting.
Happy the man whom God correcteth!
He tastes his guilt. His hope begins.
He is in league with the stones in certainty.
> [**J.B.** *pulls his rags from his head, drags himself
> around toward the voice.*]

J.B.:   *Teach me and I will hold my tongue.
Show me my transgression.*

Zophar: [*Gently*]   No.
No, my son. You show *me*.
> [*He hunches forward dropping his voice*]

Search your inmost heart! Question it!
Guilt is a deceptive secret,
The labor often of years, a work
Conceived in infancy, brought to birth
In unpredictable forms years after:
At twelve the palpable elder brother;
At seventeen, perhaps, the servant
Seen by the lamp by accident . . .

J.B.:   [*Urgently, the words forced from him*]   My
Sin! Teach me my sin! My wickedness!
Surely iniquity that suffers
Judgment like mine cannot be secret.
Mine is no childish fault, no nastiness
Concealed behind a bathroom door,
No sin a prurient virtue practices
Licking the silence from its lips
Like sugar afterwards. Mine is flagrant,
Worthy of death, of many deaths,
Of shame, loss, hurt, indignities
Such as these! Such as these!
Speak of the sin I must have sinned
To suffer what you see me suffer.

Zophar: Do we need to name our sins
To know the need to be forgiven?
Repent, my son! Repent!

J.B.:   [*An agony of earnestness*]   I sit here
Such as you see me. In my soul
I suffer what you guess I suffer.

Tell me the wickedness that justifies it.
Shall I repent of sins I have not
Sinned to understand it? Till I
Die I will not violate my integrity.

Zophar: [*A fat chuckle*]
Your integrity! Your integrity!
What integrity have you?—
A man, a miserable, mortal, sinful,
Venal man like any other.
You squat there challenging the universe
To tell you what your crime is called,
Thinking, because your life was virtuous,
It can't be called. It can. Your sin is
Simple. You were born a man!

J.B.:   What is my fault? What have I done?

Zophar: [*Thundering*]
What is your fault? Man's heart is evil!
What have you done? Man's will is evil.
Your fault, your sin, are heart and will:
The worm at heart, the wilful will
Corrupted with its foul imagining.
> [**J.B.** *crouches lower in his rags. Silence.*]

J.B.:   Yours is the cruelest comfort of them all,
Making the Creator of the Universe
The miscreator of mankind—
A party to the crimes He punishes . . .

Making my sin . . .
                    a horror . . .
                                        a deformity . . .

Zophar: [*Collapsing into his own voice*]
If it were otherwise we could not bear it . . .
Without the fault, without the Fall,
We're madmen: all of us are madmen . . .
> [*He sits staring at his hands, then repeats the
> phrase:*]

        Without the Fall
            We're madmen all.
        We watch the stars
            That creep and crawl . . .

Bildad: Like dying flies
            Across the wall
            Of night . . .

Eliphaz: and shriek . . .
            And that is all.

Zophar: Without the Fall . . .
> [*A long silence. Out of the silence at last* **J.B.'s**
> *voice, barely audible.*]

J.B.:   *God, my God, my God, answer me!*

[*Silence.*]
  [*His voice rises*]
I cry out of wrong but I am not heard . . .
I cry aloud but there is no judgment.
  [*Silence.*]
  [*Violently*]
Though He slay me, yet will I trust in Him . . .
  [*Silence.*]
  [*His voice drops*]
But I will maintain my own ways before Him . . .
  [*Silence.*]
  [*The ancient human cry*]
Oh, that I knew where I might find Him!—
That I might come even to His seat!
I would order my cause before Him
And fill my mouth with arguments.
  [*There is a rushing sound in the air.*]
                                Behold,
I go forward but He is not there,
Backward, but I cannot perceive Him . . .
  [*Out of the rushing sound, the* **Distant Voice**;
  J.B. *cowers as he hears it, his rags over his head.*]

The Distant Voice:
Who is this that darkeneth counsel
By words without knowledge? . . .

                              Where wast thou
When I laid the foundations of the earth . . .

When the morning stars sang together
And all the sons of God shouted for
Joy?
        Hast thou commanded the morning?
Hast thou entered into the springs of the sea
Or hast thou walked in the search of the depth?

Have the gates of death been opened unto thee?

Where is the way where light dwelleth?
And as for darkness, where is the place thereof?

Hast thou entered into the treasures of the snow?

By what way is the light parted
Which scattereth the east wind upon the earth?

Can'st thou bind the sweet influences of the Pleiades?

Hast thou given the horse strength?
Hast thou clothed his neck with thunder?

He saith among the trumpets, Ha, ha;
He smelleth the battle afar off,
The thunder of the captains and the shouting.

Doth the eagle mount up at thy command?

Her eyes behold afar off.
Her young ones also suck up blood:
And where the slain are, there is she . . .

  [*The rushing sound dies away. The* **Three**
  Comforters *stir uneasily, peering up into the*
  darkness. One by one they rise.]
Bildad: The wind's gone round.
Zophar: It's cold.
Bildad: I told you.
Eliphaz: I hear the silence like a sound.
Zophar: Wait for me!
Bildad: The wind's gone round.
  [*They go out as they came. Silence.* **J.B.** *sits mo-*
  tionless, his head covered. The rushing sound
  returns like the second, stronger gust of a great
  storm. **The Voice** *rises above it.*]
The Distant Voice:
Shall he that contendeth with the Almighty instruct
Him? . . .
  [*The rushing sound dies away again. The women*
  sit up, huddle together.]
Jolly Adams: [*Screaming*]
                  Mother! Mother! what was
That?
Mrs. Adams: The wind, child. Only the wind.
  Only the wind.
Jolly Adams: I heard a word.
Mrs. Adams: You heard the thunder in the
  wind.
Jolly Adams: [*Drowsy*]
  Under the wind there was a word . . .
    [**Mrs. Adams** *picks her up. The women gather*
    their newspapers and blankets and stumble out
    into the darkness through the door. For the third
    time the rushing sound returns.]
The Distant Voice:
He that reproveth God, let him answer it!
J.B.:   *Behold, I am vile; what shall I answer thee?*
  I will lay mine hand upon my mouth.
The Distant Voice:
Gird up thy loins like a man:
I will demand of thee, and declare thou unto me.
    [**J.B.** *pulls himself painfully to his knees.*]
Wilt thou disannul my judgment?
    [**J.B.** *does not answer.*]
Wilt thou condemn
Me that thou mayest be righteous?

Hast thou an arm like God? Or canst thou
Thunder with a voice like Him?

Deck thyself now with majesty and excellency
And array thyself with glory and beauty . . .

Then will I also confess unto thee
That thine own right hand can save thee.
          [**J.B.** *raises his bowed head.*]
J.B.:   [*Gently*]   *I know that thou canst do every-*
     thing. . . .
          [*The rushing sound dies away.*]
And that no thought can be withholden from thee.
Who is he that hideth counsel without knowledge?
Therefore have I uttered that I understood not:
Things too wonderful for me, which I knew not.

Hear, I beseech thee, and I will speak: . . .
          [*Silence.*]
I have heard of thee by the hearing of the ear . . .
But now . . .
          [*His face is drawn in agony*]
               mine eye seeth thee!
          [*He bows his head. His hands wring each other*]
                              Wherefore

I abhor myself . . . and repent . . .
          [*The light fades.*]

SCENE X

The Platform. As the lights come on the two
actors turn violently away from each other,
tearing their masks off. **Nickles,** with a gesture
of disgust, skims his into a corner.

Nickles: Well, that's that!
Mr. Zuss: That's . . . that!
          [*Silence. After a time* **Nickles** *looks cautiously*
          around at **Mr. Zuss.**]
Nickles: What's the matter with you?
Mr. Zuss: Nothing.
Nickles: You don't look pleased.
Mr. Zuss: Should I?
Nickles: Well,
     You were right weren't you?
Mr. Zuss: [*Too loud*]   Of course I was right.
Nickles: [*Too soft*]
     Anyway, you were magnificent.
Mr. Zuss: Thank you.

          [*He looks at the mask in his hands: puts it down*
          as though it had stung him. Silence. **Mr. Zuss**
          pretends to be busy with a shoelace.]
Mr. Zuss: Why did you say that?
Nickles: What did I say?
Mr. Zuss: Why did you say it like that?
Nickles: Like what?
Mr. Zuss: [*Imitating*]
     "Anyway!" . . .
               "Anyway, you were magnificent!"
Nickles: You know. "Anyway." Regardless.
Mr. Zuss: Regardless of
     What?
Nickles: Now, wait a minute! Wait a
     Minute! You were magnificent. I said so.
Mr. Zuss: Go on. Finish it.
Nickles: Finish what?
Mr. Zuss: Regardless of . . . ?
Nickles: . . . being right, of course.
     What's got into you, my friend? What's eating
          you?
     Being magnificent and being right
     Don't go together in this universe.
     It's being wrong—a desperate stubbornness
     Fighting the inextinguishable stars—
     Excites imagination. You were
     Right. And knew it. And were admirable.
     Notwithstanding!
          [*Snickering*]
                              anyway!
          [*A snarl*]   regardless!
Mr. Zuss: I knew you noticed.
Nickles: Of course I noticed.
     What lover of the art could fail to!
          [*Something in* **Mr. Zuss**'*s expression stops him.*]
                              Noticed
     What?
Mr. Zuss: That tone! That look he gave me!
Nickles: He misconceived the part entirely.
Mr. Zuss: Misconceived the world! Buggered
     it!
Nickles: Giving in like that! Whimpering!
Mr. Zuss: Giving in! You call that arrogant,
     Smiling, supercilious humility
     Giving in to God?
Nickles: Arrogant!
     His suppurating flesh—his children—
     Let's not talk about those children—
     Everything he ever had!

And all he asks is answers of the universe:
All he asks is reasons why—
Why? Why? And God replies to him:
God comes whirling in the wind replying—
What? That God knows more than he does.
That God's more powerful than he!—
Throwing the whole creation at him!
Throwing the Glory and the Power!
What's the Power to a broken man
Trampled beneath it like a toad already?
What's the Glory to a skin that stinks!
And this ham actor!—what does *he* do?
How does he play Job to that?

    [*Attitude*]

"Thank you!" "I'm a worm!" "Take two!"

Plays the way a sheep would play it—
Pious, contemptible, goddam sheep
Without the spunk to spit on Christmas!

    [**Mr. Zuss** *has watched* **Nickles'** *mounting rage in silence, staring at him.* **Nickles** *breaks off, shuffles, looks at* **Mr. Zuss**, *crosses to the ladder, swings a leg across the rail.*]

Well . . .

    [*He swings the other over*]

    you said he would . . .

    [*He starts down*]

        You're right.

    [*Another rung*]

I'm wrong.

    [*Another*]

    You win.

    [*Another*]

        God always wins.

    [*He peers down into the dark under the platform*]

Where did I put that . . . popcorn?

Mr. Zuss: Win!
Planets and Pleiades and eagles—
Screaming horses—scales of light—
The wonder and the mystery of the universe—
The unimaginable might of things—
Immeasurable knowledge in the waters
    somewhere
Wandering their ways—the searchless power
Burning on the hearth of stars—
Beauty beyond the feel of fingers—
Marvel beyond the maze of mind—
The whole creation! And God showed him!
God stood stooping there to show him!

Last Orion! Least sea shell! . . .
And what did Job do?

    [**Mr. Zuss** *has worked himself up into a dramatic fury equaling* **Nickles'**.]

        Job . . . just . . . sat!

    [*Silence.*]

Sat there!

    [*Silence.*]

        Dumb!

    [*Silence.*]

        Until it ended!

Then! . . . you heard him!

    [**Mr. Zuss** *chokes*]

        Then, he *calmed* me!
Gentled me the way a farmhand
Gentles a bulging, bugling bull!
Forgave me! . . .
        for the world! . . .
            for everything!

Nickles: [*Poking around in the shadow under the platform*]
Nonsense! He repented, didn't he—
The perfect and the upright man!
He repented!

Mr. Zuss: That's just it!
He repented. It was *him*—
Not the fear of God but *him*!

Nickles: Fear? Of course he feared. Why
wouldn't he?
God with all those stars and stallions!
He with little children's bones!

Mr. Zuss: [*Pursuing his mounting indignation*]
. . . As though Job's suffering were justified
Not by the Will of God but Job's
Acceptance of God's Will . . .

Nickles: Well,
What did you hope for? Hallelujahs?

Mr. Zuss: [*Not hearing*]
. . . In spite of everything he'd suffered!
In spite of all he'd lost and loved
He understood and he forgave it! . . .

Nickles: [*A contemptuous snort as he straightens to face* **Mr. Zuss** *on the platform*]
What other victory could God win?
The choice is swallowing this swill of world
Or vomiting in the trough. Job swallowed it,
That's your triumph!—that he swallowed it.

Mr. Zuss: . . . He'd heard of God and now he
    saw Him!

Who's the judge in judgment there?
Who plays the hero, God or him?
Is God to be *forgiven?*
Nickles: Isn't he?
Job was innocent, you may remember ...
      [*Silence.*]
      [*A nasty singsong*]
The perfect and the upright man!
Mr. Zuss: [*Deflated*]
Don't start that again! I'm sick of it.
Nickles: *You* are!
Mr. Zuss: I am. Sick to death.
      [*Swinging his leg over the rail and starting down
      the ladder*]
I'd rather sell balloons to children ...
Lights! ...
      [*He shouts*]
      Turn those lights on, can't you?
Want to see me break my neck?
      [*The platform lights go out. Total darkness.*]
      [*Louder.*]
Lights! Lights! That's not the end of it.
Nickles: [*In the darkness*]
Why isn't that the end? It's over.
Job has chosen how to choose.
You've made your bow? You want another?
      [*The dangling light bulbs come feebly on. By their
      light* **J.B.** *can still be seen kneeling on his broken
      table.* **Mr. Zuss** *and* **Nickles** *crawl under the
      platform after their traps. Their voices come from
      the shadow, punctuated by grunts and wheezes.*]
Mr. Zuss: You know as well as I there's
    more . . .

There's always one more scene no matter
Who plays Job or how he plays it ...

God restores him at the end.
Nickles: [*A snort*]
God restores us all. That's normal.
That's God's mercy to mankind ...

We never asked Him to be born ...

We never chose the lives we die of ...

They beat our rumps to make us breathe ...

But God, if we have suffered patiently,
Borne it in silence, stood the stench,
Rewards us ...
              gives our dirty selves back.

      [**Mr. Zuss** *emerges in his white jacket, adjusting
      his cap.*]
Mr. Zuss: Souls back!
Nickles: Selves back! Dirty selves
    We've known too well and never wanted.
Mr. Zuss: That's not this play.
      [**Nickles** *backs out with his jacket and cap and
      tray; puts them on.*]
Nickles: Hell it isn't.
      [**Mr. Zuss** *tightens his balloon belt.*]
Mr. Zuss: God restores him *here.* On earth.
Nickles: [*Balancing his tray*]
So Job gets his in cash. That's generous.
What percentage off for cash?
Mr. Zuss: Gets all he ever had and more—
    Much more.
Nickles: [*Cheerfully ironic*]
Sure. His wife. His children!
Mr. Zuss: [*Embarrassed*]
He gets his wife back, and the children ...
Follow in nature's course.
      [**Nickles,** *who has stooped to pick up a bag of
      popcorn, straightens slowly, stares at* **Mr. Zuss.**]
Nickles: [*Harshly*]   You're lying.
Mr. Zuss: I'm not lying.
Nickles: I say you're lying.
Mr. Zuss: Why should I lie. It's in the Book.
Nickles: [*Jeering*]
Wife back! Balls! He wouldn't touch her.
He wouldn't take her with a glove!
After all that filth and blood and
Fury to begin again! ...
This fetid earth! That frightened Heaven
Terrified to trust the soul
It made with Its own hands, but testing it,
Tasting it, by trial, by torture,
Over and over till the last, least town
On all this reeling, reeking earth
Stinks with a spiritual agony
That stains the stones with excrement and
    shows
In shadow on each greasy curtain!
After life like his to take
The seed up of the sad creation
Planting the hopeful world again—
He can't! ... he won't! ... he wouldn't touch
    her!
Mr. Zuss: He does though.
Nickles: [*Raging*]   Live his life again?—

Not even the most ignorant, obstinate,
Stupid or degraded man
This filthy planet ever farrowed,
Offered the opportunity to live
His bodily life twice over, would accept it—
Least of all Job, poor, trampled bastard!

> [**Mr. Zuss** *has finished fooling with his balloons.
> He straightens up and marches off without a
> glance at* **Nickles.**]

It can't be borne twice over! Can't be!

Mr. Zuss: It is though. Time and again it is—
Every blessed generation . . .

> [*His voice drifts back as he disappears*]

Time and again . . .

                        Time and again . . .

> [**Nickles** *starts to follow, looks back, sees* **J.B.**
> *kneeling in his rubble, hesitates, crosses, squats
> behind him, his vendor's cap pushed back on his
> head, his tray on his knees.*]

Nickles: J.B.!
J.B.:   Let me alone.
Nickles: It's me.

> [J.B. shrugs.]

I'm not the Father. I'm the—Friend.
J.B.:   I have no friend.
Nickles: Oh come off it.
You don't have to act with me.

> [J.B. is silent.]

O.K. Carry on.
All I wanted was to help.
Professional counsel you might call it . . .

> [J.B. is silent.]

Of course you know how all this ends? . . .

> [J.B. is silent.]

I wondered how you'd play the end.
J.B.:   Who knows what the end is, ever?
Nickles: I do. You do.
J.B.:   Then don't tell me.
Nickles: What's the worst thing you can think
of?
J.B.:   I have asked for death. Begged for it.
Prayed for it.
Nickles: Then the worst thing can't be death.
J.B.:   Ah!
Nickles: You know now.
J.B.:   No. You tell me.
Nickles: Why should I tell you when you know?
J.B.:   Then don't. I'm sick of mysteries. Sick of
them.

Nickles: He gives it back to you.
J.B.:   What back?
Nickles: All of it.
Everything He ever took:
Wife, health, children, everything.
J.B.:   I have no wife.
Nickles: She comes back to you.
J.B.:   I have no children.
Nickles: [*A nasty laugh*] You'll have better ones.
J.B.:   My skin is . . .

> [*He breaks off, staring at the skin of his naked
> arms.*]

Nickles: Oh come on! I know the
Look of grease paint!
J.B.:   . . . whole! It's healed!
Nickles: [*Heavily ironic*]
You see? You see what I mean? What He
plans for you?

> [**J.B.,** *staring at his arms, is silent.*]

Nickles: [*Leaning forward, urgently*]
Tell me how you play the end.
Any man was screwed as Job was! . . .

> [**J.B.** *does not answer.*]

I'll tell you how you play it. Listen!
Think of all the mucked-up millions
Since this buggered world began
Said, No!, said, Thank you!, took a rope's end,
Took a window for a door,
Swallowed something, gagged on some-
thing . . .

> [**J.B.** *lifts his head: he is listening but not to*
> **Nickles.**]

None of them knew the truth as Job does.
None of them had his cause to know.
J.B.:   Listen! Do you hear? There's someone . . .
Nickles: [*Violently*]
Job won't take it! Job won't touch it!
Job will fling it in God's face
With half his guts to make it spatter!
He'd rather suffocate in dung—
Choke in ordure—
J.B.:   [*Rising*]   There is someone—
Someone waiting at the door.
Nickles: [*Pulling his cap down, rising slowly*]
                        I know.

> [*The dangling lights dim out.*]

SCENE XI

A light comes from the canvas door. It increases as though day were beginning somewhere. **Nickles** has gone.

J.B.:   Who is it?
[*He crosses toward the door walking with his old ease. Stops.*]
Is there someone there?
[*There is no answer. He goes on. Reaches the door.*]
Sarah!
[*The light increases. She is sitting on the sill, a broken twig in her hand.*]
Sarah: Look, Job: the forsythia,
The first few leaves . . .
not leaves though . . .
petals . . .

J.B.:   [*Roughly*] Get up!
Sarah: Where shall I go?
J.B.:   Where you went!
Wherever!
[*She does not answer.*]
[*More gently*]
Where?
Sarah: Among the ashes.
All there is now of the town is ashes.
Mountains of ashes. Shattered glass.
Glittering cliffs of glass all shattered
Steeper than a cat could climb
If there were cats still . . .
And the pigeons—
They wheel and settle and whirl off
Wheeling and almost settling . . .
And the silence—
There is no sound there now—no wind sound—
Nothing that could sound the wind—
Could make it sing—no door—no doorway . . .
Only this.
[*She looks at the twig in her hands*]
Among the ashes!
I found it growing in the ashes,
Gold as though it did not know . . .
[*Her voice rises hysterically*]
I broke the branch to strip the leaves off—
Petals again! . . .

[*She cradles it in her arms.*]
But they so clung to it!
J.B.:   Curse God and die, you said to me.
Sarah: Yes.
[*She looks up at him for the first time, then down again.*]
You wanted justice, didn't you?
There isn't any. There's the world . . .
[*She begins to rock on the doorsill, the little branch in her arms.*]
Cry for justice and the stars
Will stare until your eyes sting. Weep,
Enormous winds will thrash the water.
Cry in sleep for your lost children,
Snow will fall . . .
snow will fall . . .
J.B.:   Why did you leave me alone?
Sarah: I loved you.
I couldn't help you any more.
You wanted justice and there was none—
Only love.
J.B.:   He does not love. He
Is.
Sarah: But we do. That's the wonder.
J.B.:   Yet you left me.
Sarah: Yes, I left you.
I thought there was a way away . . .

Water under bridges opens
Closing and the companion stars
Still float there afterwards. I thought the door
Opened into closing water.

J.B.:   Sarah!
[*He drops on his knees beside her in the doorway, his arms around her.*]
Sarah: Oh, I never could!
I never could! Even the forsythia . . .
[*She is half laughing, half crying*]
Even the forsythia beside the
Stair could stop me.
[*They cling to each other. Then she rises, drawing him up, peering at the darkness inside the door.*]
J.B.:   It's too dark to see.
[*She turns, pulls his head down between her hands and kisses him.*]
Sarah: Then blow on the coal of the heart, my darling.
J.B.:   The coal of the heart . . .

Sarah: It's all the light now.
        [**Sarah** *comes forward into the dim room,* **J.B.**
        *behind her. She lifts a fallen chair, sets it
        straight.*]
Blow on the coal of the heart.
The candles in churches are out.
The lights have gone out in the sky.
Blow on the coal of the heart
And we'll see by and by . . .
        [**J.B.** *has joined her, lifting and straightening the
        chairs.*]

                    We'll see where we are.
The wit won't burn and the wet soul
    smoulders.
Blow on the coal of the heart and we'll
    know . . .
We'll know . . .
        [*The light increases, plain white daylight from
        the door, as they work.*]

CURTAIN

It is unusually difficult to judge the theatrical effectiveness of *J.B.* from a reading. MacLeish's language and syntax are extremely complex, and a single reading of the play is usually insufficient to gain complete understanding even of the broad outline of what is happening. In a good production, the actors and their director have studied the dialogue in minute detail and can interpret it for an audience with such gestures and vocal nuances as make the meanings clear. Reading the play, however, one must do all of this work for himself. Nonetheless, after two or three readings (in order to do in the imagination what normally the actors would do in the theatre), most readers are prepared to admit that *J.B.* has power and would be moving in the theatre. Indeed, a number of successful productions, both professional and amateur, in the several years since the play was written testify to its power and effectiveness in the theatre. From what elements in the script are this power and effectiveness derived?

Utilizing the same analytical approach employed for *The Little Foxes* and *Cyrano de Bergerac,* the reader will perceive that the effectiveness of *J.B.* does not lie in its plot, for the plot is deceptively simple and is well known to everyone before the play begins. Job is a "perfect and an upright man" who has vast possessions. To test his faith, God takes all Job's possessions from him. Once Job has understood as much as man can of what has happened to him, God restores all. These three sentences sum up very simply what happens in the play, and certainly very little suspense is generated. This is not to say, of course, that the plot is uninteresting. Indeed, the events are fundamental to human life; the basic rhythm (unexpected and apparently undeserved evil coming to crush one) corresponds to the rhythm of our own lives, and interest is held through identification. But we do not base our interest upon "what happens next?", and the play's plot is clearly not the major factor that strikes a responsive chord in the depths of the soul.

Character development is not the play's major asset either. Certain of the characters are developed more fully than others, but most of them are strictly two-dimensional, cardboard figures placed there to perform a function and that is all. As was demonstrated in *Cyrano de Bergerac,* there is nothing wrong with this approach if it suits the playwright's purpose, and in this case the playwright turns the

A Discussion of the Script

shallowness of his characters into a theatrical virtue by deliberately using them to lift the play out of any realistic context. Bringing the same actors in first as soldiers, then as newspaper reporters, then as policemen, and so on, serves an important function, the same function as having Zuss and Nickles slip in and out of the characters of God and Satan. It forces the audience's attention to the fact that they are in a theatre, that this is not real life, and that they are not to suspend their disbelief, as audiences for *Cyrano de Bergerac* were expected to, but must examine critically what happens in the play, consider the skill of the actors performing it, and think about the issues the play raises. Of course the audience may not go through this evaluation consciously, but the aesthetic approach it entails underlies a major portion of the nonrealistic theatre. Zuss and Nickles are perhaps the most interesting characters in the play, and they are developed with some depth and insight, but they can hardly be described as outstanding examples of three-dimensional characterization. Job is the central figure in the play, but his characterization is remarkably shallow for one who is on stage so much. The audience knows very little more about him than that he is a perfect and an upright man. Beyond Zuss, Nickles and J.B., it is hardly necessary to comment on characterization. Each character is developed just enough to meet the playwright's needs, and that is all. Clearly, if this play depended upon character development for its power, it would be weak indeed.

MacLeish has been widely praised for showing, in John Ciardi's words, "how to write poetic drama in the twentieth century," but it would hardly be accurate to say that the playwright's use of language is the primary basis of the play's power. The language is highly effective in places, elevating what might otherwise be rather ordinary conversation into something far more meaningful and touching. On the other hand, there are also a number of spots in the script where the playwright's highly complex syntax tends to obscure meaning—especially when spoken aloud in the theatre, where the hearer cannot reread an especially difficult text. MacLeish's use of poetry undoubtedly adds a great deal to the play, but it is far from the play's most powerful element.

The factor that really lifts this play into the realm of the extraordinary is the thought content behind it—its theme. *The Little Foxes* and *Cyrano de Bergerac* have each had some telling points to make, but in neither case has the playwright's philosophical probing been nearly as important as other elements. In the case of *J.B.*, however, it is clear that the playwright was concerned above all else with some fundamental ideas that he was trying to express, and that the plot, the characters, and the language were brought together for the specific purpose of exploring these ideas as thoroughly as possible. The concept of "exploring fundamental ideas" has been carefully used above. It is relatively rare for a play (or other work of art of any merit) to try to give definitive answers. Most playwrights will evade a question like "what does your play mean?" on the grounds that the play must be allowed to speak for itself. Indeed, most important plays do not "mean" any one single thing, and the attempt to state the "theme" of a really good play in a single sentence is a pointless exercise in semantics. When a play's message can be stated in a single sentence, it is more appropriate to call it a *thesis* than a *theme*, and a thesis play usually results from a playwright's overwhelming desire to propagandize on an issue close to his heart. The majority of good plays, however, explore a complex but interconnecting series of themes, usually raising questions rather than giving answers. The really important questions of life have no easy answers, and a play that is honest in dealing with such questions will bring them up, explore them, suggest alternative solutions, point out the shortcomings of each solution, and stimulate the viewer's thinking without presuming to tell him what to think.

So it is with *J.B.* MacLeish is dealing here with some of the most fundamental questions that man has asked since the beginning of recorded time. The presence in the world of overwhelming evil defies rational explanation, especially when simple logic suggests that man could live at peace with his neighbors if only he would really adopt the Golden Rule. The paradox summed up in Nickle's jingle,

> If God is God He is not good,
> If God is good, He is not God;

is a difficult one to resolve. If God really has the power implicit in the name "God," how can He be good if He allows such evil as, for example, Hitler's murder of six million Jews? If, on the other hand, God is really good, is He an all-powerful God? Such fundamental questions clearly bothered the author of the Biblical *Book of Job* several centuries before the birth of Christ, and they are the questions MacLeish has raised in *J.B.* MacLeish does not propose an answer. The arguments between Zuss and Nickles simply explore many aspects of these questions. J. B.'s agonies illustrate the extent to which misfortune can plunge a man from the pinnacle of success into misery; the ridiculously inadequate words of the "comforters" demonstrate the emptiness of man's explanations of evil; and finally the voice out of the whirlwind reminds J. B. that God is so high above man that man can never adequately understand His ways. MacLeish claims that he is especially interested in man's eternal willingness to try again despite his inability to understand God's purposes. Man insistently says "Yes" to life even when overwhelmed with unbearable evil. Why? MacLeish's probing and pushing at these endlessly fascinating issues holds interest at a relatively high level throughout the play (although there are some structural weaknesses that tend to undermine this interest). The very richness of the play is suggested by one's inability to state fully, in expository form, the ideas that MacLeish brings up for consideration.

What does the playwright do when he has serious issues to discuss and has decided to discuss them in dramatic form? Why not just write an essay and discuss them outright? The value of the parable as a means of making truth vivid has been well known at least since Biblical times, and needs no further defense here. A story, especially one that is acted out, can serve as a metaphor, a short-hand way of stating complex concepts which have almost unlimited connotative meanings. An essay of book length probably could not state fully the ideas that are presented for consideration in *J.B.*, and certainly the essay would not be so interesting. The author with something to say who chooses the theatrical medium for saying it has chosen one of the most powerful and effective devices known to man for implanting complex concepts in the minds of an audience. He is still faced with the problem, however, of finding a story that will illustrate his ideas, and of creating characters to act out his story. His selected medium, although highly effective, is also highly demanding, for he must create his characters and his plot in such a manner as to make the play's performance interesting without losing the thematic content. In this case, of course, MacLeish found his plot and most of his characters ready-made in the Biblical story he chose to adapt. He still had the problem however of keeping the story and characters interesting in theatrical terms without detracting from the thematic content, plus the additional problem that since the Bibical story is so widely known he may depart from it only with great care. Even though some of his work was done for him, it was still no small accomplishment to tell a theatrically effective story and deal meaningfully with complex issues of life and death.

Many people, especially in America where culture has neither deep roots nor a long tradition, become uncomfortable when the thought content of a play is discussed. Often these are the same people who listen only to the latest music on the hit parade, who ignore any painting other than the strictly photographic, and read nothing more complicated than the comic strips. There are many people, however, who have developed a far deeper level of cultural appreciation in general, but are still inclined to feel that when they go to the theatre, they want "to be entertained rather than to think." Their attitude is understandable, in view of the fact that television, movies, and the Broadway theatre often cater to this taste level. This attitude can be changed, however, if they study the theatre and learn to enjoy the far greater insights of which it is capable. A taste for good literature, music, and painting is not acquired without a little study and exposure; but education in these arts is far wider spread in the public school systems than is education in theatre, and therefore many people have simply not been exposed to a very high level of theatrical values. The preference for "entertainment rather than thinking" on the part of educated people is surprising in that it presupposes a fundamental antipathy between entertainment and thinking. Most theatregoers would agree that drama must entertain to be effective; but many would also agree that intellectual stimulation when properly presented is, in fact, entertaining—and entertaining in a far more meaningful and lasting way than the latest television variety show. Think of your own reaction to *J. B.* Whatever reservations you may have had about other aspects of the play, would it be fair to say that you were bored? Probably not. And an important reason why the play is not boring is the fact that it is thought-provoking. Thinking, at least when it is provoked by a dramatic presentation, is intensely entertaining, and one need make no apologies to those who prefer their theatre to be "entertaining." If they really mean that they have sampled theatre of all kinds and genuinely prefer mindless entertainment, then one can do no more than admit that it takes all kinds of tastes to make up a world. But usually what they really mean is that they have not been exposed to the kind of entertainment that a good production of a thought-provoking play provides. This is a situation that can and should be corrected.

The playwright who is especially interested in expressing thematic concepts in his work faces the immensely complex task of incorporating these themes into a well-structured and entertaining plot. Since theme is clearly the dominant element in *J.B.*, let us examine in greater detail its plot structure to see how MacLeish deals with this difficult problem. In the first place, if one assumes that J. B. is the protagonist, it is evident that he is a singularly passive one. He is acted upon rather than acting. There is nothing that J. B. sets out to do that can be called the central action of the play. In this case, it seems more appropriate to think of God and Satan as the active agents who set out to do something—namely, to plumb the depths of Job's faith. This is the central action; God and Satan undertake it at the beginning, and when it is completed, the play is over. To identify this as the play's central action, however, is still to face some rather serious structural problems, for a central action which provides for the protagonist simply to react rather than to act is a very unusual one indeed. Some might argue that God is the true protagonist of *J.B.*, but this so completely violates our understanding of the protagonist as the central figure, who remains on stage throughout the play, that it seems more sensible to admit that J. B. is an unusually passive protagonist. A passive protagonist and a central action which consists largely of reaction strongly suggest a play in which "not much happens," and after the initial series of catastrophes that wipe out J.B.'s family and possessions, the play is notably static. As one examines the way the parts fit together to develop this central action, he encounters still further problems. It probably never was the playwright's intent to adhere to the well-made play structure, but although an inciting incident and a climax could easily be identified (respectively, Satan's proposal on page 198 to test Job and J.B.'s "I abhor myself . . . and repent" on page 218), the material which lies between these two incidents is difficult to classify. Certainly no turning point is discernible. A strong emotional impact is made by a series of catastrophes; then a long scene occurs between J.B. and the comforters in which the emotional level and the interest level fall; followed in turn by a dialogue between J.B. and a tape recorded voice—extremely difficult theatrically since almost nothing is happening on stage except J.B.'s reactions, which consist mostly of hiding his face. In short, by whatever terms one analyzes the progress of the central action, he finds that most of the intensely dramatic material is presented in the first half of the play, followed by dialogue with little action. Yet, in thematic terms, the most important parts of the play come precisely in that second half where little is happening dramatically. Evidently, the playwright was not completely successful in finding a plot structure to fit the thematic concepts he wished to discuss.

In production, a good director can do much to overcome structural problems of the sort noted above. If the director has studied the script sufficiently (as he should have) to notice that the play tends to drop in dramatic effectiveness after the series of catastrophes hits J.B., he can devote extra attention to making the last portion of the play theatrically exciting. The director should introduce as much movement as possible, provide lighting and sound effects that will enhance the visual impact, elicit from the actors a high degree of emotional intensity to balance the intensity achieved in the first half. If necessary, he can hold back the first half to avoid "pulling out all the stops," and thereby stretch the play out of balance. The treatment of the voice out of the whirlwind will be especially meaningful for such a director, since he knows that, in defiance of all the usual conventions of something happening on the stage for an audience to watch, he must create the climax for the play out of a tape-recorded voice and one actor crouched alone in the middle of the stage. It is an extremely difficult assignment, but it can be done successfully.

In addition to the central action, MacLeish has provided for *J.B.* a very important "framing action." He has caused the entire play to take place in a circus tent, and has provided two roustabouts who decide to play the roles of God and Satan. This highly theatrical device not only adds interest and visual excitement, but also removes the play from the realm of realism. (The circus as a symbol of life is a widely used metaphor, and needs no further comment here.) It is clear from the preceding analysis that using a framing action of this sort, and breaking esthetic distance constantly by having the characters speak of themselves and others as actors in a play, helps the audience to break out of the same empathic involvement that was so desirable in *The Little Foxes* and *Cyrano de Bergerac* and to think about the thematic concepts. This effect is increased by the use of masks, another antirealistic device which reminds one of the theatrical, rather than the realistic, nature of the performance. The entire story is told in advance by Zuss and Nickles before the central action even gets under way. Obviously suspense was not desired, and if suspense is eliminated, thematic issues may be emphasized.

Clearly, *J.B.* is not realistic in style, but neither does it belong to any other easily identifiable style. One must be prepared to find some plays that do not fit into preconceived pigeon-holes. It is possible, however, to place *J.B.* in a broad classification that will prove useful: the quality of communicating directly with an audience, of reminding them forcefully that they are in a theatre and must not forget it, of deliberately breaking into any emotional involvement which they may begin to feel with the play's plot—all of these elements are characteristic of what is called *presentational* theatre. Its opposite is *representational* theatre, in which the audience is made to feel that the events on stage are actually happening, and they are privileged to watch only by accident. Representational theatre is frequently associated with realism. Presentational theatre frankly presents itself to the audience, asking that it be admired for its skill rather than its credibility. Presentational theatre may include many different styles under its general heading; there are many theatrical values other than those usually associated with realism.

One last, important point about *J.B.* must be made before leaving it. The script that you have read is the original version as it was written by the playwright and produced at Yale University in 1958. In 1959, when the play was finally done on Broadway, several important changes were made in the script. Of course the playwright made these changes voluntarily, but he made them, as far as one can tell, as the result of assurances from the director and the producers that Broadway audiences would not accept the play (at least as readily) as it stood. The substantive changes were at the end of the play, when Sarah returns to her husband. J. B. asserts his individuality in a most heroic way, stating that he will not again succumb to a God who can treat him in such a fashion; he and Sarah agree that human love is the one great answer to the unanswerable questions raised in the play. This strange, new ending completely violates the thematic concepts developed in the earlier portion of the play. If human love is the answer to all problems (like the fadeout in almost every Hollywood movie), why concern oneself with issues of good and evil? Indeed, if one admits that, after all, there is a simple answer to these complex problems, has he not denied the whole point of the voice out of the whirlwind, which asserts that God's plan is too grand for men to understand? Quite simply, if one accepts an easy answer where something far more complex is obviously called for, has he not in fact surrendered his right to think deeply? If J. B. spends the whole play asserting that he loves God, and then decides at the last moment not to worship Him after all, what becomes of the whole theological foundation of the play? How the playwright would answer these questions need not concern us here. What does concern those who prefer a theatre of solid intellectual challenge is that the collective judgment of those responsible for producing *J.B.* in New York was that its thought content was too challenging for a Broadway audience—neat, simple answers had to be provided so that audiences could go away from the theatre without being too deeply disturbed. The frightening fact is that the professional judgment of the people involved was probably accurate. Many other plays are watered down before they reach Broadway, and plays that really raise profound thematic questions are often treated very gingerly. Some of these plays are produced in the resident professional companies, outside of New York, which are rapidly replacing Broadway as centers of vital theatrical activity in this country; others are produced "off-Broadway" or "off-off-Broadway;" many are first seen on the more venturesome college campuses. The slickness of Broadway's production methods is indisputable, but only a few production achieve the real, deeper distinction associated with major theatrical events. Too large a segment of the American public still prefers its entertainment mindless.

In order to pursue a discussion of the technical aspects of theatrical production, it is necessary first to define a few basic terms. For the time being, this discussion will be confined to the proscenium theatre which is most familiar to the majority of theatre-goers, but it is by no means the only type of stage arrangement in which good theatre may exist. Referring, then, to the accompanying diagrams, pages 231–232, one can name and define a number of features common to the proscenium theatre. When one enters the theatre, he normally enters through the *lobby,* buys his ticket at the *box office* and finds his seat in the *house.* Although the house obviously has a front (nearest the stage) and a back, the lobby, box office, coat rooms, rest rooms, and so on are collectively known as the *front of the house.* The house is separated from the stage area by a wall known as the *proscenium;* the audience views the play through the *proscenium opening* when the curtain is open. The *main curtain* fills the proscenium opening, and may be opened by several methods; the two most common are lifting it out of sight (in which case it is usually called a *fly curtain*) or parting it in the middle and drawing it to each side (in which case it is called a *draw curtain*). The imaginary line on the stage floor which the main curtain touches when it is closed is called the *curtain line.* The portion of the stage that juts out in front of the curtain line into the house is called the *apron;* the apron often contains *footlights,* which are simply a row of lights sunk into the floor. Often they are mounted in such a way that they can disappear beneath the stage floor when they are not needed.

Behind the curtain line, theatre people make use of the standard directions *stage right* and *stage left,* meaning the actor's right and left, respectively, as he faces the audience. Thus, no matter what theatre one enters, when a director tells an actor to move three steps stage right, he understands precisely where he is to go. By the same token, the direction *downstage* is toward the curtain line and *upstage* is away from the curtain line; these directions derive from the pre twentieth-century theatres in which the stage floor actually sloped toward the audience. The area of the stage floor roughly outlined by the proscenium opening on each side and as far upstage as the set will allow the audience to see is called the *acting area* (if a box set is used, the acting area will be the area enclosed

Nomenclature of the Stage

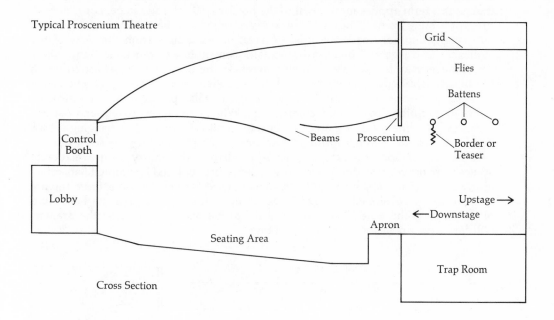

Typical Proscenium Theatre

Cross Section

by the set), and all the rest of the stage is called *backstage* or *offstage.* The acting area is arbitrarily divided into at least six imaginary areas (not shown on the diagram) which are called *down right, down center, down left, up right, up center,* and *up left.* Thus, an actor in a strange theatre can be told to enter down left and cross up center, and he knows what is expected of him. The whole area above the stage is known as the *flies,* and normally contains a complete system of pulleys and lines suitable for lifting scenery and other items directly up from the stage. To *fly* anything, then, is to attach it to ropes and lift it into the flies. The fly system, in most theatres, consists of a series of pipes or *battens* hung parallel to the curtain line by steel cables. These steel cables go directly up to pulleys attached to a framework near the roof called the *grid,* and thence to one side of the stage. There, if the theatre has a *counterweight system,* the cables attach to counterweights that can be adjusted to balance exactly the weight of the scenery; thus, to fly a large piece of scenery is an easy job for one man. In older theatres, ropes may substitute for the steel cables, in which case the ropes are terminated at a *pin rail* at the side of the stage where they are tied off to *belaying pins.* The largest item hung in the flies is often a *cyclorama,* which is a seamless expanse of stretched cloth (or occasionally something stronger), large enough to surround completely the upstage portion of the acting area. When properly lighted, a cyclorama gives an illusion of sky. When the stage floor has a series of trap doors in it, the room beneath the stage is called the *trap room.*

It will not be possible in this short space to name all the scenic devices used in the theatre, but since a complete set of draperies is the most common scenic element, the names of its parts will be useful. A *border* is a narrow cloth hung from a batten parallel to the curtain line and used to mask the audience's view of the flies. Its height is easily adjustable by the fly system. A border is also called a *teaser*, although this term applies more often to the border farthest downstage. Long, narrow draperies, hung on each side of the stage, are called *legs*. Several sets of legs, used one behind another, mask the offstage area, on each side, from the view of the audience. Two legs and one border actually constitute an adjustable frame, then, for whatever may be seen inside them; therefore, the downstage-most set, in which the border is called a teaser and the legs are called *tormentors*, may be spoken of as a *false proscenium*. Frequently, a semipermanent false proscenium is constructed out of flats or other, more solid, components. When several sets of legs and borders are used to outline the acting area, the upstage limit is delineated by hanging a draw curtain, or *traveler*, parallel to the curtain line. If a curtain which does not draw is used in this position, it is called a *drop*. In pre-twentieth-century theatre, elaborate scenes were often painted on the drop, and legs were replaced by painted flats called *wings*. The *wing-and-drop* set is still occasionally used for period flavor. From the use of these wings developed the habit of referring to the offstage areas on both sides of the stage as the *wings*. The *beams* and the *control booth* indicated on the drawing will be discussed in the section on lighting.

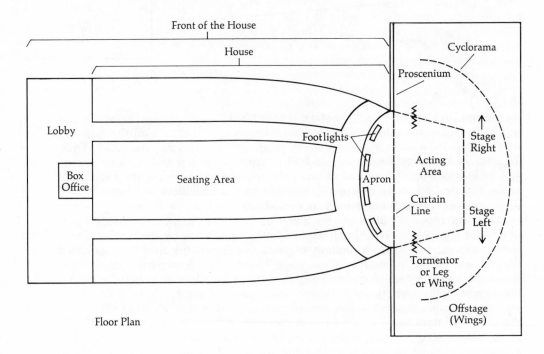

Floor Plan

The largest and most obvious visual element in most productions in a proscenium theatre is the set. A set which is at all elaborate calls for a considerable investment of money, time, and effort in design and construction. The responsibility for its design and execution are seldom borne single-handedly by a director, but are turned over to a scene designer, who in turn usually works with a large staff. Of course the scene designer works very closely with the director, and the set is a result of their combined ideas. The director must retain final artistic control over all phases of his production, but most directors rely heavily upon their designers to approach all of its visual aspects creatively.

For Broadway, construction of the settings is done under contract by a scenic studio, which works from highly detailed drawings submitted by the designer. Many other theatres, both professional and amateur, maintain a scene-construction shop, which may be under the supervision of the scene designer himself, a technical director, or another member of the technical staff. It is not necessary, at this point, to go into the details of scenic construction. It is appropriate, rather, to show the relationship of the set to the other elements of theatrical production, and to suggest a few of the ways in which sets make a positive contribution to the over-all theatrical experience. In production, of course, the set does not exist independently of the other visual elements, such as stage lights, properties, and actors wearing costumes and makeup; the over-all visual impact is a combination of all these elements. A designer who forgets this and designs a set which does not function well with the other elements is in for a great deal of trouble.

The designer begins, as do all the production artists, with the script. He must study it carefully, assimilating its structure, style, themes, and mechanical needs as thoroughly as the director. Furthermore, the designer must find out from the director what approach to the script he has chosen. Once the designer has some ideas which can be expressed in sketches, models, or other concrete forms, he checks frequently with the director to make sure they are still thinking in similar terms. As the designer begins to evolve some clear images of what the set might look like, he must keep in mind the following five functions which sets perform. (Such a list of functions cannot be perfectly conceived, and few designers would allow them-

The Set

selves to be bound by anything so arbitrary, but the functions set forth here represent with a fair degree of completeness the things that sets do, whether consciously so conceived or not.) They are listed in their usual order of importance:

1. The set must, first of all, provide an environment for the acting. It must provide such functional elements as entrances, exits, levels, steps, and other requirements indicated in the script or requested by the director. This means, of course, that the designer must study the script with great care and must understand something of the type of blocking that the director has in mind, at least for key scenes. The description of the set provided in most published modern plays will not greatly influence the imaginative designer. This description often represents the playwright's or the Broadway designer's solution to the problems the script presents. The imaginative designer will turn, rather, to the dialogue and action themselves to determine the needs of the script; and he will seek his own solution in terms of what the director hopes to accomplish in the production at hand. Some stage settings consist of nothing more than series of steps and levels, more or less complex as the needs of the script may dictate, perhaps placed in front of black draperies or a cyclorama. This provides an environment for the acting and nothing more. In J. B., the designer will see at once that the structure of the play calls for two separate acting areas, one for Zuss and Nickles, the other for the scenes involving J. B. The script calls for Zuss and Nickles to perform on and around an elevated platform, and, since a variety of levels adds visual interest to a stage picture, most designers would undoubtedly follow the script in this regard. Only one entrance to this platform is needed (a ladder visible to the audience), but the other acting area requires more than one entrance because so many actors must move in and out, and variety in their movements will be necessary. The designer will have to be careful about the exact relationship he establishes between these two acting areas: the audience must be able to see both clearly; the stage picture must be interesting; and the upper level must appear to overlook the lower one. There are many other factors, too numerous to go into here, that may affect the designer's final decision in providing a stage environment for the acting.

2. The set must express the proper mood for the play. The most obvious manifestation of this, perhaps, is the selection of light, gay colors for comedy and dark, sombre colors for tragedy, but far more is needed to set the proper mood. Color, line, mass, balance, order, proportion, harmony—all of these artistic elements may be manipulated by the imaginative designer to create mood, following, of course, the director's interpretation of the script. Many sets have been beautiful in themselves, but, by failing to capture the proper mood for the play, have done more harm than good within the context of the production. MacLeish explains, in his introductory statement to J.B., the mood he wishes the set to capture: "The feel is of a public place at late night, the audience gone, no one about but maybe a stagehand somewhere cleaning up, fooling with the lights." The designer notes, of course, that MacLeish has not said that the set must *look* like a public place late at night, but that it must *feel* like one. Sometimes a simile like this is the only effective means by which a mood can be conveyed; anyone who has ever been in an empty theatre or other public building late at night will understand. The designer who wishes to convey this mood has a problem, since, during performances, the theatre is presumably not empty nor is the hour late. He can, however, within the limits of his stage, provide as much vastness and empty space as possible. He will probably rely heavily on the lighting (MacLeish refers to the naked light bulbs "dangling from hanks of

The "circus tent" setting designed by Boris Aronson for *J. B.*, in the production directed by Elia Kazan and presented by Alfred de Liagre, Jr., at the ANTA Theatre in 1959. Photograph: Friedman-Ables.

wire") to help him create this mood. Of course, the director may have other ideas about the mood he wants to convey, too.

3. The setting may make a thematic statement about the play. Sometimes this takes a very blatant form when the setting, instead of representing the locale in which the play is supposed to take place, consists of pictures, charts, maps, or other devices which convey a message *about* the play rather than establish surroundings for it. A good example of this, to draw one from the lecture platform rather than legitimate drama, might be the political campaign speech which is delivered from a stage decorated with a huge replica of the American flag. This is an attempt, of course, to make a "thematic" statement about the candidate. But to turn again to *J.B.*, the setting envisioned by the playwright correlates to the thematic concept of the play. The selection of the circus motif as a metaphor for life is not an incidental choice, as it evokes ironic images of gaiety superimposed upon the shocking evil that J.B. has to suffer. The designer does not often find a central metaphor for his stage design so readily at hand, but in this case the playwright has taken that step for him. Few designers or directors would try to find another production image, since the circus that the playwright has called for here is so "right." Finding a way to express the thematic impact of *The Little Foxes* might be considerably more difficult, but the playwright's use of "foxes" in the title might give the designer a clue. As the play is realistic in style, he can hardly do anything so obvious as to make his stage

look like a fox, but he might well feature the color of fox's fur. If such a choice coincides with the other requirements of the play, it should serve to reinforce the thematic impact that the playwright has in mind.

4. In settings that do provide surroundings in which the play is supposed to take place, the design should help to establish the time and place of the action. An obvious example of this might be drawn from *The Little Foxes* where the set must be clearly established as the living room of Regina's home in the rural South, and the time identified as the turn of the century. This means not only that each item in the set (including properties) must be in the right period and style, but that among all the possible things that might be selected from the right period and style, those must be selected which will best convey to an audience what it needs to know about the play. A butter churn might well be of the right period, but Regina would hardly have one in her living room. In *J. B.*, both the time and the place are kept deliberately vague, although one assumes that the place is America and the time is the present. If the specific place is a circus tent, located in any part of the world, the designer will have to include elements which clearly convey the concept "circus." MacLeish suggests a tent pole and some canvas. The truncated pyramids often used for elephant acts might be included; a portion of a circus ring could surround the main action. All the elements the designer selects should help to place the action in a circus tent, since that is the motif which has been agreed upon.

5. Finally, the set often provides visual impact—beauty, spectacle, realistic detail, incredible ugliness, or a host of other possibilities. Not all plays allow the designer to go all out, but most designers welcome the opportunity when it comes. Many modern musical comedies rely heavily on the sheer spectacle that the designer can provide to keep them visually exciting. The Act I set for *Cyrano de Bergerac* should probably be as breath-taking as the designer can make it. The set for *The Little Foxes*, on the other hand, should not be beautiful, but its realistic detail might delight the spectator and help him enter into the play world, in addition to establishing time and place. The set for *J. B.* could have this kind of visual impact, and some directors might elect to emphasize some aspect of the play that would allow for such impact. Most directors, however, would agree that, in order to focus attention on *J.B.'s* thematic content, spectacle for its own sake should be minimized. The playwright evidently had this in mind when he called for so many antirealistic devices. Visual impact for its own sake can be exciting, but it has a cheapening and tasteless effect when applied indiscriminately.

When the designer is satisfied that his set performs all of the functions listed above (or at least as many of them as are appropriate to the play in question), he must combine his ideas in an over-all production plan. The manner in which he puts these elements together is termed the *style* of the set. The concept of style, as it relates to the script, has already been defined, and normally the style chosen for a particular production will be a direct reflection of the style in which the script is written. This is not always the case, however, for, as noted above, it is perfectly possible for a director to impose upon a play a production style entirely foreign to it. This may be done either to express a concept in which the director is interested, or to improve upon the style of the original to make it more compelling to an audience. A Shakespearean play, for example, might be produced in a starkly realistic style on the grounds that it will have a more immediate impact on a modern audience accustomed to realism. Thus, the style that the set designer uses must be carefully worked out with the director. Usually, the production style will not be a simple one which can be neatly labeled, but will be unique to the play. Coordination between director and designer is necessary to ensure that the unique style evolving in the mind of the one does, in fact, correspond with the unique style in the mind of the other.

Although a list of styles is necessarily a series of slots into which many plays cannot easily be fit, it is still desirable to list some of the more common production styles and note the ways in which they may be related to the technical elements of production. Consider first several varieties of realism, then a number of deliberate departures from realism, and finally several other miscellaneous styles.

1. *The varieties of realism.* It is more accurate to think of "realism" as a continuum rather than as a single, specific style. This continuum might be sketched as follows:

Naturalism

| Realism   Selective Realism

Naturalism represents a dead end on this continuum because it is as "realistic" as one can get in the theatre. In the naturalistic style, everything on the stage must be as real as may be practical. Where the real thing called for in the script may reasonably be obtained and may sensibly be used, it is. Other needs of the script are fabricated, but always with an effort to make them look as real as possible. Real rocks, trees, and shrubbery are often used; occasionally, tons of real dirt have been trucked into the theatre. Furniture must be genuinely in the right period, or constructed as closely to it as possible. Walls (both interior and exterior) are usually represented by *flats* (wooden frames covered with canvas and painted), but the painted detail work on them must look as real as possible. Often real wooden moldings, doors, windows, and other architectural features are added. The attempt always in naturalism is to adhere with complete fidelity to every detail of the environment depicted in the play. David Belasco, an American producer famous for his naturalistic settings, once bought an entire room with all its contents and had it moved into his theatre in order to achieve absolute realism. Such literal adherence to naturalistic detail is relatively rare in the modern theatre; on the surface, one expects realistic plays to be realistic, but rarely is naturalism actually employed. Realism is usually only painted detail with a few three-dimensional embellishments, creating the illusion of reality. Furniture, however, is generally arranged to face the audience in a most "unrealistic" manner, and the walls are angled in order to insure good sightlines throughout the auditorium. Real rocks and shrubbery are used sparingly, and more often than not, high-quality imitations are substituted. Sinks seldom run real water nor stoves cook real food, as naturalism would require.

As one continues to move out along the continuum, it is possible to omit more and more physical details without harming the essentially "realistic" effect. If one omits the real dirt on the stage floor that naturalism calls for, why not omit, as well, the painted rocks and grass of realism, and leave only the one painted rock the heroine sits on? The one rock might be as realistic as possible, but the rest of the set could be cut down to a bare minimum. There is, theoretically, almost no limit at this end of the continuum; one can continue to omit unnecessary realistic detail until there is hardly anything left. Where exactly naturalism stops and realism begins is hard to say; when one should stop using the label *"realism"* and start referring to the style as *selective realism* is equally difficult to determine. Take as an example *The Little Foxes*, which is essentially a realistic play. Should the director decide to do it in naturalistic style, the designer would reproduce every detail of Regina's living room as it might have appeared in the spring of 1900. The furniture (strictly selected from antiques of the period) would be arranged normally for such a room, with some pieces facing away from the audience. The walls should appear to be solid, there should be real glass in the windows, and real trees should be visible outside. If, however, the director decided on ordinary realism, the walls would still be realistically painted, with, perhaps, a wallpaper pattern stenciled on them; the furniture would be arranged to face the audience, both enhancing the effectiveness of the blocking and suggesting a real room at the same time; the window glass could be simulated by fine mesh net. Similar details would be modified in a sensible way, but the room would *appear* to be a real one of the period. As the director moved further into selective realism, he would strip away more and more of the nonessentials. Since no view out the window is necessary to the plot, the designer might simply mask behind it with a black drape. A realistic ceiling might be replaced with black borders. Properties that were not actually used by the actors might be stripped away. Ultimately, the realism might be reduced to the point where the walls themselves were cut down to three or four feet—just enough to delineate an acting area and indicate the doors and windows. Behind all this, either black drapes or a cyclorama might be hung. To strip the realism down to this degree would, of course, totally change the mood of the play. Other factors being equal, a realistic set tends to particularize the action, to make it happen in one time and at one place only, whereas the more selective realism becomes, the more universal its nature—more suitable for *J.B.*, perhaps. Few directors would wish to move very far out along this continuum for *The Little Foxes*, but would restrict it to a fairly detailed realism; whereas most directors would use a highly selective realism (if they used realism at all) for *J.B.* The decision must grow out of an understanding of the play itself.

   2. *Departures from realism.* There are a number of theatrical styles, however, that depart from this continuum altogether. Most of these have developed (or, at least, been defined and organized) since realism began to dominate the theatre, and are definite reactions against it. Proponents of these styles have argued that the deepest truths of life consist not at all in a surface realism, but in something that exists far beneath the surface, and can only be expressed through the imaginative use of other-than-realistic elements. In a sense, then, these styles are attempting to be more "realistic" than realism, since they propose to be more fundamentally truthful. They may be thought of as tangential to the realism continuum—departing from some point solidly anchored in realism, but then moving away with no further ties, limited only by the imagination of the artists involved:

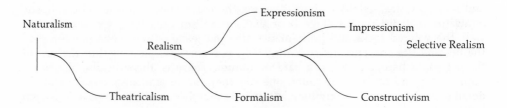

a. *Expressionism* may be simply defined here as that style in which the play world is viewed through the eyes of a character within the play, usually the protagonist. Normally, when this style is employed, the character through whose eyes the action is viewed is under severe emotional stress—he may be insane, for example—so there is a real basis for sharply distorting the world that he sees. In that case, the scenery may be designed with sharp angles, extravagant colors, and impossible proportions, expressing the character's disturbed state of mind. None of the plays studied so far lends itself to expressionistic production, but if one were arbitrarily to do the last act of *Cyrano de Bergerac* in expressionistic style, he would have an actor dressed as "Death" come in to fence with Cyrano at the end, the lights would grow very dim and finally go out altogether, the scenery might be painted in a predominantly blood-red color, if Cyrano had steps to climb, they might be several feet high so he would have to hoist himself up step by step, and so on. All would be an attempt to express Cyrano's state of mind as he forced himself to face death bravely.

b. *Impressionism* shows a distorted play world, viewed through the omniscient eyes of the playwright or the director. Any playwright has a point of view, but in this case his point of view is distorted for the purpose of making a thematic statement. He sets up a stage metaphor which is a planned distortion of superficial reality, and which provides a milieu for the entire play. Again, none of the plays studied so far lends itself easily to this style of production, but perhaps it can be illustrated by supposing that MacLeish had set up his circus metaphor in *J.B.* not as a framing action, but rather as the central meaning of the play. If the point of the play were that "life is a circus," then the entire play might be staged in a set which was an elaborate and colorful circus tent; the actors might all be costumed in fancy circus costumes and made up with clown faces, a band might play circus music at their entrances and exits, Zuss might be dressed as the ring master instead of as a balloon salesman, and the entire acting style used might be light and gay, suggesting only by indirection the tragedy underneath. Most viewers would find this a gross distortion of the play's thematic content, but it is possible to imagine a director choosing this approach.

c. *Theatricalism* is a frank use of the elements of theatre to please and delight, rather than to create an illusion of being somewhere else. In realism, the audience "believes" that the room represented (Regina's living room, for example) is what they are viewing; even in expressionism or impressionism, one is expected to suspend disbelief and enter into another world than that to which he is accustomed. In theatricalism, however, the audience is fully aware that it is in the theatre, and is simply expected to enjoy what is presented for its skill or artistry. A vaudeville revue, for example, consisting of a number of song-and-dance acts, would never create the illusion of being anywhere but in the theatre. A theatrical play would have scenery which was frankly decorative rather than representative, the actors would play directly to the audience, frankly asking them to share in the pleasure of the performance rather than to believe that they were really somewhere else. This is a style usually best adapted to comedy, and thus the best available example might be *The Importance of Being Earnest* (the next play in this volume). It would be conceivable to stage the play realistically, but far more likely that a director would decide to get the maximum fun out of it. The scenery might consist of wing-and-drop sets elaborately painted for decoration, but without trying to fool anybody that they really represented people's homes. The costumes might also be grossly overdone, unlike anything anyone has ever worn but intended as a frank exaggeration for the fun of it. The acting style might be clearly artificial, getting the most mileage out of the artificial language and aiming the *bon mots* and aphorisms directly at the audience. Theatricalism is, as its name implies, "of the theatre," and uses all the elements of theatre as effectively as possible.

d. *Formalism* provides the simple "forms" that are necessary to stage the play, and then relies almost totally on the script and the acting to convey the play's essential values. The set for such a play would simply provide an environment for the acting and nothing more. The costumes would cover the actors in a simple, dignified manner (academic gowns, for example, or formal evening dress). The other technical elements would follow the same general pattern. Again, to illustrate from among the plays already read, if *J. B.* were to be staged in a formalistic manner, the set might consist of a raised platform for Zuss and Nickles and a lower platform (or just the stage floor) for J.B.'s scenes. All of this might be arranged in front of black drapes. The actors might wear white work coats and dark trousers, typical of popcorn salesmen; the furniture might consist of a table and several plain stools which could be shifted around as needed; the lighting would provide illumination, but no special effects. Such an approach to *J.B.* would put the focus squarely on the script and the actors, and is often employed for plays in which theme is the most important element. In the case of *J.B.*, however, many directors would feel that the script (particularly in the last half) tends to be too static anyway, and that it needs all the theatrical devices that can be legitimately introduced to keep it interesting. These directors would never adopt a formalistic approach to *J.B.*; they would use formalism only when they felt that the script and the acting were so strong that nothing else would be needed to sustain interest, and, indeed, that anything else introduced might actually detract from what was being said.

e. *Constructivism* is a rather specialized style that attempts to express the harsh machine age by revealing the mechanical elements which make up the world. Anything that is not functional or is purely decorative is removed. What remains is not only necessary to the action, but is also likely to be harsh or even ugly to look at. This style in sets is likely to involve platforms in which the legs and bracing are left revealed, "cut-away" houses or rooms in which only the basic structural elements are visible, and steel-work of one sort or another, especially machinery. If *J.B.* were to be staged in constructivist style, the set might be similar to the formalist set described above, except that, where formalism would confine itself to clean, simple lines which did not draw attention to themselves, constructivism would leave the legs and bracing of the platforms revealed, the tables and stools used would be rough-hewn and ugly, and the "tent" might be indicated by a series of sections of pipe on which actors might climb. Since the harshness of the world in the machine age is not really an issue in *J.B.* (the issues are more timeless), most directors would probably not choose constructivism as the most effective style in which to stage the play, but it is a possible approach.

3. *Other styles.* At least two other styles can be mentioned here that bear no direct relationship to the realism—nonrealism continuum. Both are actually historical approaches and grow out of a desire to reproduce at least some sense of what playgoing must have been like in the times in which the scripts were written. *Classicism* is the name given to the style in which Greek tragedies are often produced, and it involves both formalism and some adherence to the way in which the tragedies were originally staged in the Theatre of Dionysus. The austerity and simplicity of

this style is sometimes applied to neoclassic and other more modern plays as well. It is discussed in greater detail in connection with the study of *Oedipus the King.* Shakespearean plays are often produced in a style which may be called simply "Shakespearean" or "Elizabethan." Again, formalism figures heavily in the style, but it is a decorated formalism which attempts to capture the spirit of the Globe Theatre in which many of Shakespeare's plays were originally performed (see the pages on *Twelfth Night* for further discussion). This style may involve actually building a replica of the Globe, or it may mean simply working out a thrust-stage arrangement with an inner below, balconies, and other necessary acting areas. Elizabethan half-timbered decor is often used, with colorful banners and other devices of the period. Costuming is usually of the Elizabethan period. Many theatre people would object to listing these two styles separately, insisting that they are merely variations of formalism, but they have such a recognizable entity of their own and are so widely accepted that they might as well be discussed separately.

The styles listed above are not neatly isolated categories. Although settings can be pure examples of a single style, it is far more common for the director and designer to work together to evolve a style distinctive to the play they are staging; it may partake of several of the recognizable styles listed above. This "distinctive style" should express the director's conception of the play. If it is merely a conglomeration of styles without a unified plan, arrived at through indecisiveness, ignorance, or poor taste, the production will be harmed rather than helped. It is often said that the style of a production must be "consistent"; that the style decided upon must be employed throughout, in the acting, sets, costumes, and all areas of technical production. Unfortunately, the truth, as usual, is more complex: one single, consistent style used throughout a production can be a very effective artistic pattern and is often used. Sometimes, however, for reasons that are consistent within the play itself, a mixture of styles may be employed—realistic costumes in a formalistic set, for example. Whether such choices are "right" or "wrong" can only be judged by discriminating critics witnessing the production itself; no "rule" about consistency can determine automatically that such a mixture of styles is a mistake.

The designer has a great deal more to think about than simply artistic considerations when he plans the sets for a play. The details of construction and rigging of scenery are beyond the scope of this book, but obviously they are matters of no small concern to the designer. It is all very well to envision a great, curving staircase sweeping down from the flies to the apron, but practical considerations may well rule out the construction of such a wonder. On Broadway sometimes money appears to be no object, and almost anything is possible in terms of construction. But most theatres, both professional and amateur, work within limited budgets, limited staffs, and limited time, and the designer has to think in terms of what is possible under the prevailing conditions. If the play involves any shifting of sets from one scene to another, the designer will be even further confined by the size and equipment of his theatre. Many proscenium theatres are built with too little fly and wing space, no trap doors, and other limitations which simply rule out what the director or designer would choose to do. Basically, scenery can be moved off the stage either up, down, or along the floor, and if down is ruled out by lack of elevators or traps, and up is ruled out by lack of fly space, then the remaining choice is rather limiting: the scenery can roll off the stage in large, castered units, or it can be broken down into smaller units and carried off by hand. Some really well-equipped theatres have built-in turntables or large wagons, so that whole sets can be rolled offstage in seconds; theatres this well-equipped are rare. Often, the hand-carrying method is the only one left open, and such an alternative will seriously limit the designer in realizing his artistic aims.

The designer, then, works out a set (or a series of sets) for the play which will work most effectively in terms of the director's plans. The sets must "work" in the artistic sense of expressing what the director wishes to express and of fitting in well with the other visual elements of the production, and they must also "work" in the practical sense of fitting within the budgetary and physical limitations of construction and of being capable of shifting as the needs of the play may dictate. The designer, as the director's chief consultant on all of the visual elements of production, will probably also have a great deal to say about the costumes, the lighting, the properties, and anything else that is seen on the stage. Each of these elements will be considered separately.

Oscar Fingall O'Flahertie Wills Wilde was born in Dublin, Ireland, on October 16, 1854. He was the son of Sir William Wilde, a surgeon noted for his large number of illegitimate children, and Jane Elgee Wilde, who, under the pen name of "Speranza," wrote poetry and pamphlets fanatically supporting the cause of a free Ireland. These unlikely factors, together with the fact that Oscar's mother delighted in dressing him as a girl, may in some measure help to account for his exceptional behavior in later life. He was educated at Trinity College in Dublin and then spent four years at Oxford, where he was evidently both an extraordinary scholar and personality. He became a leading figure in the "art for art's sake" cult which championed the pursuit of pleasure, especially esthetic pleasure, and Wilde gained notoriety for his affectations of long hair, flowing garments, and ever-present sunflower. He published some verse in these early years, and in general attracted sufficient attention to be parodied as Bunthorne in Gilbert and Sullivan's *Patience* in 1881. Capitalizing upon his extraordinary reputation, Wilde recouped his sagging financial fortunes with an eminently successful lecture tour of the United States in 1882, where he was received largely as an object of humor (especially in the rough western mining towns). He married Constance Lloyd in 1884 and fathered two sons, sustaining his family through writing and lecturing. He was accounted the wittiest conversationalist of his day, and was extremely popular at parties and social gatherings.

Much of Wilde's writing was less than memorable as he experimented with a variety of literary forms, but in 1892, with the production of *Lady Windermere's Fan*, he hit upon his metier. Wilde could operate within the dramatic forms and concepts of the period (the well-made play, the social problem play) without becoming bogged down; he was able to use and satirize them simultaneously. His witty comedies were both good theatre and social criticism, and were extremely popular. Suddenly Wilde's income was sufficient to give him all the writing time he could wish for. He produced *A Woman of No Importance* in 1893, *An Ideal Husband* in 1895, and *The Importance of Being Earnest* also in 1895. The one serious drama of this period was *Salome*, which he published in French.

At the height of Wilde's career, however, he wrecked it. His behavior, which, for a time, had

The Importance of Being Earnest by Oscar Wilde

been popularly regarded as humorously eccentric, suddenly took on another color when the father of a young man with whom he was intimately involved openly accused him of homosexuality. The Marquis of Queensbury, father of Lord Alfred Douglas, was himself eccentric and strong-willed, and Wilde foolishly sued him for slander. The case provoked an uproar in Victorian England, and, partly through suborned witnesses and partly through valid evidence of Wilde's involvement with male prostitutes, Wilde lost the case. On the evidence brought out at the trial, Wilde was charged with several criminal violations, found guilty, and sentenced to two years at hard labor in Reading Gaol. The penalty was severe, and prison conditions in England at the time made it worse. By the time Wilde emerged from prison in 1897, he was a broken man, both in spirit and health. He lived in Europe under an assumed name, published several non-theatrical works of importance, but never wrote for the theatre again. He died in Paris on November 30, 1900.

The Importance of Being Earnest was, by all odds, Wilde's finest accomplishment. When it opened on February 14, 1895, he was at the peak of his career, and his witty impudence and gay bonhomie enlivened every scene. Written in a style that few had tried and none had mastered since the eighteenth century, the play provoked laughter and delight both for the theatre-goer and for the reader. The sudden shift in Wilde's fortunes, however, resulted in the play being withdrawn from production, and for years it was rarely seen, and no polite home contained copies of his works. In more recent years, however, it has been frequently revived in both the professional and the amateur theatre—notably in an extraordinarily effective production starring John Gielgud which opened on Broadway on March 3, 1947. It is now widely regarded as a masterpiece within its rather specialized genre.

Opposite: Robert Flemyng as Algernon Moncrieff and Margaret Rutherford as Lady Bracknell in *The Importance of Being Earnest,* Act I, in the 1947 revival by the Theatre Guild and John C. Wilson in association with H. M. Tennent, Ltd., at the Royale Theatre, New York. Staged by John Gielgud, settings by Motley. Photograph: Vandamm, Theatre Collection, New York Public Library at Lincoln Center.

Page 247: Joan Greenwood (Gwendolen Fairfax) and Michael Redgrave (John Worthing) in the J. Arthur Rank film of *The Importance of Being Earnest,* 1952. Photograph courtesy of Universal-International and Janus Films, Inc.

The Importance of Being Earnest

A Trivial Comedy for Serious People by
OSCAR WILDE

John Worthing, J.P.	*Lane,* manservant
Algernon Moncrieff	*Lady Bracknell*
Rev. Canon Chasuble, D.D.	*Hon. Gwendolen Fairfax*
Merriman, butler	*Cecily Cardew*
	Miss Prism, governess

ACT I

Morning-room in **Algernon's** flat in Half-Moon Street. The room is luxuriously and artistically furnished. The sound of a piano is heard in the adjoining room.

[**Lane** *is arranging afternoon tea on the table, and after the music has ceased,* **Algernon** *enters.*]

Algernon: Did you hear what I was playing, Lane?

Lane: I didn't think it polite to listen, sir.

Algernon: I'm sorry for that, for your sake. I don't play accurately—any one can play accurately—but I play with wonderful expression. As far as the piano is concerned, sentiment is my forte. I keep science for Life.

Lane: Yes, sir.

Algernon: And, speaking of the science of Life, have you got the cucumber sandwiches cut for Lady Bracknell?

Lane: Yes, sir. [*Hands them on a salver.*]

Algernon: [*Inspects them, takes two, and sits down on the sofa*] Oh! . . . by the way, Lane, I see from your book that on Thursday night, when Lord Shoreman and Mr. Worthing were dining with me, eight bottles of champagne are entered as having been consumed.

Lane: Yes, sir; eight bottles and a pint.

Algernon: Why is it that at a bachelor's establishment the servants invariably drink the champagne? I ask merely for information.

Lane: I attribute it to the superior quality of the wine, sir. I have often observed that in married households the champagne is rarely of a first-rate brand.

Algernon: Good heavens! Is marriage so demoralizing as that?

Lane: I believe it *is* a very pleasant state, sir.

I have had very little experience of it myself up to the present. I have only been married once. That was in consequence of a misunderstanding between myself and a young person.

Algernon: [*Languidly*] I don't know that I am much interested in your family life, Lane.

Lane: No, sir; it is not a very interesting subject. I never think of it myself.

Algernon: Very natural, I am sure. That will do, Lane, thank you.

Lane: Thank you, sir.

[**Lane** *goes out.*]

Algernon: Lane's views on marriage seem somewhat lax. Really, if the lower orders don't set us a good example, what on earth is the use of them? They seem, as a class, to have absolutely no sense of moral responsibility.

[*Enter* **Lane.**]

Lane: Mr. Ernest Worthing.

[*Enter* **Jack.** **Lane** *goes out.*]

Algernon: How are you, my dear Ernest? What brings you up to town?

Jack: Oh, pleasure, pleasure! What else should bring one anywhere? Eating as usual, I see, Algy!

Algernon: [*Stiffly*] I believe it is customary in good society to take some slight refreshment at five o'clock. Where have you been since last Thursday?

Jack: [*Sitting down on the sofa*] In the country.

Algernon: What on earth do you do there?

Jack: [*Pulling off his gloves*] When one is in town one amuses onself. When one is in the country one amuses other people. It is excessively boring.

Algernon: And who are the people you amuse?

Jack: [*airly*] Oh, neighbours, neighbours.

Algernon: Got nice neighbours in your part of Shropshire?

Jack: Perfectly horrid! Never speak to one of them.

Algernon: How immensely you must amuse them! [*Goes over and takes sandwich*] By the way, Shropshire is your county, is it not?

Jack: Eh? Shropshire? Yes, of course. Hallo! Why all these cups? Why cucumber sandwiches? Why such reckless extravagance in one so young? Who is coming to tea?

Algernon: Oh! merely Aunt Augusta and Gwendolen.

Jack: How perfectly delightful!

Algernon: Yes, that is all very well; but I am afraid Aunt Augusta won't quite approve of your being here.

Jack: May I ask why?

Algernon: My dear fellow, the way you flirt with Gwendolen is perfectly disgraceful. It is almost as bad as the way Gwendolen flirts with you.

Jack: I am in love with Gwendolen. I have come up to town expressly to propose to her.

Algernon: I thought you had come up for pleasure? . . . I call that business.

Jack: How utterly unromantic you are!

Algernon: I really don't see anything romantic in proposing. It is very romantic to be in love. But there is nothing romantic about a definite proposal. Why, one may be accepted. One usually is, I believe. Then the excitement is all over. The very essence of romance is uncertainty. If ever I get married, I'll certainly try to forget the fact.

Jack: I have no doubt about that, dear Algy. The Divorce Court was specially invented for people whose memories are so curiously constituted.

Algernon: Oh! there is no use speculating on that subject. Divorces are made in Heaven—[**Jack** *puts out his hand to take a sandwich.* **Algernon** *at once interfers*] Please don't touch the cucumber sandwiches. They are ordered specially for Aunt Augusta. [*Takes one and eats it.*]

Jack: Well, you have been eating them all the time.

Algernon: That is quite a different matter. She is my aunt. [*Takes plate from below*] Have some bread and butter. The bread and butter is for Gwendolen. Gwendolen is devoted to bread and butter.

Jack: [*Advancing to table and helping himself*] And very good bread and butter it is too.

Algernon: Well, my dear fellow, you need not eat as if you were going to eat it all. You behave as if you were married to her already.

You are not married to her already, and I don't think you ever will be.

Jack: Why on earth do you say that?

Algernon: Well, in the first place, girls never marry the men they flirt with. Girls don't think it right.

Jack: Oh, that is nonsense!

Algernon: It isn't. It is a great truth. It accounts for the extraordinary number of bachelors that one sees all over the place. In the second place, I don't give my consent.

Jack: Your consent!

Algernon: My dear fellow, Gwendolen is my first cousin. And before I allow you to marry her, you will have to clear up the whole question of Cecily. [*Rings bell.*]

Jack: Cecily! What on earth do you mean? What do you mean, Algy, by Cecily? I don't know any one of the name of Cecily.

[*Enter* **Lane.**]

Algernon: Bring me that cigarette case Mr. Worthing left in the smoking-room the last time he dined here.

Lane: Yes, sir.

[**Lane** *goes out.*]

Jack: Do you mean to say you have had my cigarette case all this time? I wish to goodness you had let me know. I have been writing frantic letters to Scotland Yard about it. I was very nearly offering a large reward.

Algernon: Well, I wish you would offer one. I happen to be more than usually hard up.

Jack: There is no good offering a large reward now that the thing is found.

[*Enter* **Lane** *with the cigarette case on a salver.* **Algernon** *takes it at once.* **Lane** *goes out.*]

Algernon: I think that is rather mean of you, Ernest, I must say. [*Opens case and examines it*] However, it makes no matter, for, now that I look at the inscription inside, I find that the thing isn't yours after all.

Jack: Of course it's mine. [*Moving to him*] You have seen me with it a hundred times, and you have no right whatsoever to read what is written inside. It is a very ungentlemanly thing to read a private cigarette case.

Algernon: Oh! it is absurd to have a hard and fast rule about what one should read and what

one shouldn't. More than half of modern culture depends on what one shouldn't read.

Jack: I am quite aware of the fact, and I don't propose to discuss modern culture. It isn't the sort of thing one should talk of in private. I simply want my cigarette case back.

Algernon: Yes; but this isn't your cigarette case. This cigarette case is a present from someone of the name of Cecily, and you said you didn't know anyone of that name.

Jack: Well, if you want to know, Cecily happens to be my aunt.

Algernon: Your aunt!

Jack: Yes. Charming old lady she is, too. Lives at Tunbridge Wells. Just give it back to me, Algy.

Algernon: [*Retreating to back of sofa*] But why does she call herself little Cecily if she is your aunt and lives at Tunbridge Wells. [*Reading*] "From little Cecily with her fondest love."

Jack: [*Moving to sofa and kneeling upon it*] My dear fellow, what on earth is there in that? Some aunts are tall, some aunts are not tall. That is a matter that surely an aunt may be allowed to decide for herself. You seem to think that every aunt should be exactly like your aunt! That is absurd. For Heaven's sake give me back my cigarette case. [*Follows* **Algernon** *round the room.*]

Algernon: Yes. But why does your aunt call you her uncle? "From little Cecily, with her fondest love to her dear Uncle Jack." There is no objection, I admit, to an aunt being a small aunt, but why an aunt, no matter what her size may be, should call her own nephew her uncle, I can't quite make out. Besides your name isn't Jack at all; it is Ernest.

Jack: It isn't Ernest; it's Jack.

Algernon: You have always told me it was Ernest. I have introduced you to every one as Ernest. You answer to the name of Ernest. You look as if your name was Ernest. You are the most earnest-looking person I ever saw in my life. It is perfectly absurd your saying that your name isn't Ernest. It's on your cards. Here is one of them [*taking it from case*]. "Mr. Ernest Worthing, B.4, The Albany." I'll keep this as a proof that your name is Ernest if ever you attempt to deny it to me, or to Gwendolen, or to any one else. [*Puts the card in his pocket.*]

Jack: Well, my name is Ernest in town and Jack in the country, and the cigarette case was given to me in the country.

Algernon: Yes, but that does not account for the fact that your small Aunt Cecily, who lives at Tunbridge Wells, call you her dear uncle. Come, old boy, you had much better have the thing out at once.

Jack: My dear Algy, you talk exactly as if you were a dentist. It is very vulgar to talk like a dentist when one isn't a dentist. It produces a false impression.

Algernon: Well, that is exactly what dentists always do. Now, go on! Tell me the whole thing. I may mention that I have always suspected you of being a confirmed and secret Bunburyist, and I am quite sure of it now.

Jack: Bunburyist? What on earth do you mean by a Bunburyist?

Algernon: I'll reveal to you the meaning of that incomparable expression as soon as you are kind enough to inform me why you are Ernest in town and Jack in the country.

Jack: Well, produce my cigarette case first.

Algernon: Here it is. [*Hands cigarette case*] Now produce your explanation, and pray make it improbable. [*Sits on sofa.*]

Jack: My dear fellow, there is nothing improbable about my explanation at all. In fact it's perfectly ordinary. Old Mr. Thomas Cardew, who adopted me when I was a little boy, made me in his will guardian to his granddaughter, Miss Cecily Cardew. Cecily, who addresses me as her uncle from motives of respect that you could not possibly appreciate, lives at my place in the country under the charge of her admirable governess, Miss Prism.

Algernon: Where is that place in the country, by the way?

Jack: That is nothing to you, dear boy. You are not going to be invited. . . . I may tell you candidly that the place is not in Shropshire.

Algernon: I suspected that, my dear fellow! I have Bunburyed all over Shropshire on two separate occasions. Now, go on. Why are you Ernest in town and Jack in the country?

Jack: My dear Algy, I don't know whether you will be able to understand my real motives. You are hardly serious enough. When one is placed in the position of guardian, one has to adopt a very high moral tone on all subjects. It's one's duty to do so. And as a high moral tone can hardly be said to conduce very much to either one's health or one's happiness, in order to get up to town I have always pretended to have a younger brother of the name of Ernest, who lives in the Albany, and gets into the most dreadful scrapes. That, my dear Algy, is the whole truth pure and simple.

Algernon: The truth is rarely pure and never simple. Modern life would be very tedious if it were either, and modern literature a complete impossibility!

Jack: That wouldn't be at all a bad thing.

Algernon: Literary criticism is not your forte, my dear fellow. Don't try it. You should leave that to people who haven't been at a University. They do it so well in the daily papers. What you really are is a Bunburyist. I was quite right in saying you were a Bunburyist. You are one of the most advanced Bunburyists I know.

Jack: What on earth do you mean?

Algernon: You have invented a very useful younger brother called Ernest, in order that you may be able to come up to town as often as you like. I have invented an invaluable permanent invalid called Bunbury, in order that I may be able to go down into the country whenever I choose. Bunbury is perfectly invaluable. If it wasn't for Bunbury's extraordinary bad health, for instance, I wouldn't be able to dine with you at Willis's tonight, for I have been really engaged to Aunt Augusta for more than a week.

Jack: I haven't asked you to dine with me anywhere tonight.

Algernon: I know. You are absurdly careless about sending out invitations. It is very foolish of you. Nothing annoys people so much as not receiving invitations.

Jack: You had much better dine with your Aunt Augusta.

Algernon: I haven't the smallest intention of

doing anything of the kind. To begin with, I dined there on Monday, and once a week is quite enough to dine with one's own relations. In the second place, whenever I do dine there I am always treated as a member of the family, and sent down with either no woman at all, or two. In the third place, I know perfectly well whom she will place me next to, tonight. She will place me next to Mary Farquhar, who always flirts with her own husband across the dinner table. That is not very pleasant. Indeed, it is not even decent . . . and that sort of thing is enormously on the increase. The amount of women in London who flirt with their own husbands is perfectly scandalous. It looks so bad. It is simply washing one's clean linen in public. Besides, now that I know you to be a confirmed Bunburyist I naturally want to talk to you about Bunburying. I want to tell you the rules.

Jack: I'm not a Bunburyist at all. If Gwendolen accepts me, I am going to kill my brother, indeed I think I'll kill him in any case. Cecily is a little too much interested in him. It is rather a bore. So I am going to get rid of Ernest. And I strongly advise you to do the same with Mr. . . . with your invalid friend who has the absurd name.

Algernon: Nothing will induce me to part with Bunbury, and if you ever get married, which seems to me extremely problematic, you will be very glad to know Bunbury. A man who marries without knowing Bunbury has a very tedious time of it.

Jack: That is nonsense. If I marry a charming girl like Gwendolen, and she is the only girl I ever saw in my life that I would marry, I certainly won't want to know Bunbury.

Algernon: Then your wife will. You don't seem to realize, that in married life three is company and two is none.

Jack: [*Sententiously*] That, my dear young friend, is the theory that the corrupt French Drama has been propounding for the last fifty years.

Algernon: Yes! and that the happy English home has proved in half the time.

Jack: For heaven's sake, don't try to be cynical. It's perfectly easy to be cynical.

Algernon: My dear fellow, it isn't easy to be anything nowadays. There's such a lot of beastly competition about. [*The sound of an electric bell is heard*] Ah! that must be Aunt Augusta. Only relatives, or creditors, ever ring in that Wagnerian manner. Now, if I get her out of the way for ten minutes, so that you can have an opportunity for proposing to Gwendolen, may I dine with you tonight at Willis's?

Jack: I suppose so, if you want to.

Algernon: Yes, but you must be serious about it. I hate people who are not serious about meals. It is so shallow of them.

> [*Enter* **Lane.**]

Lane: Lady Bracknell and Miss Fairfax.

> [**Algernon** *goes forward to meet them. Enter* **Lady Bracknell** *and* **Gwendolen.**]

Lady Bracknell: Good afternoon, dear Algernon, I hope you are behaving very well.

Algernon: I'm feeling very well, Aunt Augusta.

Lady Bracknell: That's not quite the same thing. In fact the two things rarely go together. [*Sees* **Jack** *and bows to him with icy coldness.*]

Algernon: [*to* **Gwendolen**] Dear me, you are smart!

Gwendolen: I am always smart! Am I not, Mr. Worthing?

Jack: You're quite perfect, Miss Fairfax.

Gwendolen: Oh! I hope I am not that. It would leave no room for developments, and I intend to develop in many directions. [**Gwendolen** *and* **Jack** *sit down together in the corner.*]

Lady Bracknell: I'm sorry if we are a little late, Algernon, but I was obliged to call on dear Lady Harbury. I hadn't been there since her poor husband's death. I never saw a woman so altered; she looks quite twenty years younger. And now I'll have a cup of tea and one of those nice cucumber sandwiches you promised me.

Algernon: Certainly, Aunt Augusta. [*Goes over to tea-table.*]

Lady Bracknell: Won't you come and sit here, Gwendolen?

Gwendolen: Thanks, mamma, I'm quite comfortable where I am.

Algernon: [*Picking up empty plate in horror*] Good heavens! Lane! Why are there no cucumber sandwiches? I ordered them specially.

Lane: [*Gravely*] There were no cucumbers in the market this morning, sir. I went down twice.

Algernon: No cucumbers!

Lane: No, sir. Not even for ready money.

Algernon: That will do, Lane, thank you.

Lane: Thank you, sir. [*Goes out.*]

Algernon: I am greatly distressed, Aunt Augusta, about there being no cucumbers, not even for ready money.

Lady Bracknell: It really makes no matter, Algernon. I had some crumpets with Lady Harbury, who seems to me to be living entirely for pleasure now.

Algernon: I hear her hair has turned quite gold from grief.

Lady Bracknell: It certainly has changed its colour. From what cause I, of course, cannot say. [**Algernon** *crosses and hands tea*] Thank you. I've quite a treat for you tonight, Algernon. I am going to send you down with Mary Farquhar. She is such a nice woman, and so attentive to her husband. It's delightful to watch them.

Algernon: I am afraid, Aunt Augusta, I shall have to give up the pleasure of dining with you tonight after all.

Lady Bracknell: [*Frowning*] I hope not, Algernon. It would put my table completely out. Your uncle would have to dine upstairs. Fortunately he is accustomed to that.

Algernon: It is a great bore, and, I need hardly say, a terrible disappointment to me, but the fact is I have just had a telegram to say that my poor friend Bunbury is very ill again. [*Exchanges glances with* **Jack**] They seem to think I should be with him.

Lady Bracknell: It is very strange. This Mr. Bunbury seems to suffer from curiously bad health.

Algernon: Yes; poor Bunbury is a dreadful invalid.

Lady Bracknell: Well, I must say, Algernon, that I think it is high time that Mr. Bunbury made up his mind whether he was going to live or to die. This shilly-shallying with the question is absurd. Nor do I in any way approve of the modern sympathy with invalids. I consider it morbid. Illness of any kind is hardly a thing to be encouraged in others.

Health is the primary duty of life. I am always telling that to your poor uncle, but he never seems to take much notice . . . as far as any improvement in his ailments goes. I should be much obliged if you would ask Mr. Bunbury, from me, to be kind enough not to have a relapse on Saturday, for I rely on you to arrange my music for me. It is my last reception, and one wants something that will encourage conversation, particularly at the end of the season when every one has practically said whatever they had to say, which, in most cases, was probably not much.

Algernon: I'll speak to Bunbury, Aunt Augusta, if he is still conscious, and I think I can promise you he'll be all right by Saturday. Of course the music is a great difficulty. You see, if one plays good music, people don't listen, and if one plays bad music, people don't talk. But I'll run over the programme I've drawn out, if you will kindly come into the next room for a moment.

Lady Bracknell: Thank you, Algernon. It is very thoughtful of you. [*Rising, and following* **Algernon**] I'm sure the programme will be delightful, after a few expurgations. French songs I cannot possibly allow. People always seem to think that they are improper, and either look shocked, which is vulgar, or laugh, which is worse. But German sounds a thoroughly respectable language, and, indeed I believe is so. Gwendolen, you will accompany me.

Gwendolen: Certainly, mamma.

[**Lady Bracknell** *and* **Algernon** *go into the music-room;* **Gwendolen** *remains behind.*]

Jack: Charming day it has been, Miss Fairfax.

Gwendolen: Pray don't talk to me about the weather, Mr. Worthing. Whenever people talk to me about the weather, I always feel quite certain that they mean something else. And that makes me so nervous.

Jack: I do mean something else.

Gwendolen: I thought so. In fact, I am never wrong.

Jack: And I would like to be allowed to take advantage of Lady Bracknell's temporary absence. . . .

Gwendolen: I would certainly advise you to

do so. Mamma has a way of coming back suddenly into a room that I have often had to speak to her about.

Jack: [*Nervously*] Miss Fairfax, ever since I met you I have admired you more than any girl . . . I have ever met since . . . I met you.

Gwendolen: Yes, I am quite aware of the fact. And I often wish that in public, at any rate, you had been more demonstrative. For me you have always had an irresistible fascination. Even before I met you I was far from indifferent to you. [**Jack** *looks at her in amazement.*] We live, as I hope you know, Mr. Worthing, in an age of ideals. The fact is constantly mentioned in the more expensive monthly magazines, and has reached the provincial pulpits, I am told; and my ideal has always been to love some one of the name of Ernest. There is something in that name that inspires absolute confidence. The moment Algernon first mentioned to me that he had a friend called Ernest, I knew I was destined to love you.

Jack: You really love me, Gwendolen?

Gwendolen: Passionately!

Jack: Darling! You don't know how happy you've made me.

Gwendolen: My own Ernest!

Jack: But you don't really mean to say that you couldn't love me if my name wasn't Ernest?

Gwendolen: But your name is Ernest.

Jack: Yes, I know it is. But supposing it was something else? Do you mean to say you couldn't love me then?

Gwendolen: [*Glibly*] Ah! that is clearly a metaphysical speculation, and like most metaphysical speculations has very little reference at all to the actual facts of real life, as we know them.

Jack: Personally, darling, to speak quite candidly, I don't much care about the name of Ernest. . . . I don't think the name suits me at all.

Gwendolen: It suits you perfectly. It is a divine name. It has a music of its own. It produces vibrations.

Jack: Well, really, Gwendolen, I must say that I think there are lots of other much nicer names. I think Jack, for instance, a charming name.

Gwendolen: Jack? . . . No, there is very little music in the name Jack, if any at all, indeed. It does not thrill. It produces absolutely no vibrations. . . . I have known several Jacks, and they all, without exception, were more than usually plain. Besides, Jack is a notorious domesticity for John! And I pity any woman who is married to a man called John. She would probably never be allowed to know the entrancing pleasure of a single moment's solitude. The only really safe name is Ernest.

Jack: Gwendolen, I must get christened at once—I mean we must get married at once. There is no time to be lost.

Gwendolen: Married, Mr. Worthing?

Jack: [*Astounded*] Well . . . surely. You know that I love you, and you led me to believe, Miss Fairfax, that you were not absolutely indifferent to me.

Gwendolen: I adore you. But you haven't proposed to me yet. Nothing has been said at all about marriage. The subject has not even been touched on.

Jack: Well . . . may I propose to you now?

Gwendolen: I think it would be an admirable opportunity. And to spare you any possible disappointment, Mr. Worthing, I think it only fair to tell you quite frankly beforehand that I am fully determined to accept you.

Jack: Gwendolen!

Gwendolen: Yes, Mr. Worthing, what have you got to say to me?

Jack: You know what I have got to say to you.

Gwendolen: Yes, but you don't say it.

Jack: Gwendolen, will you marry me? [*Goes on his knees.*]

Gwendolen: Of course I will, darling. How long you have been about it! I am afraid you have had very little experience in how to propose.

Jack: My own one, I have never loved any one in the world but you.

Gwendolen: Yes, but men often propose for practice. I know my brother Gerald does. All my girl-friends tell me so. What wonderfully blue eyes you have, Ernest! They are quite, quite blue. I hope you will always look at me just like that, especially when there are other people present.

[*Enter* **Lady Bracknell.**]

Lady Bracknell: Mr. Worthing! Rise sir, from this semi-recumbent posture. It is most indecorous.

Gwendolen: Mamma! [*He tries to rise; she restrains him*] I must beg you to retire. This is no place for you. Besides, Mr. Worthing has not quite finished yet.

Lady Bracknell: Finished what, may I ask?

Gwendolen: I am engaged to Mr. Worthing, mamma. [*They rise together.*]

Lady Bracknell: Pardon me, you are not engaged to any one. When you do become engaged to some one, I, or your father, should his health permit him, will inform you of the fact. An engagement should come on a young girl as a surprise, pleasant or unpleasant, as the case may be. It is hardly a matter that she could be allowed to arrange for herself. . . . And now I have a few questions to put to you, Mr. Worthing. While I am making these inquiries, you, Gwendolen, will wait for me below in the carriage.

Gwendolen: [*Reproachfully*] Mamma!

Lady Bracknell: In the carriage, Gwendolen! [**Gwendolen** *goes to the door. She and* **Jack** *blow kisses to each other behind* **Lady Bracknell**'*s back.* **Lady Bracknell** *looks vaguely about as if she could not understand what the noise was. Finally turns round*] Gwendolen, the carriage!

Gwendolen: Yes, mamma. [*Goes out, looking back at* **Jack.**]

Lady Bracknell: [*Sitting down*] You can take a seat, Mr. Worthing.

   [*Looks in her pocket for notebook and pencil.*]

Jack: Thank you, Lady Bracknell, I prefer standing.

Lady Bracknell: [*Pencil and notebook in hand*] I feel bound to tell you that you are not down on my list of elgible young men, although I have the same list as the dear Duchess of Bolton has. We work together, in fact. However, I am quite ready to enter your name, should your answers be what a really affectionate mother requires. Do you smoke?

Jack: Well, yes, I must admit I smoke.

Lady Bracknell: I am glad to hear it. A man should always have an occupation of some kind. There are far too many idle men in London as it is. How old are you?

Jack: Twenty-nine.

Lady Bracknell: A very good age to be married at. I have always been of opinion that a man who desires to get married should know either everything or nothing. Which do you know?

Jack: [*After some hesitation*] I know nothing, Lady Bracknell.

Lady Bracknell: I am pleased to hear it. I do not approve of anything that tampers with natural ignorance. Ignorance is like a delicate exotic fruit; touch it and the bloom is gone. The whole theory of modern education is radically unsound. Fortunately in England, at any rate, education produces no effect whatsoever. If it did, it would prove a serious danger to the upper classes, and probably lead to acts of violence in Grosvenor Square. What is your income?

Jack: Between seven and eight thousand a year.

Lady Bracknell: [*Makes a note in her book*] In land, or in investments?

Jack: In investments, chiefly.

Lady Bracknell: That is satisfactory. What between the duties expected of one during one's lifetime, and the duties exacted from one after one's death, land has ceased to be either a profit or a pleasure. It gives one position, and prevents one from keeping it up. That's all that can be said about land.

Jack: I have a country house with some land, of course, attached to it, about fifteen hundred acres, I believe; but I don't depend on that for my real income. In fact, as far as I can make out, the poachers are the only people who make anything out of it.

Lady Bracknell: A country house! How many bedrooms? Well, that point can be cleared up afterwards. You have a town house, I hope? A girl with a simple, unspoiled nature, like Gwendolen, could hardly be expected to reside in the country.

Jack: Well, I own a house in Belgrave Square, but it is let by the year to Lady Bloxham. Of course, I can get back whenever I like, at six months' notice.

Lady Bracknell: Lady Bloxham? I don't know her.

Jack: Oh, she goes about very little. She is a lady considerably advanced in years.

Lady Bracknell: Ah, nowadays that is no guarantee of respectability of character. What number in Belgrave Square?

Jack: 149.

Lady Bracknell: [*Shaking her head*] The unfashionable side, I thought there was something. However, that could easily be altered.

Jack: Do you mean the fashion, or the side?

Lady Bracknell: [*Sternly*] Both, if necessary, I presume. What are your politics?

Jack: Well, I am afraid I really have none. I am a Liberal Unionist.

Lady Bracknell: Oh, they count as Tories. They dine with us. Or come in the evening, at any rate. Now to minor matters. Are your parents living?

Jack: I have lost both my parents.

Lady Bracknell: To lose one parent, Mr. Worthing, may be regarded as a misfortune; to lose both looks like carelessness. Who was your father? He was evidently a man of some wealth. Was he born in what the Radical papers call the purple of commerce, or did he rise from the ranks of the aristocracy?

Jack: I am afraid I really don't know. The fact is, Lady Bracknell, I said I had lost my parents. It would be nearer the truth to say that my parents seem to have lost me. . . . I don't actually know who I am by birth. I was . . . well, I was found.

Lady Bracknell: Found!

Jack: The late Mr. Thomas Cardew, an old gentleman of a very charitable and kindly disposition, found me, and gave me the name of Worthing, because he happened to have a first-class ticket for Worthing in his pocket at the time. Worthing is a place in Sussex. It is a seaside resort.

Lady Bracknell: Where did the charitable gentleman who had a first-class ticket for this seaside resort find you?

Jack: [*Gravely*] In a handbag.

Lady Bracknell: A handbag?

Jack: [*Very seriously*] Yes, Lady Bracknell. I was in a handbag— a somewhat large, black leather handbag, with handles to it—an ordinary handbag in fact.

Lady Bracknell: In what locality did this Mr. James, or Thomas, Cardew come across this ordinary handbag?

Jack: In the cloakroom at Victoria Station. It was given to him in mistake for his own.

Lady Bracknell: The cloakroom at Victoria Station?

Jack: Yes. The Brighton line.

Lady Bracknell: The line is immaterial. Mr. Worthing, I confess I feel somewhat bewildered by what you have just told me. To be born, or at any rate bred, in a handbag, whether it had handles or not, seems to me to display a contempt for the ordinary decencies of family life that reminds one of the worst excesses of the French Revolution. And I presume you know what that unfortunate movement led to? As for the particular locality in which the handbag was found, a cloakroom at a railway station might serve to conceal a social indiscretion—has probably, indeed, been used for that purpose before now—but it could hardly be regarded as an assured basis for a recognized position in good society.

Jack: May I ask you then what you would advise me to do? I need hardly say I would do anything in the world to ensure Gwendolen's happiness.

Lady Bracknell: I would strongly advise you, Mr. Worthing, to try and acquire some relations as soon as possible, and to make a definite effort to produce at any rate one parent, of either sex, before the season is quite over.

Jack: Well, I don't see how I could possibly manage to do that. I can produce the handbag at any moment. It is in my dressingroom at home. I really think that should satisfy you, Lady Bracknell.

Lady Bracknell: Me, sir! What has it to do with me? You can hardly imagine that I and Lord Bracknell would dream of allowing our only daughter—a girl brought up with the utmost care—to marry into a cloakroom, and form an alliance with a parcel. Good morning, Mr. Worthing!

[**Lady Bracknell** *sweeps out in majestic indignation.*]

Jack: Good morning! [**Algernon,** *from the other room, strikes up the Wedding March.* **Jack** *looks perfectly furious, and goes to the door*] For goodness' sake don't play that ghastly tune, Algy! How idiotic you are!

[*The music stops and* **Algernon** *enters cheerily.*]

Algernon: Didn't it go off all right, old boy? You don't mean to say Gwendolen refused you? I know it is a way she has. She is always refusing people. I think it is most ill-natured of her.

Jack: Oh, Gwendolen is as right as a trivet. As far as she is concerned, we are engaged. Her mother is perfectly unbearable. Never met such a Gorgon. . . . I don't really know what a Gorgon is like, but I am quite sure that Lady Bracknell is one. In any case, she is a monster, without being a myth, which is rather unfair. . . . I beg your pardon, Algy, I suppose I shouldn't talk about your own aunt in that way before you.

Algernon: My dear boy, I love hearing my relations abused. It is the only thing that makes me put up with them at all. Relations are simply a tedious pack of people, who haven't got the remotest knowledge of how to live, nor the smallest instinct about when to die.

Jack: Oh, that is nonsense!

Algernon: It isn't!

Jack: Well, I won't argue about the matter. You always want to argue about things.

Algernon: That is exactly what things were originally made for.

Jack: Upon my word, if I thought that, I'd shoot myself. . . . [*A pause*] You don't think there is any chance of Gwendolen becoming like her mother in about a hundred and fifty years, do you, Algy?

Algernon: All women become like their mothers. That is their tragedy. No man does. That's his.

Jack: Is that clever?

Algernon: It is perfectly phrased! and quite as true as any observation in civilized life should be.

Jack: I am sick to death of cleverness. Everybody is clever nowadays. You can't go anywhere without meeting clever people. The thing has become an absolute public nuisance. I wish to goodness we had a few fools left.

Algernon: We have.

Jack: I should extremely like to meet them. What do they talk about?

Algernon: The fools? Oh! about the clever people, of course.

Jack: What fools.

Algernon: By the way, did you tell Gwendolen the truth about your being Ernest in town, and Jack in the country?

Jack: [*In a very patronizing manner*] My dear fellow, the truth isn't quite the sort of thing one tells to a nice, sweet, refined girl. What extraordinary ideas you have about the way to behave to a woman!

Algernon: The only way to behave to a woman is to make love to her, if she is pretty, and to someone else, if she is plain.

Jack: Oh, that is nonsense.

Algernon: What about your brother? What about the profligate Ernest?

Jack: Oh, before the end of the week I shall have got rid of him. I'll say he died in Paris of apoplexy. Lots of people die of apoplexy, quite suddenly, don't they?

Algernon: Yes, but it's hereditary, my dear fellow. It's a sort of thing that runs in families. You had much better say a severe chill.

Jack: You are sure a severe chill isn't hereditary, or anything of that kind?

Algernon: Of course it isn't!

Jack: Very well, then. My poor brother Ernest is carried off suddenly, in Paris, by a severe chill. That gets rid of him.

Algernon: But I thought you said that . . . Miss Cardew was a little too much interested in your poor brother Ernest? Won't she feel his loss a good deal?

Jack: Oh, that is all right. Cecily is not a silly romantic girl, I am glad to say. She has got a capital appetite, goes on long walks, and pays no attention at all to her lessons.

Algernon: I would rather like to see Cecily.

Jack: I will take very good care you never do. She is excessively pretty, and she is only just eighteen.

Algernon: Have you told Gwendolen yet that you have an excessively pretty ward who is only just eighteen?

Jack: Oh! one doesn't blurt these things out to people. Cecily and Gwendolen are perfectly certain to be extremely great friends. I'll bet you anything you like that half an hour after they have met, they will be calling each other sister.

Algernon: Women only do that when they have called each other a lot of other things first. Now, my dear boy, if we want to get a good table at Willis's, we really must go and dress. Do you know it is nearly seven?

Jack: [*Irritably*] Oh! it always is nearly seven.

Algernon: Well, I'm hungry.

Jack: I never knew you when you weren't. . . .

Algernon: What shall we do after dinner? Go to a theatre?

Jack: Oh no! I loathe listening.

Algernon: Well, let us go to the Club?

Jack: Oh, no! I hate talking.

Algernon: Well, we might trot round to the Empire at ten?

Jack: Oh, no! I can't bear looking at things. It is so silly.

Algernon: Well, what shall we do?

Jack: Nothing!

Algernon: It is awfully hard work doing nothing. However, I don't mind hard work where there is no definite object of any kind.

[*Enter* **Lane.**]

Lane: Miss Fairfax.

[*Enter* **Gwendolen. Lane** *goes out.*]

Algernon: Gwendolen, upon my word!

Gwendolen: Algy, kindly turn your back. I have something very particular to say to Mr. Worthing.

Algernon: Really, Gwendolen, I don't think I can allow this at all.

Gwendolen: Algy, you always adopt a strictly immoral attitude towards life. You are not quite old enough to do that.

[**Algernon** *retires to the fireplace.*]

Jack: My own darling!

Gwendolen: Ernest, we may never be married. From the expression on mamma's face I fear we never shall. Few parents nowadays pay any regard to what their children say to them. The old-fashioned respect for the young is fast dying out. Whatever influence I ever had over mamma, I lost at the age of three. But although she may prevent us from becoming man and wife, and I may marry someone else, and marry often, nothing that she can possibly do can alter my eternal devotion to you.

Jack: Dear Gwendolen!

Gwendolen: The story of your romantic origin, as related to me by mamma, with unpleasing comments, has naturally stirred the deeper fibres of my nature. Your Christian name has an irresistible fascination. The simplicity of your character makes you exquisitely incomprehensible to me. Your town address at the Albany I have. What is your address in the country?

Jack: The Manor House, Woolton, Hertfordshire.

[**Algernon,** *who has been carefully listening, smiles to himself, and writes the address on his shirt-cuff. Then picks up the Railway Guide.*]

Gwendolen: There is a good postal service, I suppose? It may be necessary to do something desperate. That of course will require serious consideration. I will communicate with you daily.

Jack: My own one!

Gwendolen: How long do you remain in town?

Jack: Till Monday.

Gwendolen: Good! Algy, you may turn round now.

Algernon: Thanks, I've turned round already.

Gwendolen: You may also ring the bell.

Jack: You will let me see you to your carriage, my own darling?

Gwendolen: Certainly.

Jack: [*To* **Lane,** *who now enters*] I will see Miss Fairfax out.

Lane: Yes, sir. [**Jack** *and* **Gwendolen** *go off*]

[**Lane** *presents several letters on a salver to* **Algernon.** *It is to be surmised that they are bills, as* **Algernon,** *after looking at the envelopes, tears them up.*]

Algernon: A glass of sherry, Lane.

Lane: Yes, sir.

Algernon: Tomorrow, Lane, I'm going Bunburying.

Lane: Yes, sir.

Algernon: I shall probably not be back till Monday. You can put up my dress clothes, my smoking jacket, and all the Bunbury suits . . .

Lane: Yes, sir. [*Handing sherry.*]

Algernon: I hope tomorrow will be a fine day, Lane.

Lane: It never is, Sir.

Algernon: Lane, you're a perfect pessimist.

Lane: I do my best to give satisfaction, sir.

[*Enter* **Jack**. **Lane** *goes off.*]

Jack: There's a sensible, intellectual girl! the only girl I ever cared for in my life. [**Algernon** *is laughing immoderately*] What on earth are you so amused at?

Algernon: Oh, I'm a little anxious about poor Bunbury, that is all.

Jack: If you don't take care, your friend Bunbury will get you into a serious scrape some day.

Algernon: I love scrapes. They are the only things that are never serious.

Jack: Oh, that's nonsense, Algy. You never talk anything but nonsense.

Algernon: Nobody ever does.

[**Jack** *looks indignantly at him, and leaves the room.* **Algernon** *lights a cigarette, reads his shirt-cuff, and smiles.*]

ACT II

Garden at the Manor House. A flight of grey stone steps leads up to the house. The garden, an old-fashioned one, full of roses. Time of year, July. Basket chairs, and a table covered with books, are set under a large yew-tree.

[**Miss Prism** *discovered seated at the table.* **Cecily** *is at the back, watering flowers.*]

Miss Prism: [*Calling*] Cecily, Cecily! Surely such a utilitarian occupation as the watering of flowers is rather Moulton's duty than yours? Especially at a moment when intellectual pleasures await you. Your German grammar is on the table. Pray open it at page fifteen. We will repeat yesterday's lesson.

Cecily: [*Coming over very slowly*] But I don't like German. It isn't at all a becoming language. I know perfectly well that I look quite plain after my German lesson.

Miss Prism: Child, you know how anxious your guardian is that you should improve yourself in every way. He laid particular stress on your German, as he was leaving for town yesterday. Indeed, he always lays stress on your German when he is leaving for town.

Cecily: Dear Uncle Jack is so very serious! Sometimes he is so serious that I think he cannot be quite well.

Miss Prism: [*Drawing herself up*] Your guardian enjoys the best of health, and his gravity of demeanor is especially to be commended in one so comparatively young as he is. I know no one who has a higher sense of duty and responsibility.

Cecily: I suppose that is why he often looks a little bored when we three are together.

Miss Prism: Cecily! I am surprised at you. Mr. Worthing has many troubles in his life. Idle merriment and triviality would be out of place in his conversation. You must remember his constant anxiety about that unfortunate young man, his brother.

Cecily: I wish Uncle Jack would allow that unfortunate young man, his brother, to come down here sometimes. We might have a good influence over him, Miss Prism. I am sure you certainly would. You know German, and geology, and things of that kind influence a man very much. [**Cecily** *begins to write in her diary.*]

Miss Prism: [*Shaking her head*] I do not think that even I could produce any effect on a character that according to his own brother's admission is irretrievably weak and vacillating. Indeed I am not sure that I would desire to reclaim him. I am not in favor of this modern mania for turning bad people into good people at a moment's notice. As a man sows so let him reap. You must put away your diary, Cecily. I really don't see why you should keep a diary at all.

Cecily: I keep a diary in order to enter the wonderful secrets of my life. If I didn't write them down, I should probably forget all about them.

Miss Prism: Memory, my dear Cecily, is the diary that we all carry about with us.

Cecily: Yes, but it usually chronicles the things that have never happened, and couldn't possibly have happened. I believe that Memory is responsible for nearly all the three-volume novels that Mudie sends us.

Miss Prism: Do not speak slightingly of the three-volume novel, Cecily. I wrote one myself in earlier days.

Cecily: Did you really, Miss Prism? How wonderfully clever you are! I hope it did not end happily? I don't like novels that end happily. They depress me so much.

Miss Prism: The good ended happily, and the bad unhappily. That is what Fiction means.

Cecily: I suppose so. But it seems very unfair. And was your novel ever published?

Miss Prism: Alas! no. The manuscript unfortunately was abandoned. [**Cecily** *starts*] I used the word in the sense of lost or mislaid. To your work, child, these speculations are profitless.

Cecily: [*Smiling*] But I see dear Dr. Chasuble coming up through the garden.

Miss Prism: [*Rising and advancing*] Dr. Chasuble! This is indeed a pleasure.

[*Enter* **Canon Chasuble.**]

Chasuble: And how are we this morning? Miss Prism, you are, I trust, well?

Cecily: Miss Prism has just been complaining of a slight headache. I think it would do her so much good to have a short stroll with you in the Park, Dr. Chasuble.

Miss Prism: Cecily, I have not mentioned anything about a headache.

Cecily: No, dear Miss Prism, I know that, but I felt instinctively that you had a headache. Indeed I was thinking about that, and not about my German lesson, when the Rector came in.

Chasuble: I hope, Cecily, you are not inattentive.

Cecily: Oh, I am afraid I am.

Chasuble: That is strange. Were I fortunate enough to be Miss Prism's pupil, I would hang upon her lips. [**Miss Prism** *glares*] I spoke metaphorically.—My metaphor was drawn from bees. Ahem! Mr. Worthing, I suppose, has not returned from town yet?

Miss Prism: We do not expect him till Monday afternoon.

Chasuble: Ah yes, he usually likes to spend his Sunday in London. He is not one of those whose sole aim is enjoyment, as, by all accounts, that unfortunate young man his brother seems to be. But I must not disturb Egeria and her pupil any longer.

Miss Prism: Egeria? My name is Laetitia, Doctor.

Chasuble: [*Bowing*] A classical allusion merely, drawn from the Pagan authors. I shall see you both no doubt at Evensong?

Miss Prism: I think, dear Doctor, I will have a stroll with you. I find I have a headache after all, and a walk might do it good.

Chasuble: With pleasure, Miss Prism, with pleasure. We might go as far as the schools and back.

Miss Prism: That would be delightful. Cecily, you will read your Political Economy in my absence. The chapter on the Fall of the Rupee you may omit. It is somewhat too sensational. Even these metallic problems have their melodramatic side.

[*Goes down the garden with* **Dr. Chasuble.**]

Cecily: [*Picks up books and throws them back on table*] Horrid Political Economy! Horrid Geography! Horrid, horrid German!

[*Enter* **Merriman** *with a card on a salver.*]

Merriman: Mr. Ernest Worthing has just driven over from the station. He has brought his luggage with him.

Cecily: [*Takes the card and reads it*] "Mr. Ernest Worthing, B.4, The Albany, W." Uncle Jack's brother! Did you tell him Mr. Worthing was in town?

Merriman: Yes, Miss. He seemed very much disappointed. I mentioned that you and Miss Prism were in the garden. He said he was anxious to speak to you privately for a moment.

Cecily: Ask Mr. Ernest Worthing to come here. I suppose you had better talk to the housekeeper about a room for him.

Merriman: Yes, Miss. [**Merriman** *goes off.*]

Cecily: I have never met any really wicked person before. I feel rather frightened. I am so afraid he will look just like every one else.

[*Enter* **Algernon,** *very gay and debonnaire.*]

He does!

Algernon: [*Raising his hat*] You are my little cousin Cecily, I'm sure.

Cecily: You are under some strange mistake. I am not little. In fact, I believe I am more than usually tall for my age. [**Algernon** *is rather taken aback*] But I am your cousin Cecily. You, I see from your card, are Uncle Jack's brother, my cousin Ernest, my wicked cousin Ernest.

Algernon: Oh! I am not really wicked at all, Cousin Cecily. You mustn't think that I am wicked.

Cecily: If you are not, then you have certainly been deceiving us all in a very inexcusable manner. I hope you have not been leading a double life, pretending to be wicked and being really good all the time. That would be hypocrisy.

Algernon: [*Looks at her in amazement*] Oh! Of course I have been rather reckless.

Cecily: I am glad to hear it.

Algernon: In fact, now you mention the subject, I have been very bad in my own small way.

Cecily: I don't think you should be so proud of that, though I am sure it must have been very pleasant.

Algernon: It is much pleasanter being here with you.

Cecily: I can't understand how you are here at all. Uncle Jack won't be back till Monday afternoon.

Algernon: That is a great disappointment. I am obliged to go up by the first train on Monday morning. I have a business appointment that I am anxious . . . to miss!

Cecily: Couldn't you miss it anywhere but in London?

Algernon: No: the appointment is in London.

Cecily: Well, I know, of course, how important it is not to keep a business engagement, if one wants to retain any sense of the beauty of life, but still I think you had better wait till Uncle Jack arrives. I know he wants to speak to you about your emigrating.

Algernon: About my what?

Cecily: Your emigrating. He has gone up to buy your outfit.

Algernon: I certainly wouldn't let Jack buy my outfit. He has no taste in neckties at all.

Cecily: I don't think you will require neckties. Uncle Jack is sending you to Australia.

Algernon: Australia! I'd sooner die.

Cecily: Well, he said at dinner on Wednesday night, that you would have to choose between this world, the next world, and Australia.

Algernon: Oh, well! The accounts I have received of Australia and the next world are not particularly encouraging. This world is good enough for me, Cousin Cecily.

Cecily: Yes, but are you good enough for it?

Algernon: I'm afraid I'm not that. That is why I want you to reform me. You might make that your mission, if you don't mind, cousin Cecily.

Cecily: I'm afraid I've no time, this afternoon.

Algernon: Well, would you mind my reforming myself this afternoon?

Cecily: It is rather Quixotic of you. But I think you should try.

Algernon: I will. I feel better already.

Cecily: You are looking a little worse.

Algernon: That is because I am hungry.

Cecily: How thoughtless of me. I should have remembered that when one is going to lead an entirely new life, one requires regular and wholesome meals. Won't you come in?

Algernon: Thank you. Might I have a buttonhole first? I never have any appetite unless I have a buttonhole first.

Cecily: A Maréchal Niel? [*Picks up scissors.*]

Algernon: No, I'd sooner have a pink rose.

Cecily: Why? [*Cuts a flower.*]

Algernon: Because you are like a pink rose, Cousin Cecily.

Cecily: I don't think it can be right for you to talk to me like that. Miss Prism never says such things to me.

Algernon: Then Miss Prism is a shortsighted old lady. [**Cecily** *puts the rose in his buttonhole*] You are the prettiest girl I ever saw.

Cecily: Miss Prism says that all good looks are a snare.

Algernon: They are a snare that every sensible man would like to be caught in.

Cecily: Oh, I don't think I would care to catch a sensible man. I shouldn't know what to talk to him about.

[*They pass into the house.* **Miss Prism** *and* **Dr. Chasuble** *return.*]

Miss Prism: You are too much alone, dear Dr.

Chasuble. You should get married. A misanthrope I can understand—a womanthrope, never!

Chasuble: [*With a scholar's shudder*] Believe me, I do not deserve so neologistic a phrase. The precept as well as the practice of the Primitive Church was distinctly against matrimony.

Miss Prism: [*Sententiously*] That is obviously the reason why the Primitive Church has not lasted up to the present day. And you do not seem to realize, dear Doctor, that by persistently remaining single, a man converts himself into a permanent public temptation. Men should be more careful; this very celibacy leads weaker vessels astray.

Chasuble: But is a man not equally attractive when married?

Miss Prism: No married man is ever attractive except to his wife.

Chasuble: And often, I've been told, not even to her.

Miss Prism: That depends on the intellectual sympathies of the woman. Maturity can always be depended on. Ripeness can be trusted. Young women are green. [**Dr. Chasuble** *starts*] I spoke horticulturally. My metaphor was drawn from fruits. But where is Cecily?

Chasuble: Perhaps she followed us to the schools.

[*Enter* **Jack** *slowly from the back of the garden. He is dressed in the deepest mourning, with crepe hatband and black gloves.*]

Miss Prism: Mr. Worthing!

Chasuble: Mr. Worthing?

Miss Prism: This is indeed a surprise. We did not look for you till Monday afternoon.

Jack: [*Shakes* **Miss Prim**'*s hand in a tragic manner*] I have returned sooner than I expected. Dr. Chasuble, I hope you are well?

Chasuble: Dear Mr. Worthing, I trust this garb of woe does not betoken some terrible calamity?

Jack: My brother.

Miss Prism: More shameful debts and extravagance?

Chasuble: Still leading his life of pleasure?

Jack: [*Shaking his head*] Dead!

Chasuble: Your brother Ernest dead?

Jack: Quite dead.

Miss Prism: What a lesson for him! I trust he will profit by it.

Chasuble: Mr. Worthing, I offer you my sincere condolence. You have at least the consolation of knowing that you were always the most generous and forgiving of brothers.

Jack: Poor Ernest! He had many faults, but it is a sad, sad blow.

Chasuble: Very sad indeed. Were you with him at the end?

Jack: No. He died abroad; in Paris, in fact. I had a telegram last night from the manager of the Grand Hotel.

Chasuble: Was the cause of death mentioned?

Jack: A severe chill, it seems.

Miss Prism: As a man sows, so shall he reap.

Chasuble: [*Raising his hand*] Charity, dear Miss Prism, charity! None of us are perfect. I myself am peculiarly susceptible to draughts. Will the interment take place here?

Jack: No. He seems to have expressed a desire to be buried in Paris.

Chasuble: In Paris! [*Shakes his head*] I fear that hardly points to any very serious state of mind at the last. You would no doubt wish me to make some slight allusion to this tragic domestic affliction next Sunday. [**Jack** *presses his hand convulsively*] My sermon on the meaning of the manna in the wilderness can be adapted to almost any occasion, joyful, or, as in the present case, distressing. [*All sigh*] I have preached it at harvest celebrations, christenings, confirmations, on days of humiliation and festal days. The last time I delivered it was in the Cathedral, as a charity sermon on behalf of the Society for the Prevention of Discontent among the Upper Orders. The Bishop, who was present, was much struck by some of the analogies I drew.

Jack: Ah! that reminds me, you mentioned christenings I think, Dr. Chasuble? I suppose you know how to christen all right? [**Dr. Chasuble** *looks astounded*] I mean, of course, you are continually christening, aren't you?

Miss Prism: It is, I regret to say, one of the Rector's most constant duties in this parish. I have often spoken to the poorer classes on the subject. But they don't seem to know what thrift is.

Chasuble: But is there any particular infant in whom you are interested, Mr. Worthing? Your brother was, I believe, unmarried, was he not?

Jack: Oh yes.

Miss Prism: [*Bitterly*] People who live entirely for pleasure usually are.

Jack: But it is not for any child, dear Doctor. I am very fond of children. No! the fact is, I would like to be christened myself, this afternoon, if you have nothing better to do.

Chasuble: But surely, Mr. Worthing, you have been christened already?

Jack: I don't remember anything about it.

Chasuble: But have you any grave doubts on the subject?

Jack: I certainly intend to have. Of course I don't know if the thing would bother you in any way, or if you think I am a little too old now.

Chasuble: Not at all. The sprinkling, and, indeed, the immersion of adults is a perfectly canonical practice.

Jack: Immersion!

Chasuble: You need have no apprehensions. Sprinkling is all that is necessary, or indeed I think advisable. Our weather is so changeable. At what hour would you wish the ceremony performed?

Jack: Oh, I might trot round about five if that would suit you.

Chasuble: Perfectly, perfectly! In fact I have two similar ceremonies to perform at that time. A case of twins that occurred recently in one of the outlying cottages on your own estate. Poor Jenkins the carter, a most hardworking man.

Jack: Oh! I don't see much fun in being christened along with other babies. It would be childish. Would half-past five do?

Chasuble: Admirably! Admirably! [*Takes out watch*] And now, dear Mr. Worthing, I will not intrude any longer into a house of sorrow. I would merely beg you not to be too much bowed down by grief. What seem to us bitter trials are often blessings in disguise.

Miss Prism: This seems to me a blessing of an extremely obvious kind.

[*Enter* **Cecily** *from the house.*]

Cecily: Uncle Jack! Oh, I am pleased to see you back. But what horrid clothes you have got on. Do go and change them.

Miss Prism: Cecily!

Chasuble: My child! My child! [**Cecily** *goes toward* **Jack;** *he kisses her brow in a melancholy manner.*]

Cecily: What is the matter, Uncle Jack? Do look happy! You look as if you had toothache, and I have got such a surprise for you. Who do you think is in the dining-room? Your brother!

Jack: Who?

Cecily: Your brother Ernest. He arrived about half an hour ago.

Jack: What nonsense! I haven't got a brother.

Cecily: Oh, don't say that. However badly he may have behaved to you in the past he is still your brother. You couldn't be so heartless as to disown him. I'll tell him to come out. And you will shake hands with him, won't you, Uncle Jack? [*Runs back into the house.*]

Chasuble: These are very joyful tidings.

Miss Prism: After we had all been resigned to his loss, his sudden return seems to me peculiarly distressing.

Jack: My brother is in the dining-room? I don't know what it all means. I think it is perfectly absurd.

[*Enter* **Algernon** *and* **Cecily** *hand in hand. They come slowly up to* **Jack.**]

Jack: Good heavens! [*Motions* **Algernon** *away.*]

Algernon: Brother John, I have come down from town to tell you that I am very sorry for all the trouble I have given you, and that I intend to lead a better life in the future. [**Jack** *glares at him and does not take his hand.*]

Cecily: Uncle Jack, you are not going to refuse your own brother's hand?

Jack: Nothing will induce me to take his hand. I think his coming down here disgraceful. He knows perfectly well why.

Cecily: Uncle Jack, do be nice. There is some good in everyone. Ernest has just been telling me about his poor invalid friend Mr. Bunbury whom he goes to visit so often. And surely there must be much good in one who is kind to an invalid, and leaves the pleasures of London to sit by a bed of pain.

Jack: Oh! he has been talking about Bunbury, has he?

Cecily: Yes, he has told me all about poor Mr. Bunbury, and his terrible state of health.

Jack: Bunbury! Well, I won't have him talk to you about Bunbury or about anything else. It is enough to drive one perfectly frantic.

Algernon: Of course I admit that the faults were all on my side. But I must say that I think that Brother John's coldness to me is peculiarly painful. I expected a more enthusiastic welcome, especially considering it is the first time I have come here.

Cecily: Uncle Jack, if you don't shake hands with Ernest I will never forgive you.

Jack: Never forgive me?

Cecily: Never, never, never!

Jack: Well, this is the last time I shall ever do it. [*Shakes hands with* **Algernon** *and glares.*]

Chasuble: It's pleasant, is it not, to see so perfect a reconciliation? I think we might leave the two brothers together.

Miss Prism: Cecily, you will come with us.

Cecily: Certainly, Miss Prism. My little task of reconciliation is over.

Chasuble: You have done a beautiful action today, dear child.

Miss Prism: We must not be premature in our judgements.

Cecily: I feel very happy.

[*They all go off except*
Jack *and* **Algernon**.]

Jack: You young scoundrel, Algy, you must get out of this place as soon as possible. I don't allow any Bunburying here.

[*Enter* **Merriman**.]

Merriman: I have put Mr. Ernest's things in the room next to yours, sir. I suppose that is all right?

Jack: What?

Merriman: Mr. Ernest's luggage, sir. I have unpacked it and put it in the room next to your own.

Jack: His luggage?

Merriman: Yes sir. Three portmanteaus, a dressing-case, two hatboxes, and a large luncheon-basket.

Algernon: I am afraid I can't stay more than a week this time.

Jack: Merriman, order the dogcart at once. Mr. Ernest has been suddenly called back to town.

Merriman: Yes, sir. [*Goes back into the house.*]

Algernon: What a fearful liar you are, Jack. I have not been called back to town at all.

Jack: Yes, you have.

Algernon: I haven't heard any one call me.

Jack: Your duty as a gentleman calls you back.

Algernon: My duty as a gentleman has never interfered with my pleasures in the smallest degree.

Jack: I can quite understand that.

Algernon: Well, Cecily is a darling.

Jack: You are not to talk of Miss Cardew like that. I don't like it.

Algernon: Well, I don't like your clothes. You look perfectly ridiculous in them. Why on earth don't you go up and change? It is perfectly childish to be in deep mourning for a man who is actually staying for a whole week with you in your house as a guest. I call it grotesque.

Jack: You are certainly not staying with me for a whole week as a guest or anything else. You have got to leave . . . by the four-five train.

Algernon: I certainly won't leave you so long as you are in mourning. It would be most unfriendly. If I were in mourning you would stay with me, I suppose. I should think it very unkind if you didn't.

Jack: Well, will you go if I change my clothes?

Algernon: Yes, if you are not too long. I never saw anybody take so long to dress, and with such little result.

Jack: Well, at any rate, that is better than being always overdressed as you are.

Algernon: If I am occasionally a little overdressed, I make up for it by being always immensely overeducated.

Jack: Your vanity is ridiculous, your conduct an outrage, and your presence in my garden utterly absurd. However, you have got to catch the four-five, and I hope you will have a pleasant journey back to town. This Bunburying, as you call it, has not been a great success for you.

[*Goes into the house.*]

Algernon: I think it has been a great success. I'm in love with Cecily, and that is everything.

[*Enter* **Cecily** *at the back of the garden. She picks up the can and begins to water the flowers.*]

But I must see her before I go, and make arrangements for another Bunbury. Ah, there she is.

Cecily: Oh, I merely came back to water the roses. I thought you were with Uncle Jack.

Algernon: He's gone to order the dogcart for me.

Cecily: Oh, is he going to take you for a nice drive?

Algernon: He's going to send me away.

Cecily: Then have we got to part?

Algernon: I am afraid so. It's a very painful parting.

Cecily: It is always painful to part from people whom one has known for a very brief space of time. The absence of old friends one can endure with equanimity. But even a momentary separation from any one to whom one has just been introduced is almost unbearable.

Algernon: Thank you.

[*Enter* **Merriman.**]

Merriman: The dogcart is at the door, sir.

[**Algernon** *looks appealingly at* **Cecily.**]

Cecily: It can wait, Merriman . . . for . . . five minutes.

Merriman: Yes, miss.

[*Exit* **Merriman.**]

Algernon: I hope, Cecily, I shall not offend you if I state quite frankly and openly that you seem to me to be in every way the visible personification of absolute perfection.

Cecily: I think your frankness does you great credit, Ernest. If you will allow me, I will copy your remarks into my diary. [*Goes over to table and begins writing in diary.*]

Algernon: Do you really keep a diary? I'd give anything to look at it. May I?

Cecily: Oh no. [*Puts her hand over it*] You see, it is simply a very young girl's record of her own thoughts and impressions, and consequently meant for publication. When it appears in volume form I hope you will order a copy. But pray, Ernest, don't stop. I delight in taking down from dictation. I have reached "absolute perfection." You can go on. I am quite ready for more.

Algernon: [*Somewhat taken aback*] Ahem! Ahem!

Cecily: Oh, don't cough, Ernest. When one is dictating one should speak fluently and not cough. Besides, I don't know how to spell a cough. [*Writes as* **Algernon** *speaks.*]

Algernon: [*Speaking very rapidly*] Cecily, ever since I first looked upon your wonderful and incomparable beauty, I have dared to love you wildly, passionately, devotedly, hopelessly.

Cecily: I don't think that you should tell me that you love me wildly, passionately, devotedly, hopelessly. Hopelessly doesn't seem to make much sense, does it?

Algernon: Cecily.

[*Enter* **Merriman.**]

Merriman: The dogcart is waiting, sir.

Algernon: Tell it to come round next week, at the same hour.

Merriman: [*Looks at* **Cecily,** *who makes no sign.*] Yes, sir.

[**Merriman** *retires.*]

Cecily: Uncle Jack would be very much annoyed if he knew you were staying on till next week, at the same hour.

Algernon: Oh, I don't care about Jack. I don't care for anybody in the whole world but you. I love you, Cecily. You will marry me, won't you?

Cecily: You silly boy! Of course. Why, we have been engaged for the last three months.

Algernon: For the last three months?

Cecily: Yes, it will be exactly three months on Thursday.

Algernon: But how did we become engaged?

Cecily: Well, ever since dear Uncle Jack first confessed to us that he had a younger brother who was very wicked and bad, you of course have formed the chief topic of conversation between myself and Miss Prism. And of course a man who is much talked about is always very attractive. One feels there must be something in him, after all. I daresay it was foolish of me, but I fell in love with you, Ernest.

Algernon: Darling. And when was the engagement actually settled?

Cecily: On the 14th of February last. Worn out by your entire ignorance of my existence, I determined to end the matter one way or the other, and after a long struggle with myself I accepted you under this dear old tree here. The next day I bought this little ring in your name, and this is the little bangle with the true lovers' knot I promised you always to wear.

Algernon: Did I give you this? It's very pretty, isn't it?

Cecily: Yes, you've wonderfully good taste, Ernest. It's the excuse I've always given for your leading such a bad life. And this is the box in which I keep all your dear letters.

[*Kneels at table, opens box,
and produces letters
tied up with blue ribbon.*]

Algernon: My letters! But, my own sweet Cecily, I have never written you any letters.

Cecily: You need hardly remind me of that, Ernest. I remember only too well that I was forced to write your letters for you. I wrote always three times a week, and sometimes oftener.

Algernon: Oh, do let me read them, Cecily?

Cecily: Oh, I couldn't possibly. They would make you far too conceited. [*Replaces box*] The three you wrote me after I had broken off the engagement are so beautiful, and so badly spelled, that even now I can hardly read them without crying a little.

Algernon: But was our engagement ever broken off?

Cecily: Of course it was. On the 22nd of last March. You can see the entry if you like. [*Shows diary*] "Today I broke off my engagement with Ernest. I feel it is better to do so. The weather still continues charming."

Algernon: But why on earth did you break it off? What had I done? I had done nothing at all. Cecily, I am very much hurt indeed to hear you broke it off. Particularly when the weather was so charming.

Cecily: It would hardly have been a really serious engagement if it hadn't been broken off at least once. But I forgave you before the week was out.

Algernon: [*Crossing to her, and kneeling*] What a perfect angel you are, Cecily.

Cecily: You dear romantic boy [*He kisses her, she puts her fingers through his hair*] I hope you hair curls naturally, does it?

Algernon: Yes, darling, with a little help from others.

Cecily: I am so glad.

Algernon: You'll never break off our engagement again, Cecily?

Cecily: I don't think I could break it off now that I have actually met you. Besides, of course, there is the question of your name.

Algernon: Yes, of course. [*Nervously.*]

Cecily: You must not laugh at me, darling, but it had always been a girlish dream of mine to love some one whose name was Ernest. [**Algernon** rises, **Cecily** also] There is something in that name that seems to inspire absolute confidence. I pity any poor married woman whose husband is not called Ernest.

Algernon: But, my dear child, do you mean to say you could not love me if I had some other name?

Cecily: But what name?

Algernon: Oh, any name you like—Algernon—for instance . . .

Cecily: But I don't like the name of Algernon.

Algernon: Well, my own dear, sweet, loving little darling, I really can't see why you should object to the name of Algernon. It is not at all a bad name. In fact, it is rather an aristocratic name. Half of the chaps who get into the Bankruptcy Court are called Algernon. But seriously, Cecily . . . [*Moving to her*] if my name was Algy, couldn't you love me?

Cecily: [*Rising*] I might respect you, Ernest, I might admire your character, but I fear that I should not be able to give you my undivided attention.

Algernon: Ahem! Cecily! [*Picking up hat*] Your Rector here is, I suppose, thoroughly experienced in the practice of all the rites and ceremonials of the Church?

Cecily: Oh, yes. Dr. Chasuble is a most learned man. He has never written a single book, so you can imagine how much he knows.

Algernon: I must see him at once on a most

important christening—I mean on most important business.

Cecily: Oh!

Algernon: I shan't be away more than half an hour.

Cecily: Considering that we have been engaged since February the 14th, and that I only met you today for the first time, I think it is rather hard that you should leave me for so long a period as half an hour. Couldn't you make it twenty minutes?

Algernon: I'll be back in no time. [*Kisses her and rushes down the garden.*]

Cecily: What an impetuous boy he is! I like his hair so much. I must enter his proposal in my diary.

[*Enter* **Merriman**.]

Merriman: A Miss Fairfax just called to see Mr. Worthing. On very important business, Miss Fairfax states.

Cecily: Isn't Mr. Worthing in his library?

Merriman: Mr. Worthing went over in the direction of the Rectory some time ago.

Cecily: Pray ask the lady to come out here; Mr. Worthing is sure to be back soon. And you can bring tea.

Merriman: Yes, Miss.

[*Goes out.*]

Cecily: Miss Fairfax! I suppose one of the many good elderly women who are associated with Uncle Jack in some of his philanthropic work in London. I don't quite like women who are interested in philanthropic work. I think it is so forward of them.

[*Enter* **Merriman**.]

Merriman: Miss Fairfax.

[*Enter* **Gwendolen**. *Exit* **Merriman**.]

Cecily: [*Advancing to meet her*] Pray let me introduce myself to you. My name is Cecily Cardew.

Gwendolen: Cecily Cardew? [*Moving to her and shaking hands*] What a very sweet name! Something tells me that we are going to be great friends. I like you already more than I can say. My first impressions of people are never wrong.

Cecily: How nice of you to like me so much after we have known each other such a comparatively short time. Pray sit down.

Gwendolen: [*Still standing up*] I may call you Cecily, may I not?

Cecily: With pleasure!

Gwendolen: And you will always call me Gwendolen, won't you?

Cecily: If you wish.

Gwendolen: Then that is all quite settled, is it not?

Cecily: I hope so. [*A pause. They both sit down together.*]

Gwendolen: Perhaps this might be a favorable opportunity for my mentioning who I am. My father is Lord Bracknell. You have never heard of papa, I suppose?

Cecily: I don't think so.

Gwendolen: Outside the family circle, papa, I am glad to say is entirely unknown. I think that is quite as it should be. The home seems to me to be the proper sphere for the man. And certainly once a man begins to neglect his domestic duties he becomes painfully effeminate, does he not? And I don't like that. It makes men so very attractive. Cecily, mamma, whose views on education are remarkably strict, has brought me up to be extremely shortsighted; it is part of her system; so do you mind my looking at you through my glasses?

Cecily: Oh! not at all, Gwendolen. I am very fond of being looked at.

Gwendolen: [*After examining* **Cecily** *carefully through a lorgnette*] You are here on a short visit, I suppose.

Cecily: Oh no! I live here.

Gwendolen: [*severely*] Really? Your mother, no doubt, or some female relative of advanced years, resides here also?

Cecily: Oh no! I have no mother, nor, in fact, any relations.

Gwendolen: Indeed?

Cecily: My dear guardian, with the assistance of Miss Prism, has the arduous task of looking after me.

Gwendolen: Your guardian?

Cecily: Yes, I am Mr. Worthing's ward.

Gwendolen: Oh! it is strange he never mentioned to me that he had a ward. How secretive of him! He grows more interesting hourly. I am not sure, however, that the news inspires me with feelings of unmixed delight. [*Rising and going to her*] I am very fond of you, Cecily; I have liked you ever since I met you! But I am bound to state that now that I know that you are Mr. Worthing's ward, I cannot help expressing a wish you were—well, just a little older than you seem to be—and not quite so very alluring in appearance. In fact, if I may speak candidly—

Cecily: Pray do! I think that whenever one has anything unpleasant to say, one should always be quite candid.

Gwendolen: Well, to speak with perfect candor, Cecily, I wish that you were fully forty-two, and more than usually plain for your age. Ernest has a strong upright nature. He is the very soul of truth and honor. Disloyalty would be as impossible to him as deception. But even men of the noblest possible moral character are extremely susceptible to the influence of the physical charms of others. Modern, no less than Ancient History, supplies us with many most painful examples of what I refer to. If it were not so, indeed, History would be quite unreadable.

Cecily: I beg your pardon, Gwendolen, did you say Ernest?

Gwendolen: Yes.

Cecily: Oh, but it is not Mr. Ernest Worthing who is my guardian. It is his brother—his elder brother.

Gwendolen: [*Sitting down again*] Ernest never mentioned to me that he had a brother.

Cecily: I am sorry to say they have not been on good terms for a long time.

Gwendolen: Ah! that accounts for it. And now that I think of it I have never heard any man mention his brother. The subject seems distasteful to most men. Cecily, you have lifted a load from my mind. I was growing almost anxious. It would have been terrible if any cloud had come across a friendship like ours, would it not? Of course you are quite, quite sure that it is not Mr. Ernest Worthing who is your guardian?

Cecily: Quite sure. [*A pause*] In fact, I am going to be his.

Gwendolen: [*Inquiringly*] I beg your pardon?

Cecily: [*Rather shy and confidingly*] Dearest Gwen-

dolen, there is no reason why I should make a secret of it to you. Our little country newspaper is sure to chronicle the fact next week. Mr. Ernest Worthing and I are engaged to be married.

Gwendolen: [*Quite politely, rising*] My darling Cecily, I think there must be some slight error. Mr. Ernest Worthing is engaged to me. The announcement will appear in the *Morning Post* on Saturday at the latest.

Cecily: [*Very politely, rising*] I am afraid you must be under some misconception. Ernest proposed to me exactly ten minutes ago. [*Shows diary.*]

Gwendolen: [*Examines diary through her lorgnette carefully*] It is very curious, for he asked me to be his wife yesterday afternoon at 5:30. If you would care to verify the incident, pray do so. [*Produces diary of her own*] I never travel without my diary. One should always have something sensational to read in the train. I am so sorry, dear Cecily, if it is any disappointment to you, but I am afraid I have the prior claim.

Cecily: It would distress me more than I can tell you, dear Gwendolen, if it caused you any mental or physical anguish, but I feel bound to point out that since Ernest proposed to you he clearly has changed his mind.

Gwendolen: [*Meditatively*] If the poor fellow has been entrapped into any foolish promise I shall consider it my duty to rescue him at once, and with a firm hand.

Cecily: [*Thoughtfully and sadly*] Whatever unfortunate entanglement my dear boy may have got into, I will never reproach him with it after we are married.

Gwendolen: Do you allude to me, Miss Cardew, as an entanglement? You are presumptuous. On an occasion of this kind it becomes more than a moral duty to speak one's mind. It becomes a pleasure.

Cecily: Do you suggest, Miss Fairfax, that I entrapped Ernest into an engagement? How dare you? This is no time for wearing the shallow mask of manners. When I see a spade I call it a spade.

Gwendolen: [*Satirically*] I am glad to say that I have never seen a spade. It is obvious that our social spheres have been widely different. [*Enter* **Merriman,** *followed by the footman. He carries a salver, table cloth, and plate stand.* **Cecily** *is about to retort. The presence of the servants exercises a restraining influence, under which both girls chafe.*]

Merriman: Shall I lay tea here as usual, Miss?

Cecily: [*Sternly, in a calm voice*] Yes, as usual. [**Merriman** *begins to clear table and lay cloth. A long pause.* **Cecily** *and* **Gwendolen** *glare at each other.*]

Gwendolen: Are there many interesting walks in the vicinity, Miss Cardew?

Cecily: Oh! yes! a great many. From the top of one of the hills quite close one can see five counties.

Gwendolen: Five counties! I don't think I should like that; I hate crowds.

Cecily: [*Sweetly*] I suppose that is why you live in town? [**Gwendolen** *bites her lip, and beats her foot nervously with her parasol.*]

Gwendolen: [*Looking round*] Quite a well-kept garden this is, Miss Cardew.

Cecily: So glad you like it, Miss Fairfax.

Gwendolen: I had no idea there were any flowers in the country.

Cecily: Oh, flowers are as common here, Miss Fairfax, as people are in London.

Gwendolen: Personally I cannot understand how anybody manages to exist in the country, if anybody who is anybody does. The country always bores me to death.

Cecily: Ah! This is what the newspapers call agricultural depression, is it not? I believe the aristocracy are suffering very much from it just at present. It is almost an epidemic amongst them, I have been told. May I offer you some tea, Miss Fairfax?

Gwendolen: [*With elaborate politeness*] Thank you. [*Aside*] Detestable girl! But I require tea!

Cecily: [*Sweetly*] Sugar?

Gwendolen: [*Superciliously*] No, thank you. Sugar is not fashionable any more. [**Cecily** *looks angrily at her, takes up the tongs and puts four lumps of sugar into the cup.*]

Cecily: [*Severely*] Cake or bread and butter?

Gwendolen: [*In a bored manner*] Bread and butter, please. Cake is rarely seen at the best houses nowadays.

Cecily: [*Cuts a very large slice of cake and puts it on the tray*] Hand that to Miss Fairfax.

[**Merriman** *does so, and goes out with footman.* **Gwendolen** *drinks the tea and makes a grimace. Puts down cup at once, reaches out her hand to the bread and butter, looks at it, and finds it is cake. Rises in indignation.*]

Gwendolen: You have filled my tea with lumps of sugar, and though I asked most distinctly for bread and butter, you have given me cake. I am known for the gentleness of my disposition, and the extraordinary sweetness of my nature, but I warn you, Miss Cardew, you may go too far.

Cecily: [*Rising*] To save my poor, innocent, trusting boy from the machinations of any other girl there are no lengths to which I would not go.

Gwendolen: From the moment I saw you I distrusted you. I felt that you were false and deceitful. I am never deceived in such matters. My first impressions of people are invariably right.

Cecily: It seems to me, Miss Fairfax, that I am trespassing on your valuable time. No doubt you have many other calls of a similar character to make in the neighbourhood.

[*Enter* **Jack.**]

Gwendolen: [*Catching sight of him*] Ernest! My own Ernest!

Jack: Gwendolen! Darling! [*Offers to kiss her.*]

Gwendolen: [*Drawing back*] A moment! May I ask if you are engaged to be married to this young lady? [*Points to* **Cecily.**]

Jack: [*Laughing*] To dear little Cecily! Of course not! What could have put such an idea into your pretty little head?

Gwendolen: Thank you. You may! [*Offers her cheek.*]

Cecily: [*Very sweetly*] I knew there must be some misunderstanding, Miss Fairfax. The gentleman whose arm is at present round your waist is my dear guardian, Mr. John Worthing.

Gwendolen: I beg your pardon?

Cecily: This is Uncle Jack.

Gwendolen: [*Receding*] Jack! Oh!

[*Enter* **Algernon.**]

Cecily: Here is Ernest.

Algernon: [*Goes straight over to* **Cecily** *without noticing anyone else*] My own love! [*Offers to kiss her.*]

Cecily: [*Drawing back*] A moment, Ernest! May I ask you—are you engaged to be married to this young lady?

Algernon: [*Looking round*] To what young lady? Good heavens! Gwendolen!

Cecily: Yes: to good heavens, Gwendolen, I mean to Gwendolen.

Algernon: [*Laughing*] Of course not! What could have put such an idea into your pretty little head?

Cecily: Thank you. [*Presenting her cheek to be kissed*] You may. [**Algernon** *kisses her.*]

Gwendolen: I felt there was some slight error, Miss Cardew. The gentleman who is now embracing you is my cousin, Mr. Algernon Moncrieff.

Cecily: [*Breaking away from Algernon*] Algernon Moncrieff! Oh! [*The two girls move towards each other and put their arms round each other's waists as if for protection.*]

Cecily: Are you called Algernon?

Algernon: I cannot deny it.

Cecily: Oh!

Gwendolen: Is your name really John?

Jack: [*Standing rather proudly*] I could deny it if I liked. I could deny anything if I liked. But my name certainly is John. It has been John for years.

Cecily: [*To* **Gwendolen**] A gross deception has been practised on both of us.

Gwendolen: My poor wounded Cecily!

Cecily: My sweet wronged Gwendolen!

Gwendolen: [*Slowly and seriously*] You will call me sister, will you not? [*They embrace.* **Jack** *and* **Algernon** *groan and walk up and down.*]

Cecily: [*Rather brightly*] There is just one question I would like to be allowed to ask my guardian.

Gwendolen: An admirable idea! Mr. Worthing, there is just one question I would like to be permitted to put to you. Where is your brother Ernest? We are both engaged to be married to your brother Ernest, so it is a matter of some importance to us to know where your brother Ernest is at present.

Jack: [*Slowly and hesitatingly*] Gwendolen—Cecily —it is very painful for me to be forced to speak the truth. It is the first time in my life that I have ever been reduced to such a painful position, and I am really quite inexperienced in doing anything of the kind. However, I will tell you quite frankly that I have no brother Ernest. I have no brother at all. I never had a brother in my life, and I certainly have not the smallest intention of ever having one in the future.

Cecily: [*Surprised*] No brother at all?

Jack: [*Cheerily*] None!

Gwendolen: [*Severely*] Had you never a brother of any kind?

Jack: [*Pleasantly*] Never. Not even of any kind.

Gwendolen: I am afraid it is quite clear, Cecily, that neither of us is engaged to be married to anyone.

Cecily: It is not a very pleasant position for a young girl suddenly to find herself in. Is it?

Gwendolen: Let us go into the house. They will hardly venture to come after us there.

Cecily: No, men are so cowardly, aren't they? [*They retire into the house with scornful looks.*]

Jack: This ghastly state of things is what you call Bunburying, I suppose?

Algernon: Yes, and a perfectly wonderful Bunbury it is. The most wonderful Bunbury I have ever had in my life.

Jack: Well, you've no right whatsoever to Bunbury here.

Algernon: That is absurd. One has a right to Bunbury anywhere one chooses. Every serious Bunburyist knows that.

Jack: Serious Bunburyist? Good heavens!

Algernon: Well, one must be serious about something, if one wants to have any amusement in life. I happen to be serious about Bunburying. What on earth you are serious about I haven't got the remotest idea. About everything, I should fancy. You have such an absolutely trivial nature.

Jack: Well, the only small satisfaction I have in the whole of this wretched business is that your friend Bunbury is quite exploded. You won't be able to run down to the country quite so often as you used to do, dear Algy.

And a very good thing too.

Algernon: Your brother is a little off color, isn't he, dear Jack? You won't be able to disappear to London quite so frequently as your wicked custom was. And not a bad thing either.

Jack: As for your conduct towards Miss Cardew, I must say that your taking in a sweet, simple, innocent girl like that is quite inexcusable. To say nothing of the fact that she is my ward.

Algernon: I can see no possible defence at all for your deceiving a brilliant, clever, thoroughly experienced young lady like Miss Fairfax. To say nothing of the fact that she is my cousin.

Jack: I wanted to be engaged to Gewendolen, that is all. I love her.

Algernon: Well, I simply wanted to be engaged to Cecily. I adore her.

Jack: There is certainly no chance of your marrying Miss Cardew.

Algernon: I don't think there is much likelihood, Jack, of you and Miss Fairfax being united.

Jack: Well, that is no business of yours.

Algernon: If it was my business, I wouldn't talk about it. [*Begins to eat muffins*] It is very vulgar to talk about one's business. Only people like stockbrokers do that, and then merely at dinner parties.

Jack: How you can sit there, calmly eating muffins when we are in this horrible trouble, I can't make out. You seem to me to be perfectly heartless.

Algernon: Well, I can't eat muffins in an agitated manner. The butter would probably get on my cuffs. One should always eat muffins quite calmly. It is the only way to eat them.

Jack: I say it's perfectly heartless your eating muffins at all, under the circumstances.

Algernon: When I am in trouble, eating is the only thing that consoles me. Indeed, when I am in really great trouble, as any one who knows me intimately will tell you, I refuse everything except food and drink. At the present moment I am eating muffins because I am unhappy. Besides, I am particularly fond of muffins. [*Rising.*]

Jack: [*Rising*] Well, there is no reason why you should eat them all in that greedy way. [*Takes muffins from* **Algernon.**]

Algernon: [*Offering tea-cake*] I wish you would have tea-cake instead. I don't like tea-cake.

Jack: Good heavens! I suppose a man may eat his own muffins in his own garden.

Algernon: But you have just said it was perfectly heartless to eat muffins.

Jack: I said it was perfectly heartless of you, under the circumstances. That is a very different thing.

Algernon: That may be. But the muffins are the same. [*He seizes the muffin-dish from* **Jack.**]

Jack: Algy, I wish to goodness you would go.

Algernon: You can't possibly ask me to go without having some dinner. It's absurd. I never go without my dinner. No one ever does, except vegetarians and people like that. Besides I have just made arrangements with Dr. Chasuble to be christened at a quarter to six under the name of Ernest.

Jack: My dear fellow, the sooner you give up that nonsense the better. I made arrangements this morning with Dr. Chasuble to be christened myself at 5:30, and I naturally will take the name of Ernest. Gwendolen would wish it. We can't both be christened Ernest. It's absurd. Besides, I have a perfect right to be christened if I like. There is no evidence at all that I have ever been christened by anybody. I should think it extremely probable I never was, and so does Dr. Chasuble. It is entirely different in your case. You have been christened already.

Algernon: Yes, but I have not been christened for years.

Jack: Yes, but you have been christened. That is the important thing.

Algernon: Quite so. So I know my constitution can stand it. If you are not quite sure about your ever having been christened, I must say I think it rather dangerous your venturing on it now. It might make you very unwell. You can hardly have forgotten that someone very closely connected with you was very nearly carried off this week in Paris by a severe chill.

Jack: Yes, but you said yourself that a severe chill was not hereditary.

Algernon: It usen't to be, I know—but I daresay it is now. Science is always making wonderful improvements in things.

Jack: [*Picking up the muffin-dish*] Oh, that is nonsense; you are always talking nonsense.

Algernon: Jack, you are at the muffins again! I wish you wouldn't. There are only two left. [*Takes them*] I told you I was particularly fond of muffins.

Jack: But I hate tea-cake.

Algernon: Why on earth then do you allow tea-cake to be served up for your guests? What ideas you have of hospitality!

Jack: Algernon! I have already told you to go. I don't want you here. Why don't you go!

Algernon: I haven't quite finished my tea yet! and there is still one muffin left. [**Jack** *groans, and sinks into a chair.* **Algernon** *still continues eating.*]

ACT III

Morning-room at the Manor House. **Gwendolen** and **Cecily** are at the window, looking out into the garden.

Gwendolen: The fact that they did not follow us at once into the house, as any one else would have done, seems to me to show that they have some sense of shame left.

Cecily: They have been eating muffins. That looks like repentance.

Gwendolen: [*After a pause*] They don't seem to notice us at all. Couldn't you cough?

Cecily: But I haven't got a cough.

Gwendolen: They're looking at us. What effrontery!

Cecily: They're approaching. That's very forward of them.

Gwendolen: Let us preserve a dignified silence.

Cecily: Certainly. It's the only thing to do now. [*Enter* **Jack** *followed by* **Algernon**. *They whistle some dreadful popular air from a British Opera.*]

Gwendolen: This dignified silence seems to produce an unpleasant effect.

Cecily: A most distasteful one.

Gwendolen: But we will not be the first to speak.

Cecily: Certainly not.

Gwendolen: Mr. Worthing, I have something very particular to ask you. Much depends on your reply.

Cecily: Gwendolen, your common sense is invaluable. Mr. Moncrieff, kindly answer me the following question. Why did you pretend to be my guardian's brother?

Algernon: In order that I might have an opportunity of meeting you.

Cecily: [*To* **Gwendolen**] That certainly seems a satisfactory explanation, does it not?

Gwendolen: Yes, dear, if you can believe him.

Cecily: I don't. But that does not affect the wonderful beauty of his answer.

Gwendolen: True. In matters of grave importance, style, not sincerity, is the vital thing. Mr. Worthing, what explanation can you offer to me for pretending to have a brother? Was it in order that you might have an opportunity of coming up to town to see me as often as possible?

Jack: Can you doubt it, Miss Fairfax?

Gwendolen: I have the gravest doubts upon the subject. But I intend to crush them. This is not the moment for German scepticism. [*Moving to* **Cecily**] Their explanations appear to be quite satisfactory, especially Mr. Worthing's. That seems to me to have the stamp of truth upon it.

Cecily: I am more than content with what Mr. Moncrieff said. His voice alone inspires one with absolute credulity.

Gwendolen: Then you think we should forgive them?

Cecily: Yes. I mean no.

Gwendolen: True! I had forgotten. There are principles at stake that one cannot surrender. Which of us should tell them? The task is not a pleasant one.

Cecily: Could we not both speak at the same time?

Gwendolen: An excellent idea! I nearly always speak at the same time as other people. Will you take the time from me?

Cecily: Certainly. [**Gwendolen** *beats time with uplifted finger.*]

Gwendolen *and* **Cecily:** [*Speaking together*] Your Christian names are still an insuperable barrier. That is all!

Jack *and* **Algernon:** [*Speaking together*] Our

Christian names! Is that all? But we are going to be christened this afternoon.

Gwendolen: [*To* **Jack**] For my sake you are prepared to do this terrible thing?

Jack: I am.

Cecily: [*To* **Algernon**] To please me you are ready to face this fearful ordeal?

Algernon: I am!

Gwendolen: How absurd to talk of the equality of the sexes! Where questions of self-sacrifice are concerned, men are infinitely beyond us.

Jack: We are. [*Clasps hands with* **Algernon.**]

Cecily: They have moments of physical courage of which we women know absolutely nothing.

Gwendolen: [*To* **Jack**] Darling!

Algernon: [*To* **Cecily**] Darling! [*They fall into each other's arms.*]

[*Enter* **Merriman.** *When he enters he coughs loudly, seeing the situation.*]

Merriman: Ahem! Ahem! Lady Bracknell.

Jack: Good heavens!

[*Enter* **Lady Bracknell.** *The couples separate in alarm. Exit* **Merriman.**]

Lady Bracknell: Gwendolen! What does this mean?

Gwendolen: Merely that I am engaged to be married to Mr. Worthing, mamma.

Lady Bracknell: Come here. Sit down. Sit down immediately. Hesitation of any kind is a sign of mental decay in the young, of physical weakness in the old. [*Turns to* **Jack**] Apprised, sir, of my daughter's sudden flight by her trusty maid, whose confidence I purchased by means of a small coin, I followed her at once by a luggage train. Her unhappy father is, I am glad to say, under the impression that she is attending a more than usually lengthy lecture by the University Extension Scheme on the Influence of a Permanent Income on Thought. I do not propose to undeceive him. Indeed I have never undeceived him on any question. I would consider it wrong. But of course, you will clearly understand that all communication between yourself and my daughter must cease immediately from this moment. On this point, as indeed on all points, I am firm.

Jack: I am engaged to be married to Gwendolen, Lady Bracknell!

Lady Bracknell: You are nothing of the kind, sir. And now as regards Algernon! . . . Algernon!

Algernon: Yes, Aunt Augusta.

Lady Bracknell: May I ask if it is in this house that your invalid friend Mr. Bunbury resides?

Algernon: [*Stammering*] Oh! No! Bunbury doesn't live here. Bunbury is somewhere else at present. In fact, Bunbury is dead.

Lady Bracknell: Dead! When did Mr. Bunbury die? His death must have been extremely sudden.

Algernon: [*Airily*] Oh! I killed Bunbury this afternoon. I mean poor Bunbury died this afternoon.

Lady Bracknell: What did he die of?

Algernon: Bunbury? Oh, he was quite exploded.

Lady Bracknell: Exploded! Was he the victim of a revolutionary outrage? I was not aware that Mr. Bunbury was interested in social legislation. If so, he is well punished for his morbidity.

Algernon: My dear Aunt Augusta, I mean he was found out! The doctors found out that Bunbury could not live, that is what I mean—so Bunbury died.

Lady Bracknell: He seems to have had great confidence in the opinion of his physicians. I am glad, however, that he made up his mind at the last to some definite course of action, and acted under proper medical advice. And now that we have finally got rid of this Mr. Bunbury, may I ask, Mr. Worthing, who is that young person whose hand my nephew Algernon is now holding in what seems to me a peculiarly unnecessary manner?

Jack: That lady is Miss Cecily Cardew, my ward. [**Lady Bracknell** *bows coldly to* **Cecily.**]

Algernon: I am engaged to be married to Cecily, Aunt Augusta.

Lady Bracknell: I beg your pardon?

Cecily: Mr. Moncrieff and I are engaged to be married, Lady Bracknell.

Lady Bracknell: [*With a shiver, crossing to the sofa and sitting down*] I do not know whether there is anything peculiarly exciting in the air of this particular part of Hertfordshire, but the number of engagements that go on seems to me considerably above the proper average that statistics have laid down for our guidance. I think some preliminary inquiry on my part would not be out of place. Mr. Worthing, is Miss Cardew at all connected with any of the larger railway stations in London? I merely desire information. Until yesterday I had no idea that there were any families or persons whose origin was a Terminus. [Jack *looks perfectly furious, but restrains himself.*]

Jack: [*In a cold, clear voice*] Miss Cardew is the granddaughter of the late Mr. Thomas Cardew of 149 Belgrave Square, S.W.; Gervase Park, Dorking, Surrey; and the Sporran, Fifeshire, N..B.

Lady Bracknell: That sounds not unsatisfactory. Three addresses always inspire confidence, even in tradesmen. But what proof have I of their authenticity?

Jack: I have carefully preserved the Court Guides of the period. They are open to your inspection, Lady Bracknell.

Lady Bracknell: [*Grimly*] I have known strange errors in that publication.

Jack: Miss Cardew's family solicitors are Messrs. Markby, Markby, and Markby.

Lady Bracknell: Markby, Markby, and Markby? A firm of the very highest position in their profession. Indeed I am told that one of the Mr. Markby's is occasionally to be seen at dinner parties. So far I am satisfied.

Jack: [*Very irritably*] How extremely kind of you, Lady Bracknell! I have also in my possession, you will be pleased to hear, certificates of Miss Cardew's birth, baptism, whooping cough, registration, vaccination, confirmation, and the measles; both the German and the English variety.

Lady Bracknell: Ah! A life crowded with incident, I see; though perhaps somewhat too exciting for a young girl. I am not myself in favor of premature experiences. [*Rises, looks at her watch*] Gwendolen! the time approaches for our departure. We have not a moment to lose. As a matter of form, Mr. Worthing, I had better ask you if Miss Cardew has any little fortune?

Jack: Oh! about a hundred and thirty thousand pounds in the Funds. That is all. Good-bye, Lady Bracknell. So pleased to have seen you.

Lady Bracknell: [*Sitting down again*] A moment, Mr. Worthing. A hundred and thirty thousand pounds! And in the Funds! Miss Cardew seems to me a most attractive young lady, now that I look at her. Few girls of the present day have any really solid qualities, any of the qualities that last, and improve with time. We live, I regret to say, in an age of surfaces. [*To Cecily*] Come over here, dear. [**Cecily** *goes across*] Pretty child! your dress is sadly simple, and your hair seems almost as Nature might have left it. But we can soon alter all that. A thoroughly experienced French maid produces a really marvellous result in a very brief space of time. I remember recommending one to young Lady Lancing, and after three months her own husband did not know her.

Jack: And after six months nobody knew her.

Lady Bracknell: [*Glares at Jack for a few moments. Then bends, with a practised smile, to* **Cecily**] Kindly turn round, sweet child. [**Cecily** *turns completely round*] No, the side view is what I want. [**Cecily** *presents her profile*] Yes, quite as I expected. There are distinct social possibilities in your profile. The two weak points in our age are its want of principle and its want of profile. The chin a little higher, dear. Style largely depends on the way the chin is worn. They are worn very high, just at present. Algernon!

Algernon: Yes, Aunt Augusta!

Lady Bracknell: There are distinct social possibilities in Miss Cardew's profile.

Algernon: Cecily is the sweetest, dearest, prettiest girl in the whole world. And I don't care twopence about social possibilities.

Lady Bracknell: Never speak disrespectfully of Society, Algernon. Only people who can't get into it do that. [*To Cecily*] Dear child, of course you know that Algernon has nothing but his debts to depend upon. But I do not approve of mercenary marriages. When I married Lord Bracknell I had no fortune of any kind. But I never dreamed for a moment of allowing that to stand in my way. Well, I suppose I must give my consent.

Algernon: Thank you, Aunt Augusta.

Lady Bracknell: Cecily, you may kiss me!

Cecily: [*Kisses her*] Thank you, Lady Bracknell.

Lady Bracknell: You may also address me as Aunt Augusta for the future.

Cecily: Thank you, Aunt Augusta.

Lady Bracknell: The marriage, I think, had better take place quite soon.

Algernon: Thank you, Aunt Augusta.

Cecily: Thank you, Aunt Augusta.

Lady Bracknell: To speak frankly, I am not in favor of long engagements. They give people the opportunity of finding out each other's character before marriage, which I think is never advisable.

Jack: I beg your pardon for interrupting you, Lady Bracknell, but this engagement is quite out of the question. I am Miss Cardew's guardian, and she cannot marry without my consent until she come of age. That consent I absolutely decline to give.

Lady Bracknell: Upon what grounds, may I ask? Algernon is an extremely, I may almost say an ostentatiously, eligible young man. He has nothing, but he looks everything. What more can one desire?

Jack: It pains me very much to have to speak frankly to you, Lady Bracknell, about your nephew, but the fact is that I do not approve at all of his moral character. I suspect him of being untruthful. [**Algernon** and **Cecily** look at him in indignant amazement.]

Lady Bracknell: Untruthful! My nephew Algernon? Impossible! He is an Oxonian.

Jack: I fear there can be no possible doubt about the matter. This afternoon during my temporary absence in London on an important question of romance, he obtained admission to my house by means of the false pretence of being my brother. Under an assumed name he drank, I've just been informed by my butler, an entire pint bottle of my Perrier-Jouet, Brut, '89; wine I was specially reserving for myself. Continuing his disgraceful deception, he succeeded in the course of the afternoon in alienating the affections of my only ward. He subsequently stayed to tea, and devoured every single muffin. And what makes his conduct all the more heartless is, that he was perfectly well aware from the first

that I have no brother, that I never had a brother, and that I don't intend to have a brother, not even of any kind. I distinctly told him so myself yesterday afternoon.

Lady Bracknell: Ahem! Mr. Worthing, after careful consideration I have decided entirely to overlook my nephew's conduct to you.

Jack: That is very generous of you, Lady Bracknell. My own decision, however, is unalterable. I decline to give my consent.

Lady Bracknell: [*To* **Cecily**] Come here, sweet child. [**Cecily** *goes over*] How old are you, dear?

Cecily: Well, I am really only eighteen, but I always admit to twenty when I go to evening parties.

Lady Bracknell: You are perfectly right in making some slight alteration. Indeed, no woman should ever be quite accurate about her age. It looks so calculating. . . . [*In a meditative manner*] Eighteen, but admitting to twenty at evening parties. Well, it will not be very long before you are of age and free from the restraints of tutelage. So I don't think your guardian's consent is, after all, a matter of any importance.

Jack: Pray excuse me, Lady Bracknell, for interrupting you again, but it is only fair to tell you that according to the terms of her grandfather's will Miss Cardew does not come legally of age till she is thirty-five.

Lady Bracknell: That does not seem to me to be a grave objection. Thirty-five is a very attractive age. London society is full of women of the very highest birth who have, of their own free choice, remained thirty-five for years. Lady Dumbleton is an instance in point. To my own knowledge she has been thirty-five ever since she arrived at the age of forty, which was many years ago now. I see no reason why our dear Cecily should not be even still more attractive at the age you mention than she is at present. There will be a large accumulation of property.

Cecily: Algy, could you wait for me till I was thirty-five?

Algernon: Of course I could, Cecily. You know I could.

Cecily: Yes, I felt it instinctively, but I couldn't wait all that time. I hate waiting even five minutes for anybody. It always make me rather cross. I am not punctual myself, I know, but I do like punctuality in others, and waiting, even to be married, is quite out of the question.

Algernon: Then what is to be done, Cecily?

Cecily: I don't know, Mr. Moncrieff.

Lady Bracknell: My dear Mr. Worthing, as Miss Cardew states positively that she cannot wait till she is thirty-five—a remark which I am bound to say seems to me to show a somewhat impatient nature—I would beg of you to reconsider your decision.

Jack: But my dear Lady Bracknell, the matter is entirely in your own hands. The moment you consent to my marriage with Gwendolen, I will most gladly allow your nephew to form an alliance with my ward.

Lady Bracknell: [*Rising and drawing herself up*] You must be quite aware that what you propose is out of the question.

Jack: Then a passionate celibacy is all that any of us can look forward to.

Lady Bracknell: That is not the destiny I propose for Gwendolen. Algernon, of course, can choose for himself. [*Pulls out her watch*] Come, dear [**Gwendolen** rises], we have already missed five, if not six, trains. To miss any more might expose us to comment on the platform.

[*Enter* **Dr. Chasuble.**]

Chasuble: Everything is quite ready for the christenings.

Lady Bracknell: The christenings, sir! Is not that somewhat premature?

Chasuble: [*Looking rather puzzled, and pointing to* **Jack** *and* **Algernon**] Both these gentlemen have expressed a desire for immediate baptism.

Lady Bracknell: At their age? The idea is grotesque and irreligious! Algernon, I forbid you to be baptized. I will not hear of such excesses. Lord Bracknell would be highly displeased if he learned that that was the way in which you wasted your time and money.

Chasuble: Am I to understand then that there are to be no christenings at all this afternoon?

Jack: I don't think that, as things are now, it would be of much practical value to either of us, Dr. Chasuble.

Chasuble: I am grieved to hear such sentiments from you, Mr. Worthing. They savour of the heretical views of the Anabaptists, views that I have completely refuted in four of my unpublished sermons. However, as your present mood seems to be one peculiarly secular, I will return to the church at once. Indeed, I have just been informed by the pew-opener that for the last hour and a half Miss Prism has been waiting for me in the vestry.

Lady Bracknell: [*Starting*] Miss Prism! Did I hear you mention a Miss Prism?

Chasuble: Yes, Lady Bracknell. I am on my way to join her.

Lady Bracknell: Pray allow me to detain you for a moment. This matter may prove to be one of vital importance to Lord Bracknell and myself. Is this Miss Prism a female of repellent aspect, remotely connected with education?

Chasuble: [*Somewhat indignantly*] She is the most cultivated of ladies, and the very picture of respectability.

Lady Bracknell: It is obviously the same person. May I ask what position she holds in your household?

Chasuble: [*Severely*] I am a celibate, madam.

Jack: [*Interposing*] Miss Prism, Lady Bracknell, has been for the last three years Miss Cardew's esteemed governess and valued companion.

Lady Bracknell: In spite of what I hear of her, I must see her at once. Let her be sent for.

Chasuble: [*Looking off*] She approaches; she is nigh.

[*Enter* **Miss Prism** *hurriedly.*]

Miss Prism: I was told you expected me in the vestry, dear Canon. I have been waiting for you there for an hour and three-quarters. [*Catches sight of* **Lady Bracknell,** *who has fixed her with a stony glare.* **Miss Prism** *grows pale and quails. She looks anxiously round as if desirous to escape.*]

Lady Bracknell: [*In a severe, judicial voice*] Prism! [**Miss Prism** *bows her head in shame*] Come here, Prism! [**Miss Prism** *approaches in a humble manner*] Prism! Where is that baby? [*General consternation. The* **Canon** *starts back in horror.* **Algernon** *and* **Jack** *pretend to be anxious to shield* **Cecily** *and* **Gwendolen**

from hearing the details of a terrible public scandal] Twenty-eight years ago, Prism, you left Lord Bracknell's house, Number 104, Upper Grosvenor Square, in charge of a perambulator that contained a baby of the male sex. You never returned. A few weeks later, through the elaborate investigations of the Metropolitan police, the perambulator was discovered at midnight standing by itself in a remote corner of Bayswater. It contained the manuscript of a three-volume novel of more than usually revolting sentimentality. [**Miss Prism** *starts in involuntary indignation]* But the baby was not there. [*Every one looks at* **Miss Prism**] Prism! Where is that baby? [*A pause.*]

Miss Prism: Lady Bracknell, I admit with shame that I do not know. I only wish I did. The plain facts of the case are these. On the morning of the day you mention, a day that is for ever branded on my memory, I prepared as usual to take the baby out in its perambulator. I had also with me a somewhat old, but capacious handbag in which I had intended to place the manuscript of a work of fiction that I had written during my few unoccupied hours. In a moment of mental abstraction, for which I can never forgive myself, I deposited the manuscript in the bassinette and placed the baby in the handbag.

Jack: [*Who has been listening attentively*] But where did you deposit the handbag?

Miss Prism: Do not ask me, Mr. Worthing.

Jack: Miss Prism, this is a matter of no small importance to me. I insist on knowing where you deposited the handbag that contained that infant.

Miss Prism: I left it in the cloakroom of one of the larger railway stations in London.

Jack: What railway station?

Miss Prism: [*Quite crushed*] Victoria. The Brighton line. [*Sinks into a chair.*]

Jack: I must retire to my room for a moment. Gwendolen, wait here for me.

Gwendolen: If you are not too long, I will wait here for you all my life. [*Exit* **Jack** *in great excitement.*]

Chasuble: What do you think this means, Lady Bracknell?

Lady Bracknell: I dare not even suspect, Dr. Chasuble. I need hardly tell you that in families of high position strange coincidences are not supposed to occur. They are hardly considered the thing.

[*Noises heard overhead as if some one was throwing trunks about. Every one looks up.*]

Cecily: Uncle Jack seems strangely agitated.

Chasuble: Your guardian has a very emotional nature.

Lady Bracknell: This noise is extremely unpleasant. It sounds as if he was having an argument. I dislike arguments of any kind. They are always vulgar, and often convincing.

Chasuble: [*Looking up*] It has stopped now. [*The noise is redoubled.*]

Lady Bracknell: I wish he would arrive at some conclusion.

Gwendolen: This suspense is terrible. I hope it will last.

[*Enter* **Jack** *with a handbag of black leather in his hand.*]

Jack: [*Rushing over to* **Miss Prism**] Is this the handbag, Miss Prism? Examine it carefully before you speak. The happiness of more than one life depends on your answer.

Miss Prism: [*Calmly*] It seems to be mine. Yes, here is the injury it received through the upsetting of a Gower Street omnibus in younger and happier days. Here is the stain on the lining caused by the explosion of a temperance beverage, an incident that occurred at Leamington. And here, on the lock, are my initials. I had forgotten that in an extravagant mood I had had them placed there. The bag is undoubtedly mine. I am delighted to have it so unexpectedly restored to me. It has been a great inconvenience being without it all these years.

Jack: [*In a pathetic voice*] Miss Prism, more is restored to you than this handbag. I was the baby you placed in it.

Miss Prism: [*Amazed*] You?

Jack: [*Embracing her*] Yes . . . mother!

Miss Prism: [*Recoiling in indignant astonishment*] Mr. Worthing, I am unmarried!

Jack: Unmarried! I do not deny that is a serious blow. But after all, who has the right to cast a stone against one who has suffered? Cannot repentance wipe out an act of folly? Why should there be one law for men, and another for women? Mother, I forgive you. [*Tries to embrace her again.*]

Miss Prism: [*Still more indignant*] Mr. Worthing, there is some error. [*Pointing to* **Lady Bracknell**] There is the lady who can tell you who you really are.

Jack: [*After a pause*] Lady Bracknell, I hate to seem inquisitive, but would you kindly inform me who I am?

Lady Bracknell: I am afraid that the news I have to give you will not altogether please you. You are the son of my poor sister, Mrs. Moncrieff, and consequently Algernon's elder brother.

Jack: Algy's elder brother! Then I have a brother after all. I knew I had a brother! I always said I had a brother! Cecily—how could you have ever doubted that I had a brother? [*Seizes hold of* **Algernon**] Dr. Chasuble, my unfortunate brother. Miss Prism, my unfortunate brother. Gwendolen, my unfortunate brother. Algy, you young scoundrel, you will have to treat me with more respect in the future. You have never behaved to me like a brother in all your life.

Algernon: Well, not till today, old boy, I admit. I did my best, however, though I was out of practice.

[*Shakes hands.*]

Gwendolen: [*To* **Jack**] My own! But what own are you? What is your Christian name, now that you have become some one else?

Jack: Good heavens! . . . I had quite forgotten that point. Your decision on the subject of my name is irrevocable, I suppose?

Gwendolen: I never change, except in my affections.

Cecily: What a noble nature you have, Gwendolen!

Jack: Then the question had better be cleared up at once. Aunt Augusta, a moment. At the time when Miss Prism left me in the handbag, had I been christened already?

Lady Bracknell: Every luxury that money could buy, including christening, had been lavished on you by your fond and doting parents.

Jack: Then I was christened! That is settled.

Now, what name was I given? Let me know the worst.

Lady Bracknell: Being the eldest son you were naturally christened after your father.

Jack: [*Irritably*] Yes, but what was my father's Christian name?

Lady Bracknell: [*Meditatively*] I cannot at the present moment recall what the General's Christian name was. But I have no doubt he had one. He was eccentric, I admit. But only in later years. And that was the result of the Indian climate, and marriage, and indigestion, and other things of that kind.

Jack: Algy! Can't you recollect what our father's Christian name was?

Algernon: My dear boy, we were never even on speaking terms. He died before I was a year old.

Jack: His name would appear in the Army Lists of the period, I suppose, Aunt Augusta?

Lady Bracknell: The General was essentially a man of peace, except in his domestic life. But I have no doubt his name would appear in any military directory.

Jack: The Army Lists of the last forty years are here. These delightful records should have been my constant study. [*Rushes to bookcase and tears the books out*] M. Generals . . . Mallam, Maxbohm, Magley—what ghastly names they have—Markby, Migsby, Mobbs, Moncrieff! Lieutenant 1840, Captain, Lieutenant-Colonel, Colonel, General 1869, Christian names, Ernest John. [*Puts book very quietly down and speaks quite calmly*] I always told you, Gwendolen, my name was Ernest, didn't I? Well, it is Ernest after all. I mean it naturally is Ernest.

Lady Bracknell: Yes, I remember now that the General was called Ernest. I knew I had some particular reason for disliking the name.

Gwendolen: Ernest! My own Ernest! I felt from the first that you could have no other name!

Jack: Gwendolen, it is a terrible thing for a man to find out suddenly that all his life he has been speaking nothing but the truth. Can you forgive me?

Gwendolen: I can. For I feel that you are sure to change.

Jack: My own one!

Chasuble: [*To* **Miss Prism**] Laetitia! [*Embraces her.*]

Miss Prism: [*Enthusiastically*] Frederick! At last!

Algernon: Cecily! [*Embraces her*] At last!

Jack: Gwendolen! [*Embraces her*] At last!

Lady Bracknell: My nephew, you seem to be displaying signs of triviality.

Jack: On the contrary, Aunt Augusta, I've now realized for the first time in my life the vital Importance of Being Earnest.

THE END

The Importance of Being Earnest marks a complete shift from the plays studied previously in this volume. It is the first comedy to be dealt with; but, what is more important to our discussion, it does not depend primarily upon plot, character, or theme for its effectiveness. The plot is quite absurd and improbable, and one can hardly conceive of any of the principal events actually occurring; but this is quite in keeping with the spirit of comedy and merely adds to the delight that the play affords. The triviality of the plot suggests that it is hardly substantial enough to carry the weight of a play that does not have other very strong elements. Although the characters are comically fascinating, close analysis reveals that there is very little character development. Indeed, the characters are alike to a startling degree, full of witticisms that are reflections of Wilde's point of view rather than that of the individual characters. Because what they say is often witty, one is inclined to forgive the lack of depth and similarity of viewpoint. This is, however, a highly dangerous technique. Wilde, a playwright of genius, is able to make a success of his play despite this limitation, where many a lesser playwright has failed miserably. Clearly, the sort of characterization which lends itself to penetrating analysis is not one of Wilde's strong points. Nor is theme a particularly strong element. Admittedly, Wilde succeeds in introducing a number of witty aphorisms, some of which can offer startling new insights. However each of these is an isolated epigram, introduced for its own sake and not for the purpose of exploring great truths. There is no over-all intention to raise thought-provoking issues in Wilde's play, as there is in *J.B.* Comedy has often been described as intellectual (as opposed to the emotional quality of serious drama), but this refers more to the initial impact than to the seriousness of the issues it raises. No one could deny that theme plays some small part in the success of *The Importance of Being Earnest*, but one must look elsewhere for its primary value.

The witty aphorisms and epigrams, previously mentioned, are the real strength of *The Importance of Being Earnest*. Gwendolyn says that "in matters of grave importance, style, not sincerity, is the vital thing," and clearly the style of Wilde's dialogue creates the play's great delight. His facility with language, his ability to manipulate it, apparently

A Discussion of the Script

at will, is a quality for which Wilde is justly famous, and it is the quality of the language (rather than what is actually said) that makes this a brilliant play. Conversations, even when presumably serious issues are at stake, are series of epigrams; each character tries apparently to top the other with little concern for maintaining a consistent point of view. Algernon, for example, may praise marriage at one moment and condemn it a few lines later, if to do so allows him to express himself in a witty and urbane manner. After one such aphorism, Jack asks him if it is witty and he replies, "It is perfectly phrased! and quite as true as any observation in civilized life should be." This is the attitude of all of the characters in the play, and, indeed, the apparent attitude of Wilde himself. Whatever may be said for the attitude, it leads to some delightful manipulation of language. *Cyrano de Bergerac* and *J.B.* are extraordinary for the poetic quality of the language. *The Importance of Being Earnest* illustrates that poetry is not the only means of elevating the language of a play. Here, brilliant manipulation and the ability to extract verbal wit from almost any idea, controls the direction and success of the play, overshadowing plot, character and theme.

An analysis of the structure of *The Importance of Being Earnest* is a relatively easy task, since it fits neatly into the well-made play form. The central action, clearly, is "to win Gwendolyn." Jack announces precisely what he intends to do almost as soon as he comes on stage (page 248), and when he has accomplished this action the play is over. Jack's simple declaration of his intention is enough to make the central action clear, and Gwendolyn's arrival shortly thereafter allows him to begin. Her arrival is the incident which gets the action underway, and which consequently must be designated as the inciting incident. Prior to Gwendolyn's entrance with her mother, there is simple exposition. Having Algernon quite ignorant of Jack's double identity, and then using the cigarette case as a means of forcing out the truth, provides a sure and effective way for accomplishing this exposition without apparent strain. By the time Gwendolyn enters, one knows all that is necessary to follow the play's action.

The rising action suitably complicates the matter of winning Gwendolyn which Jack has undertaken. At first she indicates that she is in love with him, but his apparent victory is thwarted when she reveals that she can only love a man whose name is Ernest. His problems are further complicated when, in the ensuing interview with Lady Bracknell, it develops that she will not approve her daughter's marriage to anyone whose family is unknown. Jack goes to the country determined to put an end to his double existence and have himself christened "Ernest," but in the meantime Algernon, posing as Ernest, has gone to meet Cecily. The arrival of Gwendolyn at the country house further complicates the situation, and it is hardly necessary to trace the comings and goings that fill out Act II, as the four young people try to sort out their identities. By the end of the act, it has been revealed that neither Jack nor Algernon is actually named Ernest, and it appears that neither marriage will be possible. At the opening of Act III the four young people are assembled in the library; Lady Bracknell enters a few minutes later.

The arrival of Lady Bracknell is the turning point, although it comes a little late by the usual standards of the well-made play. As one reviews the central action, it is clear that, prior to her arrival, there was no apparent way for Jack to win Gwendolyn. Lady Bracknell has ruled that Gwendolyn should not marry one whose family is unknown, and Jack has no basis for assuming that he could uncover his family origins. Lady Bracknell's arrival, although it appears to make things even worse at first, is the one essential ingredient for clearing up all the problems, for it makes possible the meeting between her and Miss Prism. At this point, the rising action changes to the falling action (no further complications are introduced, and the action begins to unravel of its own accord). Lady Bracknell questions Cecily and decides she is an altogether suitable match for Algernon. Jack attempts to use his power over Cecily to force Lady Bracknell's consent to his own match, but she is adamant. Just as matters appear to be at an impasse, Prism enters, and, in due course, Jack's true identity is revealed. This major obstacle removed, Jack has only to learn his true name—Ernest—in order to overcome the last of Gwendolyn's objections and win her hand. This moment, of course, when he finally wins Gwendolyn, is the play's climax; the outcome of the central action is finally settled once and for all. A very short denouement follows in which the other couples are paired off.

Structurally, then, the play is very simple. Indeed, an outline of the plot like the one above reveals that it is almost preposterous in its simplicity. Such a plot, without the tremendous advantage of Wilde's superlative use of language, would be merely absurd. Embellished with Wilde's extraordinary wit, however, the plot can be extremely simple and straight-forward; the audience, far from worrying about its apparent inconsistencies and improbabilities, will actually find them delightful and find the play more amusing because of them. Just as form is more important than truth in the epigrams within the play, so a concise form for the entire play seems to be more important than verisimilitude within that structure.

The brittle, brilliant language and the artificial characterization and plot structure of *The Importance of Being Earnest* are not characteristic of realism. They are far more reminiscent of an era of British comedy known as Restoration Comedy (roughly 1660 to 1700) when Charles II was restored to the English throne. It also bears a resemblance to the style of certain of Molière's plays. This style is not known by a one-word name like realism or romanticism, but is often called "high comedy" because of its reliance on witty language and intellectual perception. *The Importance of Being Earnest* may, then, be termed a high comedy, although it was written in 1895. High comedy lends itself readily to the production style known as "theatricalism," in which scenery, costumes, acting techniques, and other production elements are exaggerated for theatrical impact. Scenery in this style might be obviously painted background, but highly decorative and colorful to please the eye and capture the spirit of the play. The acting would be presentational, and would depend upon appreciation of the skill with which the witty epigrams were delivered rather than total, realistic belief in the characters. It can readily be seen how a production style such as this (which would consciously be adopted by the director) could express effectively a high comedy. It should also be clear, however, that this is not an easy style to employ successfully. *The Importance of Being Earnest* is deceptive with its simple plot, readily perceived characters, and simple technical requirements, and thus is widely popular with amateur groups, but to achieve in production the brittle wit, brilliance, and artificiality that compose its high comedy style is far more difficult than may at first appear.

Costumes

Another extremely important visual element in any stage production is the costuming. If the set usually makes the first visual impact on the audience by reason of its size, the costumes normally make the most continuous impact because they are constantly in motion. On Broadway a costume designer (often the same person who designs the sets) draws up detailed specifications for the costumes and their construction is carried out under contract by a professional costume studio. Almost all other theatres, however, professional and amateur, maintain a costume department, and, because the skills necessary for the construction of costumes are so specialized, there is usually a staff member who is responsible for costuming. Costumes can be bought, rented, borrowed, or constructed, and one of the chief responsibilities of the costumer is to determine the most practical approach for each play. No matter by what means costumes may be obtained, however, the competent designer will insure that they all fit together in an artistically valid manner. When modern dress is called for, borrowing either from the actor's own wardrobe or from that of friends is often the most practical approach. For the recent past, or when ragged, unkempt clothing is needed, much can be accomplished by buying from second-hand clothing shops and making such alterations as may be necessary. When costumes of another period are needed, there are a number of costume rental houses available; but of course the director has little choice of color, line, or sometimes even of proper fit. Most continuing theatre operations, therefore, make as many of their own period costumes as possible, gradually building up a stock of their own from which selections can be made. For simplicity's sake, this discussion will proceed on the assumption that one has the happy alternative of being able to make any costumes necessary; of course, practical considerations such as money and personnel often limit this freedom even in established theatre companies.

The costume designer, then, will meet with the director and the set designer to be sure he understands precisely the approach to be taken to the play in question. The costume designer, too, begins with the script, not only studying all of the factors already mentioned which affect over-all interpretation, but also noting any specific costume requirements inherent in the script. (When Cyrano

Edmond Rostand's sketch of two costume
ideas and a suggestion of scenery for *Cyrano
de Bergerac.*

says, "Lightly I toss my hat away,/Languidly over my arm let fall/The cloak that
covers my bright array . . .," he has said something specific about his costume which
the costume designer must note.) He will coordinate all details of the costumes with
the director (to insure a uniform concept) and also with the scene designer to make
sure that the designs of one complement the designs of the other. (If the set designer
plans on red velvet upholstered furniture for Regina's living room, Regina obviously
cannot wear a red velvet dress.) As the designs for the play's costumes evolve, they
perform five functions which are closely analogous to the five functions of scenery
listed earlier. These functions of costume in terms of their contribution to the production as a whole are:

1. *To clothe the actor.* This is the one essential. Despite the current, increasing
practice of nudity on the New York stage, it still seems most improbable that costumes will be eliminated totally from the theatre. Sets can be eliminated, makeup
need not be used, properties can be pantomimed, but no one has yet learned to
pantomime a costume. The occasional productions of period plays in modern dress or
rehearsal clothes are not, of course, "no costume" productions. Costumes are still
used, and they still make some sort of visual impact, and, since this is unavoidable, it
behooves the director and his staff to decide what kind of visual impact will be best
for the show. A use of formalism (uniform gowns, for example, or evening dress) can
reduce the impact to a minimum if desired, but costume can hardly be totally removed from the production. As long as the costumer is responsible for clothing the
actor, he must accept the added responsibility for clothing him well. Costumes must

fit properly, allowing the actor freedom for any necessary violent movement without the danger of splitting open at an inopportune moment. Actors have no right to complain about uncomfortable costumes if the discomfort results from some specific need of the play (most period costumes, for example, must be made of heavy, and hence very warm, materials if they are to drape properly); but they have a legitimate complaint indeed if, aside from this, their costumes deny them the ease or peace of mind to carry out their own responsibilities.

2. *To help create mood.* The color, the line, indeed, the whole design of the costumes contribute in a material way to the establishment of the play's mood. There is no need to elaborate on this, as the costumes perform this function in precisely the same way as the sets. It would be most inappropriate to costume Regina in gay, frilly, cotton frocks (inappropriate to her character, as well as the mood of the show), and equally inappropriate to costume Cecily Cardew in a heavy dark dress, although both these characters belong to approximately the same period.

3. *To help establish theme.* Again, costumes perform this function in much the same way as sets do. If the circus motif is to be preserved in *J. B.* as a thematic statement, costumes can be used to suggest that the actors are all circus people. Such a decision would be a logical extension of the decision to make the set suggestive of a circus tent.

4. *To establish time, place, and character relationships.* Costumes often play a great part in establishing the period and location of a play. Upon seeing the first act of *Cyrano de Bergerac* one would not have to be an expert in period costume to establish its time and place. Assuming that the play is produced in a romantic style, elaborate period costumes would establish, by their line and color, the Europe of several centuries ago. Whether the typical spectator could or could not say "seventeenth-century Paris," the general impression created by the costumes would help to locate the play. The set would, of course, perform a large share of this function also. Costumes can go further, however, and help to establish relationships among the various characters. Servants' costumes are usually quite distinct from their masters'. Members of opposing armies wear different uniforms. Often, more subtly, opposing groups or families wear contrasting colors, even though "uniforms" as such are not called for. Whether clearly established in the script or simply the invention of the costumer, such establishment of character relationships by means of costuming is a tremendous aid to understanding. The battle scene in *Cyrano de Bergerac* would become very confusing if the attacking soldiers were not costumed in distinct contrast to those surrounding Cyrano.

5. *To add to the visual impact.* Sets can be used for color and spectacle, but the costumes can also perform the same function and can often do so more effectively than the sets. Although elaborate spectacle is possible for the scenery for a musical comedy, it could easily become overpowering in *The Importance of Being Earnest*. Colorful sets are called for, of course, but they cannot become so elaborate that they overpower the actors. Most designers, then, would depend heavily on the costumes in *The Importance of Being Earnest* to make the stage picture colorful and exciting. The principal characters in the play have such colorful personalities that the use of color in the costumes is, for all practical purposes, limited only by the imagination of the designer. Lady Bracknell, particularly, offers a challenge which few costume designers could resist: her brashness and overbearing determination must be expressed within the limits of high fashion which mean so much to her. Some plays

are deliberately staged on formalistic sets that provide a simple environment for the acting in order to allow colorful costumes to do almost all of the work of brightening the stage picture. Shakespearean plays are frequently produced in this manner.

In addition to the functions listed above which costumes perform for the play as a whole, costumes also perform certain functions for the individual actor. These functions are:

1. *To help him to portray his character.* If the actor is trying to create a personality other than his own, he often will need to create a new appearance. Perhaps he needs to appear older or younger than he really is. Makeup can help, of course, but clothing styles of any period differ for the young and old. If the actress who plays Miss Prism happens to be very young, a severe, plain, ankle-length dress can help a great deal in establishing her age. Sometimes an actor must appear fatter or thinner than he really is. Padding can be skillfully used and horizontal stripes can create apparent girth; conversely, vertical stripes tend to make the figure thinner. Lady Bracknell is usually pictured as a lady of imposing physical presence; unless the actress who performs the role happens to be quite large, padding or other adjustments will probably be desirable. Perhaps the actor must appear miserly, or extravagant, or possessed of poor taste. All of these things, and many more, can be suggested by a careful selection of costumes. Not only do costumes help the actor to portray his character by changing his appearance, but they also actually make him feel different. Any actor can testify that, when he puts on his costume for dress rehearsal, his whole feeling toward the character becomes clearer. If the costumes belong to another period this impact is more pronounced; but even when the costumes are modern there is something about stepping into the character's clothes which helps the actor to put his own personality aside and to assume the character's. An actor who is having difficulty capturing a character in rehearsal may use some portion of his costume to give him the right feeling. Actresses who are to play period roles often rehearse in long skirts. The actresses who are to play Gwendolyn and Cecily might well wish to rehearse in boned corsets and leg-o'-mutton sleeves. One carries oneself differently in such clothing, and actresses need to get used to it early.

2. *To enhance or disguise the actor.* This is actually part of character portrayal, but its importance warrants separate discussion. It always helps if the actress who is playing the beautiful young heroine is already beautiful, but a beautiful dress can do much to improve both her appearance and her spirits. Or if the actress simply does not look her best in green, then the design of the show as a whole should take this into account. Temperamental refusals on the part of a vain actress to wear the clothes designed for her are actually rarer in the theatre than popular fiction would suggest; but the designer who is too concerned with the over-all design of the show to consider the effect of one costume upon one actress may actually be doing the production more harm than good. On the other hand, if the character the actress is playing is not supposed to be strikingly beautiful or is supposed to have poor taste, then perhaps the deliberate choice of an inappropriate color might be desirable. By the same token, if the actress playing the beautiful heroine is a little overweight, the skilful costumer can design a dress that will disguise this fact. If the leading man, on the other hand, is too thin to wear tights to best advantage and yet the period requires him to do so, carefully applied padding may aid his appearance a great deal. In extreme cases, the costumer may even be called upon to turn the actor into some kind of monster—Caliban, in *The Tempest*, for example.

A more normal situation, however, might be drawn from *The Importance of Being Earnest.* The actresses playing Gwendolyn and Cecily need not be Miss America candidates, but both should appear to be very attractive young girls. Makeup will help a great deal, but first the costume designer must dress them as attractively as possible.

The functions of costumes, listed above, work within the framework of the style which has been established for the over-all production. The production styles listed in the discussion of settings have implications in terms of costuming as well, which were generally pointed out when the styles were discussed. If the costume designer and the set designer are the same person, the two designs will of course be coordinated (whether satisfactorily so will depend upon the talent of the designer). If there are separate designers, it is necessary for them to stay in close communication, in order that the production will be stylistically unified, and the many details, which could lead to difficulties later (the costume that clashes with drapes or upholstery, for example), can be ironed out during the planning period. The costume designer who is planning the costumes for *The Importance of Being Earnest,* and is closely in touch with the director and the scene designer, might plan roughly as follows: Canon Chasuble is a cleric and thus his costume is largely determined by the clerical attire of the period. He should be pompous and portly, however, so that some padding may be necessary if the actor is not adequately endowed. Merriman and Lane are servants; their costumes must be simple, and formal attire may be appropriate. Miss Prism is also severely plain, according to her character as established in the script. Since nearly half the characters wear black (or at least muted colors) it is important to costume the others in lively colors. Cecily appears only in the last two acts, and since the script allows for no time lapse between these acts she cannot change costumes. She has only one costume for the show. Jack, Algy, Gwendolyn, and Lady Bracknell need two costumes each, and Jack's costume for the second and third acts is clearly established as the "deepest mourning." Algy seems more scatterbrained than Jack, and can be costumed more colorfully. Cecily and Gwendolyn must both be young and beautiful; summery pastels would be appropriate. Lady Bracknell must be large and overbearing, and will need some padding unless the actress is very large.

All of the above ideas regarding *The Importance of Being Earnest* belong to the general category of "first impressions." The costumer will need to do research on the period in which the play is set to learn the details of how clothing looked in that day, and then apply these factors in reaching final decisions about costume designs. Within the general limits set by the stylistic decisions of the director and set designer, limitations imposed by the period, and what the costumer's analysis of the play has told him about its needs, he has three primary variables with which to work in establishing his final designs. These are color, line, and texture. Color has already been discussed above. Line refers primarily to the silhouette of the costume, and is the chief factor that varies from one period to another. Waist lines are high or low, necklines vary in shape and cut, hem lines are up or down, sleeves may be full or tight, and so forth. Texture refers both to the fabric (weight, feel, nap, and so on) and color. Solid colors are rarely used either in scenery or costumes. Colors seem more vibrant and interesting if they are "textured," that is, broken up by regular or irregular patterns of other colors. Scenery, painted in a solid color, may be spattered, sponged, stenciled, dry-brushed, or treated in many other ways with contrasting colors to give a more interesting effect. Costumes are also occasionally painted in this way, but usually the fabrics selected are very small prints, stripes, tweeds, etc., with built in color "texturing." Thus, the costumer must select a fabric that is heavy enough to drape in the manner he wishes, and that, both by its surface and its color pattern, will appear vibrant and alive under stage lights.

The costumer, like the other artists and craftsmen in the theatre, must keep the whole show in mind as he concentrates upon the many details of his own specialty. The audience normally sees only the over-all pattern, and may not stop to think of the costumes in isolation. This is as it should be, for neither costumes nor any other element of production should be so spectacular that it draws attention to itself at the expense of the show as a whole; on the other hand, one button that pops off or one poorly sewn hem can bring a production to a halt. The total picture must always be balanced against the attention paid to individual details.

Summary

It is now time to pause and sum up what has been achieved with the four plays studied so far. Aristotle listed six elements basic to drama; loosely translated and brought up to date, these are plot, character, theme, language, music and spectacle. He indicated that the last two could be enjoyed only in a production, but that the first four were inherent in the script and could be enjoyed through an imaginative reading of it. These first four elements, then, have provided a basis for criticism of play scripts ever since, and are the organizing principle for the preceding pages here. Aristotle, of course, had in mind only a very limited number of plays—specifically, the Greek tragedies as they were produced in Athens. Music, dance and spectacle were integral to all such productions, but do not provide a convenient organizing scheme for discussion of the transformation of a modern script in a modern production. Aristotle's analysis of the basic elements in the script, however, has been applied to much of the drama which has been written since his time. All play scripts may be analyzed in terms of the basic elements of plot, character, theme, and language, and Aristotle added that this was the order of their importance. Most plays of any merit make use of all four elements, but they are not necessarily balanced; one may dominate the other three considerably. The first four plays have illustrated the domination of each of the four elements in turn. In *The Little Foxes*, plot is clearly the dominant element; in *Cyrano de Bergerac*, character (in this case, just one character) is emphasized; in *J.B.*, the playwright's primary concern is theme; and in *The Importance of Being Earnest*, language dominates. In most great plays, one of these elements is not so clearly dominant. Usually a better balance is achieved and one has to concede that plot, character, theme and language are all outstanding in quality. The next several plays are of this sort. It will be evident in some cases that one or perhaps two elements are inferior to others in some aspects, and such observations, when supported with sufficient evidence from the texts, can form the beginning of dramatic criticism. These first four plays have also been used to study the nature of plot structure. The time has come to point out, however, that in studying a play, one must look for its broader structural foundation, not just the structure of its plot. Plot structure is important, but one may also be interested in thematic structure (the way a play's themes are woven together in a careful pattern) or the way certain pivotal characters serve structural functions within a play (a narrator, for example). In short, an approach through plot structure will very often lead directly to the over-all master plan or structure. Not every playwright works with a planned structure, and has it before him like an outline when he writes his play. On the contrary, in most cases major structural features (perhaps even the whole structural pattern) evolve as the playwright struggles with his material, and it would be impossible to say later how much of it came from conscious, premeditated plan and how much from sheer inspirational genius. Whatever its source, however, when one has penetrated a play's essence to the extent of really understanding its structure, he is well along the road to understanding the play. When one sees the essential pattern behind it, he can then see rather easily how the various parts fit into place. Of course, many plays are so structurally complex that one cannot see their patterns clearly, and established critics will argue among themselves as to exactly what the play's structure is.

A large number of plays exhibit a good, clear central action, and the preceding discussion illustrates how to determine just what that action is. Unity of action was one principle that Aristotle insisted was essential to good play structure, and a great many playwrights since his time (although by no means all) have adhered to this principle. The well-made play is one widely used play structure that does make use of a single central action. Two of the preceding plays are very clearly structured according to the principles of the well-made play and a third (*J.B.*) appears to be so structured, if only to a degree. The key features that the well-made play exhibits are exposition, inciting incident, rising action, turning point, falling action, climax, and denouement. One of the preceding plays, *Cyrano de Bergerac,* although having a central action, is loosely structured along lines unlike the well-made play. As this study proceeds with a number of plays from various periods and types of the world's greatest dramatic literature, the structure of each will be examined closely. There will be examples of other major structural patterns used extensively by playwrights, and there will be several plays which are not representative of any particular group, but have structures that are apparently unique. Always, among the several features studied in each play will be its structure, for directors and actors must make a structural analysis in order to thoroughly understand the script which they are preparing for production.

The next sections will discuss several major types of drama. Melodrama has already been defined, and some of the many complexities of tragedy will be pointed out. There are many serious plays besides those classified as melodrama or tragedy, however. Frequently they are lumped together into a general category known as *serious drama.* Many critics prefer to subdivide this catch-all category into more specific dramatic types such as romantic drama (*Cyrano de Bergerac,* for example,) social problem plays, thesis plays, and so on. In addition to the whole matter of classifying serious plays, there is still the second great area to be considered: comedy. If anything, comedy is even more difficult to classify than serious drama. High comedy was defined in discussing *The Importance of Being Earnest.* Farce is the comic counterpart of melodrama—depending primarily upon plot for its effectiveness. Usually, however, the better comedies exhibit elements of both high comedy and farce. Frequently comedies are classified as farces, high comedies, or "other comedies," depending upon the predominant type of humor. Further attempt to subdivide these categories usually leads to more confusion. Examples of each of these major types are included among the remaining plays in this volume.

Each of the four plays already discussed has been evaluated in terms of style. Style has been defined as that fundamental approach which the playwright adopts toward his material, which gives it a distinctive and characteristic mode of expression. The whole mood and attitude of a play will, in part, be outgrowths of the style, and ultimately every play has its own particular style. Nevertheless, as with comedy and tragedy, melodrama and farce, there are certain broad categories of style that may usefully be designated. The most popular style in today's theatre is realism. Realism is so prevalent today that it should be noted that only a small minority of the world's great drama is realistic: Almost all great plays, particularly those written in the past, were written with other values and other production styles in mind. It is possible, of course, to take plays that are written in another style and produce them realistically but one must distinguish between literary styles and production styles; the wise theatre-goer becomes accustomed to looking for other values besides realism both in reading plays and seeing productions of them. Many production and many literary styles are possible. Getting the possible combinations of these together into the right formula is an extremely complex problem, and one that will be probed in greater detail in connection with the remaining plays in this volume.

Although a great deal of attention has been devoted to analysis and understanding of the various scripts, consideration has also been given to their preparation for stage production by theatrical artists. It has been pointed out that production cannot reasonably be separated from script analysis, nor script analysis from production considerations. Acting, directing, and the several technical elements are, in fact, so closely related that it is difficult (perhaps even undesirable) to separate them; however, for the sake of convenient analysis, one area has been dealt with in connection with each play. Acting, directing, scenic and costume design have been examined in some detail, attempting always to single out the most important factors theatrical artists must consider and a perceptive spectator may appreciate. The intricate details of how these over-all aims are carried out are best left for other, more advanced texts. As more plays are examined, however, the remaining technical areas of theatre production will also be studied. Each must grow out of a thorough understanding of the script itself and of the director's interpretive approach to the script.

Basic Types of Drama
and Some Experimental Forms

There is no legal record of William Shakespeare's birth, but his baptism was registered in the Church of the Holy Trinity in Stratford-on-Avon, Warwickshire, on April 26, 1564. Presumably, he was only a few days old at the time. His mother, Mary Arden, was the daughter of Robert Arden, who was moderately wealthy; his father, John Shakespeare, was a self-made businessman who rose eventually to the position of bailiff, or mayor, of Stratford. William had three brothers and four sisters, although not all of these children survived infancy; William was the eldest to reach adulthood. There is no definite record of his education, but there was a free grammar school in Stratford and the son of the mayor would certainly have attended it. Several legends survive regarding Shakespeare's youthful activities, but the next official record available is the registry of certain legal documents having to do with his marriage in November of 1582 to Anne Hathaway, who came from the neighboring village of Shottery; she was eight years older than he. The records suggest some haste about the marriage and with reason, for their daughter, Susanna, was born in May, 1583. Twins, Hamnet and Judith, were born in February, 1585.

It was evidently in 1586 or 1587 that Shakespeare left Stratford and found his way to London; he probably divided his time between these two locations throughout his working life. He became an actor and later a shareholder in the leading theatrical company of the day, and by 1592 was already regarded as a promising young poet and playwright. In 1597, he had earned sufficient money through his theatrical endeavors to buy the largest house in Stratford. There are detailed records, during the ensuing years, of land purchases and other investments in the Stratford area, as well as literary and theatrical pursuits in London. These need not be discussed here except to point out that, in the early 1600's, Shakespeare was the most popular playwright in London. Relatively few of his plays were published, since they were the property of his theatrical company and too valuable to circulate in a day when no copyright laws protected the playwright. A good number were pirated and printed without his permission, however (along with a few that evidently found their way into print with the author's cooperation). His published poetry was very popular, tending, at the time, to establish his strictly literary reputation

Twelfth Night
by William
Shakespeare

more than his plays. By 1611, he seems to have been in semi-retirement in Stratford, and he died on April 23, 1616. In 1623, two of his fellow actors, from the company in which Shakespeare had enjoyed such success, published a volume containing thirty-six of Shakespeare's plays. Were it not for their efforts, presumably many of Shakespeare's best works would be lost.

There has been a great amount of pseudo-scholarly speculation as to whether Shakespeare's plays were actually written by someone else, but not a shred of solid evidence is available to support such theorizing. Records are scant on all literary and theatrical figures of this period, and there is more solid evidence regarding Shakespeare's life and work than many of his contemporaries. That a young actor from a country town should develop into the most popular playwright of his day and one of the commanding literary figures of all time may displease a few cultural snobs, but it is no less probable than that a vast and purposeless conspiracy could have fabricated the literary hoax of the millenium.

Twelfth Night, perhaps the merriest and most popular of Shakespeare's comedies, was written about 1601, performed frequently during the ensuing years, but not published until the collection of 1623. The story of Viola, Orsino, and Olivia is based upon an Italian play *Gl 'Ingannati* (The Cheated), which was widely translated, adapted, and produced, but the specific details of this plot, as well as the characterizations and the antics of the rest of the play, are Shakespeare's invention. Literary borrowing was not uncommon in Shakespeare's day, and many of his plays involve such adaptation. Except for a short period in Restoration England, *Twelfth Night* has been popular with audiences down to the present day. Viola's wit, beauty, modesty, and determination have endeared her to generations of theatre-goers; whereas Malvolio, sick from self-love and the dupe in an elaborate and rather cruel plot, has excited a great deal of controversy and misunderstanding. Modern sensibilities should not be allowed to interfere, however, with a vigorous, ribald appreciation of the fate of a bigoted puritan caught in his own conceit. Whether literally he should be understood to have belonged to one of the puritan sects then gaining power in England is beside the point; Malvolio is spiritually akin to every prig who believes that, because he is virtuous, there should be no more cakes and ale. The play offers a rollicking, fun-filled good time throughout, with beauty, love, and good humor but no serious social concerns whatsoever.

Opposite: Malvolio (Douglas Rain) shows his cross-gartering to Olivia (Frances Hyland) in the 1957 production of *Twelfth Night* at the Stratford Shakespearean Festival, Ontario, Canada directed by Tyrone Guthrie, designed by Tanya Moiseiwitsch. Photograph: Peter Smith.

Page 297: Lloyd Bocher as Orsino, Siobhan McKenna as Viola, and Bruno Gerussi as Feste in the same production of *Twelfth Night*. Photograph: Peter Smith. Both pictures courtesy of the Stratford Shakespearean Festival Foundation of Canada.

Twelfth Night,
or WHAT YOU WILL

A Comedy by
WILLIAM SHAKESPEARE

Orsino, Duke of Illyria.
Sebastian, brother to *Viola.*
Antonio, a sea captain, friend to *Sebastian.*
A Sea Captain, friend to *Viola.*
Valentine,
Curio, } gentlemen attending the Duke.
Sir Toby Belch, uncle to *Olivia.*
Sir Andrew Aguecheek.
Malvolio, steward to *Olivia.*
Fabian,
Feste, a Clown, } servants to *Olivia.*
Olivia, a countess.
Viola, sister to *Sebastian.*
Maria, attendant to *Olivia.*

Lords, a Priest, Sailors, Officers, Musicians, and Attendants.

SCENE: A city in Illyria, and the nearby seacoast.

ACT I

Scene 1. [The Duke's Palace]

[*Enter* **Orsino** (*Duke of Illyria*), **Curio** *and other* **Lords;** (*and* **Musicians**).]

Duke: If music be the food of love, play on;
Give me excess of it, that, surfeiting,
The appetite may sicken, and so die.
That strain again! It had a dying fall;[1]   5
O, it came o'er my ear like the sweet sound[2]
That breathes upon a bank of violets,
Stealing and giving odor! Enough, no more!   10
'Tis not so sweet now as it was before.
O spirit of love, how quick and fresh art thou,
That, notwithstanding thy capacity
Receiveth as the sea, naught enters there,   15

[1] Sound.
[2] Breeze.

Of what validity and pitch soe'er,

But falls into abatement and low price

Even in a minute!³ So full of shapes is fancy   20

That it alone is high fantastical.⁴

Curio: Will you go hunt, my lord?

Duke: What, Curio?

Curio: The hart.

Duke: Why, so I do, the noblest that I   25
have.⁵

O, when mine eyes did see Olivia first,

Methought she purged the air of pestilence!⁶

That instant was I turned into a hart,   30

And my desires, like fell⁷ and cruel hounds,

E'er since pursue me.⁸

     [*Enter* **Valentine.**]

     How now? What news from her?⁹

Valentine: So please my lord, I might   35
not be admitted.

But from her handmaid do return this answer:

The element itself, till seven years' heat,

Shall not behold her face at ample   40
view;¹⁰

But like a cloistress¹¹ she will veiled walk,

And water once a day her chamber round   45

With eye-offending brine: all this to season

A brother's dead love,¹² which she would keep fresh

And lasting in her sad remembrance.   50

Duke: O, she that hath a heart of that fine frame

To pay this debt of love but to a brother,

How will she love when the rich golden   55
shaft¹³

Hath killed the flock of all affections else

That live in her; when liver,¹⁴ brain, and heart,   60

These sovereign thrones, are all supplied and filled,

Her sweet perfections, with one self king!¹⁵

Away before me to sweet beds of   65
flowers!

Love-thoughts lie rich when canopied with bowers.

     [*Exeunt.*]

Scene 2. [*The seacoast*]

     [*Enter* **Viola,** *a* **Captain,** *and* **Sailors.**]

Viola: What country, friends, is this?

Captain: This is Illyria, lady.

Viola: And what should I do in Illyria?
My brother he is in Elysium.¹

Perchance he is not drowned: what   5
think you, sailors?

Captain: It is perchance that you yourself
were saved.

Viola: O my poor brother! and so perchance may he be.   10

Captain: True, madam; and, to comfort
you with chance,
Assure yourself, after our ship did split,

---

³ O spirit of love, you are so vital and alive that, although
you have an endless capacity for absorbing new concepts,
no concept may enter you without becoming, by compari-
son, valueless within a minute.

⁴ Love has so many forms that it is the ultimate in imagina-
tiveness.

⁵ A pun on "heart" and "hart" (a male deer).

⁶ It seemed that she sweetened and freshened the air with
her purity.

⁷ Fierce.

⁸ In ancient mythology, Actaeon was turned into a hart when
he accidently came upon Diana bathing, after which he
was pursued and killed by his own hounds.

⁹ Valentine is just returning from Olivia's home, where Orsino has sent him to tell Olivia of Orsino's love for her.

¹⁰ She will not leave her home for seven years.

¹¹ Nun.

¹² To keep alive the memory of her dead brother's love.

¹³ Cupid's arrow.

¹⁴ The center of passion.

¹⁵ The sense of the passage is: if she can be so moved by
a brother's love, how much more will she be moved by
a true lover.

---

¹ Heaven.

When you, and those poor number
   saved with you, 15
Hung on our driving boat, I saw your
   brother,
Most provident in peril, bind himself
(Courage and hope both teaching him
   the practice) 20
To a strong mast that lived upon the
   sea;
Where, like Arion on the dolphin's
   back,[2]
I saw him hold acquaintance with the 25
   waves
So long as I could see.
Viola: For saying so, there's gold.
Mine own escape unfoldeth to my
hope, 30
Whereto thy speech serves for
   authority,
The like of him.[3] Knowst thou this
   country?
Captain: Ay, madam, well, for I was 35
   bred and born
Not three hours' travel from this very
   place.
Viola: Who governs here?
Captain: A noble duke, in nature as in 40
   name.
Viola: What is his name?
Captain: Orsino.
Viola: Orsino! I have heard my father
   name him. 45
He was a bachelor then.
Captain: And so is now, or was so very
   late;[4]
For but a month ago I went from hence,
And then 'twas fresh in murmur (as 50
   you know
What great ones do, the less will prattle
   of)

That he did seek the love of fair Olivia.
Viola: What's she? 55
Captain: A virtuous maid, the daughter
   of a count
That died some twelvemonth since;
   then leaving her
In the protection of his son, her 60
   brother,
Who shortly also died; for whose dear
   love,
They say, she hath abjured the sight
And company of men. 65
Viola: O that I served that lady,
And might not be delivered to the
   world,
Till I had made mine own occasion
   mellow, 70
What my estate is![5]
Captain: That were hard to compass,[6]
Because she will admit no kind of suit;
No, not the Duke's.
Viola: There is a fair behavior in thee, 75
   Captain;
And though that nature with a
   beauteous wall
Doth oft close in pollution, yet of thee
I will believe thou has a mind that 80
   suits
With this thy fair and outward
   character.[7]
I prithee (and I'll pay thee
   bounteously) 85
Conceal me what I am, and be my aid
For such disguise as haply shall become
The form of my intent.[8] I'll serve this
   duke.
Thou shalt present me as an eunuch to 90
   him;

---

[2] Arion was a Greek poet who was saved from drowning by a school of dolphins who carried him to shore on their backs.
[3] My own escape, together with what you have just said, leads me to hope that he may have been saved.
[4] Recently.
[5] And my true identity might not be revealed to the world until I have an opportunity to reassess the circumstances in which I find myself.
[6] Accomplish.
[7] Although nature often conceals evil within a beautiful exterior, I will believe that your character is as handsome as your appearance.
[8] Help me to a disguise suitable for my purpose—i.e., to enter the service of Duke Orsino.

It may be worth thy pains. For I can
  sing,
And speak to him in many sorts of
  music
That will allow me very worth his
  service.
What else may hap, to time I will
  commit;⁹   60
Only shape thou thy silence to my wit.¹⁰

Captain: Be you his eunuch, and your
  mute I'll be.
When my tongue blabs, then let mine
  eyes not see.

Viola: I thank thee. Lead me on.

                                    [*Exeunt.*]

Scene 3. [Olivia's house]

  [*Enter* **Sir Toby** *and* **Maria.**]

Toby: What a plague means my niece to
  take the death of her brother thus? I am
  sure care's an enemy to life.

Maria: By my troth, Sir Toby, you must
  come in earlier o' nights. Your cousin,¹ my
  lady, takes great exceptions to your ill
  hours.

Toby: Why, let her except before excepted!²

Maria: Ay, but you must confine yourself
  within the modest limits of order.

Toby: Confine? I'll confine³ myself no finer   10
  than I am. These clothes are good enough
  to drink in, and so be these boots too. An
  they be not, let them hang themselves in
  their own straps.

Maria: That quaffing and drinking will
  undo you. I heard my lady talk of it yesterday; and of a foolish knight that you
  brought in one night here to be her wooer.

Toby: Who? Sir Andrew Aguecheek?

Maria: Ay, he.

Toby: He's as tall⁴ a man as any's in Illyria. 20

Maria: What's that to the purpose?

Toby: Why, he has three thousand ducats
  a year.

Maria: Ay, but he'll have but a year in all
  these ducats. He's a very fool and a prodi-
  gal.

Toby: Fie that you'll say so! He plays o' the
  viol de gamboys,⁵ and speaks three or four
  languages word for word without book,
  and hath all the good gifts of nature.

Maria: He hath, indeed, almost natural!⁶   30
  for, besides that he's a fool, he's a great
  quarreler; and but that he hath the gift of
  a coward to allay the gust⁷ he hath in
  quarreling, 'tis thought among the prudent
  he would quickly have the gift of a grave.

Toby: By this hand, they are scoundrels
  and substractors⁸ that say so of him. Who
  are they?

Maria: They that add, moreover, he's
  drunk nightly in your company.

Toby: With drinking healths to my niece.   40
  I'll drink to her as long as there is a passage in my throat and drink in Illyria. He's
  a coward and a coistrel⁹ that will not drink
  to my niece till his brains turn o' the toe
  like a parish top. What, wench! Castiliano
  vulgo!¹⁰ for here comes Sir Andrew Ague-
  face.

                  [*Enter* **Sir Andrew.**]

Andrew: Sir Toby Belch! How now, Sir
  Toby Belch?

Toby: Sweet Sir Andrew!

Andrew: Bless you, fair shrew.   50

Maria: And you too, sir.

Toby: Accost, Sir Andrew, accost.

Andrew: What's that?

---

⁹ I shall face whatever happens next when it happens.
¹⁰ Maintain silence regarding the disguise my wit will devise.

---

¹ Any near relative. Olivia is Toby's niece.
² A quibble on a legal phrase. Toby takes exception to Olivia's exception.
³ Dress.

---

⁴ Valiant.
⁵ Bass viol.
⁶ Like an idiot.
⁷ Gusto.
⁸ Detractors.
⁹ Knave.
¹⁰ Pretentious nonsense.

Toby: My niece's chambermaid.

Andrew: Good Mistress Accost, I desire better acquaintance.

Maria: My name is Mary, sir.

Andrew: Good Mistress Mary Accost—

Toby: You mistake, knight. "Accost" is front her, board her, woo her, assail her. 60

Andrew: By my troth, I would not undertake her in this company. Is that the meaning of "accost"?

Maria: Fare you well, gentlemen.

Toby: An thou let part so,[11] Sir Andrew, would thou mightst never draw sword again!

Andrew: An you part so, mistress, I would I might never draw sword again! Fair lady, do you think you have fools in hand?

Maria: Sir, I have not you by the hand. 70

Andrew: Marry, but you shall have! and here's my hand.

Maria: Now, sir, thought is free. I pray you, bring your hand to the buttery bar[12] and let it drink.

Andrew: Wherefore, sweetheart? What's your metaphor?

Maria: It's dry,[13] sir.

Andrew: Why, I think so. I am not such an ass but I can keep my hand dry. But what's your jest? 80

Maria: A dry jest, sir.

Andrew: Are you full of them?

Maria: Ay, sir, I have them at my fingers' ends. Marry, now I let go your hand, I am barren.   [*Exit.*]

Toby: O knight, thou lackst a cup of canary![14] When did I see thee so put down?

Andrew: Never in your life, I think, unless you see canary put me down. Methinks sometimes I have no more wit than a Christian or an ordinary man has. But I am a great eater of beef, and I believe that 90 does harm to my wit.[15]

Toby: No question.

Andrew: An I thought that, I'd forswear it. I'll ride home tomorrow, Sir Toby.

Toby: *Pourquoi*, my dear knight?

Andrew: What is *"pourquoi"*? Do, or not do? I would I had bestowed that time in the tongues that I have in fencing, dancing, and bear-baiting. O, had I but followed the arts!

Toby: Then hadst thou had an excellent 100 head of hair.

Andrew: Why, would that have mended my hair?

Toby: Past question, for thou seest it will not curl by nature.

Andrew: But it becomes me well enough, does't not?

Toby: Excellent. It hangs like flax on a distaff; and I hope to see a housewife take thee between her legs and spin it off. 110

Andrew: Faith, I'll home tomorrow, Sir Toby. Your niece will not be seen; or if she be, it's four to one she'll none of me. The Count himself here hard by woos her.

Toby: She'll none o' the Count. She'll not match above her degree, neither in estate, years, nor wit; I have heard here swear't. Tut, there's life in't,[16] man.

Andrew: I'll stay a month longer. I am a fellow o' the strangest mind i' the world. 120 I delight in masques and revels sometimes altogether.

Toby: Art thou good at these kickshawses,[17] knight?

Andrew: As any man in Illyria, whatsoever he be, under the degree of my betters; and yet I will not compare with an old man.

---

11 If you let her depart so.

12 Where drinks are served.

13 A moist palm was popularly supposed to be a sign of lechery, and a dry palm a sign of impotence.

14 A kind of wine from the Canary Islands.

---

15 It was popularly believed that eating beef would dull one's wit.

16 There is still hope for your suit.

17 Trifles.

Toby: What is thy excellence in a galliard,[18] knight?

Andrew: Faith, I can cut a caper.

Toby: And I can cut the mutton[19] to't.   130

Andrew: And I think I have the back-trick[20] simply as strong as any man in Illyria.

Toby: Wherefore are these things hid? Wherefore have these gifts a curtain before 'em? Are they like to take dust, like Mistress Mall's picture? Why dost thou not go to church in a galliard and come home in a coranto?[21] My very walk should be a jig. I would not so much as make water but in a sink-a-pace.[22] What dost thou mean? Is it a world to hide virtues in? I did think, by the excellent consti-   140 tution of thy leg, it was formed under the star of a galliard.

Andrew: Ay, 'tis strong, and it does indifferent well in a flame-colored stock.[23] Shall we set about some revels?

Toby: What shall we do else? Were we not born under Taurus?[24]

Andrew: Taurus? That's sides and heart.

Toby: No, sir; it is legs and thighs. Let me see thee caper. [**Sir Andrew** *dances*] Ha,   150 higher! Ha, ha, excellent!

> [*Exeunt.*]

Scene 4. [*The Duke's Palace*]

> [*Enter* **Valentine**, *and* **Viola** *in man's attire.*]

Valentine: If the Duke continue these favors towards you, Cesario, you are like to be much advanced. He hath known you but three days, and already you are no stranger.

Viola: You either fear his humor or my negligence, that you call in question the continuance of his love. Is he inconstant, sir, in his favors?

Valentine: No, believe me.

> [*Enter* **Duke, Curio,** *and* **Attendants.**]

Viola: I thank you. Here comes the Count.

Duke: Who saw Cesario, ho?   10

Viola: On your attendance, my lord, here.

Duke: Stand you awhile aloof.—Cesario, Thou knowst no less but all. I have unclasped
To thee the book even of my secret soul.
Therefore, good youth, address thy gait unto her;[1]
Be not denied access, stand at her doors,
And tell them there thy fixed foot shall grow
Till thou have audience.

Viola: Sure, my noble lord,
If she be so abandoned to her sorrow
As it is spoke, she never will admit me.   20

Duke: Be clamorous and leap all civil bounds
Rather than make unprofited return.

Viola: Say I do speak with her, my lord, what then?

Duke: O, then unfold the passion of my love;
Surprise[2] her with discourse of my dear faith!
It shall become thee well to act my woes.
She will attend it better in thy youth

---

18 An Elizabethan dance step.

19 A pun on "caper." Mutton might be served with capers, a side dish.

20 A dance step.

21 Another dance step.

22 Another dance step.

23 Stocking.

24 The zodiacal sign of the bull. Since it was supposed to govern the neck and throat, however, Toby and Andrew are both wrong.

---

1 Go to Olivia.

2 Overwhelm.

Than in a nuncio's of more grave
   aspect.[3]
Viola: I think not so, my lord.
Duke: Dear lad, believe it;
For they shall yet belie thy happy years   30
That say thou art a man. Diana's lip
Is not more smooth and rubious;[4] thy
   small pipe[5]
Is as the maiden's organ, shrill and
   sound,
And all is semblative a woman's part.
I know thy constellation is right apt
For this affair.[6] Some four or five attend
   him—
All, if you will; for I myself am best
When least in company. Prosper well in
   this,
And thou shalt live as freely as thy lord
To call his fortunes thine.[7]
Viola: I'll do my best   40
To woo your lady. [*Aside*] Yet a barful
   strife![8]
Whoe'er I woo, myself would be his
   wife.

                       [*Exeunt.*]

Scene 5. [Olivia's house]

      [*Enter* **Maria** *and* **Clown.**]

Maria: Nay, either tell me where thou hast
been, or I will not open my lips so wide
as a bristle may enter in way of thy excuse.
My lady will hang thee for thy absence.
Clown: Let her hang me! He that is well
hanged in this world needs to fear no
colors.[1]

---

[3] She will pay more attention to a youth than to an older
messenger.
[4] Ruby-red.
[5] Wind pipe; i.e., voice.
[6] Your stars are right for this business.
[7] If you succeed, you shall have free access to my fortune.
[8] A difficult undertaking.

---

[1] Enemy flags. The sense of the phrase is that he need fear
nothing.

Maria: Make that good.
Clown: He shall see none to fear.
Maria: A good lenten answer. I can tell
thee where that saying was born, of "I fear   10
no colors."
Clown: Where, good Mistress Mary?
Maria: In the wars; and that may you be
bold to say in your foolery.
Clown: Well, God give them wisdom that
have it; and those that are fools, let them
use their talents.
Maria: Yet you will be hanged for being
so long absent, or to be turned away—is
not that as good as a hanging to you?
Clown: Many a good hanging prevents a   20
bad marriage; and for turning away, let
summer bear it out.[2]
Maria: You are resolute then?
Clown: Not so, neither; but I am resolved
on two points.
Maria: That if one break, the other will
hold; or if both break, your gaskins fall.[3]
Clown: Apt, in good faith; very apt. Well,
go thy way! If Sir Toby would leave
drinking, thou wert as witty a piece of   30
Eve's flesh as any in Illyria.[4]
Maria: Peace, you rogue; no more o' that.
Here comes my lady. Make your excuse
wisely, you were best.   [*Exit.*]
      [*Enter* **Lady Olivia** *with* **Malvolio.**]
Clown: Wit, an't be thy will, put me into
good fooling! Those wits that think they
have thee do very oft prove fools; and I
that am sure I lack thee may pass for a
wise man. For what says Quinapalus?[5]
"Better a witty fool than a foolish wit."—   40
God bless thee, lady!
Olivia: Take the fool away.

---

[2] We'll see if, by summer, I have really been turned away.
[3] A pun on "points," the laces used to hold up one's gaskins
(trousers).
[4] This may be a sly suggestion that Maria would be a good
wife for Toby.
[5] A nonsense name.

Clown: Do you not hear, fellows? Take away the lady.

Olivia: Go to, y'are a dry fool! I'll no more of you. Besides, you grow dishonest.

Clown: Two faults, madonna, that drink and good counsel will amend. For give the dry fool drink, then is the fool not dry. Bid the dishonest man mend himself: if he mend, he is no longer dishonest; if he cannot, let the botcher[6] mend him. Anything that's mended is but patched; virtue that transgresses is but patched with sin, and sin that amends is but patched with virtue. If that this simple syllogism will serve, so; if it will not, what remedy? As there is no true cuckold but calamity, so beauty's a flower. The lady bade take away the fool; therefore, I say again, take her away.[7]   50

Olivia: Sir, I bade them take away you.   60

Clown: Misprision[8] in the highest degree! Lady, *cucullus non facit monachum.*[9] That's as much to say as, I wear not motley[10] in my brain. Good madonna, give me leave to prove you a fool.

Olivia: Can you do it?

Clown: Dexteriously, good madonna.

Olivia: Make your proof.

Clown: I must catechize you for it, madonna. Good my mouse of virtue,[11] answer me.

Olivia: Well, sir, for want of other idleness, I'll bide your proof.   70

Clown: Good madonna, why mournest thou?

Olivia: Good fool, for my brother's death.

Clown: I think his soul is in hell, madonna.

Olivia: I know his soul is in heaven, fool.

Clown: The more fool, madonna, to mourn for your brother's soul being in heaven. Take away the fool, gentlemen.

Olivia: What think you of this fool, Malvolio? Doth he not mend?   80

Malvolio: Yes, and shall do till the pangs of death shake him. Infirmity, that decays the wise, doth ever make the better fool.

Clown: God send you, sir, a speedy infirmity, for the better increasing your folly! Sir Toby will be sworn that I am no fox; but he will not pass his word for twopence that you are no fool.

Olivia: How say you to that, Malvolio?

Malvolio: I marvel your ladyship takes delight in such a barren rascal. I saw him put down the other day with[12] an ordinary fool that has no more brain than a stone. Look you now, he's out of his guard[13] already. Unless you laugh and minister occasion to him, he is gagged. I protest I take these wise men that crow so at these set kind of fools no better than the fools' zanies.[14]   90

Olivia: O, you are sick of self-love, Malvolio, and taste with a distempered appetite. To be generous, guiltless, and of free disposition, is to take those things for bird bolts[15] that you deem cannon bullets. There is no slander in an allowed fool, though he do nothing but rail; nor no railing in a known discreet man, though he do nothing but reprove.   100

Clown: Now Mercury indue thee with leasing,[16] for thou speakest well of fools!
  [*Enter* **Maria.**]

Maria: Madam, there is at the gate a young gentleman much desires to speak with you.

---

[6] One who mends clothing.

[7] This entire speech is inspired nonsense, intended to ward off the punishment that Feste fears from Olivia.

[8] Mistake.

[9] The cowl doesn't make the monk.

[10] The parti-colored costume of the jester.

[11] Familiar endearment, too saucy for an ordinary servant and hence indicative of Feste's well-established position in Olivia's household.

---

[12] By.

[13] Unable to defend himself.

[14] Dupes; i.e., the fools' fools.

[15] Relatively harmless arrows used for hunting small birds.

[16] May Mercury (the god of deceit) give you the gift of the ability to lie.

Olivia: From the Count Orsino, is it?

Maria: I know not, madam. 'Tis a fair 110 young man, and well attended.

Olivia: Who of my people hold him in delay?

Maria: Sir Toby, madam, your kinsman.

Olivia: Fetch him off, I pray you. He speaks nothing but madman. Fie on him! [*Exit* **Maria**] Go you, Malvolio. If it be a suit from the Count, I am sick, or not at home. What you will, to dismiss it. [*Exit* **Malvolio**] Now you see, sir, how your fooling grows old, and people dislike it.

Clown: Thou hast spoke for us, madonna, 120 as if thy eldest son should be a fool; whose skull Jove cram with brains!

    [*Enter* **Sir Toby**.]

for—here he comes—one of thy kin has a most weak *pia mater*.[17]

Olivia: By mine honor, half drunk! What is he at the gate, cousin?

Toby: A gentleman.

Olivia: A gentleman? What gentleman?

Toby: 'Tis a gentleman here. A plague o' these pickleherring![18] How now, sot?

Clown: Good Sir Toby! 130

Olivia: Cousin, cousin, how have you come so early by this lethargy?

Toby: Lechery? I defy lechery. There's one at the gate.

Olivia: Ay, marry, what is he?

Toby: Let him be the Devil an he will, I care not! Give me faith, say I. Well, it's all one.   [*Exit.*]

Olivia: What's a drunken man like, fool?

Clown: Like a drowned man, a fool, and a madman. One draught above heat makes him a fool, the second mads him, and a 140 third drowns him.

Olivia: Go thou and seek the crowner,[19]

and let him sit[20] o' my coz; for he's in the third degree of drink—he's drowned. Go look after him.

Clown: He is but mad yet, madonna, and the fool shall look to the madman.

    [*Enter* **Malvolio**.]

Malvolio: Madam, yond young fellow swears he will speak with you. I told him you were sick: he takes on him to understand so much, and therefore comes to speak with you. I told him you were 150 asleep: he seems to have a foreknowledge of that too, and therefore comes to speak with you. What is to be said to him, lady? He's fortified against any denial.

Olivia: Tell him he shall not speak with me.

Malvolio: Has been told so; and he says he'll stand at your door like a sheriff's post,[21] and be the supporter to a bench, but he'll speak with you.

Olivia: What kind o' man is he?

Malvolio: Why, of mankind. 160

Olivia: What manner of man?

Malvolio: Of very ill manner. He'll speak with you, will you or no.

Olivia: Of what personage and years is he?

Malvolio: Not yet old enough for a man nor young enough for a boy; as a squash[22] is before 'tis a peasecod, or a codling[23] when 'tis almost an apple. 'Tis with him in standing water,[24] between boy and man. He is very well-favored and he speaks very shrewishly. One would think his mother's milk were scarce out of him. 170

Olivia: Let him approach. Call in my gentlewoman.

Malvolio: Gentlewoman, my lady calls.

    [*Exit.*]

    [*Enter* **Maria**.]

---

[17] Brain.
[18] Toby hiccups, and then, in his drunken state, blames it on some pickled herring.
[19] Coroner.

[20] Hold an inquest.
[21] A post set before the sheriff's house.
[22] Unripe pea pod.
[23] Unripe apple.
[24] At the moment of the tide's turning.

Olivia: Give me my veil; come, throw it o'er my face. We'll once more hear Orsino's embassy.

[*Enter* **Viola.**]

Viola: The honorable lady of the house, which is she?

Olivia: Speak to me; I shall answer for her. Your will?   180

Viola: Most radiant, exquisite, and unmatchable beauty—I pray you tell me if this be the lady of the house, for I never saw her. I would be loath to cast away my speech; for, besides that it is excellently well penned, I have taken great pains to con[25] it. Good beauties, let me sustain no scorn. I am very comptible,[26] even to the least sinister usage.

Olivia: Whence came you, sir?

Viola: I can say little more than I have   190 studied, and that question's out of my part. Good gentle one, give me modest assurance if you be the lady of the house, that I may proceed in my speech.

Olivia: Are you a comedian?

Viola: No, my profound heart; and yet (by the very fangs of malice I swear) I am not that I play. Are you the lady of the house?

Olivia: If I do not usurp myself, I am.

Viola: Most certain, if you are she, you do usurp yourself; for what is yours to bestow   200 is not yours to reserve. But this is from[27] my commission. I will on with my speech in your praise and then show you the heart of my message.

Olivia: Come to what is important in't. I forgive you the praise.

Viola: Alas, I took great pains to study it, and 'tis poetical.

Olivia: It is the more like to be feigned; I pray you keep it in. I heard you were saucy at my gates; and allowed your approach   210

rather to wonder at you than to hear you. If you be not mad, be gone; if you have reason, be brief. 'Tis not that time of moon with me to make one in so skipping a dialogue.

Maria: Will you hoist sail, sir? Here lies your way.

Viola: No, good swabber;[28] I am to hull[29] here a little longer. Some mollification for your giant,[30] sweet lady!

Olivia: Tell me your mind.

Viola: I am a messenger.   220

Olivia: Sure you have some hideous matter to deliver, when the courtesy of it is so fearful. Speak your office.

Viola: It alone concerns your ear. I bring no overture of war, no taxation[31] of homage. I hold the olive in my hand. My words are as full of peace as matter.

Olivia: Yet you began rudely. What are you? What would you?

Viola: The rudeness that hath appeared in   230 me have I learned from my entertainment.[32] What I am, and what I would, are as secret as maidenhead: to your ears, divinity; to any other's, profanation.

Olivia: Give us the place alone; we will hear this divinity. [*Exit* **Maria**] Now, sir, what is your text?

Viola: Most sweet lady—

Olivia: A comfortable doctrine, and much may be said of it. Where lies your text?   240

Viola: In Orsino's bosom.

Olivia: In his bosom? In what chapter of his bosom?

Viola: To answer by the method, in the first of his heart.

Olivia: O, I have read it! it is heresy. Have you no more to say?

---

[25] Memorize.
[26] Sensitive.
[27] Aside from.

[28] Deck-washer.
[29] Drift.
[30] Ironic; there are several references throughout the play to Maria's small stature.
[31] Demand.
[32] The way I have been met.

Viola: Good madam, let me see your face.

Olivia: Have you any commission from your lord to negotiate with my face? You are now out of your text. But we will draw 250 the curtain and show you the picture. [*Unveils*] Look you, sir, such a one I was this present.[33] Is't not well done?

Viola: Excellently done, if God did all.

Olivia: 'Tis in grain,[34] sir; 'twill endure wind and weather.

Viola: 'Tis beauty truly blent, whose red and white

Nature's own sweet and cunning hand laid on.

Lady, you are the cruel'st she alive

If you will lead these graces to the grave, 260

And leave the world no copy.

Olivia: O, sir, I will not be so hard-hearted. I will give out divers schedules of my beauty. It shall be inventoried, and every particle and utensil labeled to my will:—as, item, two lips, indifferent red; item, two grey eyes, with lids to them; item, one neck, one chin, and so forth. Were you sent hither to praise[35] me?

Viola: I see you what you are—you are too proud;

But if you were the Devil, you are fair. 270

My lord and master loves you. O, such love

Could be but recompensed though you were crowned

The nonpareil of beauty!

Olivia: How does he love me?

Viola: With adorations, fertile tears,

With groans that thunder love, with sighs of fire.

Olivia: Your lord does know my mind; I cannot love him.

Yet I suppose him virtuous, know him noble,

Of great estate, of fresh and stainless youth;

In voices well divulged,[36] free, learned, and valiant,

And in dimension and the shape of nature 280

A gracious person. But yet I cannot love him.

He might have took his answer long ago.

Viola: If I did love you in my master's flame,[37]

With such a suff'ring, such a deadly[38] life,

In your denial I would find no sense;

I would not understand it.

Olivia: Why, what would you?

Viola: Make me a willow cabin at your gate

And call upon my soul within the house;

Write loyal cantons[39] of contemned love

And sing them loud even in the dead of night; 290

Halloa your name to the reverberate hills

And make the babbling gossip of the air[40]

Cry out "Olivia!" O, you should not rest

Between the elements of air and earth

But you should pity me!

Olivia: You might do much. What is your parentage?

Viola: Above my fortunes, yet my state is well.

I am a gentleman.

Olivia: Get you to your lord.

I cannot love him. Let him send no more,

---

[33] Moment (still referring to her face as a portrait).

[34] Fixed (with dye rather than paint).

[35] Appraise.

[36] Of good repute.

[37] With my master's intensity.

[38] Doomed.

[39] Songs.

[40] Echo.

Unless, perchance, you come to me
  again   300
To tell me how he takes it. Fare you
  well.
I thank you for your pains. Spend this
  for me.
Viola: I am no fee'd post,[41] lady; keep
  your purse;
My master, not myself, lacks
  recompense.
Love make his heart of flint that you
  shall love;
And let your fervor, like my master's,
  be
Placed in contempt! Farewell, fair cruelty.
                                             [*Exit.*]
Olivia: "What is your parentage?"
"Above my fortunes, yet my state is
  well.
I am a gentleman." I'll be sworn thou
  art.   310
Thy tongue, thy face, thy limbs, actions,
  and spirit
Do give thee fivefold blazon.[42] Not too
  fast! soft, soft!
Unless the master were the man. How
  now?
Even so quickly may one catch the
  plague?
Methinks I feel this youth's perfections
With an invisible and subtle stealth
To creep in at mine eyes. Well, let it
  be.
What ho, Malvolio!
        [*Enter* **Malvolio.**]
Malvolio: Here, madam, at your
  service.
Olivia: Run after that same peevish
  messenger,
The County's man. He left this ring
  behind him,   320
Would I or not. Tell him I'll none of it.

Desire him not to flatter with his lord
Nor hold him up with hopes. I am not
  for him.
If that the youth will come this way
  tomorrow,
I'll give him reasons for't. Hie thee,
  Malvolio.
Malvolio: Madam, I will.   [*Exit.*]
Olivia: I do I know not what, and fear
  to find
Mine eye too great a flatterer for my
  mind.[43]
Fate, show thy force! Ourselves we do
  not owe.[44]
What is decreed must be—and be this
  so!   330
                                             [*Exit.*]

ACT II

Scene 1. [*The seacoast.*]

    [*Enter* **Antonio** *and* **Sebastian.**]
Antonio: Will you stay no longer? nor will
  you not that I go with you?
Sebastian: By your patience, no. My stars
  shine darkly over me; the malignancy of
  my fate might perhaps distemper yours.
  Therefore I shall crave of you your leave,
  that I may bear my evils alone. It were a
  bad recompense for your love to lay any
  of them on you.
Antonio: Let me yet know of you whither
  you are bound.   10
Sebastian: No, sooth, sir. My determinate
  voyage is mere extravagancy.[1] But I perceive in you so excellent a touch of modesty that you will not extort from me what
  I am willing to keep in; therefore it charges
  me in manners the rather to express[2] my-

---

[41] Paid messenger.
[42] Proof.

[43] My mind will be unable to resist what my eyes have
  enjoyed.
[44] Own; control.

[1] My plan of travel is mere wandering.
[2] Reveal.

self. You must know of me then, Antonio,
my name is Sebastian, which I called Rod-
erigo. My father was that Sebastian of
Messaline whom I know you have heard
of. He left behind him myself and a sister,
both born in an hour.[3] If the heavens had   20
been pleased, would we had so ended! But
you, sir, altered that, for some hour before
you took me from the breach of the sea
was my sister drowned.

Antonio: Alas the day!

Sebastian: A lady, sir, though it was said
she much resembled me, was yet of many
accounted beautiful. But though I could
not with such estimable wonder overfar
believe that, yet thus far I will boldly publish her: she bore a mind that envy could   30
not but call fair.[4] She is drowned already, sir, with salt water, though I seem to
drown her remembrance again with more.

Antonio: Pardon me, sir, your bad entertainment.

Sebastian: O good Antonio, forgive me
your trouble!

Antonio: If you will not murder me for my
love, let me be your servant.[5]

Sebastian: If you will not undo what you
have done, that is, kill him whom you
have recovered, desire it not. Fare ye well
at once. My bosom is full of kindness; and   40
I am yet so near the manners of my mother
that, upon the least occasion more, mine
eyes will tell tales of me.[6] I am bound to
the Count Orsino's court. Farewell.

[*Exit.*]

Antonio: The gentleness of all the gods
go with thee!
I have many enemies in Orsino's court,
Else would I very shortly see thee there.

---

[3] In the same hour (they are twins).

[4] This passage is grammatically difficult, but its general sense
is that Sebastian is modestly denying Viola's great beauty
since she so closely resembles him, but adding that she
did, in fact, have a fine mind.

[5] I shall die if you do not let me serve you.

[6] I am so like my mother that I am on the verge of tears.

But come what may, I do adore thee so
That danger shall seem sport, and I will
go.

[*Exit.*]

Scene 2. [*A street*]

[*Enter* **Viola** *and* **Malvolio** *at several
doors.*[1]]

Malvolio: Were not you even now with
the Countess Olivia?

Viola: Even now, sir. On a moderate pace
I have since arrived but hither.

Malvolio: She returns this ring to you, sir.
You might have saved me my pains, to
have taken it away yourself. She adds,
moreover, that you should put your lord
into a desperate assurance she will none
of him. And one thing more, that you
never so hardy to come again in his affairs,   10
unless it be to report your lord's taking
of this. Receive it so.

Viola: She took the ring of me. I'll none
of it.

Malvolio: Come, sir, you peevishly threw
it to her; and her will is, it should be so
returned. If it be worth stooping for, there
it lies, in your eye; if not, be it his that
finds it.   [*Exit.*]

Viola: I left no ring with her. What
means this lady?
Fortune forbid my outside have not
charmed her!
She made good view of me; indeed, so
much   20
That methought her eyes had lost her
tongue,[2]
For she did speak in starts distractedly.
She loves me sure; the cunning of her
passion
Invites me in this churlish messenger.
None of my lord's ring? Why, he sent
her none!

---

[1] Through two separate doors (on the Elizabethan stage).

[2] Her eyes were so busy that she became tongue-tied.

I am the man. If it be so—as 'tis—
Poor lady, she were better love a
　dream!
Disguise, I see thou art a wickedness
Wherein the pregnant enemy[3] does
　much.
How easy is it for the proper false　　30
In women's waxen hearts to set their
　forms![4]
Alas, our frailty is the cause, not we!
For such as we are made of, such we
　be.
How will this fadge?[5] My master loves
　her dearly;
And I (poor monster) fond as much on
　him;
And she (mistaken) seems to dote on
　me.
What will become of this? As I am
　man,
My state is desperate for my master's
　love.
As I am woman (now alas the day!),
What thriftless sighs shall poor Olivia
　breathe!　　　　　　　　　　　　40
O Time, thou must untangle this, not I;
It is too hard a knot for me t'untie!

　　　　　　　　　　　　　[Exit.]

Scene 3. [Olivia's house]

　　[Enter Sir Toby and Sir Andrew.]
Toby:　Approach, Sir Andrew. Not to be
　abed after midnight is to be up betimes;
　and "diluculo surgere,"[1] thou knowst—
Andrew:　Nay, by my troth, I know not;
　but I know to be up late is to be up late.
Toby:　A false conclusion! I hate it as an
　unfilled can. To be up after midnight, and

to go to bed then, is early; so that to go
to bed after midnight is to go to bed
betimes. Does not our life consist of the
four elements?[2]　　　　　　　　　　10
Andrew:　Faith, so they say; but I think it
　rather consists of eating and drinking.
Toby:　Th'art a scholar! Let us therefore eat
　and drink. Marian I say! a stoup[3] of wine!
　　　　　　　　[Enter Clown.]
Andrew:　Here comes the fool, i' faith.
Clown:　How now, my hearts? Did you
　never see the picture of We Three?[4]
Toby:　Welcome, ass. Now let's have a
　catch.[5]
Andrew:　By my troth, the fool has an ex-
　cellent breast.[6] I had rather than forty
　shillings I had such a leg, and so sweet　　20
　a breath to sing, as the fool has. In sooth,
　thou wast in very gracious fooling last
　night, when thou spokest of Pigrogro-
　mitus, of the Vapians passing the equin-
　octial of Queubus.[7] Twas very good, i'
　faith. I sent thee sixpence for thy leman.[8]
　Hadst it?
Clown:　I did impeticos thy gratillity; for
　Malvalio's nose is no whipstock. My lady
　has a white hand, and the Myrmidons are
　no bottle-ale houses.[9]
Andrew:　Excellent! Why this is the best　　30
　fooling, when all is done. Now a song!
Toby:　Come on! there is sixpence for you.
　Let's have a song.
Andrew:　There's a testril[10] of me too. If one
　knight give a—

---

[3] Resourceful enemy; i.e., the Devil.
[4] How easy it is for a handsome appearance to make an
impression on a woman's soft heart.
[5] End.

---

[1] The first part of a Latin maxim meaning "to get up at
dawn is most healthy."

---

[2] Elizabethans believed that the human body was made up
of four elements: earth, water, fire, and air.
[3] Cup.
[4] A picture of two asses or fools with the inscription "We
three;" the spectator made the third.
[5] Round (a song).
[6] Voice.
[7] Probably nonsense when Feste first said it, and certainly
nonsense as Andrew repeats it.
[8] Lover.
[9] Again, the clown speaks clever nonsense.
[10] Sixpence.

Clown: Would you have a love song, or a song of good life?

Toby: A love song, a love song.

Andrew: Ay, ay! I care not for good life.
[**Clown** *sings*.]

O mistress mine, where are you roaming? 40
O, stay and hear! your truelove's coming,
  That can sing both high and low.
Trip no further, pretty sweeting;
Journeys end in lovers meeting,
  Every wise man's son doth know.

Andrew: Excellent good, i' faith!

Toby: Good, good!
[**Clown** (*sings*).]

What is love? 'Tis not hereafter;
Present mirth hath present laughter;
  What's to come is still unsure: 50
In delay there lies no plenty;
Then come kiss me, sweet and twenty!
  Youth's a stuff will not endure.

Andrew: A mellifluous voice, as I am true knight.

Toby: A contagious breath.[11]

Andrew: Very sweet and contagious, i' faith.

Toby: To hear by the nose, it is dulcet in contagion. But shall we make the welkin[12] dance indeed? Shall we rouse the night owl in a catch that will draw three souls 60 out of one weaver? Shall we do that?

Andrew: An you love me, let's do't! I am dog at a catch.

Clown: By'r Lady, sir, and some dogs will catch well.

Andrew: Most certain. Let our catch be "Thou knave."

Clown: "Hold thy peace, thou knave," knight? I shall be constrained in't to call thee knave, knight. 70

Andrew: 'Tis not the first time I have constrained one to call me knave. Begin, fool. It begins, "Hold thy peace."

Clown: I shall never begin if I hold my peace.

Andrew: Good, i' faith! Come, begin.
[*Catch sung. Enter* **Maria.**]

Maria: What a caterwauling do you keep here! If my lady have not called up her steward Malvolio and bid him turn you out of doors, never trust me.

Toby: My lady's a Cataian,[13] we are politi- 80 cians, Malvolio's a Peg-a-Ramsey[14] and [*Sings*] "Three merry men be we."[15] Am not I consanguineous? Am I not of her blood? Tilly-vally, lady! [*Sings*] "There dwelt a man in Babylon, lady, lady!"

Clown: Beshrew me, the knight's in admirable fooling.

Andrew: Ay, he does well enough if he be disposed, and so do I too. He does it with a better grace, but I do it more natural.

Toby: [*Sings*] "O' the twelfth day of De- 90 cember"—

Maria: For the love o' God, peace!
[*Enter* **Malvolio.**]

Malvolio: My masters, are you mad? or what are you? Have you no wit, manners, nor honesty, but to gabble like tinkers at this time of night? Do ye make an alehouse of my lady's house, that ye squeak out your coziers[16] catches without any mitigation or remorse of voice? Is there no respect of place, persons, nor time in you?

Toby: We did keep time, sir, in our 100 catches. Sneck up![17]

Malvolio: Sir Toby, I must be round with you. My lady bade me tell you that, though she harbors you as her kinsman, she's nothing allied to your disorders. If you can separate yourself and your mis-

---

[11] A pun on "sweet song" and "halitosis."
[12] Sky.

[13] Chinaman.
[14] An old ballad.
[15] This line and the subsequently quoted ones are snatches from popular songs of the period.
[16] Cobblers'.
[17] Go hang yourself.

demeanors, you are welcome to the house. If not, and it would please you to take leave of her, she is very willing to bid you farewell.

Toby: [*Sings*] "Farewell, dear heart, since I must needs be gone." 110

Maria: Nay, good Sir Toby!

Clown: [*Sings*] "His eyes do show his days are almost done."

Malvolio: Is't even so?

Toby: "But I will never die."

Clown: Sir Toby, there you lie.

Malvolio: This is much credit to you!

Toby: "Shall I bid him go?"

Clown: "What an if you do?"

Toby: "Shall I bid him go, and spare not?" 120

Clown: "O, no, no, no, no, you dare not!"

Toby: Out o' tune, sir? Ye lie. Art any more than a steward? Dost thou think, because thou art virtuous, there shall be no more cakes and ale?

Clown: Yes, by Saint Anne! and ginger shall be hot i' the mouth too.

Toby: Th'art i' the right.—Go, sir, rub your chain[18] with crumbs. A stoup of wine, Maria!

Malvolio: Mistress Mary, if you prized my 130 lady's favor at anything more than contempt, you would not give means for this uncivil rule. She shall know of it, by this hand.   [*Exit.*]

Maria: Go shake your ears!

Andrew: 'Twere as good a deed as to drink when a man's ahungry, to challenge him the field, and then to break promise with him and make a fool of him.

Toby: Do't, knight. I'll write thee a challenge; or I'll deliver thy indignation to him 140 by word of mouth.

Maria: Sweet Sir Toby, be patient for tonight. Since the youth of the Count's was today with my lady, she is much out of quiet. For Monsieur Malvolio, let me alone

with him. If I do not gull[19] him into a nay-word, and make him a common recreation, do not think I have wit enough to lie straight in my bed. I know I can do it.

Toby: Possess[20] us, possess us! Tell us something of him. 150

Maria: Marry, sir, sometimes he is kind of Puritan.

Andrew: O, if I thought that, I'd beat him like a dog!

Toby: What, for being a Puritan? Thy exquisite reason, dear knight?

Andrew: I have no exquisite reason for't, but I have reason good enough.

Maria: The devil a Puritan that he is, or anything constantly but a time-pleaser; an 160 affectioned[21] ass, that cons state without book[22] and utters it by great swarths; the best persuaded of himself; so crammed, as he thinks, with excellencies that it is his grounds of faith that all that look on him love him; and on that vice in him will my revenge find notable cause to work.

Toby: What wilt thou do?

Maria: I will drop in his way some obscure epistles of love, wherein by the color of his beard, the shape of his leg, the manner 170 of his gait, the expressure of his eye, forehead, and complexion, he shall find himself most feelingly personated. I can write very like my lady your niece; on a forgotten matter we can hardly make distinction of our hands.

Toby: Excellent! I smell a device.

Andrew: I have't in my nose too.

Toby: He shall think by the letters that thou wilt drop that they come from my niece, and that she's in love with him. 180

---

18 Chain of office (as steward of the household).

19 Fool.
20 Inform.
21 Affected.
22 Memorizes courtly phrases.

Maria: My purpose is indeed a horse of that color.

Andrew: And your horse now would make him an ass.

Maria: Ass, I doubt not.

Andrew: O, 'twill be admirable!

Maria: Sport royal, I warrant you. I know my physic will work with him. I will plant you two, and let the fool make a third, where he shall find the letter. Observe his construction of it. For this night, to 190 bed, and dream on the event. Farewell.

[*Exit.*]

Toby: Good night, <u>Penthesilea</u>.[23]

Andrew: Before me, she's a good wench.

Toby: She's a beagle true-bred, and one that adores me. What o' that?

Andrew: I was adored once too.

Toby: Let's to bed, knight. Thou hadst need send for more money.

Andrew: If I cannot <u>recover</u>[24] your niece, 200 I am a foul way out.

Toby: Send for money, knight. If thou hast her not i' the end, call me <u>Cut</u>.[25]

Andrew: If I do not, never trust me, take it how you will.

Toby: Come, come; I'll go <u>burn some sack</u>.[26] 'Tis too late to go to bed now. Come, knight; come, knight.

[*Exeunt.*]

Scene 4. [The Duke's Palace]

[*Enter* **Duke, Viola, Curio,** *and others.*]

Duke: Give me some music. Now—Good morrow, friends.

Now, good Cesario, but that piece of song,

That old and antique song we heard last night.

---

[23] Queen of the Amazons. Another ironic reference to Maria's small size.
[24] Win.
[25] A stupid horse.
[26] Heat some wine.

Methought it did relieve my passion much,

More than light airs and <u>recollected terms</u>[1]

Of these most brisk and giddy-paced times.

Come, but one verse.

Curio: He is not here, so please your lordship, that should sing it.

Duke: Who was it?   10

Curio: Feste the jester, my lord, a fool that the Lady Olivia's father took much delight in. He is about the house.

Duke: Seek him out. [*Exit* **Curio**] And play the tune the while.   [*Music plays.*]

Come hither, boy. If ever thou shalt love,

In the sweet pangs of it remember me;

For such as I am all true lovers are,

Unstaid and skittish in all motions else

Save in the constant image of the creature

That is beloved. How dost thou like this tune?   20

Viola: It gives a very echo to <u>the seat Where Love is throned</u>.[2]

Duke: Thou dost speak masterly.

My life upon't, young though thou art, thine eye

Hath stayed upon some favor that it loves.

Hath it not, boy?

Viola: A little, by your favor.

Duke: What kind of woman is't?

Viola: Of your complexion.

Duke: She is not worth thee then. What years, i' faith?

Viola: About your years, my lord.

Duke: Too old, by heaven! Let still the woman take   30

An elder than herself: so wears she to him,

---

[1] Studied phrases.
[2] The heart.

So sways she level in her husband's
  heart;
For, boy, however we do praise
  ourselves,
Our fancies are more giddy and unfirm,
More longing, wavering, sooner lost and
  won,
Than women's are.
Viola: I think it well, my lord.
Duke: Then let thy love be younger
  than thyself,
Or thy affection cannot hold the bent;
For women are as roses, whose fair
  flower,
Being once displayed, doth fall that
  very hour.   40
Viola: And so they are; alas, that they
  are so!
To die, even when they to perfection
  grow!
        [*Enter* **Curio** *and* **Clown.**]
Duke: O, fellow, come, the song we had
  last night.
Mark it, Cesario; it is old and plain.
The spinsters and the knitters in the
  sun,
And the free maids that weave their
  thread with bones,[3]
Do use to chant it. It is silly sooth,[4]
And dallies with the innocence of love,
Like the old age.[5]
Clown: Are you ready, sir?   50
Duke: Ay; prithee sing.   [*Music.*]

The Song

Clown: Come away, come away, death,
  And in sad cypress let me be laid.
Fly away, fly away, breath;
  I am slain by a fair cruel maid.
My shroud of white, stuck all with yew,
O, prepare it!

My part of death, no one so true
  Did share it.

Not a flower, not a flower sweet,   60
  On my black coffin let there be strown;
Not a friend, not a friend greet
  My poor corpse, where my bones shall
  be thrown.
A thousand thousand sighs to save,
  Lay me, O, where
Sad true lover never find my grave,
  To weep there!

Duke: There's for thy pains.
Clown: No pains, sir. I take pleasure in
  singing, sir.   70
Duke: I'll pay thy pleasure then.
Clown: Truly, sir, and pleasure will be
  paid one time or another.
Duke: Give me now leave to leave thee.
Clown: Now the melancholy god protect
  thee, and the tailor make thy doublet of
  changeable taffeta, for thy mind is a very
  opal! I would have men of such constancy
  put to sea, that their business might be
  everything, and their intent everywhere;
  for that's it that always makes a good   80
  voyage of nothing. Farewell.   [*Exit.*]
Duke: Let all the rest give place.
        [*Exeunt* **Curio** *and* **Attendants.**]
                    Once more, Cesario,
Get thee to yond same sovereign cruelty.
Tell her, my love, more noble than the
  world.
Prizes not quantity of dirty lands.
The parts[6] that Fortune hath bestowed
  upon her,
Tell her I hold as giddily as Fortune;
But 'tis that miracle and queen of gems
That nature pranks her in,[7] attracts my
  soul.
Viola: But if she cannot love you, sir—   90
Duke: I cannot be so answered.

---

[3] Bobbins.
[4] Simple truth.
[5] Former (simpler) times.

[6] Property.
[7] It is that beautiful body that nature has given her.

Viola: Sooth, but you must.
  Say that some lady, as perhaps there is,
  Hath for your love as great a pang of
    heart
  As you have for Olivia: You cannot
    love her;
  You tell her so. Must she not then be
    answered?
Duke: There is no woman's sides
  Can bide the beating of so strong a
    passion
  As love doth give my heart; no
    woman's heart
  So big to hold so much; they lack
    retention.
  Alas, their love may be called appetite—   100
  No motion of the liver,[8] but the palate—
  That suffers surfeit, cloyment, and
    revolt;[9]
  But mine is all as hungry as the sea
  And can digest as much. Make no
    compare
  Between that love a woman can bear
    me
  And that I owe Olivia.
Viola: Ay, but I know—
Duke: What dost thou know?
Viola: Too well what love women to
    men may owe.
  In faith, they are as true of heart as we.
  My father had a daughter loved a man   110
  As it might be perhaps, were I a
    woman,
  I should your lordship.
Duke: And what's her history?
Viola: A blank, my lord. She never told
    her love,
  But let concealment, like a worm i' the
    bud,
  Feed on her damask cheek. She pined in
    thought;
  And, with a green and yellow melancholy,
  She sat like Patience on a monument,

Smiling at grief. Was not this love
    indeed?
We men may say more, swear more; but
    indeed
Our shows are more than will; for still we
    prove   120
Much in our vows but little in our love.
Duke: But died thy sister of her love,
    my boy?
Viola: I am all the daughters of my
    father's house,
  And all the brothers too—and yet I
    know not.
  Sir, shall I to this lady?
Duke: Ay, that's the theme.
  To her in haste! Give her this jewel.
    Say
  My love can give no place, bide no
    denay.[10]
                                    [*Exeunt.*]

Scene 5. [*Olivia's garden*]

        [*Enter* **Sir Toby, Sir Andrew,** *and* **Fa-
        bian.**]
Toby: Come thy ways, Signior Fabian.
Fabian: Nay, I'll come. If I lose a scruple
  of this sport, let me be boiled to death
  with melancholy.
Toby: Wouldst thou not be glad to have
  the niggardly rascally sheepbiter come by
  some notable shame?
Fabian: I would exult, man. You know he
  brought me out o' favor with my lady
  about a bear-baiting here.   10
Toby: To anger him we'll have the bear
  again; and we will fool him black and blue.
  Shall we not, Sir Andrew?
Andrew: An we do not, it is pity of our
  lives.
        [*Enter* **Maria.**]
Toby: Here comes the little villain. How
  now, my metal of India?[1]

---

[8] The center of true passion.
[9] Satiety and revulsion.

---

[10] Denial.

---

[1] Gold.

Maria: Get ye all three into the box tree. Malvolio's coming down this walk. He has been yonder i' the sun practicing behavior to his own shadow this half hour. Observe him, for the love of mockery; for I know this letter will make a contemplative idiot of him. Close, in the name of jesting! Lie thou there [*Throws down a letter*]; for here comes the trout that must be caught with tickling.   [*Exit.*]

[*Enter* **Malvolio.**]

Malvolio: 'Tis but fortune; all is fortune. Maria once told me she[2] did affect me; and I have heard herself come thus near, that, should she fancy, it should be one of my complexion. Besides, she uses me 30 with a more exalted respect than anyone else that follows her. What should I think on't?

Toby: Here's an overweening rogue!

Fabian: O, peace! Contemplation makes a rare turkey cock of him. How he jets under his advanced plumes![3]

Andrew: Slight, I could so beat the rogue!

Fabian: Peace, I say.

Malvolio: To be Count Malvolio!   40

Toby: Ah, rogue!

Andrew: Pistol him, pistol him!

Fabian: Peace, peace!

Malvolio: There is example for't. The Lady of the Strachy married the yeoman of the wardrobe.

Andrew: Fie on him, Jezebel!

Fabian: O, peace! Now he's deeply in. Look how imagination blows him.

Malvolio: Having been three months married to her, sitting in my state—[4]   50

Toby: O for a stonebow,[5] to hit him in the eye!

Malvolio: Calling my officers about me, in

my branched[6] velvet gown; having come from a day bed, where I have left Olivia sleeping—

Toby: Fire and brimstone!

Fabian: O, peace, peace!

Malvolio: And then to have the humor of state;[7] and after a demure travel of regard[8]—telling them I know my place, as I would they should do theirs—to ask for 60 my kinsman Toby—

Toby: Bolts and shackles!

Fabian: O, peace, peace, peace! Now, now.

Malvolio: Seven of my people, with an obedient start, make out for him. I frown the while, and perchance wind up my watch, or play with my—some rich jewel. Toby approaches; curtsies there to me—

Toby: Shall this fellow live?

Fabian: Though our silence be drawn from 70 us with cars, yet peace!

Malvolio: I extend my hand to him thus, quenching my familiar smile with an austere regard of control—

Toby: And does not Toby take you a blow o' the lips then?

Malvolio: Saying, "Cousin Toby, my fortunes having cast me on your niece, give me this prerogative of speech."

Toby: What, what?   80

Malvolio: "You must amend your drunkenness."

Toby: Out, scab!

Fabian: Nay, patience, or we break the sinews of our plot.

Malvolio: "Besides, you waste the treasure of your time with a foolish knight"—

Andrew: That's me, I warrant you.

Malvolio: "One Sir Andrew"—

Andrew: I knew 'twas I, for many do call me fool.   90

Malvolio: What employment have we here?

---

[2] Olivia.
[3] He struts like a peacock as he thinks of Olivia loving him.
[4] Chair of state.
[5] A crossbow which shoots stones.

---

[6] Flowered.
[7] The high airs of authority.
[8] After looking over each member of his court.

[Picks up the letter.]

Fabian: Now is the woodcock near the gin.⁹

Toby: O, peace! and the spirit of humors intimate reading aloud to him!

Malvolio: By my life, this is my lady's hand! These be her very C's, her U's, and her T's; and thus makes she her great P's. It is, in contempt of question,¹⁰ her hand.

Andrew: Her C's, her U's, and her T's? Why that?   100

Malvolio: *[Reads]* "To the unknown beloved, this, and my good wishes." Her very phrases! By your leave, wax. Soft! and the impressure her Lucrece, with which she uses to seal!¹¹ 'Tis my lady. To whom should this be?

Fabian: This wins him, liver and all.

Malvolio: *[Reads]*

    "Jove knows I love—
      But who?
    Lips, do not move;
      No man must know."   110

"No man must know." What follows? The numbers altered!¹² "No man must know." If this should be thee, Malvolio?

Toby: Marry, hang thee, brock!¹³

Malvolio: *[Reads]*

"I may command where I adore;
    But silence, like a Lucrece knife,
With bloodless stroke my heart doth
    gore.
M. O. A. I. doth sway my life."

Fabian: A fustian¹⁴ riddle!

Toby: Excellent wench, say I.   120

Malvolio: "M.O.A.I. doth sway my life." Nay, but first, let me see, let me see, let me see.

Fabian: What dish o' poison has she dressed him!

Toby: And with what wing the staniel checks at it!¹⁵

Malvolio: "I may command where I adore." Why, she may command me: I serve her; she is my lady. Why, this is evident to any formal capacity.¹⁶ There is no obstruction in this. And the end— what should that alphabetical position   130 portend? If I could make that resemble something in me! Softly! M. O. A. I.

Toby: O, ay, make up that! He is now at a cold scent.

Fabian: Sowter will cry upon't for all this, though it be as rank as a fox.¹⁷

Malvolio: M.—Malvolio. M.—Why, that begins my name!

Fabian: Did not I say he would work it out? The cur is excellent at faults.¹⁸   140

Malvolio: M.—But then there is no consonancy¹⁹ in the sequel. That suffers under probation.²⁰ A should follow, but O does.

Fabian: And O shall end, I hope.

Toby: Ay, or I'll cudgel him, and make him cry O!

Malvolio: And then I comes behind.

Fabian: Ay, an you had any eye behind you, you might see more detraction at your heels than fortunes before you.   150

Malvolio: M, O, A, I. This simulation is not as the former;²¹ and yet, to crush this a little, it would bow to me, for every one of these letters are in my name. Soft! here follows prose.

[Reads] "If this fall into thy hand, revolve.²²

---

⁹ The woodcock, a traditionally stupid bird, is near the trap.
¹⁰ Without question.
¹¹ Malvolio starts to break the seal, then notices that the wax has the impression of Olivia's own sealing ring in it—an outline of Lucrece, noted for her chastity.
¹² The versification changes.
¹³ Badger.
¹⁴ Ridiculous.
¹⁵ The hawk turns aside to follow it. The figure is from falconry.
¹⁶ Normal intelligence.
¹⁷ The dog will follow the scent, though it be as strong as that of a fox.
¹⁸ A break in the line of a scent.
¹⁹ Consistency.
²⁰ Further scrutiny.
²¹ This riddle is not as clear as the preceding phrases.
²² Consider.

In my stars I am above thee; but be not afraid of greatness. Some are born great, some achieve greatness, and some have greatness thrust upon 'em. Thy Fates open their hands; let thy blood and spirit embrace them; and to inure thyself to what thou art like to be, cast thy humble slough[23] and appear fresh. Be opposite with a kinsman, surly with servants. Let thy tongue tang arguments of state; put thyself into the trick of singularity.[24] She thus advises thee that sighs for thee. Remember who commended thy yellow stockings and wishes to see thee ever cross-gartered.[25] I say, remember. Go to, thou art made, if thou desirest to be so. If not, let me see thee a steward still, the fellow of servants, and not worthy to touch Fortune's fingers. Farewell. She that would alter services[26] with thee,

"THE FORTUNATE UNHAPPY."

Daylight and champian[27] discovers not more, This is open. I will be proud, I will read politic authors,[28] I will baffle Sir Toby, I will wash off gross acquaintance, I will be point-device[29] the very man. I do not now fool myself, to let imagination jade[30] me; for every reason excites to this, that my lady loves me. She did commend my yellow stockings of late, she did praise my leg being cross-gartered; and in this she manifests herself to my love, and with a kind of injunction drives me to these

habits of her liking. I thank my stars, I am happy. I will be strange,[31] stout,[32] in yellow stockings, and cross-gartered, even with the swiftness of putting on. Jove and my stars be praised! Here is yet a postscript.

"Thou canst not choose but know who I am. If thou entertainst my love, let it appear in thy smiling. Thy smiles become thee well. Therefore in my presence still smile, dear my sweet, I prithee."

Jove, I thank thee. I will smile; I will do everything that thou wilt have me. [*Exit.*]

Fabian: I will not give my part of this sport for a pension of thousands to be paid from the Sophy.[33]

Toby: I could marry this wench for this device—

Andrew: So could I too.

Toby: And ask no other dowry with her but such another jest.
[*Enter* **Maria.**]

Andrew: Nor I neither.

Fabian: Here comes my noble gull-catcher.[34]

Toby: Wilt thou set thy foot o' my neck?

Andrew: Or o' mine either?

Toby: Shall I play my freedom at tray-trip[35] and become thy bondslave?

Andrew: I' faith, or I either?

Toby: Why, thou hast put him in such a dream that, when the image of it leaves him, he must run mad.

Maria: Nay, but say true, does it work upon him?

Toby: Like aqua vitae[36] with a midwife.

Maria: If you will, then, see the fruits of the sport, mark his first approach before my lady. He will come to her in yellow

---

[23] Skin (as does a snake).
[24] Be singularly yourself.
[25] An out-dated fashion in which ribbon garters were crossed behind the knees and tied in a bow in front. When Malvolio later dresses in this manner, he appears ridiculous.
[26] Exchange places.
[27] Open plains.
[28] Authors who deal in matters of politics—so that his tongue may tang arruments of state.
[29] Precisely.
[30] Trick.

[31] Stern.
[32] Haughty.
[33] Shah of Persia.
[34] Catcher of fools.
[35] A gambling game.
[36] Liquor.

stockings, and 'tis a color she abhors, and cross-gartered, a fashion she detests; and he will smile upon her, which will now be so unsuitable to her disposition, being addicted to a melancholy as she is, that it cannot but turn him into a notable contempt. If you will see it, follow me.

Toby: To the gates of Tartar,[37] thou most excellent devil of wit!

Andrew: I'll make one too.

[*Exeunt.*]

ACT III

Scene 1. [*Olivia's garden*]

[*Enter* **Viola,** *and* **Clown** (*with a tabor*[1] *and pipe*).]

Viola: Save thee, friend, and thy music! Dost thou live by thy tabor?

Clown: No, sir, I live by the church.

Viola: Art thou a churchman?

Clown: No such matter, sir. I do live by the church; for I do live at my house, and my house doth stand by the church.

Viola: So thou mayst say, the king lies by a beggar, if a beggar dwell near him; or, the church stands by thy tabor, if thy tabor stand by the church.

Clown: You have said, sir. To see this age! A sentence is but a chev'ril[2] glove to a good wit. How quickly the wrong side may be turned outward!

Viola: Nay, that's certain. They that dally nicely with words may quickly make them wanton.

Clown: I would therefore my sister had had no name, sir.

Viola: Why, man?

Clown: Why, sir, her name's a word, and to dally with that word might make my sister wanton. But indeed words are very rascals since bonds disgraced them.[3]

Viola: Thy reason, man?

Clown: Troth, sir, I can yield you none without words, and words are grown so false I am loath to prove reason with them.

Viola: I warrant thou art a merry fellow and carest for nothing.

Clown: Not so, sir; I do care for something; but in my conscience, sir, I do not care for you. If that be to care for nothing, sir, I would it would make you invisible.

Viola: Art not thou the Lady Olivia's fool?

Clown: No, indeed, sir. The Lady Olivia has no folly. She will keep no fool, sir, till she be married; and fools are as like husbands as pilchards[4] are to herrings—the husband's the bigger. I am indeed not her fool, but her corrupter of words.

Viola: I saw thee late at the Count Orsino's.

Clown: Foolery, sir, does walk about the orb[5] like the sun; it shines everywhere. I would be sorry, sir, but the fool should be as oft with your master as with my mistress. I think I saw your wisdom[6] there.

Viola: Nay, an thou pass upon[7] me, I'll no more with thee. Hold, there's expenses for thee.

[*Gives a piece of money.*]

Clown: Now Jove, in his next commodity[8] of hair, send thee a beard!

Viola: By my troth, I'll tell thee, I am almost sick for one, though I would not have it grow on my chin. Is thy lady within?

Clown: Would not a pair of these[9] have bred, sir?

---

[37] Hell.

---

[1] Small drum.
[2] Kid.
[3] Words have been disgraced since legal contracts are now needed to bind a man's word.
[4] A fish almost indistinguishable from a herring.
[5] Earth.
[6] Ironic variation of "your worship."
[7] Begin to jest about.
[8] Shipment.
[9] Referring to the coin Viola has just given him.

Viola: Yes, being kept together and put to use.

Clown: I would play Lord Pandarus of Phrygia, sir, to bring a Cressida to this Troilus.[10]

Viola: I understand you, sir. 'Tis well begged.   60

Clown: The matter, I hope, is not great, sir, begging but a beggar: Cressida was a beggar.[11] [*Viola tosses him another coin*] My lady is within, sir. I will conster[12] to them whence you come. Who you are and what you would are out of my welkin[13]—I might say "element," but the word is over-worn.
                                    [*Exit.*]

Viola: This fellow is wise enough to
         play the fool,
And to do that well craves a kind of
         wit.
He must observe their mood on whom
         he jests,
The quality of persons, and the time;   70
Not, like the haggard,[14] check at every
         feather[15]
That comes before his eye. This is a
         practice
As full of labor as a wise man's art;
For folly that he wisely shows, is fit;
But wise men, folly-fall'n, quite taint
         their wit.
                [*Enter* **Sir Toby** *and* (*Sir*) **Andrew**.]

Toby: Save you, gentleman!

Viola: And you, sir.

Andrew: *Dieu vous garde, monsieur.*[16]

Viola: *Et vous aussi; votre serviteur.*[17]   80

Andrew: I hope, sir, you are, and I am yours.

---

[10] Pandarus, Cressida's uncle, first brought Troilus and Cressida together.
[11] Cressida eventually became a beggar.
[12] Explain.
[13] *Welkin* and *element* both mean "sky."
[14] Untrained hawk.
[15] Strike at every opportunity.
[16] God save you, sir.
[17] And you also; I am your servant.

Toby: Will you encounter the house?[18] My niece is desirous you should enter, if your trade be to her.

Viola: I am bound to your niece, sir. I mean, she is the list[19] of my voyage.

Toby: Taste your legs, sir; put them to motion.

Viola: My legs do better understand me, sir, than I understand what you mean by   90 bidding me taste my legs.

Toby: I mean, to go, sir, to enter.

Viola: I will answer you with gait and entrance. But we are prevented.
                [*Enter* **Oliva** *and* **Gentlewoman** (**Maria**).]
Most excellent accomplished lady, the heavens rain odors on you!

Andrew: [*Aside*] That youth's a rare courtier. "Rain odors"—well!

Viola: My matter hath no voice, lady, but to your own most pregnant[20] and vouchsafed[21] ear.   100

Andrew: [*Aside*] "Odors," "pregnant," and "vouchsafed"—I'll get 'em all three all ready.

Olivia: Let the garden door be shut, and leave me to my hearing. [*Exeunt* **Sir Toby**, **Sir Andrew**, *and* **Maria**.] Give me your hand, sir.

Viola: My duty, madam, and most humble service.

Olivia: What is your name?

Viola: Cesario is your servant's name, fair princess.

Olivia: My servant, sir? 'Twas never merry world
Since lowly feigning was called
         compliment.   110
Y'are servant to the Count Orsino,
         youth.

Viola: And he is yours, and his must needs be yours.

---

[18] Deliberately high-flown and ridiculous language.
[19] Goal.
[20] Ready.
[21] Proffered.

Your servant's servant is your servant,
  madam.

Olivia: For him, I think not on him; for
  his thoughts,
Would they were blanks, rather than
  filled with me!

Viola: Madam, I come to whet your
  gentle thoughts
On his behalf.

Olivia: O, by your leave, I pray
  you!
I bade you never speak again of him;
But, would you undertake another suit,
I had rather hear you to solicit that   120
Than music from the spheres.

Viola: Dear lady—

Olivia: Give me leave, beseech you. I
  did send,
After the last enchantment you did
  here,
A ring in chase of you. So did I abuse
Myself, my servant, and, I fear me, you.
Under your hard construction²² must I
  sit,
To force²³ that on you in a shameful
  cunning
Which you knew none of yours. What
  might you think?
Have you not set mine honor at the
  stake
And baited²⁴ it with all the unmuzzled
  thoughts   130
That tyrannous heart can think? To one
  of your receiving²⁵
Enough is shown; a cypress, not a
  bosom,
Hides my heart. So, let me hear you
  speak.

Viola: I pity you.

Olivia: That's a degree to love.

Viola: No, not a grise;²⁶ for 'tis a vulgar²⁷
  proof
That very oft we pity enemies.

Olivia: Why then, methinks 'tis time to
  smile again.
O world, how apt the poor are to be
  proud!
If one should be a prey, how much the
  better
To fall before the lion than the wolf!   140
  [*Clock strikes.*]
The clock upbraids me with the waste
  of time.
Be not afraid, good youth, I will not
  have you;
And yet, when wit and youth is come
  to harvest,²⁸
Your wife is like to reap a proper man.
There lies your way, due west.

Viola: Then westward ho!
Grace and good disposition attend your
  ladyship!
You'll nothing, madam, to my lord by
  me?   150

Olivia: Stay.
I prithee tell me what thou thinkst of
  me.

Viola: That you do think you are not
  what you are.

Olivia: If I think so, I think the same of
  you.

Viola: Then think you right. I am not
  what I am.

Olivia: I would you were as I would
  have you be!

Viola: Would it be better, madam, than
  I am?
I wish it might; for now I am your fool.

Olivia: O, what a deal of scorn looks
  beautiful
In the contempt and anger of his lip!

---

²² Bad opinion.
²³ For forcing.
²⁴ In the popular sport of bear-baiting, a bear was tied to
  a stake and attacked by dogs.
²⁵ Intelligence.

²⁶ Step.
²⁷ Common.
²⁸ Matured.

A murd'rous guilt shows not itself more
soon
Than love that would seem hid: love's
night is noon.   160
Cesario, by the roses of the spring,
By maidhood, honor, truth, and
everything,
I love thee so that, maugre[29] all thy
pride,
Nor wit nor reason can my passion
hide.
Do not extort thy reasons from this
clause,
For that I woo, thou therefore hast no
cause;
But rather reason thus with reason
fetter:
Love sought is good, but given
unsought is better.[30]

Viola: By innocence I swear, and by my
youth,
I have one heart, one bosom, and one
truth,   170
And that no woman has; nor never
none
Shall mistress be of it, save I alone.
And so adieu, good madam. Never
more
Will I my master's tears to you deplore.

Olivia: Yet come again; for thou perhaps
mayst move
That heart which now abhors to like his
love.

[*Exeunt.*]

Scene 2. [*Olivia's house*]

[*Enter* **Sir Toby, Sir Andrew,** *and* **Fabian.**]

Andrew: No, faith, I'll not stay a jot longer.

Toby: Thy reason, dear venom; give thy
reason.

Fabian: You must needs yield your reason,
Sir Andrew.

Andrew: Marry, I saw your niece do more
favors to the Count's servingman than
ever she bestowed upon me. I saw't i' the
orchard.

Toby: Did she see thee the while, old boy?
Tell me that.   10

Andrew: As plain as I see you now.

Fabian: This was a great argument of love
in her toward you.

Andrew: 'Slight![1] will you make an ass o'
me?

Fabian: I will prove it legitimate, sir, upon
the oaths of judgment and reason.

Toby: And they have been grand-jurymen
since before Noah was a sailor.

Fabian: She did show favor to the youth
in your sight only to exasperate you, to   20
awake your dormouse valor, to put fire
in your heart and brimstone in your liver.
You should then have accosted her; and
with some excellent jests, fire-new from
the mint, you should have banged the
youth into dumbness. This was looked for
at your hand, and this was balked. The
double gilt of this opportunity you let time
wash off, and you are now sailed into the
North of my lady's opinion, where you
will hang like an icicle on a Dutchman's
beard unless you do redeem it by some   30
laudable attempt either of valor or policy.

Andrew: An't be any way, it must be with
valor; for policy I hate. I had as lief be
a Brownist[2] as a politician.

Toby: Why then, build me thy fortunes
upon the basis of valor. Challenge me the
Count's youth to fight with him; hurt him
in eleven places. My niece shall take note

---

[29] Despite.
[30] Do not, from my avowal, assume that you have no need
to woo (i.e., that I will give myself too easily); rather assume that, although it is good to woo, love freely given
is better.

---

[1] By God's light.
[2] Member of a puritanical religious sect founded by Robert
Brown; the sect was a frequent subject for satire.

of it; and assure thyself there is no love-broker in the world can more prevail in man's commendation with woman than report of valor. 40

Fabian: There is no way but this, Sir Andrew.

Andrew: Will either of you bear me a challenge to him?

Toby: Go, write it in a martial hand. Be curst[3] and brief; it is no matter how witty, so it be eloquent and full of invention. Taunt him with the license of ink. If thou thou'st[4] him some thrice, it shall not be amiss; and as many lies as will lie in thy sheet of paper, although the sheet were 50 big enough for the bed of Ware[5] in England, set 'em down. Go, about it! Let there be gall enough in thy ink, though thou write with a goose-pen, no matter. About it!

Andrew: Where shall I find you?

Toby: We'll call thee at the cubiculo.[6] Go.   [*Exit* **Sir Andrew.**]

Fabian: This is a dear manikin[7] to you, Sir Toby.

Toby: I have been dear to him, lad—some two thousand strong, or so.[8]

Fabian: We shall have a rare letter from 60 him—but you'll not deliver't?

Toby: Never trust me then; and by all means stir on the youth to an answer. I think oxen and wainropes cannot hale them together. For Andrew, if he were opened, and you find so much blood in his liver as will clog the foot of a flea, I'll eat the rest of the anatomy.

Fabian: And his opposite, the youth, bears in his visage no great presage of cruelty.
                    [*Enter* **Maria.**]

Toby: Look where the youngest wren of 70 mine comes.

Maria: If you desire the spleen,[9] and will laugh yourselves into stitches, follow me. Yond gull Malvolio is turned heathen, a very renegado; for there is no Christian that means to be saved by believing rightly can ever believe such impossible passages of grossness.[10] He's in yellow stockings!

Toby: And cross-gartered?

Maria: Most villainously; like a pedant that 80 keeps a school i' the church. I have dogged him like his murderer. He does obey every point of the letter that I dropped to betray him. He does smile his face into more lines than is in the new map with the augmentation of the Indies.[11] You have not seen such a thing as 'tis. I can hardly forbear hurling things at him. I know my lady will strike him. If she do, he'll smile, and take't for a great favor.

Toby: Come bring us, bring us where he is! 90

                    [*Exeunt omnes.*]

Scene 3. [*A street*]

                    [*Enter* **Sebastian** *and* **Antonio.**]

Sebastian: I would not by my will have troubled you;
But since you make your pleasure of your pains,
I will no further chide you.

Antonio: I could not stay behind you. My desire,
More sharp than filed steel, did spur me forth;
And not all love to see you (though so much
As might have drawn one to a longer voyage)

---

3 Surly.
4 Second person singular pronouns were used when speaking to social inferiors.
5 This famous bed was 10 feet, 9 inches square.
6 I.e., Sir Andrew's room, which was evidently quite small.
7 Doll, or toy.
8 I have cost him some two thousand ducats.

9 Fit of laughter.
10 Acts of absurdity.
11 A recently published map that was attracting considerable attention at the time this play was written.

But jealousy[1] what might befall your
    travel,
Being skilless in these parts; which to a
    stranger,
Unguided and unfriended, often prove   10
Rough and unhospitable. My willing
    love,
The rather by these arguments of fear,
Set forth in your pursuit.
Sebastian: My kind Antonio,
I can no other answer make but thanks,
And thanks, and ever thanks. Too oft
    good turns
Are shuffled off with such
    uncurrent[2] pay;
But, were my worth as is my conscience
    firm,
You should find better dealing. What's
    to do?
Shall we go see the relics of this town?
Antonio: Tomorrow, sir; best first go see
    your lodging.   20
Sebastian: I am not weary, and 'tis long
    to night.
I pray you let us satisfy our eyes
With the memorials and the things of
    fame
That do renown this city.
Antonio: Would you'ld pardon me.
I do not without danger walk these
    streets.
Once in a sea-fight 'gainst the Count
    his galleys
I did some service; of such note indeed
That, were I ta'en here, it would scarce
    be answered.[3]
Sebastian: Belike you slew great number
    of his people?
Antonio: The offense is not of such a
    bloody nature,   30

Albeit the quality of the time and
    quarrel
Might well have given us bloody
    argument.
It might have since been answered in
    repaying
What we took from them, which for
    traffic's sake
Most of our city did. Only myself stood
    out;
For which, if I be lapsed[4] in this place,
I shall pay dear.
Sebastian: Do not then walk too open.
Antonio: It doth not fit me. Hold, sir,
    here's my purse.
In the south suburbs at the Elephant[5]
Is best to lodge. I will bespeak our diet,   40
Whiles you beguile the time and feed
    your knowledge
With viewing of the town. There shall
    you have me.
Sebastian: Why I your purse?
Antonio: Haply your eye shall light
    upon some toy
You have desire to purchase; and your
    store
I think is not for idle markets,
    sir.[6]
Sebastian: I'll be your purse-bearer, and
    leave you for
An hour.
Antonio: To the Elephant.
Sebastian: I do remember.
                         [*Exeunt.*]

Scene 4. [Olivia's garden]

    [*Enter* **Olivia** *and* **Maria.**]
Olivia: I have sent after him; he says
    he'll come.

---

[1] Apprehension.
[2] Nonnegotiable.
[3] I would be in great trouble.

[4] Caught.
[5] The name of an inn.
[6] You haven't enough money for frivolous purchases.

How shall I feast him? what bestow of
him?
For youth is bought more oft than
begged or borrowed.
I speak too loud.
Where is Malvolio? He is sad[1] and civil,
And suits well for a servant with my
fortunes.
Where is Malvolio?

Maria: He's coming, madam; but in very
strange manner. He is sure possessed,
madam.

Olivia: Why, what's the matter? Does he
rave?   10

Maria: No, madam, he does nothing but
smile. Your ladyship were best to have
some guard about you if he come, for sure
the man is tainted in's wits.

Olivia: Go call him hither. [*Exit* **Maria**] I
am as mad as he,
If sad and merry madness equal be.
    [*Enter* (**Maria,** *with*) **Malvolio**]
How now, Malvolio?

Malvolio: Sweet lady, ho, ho!

Olivia: Smilest thou?
I sent for thee upon a sad occasion.   20

Malvolio: Sad, lady? I could be sad. This
does make some obstruction in the blood,
this cross-gartering; but what of that? If
it please the eye of one, it is with me as
the very true sonnet is, "Please one, and
please all."

Olivia: Why, how dost thou, man? What
is the matter with thee?

Malvolio: Not black in my mind, though
yellow in my legs. It did come to his
hands, and commands shall be executed.
I think we do know the sweet Roman   30
hand.[2]

Olivia: Wilt thou go to bed, Malvolio?

Malvolio: To bed? Ay, sweetheart; and I'll
come to thee.

Olivia: God comfort thee! Why dost thou
smile so, and kiss thy hand so oft?

Maria: How do you, Malvolio?

Malvolio: At your request? Yes, nightingales answer daws![3]

Maria: Why appear you with this ridicu- 40
lous boldness before my lady?

Malvolio: "Be not afraid of greatness."
'Twas well writ.

Olivia: What meanst thou by that, Malvolio?

Malvolio: "Some are born great"—

Olivia: Ha?

Malvolio: "Some achieve greatness"—

Olivia: What sayst thou?

Malvolio: "And some have greatness thrust
upon them."   50

Olivia: Heaven restore thee!

Malvolio: "Remember who commended
thy yellow stockings"—

Olivia: Thy yellow stockings?

Malvolio: "And wished to see thee cross-
gartered."

Olivia: Cross-gartered?

Malvolio: "Go to, thou art made, if thou
desirest to be so"—

Olivia: Am I made?

Malvolio: "If not, let me see thee a servant
still."   60

Olivia: Why, this is very midsummer madness.
    [*Enter* **Servant.**]

Servant: Madam, the young gentleman of
the Count Orsino's is returned. I could
hardly entreat him back. He attends your
ladyship's pleasure.

Olivia: I'll come to him. [*Exit Servant*] Good
Maria, let this fellow be looked to.
Where's my cousin Toby? Let some of my

---

[1] Serious.
[2] Handwriting.

[3] Ironic; Malvolio does not intend even to answer a question
from Maria, a mere servant.

people have a special care of him. I would not have him miscarry⁴ for the half of my dowry.   [*Exit* (**Olivia**; *then* **Maria**).]   70

Malvolio: O ho! do you come near⁵ me now? No worse man than Sir Toby to look to me! This concurs directly with the letter. She sends him on purpose, that I may appear stubborn to him; for she incites me to that in the letter. "Cast thy humble slough," says she; "be opposite with a kinsman, surly with servants; let thy tongue tang with arguments of state; put thyself into the trick of singularity";—and consequently sets down the manner how: as, a sad face, a reverend carriage, a slow 80 tongue, in the habit⁶ of some sir of note, and so forth. I have limed⁷ her; but it is Jove's doing, and Jove make me thankful! And when she went away now, "Let this fellow be looked to." "Fellow!" not "Malvolio," nor after my degree, but "fellow." Why, everything adheres together, that no dram of a scruple, no scruple of a scruple, no obstacle, no incredulous or unsafe circumstance—What can be said? Nothing that can be can come between me and the full prospect of my hopes. Well, Jove, 90 not I, is the doer of this, and he is to be thanked.

[*Enter (Sir)* **Toby**, **Fabian**, *and* **Maria**.]

Toby: Which way is he, in the name of sanctity? If all the devils of hell be drawn in little, and Legion⁸ himself possessed him, yet I'll speak to him.

Fabian: Here he is, here he is! How is't with you, sir? How is't with you, man?

Malvolio: Go off; I discard you. Let me enjoy my private. Go off.   100

Maria: Lo, how hollow the fiend speaks within him! Did not I tell you? Sir Toby,

my lady prays you to have a care of him.

Malvolio: Aha! does she so?

Toby: Go to, go to; peace, peace! We must deal gently with him. Let me alone. How do you, Malvolio? How is't with you? What, man! defy the devil! Consider, he's an enemy to mankind.

Malvolio: Do you know what you say?   110

Maria: La you, an you speak ill of the devil, how he takes it at heart! Pray God he be not bewitched!

Fabian: Carry his water to the wise woman.⁹

Maria: Marry, and it shall be done tomorrow morning if I live. My lady would not lose him for more than I'll say.

Malvolio: How now, mistress?

Maria: O Lord!

Toby: Prithee hold thy peace. This is not 120 the way. Do you not see you move him? Let me alone with him.

Fabian: No way but gentleness; gently, gently. The fiend is rough and will not be roughly used.

Toby: Why, how now, my bawcock?¹⁰ How dost thou, chuck?¹¹

Malvolio: Sir!

Toby: Ay, biddy,¹² come with me. What, man! 'tis not for gravity to play at cherry-pit with Satan.¹³ Hang him, foul collier!¹⁴ 130

Maria: Get him to say his prayers. Good Sir Toby, get him to pray.

Malvolio: My prayers, minx?

Maria: No, I warrant you, he will not hear of godliness.

Malvolio: Go hang yourselves all! You are idle shallow things; I am not of your element. You shall know more hereafter.

[*Exit.*]

---

⁴ Come to grief.
⁵ Understand.
⁶ Clothing.
⁷ Caught; as a bird was caught with birdlime.
⁸ See *Mark* 5:9. It was Elizabethan belief that madness was, in fact, possession by the Devil.

⁹ I.e., for urinalysis.
¹⁰ Term of affection.
¹¹ Term of affection.
¹² Term of affection.
¹³ A grave man should not play games with Satan.
¹⁴ A coal dealer, and hence black; the Devil.

Toby: Is't possible?

Fabian: If this were played upon a stage   140
now, I could condemn it as an improbable
fiction.

Toby: His very genius hath taken the infection of the device,[15] man.

Maria: Nay, pursue him now, lest the device take air and taint.[16]

Fabian: Why, we shall make him mad indeed.

Maria: The house will be the quieter.

Toby: Come, we'll have him in a dark room
and bound.[17] My niece is already in the
belief that he's mad. We may carry it thus,   150
for our pleasure and his penance, till our
very pastime, tired out of breath, prompt
us to have mercy on him; at which time
we will bring the device to the bar and
crown thee for a finder of madmen. But
see, but see!

[*Enter* **Sir Andrew.**]

Fabian: More matter for a May morning.

Andrew: Here's the challenge; read it. I
warrant there's vinegar and pepper in't.

Fabian: Is't so saucy?

Andrew: Ay, is't, I warrant him. Do but   160
read.

Toby: Give me. [*Reads*] "Youth, whatsoever
thou art, thou art but a scurvy fellow."

Fabian: Good, and valiant.

Toby: [*Reads*] "Wonder not nor admire not
in thy mind why I do call thee so, for
I will show thee no reason for't."

Fabian: A good note! That keeps you from
the blow of the law.

Toby: [*Reads*] "Thou comest to the Lady   170
Olivia, and in my sight she uses thee
kindly. But thou liest in thy throat; that
is not the matter I challenge thee for."

Fabian: Very brief, and to exceeding good
sense—less.

Toby: [*Reads*] "I will waylay thee going
home; where if it be thy chance to kill
me"—

Fabian: Good.

Toby: [*Reads*] "Thou killst me like a rogue
and a villain."   180

Fabian: Still you keep o' the windy side
of the law. Good.

Toby: [*Reads*] "Fare thee well, and God have
mercy upon one of our souls! He may have
mercy upon mine, but my hope is better;
and so look to thyself. Thy friend, as thou
usest him, and thy sworn enemy,

"ANDREW AGUECHEEK."

If this letter move him not, his legs cannot.
I'll give't him.

Maria: You may have very fit occasion   190
for't. He is now in some commerce with
my lady and will by-and-by depart.

Toby: Go, Sir Andrew! Scout me for him
at the corner of the orchard like a bum-
baily.[18] So soon as ever thou seest him,
draw; and as thou drawst, swear horrible;
for it comes to pass oft that a terrible oath,
with a swaggering accent sharply twanged
off, gives manhood more approbation than
ever proof[19] itself would have earned him.
Away!   200

Andrew: Nay, let me alone for swearing.

[*Exit.*]

Toby: Now will not I deliver his letter; for
the behavior of the young gentleman gives
him out to be of good capacity and breeding; his employment between his lord and
my niece confirms no less. Therefore this
letter, being so excellently ignorant, will
breed no terror in the youth. He will find
it comes from a clodpoll. But, sir, I will
deliver his challenge by word of mouth,
set upon Aguecheek a notable report of   210
valor, and drive the gentleman (as I know

---

[15] His very soul has caught the infection of our plot.
[16] By exposure to the air, spoil (i.e., be discovered).
[17] Madmen were simply locked in a prison for lack of more
effective treatment.

[18] A bailiff that is close behind the debtor's back.
[19] Trial.

his youth will aptly receive it) into a most hideous opinion of his rage, skill, fury, and impetuosity. This will so fright them both that they will kill one another by the look, like cockatrices.[20]

[*Enter* **Olivia** *and* **Viola.**]

Fabian: Here he comes with your niece. Give them way till he take leave, and presently after him.

Toby: I will meditate the while upon some horrid message for a challenge.   220

[*Exeunt* **Sir Toby, Fabian,** *and* **Maria.**]

Olivia: I have said too much unto a
    heart of stone
And laid mine honor too unchary[21] out.
There's something in me that reproves
    my fault;
But such a headstrong potent fault it is
That it but mocks reproof.

Viola: With the same 'havior that your
    passion bears
Goes on my master's grief.

Olivia: Here, wear this jewel for me; 'tis
    my picture.
Refuse it not; it hath no tongue to vex
    you.
And I beseech you come again
    tomorrow.   230
What shall you ask of me that I'll deny,
That honor, saved, may upon asking
    give?

Viola: Nothing but this—your true love for
    my master.

Olivia: How with mine honor may I give
    him that
Which I have given to you?

Viola: I will acquit you.

Olivia: Well, come again tomorrow. Fare
    thee well.
A fiend like thee might bear my soul
    to hell.   [*Exit.*]

[*Enter (Sir)* **Toby** *and* **Fabian.**]

Toby: Gentleman, God save thee!

Viola: And you, sir.

Toby: That defense thou hast, betake thee 240
to't. Of what nature the wrongs are thou
hast done him, I know not; but thy inter-
cepter, full of despite, bloody as the
hunter, attends thee at the orchard end.
Dismount thy tuck,[22] be yare[23] in thy preparation; for thy assailant is quick, skillful,
and deadly.

Viola: You mistake, sir. I am sure no man
hath any quarrel to me. My remembrance
is very free and clear from any image of
offense done to any man.   250

Toby: You'll find it otherwise, I assure you.
Therefore, if you hold your life at any
price, betake you to your guard; for your
opposite hath in him what youth, strength,
skill, and wrath can furnish man withal.

Viola: I pray you, sir, what is he?

Toby: He is knight, dubbed with un-
hatched[24] rapier and on carpet consideration;[25] but he is a devil in private brawl.
Souls and bodies hath he divorced three;
and his incensement at this moment is so 260
implacable that satisfaction can be none
but by pangs of death and sepulcher.
"Hob, nob" is his word; "give't or take't."

Viola: I will return again into the house
and desire some conduct[26] of the lady. I
am no fighter. I have heard of some kind
of men that put quarrels purposely on
others to taste their valor. Belike this is
a man of that quirk.

Toby: Sir, no. His indignation derives itself
out of a very competent injury; therefore 270
get you on and give him his desire. Back
you shall not to the house, unless you
undertake that with me which with as

---

[20] Serpents supposed to kill merely by a glance.
[21] Generously.

[22] Draw thy sword.
[23] Quick.
[24] Unhacked.
[25] Dubbed on a carpet for money, rather than on a battlefield for valor.
[26] Escort.

much safety you might answer him. Therefore on! or strip your sword stark naked; for meddle you must, that's certain, or forswear to wear iron about you.

Viola: This is as uncivil as strange. I beseech you do me this courteous office, as to know of the knight what my offense to him is. It is something of my negligence, nothing of my purpose.   280

Toby: I will do so. Signior Fabian, stay you by this gentleman till my return.   [*Exit.*]

Viola: Pray you, sir, do you know of this matter?

Fabian: I know the knight is incensed against you, even to a mortal arbitrament;[27] but nothing of the circumstance more.

Viola: I beseech you, what manner of man is he?

Fabian: Nothing of that wonderful prom- 290 ise, to read him by his form, as you are like to find him in the proof of his valor. He is indeed, sir, the most skillful, bloody, and fatal opposite that you could possibly have found in any part of Illyria. Will you walk towards him? I will make your peace with him if I can.

Viola: I shall be much bound to you for't. I am one that had rather go with sir priest than sir knight. I care not who knows so much of my mettle.   [*Exeunt.*] 300

[*Enter (Sir)* **Toby** *and (Sir)* **Andrew.**]

Toby: Why, man, he's a very devil; I have not seen such a virago.[28] I had a pass with him, rapier, scabbard, and all, and he gives me the stuck-in with such a mortal motion that it is inevitable; and on the answer he pays you as surely as your feet hit the ground they step on. They say he has been fencer to the Sophy.

Andrew: Pox on't, I'll not meddle with him.

Toby: Ay, but he will not now be pacified. Fabian can scarce hold him yonder.   310

Andrew: Plague on't, an I thought he had been valiant, and so cunning in fence, I'd have seen him damned ere I'd have challenged him. Let him let the matter slip, and I'll give him my horse, grey Capilet.

Toby: I'll make the motion.[29] Stand here; make a good show on't. This shall end without the perdition of souls. [*Aside*] Marry, I'll ride your horse as well as I ride you.

[*Enter* **Fabian** *and* **Viola**]

I have his horse to take up[30] the quarrel. 320 I have persuaded him the youth's a devil.

Fabian: He is as horribly conceited[31] of him; and pants and looks pale, as if a bear were at his heels.

Toby: There's no remedy, sir; he will fight with you for's oath sake. Marry, he hath better bethought him of his quarrel, and he finds that now scarce to be worth talking of. Therefore draw for the supportance of his vow. He protests he will not hurt you.   330

Viola: [*Aside*] Pray God defend me! A little thing would make me tell them how much I lack of a man.

Fabian: Give ground if you see him furious.

Toby: Come, Sir Andrew, there's no remedy. The gentleman will for his honor's sake have one bout with you; he cannot by the duello[32] avoid it; but he has promised me, as he is a gentleman and a soldier, he will not hurt you. Come on, to't! 340

Andrew: Pray God he keep his oath!

[*Draws.*]

[*Enter* **Antonio.**][33]

---

[27] Trial.
[28] Amazon. Sir Toby refers simply to great strength, but the audience knows that "Caesario" is actually a woman.

---

[29] Offer.
[30] Settle.
[31] Has as horrible a conception.
[32] Dueling code.
[33] Traditionally, there is an extended mock duel between the two unwilling antagonists before Antonio actually enters to interrupt it.

Viola: I do assure you 'tis against my
will. [*Draws.*]

Antonio: Put up your sword. If this
young gentleman
Have done offense, I take the fault on me;
If you offend him, I for him defy you.

Toby: You, sir? Why, what are you?

Antonio: [*Draws*] One, sir, that for his
love dares yet do more
Than you have heard him brag to you
he will.

Toby: Nay, if you be an undertaker,[34] I
am for you.   [*Draws.*] 350
[*Enter* **Officers.**]

Fabian: O good sir Toby, hold! Here come
the officers.

Toby: I'll be with you anon.

Viola: Pray, sir, put your sword up, if you
please.

Andrew: Marry, will I, sir; and for that I
promised you, I'll be as good as my word.
He[35] will bear you easily, and reins well.

First Officer: This is the man; do thy
office.

Second Officer: Antonio, I arrest thee at
the suit   360
Of Count Orsino.

Antonio: You do mistake me, sir.

First Officer: No, sir, no jot. I know
your favor well,
Though now you have no sea-cap on
your head.
Take him away. He knows I know him
well.

Antonio: I must obey. [*To* **Viola**] This
comes with seeking you.
But there's no remedy; I shall answer it.
What will you do, now my necessity
Makes me to ask you for my purse? It
grieves me
Much more for what I cannot do for you 370
Than what befalls myself. You stand
amazed,

But be of comfort.

Second Officer: Come, sir, away.

Antonio: I must entreat of you some of
that money.

Viola: What money, sir?
For the fair kindness you have showed
me here,
And part being prompted by your
present trouble,
Out of my lean and low ability
I'll lend you something. My having is
not much.
I'll make division of my present[36] with
you.   380
Hold, there's half my coffer.

Antonio: Will you deny me now?
Is't possible that my deserts to you
Can lack persuasion? Do not tempt my
misery,
Lest that it make me so unsound a man
As to upbraid you with those
kindnesses
That I have done for you.

Viola: I know of none,
Nor know I you by voice or any
feature.
I hate ingratitude more in a man
Than lying, vainness, babbling
drunkenness,
Or any taint of vice whose strong
corruption   390
Inhabits our frail blood.

Antonio: O heavens themselves!

Second Officer: Come, sir, I pray you
go.

Antonio: Let me speak a little. This
youth that you see here
I snatched one half out of the jaws of
death;
Relieved him with such sanctity of love,
And to his image, which methought did
promise
Most venerable worth, did I devotion.

---

[34] One who undertakes (in this case, meddles).
[35] The horse, grey Capilet.

[36] Present means.

First Officer: What's that to us? The
time goes by. Away!

Antonio: But, O, how vile an idol proves
this god!

Thou hast, Sebastian, <u>done good feature
shame</u>.[37]   400

In nature there's no blemish but the
mind;

None can be called deformed but the
unkind.

Virtue is beauty; but the beauteous
<u>evil</u>[38]

Are empty trunks, o'erflourished[39] by
the devil.

First Officer: The man grows mad.
Away with him!

Come, come, sir.

Antonio: Lead me on. [*Exit* (*with* **Officers**).]

Viola: Methinks his words do from such
passion fly

That he believes himself; so do not I.

Prove true, imagination, O, prove true,

That I, dear brother, be now ta'en for
you!   410

Toby: Come hither, knight; come hither,
Fabian.

We'll whisper o'er a couplet or two of
most sage saws.

Viola: He named Sebastian. <u>I my
brother know</u>

<u>Yet living in my glass</u>.[40] Even such and
so

In favor was my brother, and <u>he went
Still in this fashion, color, ornament</u>,[41]

For him I imitate. O, if it <u>prove</u>,[42]

Tempests are kind, and salt waves fresh
in love!   [*Exit.*]

Toby: A very dishonest paltry boy, and   420

---

[37] Belied your good appearance.
[38] Evil persons.
[39] Decorated.
[40] I seem to see my brother living again each time I look
in my mirror.
[41] Viola notes that she has dressed herself exactly as her
brother used to dress.
[42] Prove true.

more a coward than a hare. His dishonesty
appears in leaving his friend here in necessity and denying him; and for his cow-
ardship, ask Fabian.

Fabian: A coward, a most devout coward;
religious in it.

Andrew: <u>Slid</u>,[43] I'll after him again and beat
him!

Toby: Do; cuff him soundly, but never
draw thy sword.

Andrew: An I do not—   [*Exit.*] 430

Fabian: Come, let's see the event.

Toby: I dare lay any money 'twill be
nothing yet.   [*Exeunt.*]

ACT IV

Scene 1. [Before Olivia's house]

[*Enter* **Sebastian** *and* **Clown.**]

Clown: Will you make me believe that I
am not sent for you?

Sebastian: Go to, go to, thou art a foolish
fellow. Let me be clear of thee.

Clown: Well held out, i' faith! No, I do not
know you; nor I am not sent to you by
my lady, to bid you come speak with her;
nor your name is not Master Cesario; nor
this is not my nose neither. Nothing that
is so is so.

Sebastian: I prithee vent thy folly some-   10
where else. Thou knowst not me.

Clown: Vent my folly! He has heard that
word of some great man, and now applies
it to a fool. Vent my folly! I am afraid this
great lubber, the world, will prove a cock-
ney.[1] I prithee now, <u>ungird thy strange-
ness</u>,[2] and tell me what <u>I shall vent to my
lady</u>. Shall I vent to her that thou art coming?

---

[43] By God's eyelid.

---

[1] Fop.
[2] Stop acting like a stranger.

Sebastian: I prithee, foolish Greek, depart from me.

There's money for thee. If you tarry longer,   20

I shall give worse payment.

Clown: By my troth, thou hast an open hand. These wise men that give fools money get themselves a good report—after fourteen years' purchase.[3]

[Enter (Sir) Andrew, (Sir) Toby, and Fabian.]

Andrew: Now, sir, have I met you again? There's for you!

[Striking Sebastian.]

Sebastian: Why, there's for thee, and there, and there!

[Returning the blow.]

Are all the people mad?

Toby: Hold, sir, or I'll throw your dagger 30
o'er the house.

Clown: This will I tell my lady straight.[4]
I would not be in some of your coats for twopence.   *[Exit.]*

Toby: Come on, sir; hold!

Andrew: Nay, let him alone. I'll go another way to work with him. I'll have an action of battery against him, if there be any law in Illyria. Though I stroke him first, yet it's no matter for that.

Sebastian: Let go thy hand.   40

Toby: Come, sir, I will not let you go. Come, my young soldier, put up your iron. You are well fleshed. Come on.

Sebastian: I will be free from thee. What wouldst thou now?

If thou darest tempt me further, draw thy sword.

Toby: What, what? Nay then, I must have an ounce or two of this malapert[5] blood from you.   *[Draws.]*

[Enter Olivia.]

Olivia: Hold, Toby! On thy life I charge thee hold!

Toby: Madam!   50

Olivia: Will it be ever thus? Ungracious wretch,

Fit for the mountains and the barbarous caves,

Where manners ne'er were preached! Out of my sight!

Be not offended, dear Cesario.

Rudesby,[6] be gone!

[Exeunt Sir Toby, Sir Andrew, and Fabian.]

I prithee, gentle friend,

Let thy fair wisdom, not thy passion, sway

In this uncivil and unjust extent[7]

Against thy peace. Go with me to my house,

And hear thou there how many fruitless pranks

This ruffian hath botched up, that thou thereby   60

Mayst smile at this. Thou shalt not choose but go;

Do not deny. Beshrew his soul for me!

He started one poor heart of mine,[8] in thee.

Sebastian: What relish[9] is in this? How runs the stream?

Or I am mad, or else this is a dream.

Let fancy still my sense in Lethe[10] steep;

If it be thus to dream, still let me sleep!

Olivia: Nay, come, I prithee. Would thou'dst be ruled by me!

Sebastian: Madam, I will.

Olivia: O, say so, and so be!

[Exeunt.]

---

[3] At a high price.
[4] Immediately.
[5] Insolent.
[6] Ruffian.
[7] Attack.
[8] Roused my heart (with a pun on flushing out a hart in hunting).
[9] Meaning.
[10] The river of forgetfulness in Hades.

Scene 2. [*Olivia's house*]

[*Enter* **Maria** *and* **Clown**.]

Maria: Nay, I prithee put on this gown and this beard; make him believe thou art Sir Topas the curate; do it quickly. I'll call Sir Toby the whilst.   [*Exit.*]

Clown: Well, I'll put it on, and I will dissemble myself in't, and I would I were the first that ever dissembled in such a gown. I am not tall enough to become the function well, nor lean enough to be thought a good student; but to be said an honest man and a good housekeeper goes as fairly   10 as to say a careful man and a great scholar. The competitors[1] enter.

[*Enter (Sir)* **Toby** *(and* **Maria**).]

Toby: Jove bless thee, Master Parson.

Clown: *Bonos dies*[2] Sir Toby; for, as the old hermit of Prague, that never saw pen and ink, very wittily said to a niece of King Gorboduc, "That that is is"; so I, being Master Parson, am Master Parson; for what is "that" but "that," and "is" but "is"?[3]

Toby: To him, Sir Topas.   20

Clown: What ho, I say. Peace in this prison!

Toby: The knave counterfeits well; a good knave.

[**Malvolio** *within*.]

Malvolio: Who calls there?

Clown: Sir Topas the curate, who comes to visit Malvolio the lunatic.

Malvolio: Sir Topas, Sir Topas, good Sir Topas, go to my lady.

Clown: Out, hyperbolical[4] fiend! How vexest thou this man! Talkest thou nothing but of ladies?   30

Toby: Well said, Master Parson.

Malvolio: Sir Topas, never was man thus

wronged. Good Sir Topas, do not think I am mad. They have laid me here in hideous darkness.

Clown: Fie, thou dishonest Satan! I call thee by the most modest terms; for I am one of those gentle ones that will use the Devil himself with courtesy. Sayst thou that house is dark?

Malvolio: As hell, Sir Topas.

Clown: Why, it hath bay windows trans-   40 parent as barricadoes,[5] and the clerestories[6] toward the south north are as lustrous as ebony; and yet complainest thou of obstruction?

Malvolio: I am not mad, Sir Topas. I say to you this house is dark.

Clown: Madman, thou errest. I say there is no darkness but ignorance, in which thou art more puzzled than the Egyptians in their fog.[7]

Malvolio: I say this house is as dark as ignorance, though ignorance were as dark   50 as hell; and I say there was never man thus abused. I am no more mad than you are. Make the trial of it in any constant[8] question.

Clown: What is the opinion of Pythagoras concerning wild fowl?

Malvolio: That the soul of our grandam might happily inhabit a bird.

Clown: What thinkst thou of his opinion?

Malvolio: I think nobly of the soul and no way approve his opinion.   60

Clown: Fare thee well. Remain thou still in darkness. Thou shalt hold the opinion of Pythagoras ere I will allow of thy wits, and fear to kill a woodcock, lest thou dispossess the soul of thy grandam. Fare thee well.

Malvolio: Sir Topas, Sir Topas!

---

[1] Confederates.
[2] Good day.
[3] Nonsense, supposed to appear learned.
[4] Excessive.

[5] Barricades (not transparent at all).
[6] High windows.
[7] See *Exodus* 10:21.
[8] Logical.

Toby: My most exquisite Sir Topas!

Clown: Nay, I am for all waters.[9]

Malvolio: Thou mightst have done this without thy beard and gown. He sees thee not.   70

Toby: To him in thine own voice, and bring me word how thou findst him. I would we were well rid of this knavery. If he may be conveniently delivered, I would he were; for I am now so far in offense with my niece that I cannot pursue with any safety this sport to the upshot. Come by-and-by to my chamber.

[*Exit* (*with* **Maria**).]

Clown: [*Singing*] "Hey, Robin, jolly Robin, Tell me how thy lady does."

Malvolio: Fool!   80

Clown: "My lady is unkind, perdie!"

Malvolio: Fool!

Clown: "Alas, why is she so?"

Malvolio: Fool, I say!

Clown: "She loves another"—Who calls, ha?

Malvolio: Good fool, as ever thou wilt deserve well at my hand, help me to a candle, and pen, ink, and paper. As I am a gentleman, I will live to be thankful to thee for't.

Clown: Master Malvolio?   90

Malvolio: Ay, good fool.

Clown: Alas, sir, how fell you besides your five wits?

Malvolio: Fool, there was never man so notoriously abused. I am as well in my wits, fool, as thou art.

Clown: But as well? Then you are mad indeed, if you be no better in your wits than a fool.

Malvolio: They have here propertied me;[10] keep me in darkness, send ministers to   100 me, asses, and do all they can to face me out of my wits.

Clown: Advise you what you say. The minister is here.[11]—Malvolio, Malvolio, thy wits the heavens restore! Endeavor thyself to sleep and leave thy vain bibble babble.

Malvolio: Sir Topas!

Clown: Maintain no words with him, good fellow.—Who, I, sir? Not I, sir. God be wi' you, good Sir Topas!—Marry, amen.—I will, sir, I will.

Malvolio: Fool, fool, fool, I say!   110

Clown: Alas, sir, be patient. What say you, sir? I am shent[12] for speaking to you.

Malvolio: Good fool, help me to some light and some paper. I tell thee, I am as well in my wits as any man in Illyria.

Clown: Well-a-day that you were, sir!

Malvolio: By this hand, I am. Good fool, some ink, paper, and light; and convey what I will set down to my lady. It shall advantage thee more than ever the bearing of letter did.   120

Clown: I will help you to't. But tell me true, are you not mad indeed? or do you but counterfeit?

Malvolio: Believe me, I am not. I tell thee true.

Clown: Nay, I'll ne'er believe a madman till I see his brains. I will fetch you light and paper and ink.

Malvolio: Fool, I'll requite it in the highest degree. I prithee be gone.

Clown: [*Singing*]
    I am gone, sir;   130
    And anon, sir,
  I'll be with you again,
    In a trice,
    Like to the old Vice,[13]
  Your need to sustain;
  Who, with dagger of lath,

---

[9] I can do anything.

[10] Treated me as property.

[11] Feste speaks alternately in his own voice and in that of Sir Topas.

[12] Reproved.

[13] A comic figure in the Morality plays who, with his wooden dagger, attempted to pare the Devil's nails.

In his rage and his wrath,
  Cries "aha!" to the Devil.
Like a mad lad,
  "Pare thy nails, dad."   140
  Adieu, goodman Devil.

                  [*Exit.*]

Scene 3. [*Olivia's garden*]

      [*Enter* **Sebastian.**]

Sebastian: This is the air; that is the
  glorious sun;
This pearl she gave me, I do feel't and
  see't;
And though 'tis wonder that enwraps
  me thus,
Yet 'tis not madness. Where's Antonio
  then?
I could not find him at the Elephant;
Yet there he was; and there I found this
  credit,[1]
That he did range the town to seek me
  out.
His counsel now might do me golden
  service;
For though my soul disputes well with
  my sense
That this may be some error, but no
  madness,   10
Yet doth this accident and flood of
  fortune
So far exceed all instance,[2] all
  discourse,[3]
That I am ready to distrust mine eyes
And wrangle with my reason, that
  persuades me
To any other trust[4] but that I am mad,
Or else the lady's mad. Yet, if 'twere
  so,

She could not sway[5] her house,
  command her followers,
Take and give back affairs and their
  dispatch[6]
With such a smooth, discreet, and
  stable bearing
As I perceive she does. There's
  something in't   20
That is deceivable.[7] But here the lady
  comes.

      [*Enter* **Olivia** *and* **Priest.**]

Olivia: Blame not this haste of mine. If
  you mean well,
Now go with me and with this holy
  man
Into the chantry[8] by. There, before him,
And underneath that consecrated roof,
Plight me the full assurance of your
  faith,
That my most jealous and too doubtful
  soul
My live at peace. He shall conceal it
Whiles[9] you are willing it shall come to
  note,
What[10] time we will our celebration
  keep   30
According to my birth. What do you
  say?
Sebastian: I'll follow this good man and
  go with you
And having sworn truth, ever will be
  true.
Olivia: Then lead the way, good father;
  and heavens so shine
That they may fairly note this act of
  mine!

                  [*Exeunt.*]

---

[1] Belief.
[2] Previous example.
[3] Reason.
[4] Belief.
[5] Command.
[6] Undertake and discharge business.
[7] Deceptive.
[8] Chapel.
[9] Until.
[10] At which.

ACT V

Scene 1. [*Before Olivia's house*]

[*Enter* **Clown** *and* **Fabian.**]

Fabian: Now as thou lovest me, let me see his letter.

Clown: Good Master Fabian, grant me another request.

Fabian: Anything.

Clown: Do not desire to see this letter.

Fabian: This is to give a dog, and in recompense desire my dog again.

[*Enter* **Duke, Viola, Curio,** *and* **Lords.**]

Duke: Belong you to the Lady Olivia, friends?

Clown: Ay, sir, we are some of her trappings. 10

Duke: I know thee well. How dost thou, my good fellow?

Clown: Truly, sir, the better for my foes, and the worse for my friends.

Duke: Just the contrary: the better for thy friends.

Clown: No, sir, the worse.

Duke: How can that be?

Clown: Marry, sir, they praise me and make an ass of me. Now my foes tell me 20 plainly I am an ass; so that by my foes, sir, I profit in the knowledge of myself, and by my friends I am abused; so that, conclusions to be as kisses, if your four negatives make your two affirmatives, why then, the worse for my friends and the better for my foes.

Duke: Why, this is excellent.

Clown: By my troth, sir, no; though it please you to be one of my friends.

Duke: Thou shalt not be the worse for me. 30 There's gold.

Clown: But that it would be double-dealing, sir, I would you could make it another.

Duke: O, you give me ill counsel.

Clown: Put your grace in your pocket, sir, for this once, and let your flesh and blood obey it.

Duke: Well, I will be so much a sinner to be a double-dealer. There's another.

Clown: *Primo, secundo, tertio* is a good play; and the old saying is "The third pays 40 for all." The triplex,[1] sir, is a good tripping measure; or the bells of Saint Bennet, sir, may put you in mind—one, two, three.

Duke: You can fool no more money out of me at this throw. If you will let your lady know I am here to speak with her, and bring her along with you, it may awake my bounty further.

Clown: Marry, sir, lullaby to your bounty till I come again! I go, sir; but I would not have you to think that my desire of having 50 is the sin of covetousness. But, as you say, sir, let your bounty take a nap; I will awake it anon. [*Exit.*]

[*Enter* **Antonio** *and* **Officers.**]

Viola: Here comes the man, sir, that did rescue me.

Duke: That face of his I do remember well;
Yet when I saw it last, it was besmeared
As black as Vulcan[2] in the smoke of war.
A baubling[3] vessel was he captain of,
For shallow draught and bulk unprizable,[4]
With which such scathful[5] grapple did he make
With the most noble bottom[6] of our fleet 60
That very envy and the tongue of loss
Cried fame and honor on him. What's the matter?

First Officer: Orsino, this is that Antonio

---

[1] Triple time in music.
[2] The Roman god of war; a blacksmith.
[3] Trifling.
[4] Valueless.
[5] Damaging.
[6] Ship.

That took the "Phoenix" and her
   fraught[7] from Candy;[8]
And this is he that did the "Tiger"
   board
When your young nephew Titus lost
   his leg.
Here in the streets, <u>desperate of shame
   and state</u>,[9]
In private <u>brabble</u>[10] did we apprehend
   him.

Viola: He did me kindness, sir; drew on
   my side;
But in conclusion put strange speech
   upon me.   70
I know not what 'twas but distraction.

Duke: Notable pirate, thou salt-water
   thief!
What foolish boldness brought thee to
   their mercies
Whom thou in terms so bloody and so
   dear
Hast made thine enemies?

Antonio: Orsino, noble sir,
Be pleased that I shake off these names
   you give me.
Antonio never yet was thief or pirate,
Though I confess, on base and ground
   enough,
Orsino's enemy. A witchcraft drew me
   hither.
That most ingrateful boy there by your
   side   80
From the rude sea's enraged and foamy
   mouth
Did I redeem. A wrack past hope he
   was.
His life I gave him, and did thereto add
My love without retention or restraint,
All his in dedication. For his sake
Did I expose myself (pure for his love)

Into the danger of this adverse town;
Drew to defend him when he was
   beset;
Where being apprehended, his false
   cunning
(Not meaning to partake with me in
   danger)   90
Taught him to <u>face me out of his
   acquaintance</u>,[11]
And grew a twenty years removed thing
While one would wink; denied me
   mine own purse,
Which I had recommended to his use
Not half an hour before.

Viola: How can this be?

Duke: When came he to this town?

Antonio: Today, my lord; and for three
   months before,
No int'rim, not a minute's vacancy,
Both day and night did we keep
   company.

        [Enter **Olivia** *and* **Attendants.***]*

Duke: Here comes the Countess; now
   heaven walks on earth.   100
But for thee, fellow—fellow, thy words
   are madness.
Three months this youth hath tended
   upon me;
But more of that anon. Take him aside.

Olivia: What would my lord, but that
   he may not have,
Wherein Olivia may seem serviceable?
Cesario, you do not keep promise with
   me.

Viola: Madam!

Duke: Gracious Olivia—

Olivia: What do you say,
   Cesario?—Good my lord—

Viola: My lord would speak; my duty
   hushes me.   110

Olivia: If it be aught to the old tune, my
   lord,

---

[7] Freight.
[8] Crete.
[9] Unattentive to his reputation or his condition.
[10] Brawl.

[11] Pretend he didn't know me.

It is as fat and fulsome[12] to mine ear
As howling after music.
Duke: Still so cruel?
Olivia: Still so constant, lord.
Duke: What, to perverseness? You
   uncivil lady,
To whose ingrate and unauspicious
   altars
My soul the faithful'st off'rings hath
   breathed out
That e'er devotion tendered! What shall
   I do?
Olivia: Even what it please my lord, that
   shall become him.
Duke: Why should I not, had I the heart
   to do it,   120
Like to the Egyptian thief[13] at point of
   death,
Kill what I love?—a savage jealousy
That sometime savors nobly. But hear
   me this:
Since you to non-regardance cast my
   faith,
And that I partly know the instrument[14]
That screws me from my true place in
   your favor,
Live you the marble-breasted tyrant
   still.
But this your minion,[15] whom I know
   you love,
And whom, by heaven I swear, I tender
   dearly,
Him will I tear out of that cruel eye   130
Where he sits crowned in his master's
   spite,[16]
Come, boy, with me. My thoughts are
   ripe in mischief.
I'll sacrifice the lamb that I do love
To spite a raven's heart within a dove.

---

[12] Unbearable.
[13] A reference to an old story in which an outlaw tried to kill his mistress rather than let her be captured by his enemies.
[14] Cesario.
[15] Favorite.
[16] Stead.

Viola: And I, most jocund, apt, and
   willingly,
To do you rest a thousand deaths
   would die.
Olivia: Where goes Cesario?
Viola   After him I love
More than I love these eyes, more than
   my life,
More, by all mores, than e'er I shall
   love wife.
If I do feign, you witnesses above   140
Punish my life for tainting of my love!
Olivia: Ay me detested! how am I
   beguiled!
Viola: Who does beguile you? Who does
   do you wrong?
Olivia: Hast thou forgot thyself? Is it so
   long?
Call forth the holy father.
                         [*Exit an* **Attendant.**]
Duke: [*To* **Viola**] Come, away!
Olivia: Whither, my lord? Cesario,
   husband, stay.
Duke: Husband?
Olivia: Ay, husband. Can he that deny?
Duke: Her husband, sirrah?
Viola: No, my lord, not I.
Olivia: Alas, it is the baseness of thy
   fear
That makes thee strangle thy propriety.[17] 150
Fear not, Cesario; take thy fortunes up;
Be that thou knowst thou art, and then
   thou art
As great as that thou fearest.
   [*Enter* **Priest.**]
          O, welcome, father!
Father, I charge thee by thy reverence
Here to unfold—though lately we
   intended
To keep in darkness what occasion now
Reveals before 'tis ripe—what thou dost
   know

---

[17] Deny your identity.

Hath newly passed between this youth
  and me.

Priest: A contract of eternal bond of
  love,
Confirmed by mutual joinder of your
  hands,   160
Attested by the holy close of lips,
Strengthened by interchangement of
  your rings;
And all the ceremony of this compact
Sealed in my function, by my
  testimony;
Since when, my watch hath told me,
  toward my grave
I have traveled but two hours.

Duke: O thou dissembling cub! What
  wilt thou be
When time hath sowed a grizzle on thy
  case?[18]
Or will not else thy craft so quickly
  grow
That thine own trip shall be thine
  overthrow?[19]   170
Farewell, and take her; but direct thy
  feet
Where thou and I, henceforth, may
  never meet.

Viola: My lord, I do protest—

Olivia: O, do not swear!
Hold little faith,[20] though thou has too
  much fear.

          [*Enter* **Sir Andrew.**]

Andrew: For the love of God, a surgeon!
  Send one presently to Sir Toby.

Olivia: What's the matter?

Andrew: Has broke my head across, and
  has given Sir Toby a bloody coxcomb[21]
  too. For the love of God, your help! I had   180
  rather than forty pound I were at home.

Olivia: Who has done this, Sir Andrew?

Andrew: The Count's gentleman, one Ce-

sario. We took him for a coward, but he's
the very Devil incardinate.

Duke: My gentleman Cesario?

Andrew: Od's lifelings, here he is! You
broke my head for nothing; and that that
I did, I was set on to do't by Sir Toby.

Viola: Why do you speak to me? I never
  hurt you.   190
You drew your sword upon me without
  cause,
But I bespake you fair and hurt you
  not.

          [*Enter (Sir)* **Toby** *and* **Clown.**]

Andrew: If a bloody coxcomb be a hurt,
you have hurt me. I think you set nothing
by a bloody coxcomb. Here comes Sir
Toby halting—you shall hear more. But
if he had not been in drink, he would
have tickled you othergates[22] than he did.

Duke: How now, gentleman? How is't
with you?   200

Toby: That's all one! Has hurt me, and
there's the end on't.—Sot, didst see Dick
Surgeon, sot?

Clown: O, he's drunk, Sir Toby, an hour
agone. His eyes were set at eight i' the
morning.

Toby: Then he's a rogue and a passy measures pavin.[23] I hate a drunken rogue.

Olivia: Away with him! Who hath made
this havoc with them?

Andrew: I'll help you, Sir Toby, because   210
we'll be dressed[24] together.

Toby: Will you help—an ass-head and a
coxcomb and a knave—a thin-faced knave,
a gull?

Olivia: Get him to bed, and let his hurt
be looked to.

          [*Exeunt* **Sir Toby, Sir Andrew, Clown,**
          and **Fabian.**]
          [*Enter* **Sebastian.**]

---

[18] A grey beard on your face.
[19] That your own trickery will overthrow you.
[20] Hold [a] little faith.
[21] Head.

[22] Otherwise.
[23] Possibly a dance in eight measures, suggested to Toby
by Feste's reference to "eight i' the morning."
[24] Have our wounds treated.

Sebastian: I am sorry, madam, I have
hurt your kinsman;
But had it been the brother of my
blood,
I must have done no less with wit and
safety.
You throw a strange regard upon me,[25]
and by that
I do perceive it hath offended you.   220
Pardon me, sweet one, even for the
vows
We made each other but so late ago.

Duke: One face, one voice, one habit,[26]
and two persons!
A natural perspective,[27] that is and is
not!

Sebastian: Antonio! O my dear Antonio!
How have the hours racked and
tortured me
Since I have lost thee!

Antonio: Sebastian are you?

Sebastian: Fearst thou that, Antonio?

Antonio: How have you made division
of yourself?
An apple cleft in two is not more twin   230
Than these two creatures. Which is
Sebastian?

Olivia: Most wonderful!

Sebastian: Do I stand there? I never had
a brother;
Nor can there be that deity in my
nature
Of here and everywhere.[28] I had a sister,
Whom the blind waves and surges have
devoured.
Of charity, what kin are you to me?
What countryman? what name? what
parentage?

Viola: Of Messaline; Sebastian was my
father—
Such a Sebastian was my brother too;   240

So went he suited to his watery tomb.
If spirits can assume both form and
suit,
You come to fright us.

Sebastian: A spirit I am indeed,
But am in that dimension[29] grossly clad
Which from the womb I did
participate.[30]
Were you a woman, as the rest goes
even,[31]
I should my tears let fall upon your
cheek
And say, "Thrice welcome, drowned
Viola!"

Viola: My father had a mole upon his
brow—

Sebastian: And so had mine.   250

Viola: And died that day when Viola
from her birth
Had numbered thirteen years.

Sebastian: O, that record is lively in my
soul!
He finished indeed his mortal act
That day that made my sister thirteen
years.

Viola: If nothing lets[32] to make us happy
both
But this my masculine usurped attire,
Do not embrace me till each
circumstance
Of place, time, fortune do cohere and
jump[33]
That I am Viola; which to confirm,   260
I'll bring you to a captain in this town,
Where lie my maiden weeds;[34] by
whose gentle help
I was preserved to serve this noble
Count.
All the occurrence of my fortune since

---

[25] You look at me strangely.
[26] Costume.
[27] An optical illusion produced by nature.
[28] I have not a god's ability to be everywhere at once.

[29] Body.
[30] Inhabit.
[31] As all the other evidence is favorable.
[32] Intervenes.
[33] Agree.
[34] Clothing.

Hath been between this lady and this
  lord.
Sebastian: [*To* **Olivia**] So comes it, lady,
  you have been mistook.
But nature to her bias drew[35] in that.
You would have been contracted to a
  maid;
Nor are you therein, by my life,
  deceived:
You are betrothed both to a maid and
  man.   270
Duke: Be not amazed; right noble is his
  blood.
If this be so, as yet the glass[36] seems
  true,
I shall have share in this most happy
  wrack.
  [*To* **Viola**] Boy, thou hast said to me a
  thousand times
Thou never shouldst love woman like
  to me.
Viola: And all those sayings will I over
  swear,
And all those swearings keep as true in
  soul
As doth that orbed continent the fire
That severs day from night.[37]
Duke: Give me thy hand,
And let me see thee in thy woman's
  weeds.   280
Viola: The captain that did bring me
  first on shore
Hath my maid's garments. He upon
  some action
Is now in durance,[38] at Malvolio's suit,
A gentleman, and follower of my lady's.
Olivia: He shall enlarge[39] him. Fetch
  Malvolio hither.
And yet alas! now I remember me,

They say, poor gentleman, he's much
  distract.
     [*Enter* **Clown** *with a letter, and* **Fabian.**]
A most extracting[40] frenzy of mine own
From my remembrance clearly banished
  his.
How does he, sirrah?   290
Clown: Truly, madam, he holds Belzebub
  at the stave's end[41] as well as a man in
  his case may do. Has here writ a letter
  to you; I should have given't you today
  morning. [*Offers the letter*] But as a madman's epistles are no gospels, so it skills[42]
  not much when they are delivered.
Olivia: Open't and read it.
Clown: Look then to be well edified, when
  the fool delivers the madman. [*Reads loudly*]
  "By the Lord, madam"—   300
Olivia: How now? Art thou mad?
Clown: No, madam, I do but read madness. An your ladyship will have it as it
  ought to be, you must allow vox.[43]
Olivia: Prithee read i' thy right wits.
Clown: So I do, madonna; but to read his
  right wits is to read thus. Therefore per-
  pend,[44] my princess, and give ear.
Olivia: [*To* **Fabian**] Read it you, sirrah.

Fabian: [*Reads*] "By the Lord, madam, you   310
  wrong me, and the world shall know it.
  Though you have put me into darkness,
  and given your drunken cousin rule over
  me, yet have I the benefit of my senses
  as well as your ladyship. I have your own
  letter that induced me to the semblance
  I put on; with the which I doubt not but
  to do myself much right, or you much
  shame. Think of me as you please. I leave
  my duty a little unthought of, and speak
  out of my injury.
        "THE MADLY USED MALVOLIO."

---

[35] Nature followed her inclination.
[36] Mirror image.
[37] The sun.
[38] Upon some legal suit is now under arrest.
[39] Release.

[40] Distracting.
[41] He holds off the Devil (i.e., madness).
[42] Matters.
[43] Loud voice.
[44] Consider.

Olivia: Did he write this?   320
Clown: Ay, madam.
Duke: This savors not much of
distraction.
Olivia: See him delivered,[45] Fabian; bring
him hither.

[*Exit* **Fabian.**]

My lord, so please you, these things
further thought on,
To think me as well a sister as a wife,
One day shall crown the alliance on't,[46]
so please you,
Here at my house and at my proper[47]
cost.
Duke: Madam, I am most apt[48] t'
embrace your offer.
[*To* **Viola**] Your master quits[49] you; and
for your service done him,
So much against the mettle of your sex, 330
So far beneath your soft and tender
breeding,
And since you called me master, for so
long,
Here is my hand: you shall from this
time be
Your master's mistress.
Olivia: A sister! you are she.
[*Enter* (**Fabian,** *with*) **Malvolio.**]
Duke: Is this the madman?
Olivia: Ay, my lord, this same.
How now, Malvolio?
Malvolio: Madam, you have done
me wrong,
Notorious wrong.
Olivia: Have I, Malvolio? No.
Malvolio: Lady, you have, Pray you
peruse that letter.
You must not now deny it is your
hand.

Write from[50] it if you can, in hand or
phrase,   340
Or say 'tis not your seal, not your
invention.
You can say none of this. Well, grant it
then,
And tell me, in the modesty of honor,
Why you have given me such clear
lights[51] of favor,
Bade me come smiling and
cross-gartered to you,
To put on yellow stockings, and to
frown
Upon Sir Toby and the lighter[52] people;
And, acting this in an obedient hope,
Why have you suffered me to be
imprisoned,
Kept in a dark house, visited by the
priest,   350
And made the most notorious geck and
gul[53]
That e'er invention played on? Tell me
why.
Olivia: Alas, Malvolio, this is not my
writing,
Though I confess much like the
character;
But, out of question, 'tis Maria's hand.
And now I do bethink me, it was she
First told me thou wast mad. Thou
camest in smiling,
And in such forms which here were
presupposed[54]
Upon thee in the letter. Prithee be
content.
This practice hath most shrewdly
passed upon thee;   360
But when we know the grounds and
authors of it,
Thou shalt be both the plaintiff and the
judge

---

[45] Freed.
[46] That very day we'll hold the wedding ceremonies.
[47] Personal.
[48] Ready.
[49] Releases.

[50] Differently from.
[51] Signs.
[52] Lesser.
[53] Fool and dupe.
[54] Suggested.

Of thine own cause.

Fabian: Good madam, hear me speak,
And let no quarrel, nor no brawl to
    come,
Taint the condition of this present hour,
Which I have wond'red at. In hope it
    shall not,
Most freely I confess myself and Toby
Set this device against Malvolio here,
Upon some stubborn and uncourteous
    parts⁵⁵
We had conceived against him. Maria writ 370
The letter, at Sir Toby's great
    importance,⁵⁶
In recompense whereof he hath married
    her.
How with a sportful malice it was
    followed
May rather pluck on laughter than
    revenge,
If that the injuries be justly weighed
That have on both sides passed.

Olivia: Alas poor fool, how have they
baffled thee!

Clown: Why, "some are born great, some
achieve greatness, and some have greatness thrown upon them." I was one, sir, 380
in this interlude—one Sir Topas, sir; but
that's all one. "By the Lord, fool, I am
not mad!" But do you remember—
"Madam, why laugh you at such a barren
rascal? An you smile not, he's gagged"?
And thus the whirligig of time brings in
his revenges.

Malvolio: I'll be revenged on the whole
pack of you!   [*Exit.*]

Olivia: He hath been most notoriously
abused.

Duke: Pursue him and entreat him to a
peace.
He hath not told us of the captain yet. 390

When that is known, and golden time
    convents,⁵⁷
A solemn combination shall be made
Of our dear souls. Meantime, sweet
    sister,
We will not part from hence. Cesario,
    come—
For so you shall be while you are a
    man;
But when in other habits you are seen,
Orsino's mistress and his fancy's queen.
          [*Exeunt (all but the* **Clown***).*]
        [**Clown** *sings.*]
When that I was and a little tiny boy,
    With hey, ho, the wind and the rain,
A foolish thing was but a toy,   400
    For the rain it raineth every day.

But when I came to man's estate,
    With hey, ho, the wind and the rain,
'Gainst knaves and thieves men shut
    their gate,
For the rain it raineth every day.

But when I came, alas! to wive,
    With hey, ho, the wind and the rain,
By swaggering could I never thrive,
    For the rain it raineth every day.

But when I came unto my beds,   410
    With hey, ho, the wind and the rain,
With tosspots⁵⁸ still had drunken
    heads,
For the rain it raineth every day.

A great while ago the world begun,
    With hey, ho, the wind and the rain;
But that's all one, our play is done,
    And we'll strive to please you every
        day.

                              [*Exit.*]

---

⁵⁵ Characteristics.
⁵⁶ Importunity.

⁵⁷ Suits.
⁵⁸ Drunkards.

A Discussion
of the Script

The structure of *Twelfth Night* is extremely complex, and yet it is necessary that one try to understand it if he is to appreciate at all the wonderful richness with which Shakespeare has endowed the play. In the first place, *Twelfth Night,* like most Elizabethan and Jacobean drama, does not confine itself to a single central action. It was common practice in Shakespeare's day to write plays in which two entirely separate series of events take place, involving two separate sets of characters who have nothing whatsoever to do with each other. These plays with two (or sometimes even more) plots may seem a little strange now, but they represent a completely different approach to playwriting from the Aristotelian concept of unity of action. What many Elizabethan playwrights attempted, however (and what Shakespeare achieved magnificently), was to find some thematic unity in their two or more plots, and thus to lend an over-all unity to the play. It is possible to discern in *Twelfth Night* two entirely separate actions, but they are so closely connected thematically, and make such interesting use of interconnecting character relationships, that by the end of the play the two actions have been brought together and are cleared up simultaneously by the same stroke of fortune. The two basic plots revolve around two sets of figures: plot A is the story of Viola, Orsino, and Olivia, and their tangled love relationship which is eventually resolved; the action behind this plot might be summarized, "to find happiness in love," which, indeed, is the central action of most romantic comedies. Plot B is really little more than a series of jokes and carousing scenes involving Sir Toby Belch, Sir Andrew Aguecheek, Maria, and their cohorts; the unifying action of this plot might be summarized: "to find happiness in drink, mirth, and practical jokes." The attempt to state unifying actions for these two plots, however, is a bit misleading, for they are by no means as simply articulated as the structure of the well-made play. Each plot is developed in a manner analogous to the interweaving of two plots to form the whole play: one thread after another of the plot is picked up; these threads are brought together, connecting and interweaving one with the other, until an over-all pattern is produced. Perhaps this pattern can be illustrated with a line drawing resembling the type used to define the well-made play. In the Shakespearean structure, one bit of action is begun and stopped, then another, then another. Gradually, skillfully, these bits of action are brought together; once they have joined, they reinforce each other like two rivers and continue until another juncture is formed. In a highly simplified diagram this structure might be sketched as follows:

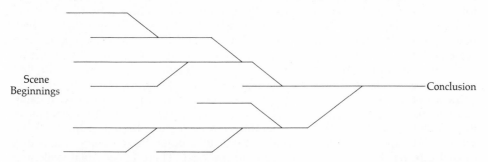

Scene
Beginnings
Conclusion

Twelfth Night, as printed here, has five acts, with one to five scenes in each, making a total of eighteen scenes; but there has been a great deal of disagreement among Shakespearean scholars as to exactly what the division into five acts may mean. The earliest printed versions of Shakespeare's plays did not show any act divisions at all. Although many of his plays were printed without his permission, it is quite likely that some of them were done with his knowledge and attention, so apparently the lack of division into acts was not just an oversight. Scholars are also reasonably sure that in Shakespeare's day plays were performed with no intermissions, so any division into acts would be purely academic and imperceptible to the audience. On the other hand, a great deal of scholarly evidence has been amassed to show that Shakespeare *thought* in terms of five acts and that his plays were written in five identifiable segments. Whatever the truth may be, two points are clear: the act divisions now standard in all printed texts are purely arbitrary, added by editors long after Shakespeare's death, and they need not have any meaning in terms of theatrical production whatsoever. In the theatre, no pause at all is needed between "acts." Rarely, if ever, are Shakespeare's plays performed today with as many as four inter- missions. On the other hand, the scene division has inescapable meaning: whenever all the characters leave the stage and a new group comes on, there is a definite *beat* or break in the action. These beats break the play into identifiable units. In a few cases, there are two or more of these units in what the editors arbitrarily called a *scene,* but for the most part, each scene represents one more unit in the interweaving of the various plot strands. These scene divisions may or may not be emphasized in production by a shift of scenery, a lighting change, a pause before the entrance of the next group of actors. In a production that flows quickly from one scene to the next, the average spectator may not think in terms of a scene break. But anyone who analyzes the script will have to confess that the division into scenic units described here is an inescapable and integral part of the structure.

Having located these units, then, one can begin to see how they fit together, one strand at a time, to make up the two basic plots referred to above. Act I, scene 1, introduces Orsino and shows that he is in love. That is all. Switch immediately to the next scene. I, 2, introduces Viola and makes clear why she is going to be in disguise for the rest of the play. I, 3, switches to plot B, and introduces three of the principal characters in it. I, 4, shows Viola, now in Orsino's court, being sent to woo Olivia. I, 5, becomes a little more complicated: Olivia and Malvolio are introduced. Some of the other characters from plot B are also part of the same household, which interweaves plot A with plot B. Then Viola woos Olivia for Orsino. Olivia falls in love with Cesario/Viola. Aside from any academic considerations, there is no need for a special break at the end of "Act I." The next scene, II, 1, follows quite naturally, with a jump to the seacoast to introduce Sebastian. Looking at the whole play in retrospect, one can see why this is especially important. Sebastian is the key to clearing up all the confusions, and the audience sees him three separate times, always moving toward a meeting with Viola, before this meeting finally occurs in the last scene and everything is straightened out. II, 1, is the first of these scenes. In II, 2, Viola learns that Olivia has fallen in love with her. In II, 3, the action is switched back to plot B to see the practical joke on Malvolio being planned. Back to plot A again in II, 4, as Orsino again sends Viola to Olivia. Notice that as plot A develops (and it is certainly the more complicated of the two) the action still jumps around from one aspect of it to another; there is very little action carried directly through from one scene to the next. There is continual switching from one group of characters to another, with Viola running back and forth between the groups: but the audience must be able to fit the plot together in their minds. Eventually, all of these characters will be brought together, and then all misunderstandings will be settled. II, 5, switches back to plot B again, as Malvolio falls into the trap Maria has laid for him. III, 1, finds Viola coming to woo Olivia the second time; again, some of the plot B characters are present to continue the connections that are building up between the two plots. III, 2, is a plot B scene, but in it definite plans are made to play a practical joke on Sir Andrew which will involve Viola, and thus the two plots are brought closer together yet. III, 3, switches back to Sebastian, reminding the audience once again that he is on the way, that he is getting closer, and his arrival will solve all the problems. III, 4, continues to intertwine the two plots, as Malvolio, as a result of the trick played on him, makes a fool of himself before Olivia and, in the latter part of the scene, the mock duel between Viola and Sir Andrew takes place. Antonio, of course, breaks up this fight, thus bringing Sebastian's arrival one step closer. In IV, 1, the audience again sees Sebastian, this time mistaken for Cesario/Viola by Olivia and all her household. IV, 2, is entirely a plot B scene, as Malvolio is tormented in his cell. IV, 3, switches back to Sebastian one more time, showing that Olivia and he are actually betrothed. It is clear that the confusion cannot last much longer. Act V, which is all one scene, finally brings everyone together, and all misunderstandings are settled. Only Malvolio is still unaccounted for, and Shakespeare takes care of him too by having Viola suddenly reveal that her sea-captain friend has been imprisoned on Malvolio's complaint; Malvolio is sent for and his difficulties, too, are cleared up.

Thus, step by step, the various parts of Shakespeare's plot structure are brought together until the whole form is complete. The way in which half a dozen or more different groups of characters can be portrayed, each in its separate scene, and all of these threads gradually picked up, as they are needed, and woven into the whole pattern is quite different from any play structure previously discussed. In fact, most of Shakespeare's plays are structured along these lines, as, indeed, are most of the English plays written between Shakespeare's first efforts and the closing of the theatres in 1642. It is one of the world's major structural forms. It doesn't possess a name like "well-made play," so for the sake of our discussion it will be called "Shakespearean structure." Evidently, it is far more complex than any structure previously studied here (it is the most complex of the major structures), and it offers infinite richness and variety to the playwright. At no other time and place in the history of Western drama have so many good playwrights produced so many good plays over such a short span of years, and there can be little doubt that one of the factors which made this possible was the richness afforded by this complex structural pattern.

A detailed critical analysis of *Twelfth Night* is far beyond the scope of this book. The play's plot, characterization, thematic structure, imagery, language, and countless other aspects have been studied in detail elsewhere. Shakespeare's works have spawned whole libraries of critical writings; he became a great playwright, not by taking new approaches to the drama, but by using the old elements of plot, character, theme, and language in superlative ways. There is neither space nor need here for a further analysis of the characters of *Twelfth Night*. Even the minor characters, with two or three exceptions, are three dimensional, living, infinitely varied human beings. Shakespeare's use of language also needs no comment, although some individual words may be obscure to modern ears; the poetry and rhythm of the whole, the intricate puns and word-plays, the facility and sweep of the iambic pentameter, the beauty of the love poems and songs, make Shakespeare's language (insofar as it can be isolated in so rich a play) a delight in the study or in performance. Perhaps the thematic content is not particularly strong in *Twelfth Night*, but some ideas are certainly raised. The blind foolishness of people in love, the self-delusion that all egocentric people practice, the happiness to be found through (1) love in plot A and (2) drink, mirth, and practical jokes in plot B—these themes and several others are discussed in detail in the wealth of critical literature available on this play.

Before one can understand the style of *Twelfth Night* and consider a style in which it might be produced one needs to know a little about play production in Shakespeare's day. The theatres in London apparently evolved from the inn yards of an earlier period, and consisted, essentially, of an area in the center open to the sky and seating facilities for the audience on all sides. Controversies rage among scholars as to the exact description of these playhouses, but there is general agreement that the stage thrust out into the open space in the center allowing the audience to stand around it on three sides. The seating area behind the standees may even have extended around all four sides, but essentially the stage was a thrust or "three-quarter round" design quite unlike the proscenium arrangements that tend to dominate the American theatre today. In the upstage wall were two doors, one on each side. Once actors entered through these doors, they almost certainly moved downstage as soon as possible in order to be seen by the whole audience. There was probably a curtained alcove up center between the doors that could be opened to reveal some pre-set scenery or a tableau, but it seems unlikely that much acting took place there as the sight-lines would be bad and audience contact would be greatly reduced. Such a theatre would necessarily lead to a presentational style of acting with a great deal of direct actor-audience contact; there would be little opportunity or need to shift sets beyond perhaps carrying in tables, some chairs, and other properties. Since performances played continuously, without intermission, it seems certain that one scene followed another with the smallest possible break between them; probably as one group of actors went out of one door, another group came in the other. It should be noted, too, that there were no actresses; women's roles were played by boys. The frequency with which girls disguise themselves in boys' clothing in Elizabethan drama suggests that audiences delighted in the double level of impersonation involved—a boy dressed up as a girl dressed up as a boy. Above all, Shakespeare's theatre was a popular theatre. existing almost entirely on box office income. All levels of society delighted in going to the theatre, and Shakespeare's plays made him a rich man. The delight that one can now find in studying these plays in great detail is well and good, but one cannot fully appreciate their effectiveness until he visualizes a popular, noisy audience enjoying them because they were the most exciting things to see in town.

The style in which *Twelfth Night* is written has no single name. As is so often the case with any aspect of Shakespeare's work, the style is far too complex to be reduced to a single concept. It is not realism, but the characters created are nonetheless wonderfully real; it is not romanticism, but certainly some of the love scenes are strongly romantic; it is a combination of the two, with a large measure of fantasy thrown in. Shakespeare's plays have proved exceptionally amenable to interpretation in a wide variety of production styles through the years: realism, expressionism, theatricalism, constructivism, and a long list of other styles have been arbitrarily applied to them, and the considerable measure of success that so often accompanies even the most esoteric of these experiments is another indication of the richness of the plays themselves. However, the current attitude among the great majority of directors and critics is that realism is not an appropriate production style for Shakespearean plays. The flowing style in which they are written, the structural pattern which calls for frequent shifting of locale, and knowledge of the forms in which they were originally staged strongly suggest that some sort of presentational quality with minimal scenery is vital to a Shakespearean production. Most directors today, even if they do not have a thrust stage available to them, try to adopt a production style which will pull the actors as close to the audience as possible (by extensive use of the apron on proscenium stages, for example) and that will demand little, if any, scene shifting. There is almost never a complete stop for scene changes. Intermissions are usually arbitrarily imposed once or twice during the playing time but, except for these, one scene flows into the next as smoothly and easily as possible. As on the Elizabethan stage, the actors may frequently carry several properties onstage with them, the first few lines of dialogue establish the locale, and the imagination of the audience, coupled with the skill of the actors, accomplishes the rest.

Clearly *Twelfth Night* is a comedy, but what kind? farce? high comedy? Once again, such arbitrary divisions as these are much too limited to encompass Shakespeare's genius. It has been pointed out earlier that many comedies lie somewhere between the extremes of farce and high comedy, and it is probably more useful, in considering such plays, to define their style of humor before trying to classify the plays themselves. Alan Reynolds Thompson has charted a hierarchy of comic effects that is especially useful in analyzing humor.[1]

FARCE	HIGH COMEDY
	6. *Comedy of ideas*
	5. *Inconsistencies of character*
	4. *Verbal wit*
	3. *Plot devices*
	2. *Physical mishaps*
1. *Obscenity*	

[1] *The Anatomy of Drama* (Berkeley 1942), p. 203. Reprinted by permission of The Regents of the University of California.

Perhaps it is unfortunate, even in this context, to suggest that one of these forms of humor is any "higher" than another, but it is certainly safe to say that a higher degree of intellectual sophistication is necessary to appreciate the humor which is at the upper end of the "ladder of comedy," and that essentially is the basis for the ranking here. *Obscenity* has always been funny, but the Puritan heritage has inculcated American sensibilities with the idea that it is evil, and thus obscenity for humor is now largely confined to pornography. In the past, obscenity was not regarded as pornographic and formed a solid basis for many excellent plays. It exists in many of Shakespeare's plays, but the evolution of the English language since Elizabethan times causes modern audiences to miss many of the puns and double-entendres that are actually present. For all practical purposes a modern production of *Twelfth Night* conveys little or no obscenity. *Physical mishaps* are a prevalent type of humor, from the pratfalls of the vaudeville comedian to the pie-in-the-face of a silent movie. The technique is widely used in television, movies, on Broadway, and can be found in the earliest Greek comedies as well. Certainly physical mishaps play a major role in plot B of *Twelfth Night,* too—not only the obvious, major scenes such as Malvolio in jail and the duel between Sir Andrew and Viola, but also the considerable amount of physical humor which most directors will add in the drinking scenes. Indeed, the opportunities for an imaginative director and actors to add physical humor are almost unlimited. Many humorous *plot devices* are also built into *Twelfth Night.* These include Olivia trying to woo Cesario/Viola (whom the audience knows to be a girl), Malvolio treating Olivia as the letter has instructed him to, Sebastian being mistaken for Cesario by everyone he meets, and so forth. *Verbal wit* is also a fundamental aspect of *Twelfth Night*; the clowning of Feste is almost entirely verbal throughout, and many of the other characters make use of puns and word plays. Unfortunately, modern audiences miss a lot of these because the vocabulary is strange to them. The phrase *inconsistencies of character* might better be interpreted as "comedy which grows out of character," for this is not always confined to inconsistencies. Malvolio is an excellent example of this kind of humor—he is funny because he is such a sour prude; when he can be put into an absurd situation, he is even funnier. Orsino can be just as funny in a more sophisticated way if the actor makes him so; his extreme pangs of love are actually pretty absurd, and are usually played that way. *Comedy of ideas,* the "highest" level on the ladder, is the kind of humor that pokes fun at political, religious, and social sacred cows. It can be devastatingly or only mildly humorous, but the thought content behind it is of major importance. This variety of humor was used to a considerable degree in *The Importance of Being Earnest,* but is less prominent in *Twelfth Night.* Elizabethan audiences could find some satirical references to current events, but these are largely lost on a modern audience. The "ladder of comedy" usually designates plays which depend on the devices in the lower part of the scale for their humor as farces, while those which depend on devices in the upper part of the scale are high comedy. *Twelfth Night,* however, makes use of all levels of the scale, with perhaps less emphasis on the scale's extremes. The spectrum of humor in *Twelfth Night* is so broad that probably one should simply call it a comedy and let it go at that.

The harnessing and controlling of electricity in the late nineteenth and early twentieth centuries has added an entirely new dimension to theatrical production. In the art of stage lighting lies the only really distinctive contribution of the modern era to the art of the theatre, for prior to the use of electricity, plays were performed either outdoors in full daylight or in a hall lighted as much in the audience area as in the acting area. During the rather brief period of gas lighting, some cumbersome dimming was attempted, and there are records from an earlier era of colored glass used in front of candles, but only by the use of electricity (and specifically the incandescent lamp) have the complicated effects of today become possible. The lighting designer has become nearly as important as and, in some cases more important than the scenic designer, and theatre designers are still only beginning to discover the possibilities inherent in controlled light. In both professional and amateur theatre, the scene designer is likely to double as the lighting designer, although many larger production companies are now depending upon separate designers to perform this function. If the lighting designer is a separate individual, it is necessary for him to work closely with the set designer and the costume designer, since the sets, the costumes, and the lights together account for most of the visual impact of a production. Beginning, as always, from the script and keeping in mind the set design, the lighting designer must plan lighting effects which will not only provide the necessary visibility but will also enhance the play's effectiveness in all its aspects. Coordination with the costumes consists mainly of being certain that the fabric colors and the lighting colors work well together, as colored light can greatly alter the appearance of a colored surface.

Some primary functions of stage lighting are listed in the approximate order of their importance. Lighting, under modern methods of control, can:

1. *Provide necessary visibility.* This is the minimal requirement, but it is a little more complex than might appear at first. Although, theoretically, it might be possible to do a play in the dark, it hardly sounds like a fruitful experiment. Very few plays are done in modern times with only natural illumination. Theatre technicians must provide whatever illumination is used. The minimum needs are not normally met by simply flooding an acting area

Lighting

with light until a satisfactory foot-candle level is achieved. A simple experiment will show what happens in these circumstances: seat someone in a chair in a darkened room and shine a light on his face. You will be able to see him, of course, but you will notice that the sharp patterns of light and shadows make it difficult to perceive his features. Now turn half a dozen lights on him from many different angles, and you will be able to see him much better. If you study his features, however, you will notice that so much light from so many angles takes away all the shadows, and his features seem to "wash out." Particularly if you try to observe him from a distance (as in a theatre), you will not actually be able to see the details of his facial expression as well as you might expect. Now light his face from two directions only, 90 degrees apart and each of the light sources placed 45 degrees above the horizontal. To make the experiment more effective, let one of the lights be a different color from the other. His face now will be optimally visible, for the two lights will have a modeling effect, much like the colors used in painting to highlight and shadow a subject supposed to appear three-dimensional. One side of the face is as brightly lighted as if it were in direct sunlight; the other side is also lighted, but more dimly, as it might appear in reflected light. The features, as a result, are not only visible, but their highlights and shadows are near enough to normal to make the facial expressions readily perceived even at a distance. When visibility is the goal, all parts of the acting area typically are lighted from two directions, each 45 degrees above the horizontal and, in the case of the proscenium stage, 45 degrees to either side of the theatre's center line. Colored plastic or cellophane-like material known as *gel* (short for "gelatin") are placed in front of each light; one of the two lights is made slightly warm in color (perhaps a very light amber) and the other is made slightly cool (perhaps a pale blue).

2. *Help establish mood.* The colors mentioned above are only for purposes of visibility; they are very pale, and thus will contribute little to the mood. The lighting designer has a large selection of colors to choose from, however, and variation in color can contribute tremendously to the establishment of a wide variety of moods. Nor is color the only variable available to the lighting designer. He can place his lights at other angles than the desirable ones mentioned above and change the mood a great deal. Lighting coming from directly beneath the face, for example, can create a weird and exciting effect. And, of course, he has the alternative of keeping the lights at a lower or higher level of brightness and thus changing the mood. The importance of creating the right mood has been discussed in connection with the set. The lighting can be a primary factor in doing this.

3. *Focus attention.* Modern lighting equipment allows for easy and quick shifts of attention from one part of the stage to another, simply by making one part brighter than another. This is very obvious in plays like *J.B.*, where the playwright has planned for the lights to fade to complete darkness on the Zuss-Nickles platform and to fade up simultaneously on the J.B. platform. No theatre spotlight is so perfectly focused (nor is reflected light so well controlled) that one area of the stage can be in total darkness while an adjacent one is brightly lighted, but attention can be focused on the brighter area so that the other *seems* to disappear. Even in more realistic plays like *The Little Foxes*, focus may be controlled by subtle changes in the lighting, and the audience may never realize what has happened. When Horace gasps for his medicine in Act III, for example, the lighting might grow more intense on the staircase which, a few moments later, will be his acting area. By the time he collapses on the staircase, this area will be brighter than the surrounding areas, and

will become dimmer after Horace is carried off up the stairs. By such a device, attention can be focused (and, incidentally, mood heightened) with little or no audience awareness of the technique. In complex productions, the lighting may change almost constantly as a means of controlling focus and mood.

4. *Heighten realism.* In realistic plays, the lighting is expected to go beyond the functions mentioned above and give the illusion of what actually occurs in real life. In an interior setting, like the one for *The Little Foxes*, this may mean finding the optimum positions of the lights in order to make it appear that all light is coming from lamps in the room. This involves less adjustment than one might think, since it is relatively easy to create the illusion, but it does become a factor in the lighting designer's plans. His choice of colors will also be influenced by the time of day and the sources of illumination available in the room. For daytime, sunlight might appear to be streaming in the window. At night, moonlight may be appropriate. Many interior settings call for a fire in the fireplace, and so on. Exterior settings are often far more difficult, for not only should they appear to be lighted by sunlight, but sky, sunset, moonrise, rainbows, and all sorts of other natural effects are often called for. Many of these are extremely difficult, and, when total realism is expected, the results are sometimes disappointing.

In order to perform the functions listed above, the lighting designer, in the properly equipped modern theatre, can vary three different properties of light:

1. *Vary intensity.* With a few minor exceptions, changes in intensity are achieved by the use of dimmers. The dimmers presently in use in this country are of several basic designs, but all of them provide the operator with the possibility of dimming one or many lights from full brightness to complete blackout in a smooth, even pattern. All but the most unsophisticated dimmer designs allow for electrical mastering, by which several dimmers may be controlled simultaneously and dimmed proportionally by the use of one handle. The more sophisticated dimmer boards also contain pre-set facilities by which a number of dimmer settings may be programmed in advance and then quickly brought into use by operating a single handle. With equipment of this sort, then, it is very easy for the lighting designer to plan a complex series of changes in intensity and, with sufficient rehearsal, to expect that they will be carried out in that planned fashion, consistently, performance after performance. A really sensitive hand on the dimmer controls can follow the action of the play not only in the relatively crude sense of executing a certain light change upon a given cue, but also far more subtly by capturing the pace and rhythm of the production and blending the lighting changes surely and meaningfully into the play. In order to do this successfully, the dimmer operator must be able to see and hear the action on the stage. For this reason, the dimmers are usually located in a control booth in the back of the house, where the operator has an unobstructed view.

2. *Vary color.* The color from a single lighting instrument can be varied by changing the piece of gel which is mounted across its front. Gel comes in a wide variety of colors, so that the lighting designer is virtually unlimited in his choice, but varying color during a performance is quite another matter. It is usually impractical for technicians to keep climbing up and changing gels; not only are the locations inaccessible, but the change could not be accomplished fast enough on a number of lights simultaneously. Automatic gel-changing mechanisms have been developed, but they are too expensive and too crude to be used widely. Thus, designers who wish to change color in a given area during a performance usually focus several instruments on the same area, and equip them with different gel colors. Color control

is then achieved by dimming out one light while another is dimming up; sometimes further variations are achieved by mixing two or three colors (using the dimmers) to create still other colors. Naturally, such a system is limited by the number of lighting instruments which the theatre owns or can acquire and by the capacities of the mounting locations and the dimmers. Total changes in color can differentiate between night and day (night is not really blue, but blue light is conventionally accepted as indicating night on the stage) or create sharply stylized effects; more subtle color changes, perhaps not perceptible to the audience, can vary mood. Again, a sensitive operator at the dimmer control board is in a position to have a great deal of influence over how the audience feels about the action which is taking place on the stage.

3. *Vary focus.* Moving spotlights are available for theatrical use, and most spotlights have some adjustments for the size and shape of their beams, but use of these devices to vary focus requires human operators at the instruments with all of the attendant problems mentioned above. For this reason, it is usual to mount separate lighting instruments covering each of the areas that must be controlled separately, and then to rely on the dimmer board operator to bring up the lights in one area and bring down those in another. Using such a system, the lighting designer can plan in terms of small, tightly controlled pools of light with the rest of the stage in darkness, or he can illuminate the entire acting area generally, and then control focus in a more subtle way by having key areas brighter than their surroundings. The focus may shift by sharp jumps from one part of the stage to another, or it may flow subtly by imperceptible dimmer changes. Again, the real

Electronic theatre-lighting-control console. Courtesy Skirpan Lighting Control Corp.

limitation lies more in the capacity and quantity of equipment available than in the sophistication of that equipment.

A production which makes full and imaginative use of the variables listed above gives the dimmer-board operator, under the direction of the lighting designer, control over the intensity, the color, and the focus of the light at every moment. He can vary the visibility, the mood, and the attention focus with a touch of his fingers, and he can create realistic special effects when they are called for. The dimmer-board operator, like the actors, has dynamic control over audience reaction from moment to moment throughout the play, and, if he is talented and well trained, he will exploit this control in support of the over-all objectives that the director has established for the play. The lighting man has a great deal to do with the establishment and maintenance of proper pace and rhythm in a production; anyone can tell if a light is turned on at a wrong time, but the more subtle mistakes of a lighting man who executes the right cues but with the wrong timing may not be so readily apparent and yet may be more destructive in the long run. No other technician has such direct, dynamic contact with the audience; the set and costumes may attract more attention, but they cannot be varied to suit the timing and mood of a given audience. Only the actors and the lighting man have this capacity.

Consider in more detail the procedures that a lighting designer might follow who found himself in charge of lighting a production of *Twelfth Night.* If the play were being staged in an arena or thrust-stage arrangement, his problems might be very different, but the assumption here is that he is operating in a proscenium theatre which has an apron large enough so that it will be an important playing area for the production. The lighting designer begins, of course, with the script. He sees at once that the play is divided into many scenes, and he anticipates that lighting changes will be required at least for every scene, and often within scenes. He confers with the director and scene designer, and learns that (for example) the set is for- malistic in order to avoid frequent shifts, but that the lighting will be expected to establish scene and mood shifts as well as to provide some of the color and spectacle that the play needs. The costumes are also supposed to be highly colorful; thus the lighting designer knows that he must keep in touch with the costume designer in order to assure that the lighting colors will go well with the costume colors. This coordination is a good deal more complicated and time-consuming than its brief mention here would indicate; in fact, the lighting designer will stay in continuous contact with the director and the scene designer all through the dress rehearsal period.

Assuming that the lighting designer takes a fairly standard, orthodox approach to the lighting for this play, one of his first steps will be to divide the total acting area into smaller subareas. If he plans to light the entire stage uniformly, he would probably use six subareas. The three upstage areas, then, would be lighted from the *first pipe,* a lighting batten hung immediately upstage of the main curtain. The three downstage areas would be lighted from the *beams,* an opening in the auditorium ceiling located to provide a good angle to the downstage portion of the acting area and the apron (see the diagram on page 231). The ideal, of course, is to hit each of these areas from two points, each 45 degrees above the horizontal and each 45 degrees to the side of the theatre's center line. Of course, the focus on each lighting instrument would have to be widened sufficiently to allow the areas to overlap a bit, because, when the lights are of uniform brightness, the audience should not be able to tell when an actor moves from one area into the next. The designer may hang additional *blending and toning* lights if he decides they are necessary to insure that the areas blend smoothly together. For a play like *Twelfth Night*, however, it might not be desirable to light the stage uniformly. It is more than likely that the set, although formalistic in nature, will be rather complex in its series of steps and levels, and will allow for playing separate scenes in various portions of the stage. In this case, the lighting designer will not divide the stage into areas on a purely arbitrary basis, but will study carefully the blocking patterns the director is using. The size and shape of each area will be determined by where the actors move within it; far more space will be needed for the fencing scene between Sir Andrew and Viola (III,4) than for the seacoast scene between Antonio and Sebastian (II,1). If lighting instruments and mounting positions are limited, the director and the lighting designer may agree to use a single lighting area for more than one scene (and such a pattern may help the audience to identify location, as, for example, the switching back and forth between Orsino's court and Olivia's home). If, however, equipment limitations do not dictate such economy, the lighting designer will probably prefer to hang separate sets of instruments for every scene in order to achieve the maximum in focus and color control. Thus, even if two scenes are played in virtually the same area, each would have its separate set of instruments.

The lighting designer would also have to select colors carefully for each scene. It is pointless to speculate about these colors here and name several arbitrarily, since they would have to be selected in coordination with the sets, the costumes, the director's wishes, and perhaps other variables. As an example, however, assume that it was decided to make the seacoast scene between Antonio and Sebastian a night scene. The intent, then, might be to make the lighting generally blue, but this might be accomplished by selecting a medium blue gel for the lights from one side and a pale lavender for those from the other to provide the desired modeling effect. A warm spot for maximum visibility might be created in the middle by gelling one light with perhaps a pale straw and then keeping it at a low dimmer setting. A floodlight, gelled in blue, might be used to wash back over the rest of the setting if the designer wished to keep it partially visible for some reason. Color and intensity changes might be required within the scene, and in that case extra instruments would have to be hung to allow for color control. Plans regarding the colors to be used would be worked out scene by scene throughout the play, with each scene treated as a separate unit and yet with the over-all production kept constantly in mind.

Once all the lights are properly hung and focused with their gels installed, the lighting designer is ready to work with the technician who will operate the control board, to set every cue properly. The designer will have worked out a very careful plan for plugging certain lights into certain dimmers in order to achieve maximum flexibility of operation. If the dimmer handles are lined up side by side on the control board, lights that go up at the same time should be plugged into adjacent dimmers for easy operation. Of course, lights that go up at the same time and *to the same level* can work from the same dimmer if it has sufficiently large capacity. Sometimes this plugging pattern is changed during the course of a performance, and in order to allow for this flexibility, most theatres have all the plugs located together in a *patch panel.* Most designers prefer to avoid replugging by keeping the operation simple and confining all changes to the dimmer settings themselves. Each lighting cue will be worked out in detail by the lighting designer and the dimmer-board operator; the designer discovers by trial and error exactly the level he wants on each dimmer and then tells the operator the speed with which the dimmers should move to that setting. As a result of this laborious process, the dimmer-board operator gradually evolves a cue sheet which will tell him precisely the dimmer settings that are needed at any point in the show, and the timing which he should use to move to the next setting. As has been pointed out earlier, even the most detailed cue sheet does not replace a sensitive awareness on the part of the operator of the pace and rhythm of the individual performance, but an accurate cue sheet is still desirable. The success of a performance of *Twelfth Night,* produced according to the pattern suggested here, would be very dependent on the work of the lighting designer and the technicians assisting him.

Jean-Baptiste Poquelin was born in Paris on or about January 15, 1622. He was the son of a well-to-do upholsterer whose official appointment in the king's service gave him a firm position both socially and financially, so that his son could be offered a good education at the Collège de Clermont. There he formed a number of friendships which were extremely valuable to him in his later career, including one with Cyrano de Bergerac. (A scene from one of Molière's plays is based on some of Cyrano de Bergerac's work; note on page 163 how Rostand uses this fact.) Young Poquelin studied law until about 1640, and in 1642 assumed some of his father's duties in the service of King Louis XIII. No doubt it was assumed that he would follow in his father's footsteps, but in 1643 he renounced his succession to his father's office in order to join a theatrical company then forming. The moving spirits within this company were a family named Béjart. Poquelin, in renouncing his heritage, renounced his name as well and took the stage name Molière, perhaps to protect his family, since acting was regarded as a frivolous and immoral profession. Molière quickly rose to the leadership of this company, but despite a great deal of energy and hard work, it failed, and Molière was imprisoned for debt.

Upon his release from prison, Molière reorganized the company and it toured the French provinces from 1645 to 1658, the actors leading a nomadic and perhaps precarious existence but training and developing themselves in their art. On October 24, 1658, they returned to Paris, where they had been invited to perform before the young King Louis XIV. According to the custom of such a solemn occasion, they opened with a tragedy. It evidently failed to please, but, after an apologetic curtain speech by Molière, they presented one of the light farces which had been pleasing the provinces for so long—Molière's own *Le Docteur amoureux*. The king was delighted, and the success of Molière's company was assured. They were placed under the personal patronage of the king's brother and allowed to share one of the major Paris theatres. The company changed its location within Paris on several occasions, and survived some rocky times during the years immediately following Molière's death, but it formed the nucleus of today's Comédie-Française, the oldest national theatre in the world.

Tartuffe
by Molière

During the fifteen years of life that remained to him, Molière headed this company in Paris, performed most of the leading roles, and wrote most of the comedies for which he is remembered. Comedy was established as a significant dramatic form in France for the first time, and Molière's work was extremely popular both in the court and with the general public. Evidently Molière never intended to publish his plays; they were written with specific actors in his company in mind and frequently revised as stage experience suggested possible improvements. Fortunately they were published nevertheless, during or shortly after his lifetime, and hence preserved.

In January of 1662, Molière married eighteen-year old Armande Béjart, the youngest sister of the family with whom he had so long been associated. The scandal mongers insisted that she was actually the daughter rather than the sister of Madeleine Béjart, Molière's former mistress, and Montfleury, a jealous rival actor, asserted before the king that Molière had married his own daughter. Louis XIV, ever Molière's protector and patron, hushed the scandal and served as godfather to Molière's first child, a son. Although a daughter was born in 1665 and another in 1672, the marriage was never a happy one; Armande was a spoiled flirt, much younger than Molière, and the two quarreled bitterly. She continued, however, to play leading roles in his plays, often as the young wife of a foolish old husband (played by Molière himself), even after the couple had separated. Molière suffered from tuberculosis and was almost constantly under a doctor's care during his declining years; he used this experience in his plays, satirizing the medical profession unmercifully. He was playing the title role in the fourth performance of *The Imaginary Invalid* (ironically again, about a hypochondriac) on the evening of February 17, 1673, when he was fatally stricken; he managed to complete the performance, but died shortly after the final curtain. Actors in seventeenth-century France were automatically excommunicated, but some managed, by a deathbed conversion, to die within the church; Molière died too quickly for this and burial in consecrated ground was refused. Again the king intervened; at least a suitable grave was provided. The church stipulated no religious rites and night burial. Thousands joined a torchlit procession to honor him.

Of Molière's many comic masterpieces, *Tartuffe* has, perhaps, the most interesting history. It was first performed in a three-act version at the court of Versailles on May 12, 1664, but some members of the religious establishment professed themselves offended by the play and succeeded in persuading the king that further performances should be banned. The *Gazette de France* described the play as "extremely harmful to religion and likely to have a most dangerous effect." Molière petitioned the king for permission to perform, insisting that the play satirized neither piety nor religion, but rather the people who were complaining, and finally in 1667 permission was granted for a public performance. Unfortunately for Molière, however, the king was away from the city when the play opened on August 5, and the mayor of Paris, secretly a member of one of the quasi-religious orders which took special umbrage at the portrayal, banned further performances. The Archbishop of Paris threatened excommunication to anyone attending a performance. After much political inveigling and rewriting of the script, Molière finally obtained clear royal permission to perform the play publicly; it reopened on February 5, 1669, and quickly became a popular hit. It is a little difficult today to imagine how such a furor could have been created over so comparatively mild a play, but it may be inferred that Molière's satire struck where it hurt the most. The word "tartuffe" has entered both the French and English languages as a common-noun synonym for "hypocrite," and the play has been one of Molière's most popular and most frequently revived.

Opposite: William Hutt (Tartuffe), Donald Davis (Orgon) in *Tartuffe*, director Jean Gascon, designer Robert Prevost, Stratford Shakespearean Festival, Stratford, Ont., 1969. *Page 361:* Angela Wood (Elmire), William Hutt (Tartuffe) in Act IV. Photographs: Douglas Spillane.

Comedy in Five Acts by

JEAN BAPTISTE POQUELIN
DE MOLIÈRE

Translated into English Verse by
RICHARD WILBUR

Mme Pernelle, Orgon's mother
Orgon, Elmire's husband
Elmire, Orgon's wife
Damis, Orgon's son, Elmire's stepson
Mariane, Orgon's daughter, Elmire's step-
    daughter, in love with Valère
Valère, in love with Mariane
Cléante, Orgon's brother-in-law
Tartuffe, a hypocrite
Dorine, Mariane's lady's-maid
M. Loyal, a bailiff
A Police Officer
Flipote, Mme Pernelle's maid

The scene throughout: Orgon's house in
    Paris

ACT I

Scene 1

[**Madame Pernelle** *and* **Flipote,** *her maid,*
Elmire, Mariane, Dorine, Damis, Cléante]

Madame Pernelle: Come, come, Flipote; it's
    time I left this place.

Elmire: I can't keep up, you walk at such a
    pace.

Madame Pernelle: Don't trouble, child; no
    need to show me out.
    It's not your manners I'm concerned about.

Elmire: We merely pay you the respect we
    owe.
    But, Mother, why this hurry? Must you
    go?

Madame Pernelle: I must. This house
    appals me. No one in it
    Will pay attention for a single minute.

Tartuffe

Children, I take my leave much vexed in
    spirit.
I offer good advice, but you won't hear it.
You all break in and chatter on and on.
It's like a madhouse with the keeper gone.

Dorine: If . . .

Madame Pernelle: Girl, you talk too much,
    and I'm afraid
You're far too saucy for a lady's-maid.
You push in everywhere and have your say.

Damis: But . . .

Madame Pernelle: You, boy, grow more
    foolish every day.
To think my grandson should be such a
    dunce!
I've said a hundred times, if I've said it
    once,
That if you keep the course on which
    you've started,
You'll leave your worthy father
    broken-hearted.

Mariane: I think . . .

Madame Pernelle: And you, his sister, seem
    so pure,
So shy, so innocent, and so demure.
But you know what they say about still
    waters.
I pity parents with secretive daughters.

Elmire: Now, Mother . . .

Madame Pernelle: And as for you, child, let
    me add
That your behavior is extremely bad,
And a poor example for these children,
    too.
Their dear, dead mother did far better than
    you.
You're much too free with money, and I'm
    distressed
To see you so elaborately dressed.
When it's one's husband that one aims to
    please,
One has no need of costly fripperies.

Cléante: Oh, Madam, really . . .

Madame Pernelle: You are her brother, Sir,
And I respect and love you; yet if I were
My son, this lady's good and pious spouse,
I wouldn't make you welcome in my
    house.

You're full of worldly counsels which, I
    fear,
Aren't suitable for decent folk to hear.
I've spoken bluntly, Sir; but it behooves us
Not to mince words when righteous fervor
    moves us.

Damis: Your man Tartuffe is full of holy
    speeches . . .

Madame Pernelle: And practises precisely
    what he preaches.
He's a fine man, and should be listened to.
I will not hear him mocked by fools like
    you.

Damis: Good God! Do you expect me to
    submit
To the tyranny of that carping hypocrite?
Must we forgo all joys and satisfactions
Because that bigot censures all our actions?

Dorine: To hear him talk—and he talks all
    the time—
There's nothing one can do that's not a
    crime.
He rails at everything, your dear Tartuffe.

Madame Pernelle: Whatever he reproves
    deserves reproof.
He's out to save your souls, and all of you
Must love him, as my son would have you
    do.

Damis: Ah no, Grandmother, I could never
    take
To such a rascal, even for my father's sake.
That's how I feel, and I shall not
    dissemble.
His every action makes me seethe and
    tremble
With helpless anger, and I have no doubt
That he and I will shortly have it out.

Dorine: Surely it is a shame and a disgrace
To see this man usurp the master's place—
To see this beggar who, when first he
    came,
Had not a shoe or shoestring to his name
So far forget himself that he behaves
As if the house were his, and we his
    slaves.

Madame Pernelle: Well, mark my words,
    your souls would fare far better
If you obeyed his precepts to the letter.

Dorine: You see him as a saint. I'm far less awed;
In fact, I see right through him. He's a fraud.
Madame Pernelle: Nonsense!
Dorine: His man Laurent's the same, or worse;
I'd not trust either with a penny purse.
Madame Pernelle: I can't say what his servant's morals may be;
His own great goodness I can guarantee.
You all regard him with distaste and fear
Because he tells you what you're loath to hear,
Condemns your sins, points out your moral flaws,
And humbly strives to further Heaven's cause.
Dorine: If sin is all that bothers him, why is it
He's so upset when folk drop in to visit?
Is Heaven so outraged by a social call
That he must prophesy against us all?
I'll tell you what I think: if you ask me,
He's jealous of my mistress' company.
Madame Pernelle: Rubbish! [*To* **Elmire**]
He's not alone, child, in complaining
Of all your promiscuous entertaining.
Why, the whole neighborhood's upset, I know,
By all these carriages that come and go,
With crowds of guests parading in and out
And noisy servants loitering about.
In all of this, I'm sure there's nothing vicious;
But why give people cause to be suspicious?
Cléante: They need no cause; they'll talk in any case.
Madam, this world would be a joyless place
If, fearing what malicious tongues might say,
We locked our doors and turned our friends away.
And even if one did so dreary a thing,
D'you think those tongues would cease their chattering?

One can't fight slander; it's a losing battle;
Let us instead ignore their tittle-tattle.
Let's strive to live by conscience' clear decrees,
And let the gossips gossip as they please.
Dorine: If there is talk against us, I know the source:
It's Daphne and her little husband, of course.
Those who have greatest cause for guilt and shame
Are quickest to besmirch a neighbor's name.
When there's a chance for libel, they never miss it;
When something can be made to seem illicit
They're off at once to spread the joyous news,
Adding to fact what fantasies they choose.
By talking up their neighbor's indiscretions
They seek to camouflage their own transgressions,
Hoping that others' innocent affairs
Will lend a hue of innocence to theirs,
Or that their own black guilt will come to seem
Part of a general shady color-scheme.
Madame Pernelle: All that is quite irrelevant. I doubt
That anyone's more virtuous and devout
Than dear Orante; and I'm informed that she
Condemns your mode of life most vehemently.
Dorine: Oh, yes, she's strict, devout, and has no taint
Of worldliness; in short, she seems a saint.
But it was time which taught her that disguise;
She's thus because she can't be otherwise.
So long as her attractions could enthrall,
She flounced and flirted and enjoyed it all,
But now that they're no longer what they were
She quits a world which fast is quitting her,
And wears a veil of virtue to conceal

Her bankrupt beauty and her lost appeal.
That's what becomes of old coquettes
    today:
Distressed when all their lovers fall away,
They see no recourse but to play the
    prude,
And so confer a style on solitude.
Thereafter, they're severe with everyone,
Condemning all our actions, pardoning
    none,
And claiming to be pure, austere, and
    zealous
When, if the truth were known, they're
    merely jealous,
And cannot bear to see another know
The pleasures time has forced them to
    forgo.

Madame Pernelle: [*Initially to* **Elmire**] That
    sort of talk is what you like to hear;
Therefore you'd have us all keep still, my
    dear,
While Madam rattles on the livelong day.
Nevertheless, I mean to have my say.
I tell you that you're blest to have Tartuffe
Dwelling, as my son's guest, beneath this
    roof;
That Heaven has sent him to forestall its
    wrath
By leading you, once more, to the true
    path;
That all he reprehends its reprehensible,
And that you'd better heed him, and be
    sensible.
These visits, balls, and parties in which
    you revel
Are nothing but inventions of the Devil.
One never hears a word that's edifying:
Nothing but chaff and foolishness and
    lying,
As well as vicious gossip in which one's
    neighbor
Is cut to bits with epee, foil, and saber.
People of sense are driven half-insane
At such affairs, where noise and folly reign
And reputations perish thick and fast.
As a wise preacher said on Sunday last,
Parties are Towers of Babylon, because
The guests all babble on with never a
    pause;

And then he told a story which, I think . . .
    [*To* **Cléante**]
I heard that laugh, Sir, and I saw that wink!
Go find your silly friends and laugh some
    more!
Enough; I'm going; don't show me to the
    door.
I leave this household much dismayed and
    vexed;
I cannot say when I shall see you next.
    [*Slapping* **Flipote**]
Wake up, don't stand there gaping into
    space!
I'll slap some sense into that stupid face.
Move, move, you slut.

Scene 2

[Cléante, Dorine]

Cléante: I think I'll stay behind;
I want no further pieces of her mind.
How that old lady . . .
Dorine: Oh, what wouldn't she say
If she could hear you speak of her that
    way!
She'd thank you for the *lady*, but I'm sure
She'd find the *old* a little premature.
Cléante: My, what a scene she made, and
    what a din!
And how this man Tartuffe has taken her
    in!
Dorine: Yes, but her son is even worse
    deceived;
His folly must be seen to be believed.
In the late troubles, he played an able part
And served his king with wise and loyal
    heart,
But he's quite lost his senses since he fell
Beneath Tartuffe's infatuating spell.
He calls him brother, and loves him as his
    life,
Preferring him to mother, child, or wife.
In him and him alone will he confide;
He's made him his confessor and his guide;
He pets and pampers him with love more
    tender
Than any pretty mistress could engender,
Gives him the place of honor when they
    dine,

Delights to see him gorging like a swine,
Stuffs him with dainties till his guts
    distend,
And when he belches, cries "God bless
    you, friend!"
In short, he's mad; he worships him; he
    dotes;
His deeds he marvels at, his words he
    quotes,
Thinking each act a miracle, each word
Oracular as those that Moses heard.
Tartuffe, much pleased to find so easy a
    victim,
Has in a hundred ways beguiled and
    tricked him,
Milked him of money, and with his
    permission
Established here a sort of Inquisition.
Even Laurent, his lackey, dares to give
Us arrogant advice on how to live;
He sermonizes us in thundering tones
And confiscates our ribbons and colognes.
Last week he tore a kerchief into pieces
Because he found it pressed in a *Life of
    Jesus:*
He said it was a sin to juxtapose
Unholy vanities and holy prose.

Scene 3

[**Elmire, Mariane, Damis, Cléante, Dorine**]

Elmire: [*To* **Cléante**] You did well not to
    follow; she stood in the door
And said *verbatim* all she'd said before.
I saw my husband coming. I think I'd best
Go upstairs now, and take a little rest.
Cléante: I'll wait and greet him here; then I
    must go.
I've really only time to say hello.
Damis: Sound him about my sister's
    wedding, please.
I think Tartuffe's against it, and that he's
Been urging Father to withdraw his
    blessing.
As you well know, I'd find that most
    distressing.
Unless my sister and Valère can marry,
My hopes to wed *his* sister will miscarry,
And I'm determined . . .
Dorine: He's coming.

Scene 4

[**Orgon, Cléante, Dorine**]

Orgon: Ah, Brother, good-day.
Cléante: Well, welcome back. I'm sorry I
    can't stay.
How was the country? Blooming, I trust,
    and green?
Orgon: Excuse me, Brother; just one moment.
    [*To* **Dorine**]
                            Dorine . . .
    [*To* **Cléante**]
To put my mind at rest, I always learn
The household news the moment I return.
    [*To* **Dorine**]
Has all been well, these two days I've been
    gone?
How are the family? What's been going on?
Dorine: Your wife, two days ago, had a bad
    fever,
And a fierce headache which refused to
    leave her.
Orgon: Ah. And Tartuffe?
Dorine: Tartuffe? Why, he's round and red,
Bursting with health, and excellently fed.
Orgon: Poor fellow!
Dorine: That night, the mistress was unable
To take a single bite at the dinner-table.
Her headache-pains, she said, were simply
    hellish.
Orgon: Ah. And Tartuffe?
Dorine: He ate his meal with relish,
And zealously devoured in her presence
A leg of mutton and a brace of pheasants.
Orgon: Poor fellow!
Dorine: Well, the pains continued strong,
And so she tossed and tossed the whole
    night long,
Now icy-cold, now burning like a flame.
We sat beside her bed till morning came.
Orgon: Ah. And Tartuffe?
Dorine: Why, having eaten, he rose
And sought his room, already in a doze,
Got into his warm bed, and snored away
In perfect peace until the break of day.
Orgon: Poor fellow!
Dorine: After much ado, we talked her
Into dispatching someone for the doctor.
He bled her, and the fever quickly fell.

Orgon: Ah. And Tartuffe?

Dorine: He bore it very well.

To keep his cheerfulness at any cost,

And make up for the blood *Madame* had lost,

He drank, at lunch, four beakers full of port.

Orgon: Poor fellow!

Dorine: Both are doing well, in short.

I'll go and tell *Madame* that you've expressed

Keen sympathy and anxious interest.

Scene 5

[Orgon, Cléante]

Cléante: That girl was laughing in your face, and though

I've no wish to offend you, even so

I'm bound to say that she had some excuse.

How can you possibly be such a goose?

Are you so dazed by this man's hocus-pocus

That all the world, save him, is out of focus?

You've given him clothing, shelter, food, and care;

Why must you also . . .

Orgon: Brother, stop right there.

You do not know the man of whom you speak.

Cléante: I grant you that. But my judgment's not so weak

That I can't tell, by his effect on others . . .

Orgon: Ah, when you meet him, you two will be like brothers!

There's been no loftier soul since time began.

He is a man who . . . a man who . . . an excellent man.

To keep his precepts is to be reborn,

And view this dunghill of a world with scorn.

Yes, thanks to him I'm a changed man indeed.

Under his tutelage my soul's been freed

From earthly loves, and every human tie:

My mother, children, brother, and wife could die,

And I'd not feel a single moment's pain.

Cléante: That's a fine sentiment, Brother; most humane.

Orgon: Oh, had you seen Tartuffe as I first knew him,

Your heart, like mine, would have surrendered to him.

He used to come into our church each day

And humbly kneel nearby, and start to pray.

He'd draw the eyes of everybody there

By the deep fervor of his heartfelt prayer;

He'd sigh and weep, and sometimes with a sound

Of rapture he would bend and kiss the ground;

And when I rose to go, he'd run before

To offer me holy-water at the door.

His serving-man, no less devout than he,

Informed me of his master's poverty;

I gave him gifts, but in his humbleness

He'd beg me every time to give him less.

"Oh, that's too much," he'd cry, "too much by twice!

I don't deserve it. The half, Sir, would suffice."

And when I wouldn't take it back, he'd share

Half of it with the poor, right then and there.

At length, Heaven prompted me to take him in

To dwell with us, and free our souls from sin.

He guides our lives, and to protect my honor

Stays by my wife, and keeps an eye upon her;

He tells me whom she sees, and all she does,

And seems more jealous than I ever was!

And how austere he is! Why, he can detect

A mortal sin where you would least suspect;

In smallest trifles, he's extremely strict.

Last week, his conscience was severely pricked

Because, while praying, he had caught a flea

And killed it, so he felt, too wrathfully.

Cléante: Good God, man! Have you lost
   your common sense—
  Or is this all some joke at my expense?
  How can you stand there and in all
   sobriety . . .
Orgon: Brother, your language savors of
   impiety.
  Too much free-thinking's made your faith
   unsteady,
  And as I've warned you many times
   already,
  'Twill get you into trouble before you're
   through.
Cléante: So I've been told before by dupes
   like you:
  Being blind, you'd have all others blind as
   well;
  The clear-eyed man you call an infidel,
  And he who sees through humbug and
   pretense
  Is charged, by you, with want of reverence.
  Spare me your warnings, Brother; I have
   no fear
  Of speaking out, for you and Heaven to
   hear,
  Against affected zeal and pious knavery.
  There's true and false in piety, as in
   bravery,
  And just as those whose courage shines the
   most
  In battle, are the least inclined to boast,
  So those whose hearts are truly pure and
   lowly
  Don't make a flashy show of being holy.
  There's a vast difference, so it seems to
   me,
  Between true piety and hypocrisy:
  How do you fail to see it, may I ask?
  Is not a face quite different from a mask?
  Cannot sincerity and cunning art,
  Reality and semblance, be told apart?
  Are scarecrows just like men, and do you
   hold
  That a false coin is just as good as gold?
  Ah, Brother, man's a strangely fashioned
   creature
  Who seldom is content to follow Nature,
  But recklessly pursues his inclination
  Beyond the narrow bounds of moderation,
  And often, by transgressing Reason's laws,

  Perverts a lofty aim or noble cause.
  A passing observation, but it applies.
Orgon: I see, dear Brother, that you're
   profoundly wise;
  You harbor all the insight of the age.
  You are our one clear mind, our only sage,
  The era's oracle, its Cato too,
  And all mankind are fools compared to you.
Cléante:
  Brother, I don't pretend to be a sage,
  Nor have I all the wisdom of the age.
  There's just one insight I would dare to
   claim:
  I know that true and false are not the
   same;
  And just as there is nothing I more revere
  Than a soul whose faith is steadfast and
   sincere,
  Nothing that I more cherish and admire
  Than honest zeal and true religious fire,
  So there is nothing that I find more base
  Than specious piety's dishonest face—
  Than these bold mountebanks, these
   histrios
  Whose impious mummeries and hollow
   shows
  Exploit our love of Heaven, and make a
   jest
  Of all that men think holiest and best;
  These calculating souls who offer prayers
  Not to their Maker, but as public wares,
  And seek to buy respect and reputation
  With lifted eyes and sighs of exaltation;
  These charlatans, I say, whose pilgrim
   souls
  Proceed, by way of Heaven, toward earthly
   goals,
  Who weep and pray and swindle and
   extort,
  Who preach the monkish life, but haunt
   the court,
  Who make their zeal the partner of their
   vice—
  Such men are vengeful, sly, and cold as
   ice,
  And when there is an enemy to defame
  They cloak their spite in fair religion's
   name,
  Their private spleen and malice being
   made

To seem a high and virtuous crusade,
Until, to mankind's reverent applause,
They crucify their foe in Heaven's cause.
Such knaves are all too common; yet, for
   the wise,
True piety isn't hard to recognize,
And, happily, these present times provide
   us
With bright examples to instruct and guide
   us.
Consider Ariston and Périandre;
Look at Oronte, Alcidamas, Clitandre;
Their virtue is acknowledged; who could
   doubt it?
But you won't hear them beat the drum
   about it.
They're never ostentatious, never vain,
And their religion's moderate and humane;
It's not their way to criticize and chide:
They think censoriousness a mark of pride,
And therefore, letting others preach and
   rave,
They show, by deeds, how Christians
   should behave.
They think no evil of their fellow man,
But judge of him as kindly as they can.
They don't intrigue and wangle and
   conspire;
To lead a good life is their one desire;
The sinner wakes no rancorous hate in
   them;
It is the sin alone which they condemn;
Nor do they try to show a fiercer zeal
For Heaven's cause than Heaven itself
   could feel.
These men I honor, these men I advocate
As models for us all to emulate.
Your man is not their sort at all, I fear:
And, while your praise of him is quite
   sincere,
I think that you've been dreadfully
   deluded.
Orgon: Now then, dear Brother, is your
   speech concluded?
Cléante: Why, yes.
Orgon: Your servant, Sir. [*He turns to go.*]
Cléante: No, Brother; wait.
   There's one more matter. You agreed of
   late

That young Valère might have your
   daughter's hand.
Orgon: I did.
Cléante: And set the date, I understand.
Orgon: Quite so.
Cléante: You've now postponed it; is that
   true?
Orgon: No doubt.
Cléante: The match no longer pleases you?
Orgon: Who knows?
Cléante: D'you mean to go back on your
   word?
Orgon: I won't say that.
Cléante: Has anything occurred
   Which might entitle you to break your
   pledge?
Orgon: Perhaps.
Cléante: Why must you hem, and haw, and
   hedge?
   The boy asked me to sound you in this
   affair . . .
Orgon: It's been a pleasure.
Cléante: But what shall I tell Valère?
Orgon: Whatever you like.
Cléante: But what have you decided?
   What are your plans?
Orgon: I plan, Sir, to be guided
   By Heaven's will.
Cléante: Come, Brother, don't talk rot.
   You've given Valère your word; will you
   keep it, or not?
Orgon: Good day.
Cléante: This looks like poor Valère's
   undoing;
   I'll go and warn him that there's trouble
   brewing.

ACT II

Scene 1

   [**Orgon, Mariane**]
Orgon: Mariane.
Mariane: Yes, Father?
Orgon: A word with you; come here.
Mariane: What are you looking for?
Orgon: [*Peering into a small closet*] Eaves-
   droppers, dear.
   I'm making sure we shan't be overheard.

Someone in there could catch our every
    word.
Ah, good, we're safe. Now, Mariane, my
    child,
You're a sweet girl who's tractable and
    mild,
Whom I hold dear, and think most highly
    of.
Mariane: I'm deeply grateful, Father, for
    your love.
Orgon: That's well said, Daughter; and you
    can repay me
If, in all things, you'll cheerfully obey me.
Mariane: To please you, Sir, is what
    delights me best.
Orgon: Good, good. Now, what d'you think
    of Tartuffe, our guest?
Mariane: I, Sir?
Orgon: Yes. Weigh your answer; think it
    through.
Mariane: Oh, dear. I'll say whatever you
    wish me to.
Orgon: That's wisely said, my Daughter.
    Say of him, then,
That he's the very worthiest of men,
And that you're fond of him, and would
    rejoice
In being his wife, if that should be my
    choice.
    Well?
Mariane: What?
Orgon: What's that?
Mariane: I . . .
Orgon: Well?
Mariane: Forgive me, pray.
Orgon: Did you not hear me?
Mariane: Of *whom*, Sir, must I say
That I am fond of him, and would rejoice
In being his wife, if that should be your
    choice?
Orgon: Why, of Tartuffe.
Mariane: But, Father, that's false, you know.
Why would you have me say what isn't
    so?
Orgon: Because I am resolved it shall be
    true.
That it's my wish should be enough for
    you.
Mariane: You can't mean, Father . . .

Orgon: Yes, Tartuffe shall be
Allied by marriage to this family,
And he's to be your husband, is that clear?
It's a father's privilege . . .

Scene 2
[Dorine, Orgon, Mariane]
Orgon: [*To* **Dorine**] What are you doing in
    here?
Is curiosity so fierce a passion
With you, that you must eavesdrop in this
    fashion?
Dorine: There's lately been a rumor going
    about—
Based on some hunch or chance remark,
    no doubt—
That you mean Mariane to wed Tartuffe.
I've laughed it off, of course, as just a
    spoof.
Orgon: You find it so incredible?
Dorine: Yes, I do.
I won't accept that story, even from you.
Orgon: Well, you'll believe it when the
    thing is done.
Dorine: Yes, yes, of course. Go on and have
    your fun.
Orgon: I've never been more serious in my
    life.
Dorine: Ha!
Orgon: Daughter, I mean it; you're to be his
    wife.
Dorine: No, don't believe your father; it's
    all a hoax.
Orgon: See here, young woman . . .
Dorine: Come, Sir, no more jokes;
You can't fool us.
Orgon: How dare you talk that way?
Dorine: All right, then: we believe you, sad
    to say.
But how a man like you, who looks so
    wise
And wears a moustache of such splendid
    size,
Can be so foolish as to . . .
Orgon: Silence, please!
My girl, you take too many liberties.
I'm master here, as you must not forget.
Dorine: Do let's discuss this calmly; don't
    be upset.

You can't be serious, Sir, about this plan.
What should that bigot want with Mariane?
Praying and fasting ought to keep him
busy.
And then, in terms of wealth and rank,
what is he?
Why should a man of property like you
Pick out a beggar son-in-law?

Orgon: That will do.
Speak of his poverty with reverence.
His is a pure and saintly indigence
Which far transcends all worldly pride and
pelf.
He lost his fortune, as he says himself,
Because he cared for Heaven alone, and so
Was careless of his interests here below.
I mean to get him out of his present straits
And help him to recover his estates—
Which, in his part of the world, have no
small fame.
Poor though he is, he's a gentleman just
the same.

Dorine: Yes, so he tells us; and, Sir, it
seems to me
Such pride goes very ill with piety.
A man whose spirit spurns this dungy earth
Ought not to brag of lands and noble
birth;
Such worldly arrogance will hardly square
With meek devotion and the life of prayer.
. . . But this approach, I see, has drawn a
blank;
Let's speak, then, of his person, not his
rank.
Doesn't it seem to you a trifle grim
To give a girl like her to a man like him?
When two are so ill-suited, can't you see
What the sad consequence is bound to be?
A young girl's virtue is imperilled, Sir,
When such a marriage is imposed on her;
For if one's bridegroom isn't to one's taste,
It's hardly an inducement to be chaste,
And many a man with horns upon his
brow
Has made his wife the thing that she is
It's hard to be a faithful wife, in short,
To certain husbands of a certain sort,
And he who gives his daughter to a man
she hates
Must answer for her sins at Heaven's gates.

Think, Sir, before you play so risky a role.

Orgon: This servant-girl presumes to save
my soul!

Dorine: You would do well to ponder what
I've said.

Orgon: Daughter, we'll disregard this
dunderhead.
Just trust your father's judgment. Oh, I'm
aware
That I once promised you to young Valére;
But now I hear he gambles, which greatly
shocks me;
What's more, I've doubts about his
orthodoxy.
His visits to church, I note, are very few.

Dorine: Would you have him go at the
same hours as you,
And kneel nearby, to be sure of being
seen?

Orgon: I can dispense with such remarks,
Dorine.
      [*To* **Mariane**]
Tartuffe, however, is sure of Heaven's
blessing,
And that's the only treasure worth
possessing.
This match will bring you joys beyond all
measure;
Your cup will overflow with every pleasure;
You two will interchange your faithful loves
Like two sweet cherubs, or two turtle-doves.
No harsh word shall be heard, no frown be
seen,
And he shall make you happy as a queen.

Dorine: And she'll make him a cuckold,
just wait and see.

Orgon: What language!

Dorine: Oh, he's a man of destiny;
He's *made* for horns, and what the stars
demand
Your daughter's virtue surely can't
withstand.

Orgon: Don't interrupt me further. Why
can't you learn
That certain things are none of your
concern?

Dorine: It's for your own sake that I
interfere.
      [*She repeatedly interrupts* **Orgon** *just as he is
      turning to speak to his daughter*]

Orgon: Most kind of you. Now, hold your
   tongue, d'you hear?

Dorine: If I didn't love you . . .

Orgon: Spare me your affection.

Dorine: I'll love you, Sir, in spite of your
   objection.

Orgon: Blast!

Dorine: I can't bear, Sir, for your honor's
   sake,
   To let you make this ludicrous mistake.

Orgon: You mean to go on talking?

Dorine: If I didn't protest
   This sinful marriage, my conscience
   couldn't rest.

Orgon: If you don't hold your tongue, you
   little shrew . . .

Dorine: What, lost your temper? A pious
   man like you?

Orgon: Yes! Yes! You talk and talk. I'm
   maddened by it.
   Once and for all, I tell you to be quiet.

Dorine: Well, I'll be quiet. But I'll be
   thinking hard.

Orgon: Think all you like, but you had
   better guard
   That saucy tongue of yours, or I'll . . .
   [*Turning back to* **Mariane**]
                                          Now, child,
   I've weighed this matter fully.

Dorine: [*Aside*] It drives me wild
   That I can't speak.
   [**Orgon** *turns his head, and she is silent.*]

Orgon: Tartuffe is no young dandy,
   But, still, his person . . .

Dorine: [*Aside*] Is as sweet as candy.

Orgon: Is such that, even if you shouldn't
   care
   For his other merits . . .
   [*He turns and stands facing* **Dorine**, *arms
   crossed.*]

Dorine: [*Aside*] They'll make a lovely pair.
   If I were she, no man would marry me
   Against my inclination, and go scot-free.
   He'd learn, before the wedding-day was
   over,
   How readily a wife can find a lover.

Orgon: [*To* **Dorine**] It seems you treat my
   orders as a joke.

Dorine: Why, what's the matter? 'Twas not
   to you I spoke.

Orgon: What *were* you doing?

Dorine: Talking to myself, that's all.

Orgon: Ah! [*Aside*] One more bit of
   impudence and gall,
   And I shall give her a good slap in the
   face.
   [*He puts himself in position to slap her;* **Dorine**,
   *whenever he glances at her, stands immobile and
   silent*]
   Daughter, you shall accept, and with good
   grace,
   The husband I've selected . . . Your
   wedding-day . . .
   [*To* **Dorine**]
   Why don't you talk to yourself?

Dorine: I've nothing to say.

Orgon: Come, just one word.

Dorine: No thank you, Sir. I pass.

Orgon: Come, speak; I'm waiting.

Dorine: I'd not be such an ass.

Orgon: [*Turning to* **Mariane**] In short, dear
   Daughter, I mean to be obeyed,
   And you must bow to the sound choice
   I've made.

Dorine: [*Moving away*] I'd not wed such a
   monster, even in jest.
   [**Orgon** *attempts to slap her, but misses.*]

Orgon: Daughter, that maid of yours is a
   thorough pest;
   She makes me sinfully annoyed and
   nettled.
   I can't speak further; my nerves are too
   unsettled.
   She's so upset me by her insolent talk,
   I'll calm myself by going for a walk.

Scene 3

[**Dorine, Mariane**]

Dorine: [*Returning*] Well, have you lost your
   tongue, girl? Must I play
   Your part, and say the lines you ought to
   say?
   Faced with a fate so hideous and absurd,
   Can you not utter one dissenting word?

Mariane: What good would it do? A
   father's power is great.

Dorine: Resist him now, or it will be too
   late.

Mariane: But . . .

Dorine: Tell him one cannot love at a
father's whim;
That you shall marry for yourself, not him;
That since it's you who are to be the bride,
It's you, not he, who must be satisfied;
And that if his Tartuffe is so sublime,
He's free to marry him at any time.

Mariane: I've bowed so long to Father's
strict control,
I couldn't oppose him now, to save my
soul.

Dorine: Come, come, Mariane. Do listen to
reason, won't you?
Valère has asked your hand. Do you love
him, or don't you?

Mariane: Oh, how unjust of you! What can
you mean
By asking such a question, dear Dorine?
You know the depth of my affection for
him;
I've told you a hundred times how I adore
him.

Dorine: I don't believe in everything I hear;
Who knows if your professions were
sincere?

Mariane: They were, Dorine, and you do
me wrong to doubt it;
Heaven knows that I've been all too frank
about it.

Dorine: You love him, then?

Mariane: Oh, more than I can express.

Dorine: And he, I take it, cares for you no
less?

Mariane: I think so.

Dorine: And you both, with equal fire,
Burn to be married?

Mariane: That is our one desire.

Dorine: What of Tartuffe, then? What of
your father's plan?

Mariane: I'll kill myself, if I'm forced to
wed that man.

Dorine: I hadn't thought of that recourse.
How splendid!
Just die, and all your troubles will be
ended!
A fine solution. Oh, it maddens me
To hear you talk in that self-pitying key.

Mariane: Dorine, how harsh you are! It's
most unfair.

You have no sympathy for my despair.

Dorine: I've none at all for people who talk
drivel
And, faced with difficulties, whine and
snivel.

Mariane: No doubt I'm timid, but it would
be wrong . . .

Dorine: True love requires a heart that's
firm and strong.

Mariane: I'm strong in my affection for
Valère,
But coping with my father is his affair.

Dorine: But if your father's brain has grown
so cracked
Over his dear Tartuffe that he can retract
His blessing, though your wedding-day was
named,
It's surely not Valère who's to be blamed.

Mariane: If I defied my father, as you
suggest,
Would it not seem unmaidenly, at best?
Shall I defend my love at the expense
Of brazenness and disobedience?
Shall I parade my heart's desires, and
flaunt . . .

Dorine: No, I ask nothing of you. Clearly
you want
To be Madame Tartuffe, and I feel bound
Not to oppose a wish so very sound.
What right have I to criticize the match?
Indeed, my dear, the man's a brilliant
catch.
Monsieur Tartuffe! Now, there's a man of
weight!
Yes, yes, Monsieur Tartuffe, I'm bound to
state,
Is quite a person; that's not to be denied;
'Twill be no little thing to be his bride.
The world already rings with his renown;
He's a great noble—in his native town;
His ears are red, he has a pink complexion,
And all in all, he'll suit you to perfection.

Mariane: Dear God!

Dorine: Oh, how triumphant you will feel
At having caught a husband so ideal!

Mariane: Oh, do stop teasing, and use your
cleverness
To get me out of this appalling mess.
Advise me, and I'll do whatever you say.

Dorine: Ah no, a dutiful daughter must obey
Her father, even if he weds her to an ape.
You've a bright future; why struggle to escape?
Tartuffe will take you back where his family lives,
To a small town aswarm with relatives—
Uncles and cousins whom you'll be charmed to meet.
You'll be received at once by the elite,
Calling upon the bailiff's wife, no less—
Even, perhaps, upon the mayoress,
Who'll sit you down in the *best* kitchen chair.
Then, once a year, you'll dance at the village fair
To the drone of bagpipes—two of them, in fact—
And see a puppet-show, or an animal act.
Your husband . . .

Mariane: Oh, you turn my blood to ice!
Stop torturing me, and give me your advice.

Dorine: [*Threatening to go*] Your servant, Madam.

Mariane: Dorine, I beg of you . . .

Dorine: No, you deserve it; this marriage must go through.

Mariane: Dorine!

Dorine: No.

Mariane: Not Tartuffe! You know I think him . . .

Dorine: Tartuffe's your cup of tea, and you shall drink him.

Mariane: I've always told you everything, and relied . . .

Dorine: No. You deserve to be tartuffified.

Mariane: Well, since you mock me and refuse to care,
I'll henceforth seek my solace in despair:
Despair shall be my counsellor and friend,
And help me bring my sorrows to an end.
   [*She starts to leave.*]

Dorine: There now, come back; my anger has subsided.
You do deserve some pity, I've decided.

Mariane: Dorine, if Father makes me undergo
This dreadful martyrdom, I'll die, I know.

Dorine: Don't fret; it won't be difficult to discover
Some plan of action . . . But here's Valère, your lover.

Scene 4

[**Valère, Mariane, Dorine**]

Valère: Madam, I've just received some wondrous news
Regarding which I'd like to hear your views.

Mariane: What news?

Valère: Your're marrying Tartuffe.

Mariane: I find
That Father does have such a match in mind.

Valère: Your father, Madam . . .

Mariane: . . . has just this minute said
That it's Tartuffe he wishes me to wed.

Valère: Can he be serious?

Mariane: Oh, indeed he can;
He's clearly set his heart upon the plan.

Valère: And what position do you propose to take,
Madam?

Mariane: Why—I don't know.

Valère: For heaven's sake—
You don't know?

Mariane: No.

Valère: Well, well!

Mariane: Advise me, do.

Valère: Marry the man. That's my advice to you.

Mariane: That's your advice?

Valère: Yes.

Mariane: Truly?

Valère: Oh, absolutely.
You couldn't choose more wisely, more astutely.

Mariane: Thanks for this counsel; I'll follow it, of course.

Valère: Do, do; I'm sure 'twill cost you no remorse.

Mariane: To give it didn't cause your heart to break.

Valère: I gave it, Madam, only for your sake.

Mariane: And it's for your sake that I take it, Sir.

Dorine: [*Withdrawing to the rear of the stage*] Let's see which fool will prove the stubborner.

Valère: So! I am nothing to you, and it was flat
Deception when you . . .

Mariane: Please, enough of that.
You've told me plainly that I should agree
To wed the man my father's chosen for me,
And since you've deigned to counsel me so wisely,
I promise, Sir, to do as you advise me.

Valère: Ah, no, 'twas not by me that you were swayed.
No, your decision was already made;
Though now, to save appearances, you protest
That you're betraying me at my behest.

Mariane: Just as you say.

Valère: Quite so. And I now see
That you were never truly in love with me.

Mariane: Alas, you're free to think so if you choose.

Valère: I choose to think so, and here's a bit of news:
You've spurned my hand, but I know where to turn
For kinder treatment, as you shall quickly learn.

Mariane: I'm sure you do. Your noble qualities
Inspire affection . . .

Valère: Forget my qualities, please.
They don't inspire you overmuch, I find.
But there's another lady I have in mind
Whose sweet and generous nature will not scorn
To compensate me for the loss I've borne.

Mariane: I'm no great loss, and I'm sure that you'll transfer
Your heart quite painlessly from me to her.

Valère: I'll do my best to take it in my stride.
The pain I feel at being cast aside
Time and forgetfulness may put an end to.
Or if I can't forget, I shall pretend to.

No self-respecting person is expected
To go on loving once he's been rejected.

Mariane: Now, that's a fine, high-minded sentiment.

Valère: One to which any sane man would assent.
Would you prefer it if I pined away
In hopeless passion till my dying day?
Am I to yield you to a rival's arms
And not console myself with other charms?

Mariane: Go then: console yourself; don't hesitate.
I wish you to; indeed, I cannot wait.

Valère: You wish me to?

Mariane: Yes.

Valère: That's the final straw.
Madam, farewell. Your wish shall be my law.
[*He starts to leave, and then returns: this repeatedly.*]

Mariane: Splendid.

Valère: [*Coming back again*] This breach, remember, is of your making;
It's you who've driven me to the step I'm taking.

Mariane: Of course.

Valère: [*Coming back again*] Remember, too, that I am merely
Following your example.

Mariane: I see that clearly.

Valère: Enough. I'll go and do your bidding, then.

Mariane: Good.

Valère: [*Coming back again*] You shall never see my face again.

Mariane: Excellent.

Valère: [*Walking to the door, then turning about*] Yes?

Mariane: What?

Valère: What's that? What did you say?

Mariane: Nothing. You're dreaming.

Valère: Ah. Well, I'm on my way.
Farewell, *Madame*.
[*He moves slowly away.*]

Mariane: Farewell.

Dorine: [*To* **Mariane**] If you ask me,
Both of you are as mad as mad can be.
Do stop this nonsense, now. I've only let you

Squabble so long to see where it would get
  you.
Whoa there, Monsieure Valère!
        [*She goes and seizes* **Valère** *by the arm; he*
        makes a great show of resistance.]
Valère: What's this, Dorine?
Dorine: Come here.
Valère: No, no, my heart's too full of
  spleen.
Don't hold me back; her wish must be
  obeyed.
Dorine: Stop!
Valère: It's too late now; my decision's
  made.
Dorine: Oh, pooh!
Mariane: [*Aside*] He hates the sight of me,
  that's plain.
I'll go, and so deliver him from pain.
Dorine: [*Leaving* **Valère,** *running after* **Mariane**]
  And now *you* run away! Come back.
Mariane: No, no.
Nothing you say will keep me here. Let go!
Valère: [*Aside*] She cannot bear my
  presence, I perceive.
To spare her further torment, I shall leave.
Dorine: [*Leaving* **Mariane,** *running after* **Valère**]
Again! You'll not escape, Sir; don't you
  try it.
Come here, you two. Stop fussing, and be
  quiet.
        [*She takes* **Valère** *by the hand, then* **Mariane,**
        and draws them together.]
Valère: [*To* **Dorine**] What do you want of me?
Mariane: [*To* **Dorine**] What is the point of
  this?
Dorine: We're going to have a little
  armistice.
        [*To* **Valère**]
Now, weren't you silly to get so overheated?
Valère: Didn't you see how badly I was
  treated?
Dorine: [*To* **Mariane**] Aren't you a simpleton,
  to have lost your head?
Mariane: Didn't you hear the hateful things
  he said?
Dorine: [*To* **Valère**] You're both great fools.
  Her sole desire, Valère,
Is to be yours in marriage. To that I'll
  swear.

        [*To* **Mariane**]
He loves you only, and he wants no wife
But you, Mariane. On that I'll stake my life.
Mariane: [*To* **Valère**] Then why you advised
  me so, I cannot see.
Valère: [*To* **Mariane**] On such a question,
  why ask advice of *me?*
Dorine: Oh, you're impossible. Give me
  your hands, you two.
        [*To* **Valère**]
Yours first.
Valère: [*Giving* **Dorine** *his hand*] But why?
Dorine: [*To* **Mariane**] And now a hand from
  you.
Mariane: [*Also giving* **Dorine** *her hand*] What are
  you doing?
Dorine: There: a perfect fit.
You suit each other better than you'll
  admit.
        [**Valère** *and* **Mariane** *holds hands for some time*
        without looking at each other.]
Valère: [*Turning toward* **Mariane**] Ah, come,
  don't be so haughty. Give a man
A look of kindness, won't you, Mariane?
        [**Mariane** *turns toward* **Valère** *and smiles.*]
Dorine: I tell you, lovers are completely mad!
Valère: [*To* **Mariane**] Now come, confess that
  you were very bad
To hurt my feelings as you did just now.
I have a just complaint, you must allow.
Mariane: *You* must allow that you were
  most unpleasant . . .
Dorine: Let's table that discussion for the
  present;
Your father has a plan which must be
  stopped.
Mariane: Advise us, then; what means must
  we adopt?
Dorine: We'll use all manner of means, and
  all at once.
        [*To* **Mariane**]
Your father's addled; he's acting like a
  dunce.
Therefore you'd better humor the old fossil.
Pretend to yield to him, be sweet and
  docile,
And then postpone, as often as necessary,
The day on which you have agreed to
  marry.

You'll thus gain time, and time will turn
   the trick.
Sometimes, for instance, you'll be taken
   sick,
And that will seem good reason for delay;
Or some bad omen will make you change
   the day—
You'll dream of muddy water, or you'll pass
A dead man's hearse, or break a
   looking-glass.
If all else fails, no man can marry you
Unless you take his ring and say "I do."
But now, let's separate. If they should find
Us talking here, our plot might be divined.
     [*To* **Valère**]
Go to your friends, and tell them what's
   occurred,
And have them urge her father to keep his
   word.
Meanwhile, we'll stir her brother into action,
And get Elmire, as well, to join our faction.
Good-bye.
Valère: [*To* **Mariane**] Though each of us will
   do his best,
It's your true heart on which my hopes
   shall rest.
Mariane: [*To* **Valère**] Regardless of what
   Father may decide,
None but Valère shall claim me as his
   bride.
Valère: Oh, how those words content me!
   Come what will . . .
Dorine: Oh, lovers, lovers! Their tongues
   are never still.
Be off, now.
Valère: [*Turning to go, then turning back*] One
   last word . . .
Dorine: No time to chat:
   You leave by this door; and *you* leave by
   that.
     [**Dorine** *pushes them, by the shoulders, toward*
     opposing doors.]

ACT III

Scene 1

[Damis, Dorine]
Damis: May lightning strike me even as I
   speak,

May all men call me cowardly and weak,
If any fear or scruple holds me back
From settling things, at once, with that
   great quack!
Dorine: Now, don't give way to violent
   emotion.
Your father's merely talked about this
   notion,
And words and deeds are far from being
   one.
Much that is talked about is left undone.
Damis: No, I must stop that scoundrel's
   machinations;
I'll go and tell him off; I'm out of patience.
Dorine: Do calm down and be practical. I
   had rather
My mistress dealt with him—and with your
   father.
She has some influence with Tartuffe, I've
   noted.
He hangs upon her words, seems most
   devoted,
And may, indeed, be smitten by her charm.
Pray Heaven it's true! 'Twould do our
   cause no harm.
She sent for him, just now, to sound him
   out
On this affair you're so incensed about;
She'll find out where he stands, and tell
   him, too,
What dreadful strife and trouble will ensue
If he lends countenance to your father's
   plan.
I couldn't get in to see him, but his man
Says that he's almost finished with his
   prayers.
Go, now. I'll catch him when he comes
   downstairs.
Damis: I want to hear this conference, and I
   will.
Dorine: No, they must be alone.
Damis: Oh, I'll keep still.
Dorine: Not you. I know your temper.
   You'd start a brawl,
And shout and stamp your foot and spoil
   it all.
Go on.
Damis: I won't; I have a perfect right . . .
Dorine: Lord, you're a nuisance! He's
   coming; get out of sight.

[**Damis** *conceals himself in a closet at the rear of the stage.*]

Scene 2

[**Tartuffe, Dorine**]

Tartuffe: [*Observing* **Dorine**, *and calling to his manservant offstage*]

Hang up my hair-shirt, put my scourge in place,

And pray, Laurent, for Heaven's perpetual grace.

I'm going to the prison now, to share

My last few coins with the poor wretches there.

Dorine: [*Aside*] Dear God, what affectation! What a fake!

Tartuffe: You wished to see me?

Dorine: Yes . . .

Tartuffe: [*Taking a handkerchief from his pocket*]

For mercy's sake,

Please take this handkerchief, before you speak.

Dorine: What?

Tartuffe: Cover that bosom, girl. The flesh is weak,

And unclean thoughts are difficult to control.

Such sights as that can undermine the soul.

Dorine: Your soul, it seems, has very poor defenses,

And flesh makes quite an impact on your senses.

It's strange that you're so easily excited;

My own desires are not so soon ignited,

And if I saw you naked as a beast,

Not all your hide would tempt me in the least.

Tartuffe: Girl, speak more modestly; unless you do,

I shall be forced to take my leave of you.

Dorine: Oh, no, it's I who must be on my way;

I've just one little message to convey.

Madame is coming down, and begs you, Sir,

To wait and have a word or two with her.

Tartuffe: Gladly.

Dorine: [*Aside*] *That* had a softening effect!

I think my guess about him was correct.

Tartuffe: Will she be long?

Dorine: No: that's her step I hear.

Ah, here she is, and I shall disappear.

Scene 3

[**Elmire, Tartuffe**]

Tartuffe: May Heaven, whose infinite goodness we adore,

Preserve your body and soul forevermore,

And bless your days, and answer thus the plea

Of one who is its humblest votary.

Elmire: I thank you for that pious wish. But please,

Do take a chair and let's be more at ease.

[*They sit down.*]

Tartuffe: I trust that you are once more well and strong?

Elmire: Oh, yes: the fever didn't last for long.

Tartuffe: My prayers are too unworthy, I am sure,

To have gained from Heaven this most gracious cure;

But lately, Madam, my every supplication

Has had for object your recuperation.

Elmire: You shouldn't have troubled so. I don't deserve it.

Tartuffe: Your health is priceless, Madam, and to preserve it

I'd gladly give my own, in all sincerity.

Elmire: Sir, you outdo us all in Christian charity.

You've been most kind. I count myself your debtor.

Tartuffe: 'Twas nothing, Madam. I long to serve you better.

Elmire: There's a private matter I'm anxious to discuss.

I'm glad there's no one here to hinder us.

Tartuffe: I too am glad; it floods my heart with bliss

To find myself alone with you like this.

For just this chance I've prayed with all my power—

But prayed in vain, until this happy hour.

Elmire: This won't take long, Sir, and I hope you'll be

Entirely frank and unconstrained with me.

Tartuffe: Indeed, there's nothing I had rather do
Than bare my inmost heart and soul to you.
First, let me say that what remarks I've made
About the constant visits you are paid
Were prompted not by any mean emotion,
But rather by a pure and deep devotion,
A fervent zeal . . .

Elmire: No need for explanation.
Your sole concern, I'm sure, was my salvation.

Tartuffe: [*Taking* **Elmire**'s *hand and pressing her fingertips*]
Quite so; and such great fervor do I feel . . .

Elmire: Ooh! Please! You're pinching!

Tartuffe: 'Twas from excess of zeal.
I never meant to cause you pain, I swear.
I'd rather . . .
[*He places his hand on* **Elmire**'s *knee.*]

Elmire: What can you hand be doing there?

Tartuffe: Feeling your gown; what soft, fine-woven stuff!

Elmire: Please, I'm extremely ticklish. That's enough.
[*She draws her chair away;* **Tartuffe** *pulls his after her.*]

Tartuffe: [*Fondling the lace collar of her gown*]
My, my, what lovely lacework on your dress!
The workmanship's miraculous, no less.
I've not seen anything to equal it.

Elmire: Yes, quite. But let's talk business for a bit.
They say my husband means to break his word
And give his daughter to you, Sir. Had you heard?

Tartuffe: He did once mention it. But I confess
I dream of quite a different happiness.
It's elsewhere, Madam, that my eyes discern
The promise of that bliss for which I yearn.

Elmire: I see: you care for nothing here below.

Tartuffe: Ah, well—my heart's not made of stone, you know.

Elmire: All your desires mount heavenward, I'm sure,
In scorn of all that's earthly and impure.

Tartuffe: A love of heavenly beauty does not preclude
A proper love for earthly pulchritude;
Our senses are quite rightly captivated
By perfect works our Maker has created.
Some glory clings to all that Heaven has made;
In you, all Heaven's marvels are displayed.
On that fair face, such beauties have been lavished,
The eyes are dazzled and the heart is ravished;
How could I look on you, O flawless creature,
And not adore the Author of all Nature,
Feeling a love both passionate and pure
For you, his triumph of self-portraiture?
At first, I trembled lest that love should be
A subtle snare that Hell had laid for me;
I vowed to flee the sight of you, eschewing
A rapture that might prove my soul's undoing;
But soon, fair being, I became aware
That my deep passion could be made to square
With rectitude, and with my bounden duty.
I thereupon surrendered to your beauty.
It is, I know, presumptuous on my part
To bring you this poor offering of my heart,
And it is not my merit, Heaven knows,
But your compassion on which my hopes repose.
You are my peace, my solace, my salvation;
On you depends my bliss—or desolation;
I bide your judgment and, as you think best,
I shall be either miserable or blest.

Elmire: Your declaration is most gallant, Sir,
But don't you think it's out of character?
You'd have done better to restrain your passion
And think before you spoke in such a fashion.

It ill becomes a pious man like you . . .

Tartuffe: I may be pious, but I'm human too:

With your celestial charms before his eyes,

A man has not the power to be wise.

I know such words sound strangely, coming from me,

But I'm no angel, nor was meant to be,

And if you blame my passion, you must needs

Reproach as well the charms on which it feeds.

Your loveliness I had no sooner seen

Than you became my soul's unrivalled queen;

Before your seraph glance, divinely sweet,

My heart's defenses crumbled in defeat,

And nothing fasting, prayer, or tears might do

Could stay my spirit from adoring you.

My eyes, my sighs have told you in the past

What now my lips make bold to say at last,

And if, in your great goodness, you will deign

To look upon your slave, and ease his pain,—

If, in compassion for my soul's distress,

You'll stoop to comfort my unworthiness,

I'll raise to you, in thanks for that sweet manna,

An endless hymn, an infinite hosanna.

With me, of course, there need be no anxiety,

No fear of scandal or of notoriety.

These young court gallants, whom all the ladies fancy,

Are vain in speech, in action rash and chancy;

When they succeed in love, the world soon knows it;

No favor's granted them but they disclose it

And by the looseness of their tongues profane

The very altar where their hearts have lain.

Men of my sort, however, love discreetly,

And one may trust our reticence completely.

My keen concern for my good name insures

The absolute security of yours;

In short, I offer you, my dear Elmire,

Love without scandal, pleasure without fear.

Elmire: I've heard your well-turned speeches to the end,

And what you urge I clearly apprehend.

Aren't you afraid that I may take a notion

To tell my husband of your warm devotion,

And that, supposing he were duly told,

His feelings toward you might grow rather cold?

Tartuffe: I know, dear lady, that your exceeding charity

Will lead your heart to pardon my temerity;

That you'll excuse my violent affection

As human weakness, human imperfection;

And that—O fairest!—you will bear in mind

That I'm but flesh and blood, and am not blind.

Elmire: Some women might do otherwise, perhaps,

But I shall be discreet about your lapse;

I'll tell my husband nothing of what's occurred

If, in return, you'll give your solemn word

To advocate as forcefully as you can

The marriage of Valère and Mariane,

Renouncing all desire to dispossess

Another of his rightful happiness,

And . . .

Scene 4

[Damis, Elmire, Tartuffe]

Damis: [*Emerging from the closet where he has been hiding*]

No! We'll not hush up this vile affair;

I heard it all inside that closet there,

Where Heaven, in order to confound the pride

Of this great rascal, prompted me to hide.

Ah, now I have my long-awaited chance

To punish his deceit and arrogance,

And give my father clear and shocking proof

Of the black character of his dear Tartuffe.

Elmire: Ah no, Damis; I'll be content if he

Will study to deserve my leniency.
I've promised silence—don't make me
    break my word;
To make a scandal would be too absurd.
Good wives laugh off such trifles, and
    forget them;
Why should they tell their husbands, and
    upset them?
Damis: You have your reasons for taking
    such a course,
And I have reasons, too, of equal force.
To spare him now would be insanely
    wrong.
I've swallowed my just wrath for far too
    long
And watched this insolent bigot bringing
    strife
And bitterness into our family life.
Too long he's meddled in my father's
    affairs,
Thwarting my marriage-hopes, and poor
    Valère's.
It's high time that my father was
    undeceived,
And now I've proof that can't be
    disbelieved—
Proof that was furnished me by Heaven
    above.
It's too good not to take advantage of.
This is my chance, and I deserve to lose it
If, for one moment, I hesitate to use it.
Elmire: Damis . . .
Damis: No, I must do what I think right.
Madam, my heart is bursting with delight,
And, say whatever you will, I'll not consent
To lose the sweet revenge on which I'm
    bent.
I'll settle matters without more ado;
And here, most opportunely, is my cue.

Scene 5

[Orgon, Damis, Tartuffe, Elmire]
Damis: Father, I'm glad you've joined us.
    Let us advise you
Of some fresh news which doubtless will
    surprise you.
You've just now been repaid with interest
For all your loving-kindness to our guest.

He's proved his warm and grateful feelings
    toward you;
It's with a pair of horns he would reward
    you.
Yes, I surprised him with your wife, and
    heard
His whole adulterous offer, every word.
She, with her all too gentle disposition,
Would not have told you of his
    proposition;
But I shall not make terms with brazen
    lechery,
And feel that not to tell you would be
    treachery.
Elmire: And I hold that one's husband's
    peace of mind
Should not be spoilt by tattle of this kind.
One's honor doesn't require it: to be
    proficient
In keeping men at bay is quite sufficient.
These are my sentiments, and I wish,
    Damis,
That you had heeded me and held your
    peace.

Scene 6

[Orgon, Damis, Tartuffe]
Orgon: Can it be true, this dreadful thing I
    hear?
Tartuffe: Yes, Brother, I'm a wicked man, I
    fear:
A wretched sinner, all depraved and
    twisted,
The greatest villain that has ever existed.
My life's one heap of crimes, which grows
    each minute;
There's naught but foulness and corruption
    in it;
And I perceive that Heaven, outraged by
    me,
Has chosen this occasion to mortify me.
Charge me with any deed you wish to
    name;
I'll not defend myself, but take the blame.
Believe what you are told, and drive
    Tartuffe
Like some base criminal from beneath your
    roof;

Yes, drive me hence, and with a
   parting curse:
I shan't protest, for I deserve far worse.

Orgon: [*To* **Damis**] Ah, you deceitful boy,
   how dare you try
To stain his purity with so foul a lie?

Damis: What? Are you taken in by such a
   bluff?
Did you not hear . . .?

Orgon: Enough, you rogue, enough!

Tartuffe: Ah, Brother, let him speak; you're
   being unjust.
Believe his story; the boy deserves your
   trust.
Why, after all, should you have faith in
   me?
How can you know what I might do, or
   be?
Is it on my good actions that you base
Your favor? Do you trust my pious face?
Ah, no, don't be deceived by hollow
   shows;
I'm far, alas, from being what men
   suppose;
Though the world takes me for a man of
   worth,
I'm truly the most worthless man on earth.
   [*To* **Damis**]
Yes, my dear son, speak out now: call me
   the chief
Of sinners, a wretch, a murderer, a thief;
Load me with all the names men most
   abhor;
I'll not complain; I've earned them all, and
   more;
I'll kneel here while you pour them on my
   head
As a just punishment for the life I've led.

Orgon: [*To* **Tartuffe**] This is too much, dear
   Brother.
   [*To* **Damis**]
Have you no heart?

Damis: Are you so hoodwinked by this
   rascal's art . . .?

Orgon: Be still, you monster.
   [*To* **Tartuffe**]
     Brother, I pray you, rise.
   [*To* **Damis**]
Villain!

Damis: But . . .

Orgon: Silence!

Damis: Can't you realize . . .?

Orgon: Just one word more, and I'll tear
   you limb from limb.

Tartuffe: In God's name, Brother, don't be
   harsh with him.
I'd rather far be tortured at the stake
Than see him bear one scratch for my poor
   sake.

Orgon: [*To* **Damis**] Ingrate!

Tartuffe: If I must beg you, on bended
   knee,
To pardon him . . .

Orgon: [*Falling to his knees, addressing* **Tartuffe**]
   Such goodness cannot be!
   [*To* **Damis**]
Now, *there's* true charity!

Damis: What, you . . .?

Orgon: Villain, be still!
I know your motives; I know you wish him
   ill:
Yes, all of you—wife, children, servants, all—
Conspire against him and desire his fall,
Employing every shameful trick you can
To alienate me from this saintly man.
Ah, but the more you seek to drive him
   away,
The more I'll do to keep him. Without
   delay,
I'll spite this household and confound its
   pride
By giving him my daughter as his bride.

Damis: You're going to force her to accept
   his hand?

Orgon: Yes, and this very night, d'you
   understand?
I shall defy you all, and make it clear
That I'm the one who gives the orders
   here.
Come, wretch, kneel down and clasp his
   blessed feet,
And ask his pardon for your black deceit.

Damis: I ask that swindler's pardon? Why,
   I'd rather . . .

Orgon: So! You insult him, and defy your
   father!
A stick! A stick! [*To* **Tartuffe**] No,
   no—release me, do.

[*To* **Damis**]

Out of my house this minute! Be off
with you,

And never dare set foot in it again.

Damis: Well, I shall go, but . . .

Orgon: Well, go quickly, then.

I disinherit you; an empty purse

Is all you'll get from me—except my curse!

Scene 7

[**Orgon, Tartuffe**]

Orgon: How he blasphemed your goodness!
What a son!

Tartuffe: Forgive him, Lord, as I've already
done.

[*To* **Orgon**]

You can't know how it hurts when someone
tries

To blacken me in my dear Brother's eyes.

Orgon: Ahh!

Tartuffe: The mere thought of such
ingratitude

Plunges my soul into so dark a mood . . .

Such horror grips my heart . . . I gasp for
breath,

And cannot speak, and feel myself near
death.

Orgon: [*He runs, in tears, to the door through
which he has just driven his son*]

You blackguard! Why did I spare you? Why
did I not

Break you in little pieces on the spot?

Compose yourself, and don't be hurt, dear
friend.

Tartuffe: These scenes, these dreadful
quarrels, have got to end.

I've much upset your household, and I
perceive

That the best thing will be for me to leave.

Orgon: What are you saying!

Tartuffe: They're all against me here;

They'd have you think me false and
insincere.

Orgon: Ah, what of that? Have I ceased
believing in you?

Tartuffe: Their adverse talk will certainly
continue,

And charges which you now repudiate

You may find credible at a later date.

Orgon: No, Brother, never.

Tartuffe: Brother, a wife can sway

Her husband's mind in many a subtle way.

Orgon: No, no.

Tartuffe: To leave at once is the solution;

Thus only can I end their persecution.

Orgon: No, no, I'll not allow it; you shall
remain.

Tartuffe: Ah, well; 'twill mean much
martyrdom and pain,

But if you wish it . . .

Orgon: Ah!

Tartuffe: Enough; so be it.

But one thing must be settled, as I see it.

For your dear honor, and for our
friendship's sake,

There's one precaution I feel bound to
take.

I shall avoid your wife, and keep away . . .

Orgon: No, you shall not, whatever they
may say.

It pleases me to vex them, and for spite

I'd have them see you with her day and
night.

What's more, I'm going to drive them to
despair

By making you my only son and heir;

This very day, I'll give to you alone

Clear deed and title to everything I own.

A dear, good friend and son-in-law-to-be

Is more than wife, or child, or kin to me.

Will you accept my offer, dearest son?

Tartuffe: In all things, let the will of
Heaven be done.

Orgon: Poor fellow! Come, we'll go draw up
the deed.

Then let them burst with disappointed
greed!

ACT IV

Scene 1

[**Cléante, Tartuffe**]

Cléante: Yes, all the town's discussing it,
and truly,

Their comments do not flatter you unduly.

I'm glad we've met, Sir, and I'll give my
view

Of this sad matter in a word or two.
As for who's guilty, that I shan't discuss;
Let's say it was Damis who caused the fuss;
Assuming, then, that you have been
    ill-used
By young Damis, and groundlessly accused,
Ought not a Christian to forgive, and
    ought
He not to stifle every vengeful thought?
Should you stand by and watch a father
    make
His only son an exile for your sake?
Again I tell you frankly, be advised:
The whole town, high and low, is
    scandalized;
This quarrel must be mended, and my
    advice is
Not to push matters to a further crisis.
No, sacrifice your wrath to God above,
And help Damis regain his father's love.

Tartuffe: Alas, for my part I should take
    great joy
In doing so. I've nothing against the boy.
I pardon all, I harbor no resentment;
To serve him would afford me much
    contentment.
But Heaven's interest will not have it so:
If he comes back, then I shall have to go.
After his conduct—so extreme, so vicious—
Our further intercourse would look
    suspicious.
God knows what people would think!
    Why, they'd describe
My goodness to him as a sort of bribe;
They'd say that out of guilt I made
    pretense
Of loving-kindness and benevolence—
That, fearing my accuser's tongue, I strove
To buy his silence with a show of love.

Cléante: Your reasoning is badly warped
    and stretched,
And these excuses, Sir, are most
    far-fetched.
Why put yourself in charge of Heaven's
    cause?
Does Heaven need our help to enforce its
    laws?
Leave vengeance to the Lord, Sir; while we
    live,

Our duty's not to punish, but forgive;
And what the Lord commands, we should
    obey
Without regard to what the world may say.
What! Shall the fear of being
    misunderstood
Prevent our doing what is right and good?
No, no; let's simply do what Heaven
    ordains,
And let no other thoughts perplex our
    brains.

Tartuffe: Again, Sir, let me say that I've
    forgiven
Damis, and thus obeyed the laws of
    Heaven;
But I am not commanded by the Bible
To live with one who smears my name
    with libel.

Cléante: Were you commanded, Sir, to
    indulge the whim
Of poor Orgon, and to encourage him
In suddenly transferring to your name
A large estate to which you have no claim?

Tartuffe: 'Twould never occur to those who
    know me best
To think I acted from self-interest.
The treasures of this world I quite despise;
Their specious glitter does not charm my
    eyes;
And if I have resigned myself to taking
The gift which my dear Brother insists on
    making,
I do so only, as he well understands,
Lest so much wealth fall into wicked
    hands,
Lest those to whom it might descend in
    time
Turn it to purposes of sin and crime,
And not, as I shall do, make use of it
For Heaven's glory and mankind's benefit.

Cléante: Forget these trumped-up fears.
    Your argument
Is one the rightful heir might well resent;
It *is* a moral burden to inherit
Such wealth, but give Damis a chance to
    bear it.
And would it not be worse to be accused
Of swindling, than to see that wealth
    misused?

I'm shocked that you allowed Orgon to
  broach
This matter, and that you feel no
  self-reproach;
Does true religion teach that lawful heirs
May freely be deprived of what is theirs?
And if the Lord has told you in your heart
That you and young Damis must dwell
  apart,
Would it not be the decent thing to beat
A generous and honorable retreat,
Rather than let the son of the house be
  sent,
For your convenience, into banishment?
Sir, if you wish to prove the honesty
Of your intentions . . .

Tartuffe: Sir, it is half-past three.
I've certain pious duties to attend to,
And hope my prompt departure won't
  offend you.

Cléante: [Alone] Damn.

Scene 2

        [Elmire, Mariane, Cléante, Dorine]
Dorine: Stay, Sir, and help Mariane, for
  Heaven's sake!
She's suffering so, I fear her heart will
  break.
Her father's plan to marry her off tonight
Has put the poor child in a desperate
  plight.
I hear him coming. Let's stand together,
  now,
And see if we can't change his mind,
  somehow,
About this match we all deplore and fear.

Scene 3

        [Orgon, Elmire, Mariane, Cléante, Dorine]
Orgon: Hah! Glad to find you all assembled
  here.
        [To **Mariane**]
This contract, child, contains your happiness,
And what it says I think your heart can guess.
Mariane: [Falling to her knees] Sir, by that
  Heaven which sees me here distressed,
  And by whatever else can move your
  breast,

Do not employ a father's power, I pray
  you,
To crush my heart and force it to obey
  you,
Nor by your harsh commands oppress me
  so
That I'll begrudge the duty which I owe—
And do not so embitter and enslave me
That I shall hate the very life you gave me.
If my sweet hopes must perish, if you
  refuse
To give me to the one I've dared to choose,
Spare me at least—I beg you, I implore—
The pain of wedding one whom I abhor;
And do not, by a heartless use of force,
Drive me to contemplate some desperate
  course.
Orgon: [Feeling himself touched by her] Be
  firm, my soul. No human weakness,
  now.
Mariane: I don't resent your love for him.
  Allow
Your heart free rein, Sir; give him your
  property,
And if that's not enough, take mine from
  me;
He's welcome to my money; take it, do,
But don't, I pray, include my person too.
Spare me, I beg you; and let me end the
  tale
Of my sad days behind a convent veil.
Orgon: A convent! Hah! When crossed in
  their amours,
All lovesick girls have the same thought as
  yours.
Get up! The more you loathe the man, and
  dread him,
The more ennobling it will be to wed him.
Marry Tartuffe, and mortify your flesh!
Enough; don't start that whimpering afresh.
Dorine: But why . . .?
Orgon: Be still, there. Speak when you're
  spoken to.
Not one more bit of impudence out of you.
Cléante: If I may offer a word of counsel
  here . . .
Orgon: Brother, in counseling you have no
  peer;
All your advice is forceful, sound, and
  clever;

I don't propose to follow it, however.

Elmire: [*To* **Orgon**] I am amazed, and don't
   know what to say;
   Your blindness simply takes my breath
      away.
   You are indeed bewitched, to take no
      warning
   From our account of what occurred this
      morning.

Orgon: Madam, I know a few plain facts,
   and one
   Is that you're partial to my rascal son;
   Hence, when he sought to make Tartuffe
      the victim
   Of a base lie, you dared not contradict
      him.
   Ah, but you underplayed your part, my pet;
   You should have looked more angry, more
      upset.

Elmire: When men make overtures, must
   we reply
   With righteous anger and a battle-cry?
   Must we turn back their amorous advances
   With sharp reproaches and with fiery
      glances?
   Myself, I find such offers merely amusing,
   And make no scenes and fusses in
      refusing;
   My taste is for good-natured rectitude,
   And I dislike the savage sort of prude
   Who guards her virtue with her teeth and
      claws,
   And tears men's eyes out for the slightest
      cause:
   The Lord preserve me from such honor as
      that,
   Which bites and scratches like an alley-cat!
   I've found that a polite and cool rebuff
   Discourages a lover quite enough.

Orgon: I know the facts, and I shall not be
   shaken.

Elmire: I marvel at your power to be
   mistaken.
   Would it, I wonder, carry weight with you
   If I could *show* you that our tale was true?

Orgon: Show me?

Elmire: Yes.

Orgon: Rot.

Elmire: Come, what if I found a way
   To make you see the facts as plain as day?

Orgon: Nonsense.

Elmire: Do answer me; don't be absurd.
   I'm not now asking you to trust our word.
   Suppose that from some hiding-place in
      here
   You learned the whole sad truth by eye
      and ear—
   What would you say of your good friend,
      after that?

Orgon: Why, I'd say . . . nothing, by
   Jehoshaphat!
   It can't be true.

Elmire: You've been too long deceived,
   And I'm quite tired of being disbelieved.
   Come now: let's put my statements to the
      test,
   And you shall see the truth made manifest.

Orgon: I'll take that challenge. Now do
   your uttermost.
   We'll see how you make good your empty
      boast.

Elmire: [*To* **Dorine**] Send him to me.

Dorine: He's crafty; it may be hard
   To catch the cunning scoundrel off his
      guard.

Elmire: No, amorous men are gullible. Their
   conceit
   So blinds them that they're never hard to
      cheat.
   Have him come down [*To* **Cléante** *and*
   Mariane] Please leave us, for a bit.

Scene 4

   [**Elmire, Orgon**]

Elmire: Pull up this table, and get under it.

Orgon: What?

Elmire: It's essential that you be
   well-hidden.

Orgon: Why there?

Elmire: Oh, Heavens! Just do as you are
   bidden.
   I have my plans; we'll soon see how they
      fare.
   Under the table, now; and once you're
      there,
   Take care that you are neither seen nor
      heard.

Orgon: Well, I'll indulge you, since I gave
   my word

To see you through this infantile charade.
Elmire: Once it is over, you'll be glad we
  played.

> [*To her husband, who is now under the table*]

I'm going to act quite strangely, now, and
  you
Must not be shocked at anything I do.
Whatever I may say, you must excuse
As part of that deceit I'm forced to use.
I shall employ sweet speeches in the task
Of making that imposter drop his mask;
I'll give encouragement to his bold desires,
And furnish fuel to his amorous fires.
Since it's for your sake, and for his
  destruction,
That I shall seem to yield to his seduction,
I'll gladly stop whenever you decide
That all your doubts are fully satisfied.
I'll count on you, as soon as you have seen
What sort of man he is, to intervene,
And not expose me to his odious lust
One moment longer than you feel you must.
Remember: you're to save me from my
  plight
Whenever . . . He's coming! Hush! Keep
  out of sight!

Scene 5

> [**Tartuffe, Elmire, Orgon**]

Tartuffe: You wish to have a word with me,
  I'm told.
Elmire: Yes. I've a little secret to unfold.
Before I speak, however, it would be wise
To close that door, and look about for
  spies.

> [**Tartuffe** *goes to the door, closes it, and returns.*]

The very last thing that must happen now
Is a repetition of this morning's row.
I've never been so badly caught off guard.
Oh, how I feared for you! You saw how
  hard
I tried to make that troublesome Damis
Control his dreadful temper, and hold his
  peace.
In my confusion, I didn't have the sense
Simply to contradict his evidence;
But as it happened, that was for the best,
And all has worked out in our interest.

This storm has only bettered your position;
My husband doesn't have the least suspicion,
And now, in mockery of those who do,
He bids me be continually with you.
And that is why, quite fearless of reproof,
I now can be alone with my Tartuffe,
And why my heart—perhaps too quick to
  yield—
Feels free to let its passion be revealed.
Tartuffe: Madam, your words confuse me.
  Not long ago,
You spoke in quite a different style, you
  know.
Elmire: Ah, Sir, if that refusal made you
  smart,
It's little that you know of woman's heart,
Or what that heart is trying to convey
When it resists in such a feeble way!
Always, at first, our modesty prevents
The frank avowal of tender sentiments;
However high the passion which inflames
  us,
Still, to confess its power somehow shames
  us.
Thus we reluct, at first, yet in a tone
Which tells you that our heart is
  overthrown,
That what our lips deny, our pulse
  confesses,
And that, in time, all noes will turn to
  yesses.
I fear my words are all too frank and free,
And a poor proof of woman's modesty;
But since I'm started, tell me, if you will—
Would I have tried to make Damis be still,
Would I have listened, calm and
  unoffended,
Until your lengthy offer of love was ended,
And been so very mild in my reaction,
Had your sweet words not given me
  satisfaction?
And when I tried to force you to undo
The marriage-plans my husband has in
  view,
What did my urgent pleading signify
If not that I admired you, and that I
Deplored the thought that someone else
  might own
Part of a heart I wished for mine alone?

Tartuffe: Madam, no happiness is so complete
As when, from lips we love, come words so sweet;
Their nectar floods my every sense, and drains
In honeyed rivulets through all my veins.
To please you is my joy, my only goal;
Your love is the restorer of my soul;
And yet I must beg leave, now, to confess
Some lingering doubts as to my happiness.
Might this not be a trick? Might not the catch
Be that you wish me to break off the match
With Mariane, and so have feigned to love me?
I shan't quite trust your fond opinion of me
Until the feelings you've expressed so sweetly
Are demonstrated somewhat more concretely,
And you have shown, by certain kind concessions,
That I may put my faith in your professions.

Elmire: [*She coughs, to warn her husband*]
Why be in such a hurry? Must my heart
Exhaust its bounty at the very start?
To make that sweet admission cost me dear,
But you'll not be content, it would appear,
Unless my store of favors is disbursed
To the last farthing, and at the very first.

Tartuffe: The less we merit, the less we dare to hope,
And with our doubts, mere words can never cope.
We trust no promised bliss till we receive it;
Not till a joy is ours can we believe it.
I, who so little merit your esteem,
Can't credit this fulfillment of my dream,
And shan't believe it, Madam, until I savor
Some palpable assurance of your favor.

Elmire: My, how tyrannical your love can be,
And how it flusters and perplexes me!
How furiously you take one's heart in hand,
And make your every wish a fierce command!
Come, must you hound and harry me to death?
Will you not give me time to catch my breath?
Can it be right to press me with such force,
Give me no quarter, show me no remorse,
And take advantage, by your stern insistence,
Of the fond feelings which weaken my resistance?

Tartuffe: Well, if you look with favor upon my love,
Why, then, begrudge me some clear proof thereof?

Elmire: But how can I consent without offense
To Heaven, toward which you feel such reverence?

Tartuffe: If Heaven is all that holds you back, don't worry.
I can remove that hindrance in a hurry.
Nothing of that sort need obstruct our path.

Elmire: Must one not be afraid of Heaven's wrath?

Tartuffe: Madam, forget such fears, and be my pupil,
And I shall teach you how to conquer scruple.
Some joys, it's true, are wrong in Heaven's eyes;
Yet Heaven is not averse to compromise;
There is a science, lately formulated,
Whereby one's conscience may be liberated,
And any wrongful act you care to mention
May be redeemed by purity of intention.
I'll teach you, Madam, the secrets of that science;
Meanwhile, just place on me your full reliance.
Assuage my keen desires, and feel no dread:
The sin, if any, shall be on my head.
        [**Elmire** *coughs, this time more loudly*]
You've a bad cough.

Elmire: Yes, yes. It's bad indeed.

Tartuffe: [*Producing a little paper bag*] A bit
of licorice may be what you need.

Elmire: No, I've a stubborn cold, it seems.
I'm sure it
Will take much more than licorice to cure
it.

Tartuffe: How aggravating.

Elmire: Oh, more than I can say.

Tartuffe: If you're still troubled, think of
things this way:
No one shall know our joys, save us alone,
And there's no evil till the act is known;
It's scandal, Madam, which makes it an
offense,
And it's no sin to sin in confidence.

Elmire: [*Having coughed once more*] Well,
clearly I must do as you require,
And yield to your importunate desire.
It is apparent, now, that nothing less
Will satisfy you, and so I acquiesce.
To go so far is much against my will;
I'm vexed that it should come to this; but
still,
Since you are so determined on it, since
you
Will not allow mere language to convince
you,
And since you ask for concrete evidence, I
See nothing for it, now, but to comply.
If this is sinful, if I'm wrong to do it,
So much the worse for him who drove me
to it.
The fault can surely not be charged to me.

Tartuffe: Madam, the fault is mine, if fault
there be,
And . . .

Elmire: Open the door a little, and peek out;
I wouldn't want my husband poking about.

Tartuffe: Why worry about the man? Each
day he grows
More gullible; one can lead him by the
nose.
To find us here would fill him with
delight,
And if he saw the worst, he'd doubt his
sight.

Elmire: Nevertheless, do step out for a
minute

Into the hall, and see that no one's in it.

Scene 6

[**Orgon, Elmire**]

Orgon: [*Coming out from under the table*]
That man's a perfect monster, I must
admit!
I'm simply stunned. I can't get over it.

Elmire: What, coming out so soon? How
premature!
Get back in hiding, and wait until you're
sure.
Stay till the end, and be convinced
completely;
We mustn't stop till things are proved
concretely.

Orgon: Hell never harbored anything so
vicious!

Elmire: Tut, don't be hasty. Try to be
judicious.
Wait, and be certain that there's no
mistake.
No jumping to conclusions, for Heaven's
sake!
[*She places* **Orgon** *behind her, as* **Tartuffe**
re-enters.]

Scene 7

[**Tartuffe, Elmire, Orgon**]

Tartuffe: [*Not seeing* **Orgon**] Madam, all
things have worked out to perfection;
I've given the neighboring rooms a full
inspection;
No one's about; and now I may at last . . .

Orgon: [*Intercepting him*] Hold on, my
passionate fellow, not so fast!
I should advise a little more restraint.
Well, so you thought you'd fool me, my
dear saint!
How soon you wearied of the saintly life—
Wedding my daughter, and coveting my
wife!
I've long suspected you, and had a feeling
That soon I'd catch you at your
double-dealing.
Just now, you've given me evidence galore;
It's quite enough; I have no wish for more.

Elmire: [*To* **Tartuffe**] I'm sorry to have
treated you so slyly,

But circumstances forced me to be wily.

Tartuffe: Brother, you can't think . . .

Orgon: No more talk from you;
Just leave this household, without more
ado.

Tartuffe: What I intended . . .

Orgon: That seems fairly clear.
Spare me your falsehoods and get out of
here.

Tartuffe: No, I'm the master, and you're the
one to go!
This house belongs to me, I'll have you
know,
And I shall show you that you can't hurt
me
By this contemptible conspiracy,
That those who cross me know not what
they do,
And that I've means to expose and punish
you,
Avenge offended Heaven, and make you
grieve
That ever you dared order me to leave.

Scene 8

[Elmire, Orgon]

Elmire: What was the point of all that
angry chatter?

Orgon: Dear God, I'm worried. This is no
laughing matter.

Elmire: How so?

Orgon: I fear I understood his drift.
I'm much disturbed about that deed of gift.

Elmire: You gave him . . .?

Orgon: Yes, it's all been drawn and signed.
But one thing more is weighing on my
mind.

Elmire: What's that?

Orgon: I'll tell you; but first let's see if
there's
A certain strong-box in his room upstairs.

ACT V

Scene 1

[Orgon, Cléante]

Cléante: Where are you going so fast?

Orgon: God knows!

Cléante: Then wait;
Let's have a conference, and deliberate
On how this situation's to be met.

Orgon: That strong-box has me utterly
upset;
This is the worst of many, many shocks.

Cléante: Is there some fearful mystery in
that box?

Orgon: My poor friend Argas brought that
box to me
With his own hands, in utmost secrecy;
'Twas on the very morning of his flight.
It's full of papers which, if they came to
light,
Would ruin him—or such is my impression.

Cléante: Then why did you let it out of
your possession?

Orgon: Those papers vexed my conscience,
and it seemed best
To ask the counsel of my pious guest.
The cunning scoundrel got me to agree
To leave the strong-box in his custody,
So that, in case of an investigation,
I could employ a slight equivocation
And swear I didn't have it, and thereby,
At no expense to conscience, tell a lie.

Cléante: It looks to me as if you're out on a
limb.
Trusting him with that box, and offering
him
That deed of gift, were actions of a kind
Which scarcely indicate a prudent mind.
With two such weapons, he has the upper
hand,
And since you're vulnerable, as matters
stand,
You erred once more in bringing him to
bay.
You should have acted in some subtler
way.

Orgon: Just think of it: behind that fervent
face,
A heart so wicked, and a soul so base!
I took him in, a hungry beggar, and
then . . .
Enough, by God! I'm through with pious
men:
Henceforth I'll hate the whole false
brotherhood,

And persecute them worse than Satan
   could.
Cléante: Ah, there you go—extravagant as
   ever!
Why can you not be rational? You never
Manage to take the middle course, it
   seems,
But jump, instead, between absurd
   extremes.
You've recognized your recent grave
   mistake
In falling victim to a pious fake;
Now, to correct that error, must you
   embrace
An even greater error in its place,
And judge our worthy neighbors as a
   whole
By what you've learned of one corrupted
   soul?
Come, just because one rascal made you
   swallow
A show of zeal which turned out to be
   hollow,
Shall you conclude that all men are
   deceivers,
And that, today, there are no true
   believers?
Let atheists make that foolish inference;
Learn to distinguish virtue from pretense,
Be cautious in bestowing admiration,
And cultivate a sober moderation.
Don't humor fraud, but also don't asperse
True piety; the latter fault is worse,
And it is best to err, if err one must,
As you have done, upon the side of trust.

Scene 2

[Damis, Orgon, Cléante]
Damis: Father, I hear that scoundrel's
   uttered threats
Against you; that he pridefully forgets
How, in his need, he was befriended by
   you,
And means to use your gifts to crucify
   you.
Orgon: It's true, my boy. I'm too distressed
   for tears.

Damis: Leave it to me, Sir; let me trim his
   ears.
Faced with such insolence, we must not
   waver.
I shall rejoice in doing you the favor
Of cutting short his life, and your distress.
Cléante: What a display of young
   hotheadedness!
Do learn to moderate your fits of rage.
In this just kingdom, this enlightened age,
One does not settle things by violence.

Scene 3

[Madame Pernelle, Mariane, Elmire,
   Dorine, Damis, Orgon, Cléante]
Madame Pernelle: I hear strange tales of
   very strange events.
Orgon: Yes, strange events which these two
   eyes beheld.
The man's ingratitude is unparalleled.
I save a wretched pauper from starvation,
House him, and treat him like a blood
   relation,
Shower him every day with my largesse,
Give him my daughter, and all that I
   possess;
And meanwhile the unconscionable knave
Tries to induce my wife to misbehave;
And not content with such extreme
   rascality,
Now threatens me with my own liberality,
And aims, by taking base advantage of
The gifts I gave him out of Christian love,
To drive me from my house, a ruined man,
And make me end a pauper, as he began.
Dorine: Poor fellow!
Madame Pernelle: No, my son, I'll never
   bring
Myself to think him guilty of such a thing.
Orgon: How's that?
Madame Pernelle: The righteous always
   were maligned.
Orgon: Speak clearly, Mother. Say what's
   on your mind.
Madame Pernelle: I mean that I can smell a
   rat, my dear.
You know how everybody hates him, here.

Orgon: That has no bearing on the case at all.

Madame Pernelle: I told you a hundred times, when you were small,

That virtue in this world is hated ever;

Malicious men may die, but malice never.

Orgon: No doubt that's true, but how does it apply?

Madame Pernelle: They've turned you against him by a clever lie.

Orgon: I've told you, I was there and saw it done.

Madame Pernelle: Ah, slanderers will stop at nothing, Son.

Orgon: Mother, I'll lose my temper ... For the last time,

I tell you I was witness to the crime.

Madame Pernelle: The tongues of spite are busy night and noon,

And to their venom no man is immune.

Orgon: You're talking nonsense. Can't you realize

I saw it; saw it; saw it with my eyes?

Saw, do you understand me? Must I shout it

Into your ears before you'll cease to doubt it?

Madame Pernelle: Appearances can deceive, my son. Dear me,

We cannot always judge by what we see.

Orgon: Drat! Drat!

Madame Pernelle: One often interprets things awry;

Good can seem evil to a suspicious eye.

Orgon: Was I to see his pawing at Elmire

As an act of charity?

Madame Pernelle: Till his guilt is clear,

A man deserves the benefit of the doubt.

You should have waited, to see how things turned out.

Orgon: Great God in Heaven, what more proof did I need?

Was I to sit there, watching, until he'd ...

You drive me to the brink of impropriety.

Madame Pernelle: No, no, a man of such surpassing piety

Could not do such a thing. You cannot shake me.

I don't believe it, and you shall not make me.

Orgon: You vex me so that, if you weren't my mother,

I'd say to you ... some dreadful thing or other.

Dorine: It's your turn now, Sir, not to be listened to;

You'd not trust us, and now she won't trust you.

Cléante: My friends, we're wasting time which should be spent

In facing up to our predicament.

I fear that scoundrel's threats weren't made in sport.

Damis: Do you think he'd have the nerve to go to court?

Elmire: I'm sure he won't: they'd find it all too crude

A case of swindling and ingratitude.

Cléante: Don't be too sure. He won't be at a loss

To give his claims a high and righteous gloss;

And clever rogues with far less valid cause

Have trapped their victims in a web of laws.

I say again that to antagonize

A man so strongly armed was most unwise.

Orgon: I know it; but the man's appalling cheek

Outraged me so, I couldn't control my pique.

Cléante: I wish to Heaven that we could devise

Some truce between you, or some compromise.

Elmire: If I had known what cards he held, I'd not

Have roused his anger by my little plot.

Orgon: [*To* **Dorine**, *as* **M. Loyal** *enters*] What is that fellow looking for? Who is he?

Go talk to him—and tell him that I'm busy.

Scene 4

[**Monsieur Loyal, Madame Pernelle, Orgon, Damis, Mariane, Dorine, Elmire, Cléante**]

Monsieur Loyal: Good day, dear sister.
  Kindly let me see
Your master.

Dorine: He's involved with company,
  And cannot be disturbed just now, I fear.

Monsieur Loyal: I hate to intrude; but what
  has brought me here
Will not disturb your master, in any event.
Indeed, my news will make him most
  content.

Dorine: Your name?

Monsieur Loyal: Just say that I bring
  greetings from
Monsieur Tartuffe, on whose behalf I've
  come.

Dorine: [*To* **Orgon**] Sir, he's a very gracious
  man, and bears
A message from Tartuffe, which, he
  declares,
Will make you most content.

Cléante: Upon my word,
  I think this man had best be seen, and
  heard.

Orgon: Perhaps he has some settlement to
  suggest.
How shall I treat him? What manner
  would be best?

Cléante: Control your anger, and if he
  should mention
Some fair adjustment, give him your full
  attention.

Monsieur Loyal: Good health to you, good
  Sir. May Heaven confound
Your enemies, and may your joys abound.

Orgon: [*Aside, to* **Cléante**] A gentle
  salutation: it confirms
My guess that he is here to offer terms.

Monsieur Loyal: I've always held your
  family most dear;
I served your father, Sir, for many a year.

Orgon: Sir, I must ask your pardon; to my
  shame,
I cannot now recall your face or name.

Monsieur Loyal: Loyal's my name; I come
  from Normandy,
And I'm a bailiff, in all modesty.
For forty years, praise God, it's been my
  boast
To serve with honor in that vital post,
And I am here, Sir, if you will permit

The liberty, to serve you with this writ . . .

Orgon: To—*what?*

Monsieur Loyal: Now, please, Sir, let us
  have no friction:
It's nothing but an order of eviction.
You are to move your goods and family
  out
And make way for new occupants, without
Deferment or delay, and give the keys . . .

Orgon: I? Leave this house?

Monsieur Loyal: Why yes, Sir, if you
  please.
This house, Sir, from the cellar to the roof,
Belongs now to the good Monsieur
  Tartuffe,
And he is lord and master of your estate
By virtue of a deed of present date,
Drawn in due form, with clearest legal
  phrasing . . .

Damis: Your insolence is utterly amazing!

Monsieur Loyal: Young man, my business
  here is not with you,
But with your wise and temperate father,
  who,
Like every worthy citizen, stands in awe
Of justice, and would never obstruct the
  law.

Orgon: But . . .

Monsieur Loyal: Not for a million, Sir,
  would you rebel
Against authority; I know that well.
You'll not make trouble, Sir, or interfere
With the execution of my duties here.

Damis: Someone may execute a smart tattoo
On that black jacket of yours, before you're
  through.

Monsieur Loyal: Sir, bid your son be silent.
  I'd much regret
Having to mention such a nasty threat
Of violence, in writing my report.

Dorine: [*Aside*] This man Loyal's a most
  disloyal sort!

Monsieur Loyal: I love all men of upright
  character,
And when I agreed to serve these papers,
  Sir,
It was your feelings that I had in mind.
I couldn't bear to see the case assigned
To someone else, who might esteem you
  less

And so subject you to unpleasantness.

Orgon: What's more unpleasant than telling a man to leave

His house and home?

Monsieur Loyal: You'd like a short reprieve?

If you desire it, Sir, I shall not press you,

But wait until tomorrow to dispossess you.

Splendid. I'll come and spend the night here, then,

Most quietly, with half a score of men.

For form's sake, you might bring me, just before

You go to bed, the keys to the front door.

My men, I promise, will be on their best

Behavior, and will not disturb your rest.

But bright and early, Sir, you must be quick

And move out all your furniture, every stick:

The men I've chosen are both young and strong,

And with their help it shouldn't take you long.

In short, I'll make things pleasant and convenient,

And since I'm being so extremely lenient,

Please show me, Sir, a like consideration,

And give me your entire cooperation.

Orgon: [*Aside*] I may be all but bankrupt, but I vow

I'd give a hundred louis, here and now,

Just for the pleasure of landing one good clout

Right on the end of that complacent snout.

Cléante: Careful; don't make things worse.

Damis: My bootsole itches

To give that beggar a good kick in the breeches.

Dorine: Monsieur Loyal, I'd love to hear the whack

Of a stout stick across your fine broad back.

Monsieur Loyal: Take care: a woman too may go to jail if

She uses threatening language to a bailiff.

Cléante: Enough, enough, Sir. This must not go on.

Give me that paper, please, and then begone.

Monsieur Loyal: Well, *au revoir.* God give you all good cheer!

Orgon: May God confound you, and him who sent you here!

Scene 5

[Orgon, Cléante, Mariane, Elmire, Madame Pernelle, Dorine, Damis]

Orgon: Now, Mother, was I right or not? This writ

Should change your notion of Tartuffe a bit.

Do you perceive his villainy at last?

Madame Pernelle: I'm thunderstruck. I'm utterly aghast.

Dorine: Oh, come, be fair. You mustn't take offense

At this new proof of his benevolence.

He's acting out of selfless love, I know.

Material things enslave the soul, and so

He kindly has arranged your liberation

From all that might endanger your salvation.

Orgon: Will you not ever hold your tongue, you dunce?

Cléante: Come, you must take some action, and at once.

Elmire: Go tell the world of the low trick he's tried.

The deed of gift is surely nullified

By such behavior, and public rage will not

Permit the wretch to carry out his plot.

Scene 6

[Valère, Orgon, Cléante, Elmire, Mariane, Madame Pernelle, Damis, Dorine]

Valère: Sir, though I hate to bring you more bad news,

Such is the danger that I cannot choose.

A friend who is extremely close to me

And knows my interest in your family

Has, for my sake, presumed to violate

The secrecy that's due to things of state,

And sends me word that you are in a plight

From which your one salvation lies in flight.

That scoundrel who's imposed upon you so

Denounced you to the King an hour ago

And, as supporting evidence, displayed
The strong-box of a certain renegade
Whose secret papers, so he testified,
You had disloyally agreed to hide.
I don't know just what charges may be
    pressed,
But there's a warrant out for your arrest;
Tartuffe has been instructed, furthermore,
To guide the arresting officer to your door.
Cléante: He's clearly done this to facilitate
His seizure of your house and your estate.
Orgon: That man, I must say, is a vicious
    beast!
Valère: Quick, Sir; you mustn't tarry in the
    least.
My carriage is outside, to take you hence;
This thousand louis should cover all
    expense.
Let's lose no time, or you shall be undone;
The sole defense, in this case, is to run.
I shall go with you all the way, and place
    you
In a safe refuge to which they'll never trace
    you.
Orgon: Alas, dear boy, I wish that I could
    show you
My gratitude for everything I owe you.
But now is not the time; I pray the Lord
That I may live to give you your reward.
Farewell, my dears; be careful . . .
Cléante: Brother, hurry.
We shall take care of things; you needn't
    worry.

Scene 7

> [The Officer, Tartuffe, Valère, Orgon, El-
> mire, Mariane, Madame Pernelle, Dorine,
> Cléante, Damis]

Tartuffe: Gently, Sir, gently; stay right
    where you are.
No need for haste; your lodging isn't far.
You're off to prison, by order of the
    Prince.
Orgon: This is the crowning blow, you
    wretch; and since
It means my total ruin and defeat,
Your villainy is now at last complete.
Tartuffe: You needn't try to provoke me;
    it's no use.

Those who serve Heaven must expect
    abuse.
Cléante: You are indeed most patient,
    sweet, and blameless.
Dorine: How he exploits the name of
    Heaven! It's shameless.
Tartuffe: Your taunts and mockeries are all
    for naught;
To do my duty is my only thought.
Mariane: Your love of duty is most
    meritorious,
And what you've done is little short of
    glorious.
Tartuffe: All deeds are glorious, Madam,
    which obey
The sovereign prince who sent me here
    today.
Orgon: I rescued you when you were
    destitute;
Have you forgotten that, you thankless
    brute?
Tartuffe: No, no, I well remember
    everything;
But my first duty is to serve my King.
That obligation is so paramount
That other claims, beside it, do not count;
And for it I would sacrifice my wife,
My family, my friend, or my own life.
Elmire: Hypocrite!
Dorine: All that we most revere, he uses
To cloak his plots and camouflage his
    ruses.
Cléante: If it is true that you are animated
By pure and loyal zeal, as you have stated,
Why was this zeal not roused until you'd
    sought
To make Orgon a cuckold, and been
    caught?
Why weren't you moved to give your
    evidence
Until your outraged host had driven you
    hence?
I shan't say that the gift of all his treasure
Ought to have damped your zeal in any
    measure;
But if he is a traitor, as you declare,
How could you condescend to be his heir?
Tartuffe: [*To the* **Officer**]
Sir, spare me all this clamor; it's growing
    shrill.

Please carry out your orders, if you will.
Officer: Yes, I've delayed too long, Sir.
   Thank you kindly.
   You're just the proper person to remind
      me.
   Come, you are off to join the other
      boarders
   In the King's prison, according to his
      orders.
Tartuffe: Who? I, Sir?
Officer: Yes.
Tartuffe: To prison? This can't be true!
Officer: I owe an explanation, but not to
      you.
      [*To* **Orgon**]
   Sir, all is well; rest easy, and be grateful.
   We serve a Prince to whom all sham is
      hateful,
   A Prince who sees into our inmost hearts,
   And can't be fooled by any trickster's arts.
   His royal soul, though generous and human,
   Views all things with discernment and
      acumen;
   His sovereign reason is not lightly swayed,
   And all his judgments are discreetly
      weighed.
   He honors righteous men of every kind,
   And yet his zeal for virtue is not blind,
   Nor does his love of piety numb his wits
   And make him tolerant of hypocrites.
   'Twas hardly likely that this man could
      cozen
   A King who's foiled such liars by the dozen.
   With one keen glance, the King perceived
      the whole
   Perverseness and corruption of his soul,
   And thus high Heaven's justice was
      displayed:
   Betraying you, the rogue stood self-betrayed.
   The King soon recognized Tartuffe as one
   Notorious by another name, who'd done
   So many vicious crimes that one could fill
   Ten volumes with them, and be writing still.
   But to be brief: our sovereign was appalled
   By this man's treachery toward you, which
      he called
   The last, worst villainy of a vile career,
   And bade me follow the imposter here
   To see how gross his impudence could be,
   And force him to restore your property.

Your private papers, by the King's
      command,
   I hereby seize and give into your hand.
   The King, by royal order, invalidates
   The deed which gave this rascal your
      estates,
   And pardons, furthermore, your grave
      offense
   In harboring an exile's documents.
   By these decrees, our Prince rewards you for
   Your loyal deeds in the late civil war,
   And shows how heartfelt is his satisfaction
   In recompensing any worthy action,
   How much he prizes merit, and how he
      makes
   More of men's virtues than of their
      mistakes.
Dorine: Heaven be praised!
Madame Pernelle: I breathe again, at last.
Elmire: We're safe.
Mariane: I can't believe the danger's past.
Orgon: [*To* **Tartuffe**] Well, traitor, now you
      see . . .
Cléante: Ah, Brother, please,
   Let's not descend to such indignities.
   Leave the poor wretch to his unhappy fate,
   And don't say anything to aggravate
   His present woes; but rather hope that he
   Will soon embrace an honest piety,
   And mend his ways, and by a true
      repentance
   Move our just King to moderate his
      sentence.
   Meanwhile, go kneel before your
      sovereign's throne
   And thank him for the mercies he has
      shown.
Orgon: Well said: let's go at once and,
      gladly kneeling,
   Express the gratitude which all are feeling.
   Then, when that first great duty has been
      done,
   We'll turn with pleasure to a second one,
   And give Valère, whose love has proven so
      true,
   The wedded happiness which is his due.

CURTAIN

A Discussion of the Script

The neoclassical period in France (roughly speaking, the middle of the seventeenth century) saw the flourishing of an altogether different structural pattern from those previously studied here. Where the Shakespearean structure was loose and free-flowing, allowing for the greatest richness and variety, the neoclassic structure was tight and constricted, demanding complete adherence to a rigid set of rules. Richness and variety were lost, of course, but dramatic intensity was enhanced to the point where it becomes almost unbearable in some of the best neoclassic tragedies. Not all of Molière's comedies are constructed according to neoclassic rules, but *Tartuffe* is, and thus it affords an opportunity to enjoy one of the world's comic masterpieces and study, at the same time, one of the theatre's important dramatic structures. In comedy, the intent of such a stringent structural pattern is to compress the action so tightly that attention is forced exclusively to the point at hand, to build expectations or suspense implacably to the highest possible point, and then to conclude as quickly as possible after the climactic moment.

All neoclassic plays were expected to adhere rigorously to the "three unities" of time, place, and action. The critics of the period had derived these unities from an erroneous interpretation of Aristotle; they believed that they were following the models of the ancient Greeks who, it was assumed, had established the best dramatic structures for all time. Unity of action has already been discussed; it is, in fact, the only one of the three which Aristotle insisted upon. The central action of *Tartuffe* is "to get Orgon out of Tartuffe's clutches;" at the beginning of the play the members of Orgon's family dedicate themselves to this end, and when it is accomplished, the play is over. All the action within the play relates directly to accomplishing this objective. Unity of place means simply that the play must take place entirely in one set which represents one location; there could be no shifting of locales as in Shakespeare's plays. *Tartuffe,* of course, takes place in one set. (*The Little Foxes* is the only play studied earlier which follows this rule.) Unity of time, in its purest form, means that the play should represent exactly as much time as its performance requires. In other words, if a performance lasts two hours, the action of the play should represent only two hours in the lives of its characters. The neoclassic critics relaxed this rule a little, however, and allowed that, at the outside, a play's action might represent twenty-four hours. This rule resulted in some extremely eventful twenty-four hour days, but *Tartuffe* operates easily within this rule—each of the five acts represents the length of time it takes to play it, and the breaks between acts represent not more than a few minutes each. The whole play represents perhaps three or four hours in the lives of its characters, perhaps six or eight, but hardly more. Neoclassic plays, according to French rules, were structured in five acts and written in alexandrine verse—a verse scheme employing iambic hexameter and rhyming couplets. *Tartuffe* meets all these requirements. In Wilbur's English version, the rhyme has been translated into pentameter (and rhymed couplets strike the ear differently in English from the way their French counterparts do, so that American readers cannot fully appreciate the effectiveness of Molière's language), but in French, at least, the rules are followed. The five acts of *Tartuffe* are altogether different from the five acts in *Twelfth Night;* act breaks made no discernible theatrical difference in *Twelfth Night,* whereas it is quite clear that the act breaks in *Tartuffe* are part of a deliberate plan. Only at the act breaks is the stage completely clear of characters; furthermore, at these points some minutes or hours of time are understood to elapse. A modern production might not have four intermissions, but a lighting change, closing the curtain, or some other device would certainly be needed to indicate the act breaks. Furthermore, the *scene* breaks have a totally different meaning in a neoclassic play than in a Shakespearean one. A Shakespearean play has a scene break each time the stage is cleared and a new group of characters enters; a new scene begins in the so-called *French scenes* system each time one character enters or leaves. It would prove extremely awkward to divide up into French scenes a play which was constructed differently; in *Tartuffe,* for example, each scene is a unit, not only because a character enters or exits, but also because some specific point is accomplished in the scene. Thus, the scene breaks in a neoclassical play, although not literally "breaks," are definite beats in the production. They clearly indicate structural units.

These structural units, existing as they do with some degree of independence and autonomy, should each contribute in a direct way to the central action; they are more likely, however, to provide a number of points of view on the central action than to move along any predetermined line in the manner of the well-made play. There is no inciting incident in *Tartuffe;* indeed, in typical neoclassical fashion, the action is already under way before the play begins. There is no turning point; the action keeps getting more and more complicated until it suddenly unwinds at the climax. One reason why definite points in the action cannot exist is that another of the neoclassical rules provided that no actual events take place on stage. The entire play was to be built around reports of incidents that had occurred elsewhere. This meant that the play could consist entirely of conversation—a strange rule, indeed, for those who believe that a theatre is a place for *seeing* things happen as well as hearing about them. Molière has dealt very adeptly with this rule, for although no violent events occur (no slapstick, no mock duels, and so on) a number of very comical things grow naturally out of the various conversational situations. The most obvious of these, perhaps, is the scene in which Orgon, under the table, eavesdrops on Tartuffe and Elmire. This scene is full of dramatic irony and is very funny, whether or not one describes it as "something happening on stage." Finally, of course, Tartuffe is arrested on stage. Molière's plays are not entirely free of incident, and certainly no modern audiences would want them to be. One big problem that they do present, however, is their "talkiness;" the director must find plenty of physical action to retain the interest of the modern audience.

A structural feature that requires special comment is the long-delayed entrance of Tartuffe. This has often been criticized on the grounds that the play's title figure should be seen long before Act III. It is evident, however, that the play's real protagonist is Orgon, not Tartuffe. Orgon is on stage in every act. Orgon is the principal person who has been deceived, and Orgon is the one who has learned something by the end of the play. If Orgon were not introduced until the third act, there would be a real problem. Tartuffe, on the other hand, is a more exciting antagonist for having been withheld so long. Molière builds to his entrance, as Rostand built to Cyrano's, so that by the time he appears he makes a strong impression. This device, therefore, is a highly effective structural feature, and adds to the over-all impact of the play.

Another feature which requires consideration is the play's ending. In the Greek theatre, there was a cranelike machine, which was sometimes used at the end of a play to lower a "god" onto the stage who would suddenly solve everybody's problems and end the play happily. This type of ending, known as *deus ex machina* (god from a machine), was considered distinctly inferior by Aristotle, and the phrase has since become a derogatory term for any ending which consists of surprising and irrational solutions to the play's problems. Clearly, the ending to *Tartuffe* is a *deus ex machina* ending, and some critics have gone to fantastic lengths in an attempt to exonerate it. The fact is, however, that nothing in the action of the play prepares one for anything so outrageous as the king simply seeing through Tartuffe's plot and quashing it. This is not to say that Molière blundered, however, for Molière was above all else an effective man of the theatre, and it is clear that in the theatre such an ending, although outrageous, can be outrageously funny. If played for all it is worth, it becomes a spoof of all other such endings, and one has only to imagine Molière performing the play before the king himself to see that an extra dimension is added to the humor. The *deus ex machina* ending, although in general a weak structural feature, is twisted around here to make the play more humorous and effective.

The plot of *Tartuffe*, then, is almost ideally structured in terms of the critical standards prevailing at the time it was written. The play may seem somewhat lacking in action to modern audiences, but this problem can be overcome if the actors and the director are sufficiently imaginative. Built right into the script and the stage directions are a number of amusing comic bits (such as Elmire's stepping out of the way to allow Tartuffe to walk into Orgon's arms), and many more can be invented. All things considered, however, it must be conceded that modern audiences will find the plot one of the play's weaker features. In French the language is a strong feature. Although rhymed iambic pentameter in English can never produce the same effect as alexandrine couplets in French, Wilbur's verse is strong and sprightly; the lines sound delightful when spoken by competent actors, and, thus, the play is enhanced by its language. Theme is strong in *Tartuffe*. The satire on a society in which hypocrisy triumphs over honesty is trenchant throughout. The foolishness of allowing oneself to be duped by outward appearances is the basis of the play's action. The hypocrisy which often seems to accompany strong religious beliefs is so severely satirized that the play ran into great difficulties with the authorities at the time of its writing (as we have already mentioned above). Comedy can be a dangerous weapon, and Molière knew how to wield it devastatingly.

Character development, however, is Molière's strong point. He has an amazing talent for breathing life into characters who would be simply stock figures in the hands of a lesser playwright; he can, also, begin from scratch and create well-rounded, original characters as well, and do either with such an economy of effort as to defy analysis. Tartuffe is an exciting, multifaceted character about whom the audience seems to know a great deal even though there are relatively few incidents in the play which characterize him. Orgon, on the other hand, is simply a new twist on an old, stock figure (the gulled old husband), but he is also handled with considerable insight. Elmire and Damis, Mariane and Dorine, are all stock figures from the popular Italian and French comedy of the sixteenth and seventeenth centuries, and yet Molière has given each just the right lines and business so that a skillful actor can make a magnificent comic portrait of the role. Again, extended analyses of the characters would fill volumes and would be out of place here; this quick outline has revealed that plot, characters, theme, and language all work together magnificently to make *Tartuffe* a comic masterpiece.

An analysis of *Tartuffe* in terms of the "ladder of comedy" on page 348 yields interesting results. There is virtually no obscenity in the play, and physical mishaps, insofar as they occur, are relatively sophisticated. There is a degree of physical indignity in Orgon's hiding under the table and Elmire stepping aside to allow Tartuffe to walk into Orgon's arms, but this level of humor is relatively rare. Plot devices used for humor are also relatively rare, the most obvious one being the *deus ex machina* ending discussed above. One cannot imagine an audience going into gales of laughter over many of the plot devices, since most of them are reported rather than actually witnessed. One must comment cautiously about verbal wit, since the play is presented here in translation. Molière's verse tends to be more utilitarian than brilliant for its own sake, however, and certainly little verbal wit has survived in this translation. It is safe to conclude, at least, that verbal wit is not one of the play's stronger features. Higher up the "ladder," however, are those areas in which *Tartuffe* is strongest: the brilliance of Molière's character development has already been discussed, and it is precisely in the juxaposition of these characters that much of the play's humor lies. Tartuffe himself is funny enough; Tartuffe brought into the presence of Dorine, Damis, or, above all, Orgon, provides an endless series of comic contrasts. The relatively sophisticated level of this comic contrast means that the play is not likely to provoke belly-laughs, but this is certainly not the only measure of comic success. The smile of understanding and the chuckle of ironic recognition are also appropriate responses to good comedy; many would argue that they represent the achievement of a quality which is reserved only for the few true comic geniuses of all time. At the top rung of the "ladder," one may observe in *Tartuffe* the comedy of ideas and satire which make the play thematically rich. Its thematic content, coupled with the character development just discussed, clearly places *Tartuffe* in the range of *high comedy*. Classification is only a convenience, however, which enables one to see *Tartuffle's* relationship to other important comedies. For example, *Tartuffle* bears certain resemblances to *The Importance of Being Earnest* that it does not bear to *Twelfth Night*.

Tartuffe's resemblance to *The Importance of Being Earnest* is mostly stylistic. Molière's play has a strong and distinctive stylistic pattern, which, to some extent, is shared by most high comedies. This is not to say that all high comedy is written in identical style, but important similarities do exist. There is a brittleness and a sense of detachment, almost a coldness, that is typical of comedy in general and that is intensified in high comedy. These qualities lead to a performance style (often theatricalism) that emphasizes the skill of the acting and allows for direct intellectual (but not emotional) contact with the audience. Settings, costumes, and other physical elements of production tend to be more decorative than realistic. Molière's genius and unique style manage to retain the high comedy and yet lift the play out of artificiality into the realm of pure humanity. Without losing a sense of comic detachment, one can still gain a real insight into the human soul from Molière's characters and plot situations. In spite of brittleness and apparent coldness, Molière brings one face to face with naked truth at the heart of his play, bridging the gap between serious and comic drama in the process. *Tartuffe* is comic, certainly, and yet the insights it offers go deeper than those of any other comic playwright. *Tartuffe* is similar to *The Importance of Being Earnest* only in the surface features of its style; at the heart of Molière's play lies a diamondlike brilliance beside which Wilde's work is only fine glass.

Indeed, this very richness has led to some confusion concerning the title character of the play. Tartuffe seems so human to some critics and directors that the play has been interpreted not as a comedy, but as a serious drama about a troubled, religious man who is misunderstood. Thus, when Tartuffe is led away to prison, the play ends on a note of defeat and tragedy. A similar interpretive battle rages about the figure of Shylock in Shakespeare's *The Merchant of Venice*, and some critics have virtually turned it into a tragedy. To prove that this sort of interpretation is erroneous would require a lengthier argument than is appropriate here. The basic rhythm of the structure of *Tartuffe* is so clearly comic that a critic would have to be sadly misled to find a tragic interpretation inherent in the script. However, it is easy to see how a production taking the tragic point of view would be *possible*. One would need merely to play Tartuffe in a more serious vein, emphasizing those elements which would make an audience identify with him. Empathy is a prime factor in most serious drama; if the audience can identify emotionally with a character's difficulties, comedy goes out the window. Suddenly, Orgon becomes a force to struggle with rather than a duped old man, and one loses the sense of perspective which is essential to comedy. Certain events seem humorous precisely because one does not identify with them. When potentially funny things happen to oneself, one does not laugh while he is emotionally involved; one laughs only at that moment when he suddenly can take the detached view and see the event in a larger perspective. To slip and fall on a banana peel is not funny at all if one has to feel the bump upon hitting the pavement; it is funny on stage only if the audience is unconcerned with the pain and concentrates on the absurdity of a human being placed in such a position. The difference between comedy and serious drama *in performance*, then, can often be reduced to identification; an audience which remains detached appreciates the comic point of view; but, as soon as empathy becomes an active force, comedy ceases and serious drama begins. Although one may view one approach as distinctly preferable to the other, it is easy to see that a play like *Tartuffe* can certainly be performed in either the comic or the serious mode. When a director wavers between the two, total chaos results. Molière has created a great play, but its very richness makes feasible a variety of production possibilities which, in the hands of an unskilled director, can create a shambles.

The term *properties* (commonly abbreviated as *props*) is sometimes a catch-all category for anything in a play production that doesn't obviously belong to another department, and the prop crew is often responsible for everything from providing offstage gun shots to sweeping the floor. Because so many of the technical areas call for highly specialized skills and training, all too often the prop job, at least in the amateur theatre, is turned over to anyone not otherwise assigned, when in fact it is a highly important area of backstage responsibility. Any actor who has been caught onstage without a key prop at the moment he needed it can testify to the importance of having a well-organized property crew. In order to define areas of responsibility backstage, it is necessary to have a working definition of what constitutes properties. It has been suggested that props fall into five general classifications[1]:

1. *Trim props* are any decorative objects which hang upon, or are attached to, the set but are not really essential to the play's action. They might include draperies and pictures for the set of *The Little Foxes,* the old clothing hanging on the platform railing in *J.B.,* or flags hanging from the tents in Act IV of *Cyrano de Bergerac.*

2. *Set props* are objects standing about the floor of the set but not large enough to be considered part of the set. The tents in *Cyrano de Bergerac,* referred to above, would probably be considered part of the set, but cannons, stagecoaches, campfires, or other such objects would be set props. The furniture in Regina's living room would be set props, as would the furniture used in *J. B.*

3. *Hand props* are any objects picked up and used by the actors, whether already in place on the set when the curtain goes up or carried on during a scene. Cyrano's sword would be a hand prop; so would Horace's bottle of medicine, J. B.'s turkey dinner, and Jack Worthing's cigarette case.

4. *Prop visual effects* are special effects such as a snowstorm, fire and smoke (when not electrical), sliding panels which mysteriously open, and so forth. Anything electrical, however, is in the province of the lighting crew.

5. *Prop sound effects* are any offstage sounds that are created by other than electrical means. The vast

[1] Harold Burris-Meyer and Edward C. Cole, *Scenery for the Theatre* (Boston, 1938), pp. 387–388.

Properties

The turkey dinner in *J.B.* Pat Hingle (J.B.), Fay Sappington, Arnold Merritt, Judith Lowry, Ciri Jacobson, Candy Moore, Merry Martin, Jeffrey Rowland, Nan Martin (Sarah), Christopher Plummer (Nickles). Production directed by Elia Kazan, designed by Boris Aronson, lighted by Tharon Musser, costumed by Lucinda Ballard. Photograph: Friedman–Ables.

majority of sound effects in the modern theatre are recorded and reproduced by high fidelity electronic equipment, but a few still remain the responsibility of the prop crew. These include gun shots, bells ringing, door slams, and other such sudden noises that must be timed more precisely than is practical for most electronically reproduced sound. The days of elaborate thunder sheets, rumble carts, and other complicated backstage noise makers are, for the most part, gone.

Since prop visual effects and sound effects are highly specialized and must be worked out in terms of the specific needs of the script at hand, little more need be said about them here. The list of trim props, set props, and hand props needed for any one show might be quite extensive, however, and a prop master is usually assigned the responsibility of locating all such props and organizing them effectively backstage (except in the Broadway theatre, where the stage manager will usually handle this matter personally). The prop master will, beginning with the script, make a complete list of all the properties needed for the production. He will check this list carefully with the director, the stage manager, and the set designer, in order to determine not only the completeness of the list but also the exact specifications of each prop. If the show in question is a production of *Tartuffe*, for example, the prop master will need to understand the period and the style in which the play is to be done as well as the colors to be employed in the setting and the costumes before he can begin to plan the props needed. Ordinarily, the set designer for *Tartuffe* will have thought of furniture as he designed the set, and will be able to give the prop master precise instructions as to period, line, color, and how much abuse a given piece of furniture might have to withstand (if an actor is going to have to stand on a table, for example). Understanding that the scene in which Orgon hides under the table is a key one in the play, the prop master would be especially careful to get a four-legged table rather than a pedestal one, and he would make sure that it would be big enough for the actor in question to hide under, and would provide a table cloth of suitable dimensions to be pulled down to conceal him. Of course there is also the possibility that, in a highly stylized production, the director and the designer may decide that all the props must be nonrealistic. In theatricalism, for example, they might all be brightly colored, simplified substitutes for the real thing, not intended to give the illusion of reality, but rather to be enjoyed as decoration. In a highly formalized production, it is even possible for all of the props to be pantomimed. Such stylistic decisions, of course, are a basic element in the over-all design of the production and must be communicated to the prop master early in the planning period so that he may organize his work accordingly. Once the property list, including all specifications, is complete and the prop master understands fully the needs of the production, he is ready to begin assembling his props.

Theatres that regularly produce plays begin to acquire a stock of all sorts of hard-to-find objects. It would be impossible to imagine a prop room so completely stocked that a prop master would never have to look elsewhere for what he needed, but on the other hand, the prop master is fortunate if he can turn to a reasonably complete prop room to begin his search. Even if the precise item he needs does not happen to be in stock, there may well be something which can be altered to suit his needs. Not only is time saved by such an arrangement, but there is a real advantage to the theatre organization as a whole in using props which it owns outright—there is less worry about breakage and damage. Once it has been determined which items from the prop list cannot be supplied out of stock, however, the prop master must consider other sources. If it is feasible to do so, the next best course of action is to manufacture the needed item or buy it outright. If the necessary furniture for *Tartuffe* can be purchased, for example, there need not be any great concern about damaging it and, furthermore, the theatre organization adds something useful to its supply of props. Period furniture can often be reupholstered or otherwise modified and used in a variety of stage situations. A few theatres maintain complete furniture-making shops where period furniture of this sort can be manufactured, but the complexity of the work involved is too much for the vast majority of theatre organizations. Thus, most theatres would fall back upon either renting or borrowing the furniture for *Tartuffe*. Since rental possibilities of this sort are very rare, the prop master is driven almost inevitably to the time-honored custom of canvassing the community in which his theatre is located in an effort to borrow the props which are needed.

At this point the prop master becomes a public relations man. No other backstage worker can do so much to help or damage the public image of a theatre organization as the prop master. Not only must he locate the properties that he needs and talk dubious owners into lending them, but he must also make definite promises about their return and see to it that these promises are honored. Furthermore, he must take extraordinary pains to see that borrowed props are carefully protected against damage; well established theatres usually make it a policy to buy outright any property that gets damaged even slightly, rather than upset the feelings of a store owner. If the prop is borrowed from a private individual, often no amount of money can compensate for damage to a valued item. The wise prop master, however, will use a system of receipts to insure that each borrowed item is accounted for when it is borrowed and when it is returned, and that borrower and lender have agreed upon its value in case of damage. A business-like approach to borrowing props, coupled with a policy of scrupulously living up to promises, can maintain good community relations for a theatre in this difficult area. More than one theatre, however, has been completely ruined by a slovenly attitude toward properties.

The prop master for *Tartuffe* would be singularly fortunate, as very few props are needed. The necessary furniture, as has been pointed out, would very likely have to be borrowed. A table cloth would certainly be necessary, and probably it should be bought, considering the abuse it must withstand. Tartuffe must have a handkerchief in Act III, although perhaps the costume crew will take the responsibility for it. The marriage contract which Orgon offers Mariane in Act IV and the eviction notice carried by M. Loyal in Act V would have to be made: good quality paper can be treated with oil to give it a parchment appearance, and dripped candle wax does very well for a seal. The licorice which Tartuffe offers to Elmire in Act IV would have to be purchased or simulated (depending upon how clearly the audience could see it); the "thousand louis" given Orgon by Valère in Act V can be only a small purse or bag, perhaps weighted with washers. Beyond these few items, only hand props required by the director and trim props needed by the designer to enchance the set will be necessary.

Once all his properties are assembled, it becomes the responsibility of the prop master to assure their smooth integration into the production. The props must be in the right place at the right time, and at all other times they must be out of the way. Props, especially small ones, have a way of disappearing just when they are needed, unless a very systematic approach to prop control and inventory is adopted. All props should be under lock and key when they are not in use. The prop master's first responsibility when he arrives at the theatre, then, is to take all the props from their storage place and put them either on stage or in their assigned places in the wings. Usually, a prop table is placed in each wing for hand props which are needed during the running of the show. As each prop is put in its place, the prop master has an opportunity to check it off his inventory; he *knows* when he is ready to begin the show. Normal backstage discipline insists that props are never touched by anyone but the prop crew and the actors who use them. This not only insures against careless damage, but also prevents idle moving of a prop after it has been properly placed for the show. During the performance, prop people may have to carry a prop to an actor who needs it in a hurry, but normally actors are expected to pick up their props from the prop table and to return them after use. If the actor playing M. Loyal is notoriously forgetful, however, the wise prop master will see to it that his legal document is placed in his hand just before he goes on. If there are set changes (or changes of props within the set) at scene breaks or at intermission, the prop crew is normally responsible for placing props as smoothly as possible. The scenery crew, of course, changes the scenery. At the end of the performance, the prop master makes sure that all props are properly returned to their storage area, and are inventoried once more as they are put away. If anything is missing or damaged, the time to discover this fact is immediately after the performance, not a few minutes before the next performance is scheduled to start. It would be easy to replace M. Loyal's legal paper, for example, if one had 24 hours in which to do it; the discovery of its loss 30 minutes before curtain, however, will cause pandemonium.

The prop master for a production of *Tartuffe* has a job which, above all else, calls for good organization and good sense. Where previously this text has dealt with theatre workers who are primarily artists, the prop master is primarily a technician. He must have enough artistic sense, however, to understand the artistic as well as the mechanical needs of the production, and to recognize, for example, which items of furniture will fit well into the set the designer is planning and which will clash. He must be a good public relations man, able to handle the borrowing and returning of other people's goods with aplomb; and he must organize well enough to make sure each prop is in its place at the right moment. As in so many things about the theatre, accuracy 99 per cent of the time (which would be an excellent record in most businesses) is not good enough. One missing prop can completely ruin the show.

Summary Note

The two plays just studied, *Twelfth Night* and *Tartuffe*, have offered at least two more important insights into the nature of comedy. Each is so richly thought-provoking that a whole book might well be devoted to its analysis. In this context, each play has been offered simply as an example of its type, its values have been examined briefly, and some of its possibilities for theatrical production have been explored. There has been no example of a pure farce, although the "plot B" scenes in *Twelfth Night* are certainly farcical in nature. The other types of comedy have been represented by at least a portion of a play, and one can see a little better, perhaps, the range and depth of which great comedy is capable. Plot, character, theme and language have been employed with such variety and imagination that no one of these elements has completely dominated the play of which it is a part, but a balanced work of art has been achieved.

Sophocles was born about 496 B.C. in the village of Colonus just outside Athens. Very little is known about his life, but a combination of legend and early documentation suggests that he belonged to a fairly well-to-do family, that he received a good education, and that he may have studied under Aeschylus, the first of the great Greek tragedians. How he became interested in the theatre or what sort of apprenticeship he may have served is not known, but in 468 B.C. he won his first victory in the annual playwriting competition; Aeschylus won second place that year. In a long and active life, Sophocles won this competition many times—one source asserts that he never finished below second place. In some sixty years of playwriting it appears that he completed about thirty of the four-play combinations which a dramatist was required to submit for the competition. None of these survives in its entirety, and only seven of the single plays are extant.

In a lifetime that spanned almost the entire fifth century B.C. (a century which encompassed the peak of Athenian civilization), Sophocles was active in public life, although it appears that he was chiefly devoted to the arts rather than to politics. He was, however, elected to several public offices and served as ambassador to other governments, as well as founding an organization devoted to the development of the arts and humanities. All the extant evidence suggests that he was a pleasant, congenial, and popular person whose intellectual insights and cultivated manners enriched and vivified the lives of those about him. He died in his native Colonus in 406 B.C., shortly before the final defeat of Athens in the Peloponnesian War put an end to the ancient Greek democracy.

Before one can understand and appreciate the Greek tragedies, one needs to know something about their original productions. The practice of performing plays evolved from Greek religious celebrations. Since accurate records do not exist, one can only speculate on how this happened, but the generally accepted version is that out of the singing and dancing which seems to have been an almost instinctive method of worship for primitive men, there arose a formally structured series of choral odes and dances. At some point, someone (tradition says his name was Thespis) "stepped out of the chorus" and demonstrated that dialogue between himself and the chorus constituted a far

Oedipus the King
by Sophocles

more flexible form than did song and dance alone. With this basic discovery, acting and playwriting were born simultaneously. Aeschylus, the first playwright whose works have survived, is credited with the discovery that using two actors instead of one allowed a far greater variety in dramatic structure and dialogue. Sophocles is said to have introduced the use of a third actor; *Oedipus the King*, it will be observed, is written for three actors, a chorus, and a few extras without lines. The three actors, of course, played more than three roles during the play, but no more than three speaking characters might be on the stage at one time.

Through a series of developments too complex to trace here, the plays which evolved in this fashion out of choral singing and dancing came to be highly popular. The performances were still religious worship, but of a different sort than that of a puritan culture. They were extremely popular, celebrating life and happiness and good times, and audiences entered into the spirit of the occasion whole-heartedly. The chief dramatic event of the year became a contest held in the spring in which each playwright submitted a series of four plays (three tragedies and a satyr play, a quasi-comic form which will not be discussed here) connected in plot, theme, or both; each playwright's work was to be performed in a single day. The three winning tetralogies were presented on three successive days in the Theatre of Dionysus at Athens, and the playwright whose work was judged best received a valuable prize, and was highly honored. Since the theatre was outdoors, depending upon the sun rather than artificial light, performances began at daybreak and lasted the better part of the day. Despite this rigorous schedule, virtually all of Athens turned out to see the plays.

Growing as it did out of a singing and dancing chorus, the drama at this stage of its development still used singing and dancing as a basic part of its structure. Reading the plays today, one's interest is likely to center upon the events which occur between choral odes—and there is little doubt that the interests of the ancient Greeks gradually moved in this direction. On the other hand, at the stage of development represented by *Oedipus the King*, the choral odes were still extremely important parts of the whole, and it is necessary to imagine complex music and dance patterns as a part of the choral activity in order to appreciate the plays as the Greek audiences did. Indeed, the successful playwright whose work was chosen among the three to be presented in the contest was expected then to serve as his own director, with particular emphasis on training the chorus. He might very well dance or act in his own show as well. These were not amateur performances, at least not in the derogatory sense of the word. The Greek audiences expected a high level of skill in the singing, dancing and acting, and a good deal of money was spent each year to assure that the actors and choruses were properly selected and well rehearsed for their performances.

The Theatre of Dionysus itself, in which these plays were performed, made certain demands on the performances—as, indeed, any physical theatre will shape a performance attempted within it. Fortunately, the ruins of the Theatre of Dionysus are still to be seen in Athens, and although the theatre was much altered by later generations, it is possible to learn a great deal about how it must have felt to witness such a performance. As in the Elizabethan theatre, the stage is essentially a thrust-stage, with the audience placed on three sides. The basic form of the theatre is outlined in the sketch on the next page, although many of the details must be understood as conjectural. The seating area indicated could accommodate some 16,000 people, which would make it comparable with many smaller football stadiums today. On

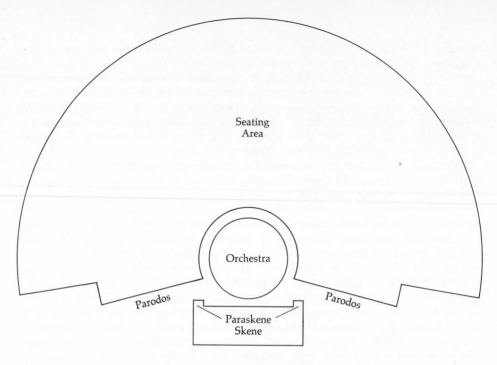

Diagram of the Theatre of Dionysos.

the other hand, this analogy can be a little misleading, for the orchestra and stage area (approximately 64 feet in diameter) are not nearly as large as a football field, and thus the distance from the performer to the back row of seats is not so great as might be imagined. Actors needed to project their voices well, but no superhuman effort was needed to assure audibility in the last row. The *skene* or scene building behind the orchestra apparently began as little more than a hut for costume changes, but it evolved into a scenic background and a place from which an actor might make a powerful entrance. There may have been a small raised stage between the *paraskenia*, but it seems certain that actors descended from it and played directly with the chorus in the orchestra area. Elaborate knowledge of this physical theatre is not necessary in order to perceive that it called for a production style differing greatly from modern realism. Probably the idea that the Greek tragedies were slow and stately in their performances has been exaggerated (people have not changed so much in 2,500 years, and nobody likes a show that drags), but on the other hand a degree of dignity and measured cadence seems almost inevitable. If everyone in such a large theatre was to see and hear properly, movement and speech would have to be larger than life and somewhat slower. Actors wore costumes that were padded and draped to make them appear larger than life (including boots that added several inches to their height), making sudden or jerky movement impossible. Perhaps most importantly, the actors wore masks. The presence of an elaborately carved and painted mask eliminated facial expression as an acting aid and set one stylized expression for at least the length of a scene.

Knowing some background in the nature of the theatre and the production methods employed at the time *Oedipus the King* was written, one is in a better position to understand and appreciate it today. The play was written between 430 and 415

B.C. The other plays written at the same time have not survived. Sophocles' other two plays involving some of the same characters (*Antigone* and *Oedipus at Colonus*) were written at widely separated times in his life and should not be treated as parts of a single tetralogy. The basic story is part of Greek legend and mythology, and the audience probably knew the story before the play began. Like Shakespeare in a later age, the Greek playwrights rarely made up their own plots, preferring to modify existing stories, whether historical or fictional. These productions were entirely audience-oriented, with little thought that any of the scripts would be read by posterity. Of the hundreds and hundreds of tragedies written during this period, only thirty-three survive today—seven by Aeschylus, seven by Sophocles, and nineteen by Euripides. Not until after Aeschylus' death, in fact, was consideration given to the possibility of repeating a performance of a really good play. Aeschylus was the first playwright honored by a revival of one of his works.

Oedipus the King is by far Sophocles' most famous play. Curiously, the tetralogy of which it was a part won only a second prize when it was first produced in the annual competition, but since the other three plays are now lost (as are the tetralogies with which it was competing), one cannot evaluate the appropriateness of the judges' decision that day. Aristotle makes frequent reference to *Oedipus the King* in the *Poetics* in contexts which make it clear that he regarded the play with the utmost esteem. Critics throughout the intervening centuries have treated it, without serious challenge, as one of the two or three finest tragedies of all time. It has been performed repeatedly in every major language and in every major country in the world, and will no doubt continue to be performed and reinterpreted as long as man aspires to tragic insights.

Page 408: Robert Goddier as Creon and Douglas Campbell as King Oedipus in *Oedipus Rex* at Stratford Shakespearean Festival, Stratford, Ontario, 1955. Directed by Tyrone Guthrie, designed by Tanya Moiseiwitsch.

Page 413: Robert Goodier as Creon, Douglas Campbell as Oedipus, and members of the Festival company as senators or elders of the Theban state (Chorus) in the same production. For this role Douglas Campbell wore the *cothurnus,* a stiltlike device of the Greek theatre that raised him six inches. Both photographs courtesy of the Stratford Shakespearean Foundation of Canada.

by
SOPHOCLES

An English Version by
JOHN GASSNER[1]

Oedipus, King of Thebes
A Priest of Zeus
Creon, brother-in-law of Oedipus and
  Jocasta's brother
Teiresias, blind prophet or seer of Thebes
Jocasta, Queen of Thebes, wife of Oedi-
  pus and widow of Laius, the former
  king
A Messenger from Corinth, an old shepherd
A Shepherd, formerly a slave in the
  palace of Thebes
A Servant from the Palace, who acts as a
  second messenger

[Line numbering follows Greek text. P.G.H.]

Oedipus the King

[1] With revisions suggested by Professor Dwight Durling.
  The dialogue has been rendered in free verse in order to
convey the lean and dramatic (occasionally even deliberately flat) quality of the original. I have tried to arrive at
a simple, forthright, and stageworthy style. I have also attempted to employ a language more direct than is usual in
the old translations, closer to idiomatic speech, but still
somewhat heightened. The choral odes are rendered in the
irregular pattern of the original strophes and antistrophes.
An attempt has been made to balance strophe and antistrophe by giving them the same number of lines and by
making each successive line of the antistrophe approximate
the length of the equivalent line of the strophe. (No rhyme
has been used, but neither is there any rhyme in classic
Greek verse.) The length of the line throughout this version is determined by the sense—whether literal, poetic, or
dramatic. The break comes where it seems to me the
breath would break, the voice would pause, or the inflec-
tion would rise with the sense, the feeling, the tone, or the
tension. The reader should also note that the word Chorus
is used both for a single speaker, the Leader of the Chorus
in the dialogue, and for the Chorus as a whole reciting in
unison. In staging the play, the director may, of course,
take some liberties. Thus, if I were to stage the play, on
[p. 437], during Oedipus' last appearance, I might consider
employing two individual speakers—the Leader of the
Chorus and a second, less sympathetic Elder of the
Chorus. Then, again, I might decide to reject this procedure, in order to give the Chorus a strict unity and make
it representative of "community." (See Francis Fergusson's
The Idea of a Theatre, Chapter I, pp. 13–41. Although disagreement is possible with some of the points Mr. Fergusson raises, his chapter is the most searching analysis
of *Oedipus the King* I have read.)—J.G.

Chorus, senators or elders of the Theban
state

NONSPEAKING CHARACTERS

Suppliants, old men, youths, and children
Antigone } daughters of Oedipus
Ismene } and Jocasta
Attendants, Servants, Suppliants

Scene—The royal palace of Thebes.

In front of the columns, *Suppliants* of
various ages sit around the altars holding
wreaths of branches. *Priests* stand among
them, and at the main altar stands the
most reverend of these, the **Priest of Zeus.**
And now **Oedipus,** King of Thebes, comes
out majestically through the central door.

Oedipus: Children, youngest brood of
   Cadmus[2] the old,
why do you sit here with branches in
   your hand
while the air is heavy with incense
and the town rings with prayer and
   lament?
Deeming it unfit to hear the reason
   from a messenger,   5
I, Oedipus, on whom men rely,
have come myself to hear you out.
      [*Turning to the* **Priest of Zeus**]
Tell me, venerable priest of Zeus,
you who can speak for these,
what do you want or fear?   10
Be sure I shall gladly help,
for hard of heart would I be
to have no pity for such suppliants.
Priest: Oedipus, ruler of my land,
you see our generations at the altar—   15
the nestlings here too weak to fly far,
the priesthood bent with age,
and the chosen young.
The rest sit with branches in the
   market-place,
before the twin altars to Pallas,   20

---
[2] The legendary founder of Thebes.

and by Ismenus who answers with
   fire.[3]
Our city—you yourself have seen!—
can no more lift prow out of the wave
   of death.
The blight lies on the blossom,
on the herds in pasture,   25
and on the women barren in labor.
The god who carries fire through the
   land,
the ferocious plague,
swoops down to empty the home of
   Cadmus
while the Grave grows more opulent
   with our weeping.   30
We, these children and I, do not call
   you a god.
But you are first among men
in the common chances of men,
and even when the contest
is with more than man.   35
For you came to Thebes and lifted the
   toll
we paid to the songstress sphinx:
we could tell you nothing, and no one
   taught you;
yet you prevailed—with the help, we
   think, of a god.
Now, Oedipus, the greatest of mortals,   40
we supplicate you to be savior again,
whether with the help of some god who
   whispers to you
or by your own wisdom as a man;
for I have learned this thing—
when men have proved themselves by
   former deeds,
they also prevail in present counsel.   45
Best of mortals,
lift up our estate once more.
Live up to your noble fame,
for now the land you rescued
calls you Savior.
Never let us remember of your reign
that as high as we rose with you
so low we were cast down thereafter.   50
Oh no, raise up our fallen city,

---
[3] An oracle which made signs by means of fire.

that it fail no more,
and brings us good fortune again.

If you are to rule this land, as you rule
it now,
surely it is better to be the lord of men
than of a waste;   55
nor walled town nor ship has any worth
when no men live in it.

Oedipus: Oh my poor children, known,
well known to me what brought you
here!
I know you suffer,   60
and yet none among you can suffer as I:
Your pain comes to each one alone for
himself,
and for none else, but I suffer for all:
for the city, for myself, and for you.
You do not rouse me, then, as one
sunk in sleep;   65
be sure I have given many tears to this
and gone wide ways in the wandering
of thought.
But the only recourse I knew I took:
I sent Menoeceus' son, Jocasta's
brother,   70
to the Pythian house,[4] to hear from
Apollo
by what word or deed I am to deliver
you.
It troubles me to count the days Creon
has been gone,   75
but when he comes I am no man of
worth
if I fail to perform what God has
ordered.

Priest: In good season you have spoken,
lord;
your servants signal that he is near.

>   [**Oedipus** *turns to see* **Creon** *approach-
> ing.*]

Oedipus: Yes, and his face is bright.   80
O King Apollo, may the words he
brings shine on us, too.

Priest: He brings good news; else he
would not come

---

[4] The temple of Apollo.

crowned with sprigs of bay.

Oedipus: He can hear me now: Prince
and kinsman,
Menoeceus' son, what news from the
God?   85

>   [**Creon** *approaches* **Oedipus.**]

Creon: Favorable news.—For even
trouble hard to bear
is well, all well, if the issue be good.

Oedipus: What says the oracle?
So far your words give us cause
for neither confidence nor despair.   90

Creon: If you will hear me now, I am
ready;
else let us go within.

Oedipus: No, speak before them,
for the grief I bear is most for them.

Creon: What the God has told I will
then tell.   95
Phoebus, our lord, speaks plainly:
Drive out, he says, pollution,
defilement harbored in the land;
drive it out nor cherish it
until it prove past cure.

Oedipus: And by what rite?

Creon: Banish the guilty man, or let
blood be shed   100
for bloodshed, since blood it is that
brought
this storm of death upon the state.

Oedipus: Who is the man for whom
God decrees doom?

Creon: King Laius was lord of Thebes
before you held the helm—

Oedipus: I know of him by hearsay;   105
I never knew him.

Creon: He was slain.
The God commands punishment
for those who slew the King.

Oedipus: And where are they? Where
shall be found
the dim trace of an ancient crime?

Creon: In this land, the God says.   110
What is sought for can be found;
only unheeded things escape.

Oedipus: Was it in house, in field, or
abroad
that Laius met death?

Creon: To Delphi⁵ he went who never
came home.   115

Oedipus: Had he companions who
witnessed the deed?

Creon: No, they perished, all but one
who fled; and of what he saw he had
but one thing to report as certain.

Oedipus: The one thing might be the
means   120
to discover all; if but a small beginning
were made—

Creon: He said that many robbers fell
on them;
the deed was not done by a single
hand.

Oedipus: And how could robbers dare
so far
unless bribed by someone in the city?   125

Creon: We thought of that, ourselves.
But Laius was dead, and our trouble,
our *other* trouble, distracted us.

Oedipus: What trouble was so great to
hinder your search
when royalty was slain?

Creon: The riddling sphinx.⁶ It made us
seek   130
an instant remedy for the instant thing
and let dark things go.

Oedipus: Well, I will start afresh
and make dark things clear.
Right was Phoebus and right are you
to give this care to the dead man's
cause,
and, as is meet, you shall find me   135
with you avenging country and God
besides.
Not on behalf of one unknown but in
my own interest,
as King, will I erase this stain,
for one who slew the old might slay
the new;
I help myself in helping Laius.   140

---

⁵ I.e., on a pilgrimage to Apollo's temple at Delphi.
⁶ The Sphinx was a monster, half woman and half lion, who
waylaid all passers and destroyed them after they failed to
answer the riddle she proposed. For answering it successfully and causing the monster to destroy itself, Oedipus
was rewarded with the throne of Thebes and the hand of
Jocasta, the widowed queen of the city.

Come, then, my children, rise from the
altar-steps
and lift up your suppliant boughs,
and let the rest of Cadmus' seed be
summoned here.
Say, nothing will be untried;
say, I will make a cleansing   145
and find for all Thebes, as God wills,
prosperity or grief.
          [**Oedipus** *goes into the palace with*
          Creon.]

Priest: My children, let us rise!
We came for this that the King
promises,
and may God Phoebus, sender of the
word, deliver us.   150
          [**The Chorus,** *composed of the* **Elders of**
          Thebes, *now enters.*]

Chorus [1st strophe]:   Oh, message of
Zeus, whose words are sweet,
with what strange portent have you
come
from the golden seat of Pytho⁷
to our glorious Theban home?
I am stretched as on the rack, and
terror shakes me,
O Delian Healer,⁸ to whom our pleas
for help are sent,
and I stand in fear of what you may
bring to pass: 155
new thing unknown or doom renewed
in the cycle of years.
Speak to me of golden hope,
Immortal Voice.

Chorus [1st antistrophe]:   I call upon
you first, divine Athene, daughter of
Zeus!
Then on your sister Artemis, the
guardian of our land   160
who sits on her throne of fame
above the circled precinct of our
market-place;
and on Phoebus, whose darts fly far.
Oh shine forth, averters of fate!
If ever before when destruction struck
the state you came,   165

---

⁷ Apollo—i.e., from Delphi, the seat of the oracle.
⁸ Apollo.

if ever you drove the fire of evil beyond
    our borders,
come to us now.

Chorus: [2ND STROPHE]:   Numberless,
    alas, the griefs I bear,
the plague on all our host,   170
with no resource of mind a shield for
    our defense.
The fruit no longer sprung from the
    glorious land
and no woman rising relieved from
    birth-labor
by issue of a child.
And one by one you may see   175
flying away, like birds on swift wing,
life after life that hastens to the
    Evening Land.

Chorus [2ND ANTISTROPHE]:   By such
    unnumbered death the great town
    perishes:
unpitied her children lie upon the
    ground, spreading pestilence,   180
while the young wives and gray-haired
    mothers
uplift a wailing, some here, some there,
bent over the altar-edge suppliant and
    moaning.   185
Prayer to God the Healer rises
but intermingled with lament.
O golden Daughter of Zeus,
send bright-faced deliverance.

Chorus [3RD STROPHE]:   And grant that
    Ares[9] the Destroyer,   190
who neither with brass shield nor
    clamor of war racks me,
may speed from our land to the
    caverns of Amphitrite[10]
below the wave   195
or to the Thracian sea where no haven
    is,
for whosoever escape the night
may find relief at last when the
    day-break comes.
O Zeus, Father, who wields the
    fire-fraught lightning,   200
destroy Death with your bolt.

Chorus [3RD ANTISTROPHE]:   Next, Lycean
    King, Apollo, I were glad too
that the arrows from your bow-string
    of woven gold   205
winged forth in their might to
    confound the foe.
Yes, and that the beams of fire
Artemis[11] sends through the hills
    brought aid.   210
And I call the God
whose hair is bound with gold, flushed
    Bacchus with Maenad band,[12]
to draw near with his torch and defeat
the god unhonored among the gods.[13]   215
    [**Oedipus** *returns*.]

Oedipus: You are at prayer, and in
    answer,
if you will heed my words
and minister to your own disease,
you may hope for help and win relief.
These words I say who have been a
    stranger
to your report and to the deed,   220
for I were not now on the track of it
without your aid.
But made a citizen among you after the
    deed,
I now proclaim to all of Thebes:
Whoever among you knows the
    murderer   225
at whose hand King Laius died,
I command he tell the truth.
For though he fear blame, I say,
exempt shall he be from punishment
and leave the land unhurt,
enduring no other harm.   230
Or if anyone know the assassin
to be alien, of a foreign state,
let him not be silent,
for I will pay him a reward
and favor him forever.

But if he hold back from fear,
attempt to screen another or himself,
give ear to what I intend: 235

---

[9] Mars, the war god.
[10] Wife of Poseidon and goddess of the sea.

[11] Diana, goddess of the moon.
[12] The women worshippers of Bacchus or Dionysus were
called Bacchantes or Maenads.
[13] Ares, or Mars, the god of war and destruction.

I order that no one in this land I rule
give shelter or speak word to the
　　murderer
whoever he be,
nor make him partner to a prayer or a
　　sacrifice,
nor serve him with water for his hand　240
in lustral rite.
And I command that the slayer
whosoever he be,
whether he alone be guilty or had
　　confederates,　　　　　　　　　　　　245
evilly, as he is evil, wear out his life
unblest in misery.
And for myself I pray:
If knowingly I succor him
as inmate of my household,
let me too endure the curse invoked on
　　you.　　　　　　　　　　　　　　　　250

This charge I lay upon you:
Make good my words—
for my sake,
for the sake of the God,
and for the sake of the land
so blasted and barren under wrathful
　　heaven.
For even without ordinance from God,　255
it was not right to leave the guilt
　　unpurged
when one so noble, your own king, was
　　dead.
You must search it out!
And now, since I hold the power he
　　once held,
possess his marriage bed and wife,　　260
and since, had his hope of issue not
　　miscarried,
he and I would have had children from
　　one mother
and so been bound by more ties still,
except that Fate came heavy upon his
　　head—
on this account I, as for my own father,　265
will leave nothing unattempted
to ferret out those who shed his blood.
I will fight for the scions of Labdacus
　　and Polydorus

and for the earlier ancestors, Cadmus
　　and Agenor of old.[14]
And for those who disobey me, I pray　270
the gods give them no harvest of earth
　　and no fruit of the womb;
waste be their lot—and a destiny still
　　more dire.
But you, the loyal men of Cadmus who
　　my intent approve,
may Justice, our ally, and all the gods
forever proffer you their blessings.　　275

Chorus:　As you have put an oath upon
　　me,
on oath, my King, I say:
I am not the slayer, nor knew him who
　　slew.—
From Phoebus, himself, who set the
　　quest, should come to answer.

Oedipus:　You speak well,　　　　　　280
but against their will
no man has the power to constrain the
　　gods.

Chorus:　I would propose, if I may, a
　　second course—

Oedipus:　—and I should listen to a third
　　course, too,
if it were proposed.

Chorus:　Teiresias above all men
is known to see what Phoebus sees.　　285
The clearest answer could come from
　　him,
if one sought it.

Oedipus:　Not even this chance have I
　　overlooked:
Advised by Creon, I have twice sent
　　for the seer;
I am perturbed he has not come.

Chorus:　There are other reports besides:　290
faint, fading rumors to explore.

Oedipus:　What rumors? I am ready to
　　weigh every tale.

Chorus:　Certain wayfarers, it was said,
　　killed Laius.

Oedipus:　That, too, I heard,
but he who saw it is himself unseen.

---

[14] Labdacus was the father of Laius; Agenor was the father
of Cadmus; Cadmus was the father of Polydorus.

Chorus: But if he has a grain of fear in
   his heart
he will step forth, knowing your curse.   295
Oedipus: My words will not frighten a
   man
who was not afraid to perform the
   deed.
Chorus: Then there is one to expose
   him, and he comes:
Here they bring the godlike prophet
in whom truth lives.
          [**Teiresias,** *led by a* **Boy,** *arrives.*]
Oedipus: Teiresias, whose mind can
   search all things,   300
the utterable and the unutterable alike,
secret of heaven and what lies on
   earth,
though you cannot see, you must know
   how the plague
afflicts the land.
Our prophet, in you alone we find a
   protector,
the only savior.   305
Perhaps you have not been told,
but Phoebus, when consulted, declared
we must discover the slayers of Laius
and slay or drive them out.
Do not, then, spare augury of birds   310
or any other form of divination you
   possess
to save yourself and the state,
and to save me and all who are defiled
   by the deed.
Man's noblest deed is to bring aid by
   what means he has,
and you alone can help.   315
Teiresias: O fate! How terrible it is to
   know
When nothing good can come of
   knowing.
I knew of the matter but it slipped out
   of mind;
else I would not have come.
Oedipus: What now? How can you
   regret your coming?
Teiresias: Let me go home. You will   320
   bear your burden easier then,
and I mine, too.

Oedipus: What! You have not spoken
   loyally or kindly,
giving no answer with strange words.
Teiresias: Because your own words miss
   the mark,
do not expect mine to hit it safely.   325
Oedipus: For the love of God, if you
   know,
do not turn away.
We bend before you; we are your
   suppliants.
Teiresias: You ask only because you
   know nothing.
I will not reveal my grief—I call it
   mine, not yours.
Oedipus: What do you know and
   refuse to tell?   330
You are a traitor if you allow the state
   to be destroyed.
Teiresias: Since I want no harm for you
   or myself,
why do you ask vain questions?
I will tell you nothing.
Oedipus: Worst of traitors,
you would rouse a stone to wrath!   335
Will you never speak out, be stirred by
   nothing,
be obstinate to the end?
Teiresias: You see the fault in me but
   not in yourself.
So it is me you blame?
Oedipus: Who would not take offense   340
hearing you flout the city?
Teiresias: It will come of itself—
the thing that must,
although I breathe no word.
Oedipus: Since it must come,
surely you can tell me what it is!
Teiresias: I say no more. Storm at me if
   you will,
you'll hear no more.
Oedipus: And being in such anger, I,   345
   for my part,
will hold back nothing, be sure.
I'll speak my thought:
Know then I suspect you of having
   plotted the deed yourself
and of having done it

short of killing with own hand;
and if you had eyesight,
I would declare the doing too your
    own.
Teiresias: Was it so?   350
Well then I charge you to abide by
    your own decree
and from this day on speak neither to
    me nor them,
being *yourself* the defiler of the land.
Oedipus: So this is your taunt!
And you expect to go scot-free?   355
Teiresias: I *am* free,
for the truth has made me so.
Oedipus: Tell me at least who is in
    league with you?
For surely this lie was not of your own
    making!
Teiresias: Yours is the blame,
who spurred me on to speak against
    my will.
Oedipus: Speak again:
Perhaps I did not understand you.
Teiresias: Did you not understand at   360
    first hearing?
Or are you bent on provoking me
    again?
Oedipus: No, I did not grasp your
    meaning.
Speak again!
Teiresias: I say that *you* are the
    murderer—
he whom you seek.
Oedipus: Now at last, now you have
    spoken twice,
you shall rue your words.
Teiresias: Shall I speak on
and incense you more?
Oedipus: Say what you will; it will be   365
    said in vain.
Teiresias: I say, then, you have lived in
    unsuspected shame
with one who is your nearest,
and you do not yet see the plight you
    are in.
Oedipus: And you expect to go on
    ranting
without smarting for it?

Teiresias: Yes, certainly, if there is
    strength in truth.
Oedipus: Why, so there is—   370
except for you; you have no truth,
blind as you are in ears, in mind—and
    eyes.
Teiresias: Wretched man,
you utter taunts that everyone will
    soon heap
upon none other than yourself.
Oedipus: Night, an endless night is
    your prison;
you cannot hurt me or any man who
    can see the sun.   375
Teiresias: No, it is not your doom to be
    hurt by me;
Apollo's is the work ahead,
and Apollo's work is enough.
Oedipus: Are these inventions yours or
    Creon's?
Teiresias: Creon is not your enemy;
you are your own foe.
Oedipus: Oh riches and dominion and   380
    the craft
surpassing others' craft in an envied
    life,
how deep is the source of jealousy
if for the sake of the power the city put
    into my hand,
a gift unsought by me,
trusty Creon, my old friend, creeps by   385
    stealth upon me,
seeks to unseat me,
and has suborned this quack and
    scheming juggler
who has an eye only for gain but
    whose divining skill is blind!

Yes, blind, I say:
For tell me, my prophet, when have
    you ever seen clear?   390
Where was your deliverance when the
    monster-woman wove dark song?
Surely the unriddling of the riddle
was not for a chance traveler like me
but for you with your skill of
    divination!
Yet no help came from you, neither

from watching the flight of birds   395
nor talking to any god.

No, I came,
I the ignorant who had no miraculous
  aid.
I, by my own wit, made answer,
  untaught of birds,
and I stopped the monster's breath.
And now it is me you would thrust
  out,
thinking to stand by Creon's side when
  he takes the throne.   400
But I think you will regret your
  proffered purge for the land,
you and that other plotter;
and, dotard, you would have been
  punished already
if I had no regard for age however
  arrogant.
Chorus: O, Oedipus, to our mind,
both this man's words and your own   405
have been spoken in anger.
Our need is not for these
  recriminations,
but for guidance on how best to abide
  by God's command.
Teiresias: King though you be,
the right of reply, at least, belongs to
  us both;
I am your peer,
for I am Apollo's servant, not yours.   410
Nor will you find me in Creon's
  service.
And I tell you, who have taunted me
  with blindness,
you that have sight
do not see your plight, where you
  dwell,
and with whom.
You do not even know what stock you
  came from,   415
nor that, unknowing, you have been
foe to your own kin
both above the earth
and below, among the shades.
You, the double curse of mother and
  father,

shall leave your land one day in
  painful haste
with darkness on the eyes that now see
  so straight.

And what are the places that shall not
  hear your cry,   420
what Cithaeron-crag shall not resound
  with it soon,
when you have learned what
  marriage-song
wafted you on a fair voyage to a foul
  haven
in your own house!
What multitudinous evils you cannot
  guess
shall level you down to yourself
and to your own brood of children!   425
So heap all your scorn on Creon and
  my words,
but know this: no man shall be
  crushed
more utterly than you.
Oedipus: Is this to be endured? Go
  quickly,
and my curse go with you.   430
Back from these walls of my home,
back to your own.
Teiresias: I should never have come had
  you not sent for me.
Oedipus: You would have waited long
  to be called
if I had known you for a fool.
Teiresias: Yes, I am a fool to you   435
whose parents thought me wise.
Oedipus: Parents, you say? Don't go!
Who were they? Who gave me birth?
Teiresias: This day shall give you both
  birth and ruin.
Oedipus: Riddles, always riddles! You
  darken everything.
Teiresias: Does that disturb you
who were so adept at unriddling?   440
Oedipus: Yes, cast it in my teeth,
that which lifted me high—
Teiresias: —and will soon bring you low!
Your fortune, Oedipus, has been your
  misfortune.

Oedipus: If misfortune must befall me
for having saved the city,
I say I do not care.
Teiresias: Well, I will go then.
You, boy, lead me home.
Oedipus: Yes, let him take you out of   445
my sight.
Here you are only a hindrance and a
trouble,
and when you are gone you will vex
me no more.
Teiresias: I will go, having said what I
came to say,
and not because I fear your anger, for
you possess
no power to destroy me. But I tell you
this now, King:
The man you have sought with threats
and proclamation,   450
that man is here!
Believed to be of foreign birth, he shall
soon be found
Theban-born, and he shall take no joy
in the discovery.
Blind, he who still has sight,
a beggar, he who is still wealthy,   455
he shall turn his face toward an alien
land,
tapping the ground before him with a
staff.
And he shall be found at once brother
and father to the children in his house,
son and husband to the woman who
bore him,
and fellow-sower in the bed of his
father,
whom he slew.
Go into your palace and ponder upon
all this—   460
and if I am proved wrong,
henceforth say that I have no skill in
prophecy.
[**Teiresias** *departs, led by the* **Boy,** *while*
Oedipus *goes into the palace.*]
Chorus [1ST STROPHE]:   Who is he whom
the divine voice of the Delian rock
has pronounced guilty with red hands,   465
perpetrator of horrors no tongue dare
name?

Now is his time to run faster than
steeds that gallop with the wind.
For upon him leaps the son of Zeus,[15]
armed with flame of lightning   470
and followed by the dread unerring
Fates
that never tire in pursuit.
Chorus [1ST ANTISTROPHE]:   For a word
but now blazed from snow-covered
Parnassus   475
orders us to look for the unknown
man who,
hidden in the wild-grown forest, slinks
or roams,
fierce as a bull and forlorn, on a
joyless path
through cave and crag to avoid
the doom pronounced at earth's central
seat.   480
Yet that never-ending doom continues
to follow and to beat wings
over him in pursuit.
Chorus [2ND STROPHE]:   In truth I am in
dread with darkest thought
aroused by the seer, the wise,
though I cannot approve or deny what   485
he said.
I do not know what to say,
but I am uneasy with foreboding,
having no clear vision in the present or
into the future.   490
For never in past years or now did I
hear
the house of Labdacus had reason
to fear hurt from a son of Polybus[16]
that I should arraign the good repute
of Oedipus   495
to avenge the line of Labdacus for an
unknown crime.
Chorus [2ND ANTISTROPHE]:   True, Zeus
indeed and Apollo are wise
and know the things of human
concern,   500
but that a mere mortal man, though he
be a seer,

---

[15] Apollo, or Phoebus.
[16] The supposed father of Oedipus.

can have certain knowledge above
    mine—
of this there is no clear proof.
One man may surpass another in
    wisdom,   505
yet until I see the prophet's word
    proved true
never will I agree when Oedipus is
    blamed;
for once the winged maiden[17] came
    against him
and he showed himself wise by the test
    and good to the state.   510
So never shall verdict of mine turn
    against him to accuse him of crime.

        [**Creon** *appears and addresses the*
        Chorus.]

Creon: My fellow-citizens, having heard
    that Oedipus makes a charge
against me that is vile, I come here
    indignant:
if in the present trouble he believes he
    was wronged   515
by me in some word or action,
then I willingly forego my term of
    years to come
rather than bear this blame.
For the rumor, having spread, wrongs
    me in all respects   520
if I am considered a traitor by the
    populace,
by you and by all friends.

Chorus: The reproach came, we think,
    under the stress of anger,
not from the heart.

Creon: Has it not been said that I
    counseled the seer to deliver   525
    falsehoods?

Chorus: So it was said, though I cannot
    understand to what purpose.

Creon: Did the king make his charge
    directly,
with steady eyes and a steadfast mind?

Chorus: That I could not tell; it is my
    rule not to look closely   530
at what my masters do. But here he is,
the lord of the house.

---

[17] The Sphinx.

[**Oedipus** *comes out, in a rage.*]

Oedipus: So, you have come with a
    bold face to my house
who would make yourself assassin of
    its master
and brazen pilferer of his crown?   535
Come, tell me, in the name of all the
    gods,
what cowardice or dotage you found in
    Oedipus
that you dared to lay a plot against
    him.
How could you believe I would fail to
    notice
your creeping upon me by stealth
or, discovering your designs, I would
    not defend myself?
Now was it not folly, this attempt of
    yours,   540
without a following, without a troop of
    friends, to seize the throne?
It is a thing to be achieved, as you
    ought to know,
with followers and with support of
    wealth.

Creon: I beg you fairly to hear a fair
    reply and then decide.

Oedipus: Are you so quick, then, to
    explain? You should be forewarned,   545
I shall be slow to understand you;
I have found you a malignant enemy.

Creon: But hear my explanation—

Oedipus: Explain but this—this one
    thing:
Tell me you are not a villain.

Creon: You are not wise if you believe
    unreasoning obstinacy is good.   550

Oedipus: And you are not sane if you
    believe
kinsmen who wrong kinsmen are not
    punished.

Creon: What you say is just, of course,
but what is my offense?

Oedipus: Did you or did you not advise
    me   555
to send for the canting prophet?

Creon: Yes, and I still believe I did
    right.

Oedipus: How long ago is it since Laius—

Creon: —since Laius . . . ? I do not
  understand—
Oedipus: —disappeared from men's
  sight by violence?   560
Creon: The count of years goes far into
  the past.
Oedipus: This seer of yours, did he
  practice his craft even then?
Creon: Yes. He was honored, as he is
  now.
Oedipus: Did he mention me at that
  time even once?
Creon: He did not. Never, certainly, in
  my presence.   565
Oedipus: And you never searched for
  the man who died?
Creon: We searched, of course; we
  discovered nothing.
Oedipus: Why did not this wise seer
  tell his story then?
Creon: It is not my wont to speak of
  things I do not know.
Oedipus: This much at least you know
  and will declare if you are wise—   570
Creon: What? If I know, I will make no
  denial.
Oedipus: That if he had not conspired
  with you,
  he would never have declared the King
  was slain by *me!*
Creon: You must know best whether
  this was said by him;
  but here I require enlightenment of
  you as you have required of me.   575
Oedipus: Learn this then:
  Never shall I be found guilty of the
  blood of Laius.
Creon: Learn this then!
  You have my sister to wife?
Oedipus: That there is no denying.
Creon: And she has equal rights with
  you in the state?
Oedipus: Yes, and she obtains
  everything she desires.   580
Creon: And I as a third owner of the
  land, am I not the equal of you two?
Oedipus: Ah!—and there, in that
  thought, appears the falseness of
  your friendship!

Creon: Not if you reason with yourself
  as I reason!
  Weigh this first:
  Would I rather choose burdensome
  sovereignty like yours   585
  and be uneasy with fear
  than equal power but power shared in
  untroubled peace?
  I am not by nature covetous of kingly
  rule
  but only of kingly worth, as befits a
  sober mind.

  At present I have all needful things
  from you and none of your anxieties.   590
  But were I the ruler of the city, as you
  are now,
  I should have to do many things
  against my inclination.
  How would a throne, then, be
  pleasanter to me
  than painless sovereignty?
  I am not yet so bemused to want
  honors that afford no profit.   595
  Every man is my friend now. He greets
  me,
  and wishes me well. And whosoever
  has a boon to ask of you
  first he speaks with me to favor his
  cause.
  Why, then, should I exchange my life
  for yours?
  I should have to take leave of sense to
  want to dethrone you;   600
  I have no love for such designs at all,
  nor could I bear to act with one who
  plotted them.
  And for proof of this, first, go to Delphi
  and inquire if I did not report the
  oracle
  as it was given.
  Next, if you discover I plotted with the
  seer,   605
  seize me and slay me,—
  and do this, not with your sentence
  alone,
  but with mine, here given.
  But do not place guilt on me by
  conjecture,

lacking all proof.
It is not just to judge a bad man good
and a good man bad;   610
and to cast away a friend is like
    throwing away
one's own life, which one values most.
Ah well! only in time will you learn
    this thing,
for time alone reveals the honest man
while a single day is long enough to
    disclose the knave.   615
Chorus: His words ring true, my King.
    Quick judgment is unsafe.
Oedipus: Quick? When a plotter moves
    against me
I must be quick with counterplot;
if I delay until he acts, he gains his
    ends   620
and I miss mine.
Creon: What is it, then, you want?
    To expel me from my country?
Oedipus: By no means:
I want your death, not banishment;
to teach the world what danger there is
    in jealousy.
Creon: You speak as one resolved to
    believe nothing.   625
Oedipus: Because you deserve no belief.
Creon: You talk as one bereft of sense.
Oedipus: I have sense enough where
    my interest lies.
Creon: You should consider my interest
    too.
Oedipus: Never! You are false.
Creon: But if your judgment is
    mistaken?
Oedipus: Be that as it may, I must
    remain the ruler of this city.
Creon: But not if you rule wrongly.
Oedipus: This city is my city!
Creon: Yours only? The city is mine   630
    too.
Chorus: Have done, my lords, have
    done!
Here is Jocasta in good time; I see her
    coming
whose voice will compose your quarrel.
            [**Jocasta** *arrives.*]
Jocasta: Misguided men, for shame,

what has stirred up trouble among you   635
with strife of tongues while the land is
    so afflicted?
        [*To* **Oedipus**]
Come into the palace,
and you, Creon, go home, go home;
push no mere nothing into a calamity.
Creon: Sister, your Oedipus threatens
    me: 640
he has only to decide whether to drive
    me from the city or kill me!
Oedipus: That is true! For I have found
    him out, finding him
conspiring against my person.
Creon: May I never know happiness
    and die accursed by God
if there is any truth in what you charge
    against me!   645
Jocasta: Oedipus, in Heaven's name
    believe him,
first for the awful oath he has sworn
    by the gods,
and next for my sake and for the sake
    of all these men.
Chorus: Hear her, our King. With
    wisdom reflect upon this
and be gracious, we pray you. Grant it.
Oedipus: What shall I grant?   650
Chorus: Accept his word; he was never
    before found in folly,
and his oath is a weighty one.
Oedipus: Do you know what you ask?
Chorus: Yes.
Oedipus: Declare it then.   655
Chorus: Use no unproved conjecture
    against the man
who has been your friend and who has
    given his oath.
Oedipus: Then be very sure you know
    that in asking this
you call destruction or exile upon
    myself.
Chorus: Oh no! By God the Sun, who
    stands   660
foremost in the heavens,
unblessed and accursed may I be,
cast in utter darkness, my lord,
if I have any such thought!
But the withering of the land wears

down my unhappy heart   665
and this new trouble, strife between
  you,
is too heavy to bear.
Oedipus: Then let him go free,
  though his freedom work my death or
  my doom
  to be thrust out dishonored from
  Thebes.   670
Your lips, not his, have moved me to
  compassion.
But wherever he is he shall still have
  my hatred.
Creon: How sullen you are in yielding
  and vehement in temper when moved!
  Such natures are, not without justice,
  the heaviest burden to themselves.   675
Oedipus: Will you not leave in peace
  and go away!
Creon: I will; but though you misjudge
  me, these men know I am innocent.
      [**Creon** *leaves.* **Oedipus** *stands shaken
      with rage.*]
Chorus: O Lady, will you take him
  within?
Jocasta: I will when I have learned what
  chanced.   680
Chorus: A blind conjecture arose on
  one side,
  bred of rash words;
  and on the other side, the sting of
  injustice
  brought strife.
Jocasta: So both sides were wrong?
Chorus: We think so.
Jocasta: What was the story that started
  this?
Chorus: Enough, enough!   685
  Let it rest, now it has ended;
  our land is vexed enough without it.
Oedipus: But do you see where your
  good purpose
  has now carried you in blunting my
  anger?
Chorus: King, I have said this before,
  and I say again: 690
  I should be a madman, devoid of
  counsel, to put away
  the man who steered a good course in

my country's trouble   695
and who shall yet, may God grant it,
lead us again to safety.
Jocasta: In the name of the gods,
  husband, I beg of you, what was the
  tale?
  What put you in a rage? Tell me.
Oedipus: I will; I honor you more than
  I honor them: 700
  Creon has laid a plot against me.
Jocasta: Husband, be plainer—
Oedipus: He declares I am guilty of the
  blood of Laius.
Jocasta: So? Did he say he heard it,
  or does he claim to know it himself?
Oedipus: Neither: *He* keeps his own
  mouth unsoiled;   705
  he made the rogue of a seer his
  mouthpiece.
Jocasta: If that is all, prepare yourself to
  put it out of mind
  at once. Listen to me and learn
  that no one born of woman is capable
  of divination—
  as I myself discovered: 710
  To Laius once came an oracle—
  I will not say directly from Apollo,
  but from his ministers—
  that he should die by the hand of a
  son born of him and me.
  But you must know that Laius, as
  reported,   715
  was waylaid by robbers
  where three highways meet,
  and our child, who should have slain
  him,
  if the oracle was true,
  was barely three days old when Laius
  pinned its ankles together
  and had it cast out by servants
  on a pathless mountain.
  So Apollo did not bring it to pass   720
  that the child should be the slayer of
  the man
  and that Laius should suffer
  the thing he dreaded—
  death from the hand of the son.
  The oracle was clear, yet was proved
  false, as you see.

So much then for the power of the
  seers!
What God desires us to know,
be sure he will reveal it himself.   725
Oedipus: Oh wife, wife!
  you cannot know what your report has
    done to me.
  What anguish—
Jocasta: What disturbs you now?
Oedipus: I thought I heard you say
  Laius was slain where three roads
    meet—   730
Jocasta: Yes, so the report went and so
  it goes still.
Oedipus: And where is this place,
  Jocasta?
Jocasta: In Phocis.
  Two roads, one from Delphi and one
    from Daulia, meet.
Oedipus: How long ago did all this
  happen?   735
Jocasta: The news was brought to the
  city
  a short time before you became the
    king.
Oedipus: O Zeus! what fate have you
  stored up for me?
Jocasta: What is troubling you?
Oedipus: No! No questions yet! Tell me
  only   740
  what sort of man was he? How tall was
    Laius?
  How old?
Jocasta: He was no longer young—his
  hair was turning white,
  and he was tall, his figure not unlike
    your own.
Oedipus: I am a miserable man.
  An ignorant man, Jocasta, I fear
  I have laid myself under my own
    curse.   745
Jocasta: You terrify me, Oedipus. What
  are you saying?
Oedipus: I have a misgiving the seer
  can see. Just that!
  But you can make something plainer.
  Tell me—
Jocasta: What? Something makes me
  tremble, yet I must answer.

Oedipus: Did Laius have few
  attendants,   750
  or did he travel with a host, as a
    prince should?
Jocasta: There were five of them, one a
  herald;
  there was one carriage, for the King.
Oedipus: All plain—too plain!
  Who told you this, Jocasta?   755
Jocasta: The survivor who returned
  alone. A servant.
Oedipus: Is he still in service?
Jocasta: No longer. When he found you
  king here on his return
  in the place of Laius,
  he touched my hand and petitioned me   760
  to send him to the fields to pasture
    flocks.
  He asked it as one who found himself
    ill at ease
  in the city and would be far from it.
  He deserved more than this
    consideration,
  for, as slaves go, he was a worthy man.
  I could not refuse his request.
Oedipus: If only we could have him
  back here quickly!   765
Jocasta: He can be brought,
  but why do you wish to see him?
Oedipus: I fear, Jocasta, I have already
  said too much;
  I must see him first.
Jocasta: He shall come, then.
  But unburden your heart to me first;
  I deserve your confidence.   770
Oedipus: I shall not keep anything from
  you
  since my forebodings have carried me
    so far.
  In whom should I confide more,
  passing through such a peril,
  than you, my wife, who are dear to me?

  My father, as you know, was Polybus
    of Corinth,
  my mother, Merope, the Dorian,   775
  and I was counted the first in the city.
  Then something occurred—a startling
    thing,

although it should not have put me
    into such a passion:
At the banquetboard, a man in his
    cups
said I was no true son of my mother
    and father.   780
For all my fury I checked my temper,
but the morning after, I went to my
    parents
and taxed them with it.
Their anger at the fellow who flung the
    taunt
was so great that I felt reassured;   785
yet the thing still galled me, for the
    rumor crept on.
So, unknown to father and mother, I
    went to Delphi.
Phoebus, it is true, left dark what I
    came to know,
but his answer was full of other things
    terrible to hear;
I was fated, he said, to defile my
    mother's bed   790
and bring forth a progeny intolerable
    to the light,
and to be my natural father's slayer,
    too.

So, having heard, I put Corinth far
    behind me,
thereafter measuring the way where the
    city lies
by the stars only,   795
seeking a place where I could never
    expect
the foretold infamies to be fulfilled.
But as I journeyed on
I found myself upon the very spot
    where, you say, Laius perished.   800

Worse still, when I was near those
    three roads,
I saw a herald advancing and a man in
    a carriage drawn by colts;
and both, the man in front and the old
    man,
wanted to edge me rudely off the road.   805
Enraged, I struck the man who thrust
    me aside,

whereupon the seated elder, biding
    time as I passed him,
leaned out and brought his goad with
    two toothpoints
down hard on my head.
I repaid the blow at once,   810
striking with my staff so hard that with
    one stroke
I rolled him out of the carriage into the
    road;
and then with my sword I struck down
    every man of them.
So, if there is reason to connect this
    nameless man with Laius,
you see before you a man more
    miserable than any man before.   815
For, then, what man could be more
    hated by the gods?—
a man whom no citizen and no
    stranger in Thebes may receive,
whom no man may welcome but must
    drive out of doors.
And none other than I, laid this curse
    on myself.   820

And hear me once more: If this is so,
with the hands that slew I pollute the
    bed
of him who was slain.
Am I not then loathsome and all
    unclean?

And think of it, it was only to be
    driven out of Thebes
that I had to flee before
in self-banishment, forsake my own
    people,
and never set foot again in Corinth my
    native city   825
lest I be fated to be yoked with my
    mother
and kill my father, the good Polybus
    who begot and reared me.

Would not a man then speak correctly
    who in judging of this said
that a god of evil is my enemy?
Never, you pure and sacred majesties
    of Heaven, never   830

may I behold that day. Let me pass out
of men's sight
before I see myself brought low by a
destiny so vile.
Chorus: We, too, are fearful, Prince. Yet
do not lose hope.
Await the man who saw the deed and   835
can reveal all.
Oedipus: Yes, I still hold on to hope
until he arrives.
Jocasta: [*Troubled*] And when—when he
appears,
what will you ask him?
Oedipus: I will tell you:
If his tale will tally with yours
I am clear at least of *this* disaster.   840
Jocasta: How so? What did you hear me
say that must tally?
Oedipus: You were saying that he
spoke of *robbers.*
Why, then, if he still speaks of several
men,
I am not the slayer!
One is not the same as *many.*   845
But if he speaks of one man traveling
alone,
then veritably the guilt leans toward
me.
Jocasta: Of this be assured at least,
so the tale was told by him; he cannot
revoke it
when the city, not I alone, heard him
tell it so.   850
Yet even if he shifts from it, of this be
sure—
he cannot make the death of Laius
square with the prophecy.
Plain were Apollo's words:
Laius was to be slain by a son born of
me.
And, after all, the poor thing never
killed him   855
but died itself before! so henceforth
I do not mean to look to left or right
for fear of divination.
Oedipus: You have reassured me, I
think; yet send for the slave, I pray
you.
See that it is done.   860

Jocasta: Since you desire this,
I will send someone quickly, to please
you, as in everything.
And now let us go within.
  [**Oedipus** and **Jocasta** *go into the palace.*]
Chorus [1ST STROPHE]: Mine be a way of
life that keeps
the holy purity of word and deed,
prescription of the laws that are
sublime,   865
born in the regions of the sky,
whose only begetter is Olympian Zeus.

No mortal begot the laws
and no forgetfulness shall put them to
sleep.
Ever-wakeful, the God lives great in
them,   870
and He never grows old.
Chorus [1ST ANTISTROPHE]: Pride begets
the tyrant,
and Insolence, puffed with vain wealth,
climbs and climbs to the topmost
height   875
only to be flung down to horrible
doom
where no foothold serves.
Only ambition that serves the whole
state
is ever worthy and propitious,
and only rivalry that benefits all may
God,   880
our defender, never quell.
Chorus [2ND STROPHE]: But may an evil
fate afflict
him who in ill-starred pride
proceeds with his arrogance by word
or deed,   885
despising Justice
and the holy images of God.
May he be doomed
who seeks an advantage unfairly
and does not abstain from unholiness,   890
profaning inviolable things.

When such things are done what
mortal may boast
he shall ward off the shafts of God
from his life?

When such behavior is honored,   895
why, then, should we keep our sacred
    dance?
Chorus [2ND ANTISTROPHE]:   Never to the
    inviolate hearth
at the navel of the world,
nor to Abae's shrine or Olympia   900
will I go in prayer,
if the oracles are proved untrue
for each man's finger to point at with
    scorn.
No, Zeus, if you are rightly called King
of the world, let not this issue
leave your ever-deathless hands.   905

For already men set at nought
the old prophecy for Laius, now faded,
and nowhere does Apollo receive his
    due honor:
Worship vanishes from the earth.   910
        [Jocasta *comes out of the palace with* **At-**
        tendants.]
Jocasta: Princes of the land, it occurred
    to me
to visit the temples of the deities,
bringing in my hand these garlands
    and this incense.
For Oedipus lends his mind too much
    to alarms,
nor, like a sober person, measures   915
a new conjecture by past experience,
but is at the mercy of whoever speaks
    to him
of terrors at hand. I can do nothing
    with him.
So to Apollo I mean to go,
to you, Lycean God, to us the nearest,   920
a suppliant with offerings,
that you afford us some deliverance.
For now we are all frightened, seeing
    him, Oedipus,
helmsman of our ship, in fright.
        [*A* **Messenger** *appears.*]
Messenger: Strangers, may I learn of
    you, where is the palace
of Oedipus the King? or better, where   925
is he himself, if you know?
An Elder of the Chorus: Stranger, this
    is his dwelling

and he is within;   895
and this lady is the mother of his
    children.
Messenger: May she be blessed in a
    happy home
since she is his queen.   930
Jocasta: May you be blessed too for the
    kind greeting.
Say what you have to seek or tell.
Messenger: Good news, my lady, to
    your house and husband.
Jocasta: What is your news? And from
    whom have you come?   935
Messenger: From Corinth. What I am to
    say
will please you, if not without some
    pain.
Jocasta: What can this mean, a
    double-faced report?
Messenger: The people of the Isthmus,
    the Corinthians,
intend to make him king.   940
Jocasta: What! Does not Polybus, the
    old king, still rule?
Messenger: No longer; he is death's
    subject in the pit.
Jocasta: The father of Oedipus is dead?
Messenger: May I be reft of life myself
if my report is untrue.
Jocasta: [*To an* **Attendant**] Run, girl; tell
    your master instantly.   945
        [*The* **Attendant** *goes into the palace*]
O oracles of the gods, where are you
    now?
Oedipus fled long since from the man's
    presence,
fearing to become his murderer, and
    instead
the man has died a natural death; he
    was not killed by Oedipus
        [**Oedipus** *appears.*]
Oedipus: [*Anxiously*] Jocasta, dear wife,
    why have you sent for me?   950
Jocasta: To hear this man speak.
And as you listen, mark well to what a
    pass
your dark oracles have come.
Oedipus: Who is this? And what does
    he say?

Jocasta: He comes from Corinth   955
to report that Polybus, your father, is
gone.

Oedipus: Is this true? Stranger,
let me have your news from your own
mouth!

Messenger: To make the report plainer,
I tell you, King, that our king is dead.

Oedipus: Oh! Did he die by traitorous   960
assault or by illness?

Messenger: A light thing in the scale of
life brings the old to their rest.

Oedipus: Then he died, it seems, of
illness.

Messenger: Yes, and of the long years
he had lived.

Oedipus: [*Triumphantly*] Oh, oh! Why
should one look to the hearth of
Pytho
and to the birds that scream overhead   965
on whose showing I was to slay my
father?
He is dead and already under earth,
and I have been here, not there, and
have not put my hand to the spear.—
Unless he died through longing
and in this sense is dead because of
me.   970
So Polybus is gone,
and all those oracles as they stood
have been laid to rest with him in
Hades,
and have been proved of no account.

Jocasta: Did I not foretell all this?

Oedipus: You did, but my fear led me
astray.

Jocasta: And so let none of these
predictions weigh you down further.   975

Oedipus: Yet—yet how can I help still
dreading my mother's bed?

Jocasta: Now, why should a man be so
fearful
when he knows that Chance rules
everything
and man foreknows nothing on earth?
To have a carefree mind is therefore
best.
As for that mother marriage-bed—
have no fear of it, my dear.   980

Many men before have dreamed of   955
such a marriage,
but he who gives no weight to these
fantasies
is most at ease in his life.

Oedipus: All that you say would be
well
if my mother were not living. But since
she is alive   985
I have reason for my fears.

Jocasta: Your father's death—does not
this allay them?

Oedipus: But my fear concerns the
living.

Messenger: [*Puzzled*] Who is this, the
woman you dread?

Oedipus: Merope, old man, the consort
of Polybus.   990

Messenger: But what disturbs you?

Oedipus: An oracle from the gods,
appalling in import.

Messenger: May it be told?
Or is it unlawful for another to know?

Oedipus: I may tell it.
The gods declared that I should marry
my mother,   995
and with my own hands shed the
blood of my father.
Corinth, my home, has not seen me for
no other reason:
I have won great happiness here,
yet, you know, it is sweet to see the
face of one's parents.

Messenger: This, then, was the fear that
kept you away?   1000

Oedipus: Old man, I did not want to
slay my father!

Messenger: Why should I not then free
you of this fear, my King,
since my coming here was well meant?

Oedipus: And a good reward would be
yours.

Messenger: In truth, it was for this I
came; mainly   1005
that I should reap some favor on your
return to the city.

Oedipus: [*Frantically*] Return? Oh no!
Never!
I'll never go anywhere near my parents.

Messenger: O son, it is plain
you cannot know what you are doing.

Oedipus: In what way, old man? In
God's name, tell me.

Messenger: That is, if I understand your
reasons.   1010

Oedipus: Yes, old man, these reasons
hold me back—
I fear that Phoebus may somehow
prove a true prophet.

Messenger: You fear to stain yourself
with guilt through parents?

Oedipus: Even so—the thought appalls
me.

Messenger: Then know your fears to be
baseless.

Oedipus: But how—if I am their son?   1015

Messenger: Because there is no
blood-tie.

Oedipus: What are you saying? Was
not Polybus my begetter?

Messenger: No more than I who speak
to you,
or so much as I, in fact, and no more.

Oedipus: How, my own sire no more to
me than a hireling?

Messenger: Yes. He did not beget you,
no more than I.   1020

Oedipus: Then why did he call me his
son?

Messenger: Know this: he had you as a
gift from me.

Oedipus: And he could love me so
much, though I came from another's
hand!

Messenger: His many seasons of
childlessness drew him to you.

Oedipus: Was I an infant you found—or
purchased?   1025

Messenger: In Cithaeron's wooded
valley—there I found you.

Oedipus: What took you up there?

Messenger: I tended flocks on the
mountain.

Oedipus: You were a shepherd then,
wandering for hire?

Messenger: But your preserver, my son,
and I came in good time.   1030

Oedipus: In good time? What was my
plight?

Messenger: Your ankles might tell you.

Oedipus: Yes, that is an old affliction.

Messenger: I loosed you;
your ankles had been pierced and were
pinned together.

Oedipus: Yes, I have borne a shameful
mark on them from my cradle.   1035

Messenger: And it is from this you bear
the name of Oedipus
given to you for your swollen feet.[18]

Oedipus: Tell me this, by Heaven! Was
it done by my father—or my mother?

Messenger: I have no knowledge of the
deed.
He that gave you to me can tell you, I
think.

Oedipus: What! You had me from
another? You did not light on me
yourself?

Messenger: Another shepherd gave you
to me.   1040

Oedipus: Who was he? Do you know
him?

Messenger: I think the man belonged to
Laius.

Oedipus: The king who ruled this city?

Messenger: The same. The man was a
shepherd in his service.

Oedipus: Do you know whether he is
alive? Can I see the man?   1045

Messenger: You must know that best
who live in this land.

Oedipus: [*Addressing the crowd*] Is there
anyone present
who knows the herdsman of whom he
speaks,
who has seen him in pasture or in the
city?
If anyone knows, let him answer:
the hour has come for everything to be
made clear.   1050

Chorus: The Corinthian speaks of no
other, I think,

---

[18] *Oidipous* (or Oedipus) was taken to mean "swell-foot" or
club-foot.

than the peasant you asked to see;
but Jocasta is the one who would know best.

Oedipus: Jocasta, do you remember him you sent for?
Are he and this herdsman one man?   1055

Jocasta: [*Greatly troubled*] Why ask of whom the Corinthian speaks?
Give no heed to this—waste no thought on it—
it is of no importance—

Oedipus: Importance? Can anything be more important!
With the clue close at hand,
should I not pursue the matter of my parentage
and let it come to light?

Jocasta: Oedipus, for the sake of all the gods   1060
if you have any care for your own life,
let the old things alone;
I am sick of all this—I have had enough!

Oedipus: Have no fear, Jocasta. Even if I am proved a slave,
three times a slave, and if my mother were threedeep a slave,
you will not be considered a slave too.

Jocasta: Dearest, let me persuade you,
I beseech you, no more questions!

Oedipus: Do not beseech me
to let the occasion slide; I must have light!   1065

Jocasta: [*Desperately*] I have your interest at heart—my fears are for you—
my advice, my dear, is best.

Oedipus: Then this best advice—
I am out of patience with it.

Jocasta: O Oedipus, Oedipus,
God keep you, ill-fated one, from learning who you are.

Oedipus: Will someone go at once and fetch the herdsman,
and leave this woman to glory in her noble stock!   1070

Jocasta: O miserable one, unhappy one—
that is all I can say—now and forever.

[**Jocasta** *rushes into the palace in desperation.*]

Chorus: Why has our lady run into the palace wild with grief?
A premonition shakes me:
it was terror that sealed her lips.   1075

Oedipus: Let come what will.
Be my descent ever so lowly, I still must know.
Perhaps the woman, who is proud with a woman's towering pride,
finds my origin too humble for her.
As for me,
I hold myself to be the child of gracious Fortune,   1080
and take no dishonor from this:
Fortune is the mother from whom I sprang,
and I call the months my brothers,
they that sometimes found me cast down
and then set high again.
With such a lineage,
I shall never be found ashamed
and falter in searching into my birth.   1085
[*The* **Chorus** *is filled with confidence on hearing him.*]

Chorus [strophe]:   If I am a seer or wise of heart at all,
mountain nurse, Cithaeron,
you shall not fail by Heaven   1090
to know at tomorrow's full moon
that Oedipus honors you as his foster-mother
and that you are honored in the dance by us
as one favored by our monarch.   1095
Phoebus, to whom we call, favor these things too!

Chorus [antistrophe]:   Who was it, child? which of the ageless goddesses
bore you to Pan the father,   1100
who roams the pasture hills?
Or was she bride to Phoebus? *He* the father?
Or to Cyllene's lord?[19]

---

[19] Hermes (or Mercury), said to have been born in Cyllene.

Or the Bacchantes'[20] god,   1105
a dweller on the hill-tops, was it *He*
who received you his new-born joy
   from one of the oreads[21]
with whom he mostly sports?
            [**Attendants** *appear, leading a* **Shepherd,**
            an old man.]

Oedipus: [*To the Corinthian* **Messenger**] If I
   may guess, who never saw him,   1110
here is your herdsman.
   His ripe years measure with yours,
   and the men who bring him are of my
      household.   1115
   But you, if you have seen him before,
      can tell me.

Chorus: I recognize him—
   trustiest of the servants Laius had in
      his house.

Oedipus: Now, Corinthian stranger:
   Is it he?

Messenger: This is the man.   1120

Oedipus: [*To the old* **Shepherd**] Well
   then—old man! Look at me!
   Tell me—you served Laius?

Shepherd: I was his slave.
   Not bought by him, but reared in his
      house.

Oedipus: Doing what work? What was
   your way of life?

Shepherd: For the best part of my life I
   tended flocks.   1125

Oedipus: Where did they graze?

Shepherd: Sometimes *on* Cithaeron,
   sometimes *near* the mountain.

Oedipus: [*Pointing out the* **Messenger**] This
   man—do you recall having ever met
   him there?   1130

Shepherd: Not to say off-hand, from
   memory.

Messenger: And no wonder, master!
   but he will when I remind him. We
      kept pasture there
   three half-years,
   he with his two flocks, I with one. 1135
   They grazed together from spring-time
   to the rise of Arcturus in the fall.

---

[20] See footnote 12.
[21] Mountain nymphs.

Then I drove my sheep to our fold at
   home
and he brought his back to Laius.
            [*To the* **Shepherd**]
Was this so as I tell it or not?   1140

Shepherd: It was—but it was a long
   time ago.

Messenger: And tell me now, do you
   remember giving me a boy,
   an infant then, to rear as my own?

Shepherd: [*Frightened*] What do you
   mean? Why do you ask me that?

Messenger: [*Pointing to* **Oedipus**] Here is
   the man, my friend, who was then   1145
   the child.

Shepherd: [*Violently*] The plague take
   you! Hold your tongue!

Oedipus: How now? You have no right
   to blame him.
   The words that offend are yours.

Shepherd: Offend? How have I
   offended, master?

Oedipus: In not telling us about the
   child.   1150

Shepherd: He busies himself with no
   business of his own.
   He speaks without knowing.

Oedipus: Herdsman! if you will not
   speak to please me,
   you shall be forced.

Shepherd: For God's love, master, do
   not harm an old man!

Oedipus: [*To his* **Servants**] Hold him fast;
   twist his arms behind him!

Shepherd: Wretch that I am! What do
   you want to know?   1155

Oedipus: You gave him a child? The
   child he asks about?

Shepherd: I gave it. Would I had died
   before!

Oedipus: You will now, if you do not
   speak the truth.

Shepherd: And it will be the worse
   with me if I speak it.

Oedipus: The fellow trifles with us
   still—evades the question . . .   1160

Shepherd: [*As the* **Servants** *twist his arms*]
   No, no! I have told you that I gave
   him the child.

Oedipus: From whom did you have it?
Did someone give it to you,
or was it your own?
Shepherd: It was not mine.
Another gave it to me.
Oedipus: Which of these citizens? From
whose home?
Shepherd: Master, I beg of you—
I beg you, do not ask it. 1165
Oedipus: You are a dead man if I ask
again.
Shepherd: It was a child, then—of the
house of Laius.
Oedipus: A slave's child? Or born of
the King's own family?
Shepherd: I stand on the knife-edge of
dreadful words; I fear to speak.
Oedipus: And I, to hear. Yet I must! 1170
Shepherd: The child was called his son;
but she within, your lady, could best
say how that was.
Oedipus: Did she then give it to you?
Shepherd: So it was, my King.
Oedipus: For what purpose? Speak!
Shepherd: That I should do away with
it.
Oedipus: Wretched woman! Her own
child?
Shepherd: Yes, from fear of the evil
prophecies. 1175
Oedipus: What prophecies?
Shepherd: That he should kill his
parents, it was said.
Oedipus: Why, then, did you give him
to this old man?
Shepherd: Through pity, master.
I gave him the child,
thinking he would take it to another
land, his own.
He did so but, alas, he saved it for the
worst of sorrows.
For, if you are the man he says you
are, 1180
then surely you were born to great
misery!
Oedipus: [*Uttering the cry of a wounded
animal*] Oh—oh—oh!
Everything is proved true—everything
has come to pass!

Light of the sun,
never shall I look on you again,
I who am revealed
damned by the light I saw at birth,
damned by my marriage,
damned by the blood I shed. 1185
[**Oedipus** *rushes frantically into the palace.*]
Chorus [1ST STROPHE]: O generations of
men
how I account your lives no better
than not living at all!
Where is to be found the man 1190
who attains more happiness than a
mere seeming
and after the seeming, a falling away!
Yours is the fate that warns me—
luckless, unhappy Oedipus!— 1195
to call no creature living on earth
enviable.
Chorus [1ST ANTISTROPHE]: For this is he,
o Zeus,
who speeding his bolt far beyond the
rest
won the prize of all-engrossing
prosperity.
He slew the darkly singing maiden,
her of the crooked talons; 1200
he stood as a tower between death and
our land,
and thereafter was called king,
received unrivaled honor
and next to none ruled great Thebes.
Chorus [2ND STROPHE]: But now, O Zeus,
whose is the story more grievous to
hear,
and who is more yoked to misfortune 1205
now his entire life is reversed?
O, renowned prince Oedipus,
who, on the nuptial bed,
sought the same source
as father that you had as son, 1210
how could the soil your father sowed
before
suffer you, unhappy one, in peace so
long!
Chorus [2ND ANTISTROPHE]: Time,
all-revealing, that has found you
guilty without intent,

arraigns you now for a monstrous
    marriage   1215
in which begetter and begotten are
    one.
O child of Laius,
I wish that I had never beheld your
    face!
True, I must lament your fate
with a dirge that pours from my lips,   1220
and yet, though I got new life from
    you at first,[22]
you have dropped a great darkness on
    my eyes.

        [*A* **Servant** *rushes out of the palace.*]

Servant: O you, most honored in the
    land,
what things you have to hear, what
    sights to see,
what sorrow to endure, if you still
    cherish   1225
the house of Labdacus, true to your
    oath!
For neither the waves of Ister, I fear,
    nor Phasis[23]
can wash this house clean,
so many the evils it covers and shall
    soon disclose.
Yes, evils self-inflicted,   1230
which are the worst to bear.
Chorus: There was no lack of suffering
    before;
what report can cause more
    lamentation?
Servant: To tell the shortest tale,
our royal lady, Jocasta, is dead.   1235
Chorus: Unhappy woman! How did she
    die?
Servant: By her own hand.
It cannot be so terrible to you as to
    one who witnessed it,
but as far as I can tell, you shall hear: 1240
When she passed into the vestibule,
    frantic,
she ran straight to the bedchamber

---

[22] Because Oedipus relieved Thebes of the Sphinx, which
destroyed its citizens.
[23] Ister or Istros, the lower reaches of the Danube; Phasis, a
river in eastern Asia that empties into the Black Sea.

with her fingers tearing at her hair.
She dashed the doors shut behind her,
called upon dead Laius,   1245
mindful of the begotten son
by whom, she said, he died
and by whom she bore unholy
    offspring.
So she bewailed the nuptial bed
on which she had brought forth a
    twofold brood—
a husband by her husband, and
    children by her son.   1250
What happened next, how she died,
is more than I can tell, for Oedipus
    burst in
and we could not behold her end,
our eyes being fixed on him. For he
    went about raging,
calling for a sword, and demanding   1255
where he could find the wife who was
    no wife
but the mother-soil of both himself
    and his children.
And while he was raging, some power
    guided him to her;
for with a dreadful cry, as though led
    on,   1260
he flung himself at the closed doors,
unhinging their bolts with his bare
    hands.

Going in after him, we saw the lady,
    her neck
in a twisted rope and swinging.
Then he, giving a dreadful cry,   1265
loosed her halter and when she lay on
    the ground,
how awful the sequel we saw!
For tearing from the raiment the
    golden brooches of her robe,
he raised them high and struck them
    into his eyes,
calling out, as he smote: 1270
"No longer, my eyes, shall you behold
    the horror
I suffered and performed! Too long
have you looked on those on whom
    you should not have looked

while failing to see what you should
  have seen.
Henceforth, therefore, be dark!"
With words like these, not once but
  many times   1275
he struck at his eyes with the lifted pins,
and at each blow the eyes streamed
  blood on his beard
like crimson rain.

These are the evils that from a two-fold
  source,   1280
not one alone, but from woman and
  husband,
have burst forth. The fortune of the old
  house
was once a rare happiness, but in this
  hour
of shame and ruin, lamentation and
  death,
of all earthly suffering that can be
  named
nothing was spared.   1285
Chorus: Is he eased of his misery now
  and quiet?
Servant: He calls for someone to unbar
  the doors
and show him to all the Thebans as his
  father's slayer
and his mother's—but no, the unholy
  word shall not pass my lips.
He proposes to cast himself out of the
  land   1290
and no longer to burden the
house with his curse.
Yet he lacks strength and has no one
  to guide his steps,
for no one can bear to go near him.
But you will see for yourselves now,
  for the bolts are being drawn,
and he will come out, revealing   1295
what even he who shrinks from the
  horror will pity.
         [**Oedipus** *comes out of the palace, his eyes*
         blood-stained and horrible.]
Chorus: O dreadful sight,
  most dreadful that my eyes have ever
  looked upon!

Unhappy one, what madness came
  upon you?
Who is the demon, the foe to man,   1300
that with a spring beyond mortal
  power
leaped upon your ill-fated life as its
  prey?
Hapless one, although there is more I
  would ask you
and I am drawn to you with pitying
  sorrow,
I cannot even bring myself to look
  again;   1305
you fill me with such shuddering.
Oedipus: Wretched that I am! Oh! Oh!
Where am I going in my misery,
and where is my voice borne on the
  wings of air?   1310
Fate, have you brought me so far?
Chorus: To a destiny terrible to men's
  ears
and terrible to their sight!
Oedipus: Horror of darkness that
  envelops me!
Dreadful visitant, resistless and
  unspeakable,
whom a too fair breeze of fortune sped
  against me,   1315
how my soul is stabbed, first by the
  present pain
and again by the memory of fearful
  deeds!
Chorus: [*Sympathetically*] Amid troubles so
  many
you may well bear and mourn a
  two-fold pain.   1320
Oedipus: Oh friend, you still are
  steadfast,
still ready to tend and to endure me,
a blind man!
Your presence is not hidden from me;   1325
in my darkness I know your voice.
Chorus: Yet, man of dreadful deed,
how could you bear to extinguish your
  sight?
What inhuman power drove you?
Oedipus: Apollo, friends,
Apollo brought these woes to pass;   1330

but it was my own hand that struck.
My own hand alone, man of misery
    that I am!
I did not want to see when sight could
    show me nothing good.   1335
Chorus: It is true, alas.
Oedipus: What was left to see?
What to love?
What greeting to hear with pleasure?
Hurry, lead me out of the land,   1340
lead away the lost one, the most
    damned of men,   1345
the man most abhorred by the gods.
Chorus: Unhappy equally in misfortune
and in too keen consciousness of
    horror,
it were better that you had never lived.
Oedipus: A curse on the man who
    freed me in the pasture,
who unbound my feet   1350
and saved me from death
and brought me to a life such as this.
Had I died then, on Cithaeron's slope,
I should have brought no grief
both to my friends and myself.   1355
Chorus: I, too, could wish it had been
    so.
Oedipus: I would not have come to
    shed my father's blood,
nor been known among men as my
    mother's husband.
But now I am forsaken by the gods,
the son of a defiled mother, and
    successor   1360
in the bed of him who gave me
    miserable life.
If there is any evil that exceeds all evil, 1365
that has been the fate of Oedipus.
Chorus: Yet I cannot say you have done
    well.
To have died would have been better
    than to be blind and living.
Oedipus: I have done what I thought
    best; I'll have no counsel in this.   1370
Had I retained my sight, with what
    eyes
in the land of shades underground
could I have looked on my father and

my wretched mother—
those two against whom I have done
    such things
that no halter could punish the crime.
And would the children born to me   1375
have been an endurable sight? Not to
    these eyes—never.
Nor could I look upon this city, with
    its citadel and shrines,
from which I cut myself off, I of
    Thebes the greatest,   1380
when I myself pronounced the doom to
    drive *him* out,
the criminal revealed now by the gods
    as the hateful seed of Laius.
Bearing this stain upon me,
could I have looked with unaverted
    eyes on my people?   1385
Never. And had there been some way
to seal the fountain of hearing, too,
I should have cast this wretched body
    into a still closer prison,
secure from all sound as well as sight,
for it is sweet to be beyond the stab of
    pain.   1390

Oh, Cithaeron, why did you shelter me
who came to you an infant?
Why not have destroyed me at once,
leaving my birth unrevealed?
And you Polybus and Corinth
and the ancient house I called the
    home of my fathers,   1395
how fair a nursling you fostered
and how foul a man
festered within the child,
doomed to be
found evil and of evil birth.

And you crossroads—
hidden glen, thicket and narrow way   1400
where the three paths met,
you that drank from my murdering
    hands
a father's blood,
do you still remember what you saw
    me do?

And, then, the deeds I went on to
    perform!

O, marriage, marriage,
You brought me forth,
then brought children to your child.   1405
In a kinship of fathers, brothers, sons,
and of brides, wives, and mothers,
you compounded the foulest shame a
     man can know,
ghastly incest.
But no, it is unfit to utter what it is
     unfit to do!
Hurry, friends, and in God's name,
     hide me somewhere beyond this
     land.   1410
Or kill me;
or cast me into the sea where you may
     never look upon me again.

Approach; take hold of me.
Have no fear of contamination;
my plague will touch no one else.   1415
     [**Creon** *is seen approaching.*]
Chorus: No! Creon approaches in good
     time
to advise and perform what must be.
He is left sole guardian of the land.
Oedipus: Creon! How shall I speak?
How can I request anything from him,   1420
having proved unjust in what passed
     between us?
     [**Creon** *appears with* **Attendants.**]
Creon: I have come, Oedipus, not in
     mockery
nor with intended reproaches for past
     words.
But if you have no regard for the
     children of men,
respect, at least, the all-sustaining
     flame   1425
of our Lord the Sun!
Spare Him the sight of naked pollution
that not earth, nor holy rain, nor light
     can welcome.
     [*To the* **Attendants**]
Come! Take him inside quickly.
It is seemly that kinsfolk alone   1430
should see and hear a kinsman's grief.
Oedipus: For the God's sake, since you
     have come to me,

a man so vile, with so noble a spirit,
grant me one request.
For your own good I ask it, not for
     mine.
Creon: Ask what you wish.   1435
Oedipus: Cast me out of this land,
speed me to a land where no man may
     greet me.
Creon: I should have done this, be sure,
if I had not wanted to learn first what
     the God decrees.
Oedipus: Surely his oracle was clear—   1440
to let the parricide and defiler die.
Creon: That was said.
But in our present plight it is well to
     ask the God again.
Oedipus: How can you expect a
     response from God
on behalf of so frightful a man as
     Oedipus?
Creon: Even you must now put your
     faith in the God.   1445
Oedipus: Even so! And I entreat you
to order a burial that befits her who
     lies within;
she is your own,
for whom you should properly perform
     the rites.
But for me, never should my father's
     city
have to behold me dwelling in it while
     I live.   1450

Let me go to the hills,
there where my mountain Cithaeron
     rises,
once appointed to be my tomb by
     mother and father.
Dying there,
I shall die as by their decree who
     rightly doomed me at my birth.

Yet I also know there is more to come.   1455
Neither an illness nor anything else
     will destroy me.
I should never have been snatched
     from death there

but for a strange, still uncompleted,
    destiny.[24]
Well, then, let my fate, whatever it be,
take me where it will! But my children,
    Creon!
My sons require none of your care,   1460
being grown men who will not lack the
    means to live.
Creon, I pray you, take care of my
    daughters,[25]
my two poor unhappy girls,
who never ate at a separate table away
    from me or lacked my presence
and ever shared all things with me.   1465
Grant them your protection.

And suffer me, if you will, to touch
    them
and share my grief with them.
Grant me this, Prince,
grant it, noble one,
that in touching them I may feel
they are with me, as when I still had
    my sight.   1470
    [*Led out by* **Servants, Antigone** *and* **Is-
    mene,** *the young daughters, come out of
    the palace, sobbing.*]
Oedipus: [*Hearing them*] O heavenly
    powers, are those my children,
    sobbing?
Can it be that Creon, pitying me,
sends me the children, the dear ones?
Have you done that?   1475
Creon: I have, seeing what joy you took
    in them before.
May they give you comfort.
Oedipus: Then a blessing be your
    reward.
May Heaven prove a kinder guide on
    your road of life[26]
than it was to me.
Oh, my children, where are you?   1480
Come here—here to the hands of him
whose mother was your own,
the hands that put out your father's
    once clear eyes,
which seeing nothing, understanding
    nothing,
brought him to her from whom he
    sprang   1485
to become your father.
For you, too, I weep,
though I cannot see your faces,
knowing the bitter life men will make
    for you
in the days to come. For,
to what gathering of citizens will you
    go,   1490
to what festival,

---

[24] Oedipus, according to Sophocles' later play, *Oedipus at Colonus,* was to be invested with a mysterious power after his present suffering. Creon was to try to bring him back to Thebes, in order that in dying and being buried there Oedipus should sanctify the land, or, as Oedipus says in the later tragedy, "that the city may escape unscathed" in a later war with Athens. Oedipus was to be endowed with some mystic power or magical *mana* to safeguard the land in which he might be buried. In *Oedipus at Colonus,* choosing to die on Athenian soil and to be buried in Sophocles' native village, Colonus (Sophocles having altered the old legend for reasons of patriotism), Oedipus blesses Athens and promises it safety in gratitude for the kind reception accorded him by Theseus, the legendary ruler of the Athenian state. A mysterious heavenly voice calls him, and his death is a mystic experience witnessed only by Theseus, who will not reveal what he saw. The Messenger in *Oedipus at Colonus* only reports:
"No fiery thunderbolt of the god removed him in that hour, nor any rising of storm from the sea, but either a messenger from the gods, or the world of the dead, the nether adamant, riven for him in love, without pain; for the passing of the man was not with lamentation, or in sickness and suffering, but, above mortal's, wonderful." (Translation by Richard C. Jebb)

[25] There is tragic irony in this, as a Greek audience would have known. Creon was to condemn Antigone to death for burying one of her brothers, Polyneices, who besieged Thebes after being deprived of his royal rights by the other brother, Eteocles. Sophocles had dramatized this part of the Oedipus legend in his play *Antigone,* produced earlier. And there is, of course, further irony in the confidence with which Oedipus considers the future of his sons when, actually, they would soon engage in a furious rivalry that would end in their killing each other in a duel waged over the throne they inherit from Oedipus. (This rivalry is the subject of still another extant Greek tragedy that Sophocles' audience must have known—*The Seven Against Thebes,* by Aeschylus.)

---

[26] In the light of future events, known to Sophocles' audience, this wish adds more tragic irony to the play and sustains the point that man's life is full of uncertainties. Both Creon's wife and son were to kill themselves after Antigone's death; the son because he loved Antigone, the wife because her son was dead. See Sophocles' *Antigone.*

from which you will not come back in
    tears?
Where will be found the man
willing to assume the disgrace that
    clings to my offspring
and that would to yours?   1495
For what reproach is lacking?
"Your father slew his father,
and planted you in the womb of his
    own being."
Such will be the taunts you must hear!
The man who would marry you does
    not live;   1500
you must wither away in barrenness.

O Creon, son of Menoeceus, hear me!
You are the only father left to them,
both their parents lost—both!
Do not allow my children, who are
    your kinswomen too,   1505
to wander about in beggary, unwed.[27]
Do not let them sink down to my
    misery.
Pity them when you see them forlorn,
so utterly forlorn in their young years.
Give me your promise with the touch
    of your hand!   1510

And to you, my children,
I could give much counsel if you were
    older.
As it is, I can only make this prayer:
May you find some place where you
    can live in quiet,
and may you have a better life than
    your father's.
Creon: Enough lamentation! Pass into
    the house, Oedipus.   1515
Oedipus: I must obey, though it is
    hard.

Creon: To everything there is a season.
Oedipus: Know, then, on what
    conditions I go within.
Creon: Name them, and I shall know.
Oedipus: See to it that I am cast out of
    Thebes. Banish me!
Creon: That must be as the God
    decrees.
Oedipus: But surely you understand
    that I am hateful to the God!
Creon: If so, you will obtain your desire
    soon enough.
Oedipus: So you consent.
Creon: I have said as I mean.   1520
Oedipus: [Still holding on to his daughters]
    Then it is time for me to be led
    within.
Creon: Go then, but let the children go.
Oedipus: [Clinging passionately to them] No,
    do not take them from me.
Creon: [Severely] Do not seek to be the
    master in everything,
for everything you mastered fell away
    from you.
        [Oedipus is led into the palace by an
        Attendant. Then Creon goes in with An-
        tigone and Ismene, leaving the Chorus
        outside.]
Chorus: Dwellers in Thebes,
behold, this is Oedipus,
who unriddled the famous riddle
and was a man most notable.   1525
What Theban did not envy his good
    fortune?
Yet behold into what a whirlwind of
    trouble he was hurled!

Therefore, with eyes fixed on the end
    destined for all,
count no one of the race of man happy
until he has crossed life's border free
    from pain.   1530
        [The Chorus retires.]

---

[27] In Sophocles' *Antigone,* Creon does betroth Antigone to
his son Haemon. But the consequences are tragic for Creon.

The structure of Greek tragedy had, by the time *Oedipus the King* was written, become firmly established in a fairly rigid pattern. Within the pattern, playwrights of genius like Aeschylus, Sophocles, and Euripides still found rich variety, and each made a few changes and departures from the structural pattern as he received it, but the over-all outlines remained firmly fixed throughout the period covered by all the surviving scripts. Each play opened with a *prologue,* which, in some plays, might have been direct address to the audience telling them what they needed to know before the play began. This was followed by the *parodos,* the entrance song of the chorus. The chorus normally approached the orchestra by means of one of the side entrances (around the end of the paraskene), and they remained on stage throughout the play. After the chorus was on stage, the first *episode* might begin, which, in its simplest form, would be an exchange between the protagonist and one other actor. At the conclusion of this episode, one or both actors would leave the stage and the chorus would sing an ode. Each ode was carefully structured according to a complex set of principles, but it is not necessary to analyze these odes in detail here. The body of the play, then, was made up of alternating odes and episodes, with the provision that the typical play would consist of five episodes (for centuries thereafter, five was considered the proper number of acts for any play). At the end of the fifth episode, the chorus normally had a song consisting of just a few lines to provide for its exit. The fifth episode and this choral exit combined were known as the *exodos.* Originally, each episode consisted of an exchange between the protagonist (the central figure of the play) and one other actor. Sophocles' introduction of the third actor considerably complicated this scheme, and although each episode still contained the protagonist, it might have one or two other characters either together or separately. According to the basic rule, each episode had one task to accomplish, after which there was a choral ode.

The structural pattern of *Oedipus the King* adheres neatly to what is outlined above, illustrating the standard Greek tragedy structure (another of the theatre's principal structural patterns). The prologue extends from line 1 to line 150, with an exchange of dialogue among Oedipus, Creon, and

A Discussion of the Script

the Priest essentially serving the function of exposition. The playwright who first thought of substituting dialogue for the simple business of telling the audience what has happened before the curtain goes up added a new and exciting dimension to drama which Sophocles exploits here. The audience learns that a plague hangs over the city, that Oedipus has sent Creon to the Oracle at Delphi to learn what has displeased the gods and how the plague may be lifted. Creon returns to inform Oedipus that the murder of the former king, Laius, has gone unpunished, and that the killer must be driven out of Thebes before the plague will leave them. Oedipus resolves at once to find the killer of Laius. This is the central action of *Oedipus the King.* With the exposition completed and the central action established, the prologue can be brought to a conclusion. Note that the suppliants who are on stage throughout this prologue are not the chorus; they are merely extras. The chorus enters during the parodos which now begins, extending from line 151 to line 215. This ode bewails the terrible plague affecting Thebes, and then calls upon the gods to smite the unseen enemy who has brought this suffering upon them. Episode one (lines 216 to 462) begins with Oedipus entering alone to issue his proclamation condemning the unknown killer of Laius. Teiresias, the blind seer, enters and there is a monumental quarrel in which Teiresias accuses Oedipus, himself, of being the killer and adds that Oedipus will soon find out that he has killed his father and is the husband of his own mother. As the quarrel ends and both leave the stage, there is a choral ode extending from line 463 to 512. This ode comments on the action which has just passed, and expresses confidence in Oedipus. Episode two (lines 513 to 862) begins with the confrontation between Oedipus and Creon in which Creon is accused of treason. Jocasta enters to interrupt their quarrel, and, after Creon leaves, she describes to Oedipus, apparently more fully than she ever has before, the manner of Laius' death. Oedipus is struck, for the first time, with the possibility that he may be guilty, and they send for the shepherd who can clear up the mystery. The ode that follows (lines 863 to 910) warns against pride and insolence in daring to challenge the will of the gods, but at the same time expresses some lack of faith in the gods' oracles, since it appears that they may not be depended upon. As Episode three (lines 911 to 1085) opens, the Messenger brings Jocasta the news of Polybus' death. After Oedipus joins them, the Messenger also reveals that Polybus and Merope were not Oedipus' parents, and tells enough of his true origin that the whole awful truth becomes apparent to Jocasta. She exits (line 1072) to kill herself, but Oedipus, convinced that she merely fears that he is of lowly birth, pushes onward to learn the truth for himself. The next chorale ode (lines 1086 to 1109) expresses the hope that Oedipus may prove to be the child of some god. Finally, in Episode four, (lines 1110 to 1185) the arrival of the shepherd brings the whole horrible truth to light, and Oedipus rushes into the palace. Thus, the central action is completed. Typical of Greek tragic structure, the fifth episode is reserved for the tragic lamentations toward which the entire play has been pointing. This would be far too long a denouement for a well-made play, but, in Greek structure, it fulfills the whole purpose of this play. Ode 4, then, (lines 1186 to 1222) is a lament for Oedipus, and Episode five extends from line 1223 to line 1523—not including the final chorus lines which start at line 1524 and end the play on line 1530. Particularly interesting is the device by which a servant relates Jocasta's death and Oedipus' blinding himself before Oedipus reappears on stage. This is typical of Greek tragedy: violence was never portrayed on the stage, but was always reported.

Aristotle uses *Oedipus the King* in his *Poetics* as an example of an excellently plotted play, and through the centuries it has been regarded as the nonpareil against which other tragedies are measured. Not only is it brilliantly structured according to the principles governing all Greek tragedy, but it also tells a cracking good story for any time or structure. Modern audiences, as well as the Greek ones, come to this play already knowing its outcome, for everyone knows Oedipus killed his father and married his mother. The beauty of the plot lies not in its suspense, for there is none, but rather in the economy with which the bits of evidence drop into place, piece by piece, until Oedipus is suddenly confronted with the awful truth, which the audience knew all along. Only two objections of any significance have been raised by way of criticism of the plot: one is that the shepherd's original story that Laius was killed by several robbers is never satisfactorily explained. Surely the reason for this is obvious, however, for it is established at line 759 that when the shepherd returned Oedipus was already on the throne; it is certainly reasonable to assume that the shepherd, recognizing Oedipus, would have sense enough to make up a story and then get out of sight as fast as his legs would take him, which is precisely what he did. The other objection maintains that it is inconceivable that Jocasta and Oedipus could have lived together all these years without discussing the death of Laius. This is a point well taken, and probably a weakness in the plot, but during a performance of the play there is little likelihood that an audience would worry much about it.

Far more to the point is the craftsmanship with which one incident skillfully leads to the next, always letting the audience know more than Oedipus so that it may experience the delicious horror of dramatic irony. Indeed, *Oedipus the King* is such a supreme example of dramatic irony, that this form has often been called Sophoclean irony. Hardly a moment passes in the play when this force is not at work, but perhaps especially worthy of mention is the curse which Oedipus puts on the unknown killer (lines 216 to 275), while the audience knows that Oedipus himself is the killer. This irony reaches its peak, perhaps, in lines 249 to 250 when Oedipus says: "If knowingly I succor him/as inmate of my household/ let me too endure the curse invoked on you." Also notable is the manner in which Jocasta tells of having her son put out on the mountain with his ankles pierced (lines 717 to 719). It is important here that the actor playing Oedipus react violently to the mention in line 716 of the place "where three highways meet." (Note that he indicates at line 730 that this jarred him.) Thus it can be made plain in performance that Oedipus does not hear the business about Jocasta's son, and the dramatic irony is intensified once again at the lines following 1026, as the Messenger tells Oedipus of finding such a baby. Jocasta understands fully, but Oedipus does not. Probably several dozen specific examples could be pointed out in which dramatic irony is used for maximum effect in this play.

Plot is by no means the only praiseworthy element in *Oedipus the King*. The characters, too, are developed in such a fashion that one can recognize them as human in both their strengths and their weaknesses. In keeping with the formal, ritualistic style of the play, the characters are not delineated in such a way that one knows them as intimately as close friends, but they are distinctly human nevertheless—rather in the manner of public figures whom one feels one knows and respects even though they are not personal friends. Oedipus, stubborn in his insistence that he will learn the full truth no matter who gets hurt, is all too recognizable. Creon is portrayed almost as an exact opposite to Oedipus, unwilling to act on any matter until he has carefully considered all sides of the problem. Jocasta, proud of her assurance early in the play that oracles are nonsense, becomes a pitiful figure unable to speak a word when the full horror of her situation becomes apparent to her. Even the Shepherd and the Messenger are warmly human figures; the Shepherd is often played with comic touches that, at the crucial moment of his entrance, relieve the strain a bit. Only the chorus is left, intentionally, with very little to characterize it, for the chorus represents the middle way among all the extremes of the play: Mr. Average Greek Citizen—intelligent, sensitive, but unwilling to disturb the status quo.

Thematically the play is also very powerful. Too often the last lines of the chorus, "Count no one of the race of man happy/ until he has crossed life's border free from pain," are glibly cited as though *Oedipus the King* were a thesis play and this were its message. Certainly the idea that one great disaster may deprive a man of all that once made him happy is forcefully expressed, but to stop with this theme is to oversimplify the play. *Oedipus the King* also explores the horror of incest, a basic taboo of every civilization the world has known. Oedipus, himself, does not suffer from the famous complex which bears his name, but the nature of his guilt is probed from every side. Is it fair for him to be punished for what he made every conceivable effort to avoid? How, indeed, can one live in a universe where the gods themselves seem to conspire against one? Everyone has known times when he seemed predestined, in spite of tremendous effort, not to achieve a cherished goal. Are some people damned before they are born? These and a number of related ideas are explored to the extent that, by the end of the play, the audience should feel that it has been face to face with some of the most fundamental questions man can ask. Why are we here, and what is our proper relationship to ourselves, to the universe, and to God?

One must take into consideration when discussing the language of *Oedipus the King* that the play is being studied in translation. The entire play is written in verse, however, with the verse structure varying according to its position within the play. The original verse is widely admired for its extraordinary beauty. Even in translation, one can appreciate an aspect of the language that characterizes any poetic play, but which is especially significant in *Oedipus the King*—the imagery. Imagery in any literature is simple enough in its basic concept. Similies and metaphors compare one thing with another: her teeth are like the stars, or "the road was a ribbon of moonlight." The images chosen throughout a literary work may fit together into a recognizable pattern. The patterns of imagery in Shakespeare's works have been studied at great length, and it may be instructive to go back and look again at *Twelfth Night* to see how complex these patterns may become. *Oedipus the King* is a classic model of imagery patterns in many respects. The over-all pattern used here is the contrast between light and darkness, between blindness and seeing. At its most obvious level, it is evident that Teiresias, the blind prophet, is the only one at the beginning of the play who "sees" clearly. Oedipus, by the end of the play, has blinded himself because he cannot bear what he has forced himself to see. Only in blindness can Oedipus see himself clearly. And so on. Supporting this obvious level of symbolic meaning are the similies and metaphors used throughout the play, from the first moment when Oedipus resolves to "make dark things clear" (line 132). His great quarrel with Teiresias is full of light/dark imagery, as is the final scene of the play in which Oedipus is already blind. Significantly, the god whose oracle exerts a controlling influence throughout the play is Phoebus Apollo, the god of the sun. It is hardly necessary to trace all of the examples in the play to show that the pattern of imagery employed here is very carefully worked out and envelops the entire play. It represents another level of meaning which, although it will probably not be overtly apparent to an audience, unquestionably adds subliminally to the richness of the play as a whole.

Oedipus the King is one of a handful of supreme examples of tragedy in Western literature. Plot, character, theme, and language are all superlatively effective and fit together to form one of the great plays of all time. It would be presumptuous to try to classify it; on the contrary plays like *Oedipus the King* are the criteria for establishing reasonable classifications. *Oedipus the King* is a tragedy by definition; now, what characteristics does this play exhibit that can be used in classifying other plays? Among the clichés of dramatic criticism are the dicta that a tragedy is any play which ends unhappily, or in which the hero dies or is a great man with a "tragic flaw." The latest soap opera on television meets these criteria, but what is Oedipus' tragic flaw? The usual answer to this question is "pride," or "arrogance," and it is true that Oedipus suffers from these faults to some extent. He is too stubborn for his own good in pursuing the truth, but is this really the *cause* of his downfall? Would he be any less guilty of murder and incest if he did not pursue the knowledge of it in so relentless a fashion? Clearly, this superficial criterion does not touch the fundamental basis of tragedy. Critics have been trying for twenty-five hundred years without success to distill the essence of tragedy; undoubtedly no effort here will be completely successful either; but at least several distinctive features, which seem to make *Oedipus the King* a tragedy, can be pointed out, and from these the student can begin to form his own basis for judgment.

Consider the problem from the perspective of the four basic elements of drama. The *plot* of a tragedy must be serious, leading ultimately to the utter defeat and crushing of the central figure. The contending forces must be of considerable magnitude, so that there is no easy way out; all choices open to the protagonist are undesirable, and he must weigh ultimate good against ultimate evil. The *character* of the tragic hero must be inspiring in its humanity; not only should one identify with this protagonist, but be proud to do so. Even if the protagonist has much evil in him, he must also have strengths which make the human race nobler for his having "lived." Most important of all, he must have a clear perception, by the play's end, of the forces that have crushed him and their meaning. The *themes* of a tragedy must explore questions of fundamental importance to mankind, bringing the audience face to face with ultimate good and evil and with the terrible, unanswerable questions of life and death. The profundity of the issues raised in tragedy almost demand a tragic treatment. The *language* of tragedy must be sufficiently elevated by means of verse, imagery, or other devices, to lift the play out of an everyday context and suggest its universal significance. Ultimately, the plot, character, theme, and language of a tragedy must work together to produce in the audience an experience that Aristotle called "catharsis," which is a sense of being totally drained and cleansed emotionally and, at the same time, spiritually uplifted. Certainly the experiences through which one passes with Oedipus are so horrible that they leave one "purged of pity and fear" by the end of the play; and yet in the midst of this purgation a sense of nobility is felt that lifts one above himself and brings him a little nearer to the gods. The effecting of this catharsis is the ultimate test of true tragedy.

Tragedy is often regarded as the "highest" dramatic form, perhaps because it is the most difficult to achieve. Everyone seems to sense somewhere within himself the essence of tragedy, but a succinct definition has never been found which will satisfy everyone. The foregoing characteristics sum up the nature of tragedy, and they are intended to be exclusive; any play that does not measure up to *all* the qualifications cannot truly be said to be a tragedy. A few plays, like *Oedipus the King*, represent such supreme achievements in artistry and in audience impact that one would like to be able to distill from them whatever it is that makes them so powerful. This essence is what men have named *tragedy*.

Because of the unusually tight-knit structure of Greek tragedy, and the many similarities in treatment of character, theme, and language exhibited by the surviving Greek tragedies, all of them are said to be written in a style called *classicism*. The classic style is characterized by formality, simplicity, and restraint, rarely yielding to excess in any form. The Greek ideal has often been described as moderation in all things; the moderation of classicism in playwriting is one of its more notable features. Plot, character, theme, and language seem to work together in harmony and beauty even when ugliness and evil are the subject matter. The production of a Greek tragedy raises several key questions which are not answered by a simple decision to adhere to classic style. Decisions have to be made about the chorus, for example; although, historically, they sang and danced in complex patterns, this may not be the most effective means to convey the script's values to a modern audience. Classic style may well be described as "formal," but to what extent should the acting, for example, be formalized and thus removed from the realistic portrayal of emotion? The use of masks, padded costumes, and other historically justifiable devices may add to the formal effect, or they may merely suggest a kind of perverted realism. The classic style of the scripts of *Oedipus the King* and other Greek tragedies may be described easily, but the best production style for the modern age is a matter for lively debate.

Makeup is popularly supposed to be the quintessential theatrical art, but in fact really complex and detailed makeup is infrequently used on the stage. In the movies, superior jobs of makeup are often seen, for the camera views the face so closely that even the slightest blemish could not be tolerated, and movie makeup artists can afford to spend several hours preparing a really elaborate makeup. In the theatre, however, makeup is usually left to the individual actor, although in most amateur and a few professional theatres there is a makeup supervisor who teaches some basic techniques to neophytes. The simple fact is that really elaborate makeup calls for more time and money than most theatres or individual actors can invest in it. The job of making a young person really look old involves several hours of work with fairly sophisticated materials, and few actors are willing to begin in the middle of the afternoon to prepare for an evening performance. Rubber prostheses, wigs, beards, and other such devices should be custom made to fit the actor who is to wear them, but this can easily run into several hundred dollars' worth of material and labor. The result, at least in the United States, is that even in the New York theatre elaborate makeups are not often seen, and outside New York they are almost totally unknown. Where type casting can eliminate the need for complex makeup, it is often used; otherwise, the imagination of the audience is simply stretched to the point that actors are accepted for the characters they represent. Good acting has always been far more important than external details in making a play come alive on the stage. It is unfortunate, however, that better makeup techniques are not more widely practiced; many plays are enhanced by achieving the best possible illusion of reality.

Some makeup is almost always used on the American stage, however. Caucasian actors look pale and lifeless without it. Listed below are several basic functions which makeup can perform; the needs vary so much from one play to another that it is impossible to list them in order of importance. Makeup can:

1. *Help make the features visible.* Even the very best of stage lighting tends to wash out the features, particularly in a theatre where the actors are some distance from the audience. Makeup can be used to highlight and shadow the facial features,

Makeup

to make the eyebrows darker and the lips and cheeks redder, so the audience can see the actor's face very clearly and perceive his facial expressions. In most plays, an actor's face is his most expressive instrument for conveying ideas visually; makeup can enhance the effectiveness of this instrument.

2. *Help portray character.* This is the primary function commonly associated with makeup. It is especially applicable, of course, when an actor is playing a character totally different from himself. The actor must study the character he is portraying, as well as his own face, and then do what he can to change his own face to resemble the character's. Some of the techniques involved will be discussed presently.

3. *Add to the mood, theme, and visual impact of the production.* If the play is produced in realistic style, of course, the makeup will do very little in the way of mood or theme, and will simply be in harmony with the desired visual impact. If non-realistic styles are used, however, it is possible to create special makeups which have a definite impact of their own. Traditional ballet makeup is an example of this. *Oedipus the King* might well lend itself to special nonrealistic makeup techniques in place of the masks used in the Greek theatre.

4. *Help beautify or disguise the actor.* Often an actor resembles the character he is playing and would simply like to look his best. Alternatively, he may be playing a character like himself but not wish to be recognized (if he is doubling in two roles, for example). In these situations, makeup becomes a matter of enhancing certain facial features and suppressing others. For women, this may simply involve enhancing their regular street makeup. In any case, makeup of this sort begins with the actor's own features and works from there.

To help carry out the functions listed above, the makeup artist has several basic techniques at his disposal, supplemented by many specialized devices too complex for discussion here. In the first place, he has his own face (makeup can be applied to any part of the body, but this discussion will be limited to the face). Actors must study their own faces before applying makeup, learn their bone structure, their strong and weak features, areas of loose skin that will sag with age, and so on. Realistic makeup is usually most effective when it utilizes the actor's own features, rather than attempting to create an entirely new appearance that is not even hinted at to start with. Most makeups begin with a "base" which may be the traditional grease paint or the more modern pancake. Since pancake does not provide a good base for the infinite detail of complex makeups, it is usually used in the theatre only for "straight" makeups—that is, those in which the actor does not expect to greatly alter his appearance. Either grease paint or pancake is spread lightly but uniformly across all exposed skin areas to hide any blemishes and to provide a smooth, even surface upon which to build. After the base, a straight makeup may consist of little more than darkening the eyebrows and lashes (eyebrow pencils and mascara are used) and reddening the lips and cheeks. If this is overdone, it can look as absurd on stage as it does in real life (especially on men), but if it is done subtly it can enhance the features just enough to aid them in conveying emotion to an audience and in making the actor as attractive as possible. Experienced actors learn to apply makeup in amounts varying according to the size of the house in which they are playing. If the audience is close, less makeup is needed than if features must be seen from a greater distance. If grease paint has been used for the base, the last step is to apply powder to "set" the makeup and keep it from smearing.

For a "character" makeup (one in which the actor must change his appearance materially, usually to increase his age), far more detailed work is needed. Hair and

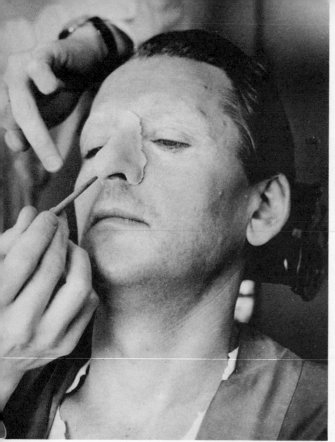

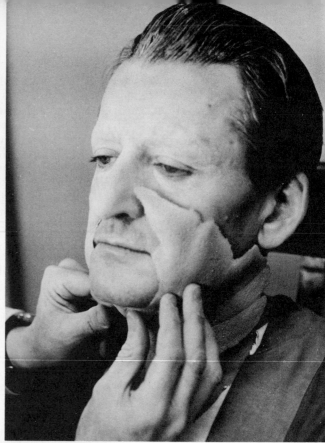

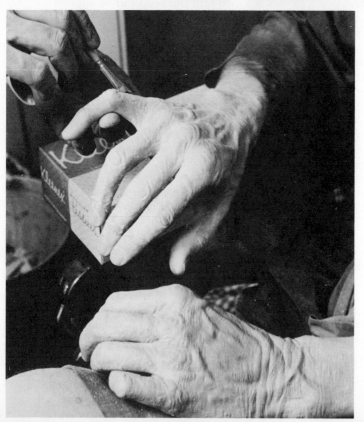

Hal Holbrook being made up for TV production of *Mark Twain Tonight* by specialist Dick Smith. *Top left:* Attaching foam latex nose with spirit gum. Eyebrows have been covered with thin latex pieces. *Right:* Larger foam latex appliance being positioned. Bags and chin pieces will follow. *Left:* Backs of hands are covered with appliances and non-smear paint to protect costume.

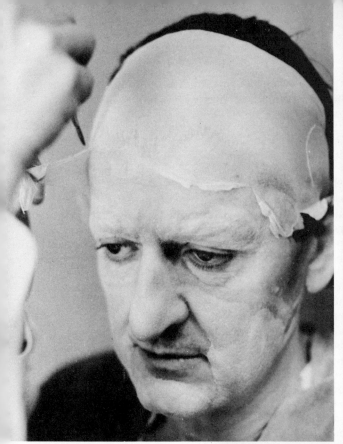

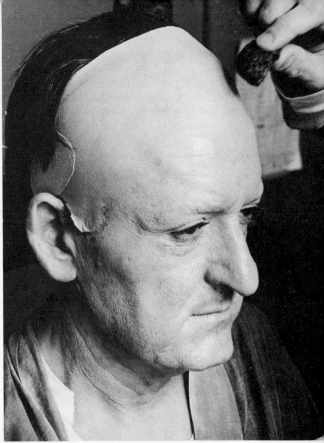

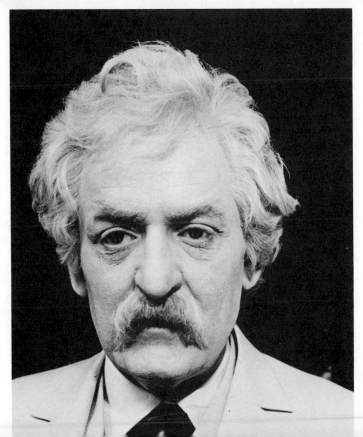

Top left: Plastic bald forehead permits use of wig with higher, thinner hairline. *Right:* A rubber mask greasepaint base covers all appliances. Pigment spots are stippled over it. *Right:* Hairpieces, shoulder hump and costume complete five-hour makeup for character of Mark Twain. New appliances are used each day. Photographs courtesy of Mr. Smith.

eyebrows may be whitened with special whitener, or a wig may be used. Often a beard, mustache, or other false hair is added. Most theatres purchase ready-made wigs, but beards and mustaches using crepe hair are built on the actor. Wrinkles in the face, including those on the forehead, may be highlighted and shadowed using light and dark colors of paint. (Accenting these wrinkles with an eyebrow pencil is also a possible technique, but it usually looks hopelessly artificial.) A more thorough makeup job can be done if the actor varies the color of his base by actually painting his face in light and dark colors, highlighting bony areas and shadowing depression areas such as the cheeks and under the chin. Viewed from close up, the face may resemble a death's head, but at a distance, skillful highlighting and shadowing can give an excellent suggestion of age. Putty may be used to change the shape of the nose or to build up other areas. Scars and other malformations can be specially created. It takes both imagination and skill to create a good character makeup.

If a unified plan for the makeup for an entire production is to be worked out, someone must be charged with the responsibility. If all the makeups are to be more or less realistic, the makeup supervisor will have little more to do than to see that all of the actors have the necessary materials, and then be prepared to lend his skill to such actors as may be unable to do a satisfactory job themselves. If, on the other hand, non-realistic techniques are to be employed, the supervision of makeup may actually involve doing every actor's makeup for him. Alternatively, an artist may make sketches of how the makeup should look, after which each actor is expected to do his own makeup to conform to the sketch. Either way, the planning of the makeup becomes more than simply a backstage chore to be performed, it becomes a positive artistic contribution to the production. In a production of *Oedipus the King,* for example, several approaches might be possible. In the first place, the director might decide to use masks, approximating the production conditions of the original staging. If he did so, someone would have to be charged with the special responsibility of designing and constructing the masks, but no makeup would be needed. Alternatively, the director might decide on a relatively realistic production, in which each actor was expected to make himself up (under the general direction of the makeup supervisor) to look as much as possible like the role he was playing. A decision would have to be made about Oedipus' age (25? 35? The script is not clear on this point), and then Jocasta would have to be at least 15 or 20 years older, since she is his mother. But if Jocasta really looks 55 to Oedipus' 35, will they not look rather strange as husband and wife? Realism in a play like *Oedipus the King* can lead to some awkward stage situations. Still, a production along these lines would certainly be possible, and the makeup supervisor's job would be a fairly standard one.

A somewhat more likely approach to a modern production of *Oedipus the King* would be to choose an exaggerated, nonrealistic makeup style which would be suggestive of the historical masks and yet leave the actor's face free to express emotion. The style selected here, of course, would depend upon the style of the rest of the production; the makeup supervisor, in conference with the director, would create makeups for the various characters which would be visually exciting and would enhance the production. Such a departure from realism (providing, of course, that it was in harmony with the rest of the production), could go much further than simple realism toward expressing the fundamental themes of the play and could avoid some of the difficult issues, like Oedipus' age, which realism would inevitably raise. The makeup could even be radically changed between episodes in order to express Oedipus' increasing anxiety and final despair. (There is reason to believe that the Greek actors changed masks for precisely this effect.) Such an approach would also solve the difficult problem of how to treat Oedipus' eyes for his final entrance: realism would call for something tastelessly gory, whereas a more stylized approach might express the horror of his blindness without violating the bounds of good taste. Perhaps spots of red paint would be enough.

It would be pointless to speculate in greater detail on how the makeup for *Oedipus the King* might be carried out. Too much depends upon other phases of the production to allow makeup to be created on a purely theoretical basis. Good makeup can, however, make a material contribution to the success of any play, and a definite, planned approach to makeup for the whole play (especially in nonrealistic styles) can be extraordinarily effective in reinforcing the values inherent in the script.

Arthur Miller was born in Manhattan on October 17, 1915, the son of Isador and Augusta (Barnett) Miller. He was educated in the elementary and secondary schools of Manhattan and Brooklyn, and graduated from high school in 1932. The depression years were sufficiently difficult for his family to prevent Miller from going directly to college, and he therefore worked for a time in the New York area. He finally enrolled at the University of Michigan, and received the Bachelor of Arts degree in 1938 after an exceptionally successful college career. He received several awards for playwriting during his college years, and saw some of his first plays produced at the University of Michigan. After graduating, Miller wrote for the Federal Theatre project and for the radio networks. He married Mary Grace Slattery on August 5, 1940, and, being rejected for military service for physical reasons, spent the war years writing and working for a time at the Brooklyn Navy Yard. Toward the end of World War II, he published several books of which his novel, *Focus* (1945), was perhaps most notable.

Miller's first professionally produced play was *The Man Who Had All the Luck*, which opened on Broadway in November of 1944. The play had moments of power, but it was uneven and ultimately ineffectual. It closed after only four performances. In February of 1947, however, Miller's second play, *All My Sons*, scored a major success, and won the New York Drama Critics' Circle Award for that year. The play centers on the activities of a manufacturer and profiteer who sells defective airplane parts to the government, and it was extraordinarily effective at a time when the nation was still close enough to World War II to be emotionally involved with its major issues and concerns. Today the play is still moving, but seems somewhat contrived. *Death of a Salesman* opened on February 10, 1949, and was immediately acclaimed as Miller's masterpiece. It again won the New York Drama Critics' Circle Award and, later, the Pulitzer Prize, and has been produced repeatedly by professional and amateur groups around the world. Miller was aiming at timeless tragedy, but *Death of a Salesman* produced dissension among the critics as to its universality and its claim to the rubric of tragedy. Miller devoted himself anew to capturing these qualities. His next effort, *An Enemy of the People* (1950), was an adaptation of Ibsen's play of the same title, but

A View from the Bridge by Arthur Miller

The Crucible (1953) was another major attempt at tragedy which many critics rank with *Death of a Salesman*. Its plot dealt with the New England witchcraft trials of 1692, but it was widely interpreted, during its initial production, as an allegorical attack upon McCarthyism, then its heyday in the United States. This unfortunate political connection has tended to obscure the play's true dramatic effectiveness until recent years, but *The Crucible* has enjoyed many productions and a critical reappraisal during the last decade, and may yet emerge with more universal appeal than *Death of a Salesman*.

Perhaps Miller's closest approach to true classical tragedy has been *A View from the Bridge*, which was first produced in New York on September 29, 1955. At the time of this first production, it was a rather austere one-act play, performed on the same bill with a short piece entitled *A Memory of Two Mondays*. *A View from the Bridge* won the New York Drama Critics' Circle Award for that year, yet was not fully successful as a production for reasons that Miller analyzes brilliantly in his introduction to the original printed version of the play. He re-wrote the script into a full-length, two-act work before the London production which opened on October 11, 1956; it is the latter version which is reprinted here. Perhaps the chief change evident in the revised script is the fuller development of the secondary characters into believable human beings; the net effect of these changes was to create a play less tied to Miller's version of the austere characteristics of classical tragedy and more believable simply as human drama. Also, the free verse of the earlier version was changed to prose.

Miller was called upon to testify before the House Un-American Activities Committee in 1956, at which time he confessed to several tenuous connections with communist organizations during his youth, but refused to implicate other members whom he might have known. He was prosecuted and convicted for contempt of Congress in 1957, but his conviction was reversed on appeal in 1958. As the McCarthy era faded, it became more evident that such vague communist connections as Miller or his associates may have had in the 1930s were quite irrelevant in the late 1950s.

There followed a hiatus in Miller's playwriting, however, which may or may not have been connected with the strain of those years. He published his *Collected Plays* in 1957, including in that volume a most penetrating analysis of the plays themselves and of his theories of tragedy. He produced *After the Fall* in 1964, followed shortly by *Incident at Vichy*. *The Price* was first performed in 1968. None of these late plays, however, has achieved the success of his earlier ones, and it remains to be seen whether Miller will again be able to write with the penetrating insights and dramatic power of *Death of a Salesman* and *A View from the Bridge*.

He was married for a time to motion-picture actress Marilyn Monroe, and is now married to Ingeborg Morath. He resides in New York.

Page 454: *A View from the Bridge* produced by Kermit Bloomgarden, Robert Whitehead, and Roger L. Stevens, Coronet Theatre, 1955; scenery by Boris Aronson, costumes by Helene Pons, lighting by Leland Watson. Alfieri, the lawyer, who frequently acts as narrator during the play, is shown in the orchestra pit bottom left, (J. Carrol Naish). Photograph: Gordon Parks, *Life* Magazine © Time Inc.

Page 458: Eileen Heckart (Beatrice), Gloria Marlowe (Catherine), Richard Davalos (Rodolpho), and Van Heflin (Eddie) in the same production. Photograph: Alfredo Valente.

by
ARTHUR MILLER

Louis	*Rodolpho*
Mike	*First Immigration Officer*
Alfieri	*Second Immigration Officer*
Eddie	*Mr. Lipari*
Catherine	*Mrs. Lipari*
Beatrice	*Two "Submarines"*
Marco	*Neighbors*
Tony	

ACT I

The street and house front of a tenement building. The front is skeletal entirely. The main acting area is the living room—dining room of **Eddie**'s apartment. It is a worker's flat, clean, sparse, homely. There is a rocker down front; a round dining table at center, with chairs; and a portable phonograph.

At back are a bedroom door and an opening to the kitchen; none of these interiors are seen.

At the right, forestage, a desk. This is **Mr. Alfieri**'s law office.

There is also a telephone booth. This is not used until the last scenes, so it may be covered or left in view.

A stairway leads up to the apartment, and then farther up to the next story, which is not seen.

Ramps, representing the street, run upstage and off to right and left.

As the curtain rises, **Louis** and **Mike**, longshoremen, are pitching coins against the building at left.

A distant foghorn blows.

[*Enter* **Alfieri**, *a lawyer in his fifties turning gray; he is portly, good-humored, and thoughtful. The two pitchers nod to him as he passes. He crosses the stage to his desk, removes his hat, runs his fingers through his hair, and grinning, speaks to the audience.*]

Alfieri: You wouldn't have known it, but something amusing has just happened. You see how uneasily they nod to me? That's because I am a lawyer. In this neighborhood to

A View From
The Bridge

457

meet a lawyer or a priest on the street is un-lucky. We're only thought of in connection with disasters, and they'd rather not get too close.

I often think that behind that suspicious little nod of theirs lie three thousand years of distrust. A lawyer means the law, and in Sic-ily, from where their fathers came, the law has not been a friendly idea since the Greeks were beaten.

I am inclined to notice the ruins in things, perhaps because I was born in Italy. . . . I only came here when I was twenty-five. In those days, Al Capone, the greatest Carthaginian of all, was learning his trade on these pavements, and Frankie Yale himself was cut precisely in half by a machine gun on the corner of Union Street, two blocks away. Oh, there were many here who were justly shot by unjust men. Jus-tice is very important here.

But this is Red Hook, not Sicily. This is the slum that faces the bay on the seaward side of Brooklyn Bridge. This is the gullet of New York swallowing the tonnage of the world. And now we are quite civilized, quite Ameri-can. Now we settle for half, and I like it better. I no longer keep a pistol in my filing cabinet.

And my practice is entirely unromantic.

My wife has warned me, so have my friends; they tell me the people in this neigh-borhood lack elegance, glamour. After all, who have I dealt with in my life? Longshore-men and their wives, and fathers and grand-fathers, compensation cases, evictions, family squabbles—the petty troubles of the poor— and yet . . . every few years there is still a case, and as the parties tell me what the trouble is, the flat air in my office suddenly washes in with the green scent of the sea, the dust in this air is blown away and the thought comes that in some Caesar's year, in Calabria per-haps or on the cliff at Syracuse, another law-yer, quite differently dressed, heard the same complaint and set there as powerless as I, and watched it run its bloody course.

[Eddie *has appeared and has been pitching coins with the men and is highlighted among them. He is forty—a husky, slightly overweight longshore-man*]

This one's name was Eddie Carbone, a longshoreman working the docks from Brooklyn Bridge to the breakwater where the open sea begins.

[Alfieri *walks into darkness.*]

Eddie: [*Moving up steps into doorway*] Well, I'll see ya, fellas.

[Catherine *enters from kitchen, crosses down to window, looks out.*]

Louis: You workin' tomorrow?

Eddie: Yeah, there's another day yet on that ship. See ya, Louis.

[Eddie *goes into the house, as light rises in the apartment.*]

[Catherine *is waving to* Louis *from the window and turns to him.*]

Catherine: Hi, Eddie!

[Eddie *is pleased and therefore shy about it; he hangs up his cap and jacket.*]

Eddie: Where you goin' all dressed up?

Catherine: [*Running her hands over her skirt*] I just got it. You like it?

Eddie: Yeah, it's nice. And what happened to your hair?

Catherine: You like it? I fixed it different. [*Calling to kitchen*] He's here, B.!

Eddie: Beautiful. Turn around, lemme see in the back. [*She turns for him*] Oh, if your mother was alive to see you now! She wouldn't be-lieve it.

Catherine: You like it, huh?

Eddie: You look like one of them girls that went to college. Where you goin'?

Catherine: [*Taking his arm*] Wait'll B. comes in, I'll tell you something. Here, sit down. [*She is walking him to the armchair. Calling offstage*] Hurry up, will you, B.?

Eddie: [*Sitting*] What's goin' on?

Catherine: I'll get you a beer, all right?

Eddie: Well, tell me what happened. Come over here, talk to me.

Catherine: I want to wait till B. comes in. [*She sits on her heels beside him*] Guess how much we paid for the skirt.

Eddie: I think it's too short, ain't it?

Catherine: [*Standing*] No! not when I stand up.

Eddie: Yeah, but you gotta sit down some-times.

Catherine: Eddie, it's the style now. [*She walks

to show him] I mean, if you see me walkin' down the street—

Eddie: Listen, you been givin' me the willies the way you walk down the street, I mean it.

Catherine: Why?

Eddie: Catherine, I don't want to be a pest, but I'm tellin' you you're walkin' wavy.

Catherine: I'm walkin' wavy?

Eddie: Now don't aggravate me, Katie, you are walkin' wavy! I don't like the looks they're givin' you in the candy store. And with them new high heels on the sidewalk—clack, clack, clack. The heads are turnin' like windmills.

Catherine: But those guys look at all the girls, you know that.

Eddie: You ain't "all the girls."

Catherine: [*Almost in tears because he disapproves*] What do you want me to do? You want me to—

Eddie: Now don't get mad, kid.

Catherine: Well, I don't know what you want from me.

Eddie: Katie, I promised your mother on her deathbed. I'm responsible for you. You're a baby, you don't understand these things. I mean like when you stand here by the window, wavin' outside.

Catherine: I was wavin' to Louis!

Eddie: Listen, I could tell you things about Louis which you wouldn't wave to him no more.

Catherine: [*Trying to joke him out of his warning*] Eddie, I wish there was one guy you couldn't tell me things about!

Eddie: Catherine, do me a favor, will you? You're gettin' to be a big girl now, you gotta keep yourself more, you can't be so friendly, kid. [*Calls*] Hey, B., what're you doin' in there? [*To* **Catherine**] Get her in here, will you? I got news for her.

Catherine: [*Starting out*] What?

Eddie: Her cousins landed.

Catherine: [*Clapping her hands together*] No! [*She turns instantly and starts for the kitchen*] B.! Your cousins!

[**Beatrice** *enters, wiping her hands with a towel.*]

Beatrice: [*In the face of* **Catherine**'s *shout*] What?

Catherine: Your cousins got in!

Beatrice: [*Astounded, turns to* **Eddie**] What are you talkin' about? Where?

Eddie: I was just knockin' off work before and Tony Bereli come over to me; he says the ship is in the North River.

Beatrice: [*Her hands are clasped at her breast; she seems half in fear, half in unutterable joy*] They're all right?

Eddie: He didn't see them yet, they're still on board. But as soon as they get off he'll meet them. He figures about ten o'clock they'll be here.

Beatrice: [*Sits, almost weak from tension*] And they'll let them off the ship all right? That's fixed, heh?

Eddie: Sure, they give them regular seamen papers and they walk off with the crew. Don't worry about it, B., there's nothin' to it. Couple of hours they'll be here.

Beatrice: What happened? They wasn't supposed to be till next Thursday.

Eddie: I don't know; they put them on any ship they can get them out on. Maybe the other ship they was supposed to take there was some danger— What you cryin' about?

Beatrice: [*Astounded and afraid*] I'm— I just—I can't believe it! I didn't even buy a new tablecloth; I was gonna wash the walls—

Eddie: Listen, they'll think it's a millionaire's house compared to the way they live. Don't worry about the walls. They'll be thankful. [*To* **Catherine**] Whyn't you run down buy a tablecloth. Go ahead, here. [*He is reaching into his pocket.*]

Catherine: There's no stores open now.

Eddie: [*To* **Beatrice**] You was gonna put a new cover on the chair.

Beatrice: I know—well, I thought it was gonna be next week! I was gonna clean the walls, I was gonna wax the floors. [*She stands disturbed.*]

Catherine: [*Pointing upward*] Maybe Mrs. Dondero upstairs—

Beatrice: [*Of the tablecloth*] No, hers is worse than this one. [*Suddenly*] My God; I don't even have nothin' to eat for them! [*She starts for the kitchen.*]

Eddie: [*Reaching out and grabbing her arm*] Hey, hey! Take it easy.

Beatrice: No, I'm just nervous, that's all. [*To* **Catherine**] I'll make the fish.

Eddie: You're savin' their lives, what're you worryin' about the tablecloth? They probably didn't see a tablecloth in their whole life where they come from.

Beatrice: [*Looking into his eyes*] I'm just worried about you, that's all I'm worried.

Eddie: Listen, as long as they know where they're gonna sleep.

Beatrice: I told them in the letters. They're sleepin' on the floor.

Eddie: Beatrice, all I'm worried about is you got such a heart that I'll end up on the floor with you, and they'll be in our bed.

Beatrice: All right, stop it.

Eddie: Because as soon as you see a tired relative, I end up on the floor.

Beatrice: When did you end up on the floor?

Eddie: When your father's house burned down I didn't end up on the floor?

Beatrice: Well, their house burned down!

Eddie: Yeah, but it didn't keep burnin' for two weeks!

Beatrice: All right, look, I'll tell them to go someplace else. [*She starts into the kitchen.*]

Eddie: Now just a minute. Beatrice! [*She halts. He goes to her*] I just don't want you bein' pushed around, that's all. You got too big a heart. [*He touches her hand*] What're you so touchy?

Beatrice: I'm just afraid if it don't turn out good you'll be mad at me.

Eddie: Listen, if everybody keeps his mouth shut, nothin' can happen. They'll pay for their board.

Beatrice: Oh, I told them.

Eddie: Then what the hell. [*Pause. He moves*] It's an honor, B. I mean it. I was just thinkin' before, comin' home, suppose my father didn't come to this country, and I was starvin' like them over there . . . and I had people in America could keep me a couple of months? The man would be honored to lend me a place to sleep.

Beatrice: [*There are tears in her eyes. She turns to* **Catherine**] You see what he is? [*She turns and grabs* **Eddie***'s face in her hands*] Mmm! You're an angel! God'll bless you. [*He is gratefully smiling*] You'll see, you'll get a blessing for this!

Eddie: [*Laughing*] I'll settle for my own bed.

Beatrice: Go, Baby, set the table.

Catherine: We didn't tell him about me yet.

Beatrice: Let him eat first, then we'll tell him. Bring everything in. [*She hurries* **Catherine** *out.*]

Eddie: [*Sitting at the table*] What's all that about? Where's she goin'?

Beatrice: Noplace. It's very good news, Eddie. I want you to be happy.

Eddie: What's goin' on?

[**Catherine** *enters with plates, forks.*]

Beatrice: She's got a job.

[*Pause.* **Eddie** *looks at* **Catherine**, *then back to* **Beatrice**.]

Eddie: What job? She's gonna finish school.

Catherine: Eddie, you won't believe it—

Eddie: No—no, you gonna finish school. What kinda job, what do you mean? All of a sudden you—

Catherine: Listen a minute, it's wonderful.

Eddie: It's not wonderful. You'll never get nowheres unless you finish school. You can't take no job. Why didn't you ask me before you take a job?

Beatrice: She's askin' you now, she didn't take nothin' yet.

Catherine: Listen a minute! I came to school this morning and the principal called me out of the class, see? To go to his office.

Eddie: Yeah?

Catherine: So I went in and he says to me he's got my records, y'know? And there's a company wants a girl right away. It ain't exactly a secretary, it's a stenographer first, but pretty soon you get to be secretary. And he says to me that I'm the best student in the whole class—

Beatrice: You hear that?

Eddie: Well why not? Sure she's the best.

Catherine: I'm the best student, he says, and if I want, I should take the job and the end of the year he'll let me take the examination and he'll give me the certificate. So I'll save practically a year!

Eddie: [*Strangely nervous*] Where's the job? What company?

Catherine: It's a big plumbing company over Nostrand Avenue.

Eddie: Nostrand Avenue and where?

Catherine: It's someplace by the Navy Yard.

Beatrice: Fifty dollars a week, Eddie.

Eddie: [*To* **Catherine**, *surprised*] Fifty?

Catherine: I swear.

> [*Pause.*]

Eddie: What about all the stuff you wouldn't learn this year, though?

Catherine: There's nothin' more to learn, Eddie, I just gotta practice from now on. I know all the symbols and I know the keyboard. I'll just get faster, that's all. And when I'm workin' I'll keep gettin' better and better, you see?

Beatrice: Work is the best practice anyway.

Eddie: That ain't what I wanted, though.

Catherine: Why! It's a great big company—

Eddie: I don't like that neighborhood over there.

Catherine: It's a block and a half from the subway, he says.

Eddie: Near the Navy Yard plenty can happen in a block and a half. And a plumbin' company! That's one step over the water front. They're practically longshoremen.

Beatrice: Yeah, but she'll be in the office, Eddie.

Eddie: I know she'll be in the office, but that ain't what I had in mind.

Beatrice: Listen, she's gotta go to work sometime.

Eddie: Listen, B., she'll be with a lotta plumbers? And sailors up and down the street? So what did she go to school for?

Catherine: But it's fifty a week, Eddie.

Eddie: Look, did I ask you for money? I supported you this long I support you a little more. Please, do me a favor, will ya? I want you to be with different kind of people. I want you to be in a nice office. Maybe a lawyer's office someplace in New York in one of them nice buildings. I mean if you're gonna get outa here then get out; don't go practically in the same kind of neighborhood.

> [*Pause.* **Catherine** *lowers her eyes.*]

Beatrice: Go, Baby, bring in the supper. [**Catherine** *goes out*] Think about it a little bit, Eddie. Please. She's crazy to start work. It's not a little shop, it's a big company. Some day she could be a secretary. They picked her out of the whole class. [*He is silent, staring down at the tablecloth, fingering the pattern*] What are you worried about? She could take care of herself. She'll get out of the subway and be in the office in two minutes.

Eddie: [*Somehow sickened*] I know that neighborhood, B., I don't like it.

Beatrice: Listen, if nothin' happened to her in this neighborhood it ain't gonna happen noplace else. [*She turns his face to her*] Look, you gotta get used to it, she's no baby no more. Tell her to take it. [*He turns his head away*] You hear me? [*She is angering*] I don't understand you; she's seventeen years old, you gonna keep her in the house all her life?

Eddie: [*Insulted*] What kinda remark is that?

Beatrice: [*With sympathy but insistent force*] Well, I don't understand when it ends. First it was gonna be when she graduated high school, so she graduated high school. Then it was gonna be when she learned stenographer, so she learned stenographer. So what're we gonna wait for now? I mean it, Eddie, sometimes I don't understand you; they picked her out of the whole class, it's an honor for her.

> [**Catherine** *enters with food, which she silently sets on the table. After a moment of watching her face,* **Eddie** *breaks into a smile, but it almost seems that tears will form in his eyes.*]

Eddie: With your hair that way you look like a madonna, you know that? You're the madonna type. [*She doesn't look at him, but continues ladling out food onto the plates*] You wanna go to work, heh, Madonna?

Catherine: [*Softly*] Yeah.

Eddie: [*With a sense of her childhood, her babyhood, and the years*] All right, go to work. [*She looks at him, then rushes and hugs him*] Hey, hey! Take it easy! [*He holds her face away from him to look at her*] What're you cryin' about? [*He is affected by her, but smiles his emotion away.*]

Catherine: [*Sitting at her place*] I just—[*Bursting out*] I'm gonna buy all new dishes with my first pay! [*They laugh warmly*] I mean it. I'll fix up the whole house! I'll buy a rug!

Eddie: And then you'll move away.

Catherine: No, Eddie!

Eddie: [*Grinning*] Why not? That's life. And you come visit on Sundays, then once a month, then Christmas and New Year's, finally.

Catherine: [*Grasping his arm to reassure him and to erase the accusation*] No, please!

Eddie: [*Smiling but hurt*] I only ask you one thing —don't trust nobody. You got a good aunt but she's got too big a heart, you learned bad from her. Believe me.

Beatrice: Be the way you are, Katie, don't listen to him.

Eddie: [*To* **Beatrice**—*strangely and quickly resentful*] You lived in a house all your life, what do you know about it? You never worked in your life.

Beatrice: She likes people. What's wrong with that?

Eddie: Because most people ain't people. She's goin' to work; plumbers; they'll chew her to pieces if she don't watch out. [*To* **Catherine**] Believe me, Katie, the less you trust, the less you be sorry.

[**Eddie** *crosses himself and the women do the same, and they eat.*]

Catherine: First thing I'll buy is a rug, heh, B.?

Beatrice: I don't mind. [*To* **Eddie**] I smelled coffee all day today. You unloadin' coffee today?

Eddie: Yeah, a Brazil ship.

Catherine: I smelled it too. It smelled all over the neighborhood.

Eddie: That's one time, boy, to be a longshoreman is a pleasure. I could work coffee ships twenty hours a day. You go down in the hold, y'know? It's like flowers, that smell. We'll bust a bag tomorrow, I'll bring you some.

Beatrice: Just be sure there's no spiders in it, will ya? I mean it. [*She directs this to* **Catherine**, *rolling her eyes upward*] I still remember that spider coming out of that bag he brung home. I nearly died.

Eddie: You call that a spider? You oughta see what comes outa the bananas sometimes.

Beatrice: Don't talk about it!

Eddie: I seen spiders could stop a Buick.

Beatrice: [*Clapping her hands over her ears*] All right, shut up!

Eddie: [*Laughing and taking a watch out of his pocket*] Well, who started with spiders?

Beatrice: All right, I'm sorry, I didn't mean it.

Just don't bring none home again. What time is it?

Eddie: Quarter nine. [*Puts watch back in his pocket. They continue eating in silence.*]

Catherine: He's bringin' them ten o'clock, Tony?

Eddie: Around, yeah. [*He eats.*]

Catherine: Eddie, suppose somebody asks if they're livin' here. [*He looks at her as though already she had divulged something publicly. Defensively*] I mean if they ask.

Eddie: Now look, Baby, I can see we're gettin' mixed up again here.

Catherine: No, I just mean . . . people'll see them goin' in and out.

Eddie: I don't care who sees them goin' in and out as long as you don't see them goin' in and out. And this goes for you too, B. You don't see nothin' and you don't know nothin'.

Beatrice: What do you mean? I understand.

Eddie: You don't understand; you still think you can talk about this to somebody just a little bit. Now lemme say it once and for all, because you're makin' me nervous again, both of you. I don't care if somebody comes in the house and sees them sleepin' on the floor, it never comes out of your mouth who they are or what they're doin' here.

Beatrice: Yeah, but my mother'll know—

Eddie: Sure she'll know, but just don't you be the one who told her, that's all. This is the United States government you're playin' with now, this is the Immigration Bureau. If you said it you knew it, if you didn't say it you didn't know it.

Catherine: Yeah, but Eddie, suppose somebody—

Eddie: I don't care what question it is. You— don't—know—nothin'. They got stool pigeons all over this neighborhood they're payin' them every week for information, and you don't know who they are. It could be your best friend. You hear? [*To* **Beatrice**] Like Vinny Bolzano, remember Vinny?

Beatrice: Oh, yeah. God forbid.

Eddie: Tell her about Vinny. [*To* **Catherine**] You think I'm blowin' steam here? [*To* **Beatrice**] Go ahead, tell her. [*To* **Catherine**] You was a baby then. There was a family next door to her mother, he was about sixteen—

Beatrice: No, he was no more than fourteen, cause I was to his confirmation in Saint Agnes. But the family had an uncle that they were hidin' in the house, and he snitched to the Immigration.

Catherine: The kid snitched?

Eddie: On his own uncle!

Catherine: What, was he crazy?

Eddie: He was crazy after, I tell you that, boy.

Beatrice: Oh, it was terrible. He had five brothers and the old father. And they grabbed him in the kitchen and pulled him down the stairs—three flights his head was bouncin' like a coconut. And they spit on him in the street, his own father and his brothers. The whole neighborhood was cryin'.

Catherine: Ts! So what happened to him?

Beatrice: I think he went away. [*To* **Eddie**] I never seen him again, did you?

Eddie: [*Rises during this, taking out his watch*] Him? You'll never see him no more, a guy do a thing like that? How's he gonna show his face? [*To* **Catherine,** *as he gets up uneasily*] Just remember, kid, you can quicker get back a million dollars that was stole than a word that you gave away. [*He is standing now, stretching his back.*]

Catherine: Okay, I won't say a word to nobody, I swear.

Eddie: Gonna rain tomorrow. We'll be slidin' all over the decks. Maybe you oughta put something on for them, they be here soon.

Beatrice: I only got fish, I hate to spoil it they ate already. I'll wait, it only takes a few minutes; I could broil it.

Catherine: What happens, Eddie, when that ship pulls out and they ain't on it, though? Don't the captain say nothin'?

Eddie: [*Slicing an apple with his pocket knife*] Captain's pieced off, what do you mean?

Catherine: Even the captain?

Eddie: What's the matter, the captain don't have to live? Captain gets a piece, maybe one of the mates, piece for the guy in Italy who fixed the papers for them, Tony here'll get a little bite. . . .

Beatrice: I just hope they get work here, that's all I hope.

Eddie: Oh, the syndicate'll fix jobs for them; till they pay 'em off they'll get them work every day. It's after the pay-off, then they'll have to scramble like the rest of us.

Beatrice: Well, it be better than they got there.

Eddie: Oh sure, well, listen. So you gonna start Monday, heh, Madonna?

Catherine: [*Embarrassed*] I'm supposed to, yeah. [**Eddie** *is standing facing the two seated women. First* **Beatrice** *smiles, then* **Catherine,** *for a powerful emotion is on him, a childish one and a knowing fear, and the tears show in his eyes— —and they are shy before the avowal.*]

Eddie: [*Sadly smiling, yet somehow proud of her*] Well . . . I hope you have good luck. I wish you the best. You know that, kid.

Catherine: [*Rising, trying to laugh*] You sound like I'm goin' a million miles!

Eddie: I know. I guess I just never figured on one thing.

Catherine: [*Smiling*] What?

Eddie: That you would ever grow up. [*He utters a soundless laugh at himself, feeling his breast pocket of his shirt*] I left a cigar in my other coat, I think. [*He starts for the bedroom.*]

Catherine: Stay there! I'll get it for you. [*She hurries out. There is a slight pause, and* **Eddie** *turns to* **Beatrice,** *who has been avoiding his gaze.*]

Eddie: What are you mad at me lately?

Beatrice: Who's mad? [*She gets up, clearing the dishes*] I'm not mad. [*She picks up the dishes and turns to him*] You're the one is mad. [*She turns and goes into the kitchen as* **Catherine** *enters from the bedroom with a cigar and a pack of matches.*]

Catherine: Here! I'll light it for you! [*She strikes a match and holds it to his cigar. He puffs. Quietly*] Don't worry about me, Eddie, heh?

Eddie: Don't burn yourself. [*Just in time she blows out the match*] You better go in help her with the dishes.

Catherine: [*Turns quickly to the table, and, seeing the table cleared, she says almost guiltily*] Oh! [*She hurries into the kitchen, and as she exits there*] I'll do the dishes, B.!
[*Alone, Eddie stands looking toward the kitchen for a moment. Then he takes out his watch, glances at it, replaces it in his pocket, sits in the*

armchair, *and stares at the smoke flowing out of his mouth.*]

[*The lights go down, then come up on* **Alfieri,** *who has moved onto the forestage.*]

Alfieri: He was as good a man as he had to be in a life that was hard and even. He worked on the piers when there was work, he brought home his pay, and he lived. And toward ten o'clock of that night, after they had eaten, the cousins came.

[*The lights fade on* **Alfieri** *and rise on the street. Enter* **Tony,** *escorting* **Marco** *and* **Rodolpho,** *each with a valise.* **Tony** *halts, indicates the house. They stand for a moment looking at it.*]

Marco: [*He is a square-built peasant of thirty-two, suspicious, tender, and quiet voiced*] Thank you.

Tony: You're on your own now. Just be careful that's all. Ground floor.

Marco: Thank you.

Tony: [*Indicating the house*] I'll see you on the pier tomorrow. You'll go to work.

[**Marco** *nods.* **Tony** *continues on walking down the street.*]

Rodolpho: This will be the first house I ever walked into in America! Imagine! She said they were poor!

Marco: Ssh! Come. [*They go to door.*]

[**Marco** *knocks. The lights rise in the room.* **Eddie** *goes and opens the door. Enter* **Marco** *and* **Rodolpho,** *removing their caps.* **Beatrice** *and* **Catherine** *enter from the kitchen. The lights fade in the street.*]

Eddie: You Marco?

Marco: Marco.

Eddie: Come on in! [*He shakes* **Marco***'s hand.*]

Beatrice: Here, take the bags!

Marco: [*Nods, looks to the women and fixes on* **Beatrice.** *Crosses to* **Beatrice**] Are you my cousin? [*She nods. He kisses her hand.*]

Beatrice: [*Above the table, touching her chest with her hand*] Beatrice. This is my husband, Eddie. [*All nod*] Catherine, my sister Nancy's daughter. [*The brothers nod.*]

Marco: [*Indicating* **Rodolpho**] My brother. Rodolpho. [**Rodolpho** *nods.* **Marco** *comes with a certain formal stiffness to* **Eddie**] I want to tell you now Eddie—when you say go, we will go.

Eddie: Oh, no . . . [*Takes* **Marco***'s bag.*]

Marco: I see it's a small house, but soon, maybe, we can have our own house.

Eddie: You're welcome, Marco, we got plenty of room here. Katie, give them supper, heh? [*Exits into bedroom with their bags.*]

Catherine: Come here, sit down. I'll get you some soup.

Marco: [*As they go to the table*] We ate on the ship. Thank you. [*To* **Eddie,** *calling off to bedroom*] Thank you.

Beatrice: Get some coffee. We'll all have coffee. Come sit down.

[**Rodolpho** *and* **Marco** *sit, at the table.*]

Catherine: [*Wondrously*] How come he's so dark and you're so light, Rodolpho?

Rodolpho: [*Ready to laugh*] I don't know. A thousand years ago, they say, the Danes invaded Sicily.

[**Beatrice** *kisses* **Rodolpho.** *They laugh as* **Eddie** *enters.*]

Catherine: [*To* **Beatrice**] He's practically blond!

Eddie: How's the coffee doin'?

Catherine: [*Brought up*] I'm gettin' it. [*She hurries out to kitchen.*]

Eddie: [*Sits on his rocker*] Yiz have a nice trip?

Marco: The ocean is always rough. But we are good sailors.

Eddie: No trouble gettin' here?

Marco: No. The man brought us. Very nice man.

Rodolpho: [*To* **Eddie**] He says we start to work tomorrow. Is he honest?

Eddie: [*Laughing*] No. But as long as you owe them money, they'll get you plenty of work. [*To* **Marco**] Yiz ever work on the piers in Italy?

Marco: Piers? Ts!—no.

Rodolpho: [*Smiling at the smallness of his town*] In our town there are no piers, only the beach, and little fishing boats.

Beatrice: So what kinda work did yiz do?

Marco: [*Shrugging shyly, even embarrassed*] Whatever there is, anything.

Rodolpho: Sometimes they build a house, or if they fix the bridge—Marco is a mason and I bring him the cement. [*He laughs*] In harvest time we work in the fields . . . if there is work. Anything.

Eddie: Still bad there, heh?

Marco: Bad, yes.

Rodolpho: [*Laughing*] It's terrible! We stand around all day in the piazza listening to the fountain like birds. Everybody waits only for the train.

Beatrice: What's on the train?

Rodolpho: Nothing. But if there are many passengers and you're lucky you make a few lire to push the taxi up the hill.

> [*Enter* **Catherine**; *she listens.*]

Beatrice: You gotta push a taxi?

Rodolpho: [*Laughing*] Oh, sure! It's a feature in our town. The horses in our town are skinnier than goats. So if there are too many passengers we help push the carriages up to the hotel. [*He laughs*] In our town the horses are only for show.

Catherine: Why don't they have automobile taxis?

Rodolpho: There is one. We push that too. [*They laugh.*] Everything in our town, you gotta push!

Beatrice: [*To* **Eddie**] How do you like that!

Eddie: [*To* **Marco**] So what're you wanna do, you gonna stay here in this country or you wanna go back?

Marco: [*Surprised*] Go back?

Eddie: Well, you're married, ain't you?

Marco: Yes. I have three children.

Beatrice: Three! I thought only one.

Marco: Oh, no. I have three now. Four years, five years, six years.

Beatrice: Ah . . . I bet they're cryin' for you already, heh?

Marco: What can I do? The older one is sick in his chest. My wife—she feeds them from her own mouth. I tell you the truth, if I stay there they will never grow up. They eat the sunshine.

Beatrice: My God. So how long you want to stay?

Marco: With your permission, we will stay maybe a—

Eddie: She don't mean in this house, she means in the country.

Marco: Oh. Maybe four, five, six years, I think.

Rodolpho: [*Smiling*] He trusts his wife.

Beatrice: Yeah, but maybe you'll get enough, you'll be able to go back quicker.

Marco: I hope. I don't know. [*To* **Eddie**] I understand it's not so good here either.

Eddie: Oh, you guys'll be all right—till you pay them off, anyway. After that, you'll have to scramble, that's all. But you'll make better here than you could there.

Rodolpho: How much? We hear all kinds of figures. How much can a man make? We work hard, we'll work all day, all night—

> [**Marco** *raises a hand to hush him.*]

Eddie: [*He is coming more and more to address* **Marco** *only*] On the average a whole year? Maybe—well, it's hard to say, see. Sometimes we lay off, there's no ships three four weeks.

Marco: Three, four weeks!—Ts!

Eddie: But I think you could probably—thirty, forty a week, over the whole twelve months of the year.

Marco: [*Rises, crosses to* **Eddie**] Dollars.

Eddie: Sure dollars.

> [**Marco** *puts an arm around* **Rodolpho** *and they laugh.*]

Marco: If we can stay here a few months, Beatrice—

Beatrice: Listen, you're welcome, Marco—

Marco: Because I could send them a little more if I stay here.

Beatrice: As long as you want, we got plenty a room.

Marco: [*His eyes are showing tears*] My wife—[*To* **Eddie**] My wife—I want to send right away maybe twenty dollars—

Eddie: You could send them something next week already.

Marco: [*He is near tears*] Eduardo . . . [*He goes to* **Eddie**, *offering his hand.*]

Eddie: Don't thank me. Listen, what the hell, it's no skin off me. [*To* **Catherine**] What happened to the coffee?

Catherine: I got it on. [*To* **Rodolpho**] You married too? No.

Rodolpho: [*Rises*] Oh, no . . .

Beatrice: [*To* **Catherine**] I told you he—

Catherine: I know, I just thought maybe he got married recently.

Rodolpho: I have no money to get married. I have a nice face, but no money. [*He laughs.*]

Catherine: [*To* **Beatrice**] He's a real blond!

Beatrice: [*To* **Rodolpho**] You want to stay here too, heh? For good?

Rodolpho: Me? Yes, forever! Me, I want to be an American. And then I want to go back to Italy when I am rich, and I will buy a motorcycle. [*He smiles.* **Marco** *shakes him affectionately.*]

Catherine: A motorcycle!

Rodolpho: With a motorcycle in Italy you will never starve any more.

Beatrice: I'll get you coffee. [*She exits to the kitchen.*]

Eddie: What you do with a motorcycle?

Marco: He dreams, he dreams.

Rodolpho: [*To* **Marco**] Why? [*To* **Eddie**] Messages! The rich people in the hotel always need someone who will carry a message. But quickly, and with a great noise. With a blue motorcycle I would station myself in the courtyard of the hotel, and in a little while I would have messages.

Marco: When you have no wife you have dreams.

Eddie: Why can't you just walk, or take a trolley or sump'm?

[*Enter* **Beatrice** *with coffee.*]

Rodolpho: Oh, no, the machine, the machine is necessary. A man comes into a great hotel and says, I am a messenger. Who is this man? He disappears walking, there is no noise, nothing. Maybe he will never come back, maybe he will never deliver the message. But a man who rides up on a great machine, this man is responsible, this man exists. He will be given messages. [*He helps* **Beatrice** *set out the coffee things*] I am also a singer, though.

Eddie: You mean a regular—?

Rodolpho: Oh, yes. One night last year Andreola got sick. Baritone. And I took his place in the garden of the hotel. Three arias I sang without a mistake! Thousand-lire notes they threw from the tables, money was falling like a storm in the treasury. It was magnificent. We lived six months on that night, eh, Marco?

[**Marco** *nods doubtfully.*]

Marco: Two months.

[**Eddie** *laughs.*]

Beatrice: Can't you get a job in that place?

Rodolpho: Andreola got better. He's a baritone, very strong.

[**Beatrice** *laughs.*]

Marco: [*Regretfully, to* **Beatrice**] He sang too loud.

Rodolpho: Why too loud?

Marco: Too loud. The guests in that hotel are all Englishmen. They don't like too loud.

Rodolpho: [*To* **Catherine**] Nobody ever said it was too loud!

Marco: I say. It was too loud. [*To* **Beatrice**] I knew it as soon as he started to sing. Too loud.

Rodolpho: Then why did they throw so much money?

Marco: They paid for your courage. The English like courage. But once is enough.

Rodolpho: [*To all but* **Marco**] I never heard anybody say it was too loud.

Catherine: Did you ever hear of jazz?

Rodolpho: Oh, sure! I *sing* jazz.

Catherine: [*Rises*] You could sing jazz?

Rodolpho: Oh, I sing Napolidan, jazz, bel canto—I sing "Paper Doll," you like "Paper Doll"?

Catherine: Oh, sure, I'm crazy for "Paper Doll." Go ahead, sing it.

Rodolpho: [*Takes his stance after getting a nod of permission from* **Marco,** *and with a high tenor voice begins singing*]

"I'll tell you boys it's tough to be alone,
And it's tough to love a doll that's not your own.
I'm through with all of them,
I'll never fall again,
Hey, boy, what you gonna do?
I'm gonna buy a paper doll that I can call my own,
A doll that other fellows cannot steal.

[**Eddie** *rises and moves upstage.*]

And then those flirty, flirty guys
With their flirty, flirty eyes
Will have to flirt with dollies that are real—

Eddie: Hey, kid—hey, wait a minute—

Catherine: [*Enthralled*] Leave him finish, it's beautiful! [*To* **Beatrice**] He's terrific! It's terrific, Rodolpho.

Eddie: Look, kid; you don't want to be picked up, do ya?

Marco: No—no! [*He rises.*]

Eddie: [*Indicating the rest of the building*] Because we never had no singers here . . . and all of a sudden there's a singer in the house, y'know what I mean?

Marco: Yes, yes. You'll be quiet, Rodolpho.

Eddie: [*He is flushed*] They got guys all over the place, Marco. I mean.

Marco: Yes. He'll be quiet. [*To* **Rodolpho**] You'll be quiet.

> [**Rodolpho** *nods.*]
>
> [**Eddie** *has risen, with iron control, even a smile. He moves to* **Catherine.**]

Eddie: What's the high heels for, Garbo?

Catherine: I figured for tonight—

Eddie: Do me a favor, will you? Go ahead.

> [*Embarrassed now, angered,* **Catherine** *goes out into the bedroom.* **Beatrice** *watches her go and gets up; in passing, she gives* **Eddie** *a cold look, restrained only by the strangers, and goes to the table to pour coffee.*]

Eddie: [*Striving to laugh, and to* **Marco,** *but directed as much to* **Beatrice**] All actresses they want to be around here.

Rodolpho: [*Happy about it*] In Italy too! All the girls.

> [**Catherine** *emerges from the bedroom in low-heel shoes, comes to the table.* **Rodolpho** *is lifting a cup.*]

Eddie: [*He is sizing up* **Rodolpho,** *and there is a concealed suspicion*] Yeah, heh?

Rodolpho: Yes! [*Laughs, indicating* **Catherine**] Especially when they are so beautiful!

Catherine: You like sugar?

Rodolpho: Sugar? Yes! I like sugar very much!

> [**Eddie** *is downstage, watching as she pours a spoonful of sugar into his cup, his face puffed with trouble, and the room dies.*]
>
> [*Lights rise on* **Alfieri.**]

Alfieri: Who can ever know what will be discovered? Eddie Carbone had never expected to have a destiny. A man works, raises his family, goes bowling, eats, gets old, and then he dies. Now, as the weeks passed, there was a future, there was a trouble that would not go away.

> [*The lights fade on* **Alfieri,** *then rise on* **Eddie** *standing at the doorway of the house.* **Beatrice** *enters on the street. She sees* **Eddie,** *smiles at him. He looks away. She starts to enter the house when* **Eddie** *speaks.*]

Eddie: It's after eight.

Beatrice: Well, it's a long show at the Paramount.

Eddie: They must've seen every picture in Brooklyn by now. He's supposed to stay in the house when he ain't working. He ain't supposed to go advertising himself.

Beatrice: Well that's his trouble, what do you care? If they pick him up they pick him up, that's all. Come in the house.

Eddie: What happened to the stenography? I don't see her practice no more.

Beatrice: She'll get back to it. She's excited, Eddie.

Eddie: She tell you anything?

Beatrice: [*Comes to him, now the subject is opened*] What's the matter with you? He's a nice kid, what do you want from him?

Eddie: That's a nice kid? He gives me the heeby-jeebies.

Beatrice: [*Smiling*] Ah, go on, you're just jealous.

Eddie: Of him? Boy, you don't think much of me.

Beatrice: I don't understand you. What's so terrible about him?

Eddie: You mean it's all right with you? That's gonna be her husband?

Beatrice: Why? He's a nice fella, hard workin', he's a good-lookin' fella.

Eddie: He sings on the ships, didja know that?

Beatrice: What do you mean, he sings?

Eddie: Just what I said, he sings. Right on the deck, all of a sudden, a whole song comes out of his mouth—with motions. You know what they're calling him now? Paper Doll they're callin' him, Canary. He's like a weird. He comes out on the pier, one-two-three, it's a regular show.

Beatrice: Well, he's a kid; he don't know how to behave himself yet.

Eddie: And with that wacky hair; he's like a chorus girl or sump'n.

Beatrice: So he's blond, so—

Eddie: I just hope that's his regular hair, that's all I hope.

Beatrice: You crazy or sump'n? [*She tries to turn him to her.*]

Eddie: [*He keeps his head turned away*] What's so crazy? I don't like his whole way.

Beatrice: Listen, you never seen a blond guy in your life? What about Whitey Balso?

Eddie: [*Turning to her victoriously*] Sure, but

Whitey don't sing; he don't do like that on the ships.

Beatrice: Well, maybe that's the way they do in Italy.

Eddie: Then why don't his brother sing? Marco goes around like a man; nobody kids Marco. [*He moves from her, halts. She realizes there is a campaign solidified in him*] I tell you the truth I'm surprised I have to tell you all this. I mean I'm surprised, B.

Beatrice: [*She goes to him with purpose now*] Listen, you ain't gonna start nothin' here.

Eddie: I ain't startin' nothin', but I ain't gonna stand around lookin' at that. For that character I didn't bring her up. I swear, B., I'm surprised at you; I sit there waitin' for you to wake up but everything is great with you.

Beatrice: No, everything ain't great with me.

Eddie: No?

Beatrice: No. But I got other worries.

Eddie: Yeah. [*He is already weakening.*]

Beatrice: Yeah, you want me to tell you?

Eddie: [*In retreat*] Why? What worries you got?

Beatrice: When am I gonna be a wife again, Eddie?

Eddie: I ain't been feelin' good. They bother me since they came.

Beatrice: It's almost three months you don't feel good; they're only here a couple of weeks. It's three months, Eddie.

Eddie: I don't know, B. I don't want to talk about it.

Beatrice: What's the matter, Eddie, you don't like me, heh?

Eddie: What do you mean, I don't like you? I said I don't feel good, that's all.

Beatrice: Well, tell me, am I doing something wrong? Talk to me.

Eddie: [*Pause. He can't speak, then*] I can't. I can't talk about it.

Beatrice: Well tell me what—

Eddie: I got nothin' to say about it!

[*She stands for a moment; he is looking off; she turns to go into the house.*]

Eddie: I'll be all right, B; just lay off me, will ya? I'm worried about her.

Beatrice: The girl is gonna be eighteen years old, it's time already.

Eddie: B., he's taking her for a ride!

Beatrice: All right, that's her ride. What're you gonna stand over her till she's forty? Eddie, I want you to cut it out now, you hear me? I don't like it! Now come in the house.

Eddie: I want to take a walk, I'll be in right away.

Beatrice: They ain't goin' to come any quicker if you stand in the street. It ain't nice, Eddie.

Eddie: I'll be in right away. Go ahead. [*He walks off.*]

[*She goes into the house.* **Eddie** *glances up the street, sees* **Louis** *and* **Mike** *coming, and sits on an iron railing.* **Louis** *and* **Mike** *enter.*]

Louis: Wanna go bowlin' tonight?

Eddie: I'm too tired. Goin' to sleep.

Louis: How's your two submarines?

Eddie: They're okay.

Louis: I see they're gettin' work allatime.

Eddie: Oh, yeah, they're doin' all right.

Mike: That's what we oughta do. We oughta leave the country and come in under the water. Then we get work.

Eddie: You ain't kiddin'.

Louis: Well, what the hell. Y'know?

Eddie: Sure.

Louis: [*Sits on railing beside* **Eddie**] Believe me, Eddie, you got a lotta credit comin' to you.

Eddie: Aah, they don't bother me, don't cost me nutt'n.

Mike: That older one, boy, he's a regular bull. I seen him the other day liftin' coffee bags over the Matson Line. They leave him alone he woulda load the whole ship by himself.

Eddie: Yeah, he's a strong guy, that guy. Their father was a regular giant, supposed to be.

Louis: Yeah, you could see. He's a regular slave.

Mike: [*Grinning*] That blond one, though—[**Eddie** *looks at him*] He's got a sense of humor. [**Louis** *snickers.*]

Eddie: [*Searchingly*] Yeah. He's funny—

Mike: [*Starting to laugh*] Well he ain't exactly funny, but he's always like makin' remarks like, y'know? He comes around, everybody's laughin'. [**Louis** *laughs.*]

Eddie: [*Uncomfortably, grinning*] Yeah, well . . . he's got a sense of humor.

Mike: [*Laughing*] Yeah, I mean, he's always makin' like remarks, like, y'know?

Eddie: Yeah, I know. But he's a kid yet, y'know? He—he's just a kid, that's all.

Mike: [*Getting hysterical with* **Louis**] I know. You take one look at him—everybody's happy. [**Louis** *laughs*] I worked one day with him last week over the Moore-MacCormack Line, I'm tell' you they was all hysterical. [**Louis** *and he explode in laughter.*]

Eddie: Why? What'd he do?

Mike: I don't know . . . he was just humorous. You never can remember what he says, y'know? But it's the way he says it. I mean he gives you a look sometimes and you start laughin'!

Eddie: Yeah. [*Troubled*] He's got a sense of humor.

Mike: [*Gasping*] Yeah.

Louis: [*Rising*] Well, we see ya, Eddie.

Eddie: Take it easy.

Louis: Yeah. See ya.

Mike: If you wanna come bowlin' later we're goin' Flatbush Avenue.

[*Laughing, they move to exit, meeting* **Rodolpho** *and* **Catherine** *entering on the street. Their laughter rises as they see* **Rodolpho**, *who does not understand but joins in.* **Eddie** *moves to enter the house as* **Louis** *and* **Mike** *exit.* **Catherine** *stops him at the door.*]

Catherine: Hey, Eddie—what a picture we saw! Did we laugh!

Eddie: [*He can't help smiling at sight of her*] Where'd you go?

Catherine: Paramount. It was with those two guys, y'know? That—

Eddie: Brooklyn Paramount?

Catherine: [*With an edge of anger, embarrassed before* **Rodolpho**] Sure, the Brooklyn Paramount. I told you we wasn't goin' to New York.

Eddie: [*Retreating before the threat of her anger*] All right, I only asked you. [*To* **Rodolpho**] I just don't want her hangin' around Times Square, see? It's full of tramps over there.

Rodolpho: I would like to go to Broadway once, Eddie. I would like to walk with her once where the theaters are and the opera. Since I was a boy I see pictures of those lights.

Eddie: [*His little patience waning*] I want to talk to her a minute, Rodolpho. Go inside, will you?

Rodolpho: Eddie, we only walk together in the streets. She teaches me.

Catherine: You know what he can't get over? That there's no fountains in Brooklyn!

Eddie: [*Smiling unwillingly*] Fountains? [**Rodolpho** *smiles at his own naïveté.*]

Catherine: In Italy he says, every town's got fountains, and they meet there. And you know what? They got oranges on the trees where he comes from, and lemons. Imagine—on the trees? I mean it's interesting. But he's crazy for New York.

Rodolpho: [*Attempting familiarity*] Eddie, why can't we go once to Broadway—?

Eddie: Look, I gotta tell her something—

Rodolpho: Maybe you can come too. I want to see all those lights. [*He sees no response in* **Eddie**'s *face. He glances at* **Catherine**] I'll walk by the river before I go to sleep. [*He walks off down the street.*]

Catherine: Why don't you talk to him, Eddie? He blesses you, and you don't talk to him hardly.

Eddie: [*Enveloping her with his eyes*] I bless you and you don't talk to me. [*He tries to smile.*]

Catherine: I don't talk to you? [*She hits his arm*] What do you mean?

Eddie: I don't see you no more. I come home you're runnin' around someplace—

Catherine: Well, he wants to see everything, that's all, so we go. . . . You mad at me?

Eddie: No. [*He moves from her, smiling sadly*] It's just I used to come home, you was always there. Now, I turn around, you're a big girl. I don't know how to talk to you.

Catherine: Why?

Eddie: I don't know, you're runnin', you're runnin', Katie. I don't think you listening any more to me.

Catherine: [*Going to him*] Ah, Eddie, sure I am. What's the matter? You don't like him? [*Slight pause.*]

Eddie: [*Turns to her*] You like him, Katie?

Catherine: [*With a blush but holding her ground*] Yeah. I like him.

Eddie: [*His smile goes*] You like him.

Catherine: [*Looking down*] Yeah. [*Now she looks at him for the consequences, smiling but tense. He looks at her like a lost boy*] What're you got against him? I don't understand. He only blesses you.

Eddie: [*Turns away*] He don't bless me, Katie.

Catherine: He does! You're like a father to him!

Eddie: [*Turns to her*] Katie.

Catherine: What, Eddie?

Eddie: You gonna marry him?

Catherine: I don't know. We just been ... goin' around, that's all. [*Turns to him*] What're you got against him, Eddie? Please, tell me. What?

Eddie: He don't respect you.

Catherine: Why?

Eddie: Katie ... if you wasn't an orphan, wouldn't he ask your father's permission before he run around with you like this?

Catherine: Oh, well, he didn't think you'd mind.

Eddie: He knows I mind, but it don't bother him if I mind, don't you see that?

Catherine: No, Eddie, he's got all kinds of respect for me. And you too! We walk across the street he takes my arm—he almost bows to me! You got him all wrong, Eddie; I mean it, you—

Eddie: Katie, he's only bowin' to his passport.

Catherine: His passport!

Eddie: That's right. He marries you he's got the right to be an American citizen. That's what's goin' on here. [*She is puzzled and surprised*] You understand what I'm tellin' you? The guy is lookin' for his break, that's all he's lookin' for.

Catherine: [*Pained*] Oh, no, Eddie, I don't think so.

Eddie: You don't think so! Katie, you're gonna make me cry here. Is that a workin' man? What does he do with his first money? A snappy new jacket he buys, records, a pointy pair new shoes and his brother's kids are starvin' over there with tuberculosis? That's a hit-and-run guy, baby; he's got bright lights in his head, Broadway. Them guys don't think of nobody but theirself! You marry him and the next time you see him it'll be for divorce!

Catherine: [*Steps toward him*] Eddie, he never said a word about his papers or—

Eddie: You mean he's supposed to tell you that?

Catherine: I don't think he's even thinking about it.

Eddie: What's better for him to think about! He could be picked up any day here and he's back pushin' taxis up the hill!

Catherine: No, I don't believe it.

Eddie: Katie, don't break my heart, listen to me.

Catherine: I don't want to hear it.

Eddie: Katie, listen ...

Catherine: He loves me!

Eddie: [*With deep alarm*] Don't say that, for God's sake! This is the oldest racket in the country—

Catherine: [*Desperately, as though he had made his imprint*] I don't believe it! [*She rushes to the house.*]

Eddie: [*Following her*] They been pullin' this since the Immigration Law was put in! They grab a green kid that don't know nothin' and they—

Catherine: [*Sobbing*] I don't believe it and I wish to hell you'd stop it!

Eddie: Katie!

[*They enter the apartment. The lights in the living room have risen and* **Beatrice** *is there. She looks past the sobbing* **Catherine** *at* **Eddie**, *who in the presence of his wife, makes an awkward gesture of eroded command, indicating* **Catherine**.]

Eddie: Why don't you straighten her out?

Beatrice: [*Inwardly angered at his flowing emotion which in itself alarms her*] When are you going to leave her alone?

Eddie: B., the guy is no good!

Beatrice: [*Suddenly, with open fright and fury*] You going to leave her alone? Or you gonna drive me crazy? [*He turns, striving to retain his dignity, but nevertheless in guilt walks out of the house, into the street and away.* **Catherine** *starts into a bedroom.*] Listen, Catherine. [**Catherine** *halts, turns to her sheepishly*] What are you going to do with yourself?

Catherine: I don't know.

Beatrice: Don't tell me you don't know; you're not a baby any more, what are you going to do with yourself?

Catherine: He won't listen to me.

Beatrice: I don't understand this. He's not your father, Catherine. I don't understand what's going on here.

Catherine: [*As one who herself is trying to rationalize a buried impulse*] What am I going to do, just kick him in the face with it?

Beatrice: Look, honey, you wanna get married, or don't you wanna get married? What are you worried about, Katie?

Catherine: [*Quietly, trembling*] I don't know B. It just seems wrong if he's against it so much.

Beatrice: [*Never losing her aroused alarm*] Sit down, honey, I want to tell you something. Here, sit down. Was there ever any fella he liked for you? There wasn't, was there?

Catherine: But he says Rodolpho's just after his papers.

Beatrice: Look, he'll say anything. What does he care what he says? If it was a prince came here for you it would be no different. You know that, don't you?

Catherine: Yeah, I guess.

Beatrice: So what does that mean?

Catherine: [*Slowly turns her head to* **Beatrice**] What?

Beatrice: It means you gotta be your own self more. You still think you're a little girl, honey. But nobody else can make up your mind for you any more, you understand? You gotta give him to understand that he can't give you orders no more.

Catherine: Yeah, but how am I going to do that? He thinks I'm a baby.

Beatrice: Because *you* think you're a baby. I told you fifty times already, you can't act the way you act. You still walk around in front of him in your slip—

Catherine: Well I forgot.

Beatrice: Well you can't do it. Or like you sit on the edge of the bathtub talkin' to him when he's shavin' in his underwear.

Catherine: When'd I do that?

Beatrice: I seen you in there this morning.

Catherine: Oh ... well, I wanted to tell him something and I—

Beatrice: I know, honey. But if you act like a baby and he be treatin' you like a baby. Like when he comes home sometimes you throw yourself at him like when you was twelve years old.

Catherine: Well I like to see him and I'm happy so I—

Beatrice: Look, I'm not tellin' you what to do honey, but—

Catherine: No, you could tell me, B.! Gee, I'm all mixed up. See, I—He looks so sad now and it hurts me.

Beatrice: Well look Katie, if it's goin' to hurt you so much you're gonna end up an old maid here.

Catherine: No!

Beatrice: I'm telling you, I'm not makin' a joke. I tried to tell you a couple of times in the last year or so. That's why I was so happy you were going to go out and get work, you wouldn't be here so much, you'd be a little more independent. I mean it. It's wonderful for a whole family to love each other, but you're a grown woman and you're in the same house with a grown man. So you'll act different now, heh?

Catherine: Yeah, I will. I'll remember.

Beatrice: Because it ain't only up to him, Katie, you understand? I told him the same thing already.

Catherine: [*Quickly*] What?

Beatrice: That he should let you go. But, you see, if only I tell him, he thinks I'm just bawlin' him out, or maybe I'm jealous or somethin', you know?

Catherine: [*Astonished*] He said you was jealous?

Beatrice: No, I'm just sayin' maybe that's what he thinks. [*She reaches over to* **Catherine**'*s hand; with a strained smile*] You think I'm jealous of you, honey?

Catherine: No! It's the first I thought of it.

Beatrice: [*With a quiet sad laugh*] Well you should have thought of it before ... but I'm not. We'll be all right. Just give him to understand; you don't have to fight, you're just— You're a woman, that's all, and you got a nice boy, and now the time came when you said good-by. All right?

Catherine: [*Strangely moved at the prospect*] All right. ... If I can.

Beatrice: Honey ... you gotta.

[**Catherine,** *sensing now an imperious demand, turns with some fear, with a discovery, to* **Beatrice.** *She is at the edge of tears, as though a familiar world had shattered.*]

Catherine: Okay.

[*Lights out on them and up on* **Alfieri,** *seated behind his desk.*]

Alfieri: It was at this time that he first came to me. I had represented his father in an accident case some years before, and I was acquainted with the family in a casual way. I remember him now as he walked through my doorway— [*Enter* **Eddie** *down right ramp.*] His eyes were like tunnels; my first thought was that he had committed a crime.

[**Eddie** *sits beside the desk, cap in hand, looking out.*]

but soon I saw it was only a passion that had moved into his body, like a stranger. [**Alfieri** *pauses, looks down at his desk, then to* **Eddie** *as though he were continuing a conversation with him*] I don't quite understand what I can do for you. Is there a question of law somewhere?

Eddie: That's what I want to ask you.

Alfieri: Because there's nothing illegal about a girl falling in love with an immigrant.

Eddie: Yeah, but what about it if the only reason for it is to get his papers?

Alfieri: First of all you don't know that.

Eddie: I see it in his eyes; he's laughin' at her and he's laughin' at me.

Alfieri: Eddie, I'm a lawyer. I can only deal in what's provable. You understand that, don't you? Can you prove that?

Eddie: I know what's in his mind, Mr. Alfieri!

Alfieri: Eddie, even if you could prove that—

Eddie: Listen ... will you listen to me a minute? My father always said you was a smart man. I want you to listen to me.

Alfieri: I'm only a lawyer, Eddie.

Eddie: Will you listen a minute? I'm talkin' about the law. Lemme just bring out what I mean. A man, which he comes into the country illegal, don't it stand to reason he's gonna take every penny and put it in the sock? Because they don't know from one day to another, right?

Alfieri: All right.

Eddie: He's spendin'. Records he buys now. Shoes. Jackets. Y'understand me? This guy ain't worried. This guy is *here.* So it must be that he's got it all laid out in his mind already—he's stayin'. Right?

Alfieri: Well? What about it?

Eddie: All right. [*He glances at* **Alfieri,** *then down to the floor*] I'm talking to you confidential, ain't I?

Alfieri: Certainly.

Eddie: I mean it don't go no place but here. Because I don't like to say this about anybody. Even my wife I didn't exactly say this.

Alfieri: What is it?

Eddie: [*Takes a breath and glances briefly over each shoulder*] The guy ain't right, Mr. Alfieri.

Alfieri: What do you mean?

Eddie: I mean he ain't right.

Alfieri: I don't get you.

Eddie: [*Shifts to another position in the chair*] Dja ever get a look at him?

Alfieri: Not that I know of, no.

Eddie: He's a blond guy. Like ... platinum. You know what I mean?

Alfieri: No.

Eddie: I mean if you close the paper fast—you could blow him over.

Alfieri: Well that doesn't mean—

Eddie: Wait a minute, I'm tellin' you sump'm. He sings, see. Which is— I mean it's all right, but sometimes he hits a note, see. I turn around. I mean—high. You know what I mean?

Alfieri: Well, that's a tenor.

Eddie: I know a tenor, Mr. Alfieri. This ain't no tenor. I mean if you came in the house and you didn't know who was singin', you wouldn't be lookin' for him you be lookin' for her.

Alfieri: Yes, but that's not—

Eddie: I'm tellin' you sump'm, wait a minute. Please, Mr. Alfieri. I'm tryin' to bring out my thoughts here. Couple of nights ago my niece brings out a dress which it's too small for her, because she shot up like a light this last year. He takes the dress, lays it on the table, he cuts it up; one-two-three, he makes a new dress. I mean he looked so sweet there, like an angel—you could kiss him he was so sweet.

Alfieri: Now look, Eddie—

Eddie: Mr. Alfieri, they're laughin' at him on the piers. I'm ashamed. Paper Doll they call him. Blondie now. His brother thinks it's because he's got a sense of humor, see—which he's got—but that ain't what they're laughin'. Which they're not goin' to come out with it because they know he's my relative, which they have to see me if they make a crack, y'know? But I know what they're laughin' at, and when I think of that guy layin' his hands on her I could— I mean it's eatin' me out, Mr. Alfieri, because I struggled for that girl. And now he comes in my house and—

Alfieri: Eddie, look—I have my own children. I understand you. But the law is very specific. The law does not ...

Eddie: [*With a fuller flow of indignation*] You mean to tell me that there's no law that a guy which he ain't right can go to work and marry a girl and—?

Alfieri: You have no recourse in the law, Eddie.

Eddie: Yeah, but if he ain't right, Mr. Alfieri, you mean to tell me—

Alfieri: There is nothing you can do, Eddie, believe me.

Eddie: Nothin'.

Alfieri: Nothing at all. There's only one legal question here.

Eddie: What?

Alfieri: The manner in which they entered the country. But I don't think you want to do anything about that, do you?

Eddie: You mean—?

Alfieri: Well, they entered illegally.

Eddie: Oh, Jesus, no, I wouldn't do nothin' about that, I mean—

Alfieri: All right, then, let me talk now, eh?

Eddie: Mr. Alfieri, I can't believe what you tell me. I mean there must be some kinda law which—

Alfieri: Eddie, I want you to listen to me. [*Pause.*] You know, sometimes God mixes up the people. We all love somebody, the wife, the kids—every man's got somebody that he loves, heh? But sometimes ... there's too much. You know? There's too much, and it goes where it mustn't. A man works hard, he brings up a child, sometimes it's a niece, sometimes even a daughter, and he never realizes it, but through the years—there is too much love for the daughter, there is too much

love for the niece. Do you understand what I'm saying to you?

Eddie: [*Sardonically*] What do you mean, I shouldn't look out for her good?

Alfieri: Yes, but these things have to end, Eddie, that's all. The child has to grow up and go away, and the man has to learn to forget. Because after all, Eddie—what other way can it end? [*Pause*] Let her go. That's my advice. You did your job, now it's her life; wish her luck, and let her go. [*Pause*] Will you do that? Because there's no law, Eddie; make up your mind to it; the law is not interested in this.

Eddie: You mean to tell me, even if he's a punk? If he's—

Alfieri: There's nothing you can do.
  [**Eddie** *stands.*]

Eddie: Well, all right, thanks. Thanks very much.

Alfieri: What are you going to do?

Eddie: [*With a helpless but ironic gesture*] What can I do? I'm a patsy, what can a patsy do? I worked like a dog twenty years so a punk could have her, so that's what I done. I mean, in the worst times, in the worst, when there wasn't a ship comin' in the harbor, I didn't stand around lookin' for relief—I hustled. When there was empty piers in Brooklyn I went to Hoboken, Staten Island, the West Side, Jersey, all over—because I made a promise. I took out of my own mouth to give to her. I took out of my wife's mouth. I walked hungry plenty days in this city! [*It begins to break through*] And now I gotta sit in my house and look at a son-of-a-bitch punk like that—which he came out of nowhere! I give him my house to sleep! I take the blankets off my bed for him, and he takes and puts his dirty filthy hands on her like a goddam thief!

Alfieri: [*Rising*] But, Eddie, she's a woman now.

Eddie: He's stealing from me!

Alfieri: She wants to get married, Eddie. She can't marry you, can she?

Eddie: [*Furiously*] What're you talkin' about, marry me! I don't know what the hell you're talkin' about!
  [*Pause.*]

Alfieri: I gave you my advice. Eddie. That's it.

[**Eddie** *gathers himself. A pause.*]

Eddie: Well, thanks. Thanks very much. It just—it's breakin' my heart, y'know. I—

Alfieri: I understand. Put it out of your mind. Can you do that?

Eddie: I'm—[*He feels the threat of sobs, and with a helpless wave*] I'll see you around. [*He goes out up the right ramp.*]

Alfieri: [*Sits on desk*] There are times when you want to spread an alarm, but nothing has happened. I knew, I knew then and there—I could have finished the whole story that afternoon. It wasn't as though there was a mystery to unravel. I could see every step coming, step after step, like a dark figure walking down a hall toward a certain door. I knew where he was heading for, I knew where he was going to end. And I sat here many afternoons asking myself why, being an intelligent man, I was so powerless to stop it. I even went to a certain old lady in the neighborhood, a very wise old woman, and I told her, and she only nodded, and said, "Pray for him ..." And so I—waited here.

[*As lights go out on* **Alfieri**, *they rise in the apartment where all are finishing dinner.* **Beatrice** *and* **Catherine** *are clearing the table.*]

Catherine: You know where they went?

Beatrice: Where?

Catherine: They went to Africa once. On a fishing boat. [**Eddie** *glances at her*] It's true, Eddie.

[**Beatrice** *exits into the kitchen with dishes.*]

Eddie: I didn't say nothin'. [*He goes to his rocker, picks up a newspaper.*]

Catherine: And I was never even in Staten Island.

Eddie: [*Sitting with the paper*] You didn't miss nothin'. [*Pause.* **Catherine** *takes dishes out*] How long that take you, Marco—to get to Africa?

Marco: [*Rising*] Oh ... two days. We go all over.

Rodolpho: [*Rising*] Once we went to Yugoslavia.

Eddie: [*To* **Marco**] They pay all right on them boats?

[**Beatrice** *enters. She and* **Rodolpho** *stack the remaining dishes.*]

Marco: If they catch fish they pay all right. [*Sits on a stool.*]

Rodolpho: They're family boats, though. And nobody in our family owned one. So we only worked when one of the families was sick.

Beatrice: Y'know, Marco, what I don't understand—there's an ocean full of fish and yiz are all starvin'.

Eddie: They gotta have boats, nets, you need money.

[**Catherine** *enters.*]

Beatrice: Yeah, but couldn't they like fish from the beach? You see them down Coney Island—

Marco: Sardines.

Eddie: Sure. [*Laughing*] How you gonna catch sardines on a hook?

Beatrice: Oh, I didn't know they're sardines. [*To* **Catherine**] They're sardines!

Catherine: Yeah, they follow them all over the ocean, Africa, Yugoslavia ... [*She sits and begins to look through a movie magazine.* **Rodolpho** *joins her.*]

Beatrice: [*To* **Eddie**] It's funny, y'know. You never think of it, that sardines are swimming in the ocean! [*She exits to kitchen with dishes.*]

Catherine: I know. It's like oranges and lemons on a tree. [*To* **Eddie**] I mean you ever think of oranges and lemons on a tree?

Eddie: Yeah, I know. It's funny. [*To* **Marco**] I heard that they paint the oranges to make them look orange.

[**Beatrice** *enters.*]

Marco: [*He has been reading a letter*] Paint?

Eddie: Yeah, I heard that they grow like green.

Marco: No, in Italy the oranges are orange.

Rodolpho: Lemons are green.

Eddie: [*Resenting his instruction*] I know lemons are green, for Christ's sake, you see them in the store they're green sometimes. I said oranges they paint, I didn't say nothin' about lemons.

Beatrice: [*Sitting; diverting their attention*] Your wife is gettin' the money all right, Marco?

Marco: Oh, yes. She bought medicine for my boy.

Beatrice: That's wonderful. You feel better, heh?

Marco: Oh, yes! But I'm lonesome.

Beatrice: I just hope you ain't gonna do like some of them around here. They're here twenty-five years, some men, and they didn't get enough together to go back twice.

Marco: Oh, I know. We have many families in our town, the children never saw the father. But I will go home. Three, four years, I think.

Beatrice: Maybe you should keep more here. Because maybe she thinks it comes so easy you'll never get ahead of yourself.

Marco: Oh, no, she saves. I send everything. My wife is very lonesome. [*He smiles shyly.*]

Beatrice: She must be nice. She pretty? I bet, heh?

Marco: [*Blushing*] No, but she understand everything.

Rodolpho: Oh, he's got a clever wife!

Eddie: I betcha there's plenty surprises sometimes when those guys get back there, heh?

Marco: Surprises?

Eddie: [*Laughing*] I mean, you know—they count the kids and there's a couple extra than when they left?

Marco: No—no . . . The women wait, Eddie. Most. Most. Very few surprises.

Rodolpho: It's more strict in our town. [*Eddie looks at him now.*] It's not so free.

Eddie: [*Rises, paces up and down*] It ain't so free here either, Rodolpho, like you think. I seen greenhorns sometimes get in trouble that way —they think just because a girl don't go around with a shawl over her head that she ain't strict, y'know? Girl don't have to wear black dress to be strict. Know what I mean?

Rodolpho: Well, I always have respect—

Eddie: I know, but in your town you wouldn't just drag off some girl without permission, I mean. [*He turns*] You know what I mean, Marco? It ain't that much different here.

Marco: [*Cautiously*] Yes.

Beatrice: Well, he didn't exactly drag her off though, Eddie.

Eddie: I know, but I seen some of them get the wrong idea sometimes. [*To* **Rodolpho**] I mean it might be a little more free here but it's just as strict.

Rodolpho: I have respect for her, Eddie. I do anything wrong?

Eddie: Look, kid, I ain't her father, I'm only her uncle—

Beatrice: Well then, be an uncle then. [**Eddie** *looks at her, aware of her criticizing force*] I *mean.*

Marco: No, Beatrice, if he does wrong you must tell him. [*To* **Eddie**] What does he do wrong?

Eddie: Well, Marco, till he came here she was never out on the street twelve o'clock at night.

Marco: [*To* **Rodolpho**] You come home early now.

Beatrice: [*To* **Catherine**] Well, you said the movie ended late, didn't you?

Catherine: Yeah.

Beatrice: Well, tell him, honey. [*To* **Eddie**] The movie ended late.

Eddie: Look, B., I'm just sayin'—he thinks she always stayed out like that.

Marco: You come home early now, Rodolpho.

Rodolpho: [*Embarrassed*] All right, sure. But I can't stay in the house all the time, Eddie.

Eddie: Look, kid, I'm not only talkin' about her. The more you run around like that the more chance you're takin'. [*To* **Beatrice**] I mean suppose he gets hit by a car or something. [*To* **Marco**] Where's his papers, who is he? Know what I mean?

Beatrice: Yeah, but who is he in the daytime, though? It's the same chance in the daytime.

Eddie: [*Holding back a voice full of anger*] Yeah, but he don't have to go lookin' for it, Beatrice. If he's here to work, then he should work; if he's here for a good time then he could fool around! [*To* **Marco**] But I understood, Marco, that you was both comin' to make a livin' for your family. You understand me, don't you, Marco? [*He goes to his rocker.*]

Marco: I beg your pardon, Eddie.

Eddie: I mean, that's what I understood in the first place, see.

Marco: Yes. That's why we came.

Eddie: [*Sits on his rocker*] Well, that's all I'm askin'.

> [**Eddie** *reads his paper. There is a pause, an awkwardness. Now* **Catherine** *gets up and puts a record on the phonograph—"Paper Doll."*]

Catherine: [*Flushed with revolt*] You wanna dance, Rodolpho?

> [**Eddie** *freezes.*]

Rodolpho: [*In deference to* **Eddie**] No, I—I'm tired.

Beatrice: Go ahead, dance, Rodolpho.

Catherine: Ah, come on. They got a beautiful quartet, these guys. Come.

> [*She has taken his hand and he stiffly rises, feeling* **Eddie***'s eyes on his back, and they dance.*]

Eddie: [*To* **Catherine**] What's that, a new record?

Catherine: It's the same one. We bought it the other day.

Beatrice: [*To* **Eddie**] They only bought three records. [*She watches them dance;* **Eddie** *turns his head away.* **Marco** *just sits there waiting. Now* **Beatrice** *turns to* **Eddie**] Must be nice to go all over in one of them fishin' boats. I would like that myself. See all them other countries?

Eddie: Yeah.

Beatrice: [*To* **Marco**] But the women don't go along, I bet.

Marco: No, not on the boats. Hard work.

Beatrice: What're you got, a regular kitchen and everything?

Marco: Yes, we eat very good on the boats—especially when Rodolpho comes along; everybody gets fat.

Beatrice: Oh, he cooks?

Marco: Sure, very good cook. Rice, pasta, fish, everything.

> [**Eddie** *lowers his paper.*]

Eddie: He's a cook, too! [*Looking at* **Rodolpho**] He sings, he cooks . . .

> [**Rodolpho** *smiles thankfully.*]

Beatrice: Well, it's good, he could always make a living.

Eddie: It's wonderful. He sings, he cooks, he could make dresses.

Catherine: They get some high pay, them guys. The head chefs in all the big hotels are men. You read about them.

Eddie: That's what I'm sayin'.

> [**Catherine** *and* **Rodolpho** *continue dancing.*]

Catherine: Yeah, well, I mean.

Eddie: [*To* **Beatrice**] He's lucky, believe me. [*Slight pause. He looks away, then back to* **Beatrice**] That's why the water front is no place for him. [*They stop dancing.* **Rodolpho** *turns off phonograph*] I mean like me—I can't cook, I can't sing, I can't make dresses, so I'm on the water front. But if I could cook, if I could sing, if I could make dresses, I wouldn't be on the water front. [*He has been unconsciously twisting the newspaper into a tight roll. They are all regarding him now; he senses he is exposing the issue and he is driven on*] I would be someplace else. I would be like in a dress store. [*He has bent the rolled paper and it suddenly tears in two. He suddenly gets up and pulls his pants up over his belly and goes to* **Marco**] What do you say, Marco, we go to the bouts next Saturday night. You never seen a fight, did you?

Marco: [*Uneasily*] Only in the moving pictures.

Eddie: [*Going to* **Rodolpho**] I'll treat yiz. What do you say, Danish? You wanna come along? I'll buy the tickets.

Rodolpho: Sure. I like to go.

Catherine: [*Goes to* **Eddie***; nervously happy now*] I'll make some coffee, all right?

Eddie: Go ahead, make some! Make it nice and strong. [*Mystified, she smiles and exits to kitchen. He is weirdly elated, rubbing his fists into his palms. He strides to* **Marco**] You wait, Marco, you see some real fights here. You ever do any boxing?

Marco: No, I never.

Eddie: [*To* **Rodolpho**] Betcha you have done some, heh?

Rodolpho: No.

Eddie: Well, come on, I'll teach you.

Beatrice: What's he got to learn that for?

Eddie: Ya can't tell, one a these days somebody's liable to step on his foot or sump'm. Come on, Rodolpho, I show you a couple a passes. [*He stands below table.*]

Beatrice: Go ahead, Rodolpho. He's a good boxer, he could teach you.

Rodolpho: [*Embarrassed*] Well, I don't know how to—[*He moves down to* **Eddie**.]

Eddie: Just put your hands up. Like this, see? That's right. That's very good, keep your left up, because you lead with the left, see, like this. [*He gently moves his left into* **Rodolpho***'s face*] See? Now what you gotta do is you gotta block me, so when I come in like that you—[**Rodolpho** *parries his left*] Hey, that's very good! [**Rodolpho** *laughs*] All right, now come into me. Come on.

Rodolpho: I don't want to hit you, Eddie.

Eddie: Don't pity me, come on. Throw it, I'll

show you how to block it. [**Rodolpho** *jabs at him, laughing. The others join*] 'At's it. Come on again. For the jaw right here. [**Rodolpho** *jabs with more assurance*] Very good!

Beatrice: [*To* **Marco**] He's very good!

[**Eddie** *crosses directly upstage of* **Rodolpho.**]

Eddie: Sure, he's great! Come on, kid, put sump'm behind it, you can't hurt me. [**Rodolpho,** *more seriously, jabs at* **Eddie**'s *jaw and grazes it*] Attaboy.

[**Catherine** *comes from the kitchen, watches.*]

Now I'm gonna hit you, so block me, see?

Catherine: [*With beginning alarm*] What are they doin'?

[*They are lightly boxing now.*]

Beatrice: [*She senses only the comradeship in it now*] He's teachin' him; he's very good!

Eddie: Sure, he's terrific! Look at him go! [**Rodolpho** *lands a blow*] 'At's it! Now, watch out, here I come, Danish! [*He feints with his left hand and lands with his right. It mildly staggers* **Rodolpho.** **Marco** *rises.*]

Catherine: [*Rushing to* **Rodolpho**] Eddie!

Eddie: Why? I didn't hurt him. Did I hurt you, kid? [*He rubs the back of his hand across his mouth.*]

Rodolpho: No, no, he didn't hurt me. [*To* **Eddie** *with a certain gleam and a smile*] I was only surprised.

Beatrice: [*Pulling* **Eddie** *down into the rocker*] That's enough, Eddie; he did pretty good, though.

Eddie: Yeah. [*Rubbing his fists together*] He could be very good, Marco. I'll teach him again.

[**Marco** *nods at him dubiously.*]

Rodolpho: Dance, Catherine. Come. [*He takes her hand; they go to phonograph and start it. It plays "Paper Doll."*]

[**Rodolpho** *takes her in his arms. They dance.* **Eddie** *in thought sits in his chair, and* **Marco** *takes a chair, places it in front of* **Eddie,** *and looks down at it.* **Beatrice** *and* **Eddie** *watch him.*]

Marco: Can you lift this chair?

Eddie: What do you mean?

Marco: From here. [*He gets on one knee with one hand behind his back, and grasps the bottom of one of the chair legs but does not raise it.*]

Eddie: Sure, why not? [*He comes to the chair, kneels, grasps the leg, raises the chair one inch, but it leans over to the floor*] Gee, that's hard, I never knew

that. [*He tries again, and again fails*] It's on an angle, that's why, heh?

Marco: Here. [*He kneels, grasps, and with strain slowly raises the chair higher and higher, getting to his feet now.* **Rodolpho** *and* **Catherine** *have stopped dancing as* **Marco** *raises the chair over his head.*]

[**Marco** *is face to face with* **Eddie,** *a strained tension gripping his eyes and jaw, his neck stiff, the chair raised like a weapon over* **Eddie**'s *head—and he transforms what might appear like a glare of warning into a smile of triumph, and* **Eddie**'s *grin vanishes as he absorbs his look.*]

CURTAIN

ACT II

[*Light rises on* **Alfieri** *at his desk.*]

Alfieri: On the twenty-third of that December a case of Scotch whisky slipped from a net while being unloaded—as a case of Scotch whisky is inclined to do on the twenty-third of December on Pier Forty-one. There was no snow, but it was cold, his wife was out shopping. Marco was still at work. The boy had not been hired that day; Catherine told me later that this was the first time they had been alone together in the house.

[*Light is rising on* **Catherine** *in the apartment.* **Rodolpho** *is watching as she arranges a paper pattern on cloth spread on the table.*]

Catherine: You hungry?

Rodolpho: Not for anything to eat. [*Pause*] I have nearly three hundred dollars. Catherine?

Catherine: I heard you.

Rodolpho: You don't like to talk about it any more?

Catherine: Sure, I don't mind talkin' about it.

Rodolpho: What worries you, Catherine?

Catherine: I been wantin' to ask you about something. Could I?

Rodolpho: All the answers are in my eyes, Catherine. But you don't look in my eyes lately. You're full of secrets. [*She looks at him. She seems withdrawn*] What is the question?

Catherine: Suppose I wanted to live in Italy.

Rodolpho: [*Smiling at the incongruity*] You going to marry somebody rich?

Catherine: No, I mean live there—you and me.

Rodllpho: [*His smile vanishing*] When?

Catherine: Well ... when we get married.

Rodolpho: [*Astonished*] You want to be an Italian?

Catherine: No, but I could live there without being Italian. Americans live there.

Rodolpho: Forever?

Catherine: Yeah.

Rodolpho: [*Crosses to rocker*] You're fooling.

Catherine: No, I mean it.

Rodolpho: Where do you get such an idea?

Catherine: Well, you're always saying it's so beautiful there, with the mountains and the ocean and all the—

Rodolpho: You're fooling me.

Catherine: I mean it.

Rodolpho: [*Goes to her slowly*] Catherine, if I ever brought you home with no money, no business, nothing, they would call the priest and the doctor and they would say Rodolpho is crazy.

Catherine: I know, but I think we would be happier there.

Rodolpho: Happier! What would you eat? You can't cook the view!

Catherine: Maybe you could be a singer, like in Rome or—

Rodolpho: Rome! Rome is full of singers.

Catherine: Well, I could work then.

Rodolpho: Where?

Catherine: God, there must be jobs somewhere!

Rodolpho: There's nothing! Nothing, nothing, nothing. Now tell me what you're talking about. How can I bring you from a rich country to suffer in a poor country? What are you talking about? [*He searches for words*] I would be a criminal stealing your face. In two years you would have an old, hungry face. When my brother's babies cry they give them water, water that boiled a bone. Don't you believe that?

Catherine: [*Quietly*] I'm afraid of Eddie here.

   [*Slight pause.*]

Rodolpho: [*Steps closer to her*] We wouldn't live here. Once I am a citizen I could work anywhere and I would find better jobs and we would have a house, Catherine. If I were not afraid to be arrested I would start to be something wonderful here!

Catherine: [*Steeling herself*] Tell me something. I mean just tell me, Rodolpho—would you still want to do it if it turned out we had to go live in Italy? I mean just if it turned out that way.

Rodolpho: This your question or his question?

Catherine: I would like to know, Rodolpho. I mean it.

Rodolpho: To go there with nothing.

Catherine: Yeah.

Rodolpho: No. [*She looks at him wide-eyed*] No.

Catherine: You wouldn't?

Rodolpho: No; I will not marry you to live in Italy. I want you to be my wife, and I want to be a citizen. Tell him that, or I will. Yes. [*He moves about angrily*] And tell him also, and tell yourself, please, that I am not a beggar, and you are not a horse, a gift, a favor for a poor immigrant.

Catherine: Well, don't get mad!

Rodolpho: I am furious! [*Goes to her*] Do you think I am so desperate? My brother is desperate, not me. You think I would carry on my back the rest of my life a woman I didn't love just to be an American? It's so wonderful? You think we have no tall buildings in Italy? Electric lights? No wide streets? No flags? No automobiles? Only work we don't have. I want to be an American so I can work, that is the only wonder here—work! How can you insult me, Catherine?

Catherine: I didn't mean that—

Rodolpho: My heart dies to look at you. Why are you so afraid of him?

Catherine: [*Near tears*] I don't know!

Rodolpho: Do you trust me, Catherine? You?

Catherine: It's only that I— He was good to me, Rodolpho. You don't know him; he was always the sweetest guy to me. Good. He razzes me all the time but he don't mean it. I know. I would—just feel ashamed if I made him sad. 'Cause I always dreamt that when I got married he would be happy at the wedding, and laughin'—and now he's—mad all the time and nasty— [*She is weeping*] Tell him you'd live in Italy—just tell him, and maybe he would start to trust you a little, see? Because

I want him to be happy; I mean—I like him, Rodolpho—and I can't stand it!

Rodolpho: Oh, Catherine—oh, little girl.

Catherine: I love you, Rodolpho, I love you.

Rodolpho: Then why are you afraid? That he'll spank you?

Catherine: Don't, don't laugh at me! I've been here all my life . . . Every day I saw him when he left in the morning and when he came home at night. You think it's so easy to turn around and say to a man he's nothin' to you no more?

Rodolpho: I know, but—

Catherine: You don't know; nobody knows! I'm not a baby, I know a lot more than people think I know. Beatrice says to be a woman, but—

Rodolpho: Yes.

Catherine: Then why don't she be a woman? If I was a wife I would make a man happy instead of goin' at him all the time. I can tell a block away when he's blue in his mind and just wants to talk to somebody quiet and nice. . . . I can tell when he's hungry or wants a beer before he even says anything. I know when his feet hurt him, I mean I *know* him and now I'm supposed to turn around and make a stranger out of him? I don't know why I have to do that, I mean.

Rodolpho: Catherine. If I take in my hands a little bird. And she grows and wishes to fly. But I will not let her out of my hands because I love her so much, is that right for me to do? I don't say you must hate him; but anyway you must go, mustn't you? Catherine?

Catherine: [*Softly*] Hold me.

Rodolpho: [*Clasping her to him*] Oh, my little girl.

Catherine: Teach me. [*She is weeping*] I don't know anything, teach me, Rodolpho, hold me.

Rodolpho: There's nobody here now. Come inside. Come. [*He is leading her toward the bedrooms*] And don't cry any more.

[*Light rises on the street. In a moment* **Eddie** *appears. He is unsteady, drunk. He mounts the stairs. He enters the apartment, looks around, takes out a bottle from one pocket, puts it on the table. Then another bottle from another pocket, and a third from an inside pocket. He sees the*

pattern and cloth, goes over to it and touches it, and turns toward upstage.]

Eddie: Beatrice? [*He goes to the open kitchen door and looks in*] Beatrice? Beatrice?

[**Catherine** *enters from bedroom; under his gaze she adjusts her dress.*]

Catherine: You got home early.

Eddie: Knocked off for Christmas early. [*Indicating the pattern*] Rodolpho makin' you a dress?

Catherine: No, I'm makin' a blouse.

[**Rodolpho** *appears in the bedroom doorway.* **Eddie** *sees him and his arm jerks slightly in shock.* **Rodolpho** *nods to him testingly.*]

Rodolpho: Beatrice went to buy present for her mother.

[*Pause.*]

Eddie: Pack it up. Go ahead. Get your stuff and get outa here. [**Catherine** *instantly turns and walks toward the bedroom, and* **Eddie** *grabs her arm*] Where you goin'?

Catherine: [*Trembling with fright*] I think I have to get out of here, Eddie.

Eddie: No, you ain't goin' nowheres, he's the one.

Catherine: I think I can't stay here no more. [*She frees her arm, steps back toward the bedroom*] I'm sorry, Eddie. [*She sees the tears in his eyes*] Well, don't cry. I'll be around the neighborhood; I'll see you. I just can't stay here no more. You know I can't. [*Her sobs of pity and love for him break her composure*] Don't you know I can't? You know that, don't you? [*She goes to him*] Wish me luck. [*She clasps her hands prayerfully*] Oh, Eddie, don't be like that!

Eddie: You ain't goin' nowheres.

Catherine: Eddie, I'm not gonna be a baby any more! You—

[*He reaches out suddenly, draws her to him, and as she strives to free herself he kisses her on the mouth.*]

Rodolpho: Don't! [*He pulls* **Eddie***'s arm*] Stop that! Have respect for her!

Eddie: [*Spun around by* **Rodolpho**] You want something?

Rodolpho: Yes! She'll be my wife. That is what I want. My wife!

Eddie: But what're you gonna be?

Rodolpho: I show you what I be!

Catherine: Wait outside; don't argue with him!

Eddie: Come on, show me! What're you gonna be? Show me!

Rodolpho: [*With tears of rage*] Don't say that to me!

[*Rodolpho flies at him in attack. Eddie pins his arms, laughing, and suddenly kisses him.*]

Catherine: Eddie! Let go, ya hear me! I'll kill you! Leggo of him!

[*She tears at Eddie's face and Eddie releases Rodolpho. Eddie stands there with tears rolling down his face as he laughs mockingly at Rodolpho. She is staring at him in horror. Rodolpho is rigid. They are like animals that have torn at one another and broken up without a decision, each waiting for the other's mood.*]

Eddie: [*To Catherine*] You see? [*To Rodolpho*] I give you till tomorrow, kid. Get outa here. Alone. You hear me? Alone.

Catherine: I'm going with him, Eddie. [*She starts toward Rodolpho.*]

Eddie: [*Indicating Rodolpho with his head*] Not with that. [*She halts, frightened. He sits, still panting for breath, and they watch him helplessly as he leans toward them over the table*] Don't make me do nuttin', Catherine. Watch your step, submarine. By rights they oughta throw you back in the water. But I got pity for you. [*He moves unsteadily toward the door, always facing Rodolpho*] Just get outa here and don't lay another hand on her unless you wanna go out feet first. [*He goes out of the apartment.*]

[*The lights go down, as they rise on Alfieri.*]

Alfieri: On December twenty-seventh I saw him next. I normally go home well before six, but that day I stay around looking out my window at the bay, and when I saw him walking through my doorway, I knew why I had waited. And if I seem to tell this like a dream, it was that way. Several moments arrived in the course of the two talks we had when it occurred to me how—almost transfixed I had come to feel. I had lost my strength somewhere. [*Eddie enters, removing his cap, sits in the chair, looks thoughtfully out*] I looked in his eyes more than I listened—in fact, I can hardly re-

member the conversation. But I will never forget how dark the room became when he looked at me; his eyes were like tunnels. I kept wanting to call the police, but nothing had happened. Nothing at all had really happened. [*He breaks off and looks down at the desk. Then he turns to Eddie*] So in other words, he won't leave?

Eddie: My wife is talkin' about renting a room upstairs for them. An old lady on the top floor is got an empty room.

Alfieri: What does Marco say?

Eddie: He just sits there. Marco don't say much.

Alfieri: I guess they didn't tell him, heh? What happened?

Eddie: I don't know; Marco don't say much.

Alfieri: What does your wife say?

Eddie: [*Unwilling to pursue this*] Nobody's talkin' much in the house. So what about that?

Alfieri: But you didn't prove anything about him. It sounds like he just wasn't strong enough to break your grip.

Eddie: I'm tellin' you I know—he ain't right. Somebody that don't want it can break it. Even a mouse, if you catch a teeny mouse and you hold it in your hand, that mouse can give you the right kind of fight. He didn't give me the right kind of fight, I know it, Mr. Alfieri, the guy ain't right.

Alfieri: What did you do that for, Eddie?

Eddie: To show her what he is! So she would see, once and for all! Her mother'll turn over in the grave! [*He gathers himself almost peremptorily*] So what do I gotta do now? Tell me what to do.

Alfieri: She actually said she's marrying him?

Eddie: She told me, yeah. So what do I do?

[*Slight pause.*]

Alfieri: This is my last word, Eddie, take it or not, that's your business. Morally and legally you have no rights, you cannot stop it; she is a free agent.

Eddie: [*Angering*] Didn't you hear what I told you?

Alfieri: [*With a tougher tone*] I heard what you told me, and I'm telling you what the answer is. I'm not only telling you now, I'm warning you—the law is nature. The law is only a word for what has a right to happen. When the law is wrong it's because it's unnatural, but in this case it is natural and a river will drown you if you buck it. Let her go. And bless her. [*A phone booth begins to glow on the opposite side of the stage; a faint, lonely blue.* **Eddie** *stands up, jaws clenched*] Somebody had to come for her, Eddie, sooner or later. [**Eddie** *starts turning to go and* **Alfieri** *rises with new anxiety*] You won't have a friend in the world, Eddie! Even those who understand will turn against you, even the ones who feel the same will despise you! [**Eddie** *moves off*] Put it out of your mind! Eddie! [*He follows into the darkness, calling desperately.*]

> [**Eddie** *is gone. The phone is glowing in light now. Light is out on* **Alfieri.** **Eddie** *has at the same time appeared beside the phone.*]

Eddie: Give me the number of the Immigration Bureau. Thanks. [*He dials*] I want to report something. Illegal immigrants. Two of them. That's right. Four-forty-one Saxon Street, Brooklyn, yeah. Ground floor. Heh? [*With greater difficulty*] I'm just around the neighborhood, that's all. Heh?

> [*Evidently he is being questioned further, and he slowly hangs up. He leaves the phone just as* **Louis** *and* **Mike** *come down the street.*]

Louis: Go bowlin', Eddie?

Eddie: No, I'm due home.

Louis: Well, take it easy.

Eddie: I'll see yiz.

> [*They leave him, exiting right, and he watches them go. He glances about, then goes up into the house. The lights go on in the apartment.* **Beatrice** *is taking down Christmas decorations and packing them in a box.*]

Eddie: Where is everybody? [**Beatrice** *does not answer*] I says where is everybody?

Beatrice: [*Looking up at him, wearied with it, and concealing a fear of him*] I decided to move them upstairs with Mrs. Dondero.

Eddie: Oh, they're all moved up there already?

Beatrice: Yeah.

Eddie: Where's Catherine? She up there?

Beatrice: Only to bring pillow cases.

Eddie: She ain't movin' in with them.

Beatrice: Look, I'm sick and tired of it. I'm sick and tired of it!

Eddie: All right, all right, take it easy.

Beatrice: I don't wanna hear no more about it, you understand? Nothin'!

Eddie: What're you blowin' off about? Who brought them in here?

Beatrice: All right, I'm sorry; I wish I'd a drop dead before I told them to come. In the ground I wish I was.

Eddie: Don't drop dead, just keep in mind who brought them in here, that's all. [*He moves about restlessly*] I mean I got a couple of rights here. [*He moves, wanting to beat down her evident disapproval of him*] This is my house here not their house.

Beatrice: What do you want from me? They're moved out; what do you want now?

Eddie: I want my respect!

Beatrice: So I moved them out, what more do you want? You got your house now, you got your respect.

Eddie: [*He moves about biting his lip*] I don't like the way you talk to me, Beatrice.

Beatrice: I'm just tellin' you I done what you want!

Eddie: I don't like it! The way you talk to me and the way you look at me. This is my house. And she is my niece and I'm responsible for her.

Beatrice: So that's why you done that to him?

Eddie: I done what to him?

Beatrice: What you done to him in front of her; you know what I'm talkin' about. She goes around shakin' all the time, she can't go to sleep! That's what you call responsible for her?

Eddie: [*Quietly*] The guy ain't right, Beatrice. [*She is silent*] Did you hear what I said?

Beatrice: Look, I'm finished with it. That's all. [*She resumes her work.*]

Eddie: [*Helping her to pack the tinsel*] I'm gonna have it out with you one of these days, Beatrice.

Beatrice: Nothin' to have out with me, it's all settled. Now we gonna be like it never happened, that's all.

Eddie: I want my respect, Beatrice, and you know what I'm talkin' about.

Beatrice: What?

> [*Pause.*]

Eddie: [*Finally his resolution hardens*] What I feel like doin' in the bed and what I don't feel like doin'. I don't want no—

Beatrice: When'd I say anything about that?

Eddie: You said, you said, I ain't deaf. I don't want no more conversations about that, Beatrice. I do what I feel like doin' or what I don't feel like doin'.

Beatrice: Okay.

[*Pause.*]

Eddie: You used to be different, Beatrice. You had a whole different way.

Beatrice: *I'm* no different.

Eddie: You didn't used to jump me all the time about everything. The last year or two I come in the house I don't know what's gonna hit me. It's a shootin' gallery in here and I'm the pigeon.

Beatrice: Okay, okay.

Eddie: Don't tell me okay, okay, I'm tellin' you the truth. A wife is supposed to believe the husband. If I tell you that guy ain't right don't tell me he is right.

Beatrice: But how do you know?

Eddie: Because I know. I don't go around makin' accusations. He give me the heeby-jeebies the first minute I seen him. And I don't like you sayin' I don't want her marryin' anybody. I broke my back payin' her stenography lessons so she could go out and meet a better class of people. Would I do that if I didn't want her to get married? Sometimes you talk like I was a crazy man or sump'm.

Beatrice: But she likes him.

Eddie: Beatrice, she's a baby, how is she gonna know what she likes?

Beatrice: Well, you kept her a baby, you wouldn't let her go out. I told you a hundred times.

[*Pause.*]

Eddie: All right. Let her go out, then.

Beatrice: She don't wanna go out now. It's too late, Eddie.

[*Pause.*]

Eddie: Suppose I told her to go out. Suppose I—

Beatrice: They're going to get married next week, Eddie.

Eddie: [*His head jerks around to her*] She said that?

Beatrice: Eddie, if you want my advice, go to her and tell her good luck. I think maybe now that you had it out you learned better.

Eddie: What's the hurry next week?

Beatrice: Well, she's been worried about him bein' picked up; this way he could start to be a citizen. She loves him, Eddie. [*He gets up, moves about uneasily, restlessly*] Why don't you give her a good word? Because I still think she would like you to be a friend, y'know? [*He is standing, looking at the floor*] I mean like if you told her you'd go to the wedding.

Eddie: She asked you that?

Beatrice: I know she would like it. I'd like to make a party for her. I mean there oughta be some kinda send-off. Heh? I mean she'll have trouble enough in her life, let's start it off happy. What do you say? Cause in her heart she still loves you, Eddie. I know it. [*He presses his fingers against his eyes*] What're you, cryin'? [*She goes to him, holds his face*] Go . . . whyn't you go tell her you're sorry? [*Catherine is seen on the upper landing of the stairway, and they hear her descending*] There . . . she's comin' down. Come on, shake hands with her.

Eddie: [*Moving with suppressed suddenness*] No, I can't, I can't talk to her.

Beatrice: Eddie, give her a break; a wedding should be happy!

Eddie: I'm goin', I'm goin' for a walk.

[*He goes upstage for his jacket.* **Catherine** *enters and starts for the bedroom door.*]

Beatrice: Katie? . . . Eddie, don't go, wait a minute. [*She embraces* **Eddie**'s *arm with warmth*] Ask him, Katie. Come on, honey.

Eddie: It's all right, I'm—[*He starts to go and she holds him.*]

Beatrice: No, she wants to ask you. Come on, Katie, ask him. We'll have a party! What're we gonna do, hate each other? Come on!

Catherine: I'm gonna get married, Eddie. So if you wanna come, the wedding be on Saturday.

[*Pause.*]

Eddie: Okay. I only wanted the best for you, Katie. I hope you know that.

Catherine: Okay. [*She starts out again.*]

Eddie: Catherine? [*She turns to him*] I was just tellin' Beatrice . . . if you wanna go out, like

... I mean I realize maybe I kept you home too much. Because he's the first guy you ever knew, y'know? I mean now that you got a job, you might meet some fellas, and you get a different idea, y'know? I mean you could always come back to him, you're still only kids, the both of yiz. What's the hurry? Maybe you'll get around a little bit, you grow up a little more, maybe you'll see different in a couple of months. I mean you be surprised, it don't have to be him.

Catherine: No, we made it up already.

Eddie: [*With increasing anxiety*] Katie, wait a minute.

Catherine: No, I made up my mind.

Eddie: But you never knew no other fella, Katie! How could you make up your mind?

Catherine: Cause I did. I don't want nobody else.

Eddie: But, Katie, suppose he gets picked up.

Catherine: That's why we gonna do it right away. Soon as we finish the wedding he's goin' right over and start to be a citizen. I made up my mind, Eddie. I'm sorry. [*To* **Beatrice**] Could I take two more pillow cases for the other guys?

Beatrice: Sure, go ahead. Only don't let her forget where they came from.

[**Catherine** *goes into a bedroom.*]

Eddie: She's got other boarders up there?

Beatrice: Yeah, there's two guys that just came over.

Eddie: What do you mean, came over?

Beatrice: From Italy. Lipari the butcher—his nephew. They come from Bari, they just got here yesterday. I didn't even know till Marco and Rodolpho moved up there before. [**Catherine** *enters, going toward exit with two pillow cases*] It'll be nice, they could all talk together.

Eddie: Catherine! [*She halts near the exit door. He takes in* **Beatrice** *too*] What're you, got no brains? You put them up there with two other submarines?

Catherine: Why?

Eddie: [*In a driving fright and anger*] Why! How do you know they're not trackin' these guys? They'll come up for them and find Marco and Rodolpho! Get them out of the house!

Beatrice: But they been here so long already—

Eddie: How do you know what enemies Lipari's got? Which they'd love to stab him in the back?

Catherine: Well what'll I do with them?

Eddie: The neighborhood is full of rooms. Can't you stand to live a couple of blocks away from him? Get them out of the house!

Catherine: Well maybe tomorrow night I'll—

Eddie: Not tomorrow, do it now. Catherine, you never mix yourself with somebody's else's family! These guys get picked up, Lipari's liable to blame you or me and we got his whole family on our head. They got a temper, that family.

[*Two men in overcoats appear outside, start into the house.*]

Catherine: How'm I gonna find a place tonight?

Eddie: Will you stop arguin' with me and get them out! You think I'm always tryin' to fool you or sump'm? What's the matter with you, don't you believe I could think of your good? Did I ever ask sump'm for myself? You think I got no feelin's? I never told you nothin 'in my life that wasn't for your good. Nothin'! And look at the way you talk to me! Like I was an enemy! Like I—[*A knock on the door. His head swerves. They all stand motionless. Another knock.* **Eddie,** *in a whisper, pointing upstage*] Go up the fire escape, get them out over the back fence.

[**Catherine** *stands motionless, uncomprehending.*]

First Officer: [*In the hall*] Immigration! Open up in there!

Eddie: Go, go. Hurry up! [*She stands a moment staring at him in a realized horror*] Well, what're you lookin' at!

First Officer: Open up!

Eddie: [*Calling toward door*] Who's that there?

First Officer: Immigration, open up.

[**Eddie** *turns, looks at* **Beatrice.** *She sits. Then he looks at* **Catherine.** *With a sob of fury* **Catherine** *streaks into a bedroom.*]

[*Knock is repeated.*]

Eddie: All right, take it easy, take it easy. [*He goes and opens the door. The* **Officer** *steps inside*] What's all this?

First Officer: Where are they?

[**Second Officer** *sweeps past and, glancing about, goes into the kitchen.*]

Eddie: Where's who?

First Officer: Come on, come on, where are they? [*He hurries into the bedrooms.*]

Eddie: Who? We got nobody here. [*He looks at* **Beatrice**, *who turns her head away. Pugnaciously, furious, he steps toward* **Beatrice**] What's the matter with *you?*

[**First Officer** *enters from the bedroom, calls to the kitchen.*]

First Officer: Dominick?

[*Enter* **Second Officer** *from kitchen.*]

Second Officer: Maybe it's a different apartment.

First Officer: There's only two more floors up there. I'll take the front, you go up the fire escape. I'll let you in. Watch your step up there.

Second Officer: Okay, right, Charley. [**First Officer** *goes out apartment door and runs up the stairs*] This is Four-forty-one, isn't it?

Eddie: That's right.

[**Second Officer** *goes out into the kitchen.*]

[**Eddie** *turns to* **Beatrice**. *She looks at him now and sees his terror.*]

Beatrice: [*Weakened with fear*] Oh, Jesus, Eddie.

Eddie: What's the matter with *you?*

Beatrice: [*Pressing her palms against her face*] Oh, my God, my God.

Eddie: What're you, accusin' me?

Beatrice: [*Her final thrust is to turn toward him instead of running from him*] My God, what did you do?

[*Many steps on the outer stair draw his attention. We see the* **First Officer** *descending, with* **Marco**, *behind him* **Rodolpho**, *and* **Catherine** *and the two strange* **Immigrants**, *followed by* **Second Officer. Beatrice** *hurries to door.*]

Catherine: [*Backing down stairs, fighting with* **First Officer**; *as they appear on the stairs*] What do yiz want from them? They work, that's all. They're boarders upstairs, they work on the piers.

Beatrice: [*To* **First Officer**] Ah, Mister, what do you want from them, who do they hurt?

Catherine: [*Pointing to* **Rodolpho**] They ain't no submarines, he was born in Philadelphia.

First Officer: Step aside, lady.

Catherine: What do you mean? You can't just come in a house and—

First Officer: All right, take it easy. [*To* **Rodolpho**] What street were you born in Philadelphia?

Catherine: What do you mean, what street? Could you tell me what street you were born?

First Officer: Sure. Four blocks away, one-eleven Union Street. Let's go fellas.

Catherine: [*Fending him off* **Rodolpho**] No, you can't! Now, get outa here!

First Officer: Look, girlie, if they're all right they'll be out tomorrow. If they're illegal they go back where they came from. If you want, get yourself a lawyer, although I'm tellin' you now you're wasting your money. Let's get them in the car, Dom. [*To the men*] Andiamo, Andiamo, let's go.

[*The men start, but* **Marco** *hangs back.*]

Beatrice: [*From doorway*] Who're they hurtin', for God's sake, what do you want from them? They're starvin' over there, what do you want! Marco!

[**Marco** *suddenly breaks from the group and dashes into the room and faces* **Eddie; Beatrice** *and* **First Officer** *rush in as* **Marco** *spits into* **Eddie**'s *face.*]

[**Catherine** *runs into hallway and throws herself into* **Rodolpho**'s *arms.* **Eddie**, *with an enraged cry, lunges for* **Marco**.]

Eddie: Oh, you mother's—!

[**First Officer** *quickly intercedes and pushes* **Eddie** *from* **Marco**, *who stands there accusingly.*]

First Officer: [*Between them, pushing* **Eddie** *from* **Marco**] Cut it out!

Eddie: [*Over the* **First Officer**'s *shoulder, to* **Marco**] I'll kill you for that, you son of a bitch!

First Officer: Hey! [*Shakes him*] Stay in here now, don't come out, don't bother him. You hear me? Don't come out, fella.

[*For an instant there is silence. Then* **First Officer** *turns and takes* **Marco**'s *arm and then gives a last, informative look at* **Eddie**. *As he and* **Marco** *are going out into the hall,* **Eddie** *erupts.*]

Eddie: I don't forget that, Marco! You hear what I'm sayin'?

[*Out in the hall,* **First Officer** *and* **Marco** *go down the stairs. Now, in the street,* **Louis, Mike**, *and several neighbors including the butcher,* **Lipari**—*a stout, intense, middle-aged man—are gathering around the stoop.*]

[**Lipari**, *the butcher, walks over to the two strange men and kisses them.* **His wife**, *keening, goes and* *kisses their hands.* **Eddie** *is emerging from the house shouting after* **Marco. Beatrice** *is trying to restrain him.*]

Eddie: That's the thanks I get? Which I took the blankets off my bed for yiz? You gonna apologize to me, Marco! *Marco!*

First Officer: [*In the doorway with* **Marco**] All right, lady, let them go. Get in the car, fellas, it's over there.

[**Rodolpho** *is almost carrying the sobbing* **Catherine** *off up the street, left.*]

Catherine: He was born in Philadelphia! What do you want from him?

First Officer: Step aside, lady, come on now . . .

[*The* **Second Officer** *has moved off with the two strange men.* **Marco,** *taking advantage of the* **First Officer**'s *being occupied with* **Catherine,** *suddenly frees himself and points back at* **Eddie.**]

Marco: That one! I accuse that one!

[**Eddie** *brushes* **Beatrice** *aside and rushes out to the stoop.*]

First Officer: [*Grabbing him and moving him quickly off up the left street*] Come on!

Marco: [*As he is taken off, pointing back at* **Eddie**] That one! He killed my children! That one stole the food from my children!

[**Marco** *is gone. The crowd has turned to* **Eddie.**]

Eddie: [*To* **Lipari** *and* **wife**] He's crazy! I give them the blankets off my bed. Six months I kept them like my own brothers!

[**Lipari,** *the butcher, turns and starts up left with his arm around his wife.*]

Eddie: Lipari! [*He follows* **Lipari** *up left*] For Christ's sake, I kept them, I give them the blankets off my bed!

[**Lipari** *and* **wife** *exit.* **Eddie** *turns and starts crossing down right to* **Louis** *and* **Mike.**]

Eddie: Louis! *Louis!*

[*Louis barely turns, then walks off and exits down right with* **Mike.** *Only* **Beatrice** *is left on the stoop.* **Catherine** *now returns, blank-eyed, from offstage and the car.* **Eddie** *calls after* **Louis** *and* **Mike.**]

Eddie: He's gonna take that back. He's gonna take that back or I'll kill him! You hear me? I'll kill him! I'll kill him! [*He exits up street calling.*]

[*There is a pause of darkness before the lights rise, on the reception room of a prison.* **Marco**

is seated; **Alfieri, Catherine,** *and* **Rodolpho** *standing.*]

Alfieri: I'm waiting, Marco, what do you say?

Rodolpho: Marco never hurt anybody.

Alfieri: I can bail you out until your hearing comes up. But I'm not going to do it, you understand me? Unless I have your promise. You're an honorable man, I will believe your promise. Now what do you say?

Marco: In my country he would be dead now. He would not live this long.

Alfieri: All right, Rodolpho—you come with me now.

Rodolpho: No! Please, Mister. Marco—promise the man. Please, I want you to watch the wedding. How can I be married and you're in here? Please, you're not going to do anything; you know you're not.

[**Marco** *is silent.*]

Catherine: [*Kneeling left of* **Marco**] Marco, don't you understand? He can't bail you out if you're gonna do something bad. To hell with Eddie. Nobody is gonna talk to him again if he lives to a hundred. Everybody knows you spit in his face, that's enough, isn't it? Give me the satisfaction—I want you at the wedding. You got a wife and kids, Marco. You could be workin' till the hearing comes up, instead of layin' around here.

Marco: [*To* **Alfieri**] I have no chance?

Alfieri: [*Crosses to behind* **Marco**] No, Marco. You're going back. The hearing is a formality, that's all.

Marco: But him? There is a chance, eh?

Alfieri: When she marries him he can start to become an American. They permit that, if the wife is born here.

Marco: [*Looking at* **Rodolpho**] Well—we did something. [*He lays a palm on* **Rodolpho**'s *arm and* **Rodolpho** *covers it.*]

Rodolpho: Marco, tell the man.

Marco: [*Pulling his hand away*] What will I tell him? He knows such a promise is dishonorable.

Alfieri: To promise not to kill is not dishonorable.

Marco: [*Looking at* **Alfieri**] No?

Alfieri: No.

Marco: [*Gesturing with his head—this is a new idea*]

Then what is done with such a man?

Alfieri: Nothing. If he obeys the law, he lives. That's all.

Marco: [*Rises, turns to* **Alfieri**] The law? All the law is not in a book.

Alfieri: Yes. In a book. There is no other law.

Marco: [*His anger rising*] He degraded my brother. My blood. He robbed my children, he mocks my work. I work to come here, mister!

Alfieri: I know, Marco—

Marco: There is no law for that? Where is the law for that?

Alfieri: There is none.

Marco: [*Shaking his head, sitting*] I don't understand this country.

Alfieri: Well? What is your answer? You have five or six weeks you could work. Or else you sit here. What do you say to me?

Marco: [*Lowers his eyes. It almost seems he is ashamed*] All right.

Alfieri: You won't touch him. This is your promise.

[*Slight pause.*]

Marco: Maybe he wants to apologize to me.

[**Marco** *is staring away.* **Alfieri** *takes one of his hands.*]

Alfieri: This is not God, Marco. You hear? Only God makes justice.

Marco: All right.

Alfieri: [*Nodding, not with assurance*] Good! Catherine, Rodolpho, Marco, let us go.

[**Catherine** *kisses* **Rodolpho** *and* **Marco,** *then kisses* **Alfieri**'*s hand.*]

Catherine: I'll get Beatrice and meet you at the church. [*She leaves quickly.*]

[**Marco** *rises.* **Rodolpho** *suddenly embraces him.* **Marco** *pats him on the back and* **Rodolpho** *exits after* **Catherine.** **Marco** *faces* **Alfieri.**]

Alfieri: Only God, Marco.

[**Marco** *turns and walks out.* **Alfieri** *with a certain processional tread leaves the stage. The lights dim out.*]

[*The lights rise in the apartment.* **Eddie** *is alone in the rocker, rocking back and forth in little surges. Pause. Now* **Beatrice** *emerges from a bedroom. She is in her best clothes, wearing a hat.*]

Beatrice: [*With fear, going to* **Eddie**] I'll be back in about an hour, Eddie. All right?

Eddie: [*Quietly, almost inaudibly, as though drained*] What, have I been talkin' to myself?

Beatrice: Eddie, for God's sake, it's her wedding.

Eddie: Didn't you hear what I told you? You walk out that door to that wedding you ain't comin' back here, Beatrice.

Beatrice: Why! What do you want?

Eddie: I want my respect. Didn't you ever hear of that? From my wife?

[**Catherine** *enters from bedroom.*]

Catherine: It's after three; we're supposed to be there already, Beatrice. The priest won't wait.

Beatrice: Eddie. It's her wedding. There'll be nobody there from her family. For my sister let me go. I'm goin' for my sister.

Eddie: [*As though hurt*] Look, I been arguin' with you all day already, Beatrice, and I said what I'm gonna say. He's gonna come here and apologize to me or nobody from this house is goin' into that church today. Now if that's more to you than I am, then go. But don't come back. You be on my side or on their side, that's all.

Catherine: [*Suddenly*] Who the hell do you think you are?

Beatrice: Sssh!

Catherine: You got no more right to tell nobody nothin'! Nobody! The rest of your life, nobody!

Beatrice: Shut up, Katie! [*She turns* **Catherine** *around.*]

Catherine: You're gonna come with me!

Beatrice: I can't Katie, I can't . . .

Catherine: How can you listen to him? This rat!

Beatrice: [*Shaking* **Catherine**] Don't you call him that!

Catherine: [*Clearing from* **Beatrice**] What're you scared of? He's a rat! He belongs in the sewer!

Beatrice: Stop it!

Catherine: [*Weeping*] He bites people when they sleep! He comes when nobody's lookin' and poisons decent people. In the garbage he belongs!

[**Eddie** *seems about to pick up the table and fling it at her.*]

Beatrice: No, Eddie! Eddie! [*To* **Catherine**] Then we all belong in the garbage. You, and me too. Don't say that. Whatever happened we all done it, and don't you ever forget it, Catherine. [*She goes to* **Catherine**] Now go, go to your wedding, Katie, I'll stay home. Go. God bless you, God bless your children.

[*Enter* **Rodolpho.**]

Rodolpho: Eddie?

Eddie: Who said you could come in here? Get outa here!

Rodolpho: Marco is coming, Eddie. [*Pause. Beatrice raises her hands in terror*] He's praying in the church. You understand? [*Pause.* **Rodolpho** *advances into the room*] Catherine, I think it is better we go. Come with me.

Catherine: Eddie, go away, please.

Beatrice: [*Quietly*] Eddie. Let's go someplace. Come. You and me. [*He has not moved*] I don't want you to be here when he comes. I'll get your coat.

Eddie: Where? Where am I goin'? This is my house.

Beatrice: [*Crying out*] What's the use of it! He's crazy now, you know the way they get, what good is it. You got nothin' against Marco, you always liked Marco!

Eddie: I got nothin' against Marco? Which he called me a rat in front of the whole neighborhood? Which he said I killed his children! Where you been?

Rodolpho: [*Quite suddenly, stepping up to* **Eddie**] It is my fault, Eddie. Everything. I wish to apologize. It was wrong that I do not ask your permission. I kiss your hand. [*He reaches for* **Eddie**'s *hand, but* **Eddie** *snaps it away from him.*]

Beatrice: Eddie, he's apologizing!

Rodolpho: I have made all our troubles. But you have insult me too. Maybe God understand why you did that to me. Maybe you did not mean to insult me at all—

Beatrice: Listen to him! Eddie, listen what he's tellin' you!

Rodolpho: I think, maybe when Marco comes, if we can tell him we are comrades now, and we have no more argument between us. Then maybe Marco will not—

Eddie: Now, listen—

Catherine: Eddie, give him a chance!

Beatrice: What do you want! Eddie, what do you want!

Eddie: I want my name! He didn't take my name; he's only a punk. Marco's got my name —[*to* **Rodolpho**] and you can run tell him, kid, that he's gonna give it back to me in front of this neighborhood, or we have it out. [*Hoisting up his pants*] Come on, where is he? Take me to him.

Beatrice: Eddie, listen—

Eddie: I heard enough! Come on, let's go!

Beatrice: Only blood is good? He kissed your hand!

Eddie: What he does don't mean nothin' to nobody! [*To* **Rodolpho**] Come on!

Beatrice: [*Barring his way to the stairs*] What's gonna mean somethin'? Eddie, listen to me. Who could give you your name? Listen to me, I love you, I'm talkin' to you, I love you; if Marco'll kiss your hand outside, if he goes on his knees, what is he got to give you? That's not what you want.

Eddie: Don't bother me!

Beatrice: You want somethin' else, Eddie, and you can never have her!

Catherine: [*In horror*] B.!

Eddie: [*Shocked, horrified, his fists clenching*] Beatrice!

[**Marco** *appears outside, walking toward the door from a distant point.*]

Beatrice: [*Crying out, weeping*] The truth is not as bad as blood, Eddie! I'm tellin' you the truth—tell her good-by forever!

Eddie: [*Crying out in agony*] That's what you think of me—that I would have such a thought? [*His fists clench his head as though it will burst.*]

Marco: [*Calling near the door outside*] Eddie Carbone!

[**Eddie** *swerves about; all stand transfixed for an instant. People appear outside.*]

Eddie: [*As though flinging his challenge*] Yeah, Marco! Eddie Carbone. Eddie Carbone. Eddie Carbone. [*He goes up the stairs and emerges from the apartment.* **Rodolpho** *streaks up and out past him and runs to* **Marco.**]

Rodolpho: No, Marco, please! Eddie, please, he has children! You will kill a family!

Beatrice: Go in the house! Eddie, go in the house!

Eddie: [*He gradually comes to address the people*] Maybe he comes to apologize to me. Heh, Marco? For what you said about me in front of the neighborhood? [*He is incensing himself and little bits of laughter even escape him as his eyes are murderous and he cracks his knuckles in his hands with a strange sort of relaxation*] He knows that ain't right. To do like that? To a man? Which I put my roof over their head and my food in their mouth? Like in the Bible? Strangers I never seen in my whole life? To come out of the water and grab a girl for a passport? To go and take from your own family like from the stable—and never a word to me? And now accusations in the bargain! [*Directly to* **Marco**] Wipin' the neighborhood with my name like a dirty rag! I want my name, Marco. [*He is moving now, carefully, toward* **Marco**] Now gimme my name and we go together to the wedding.

Beatrice *and* **Catherine:**   [*Keening*] Eddie! Eddie, don't! Eddie!

Eddie: No, Marco knows what's right from wrong. Tell the people, Marco, tell them what a liar you are! [*He has his arms spread and* **Marco** *is spreading his*] Come on, liar, you know what you done! [*He lunges for* **Marco** *as a great hushed shout goes up from the people.*]

   [**Marco** *strikes* **Eddie** *beside the neck.*]

Marco: Animal! You go on your knees to me! [**Eddie** *goes down with the blow and* **Marco** *starts to raise a foot to stomp him when* **Eddie** *springs a knife into his hand and* **Marco** *steps back.* **Louis** *rushes in toward* **Eddie.**]

Louis: Eddie, for Christ's sake!

   [**Eddie** *raises the knife and* **Louis** *halts and steps back.*]

Eddie: You lied about me, Marco. Now say it. Come on now, say it!

Marco: Anima-a-a-l!

   [**Eddie** *lunges with the knife.* **Marco** *grabs his arm, turning the blade inward and pressing it home as the women and* **Louis** *and* **Mike** *rush in and separate them, and* **Eddie,** *the knife still in his hand, falls to his knees before* **Marco.** *The two women support him for a moment, calling his name again and again.*]

Catherine: Eddie I never meant to do nothing bad to you.

Eddie: Then why—Oh, B.!

Beatrice: Yes, yes!

Eddie: My B.!

   [*He dies in her arms, and* **Beatrice** *covers him with her body.* **Alfieri,** *who is in the crowd, turns out to the audience. The lights have gone down, leaving him in a glow, while behind him the dull prayers of the people and the keening of the women continue.*]

Alfieri: Most of the time now we settle for half and I like it better. But the truth is holy, and even as I know how wrong he was, and his death useless, I tremble, for I confess that something perversely pure calls to me from his memory—not purely good, but himself purely, for he allowed himself to be wholly known and for that I think I will love him more than all my sensible clients. And yet, it is better to settle for half, it must be! And so I mourn him—I admit it—with a certain . . . alarm.

CURTAIN

*A Discussion
of the Script*

In the long run, whether a play may or may not be properly termed a tragedy is far less important than its effectiveness in the theatre. How effective is *A View from the Bridge?* Most theatregoers have found it deeply moving indeed, and much of this theatrical power is communicated in the reading. Clearly interest centers on Eddie Carbone, the play's protagonist—on what he is trying to do, the means by which he tries to do it, and the final defeat which engulfs him. Arthur Miller has indicated that his chief interest as a playwright lies in placing a human being in circumstances under which he is prepared, if necessary, to risk everything, including his very life. "It is necessary ... not only to depict why a man does what he does, or why he nearly didn't do it, but why he cannot simply walk away and say to hell with it." Miller asserts that the most penetrating drama lies in the depiction of such moments. Certainly this is true of Eddie Carbone. Eddie achieves true stature and dignity as a human being precisely as he moves inevitably towards his own doom; he devotes his life to certain principles, and lays down his life when these principles come into irresolvable conflict. Even though few would pursue these same values as relentlessly as Eddie does, one can admire him for his devotion, suffer with him for his agony, and stand in awe of the overpowering forces which ultimately defeat him.

The structure of *A View from the Bridge* is more than usually interesting, for it may be analyzed in two totally different, and yet equally penetrating, ways. On the one hand, the play yields rather easily to analysis as a well-made play. The central action may simply be stated as "to keep Catherine," since Eddie devotes himself utterly to this goal throughout the play, and the other characters react in their various capacities to the same goal. The play begins with exposition, as the situation in which Eddie and his family find themselves, before the arrival of their cousins, is clearly established. The fact that Catherine has just been offered a job is used as a device to allow the audience to see Eddie's overprotective attitude toward her, and his concern with the way she dresses, the way she behaves, and the people she associates with may give some early insight into Eddie's barely suppressed incestuous craving. The "incest" is perhaps somewhat mitigated by the fact that Catherine is technically his niece rather than his daughter, but the father-daughter relationship, in which they have lived for so many years, is clearly established, precisely for the purpose of portraying the shock with which it will be violated. As soon as these relationships are fully established and the necessary background information has been supplied, the playwright is ready for his inciting incident—the introduction of Marco and Rodolpho into the Carbone household. From this moment the central action is clearly under way, for Eddie senses at once the threat that Rodolpho constitutes for him and moves to counteract this threat—to keep Catherine.

The rising action consists of the many complications which necessarily arise from the presence of Marco and Rodolpho. As Catherine and Rodolpho begin to fall in love with each other, as Eddie and Marco come more and more into conflict, as Beatrice moves rather ineffectually to deal with the crisis which she sees approaching, as Eddie actually drives the young lovers toward each other by his frantic efforts to keep them apart, the plot builds with an awful sense of inevitability toward its turning point. Eddie has one possible way to get his cousins out of his home, but an action of this kind violates the moral code which has been so clearly established from the beginning of the play. Even law-abiding spectators are made to feel that to report an illegal immigrant to the governmental authorities is an act of cowardice and betrayal which totally violates the mores of the community. Yet, Eddie takes this ultimate step when he finds himself with no viable alternative, and, once he has done so, the action rushes precipitately towards its inevitable climax. The falling action of the play captures most effectively Eddie's horror as he struggles with the knowledge of what he has done—of the inevitable results, not only for Marco and Rodolpho, but also for Lipari's two relatives and, ultimately, for Catherine, whom he genuinely loves. Eddie is powerless to do anything constructive at this point, however, and he merely succeeds in betraying his own guilt. The immigrants are arrested, Eddie is accused, and, in a final confrontation with Marco, Eddie virtually commits suicide in a vain search for his lost honor. The moment of Eddie's death is the play's climax, and the greatly abbreviated denouement simply allows for a gradual release of tension before the play's conclusion. An analysis, in these terms, reveals Miller as a competent and effective craftsman of the well-made play, and *A View from the Bridge* may be said to gain a great deal of its effectiveness from the skillful way in which Miller has made use of the fundamental elements of this structure.

The structure of *A View from the Bridge*, however, may be viewed in another perspective altogether—one which in no way negates the analysis performed above, but which amplifies and enriches it. Miller's fascination with classical tragedy has led him to the use of several elements of that form, and these elements relate the play in a remarkable way to the foregoing study of *Oedipus the King*. In order to analyze *A View from the Bridge* as a well-made play, one must completely ignore the function of Alfieri. The lawyer actually participates in the action at several key points; but more significantly he serves as a narrator and commentator, explaining the significance of what the audience is seeing, commenting on its meaning in relation to the over-all themes of the play, and expressing his own anguish at his inability to deal effectively with Eddie's problems. Alfieri, in other words, represents an average, middleclass point of view, one which can assert at the close of the play that "most of the time now we settle for half and I like it better." What is Alfieri, in fact, but a chorus? Modern serious drama rarely makes use of a large group of chorus people singing, dancing, or chanting in unison, but there exist countless examples of one or two characters within a play whose structural function remains that of the Greek chorus. Seen in this light, Alfieri becomes much more than a narrator, and certainly more than the impediment to the action which some critics have called him. It behooves the actor playing Alfieri (as well as his director) to insure that Alfieri is not out of place or obtrusive, but rather provides the audience with a direct link to Miller's omniscient view of the significance of the action.

The parallels to Greek drama, however, do not stop at this point. *A View from the Bridge* can actually be analyzed in terms of "odes" and "episodes," and proves to be remarkably similar to the form already observed in *Oedipus the King*. Alfieri's opening speech, which sets the mood and universalizes the action, has no parallel in Greek tragedy. The first scene, however, involving Eddie, Catherine, and Beatrice may be regarded as the *prologue*, for in this scene the exposition is accomplished. When Eddie finally concedes to Catherine taking a job, the way is fully prepared for the central action to begin, and Alfieri's brief "choral ode" beginning "He was as good a man as he had to be" provides the necessary break before the first *episode*: Marco and Rodolpho enter Eddie's house. Almost from the first moment, Rodolpho and Catherine are attracted to each other, and the complications of the plot are under way. Again, as soon as the business of the episode has been completed, Alfieri as chorus provides the *ode*—the break in the action—beginning "Who can ever know what will be discovered?" The second episode is devoted largely to establishing the fact of Eddie's incestuous love, and the degree to which Beatrice and Catherine must share the responsibility for its existence. The end of this episode is marked by Alfieri's "It was at this time that he first came to me." On this occasion, however, the "choral ode" is varied by a device very commonly used in Greek tragedy, known as a *commos*—an exchange of musical lines between the protagonist and the chorus—in effect, a duet. In *A View from the Bridge*, of course, this exchange is not sung, but it provides, nevertheless, an important and necessary interlude before the third episode, and hence is structurally comparable to a commos.

The third episode brings the contest of wills among the principal characters to its peak of intensity, and sets the stage for the awful results that are quite evidently on their way. This episode concludes what Miller has called Act I, but even the most casual observer can note that there is no more structural reason for an intermission here than at the conclusion of any of the other episodes. Miller himself has spoken of "inserting" an intermission at the time the play was expanded from its one-act version, and it is apparent that, in structural terms, the intermission is, indeed, simply inserted as a concession to the physical needs of the audience rather than any significant break in the play's action. The chorus opens Act II, thus maintaining the ode-episode pattern.

Episode four finally sees matters brought to a head, as Eddie finds Catherine and Rodolpho in the bedroom together, attempts to brand Rodolpho a homosexual, climaxes his own passion for Catherine by virtually attacking her, and finally orders Rodolpho out of the house. Again, episodes four and five are separated by a commos, as Alfieri tries desperately to warn Eddie of the doom toward which he is rushing; but the commos concludes as Eddie takes the fateful step of calling the Immigration Bureau. Finally, the remainder of the play, including the last choral lines by Alfieri, constitute the *exodos*: the action is worked out to its tragic conclusion, the protagonist dies, and the play ends.

It would be inappropriate to argue that either of the analyses of plot structure offered above is "right" and the other "wrong." Probably Miller did not consciously dedicate himself to either structural pattern before beginning his work, but rather allowed his material to lead him to a form that seemed to work best for what he was trying to accomplish. Both of the above analyses are useful, however, in giving one a better understanding of the plot and how it is constructed. One sees a very careful arrangement of details, nothing missing, nothing extraneous, building up in either pattern to a gripping climax. Aristotle insisted that plot is the soul of drama, and certainly Miller has, in *A View from the Bridge*, engineered a masterly plot around which to build his play.

Characterization is also strong in *A View from the Bridge*. Interest centers primarily in Eddie Carbone, and Miller has created a penetrating portrait of a nonintrospective man who cannot understand what is happening to him. Eddie genuinely loves both his wife and his niece, and has made many sacrifices for them over the years. He has a strong sense of hospitality and generosity, in which he includes Beatrice's cousins, and wishes nothing less than the best for all concerned. His love for Catherine, however, has gone awry to the point where he cannot bear to let her go as she grows into womanhood, and he soon finds himself, against his will and without his full understanding, wanting to possess her sexually and dreading to see her in the arms of another. As the play progresses, Eddie does gain some understanding of his own suppressed desires, but he refuses to allow himself to face them squarely, as they so totally violate the acceptable norms with which he is familiar. Finally, Eddie is driven by his passion to inform the authorities of the illegal immigrants in his house, which is such a revolting violation of his own code that he is totally incapable of thinking rationally throughout the remainder of the play. Indeed, he may almost be described as committing suicide, for it is evident that he goes to meet Marco in the last scene with little thought but to secure an apology (which he knows, of course, that he is not due) or to fight a man already established as stronger than himself: death is, by this time, a desirable option.

Catherine and Beatrice are also reasonably well developed human beings. Catherine is a young woman not yet fully aware of who she is or what her place in the world might be, and she vacillates between childish and adult ways. She is sufficiently naive not to have any clear insight into what is happening to Eddie, and even to aggravate it (innocently enough) by the way she behaves toward him. Yet she is woman enough to sense Eddie's needs and hungers in the way of companionship and understanding more effectively than Beatrice (or, at least, so she tells Rodolpho). Beatrice understands Eddie's psychological problem better than Catherine does, but Beatrice feels trapped by the customs of her society which prescribe that the husband rule in the home, and she cannot take effective action to help him. In trying to warn him, she becomes a nag to the point of driving Eddie even more toward Catherine. Beatrice has, by the time of her confrontation with Catherine, seen in her a dangerous rival, but she also loves her almost as a daughter and is torn by her conflicting emotions. Ultimately, Beatrice has a clearer insight than either of the other two into what has happened and who is at fault. "Whatever happened we all done it," Beatrice points out near the end of the play.

The other characters are less fully developed, although they are certainly adequate in terms of the play. Rodolpho, although he is a pivotal figure, has relatively little to distinguish him from the young male lover in a thousand other plays, and Marco's prototype, too, is often encountered in drama. Alfieri has been described by one critic as a cross between a Greek chorus and Mary Worth, and it is fair to say that his characterization goes no deeper. The other people are merely extras, with few distinguishing characteristics. In his three central figures, Miller has done an excellent job of creating believable human beings; in other cases he has felt free to make use of stock characters or to leave characters totally undeveloped, as the needs of his script seemed to dictate.

Thematically, *A View from the Bridge* may be either rich or lean, depending upon one's point of view. Many critics hold that the fundamental forces of fate, destiny, and the gods, against which ancient tragic heroes struggled, have been replaced in the modern era by economic, social, political, and psychological forces which act upon the individual. Miller's play is devoted almost entirely to an exploration of the psychological forces that are destroying Eddie from within; there are, also, outside pressures from the community in which he lives. These psychological and social concepts are engagingly and perceptively explored, and insofar as one is satisfied with thematic material based on these values, the play is rich and meaningful. However, important as these issues are to modern life, they are not the most fundamental questions which man must answer. It may be a measure of the pettiness of modern man that he concentrates too fully upon economic, social, and political questions, when the truly vital issues of all ages consist of a renewed exploration of man's relationship to what is eternal in the universe. Whether or not he professes a specific religious faith, man forever questions the fundamental meaning and purpose of life. Not every play is obligated to deal with these more profound issues, but Miller has professed himself awed by the inevitability of the "fate" which pursues Eddie, and yet has not come to grips with this fate in his play. The play is thematically stirring, but not nearly as profound as it might be.

The language of *A View from the Bridge* is workmanlike and effective. Miller captures with rare success the argot of the waterfront, and creates a protagonist, inarticulate by nature, who nevertheless manages to make some eloquent statements about the common man. On the other hand, the language can hardly be described as elevated. Even in the earlier version, which was printed in free verse, the language form had little or no effect on the ear; in the present version, it is entirely adequate, but that is all.

Is *A View from the Bridge* a tragedy? It is not an Aristotelian tragedy, for Aristotle made it quite clear in his *Poetics* that the tragic hero must be of a noble family, and Eddie is a common man. But many critics have argued that Aristotle's definition is no longer valid, that in a democratic era any man is "noble" simply by virtue of being a man. As Miller himself has pointed out, "If rank or nobility of character was indispensable, then it would follow that the problems of those with rank were the particular problems of tragedy." Clearly, Miller argues, this has never been true. There are some far more fundamental issues involved in what constitutes tragedy than the nobility of the protagonist, and it is against these criteria (established on pages 446–447) that *A View from the Bridge* must be measured. Its plot is, indeed, of a serious nature, leading to the defeat of the protagonist, and the forces involved are of great magnitude. Eddie's character has much about it which is admirable, for he is willing to sacrifice his very life to uphold certain principles which he believes to be valid. It is far more important, however, that Eddie, even at the play's end, has no real perception of the forces which have crushed him; Beatrice has some inkling of this perception, but Eddie clearly does not. The thematic content of the play has been questioned as lacking in the profundity which would be appropriate to high tragedy; the issues are real and moving, but they are not the issues of tragedy, which must be supreme, almost sublime in their impact. The play's language is hardly elevated in the manner one expects from tragedy, although it has been argued that if one admits that a common man may be the subject of tragedy, he must also admit the language of the common man as a medium for that tragedy. The most stringent test of tragedy, however, is its emotional effect upon its audience. Certainly Eddie's predicament elicits a great deal of pity from an audience, certainly they feel fear as his inevitable doom approaches, and there is certainly some sense of being uplifted, ennobled, cleansed at Eddie's death. Catharsis is, indeed, achieved. Some critics have argued that genuine tragedy is impossible in the modern era, but *A View from the Bridge* only partially supports this view. In the strictest sense, it fails to meet certain of the fundamental criteria which mark tragedy, and hence it must at best be regarded as flawed. On the other hand, the play does achieve a degree of catharsis, it does create a powerful tragic effect in the theatre, and such an accomplishment cannot be gainsaid. *A View from the Bridge* exhibits certain strengths in common with *Oedipus the King,* but falls short of that high model in other important ways. Whether one should apply the term "tragedy" to so ambitious, but flawed, an effort is not nearly as important as being able to discern which elements constitute the play's strengths, and which its weaknesses. Such insights can be gained by measuring the play against the criteria which form a basis for judging tragedy.

Before the development of high-fidelity electronic amplification equipment, "sound" in the theatre was almost entirely a function of the property crew. Every theatre had a "thunder sheet"—a large piece of sheet metal hung in the flies—which a prop man would rattle when thunder was called for. Every theatre had rumble carts, crash boxes, door-slam devices, and numerous other special pieces of equipment for producing the sound effects which might be called for in a wide variety of plays. In addition, a great deal of imagination and effort was often required of the prop master to find ways to produce the special sound effects needed in a new play which might not be in the standard "repertoire" of sounds. Even the electronic equipment of the early part of this century did not have a marked effect on theatrical sound devices, because the reproduction quality of that equipment was so poor that more effective sounds could still be created by the traditional methods. In more recent years, however, electronic equipment has been refined to the point where, assuming a theatre can afford to buy high quality components, sound effects can be reproduced with real "living presence;" the audience cannot tell whether the sound was produced electronically or not. Assuming the availability of such equipment, there is no question that recording the necessary sounds and then playing them back is infinitely easier, more reliable, and cheaper than the use of elaborate backstage mechanisms, and thus sound equipment and a sound crew have become a permanent part of the theatrical production team. The use of such equipment has also eliminated the need for a pit orchestra to provide incidental music (which used to be a standard feature of every playhouse), and the sound crew now provides such recorded music as the director may require. Now, only theatrical productions in which music is a major factor (such as musical comedies and operettas) employ pit orchestras.

It would be inappropriate, here, to go into the complex engineering details of modern high-fidelity equipment, but it is still possible to point out the fundamentals of a typical sound system. Referring to the accompanying diagram, one can see that a signal begins at any one of several *inputs*. An input may be a microphone, which is a device for converting the vibrations of the human voice directly into very low voltage electrical signals. An input may be a tape-recorder deck, which is a de-

Sound

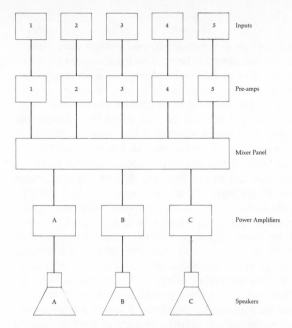

Inputs

Pre-amps

Mixer Panel

Power Amplifiers

Speakers

Schematic diagram of a
typical sound system.

vice for picking up impulses which have been stored on magnetic tape and converting
them into low voltage electrical signals. An input may be a record-player turntable,
which is a device for picking up mechanical vibrations from the grooves of a record
and converting them into low voltage electrical signals. The point is that, whatever
type of input may be involved, sound vibrations are converted into variable electrical
signals which are fed into the system. The components of the system act upon these
signals in various ways. Because these signals are very weak, they must be amplified,
and thus every input is connected directly to a small amplifier called a *pre-amplifier,*
normally shortened to *pre-amp.* Once the signal has passed through the pre-amp,
it is strong enough to be switched around and modified, as required. It is fed from
the pre-amp to the *mixer panel.* The *mixer panel* is centrally located, containing a
switching network which allows the operator to take the signal from any input and
put it into any of the output lines. If a sound system has a large number of inputs
and output lines, the mixer panel may appear to be very complicated, but actually
it performs one simple operation repeated many times. The mixer panel usually
contains volume controls, also, for each of the pre-amps, as well as volume controls
for the *power amplifiers* described below. In a more sophisticated system, the mixer
panel may also house tone controls and other more complicated devices for modify-
ing the basic signals in ways which may from time to time be desirable. The output
lines from the mixer panel lead directly to *power amplifiers,* which are high-quality
amplifiers, stepping up the signal to its final level; the signal goes from the power
amplifier directly to the *speakers* which may be located anywhere in the building.
A speaker is simply a device for converting an electrical signal back into the mechanical vibrations of sound waves. One additional modification which may appear to
complicate a very elaborate sound system is the installation of a *patch panel,* not unlike
a telephone switch board, which allows any input to be plugged into any pre-amp,
any power amplifier to be plugged into any speaker, and so forth. A panel of this
kind greatly increases the flexibility of the sound system, although a beginner may
find it incredibly complex.

For practical purposes, a sound system in a well-equipped theatre may involve many more inputs than are shown in the diagram here. The building may well be wired with microphone jacks in a number of handy locations, each terminating at the patch panel; at least two turntables and two tape decks would be useful, as well. What really makes a theatre sound system different from almost any other in common use, however, is the necessity for a large number of speaker lines capable of switching instantly from one signal to another. Consider the sound problems in producing *A View from the Bridge*, for example. There is only one sound effect which is absolutely required by the script—the music of "Paper Doll" coming from the phonograph on two occasions near the end of the first act. Miller has also called for the sound of a distant foghorn at the opening of the show, and it is entirely possible that a director might decide to add traffic or other street noises during the scenes that are supposed to take place in front of the Carbone apartment. The sound of a departing automobile might be especially appropriate at the moment when Marco, Rodolpho, and the others are taken away by the immigration authorities. Many directors would also wish to use recorded music at several points, especially as overture and entr'acte. When such a variety of effects is used, sound becomes vitally important in establishing the mood and style of the play; it must come in exactly on cue, and must be of the very highest reproduction quality. Musical recordings might well be played in the auditorium before the curtain goes up. As the lights come up on the set, perhaps the music should fade from the auditorium speakers to speakers on the stage. The foghorn effect should certainly come from a speaker located at some considerable distance from the acting area—probably far backstage. Traffic noises would need to originate off right or off left or both, depending upon the exact design of the set and where the street is supposed to be. The music "Paper Doll" must come from a phonograph actually seen on stage, and, although this could be accomplished by using a real phonograph and letting the actors control it, there is a high risk of an accident or a missed cue. It is better to have the actors only pretend to play it while the sound crew, who are located in the control booth (usually at the rear of the house) and therefore able to see the action, actually control it, as they can be sure that the right cue comes at the right time. Thus, there are at least six different locations in which speakers will be needed, and some of these locations will, in the interest of high fidelity, actually require the use of more than one speaker. The theatre sound system, then, must accommodate an extraordinarily large number of speaker lines; it is quite unlike a typical public address system which normally accommodates only one or two.

The technician in charge of sound for *A View from the Bridge* would have a fairly complicated job. Some of the speakers listed above would no doubt be permanently installed in the theatre, but others would have to be specially located with lines running to convenience outlets, or to the control booth itself. The sound effects needed for this play are all available through professional agencies, but for many plays the sound technician would have the additional problem of choosing appropriate effects and recording them. In whatever way he acquired the necessary recorded effects, the sound technician would still face the task of setting them up in the most convenient order for use in the control booth. Modern practice, almost universally, favors the use of tape recorders as they can be set for a given cue more easily and precisely than a disc. Furthermore, tape can easily be cut and spliced in order to rearrange cues to suit individual needs; a whole tape can be erased and done over with relatively little difficulty. For shows involving a large number of sound

Sound-amplification console at the New York State Theater, Lincoln Center. *The New York Times*, February 6, 1966.

cues, particularly where one follows the other with very little time lag, two tape recorders are often used, with the second tape carefully planned to contain only those sounds which must follow instantly upon sounds recorded on the first tape. By this means, the technician can fade one sound effect out and another up with no delay whatsoever, and then use the time while the second is playing to re-cue his first tape. Running one tape continuously would be easier, but often the delicate timing involved in coordinating the tape with the actors' movements precludes this convenience. For example, at the opening of the first act of *A View from the Bridge* there may well be music playing and yet simultaneously, or immediately following, the sound of a foghorn must be heard. If the foghorn were on the same tape with the music, the burden would be on all the actors and technicians to time their movements to the inexorable movement of the tape recorder, and the sound crew would have the additional problem of switching from front speakers to the distant backstage speaker at precisely the moment when the foghorn came in. With the foghorn on a separate tape, however, and its signal feeding through a separate system to the backstage speaker, the sound technician can bring the foghorn in precisely on cue, fading the music out according to prearranged plan.

Once all the procedures have been worked out in detail, the actual operation of the sound console for a production becomes a fairly straight-forward matter. Volume levels, tone levels, and timing cues need to be worked out during special technical rehearsals in much the same manner as light cues are set, and the sound technician will evolve a cue sheet that tells him, in the fullest possible detail, what to do at every moment throughout the show. The sound technician is very much like the lighting technician in that he must pay attention to the way the show is running and be sensitive to its pace and rhythm. Most sound cues are not as obvious to the audience as light cues are, for music usually fades in and out so gradually that the average spectator is not even aware of its starting and stopping. The cue for the "Paper Doll" music from the phonograph, however, is highly critical in its timing, and a sensitive sound technician can strongly reinforce this climatic moment in the first act. On the other hand, even a split second's error as the actor turns away from the phonograph could be disastrous. Thus, although the sound requirements for *A View from the Bridge* are not unduly complex, they are clearly of major importance in the over-all production. Sound is the sixth of the crucial technical areas involved in staging a play.

Many theatre artists are dissatisfied with the forms which dominate the twentieth-century theatre. They are seeking new and more effective devices to express current theatrical ideas. These devices are to be found, some believe, by returning to the roots of the several other structures which have dominated the theatre at one time or another in the past. Other artists are seeking new approaches by over-throwing much that has been used in the past. Certain modern playwrights hope, as a result of a deliberate search for new forms, to start the theatre moving again in a new and more exciting direction. The next two plays in this book are examples of radical departures from playwriting tradition. One is already established among the masterpieces of this century, the other must be regarded as distinctly experimental. One of them might turn out to be a landmark in the development of drama, heralding the discovery of an altogether new theatrical form. Despite the novelty of the forms, it will still be possible to apply old standards in evaluating their theatrical effectiveness.

Some Experimental Forms: Introductory Note

Berthold Eugen Friedrich Brecht (he changed the spelling of his first name later in life) was born in Augsburg, Germany, on February 10, 1898, the son of a paper manufacturer of considerable wealth and influence. He attended elementary and secondary schools in Augsburg and began medical studies there, but was drafted into a military hospital in 1918. His view of World War I was from this perspective; he entered the war a dedicated pacifist, and emerged from it with cynical contempt for the economic and social forces which so often have led mankind to destroy each other.

Brecht had published his first poems at the age of sixteen. After the war, he continued his literary pursuits, and at the same time became active in several of the radical political movements which swept post-war Germany. He wrote his first play, the wildly expressionistic *Baal,* in 1918; in 1919 he was elected to the Council of Workers and Soldiers of Augsburg and served as theatre critic for a Communist newspaper in the same city. This juxtaposition of politics and theatre continued throughout much of his life (Brecht usually espousing a Marxist point of view), although it is doubtful whether he was ever a member of the Communist party. He was highly critical of capitalism and free enterprise, but his artistic integrity led him to present in his works so well-rounded a criticism of these systems that it is the western world which, since World War II, has responded most enthusiastically to his works.

Throughout the 1920s and early 1930s Brecht wrote, directed, and produced plays in Augsburg, Munich, Berlin, and throughout Europe. Perhaps the best known of these in this country is *The Threepenny Opera,* which Brecht wrote with Kurt Weill in 1928, although even this play was barely known in America until its very successful off-Broadway run in the 1950s. Evidently Brecht was too well known in Germany, however, for as early as 1923 Hitler listed him among those to be eliminated, and by 1933 he was being actively sought for high treason. On the day after the Reichstag fire, Brecht escaped from Germany with his family, leaving the Nazis to burn his books and revoke his citizenship. He settled in Denmark, from which base he continued to write and to travel throughout Europe, producing his own plays and those of others. As the Nazis invaded Denmark in 1940, Brecht escaped to Finland; when the Stormtroopers

Galileo
by Bertolt Brecht

moved in there too, he traveled across Russia and sailed for California, where he settled for the duration of the war.

While living near Hollywood Brecht met Charles Laughton and collaborated with him on an English version of *Galileo*, which Brecht had written in its original form in 1938. Brecht frequently worked with collaborators, and changed his scripts as a result of the insight gained in rehearsals and performances; he adapted material from other writers and constantly revised his own, so that it is virtually impossible to settle upon an authoritative text of any of his plays. Nevertheless, the version of *Galileo* presented here may be assumed to be as nearly authoritative as anything of Brecht's in English, as it was prepared under his own direction and at a time when he was fairly familiar with the language. It was first performed on July 31, 1947, in Hollywood with Laughton in the title role, and later moved to New York. The times were inauspicious for a Brecht play in this country, however, and it did not enjoy a long run. Shortly before the play opened in New York, Brecht was invited to testify before the House Un-American Activities Committee in Washington because of his alleged Communist connections. He was congratulated by the committee's chairman for being a cooperative witness, but he left the United States for Switzerland within a few days. He waited in Zurich for several months for permission to settle in Munich, but when that was not forthcoming he obtained a Czech passport and a Swiss bank account and emigrated to East Berlin, where he soon became a leading cultural figure. His Berliner Ensemble was one of the outstanding theatrical companies of postwar Europe, and it was there that, with his wife Helene Weigel in several of the leading roles, he staged the remaining works on which his fame chiefly rests.

Brecht is important in the twentieth-century theatre not only as playwright, director, and producer, but also as a theoretician. His writings about the theatre are much too complex to be analyzed here. He often took extreme theoretical positions which his practice did not bear out, but his theories still constitute an important key to the full understanding of his plays, and certain aspects of them will be touched upon in connection with the discussion of *Galileo*. Brecht was restless under a Communist regime despite his impassioned advocacy of many Marxist theories, and he was evidently preparing once again to emigrate to Denmark, when the tuberculosis with which he had been stricken during his early years finally ended his life. He died at his home in East Berlin on August 14, 1956, after attending a performance of *Galileo*.

Page 502: Galileo, scene IV. Aline McMahon (Mrs. Sarti), Charles Abruzzo (Prince Cosimo de Medici), Anthony Quayle (Galileo Galilei), Alan Cabal (Andrea Sarti), Robert Symonds (Federzoni) in the Charles Laughton version staged by John Hirsch, settings by Robin Wagner, costumes by James Hart Stearns, lighting by Martin Aronstein, presented by The Repertory Theater of Lincoln Center, 1967. Photograph: Martha Swope.

Page 506: Galileo, scene XI, from the same production. The Cardinal Inquistor (Sheppard Strudwick) stands with his back to Cardinal Barberini (Ted van Griethuysen) as he waits for the monks (at rear) to dress him as Pope. Photograph: Martha Swope.

Galileo

BERTOLT BRECHT

English Version by
CHARLES LAUGHTON

It is my opinion that the earth is very noble and admirable by reason of so many and so different alterations and generations which are incessantly made therein.

—GALILEO GALILEI

Galileo Galilei
Andrea Sarti, two actors: boy and man
Mrs. Sarti
Ludovico Marsili
Priuli, the Curator
Sagredo, Galileo's friend
Virginia Galilei
Two Senators
Matti, an iron founder
Philosopher, later, Rector of the University
Elderly Lady
Young Lady
Federzoni, assistant to Galileo
Mathematician
Lord Chamberlain
Fat Prelate
Two Scholars
Two Monks
Infuriated Monk
Old Cardinal
Attendant Monk
Christopher Clavius
Fulganzio, the Little Monk
Two Secretaries
Cardinal Bellarmin
Cardinal Barberini, later, Pope Urban VIII
Cardinal Inquisitor
Young Girl
Her Friend
Giuseppe
Ballad Singer
His Wife
Reveller
A Loud Voice
Informer
Town Crier
Official
Peasant

Customs Officer
Boy
Senators, Officials, Professors, Artisans, Ladies,
Guests, Children

There are two wordless roles: The *Doge* in
Scene II and *Prince Cosimo De' Medici* in
Scene IV. The ballad of Scene IX is filled
out by a pantomime: among the individuals in the pantomimic crowd are three
extras (including the *"King of Hungary"*),
*Cobbler's Boy, Three Children, Peasant
Woman, Monk, Rich Couple, Dwarf, Beggar,*
and *Girl.*

SCENE I

In the year sixteen hundred and nine
Science' light began to shine.
At Padua City, in a modest house,
Galileo Galilei set out to prove
The sun is still, the earth is on the move.

GALILEO'S SCANTILY FURNISHED STUDY.   Morning.
Galileo is washing himself. A barefooted boy,
Andrea, son of his housekeeper, **Mrs. Sarti,**
enters with a big astronomical model.

Galileo: Where did you get that thing?
Andrea: The coachman brought it.
Galileo: Who sent it?
Andrea: It said "From the Court of Naples" on
the box.
Galileo: I don't want their stupid presents. Illuminated manuscripts, a statue of Hercules
the size of an elephant—they never send
money.
Andrea: But isn't this an astronomical instrument, Mr. Galilei?
Galileo: That is an antique too. An expensive
toy.
Andrea: What's it for?
Galileo: It's a map of the sky according to the
wise men of ancient Greece. Bosh! We'll try
and sell it to the university. They still teach
it there.
Andrea: How does it work, Mr. Galilei?
Galileo: It's complicated.

Andrea: I think I could understand it.
Galileo: [*Interested*] Maybe. Let's begin at the
beginning. Description!
Andrea: There are metal rings, a lot of them.
Galileo: How many?
Andrea: Eight.
Galileo: Correct. And?
Andrea: There are words painted on the
bands.
Galileo: What words?
Andrea: The names of stars.
Galileo: Such as?
Andrea: Here is a band with the sun on it and
on the inside band is the moon.
Galileo: Those metal bands represent crystal
globes, eight of them.
Andrea: Crystal?
Galileo: Like huge soap bubbles one inside the
other and the stars are supposed to be tacked
onto them. Spin the band with the sun on it.
[**Andrea** *does so*] You see the fixed ball in the
middle?
Andrea: Yes.
Galileo: That's the earth. For two thousand
years man has chosen to believe that the sun
and all the host of stars revolve about him.
Well. The Pope, the cardinals, the princes, the
scholars, captains, merchants, housewives,
have pictured themselves squatting in the
middle of an affair like that.
Andrea: Locked up inside?
Galileo: [*Triumphant*] Ah!
Andrea: It's like a cage.
Galileo: So you sensed that. [*Standing near the
model*] I like to think the ships began it.
Andrea: Why?
Galileo: They used to hug the coasts and then
all of a sudden they left the coasts and spread
over the oceans. A new age was coming. I was
onto it years ago. I was a young man, in Siena.
There was a group of masons arguing. They
had to raise a block of granite. It was hot. To
help matters, one of them wanted to try a
new arrangement of ropes. After five minutes'
discussion, out went a method which had
been employed for a thousand years. The
millennium of faith is ended, said I, this is the
millennium of doubt. And we are pulling out
of that contraption. The sayings of the wise

men won't wash any more. Everybody, at last, is getting nosy. I predict that in our time astronomy will become the gossip of the market place and the sons of fishwives will pack the schools.

Andrea: You're off again, Mr. Galilei. Give me the towel.

[*He wipes some soap from* **Galileo's** *back.*]

Galileo: By that time, with any luck, they will be learning that the earth rolls round the sun, and that their mothers, the captains, the scholars, the princes, and the Pope are rolling with it.

Andrea: That turning-around business is no good. I can see with my own eyes that the sun comes up one place in the morning and goes down in a different place in the evening. It doesn't stand still—I can see it move.

Galileo: You see nothing, all you do is gawk. Gawking is not seeing. [*He puts the iron washstand in the middle of the room*] Now—that's the sun. Sit down. [**Andrea** *sits on a chair.* **Galileo** *stands behind him*] Where is the sun, on your right or on your left?

Andrea: Left.

Galileo: And how will it get to the right?

Andrea: By your putting it there, of course.

Galileo: Of course? [*He picks* **Andrea** *up, chair and all, and carries him round to the other side of the washstand*] Now where is the sun?

Andrea: On the right.

Galileo: And did it move?

Andrea: I did.

Galileo: Wrong. Stupid! The chair moved.

Andrea: But I was on it.

Galileo: Of course. The chair is the earth, and you're sitting on it.

[**Mrs. Sarti,** *who has come in with a glass of milk and a roll, has been watching.*]

Mrs. Sarti: What are you doing with my son, Mr. Galilei?

Andrea: Now, mother, you don't understand.

Mrs. Sarti: You understand, don't you? Last night he tried to tell me that the earth goes round the sun. You'll soon have him saying that two times two is five.

Galileo: [*Eating his breakfast*] Apparently we are on the threshold of a new era, Mrs. Sarti.

Mrs. Sarti: Well, I hope we can pay the milkman in this new era. A young gentleman is here to take private lessons and he is well-dressed and don't you frighten him away like you did the others. Wasting your time with Andrea! [*To* **Andrea**] How many times have I told you not to wheedle free lessons out of Mr. Galilei? [*She goes.*]

Galileo: So you thought enough of the turning-around business to tell your mother about it.

Andrea: Just to surprise her.

Galileo: Andrea, I wouldn't talk about our ideas outside.

Andrea: Why not?

Galileo: Certain of the authorities won't like it.

Andrea: Why not, if it's the truth?

Galileo: [*Laughs*] Because we are like the worms who are little and have dim eyes and can hardly see the stars at all, and the new astronomy is a framework of guesses or very little more—yet.

[**Mrs. Sarti** *shows in* **Ludovico Marsili,** *a presentable young man.*]

Galileo: This house is like a market place. [*Pointing to the model*] Move that out of the way! Put it down there!

[**Ludovico** *does so.*]

Ludovico: Good morning, sir. My name is Ludovico Marsili.

Galileo: [*Reading a letter of recommendation he has brought*] You came by way of Holland and your family lives in the Campagna? Private lessons, thirty scudi a month.

Ludovico: That's all right, of course, sir.

Galileo: What is your subject?

Ludovico: Horses.

Galileo: Aha.

Ludovico: I don't understand science, sir.

Galileo: Aha.

Ludovico: They showed me an instrument like that in Amsterdam. You'll pardon me, sir, but it didn't make sense to me at all.

Galileo: It's out of date now.

[**Andrea** *goes.*]

Ludovico: You'll have to be patient with me, sir. Nothing in science makes sense to me.

Galileo: Aha.

Ludovico: I saw a brand-new instrument in Amsterdam. A tube affair. "See things five times as large as life!" It had two lenses, one at each end, one lens bulged and the other was like that. [*Gesture*] Any normal person would think that different lenses cancel each other out. They didn't! I just stood and looked a fool.

Galileo: I don't quite follow you. What does one see enlarged?

Ludovico: Church steeples, pigeons, boats. Anything at a distance.

Galileo: Did you yourself—see things enlarged?

Ludovico: Yes, sir.

Galileo: And the tube had two lenses? Was it like this?

> [*He has been making a sketch.*]
> [**Ludovico** *nods.*]

Galileo: A recent invention?

Ludovico: It must be. They only started peddling it on the streets a few days before I left Holland.

Galileo: [*Starts to scribble calculations on the sketch; almost friendly*] Why do you bother your head with science? Why don't you just breed horses?

> [*Enter* **Mrs. Sarti.** **Galileo** *doesn't see her. She listens to the following.*]

Ludovico: My mother is set on the idea that science is necessary nowadays for conversation.

Galileo: Aha. You'll find Latin or philosophy easier. [**Mrs. Sarti** *catches his eye*] I'll see you on Tuesday afternoon.

Ludovico: I shall look forward to it, sir.

Galileo: Good morning. [*He goes to the window and shouts into the street*] Andrea! Hey, Redhead, Redhead!

Mrs. Sarti: The curator of the museum is here to see you.

Galileo: Don't look at me like that. I took him, didn't I?

Mrs. Sarti: I caught your eye in time.

Galileo: Show the curator in.

> [*She goes. He scribbles something on a new sheet of paper. The* **Curator** *comes in.*]

Curator: Good morning, Mr. Galilei.

Galileo: Lend me a scudo. [*He takes it and goes to the window, wrapping the coin in the paper on which he has been scribbling*] Redhead, run to the spectacle-maker and bring me two lenses; here are the measurements. [*He throws the paper out the window. During the following scene* **Galileo** *studies his sketch of the lenses.*]

Curator: Mr. Galilei, I have come to return your petition for an honorarium. Unfortunately I am unable to recommend your request.

Galileo: My good sir, how can I make ends meet on five hundred scudi?

Curator: What about your private students?

Galileo: If I spend all my time with students, when am I to study? My particular science is on the threshold of important discoveries. [*He throws a manuscript on the table*] Here are my findings on the laws of falling bodies. That should be worth two hundred scudi.

Curator: I am sure that any paper of yours is of infinite worth, Mr. Galilei. . . .

Galileo: I was limiting it to two hundred scudi.

Curator: [*Cool*] Mr. Galilei, if you want money and leisure, go to Florence. I have no doubt Prince Cosimo de' Medici will be glad to subsidize you, but eventually you will be forbidden to think—in the name of the Inquisition. [**Galileo** *says nothing*] Now let us not make a mountain out of a molehill. You are happy here in the Republic of Venice but you need money. Well, that's human, Mr. Galilei. May I suggest a simple solution? You remember that chart you made for the army to extract cube roots without any knowledge of mathematics? Now that was practical!

Galileo: Bosh!

Curator: Don't say bosh about something that astounded the Chamber of Commerce. Our city elders are businessmen. Why don't you invent something useful that will bring them a little profit?

Galileo: [*Playing with the sketch of the lenses; suddenly*] I see. Mr. Priuli, I may have something for you.

Curator: You don't say so.

Galileo: It's not quite there yet, but . . .

Curator: You've never let me down yet, Galilei.

Galileo: You are always an inspiration to me, Priuli.

Curator: You are a great man: a discontented man, but I've always said you are a great man.

Galileo: [*Tartly*] My discontent, Priuli, is for the most part with myself. I am forty-six years of age and have achieved nothing which satisfies me.

Curator: I won't disturb you any further.

Galileo: Thank you. Good morning.

Curator: Good morning. And thank you.

> [*He goes.* **Galileo** *sighs.* **Andrea** *returns, bringing lenses.*]

Andrea: One scudo was not enough. I had to leave my cap with him before he'd let me take them away.

Galileo: We'll get it back someday. Give them to me. [*He takes the lenses over to the window, holding them in the relation they would have in a telescope.*]

Andrea: What are those for?

Galileo: Something for the Senate. With any luck, they will rake in two hundred scudi. Take a look!

Andrea: My, things look close! I can read the copper letters on the bell in the Campanile. And the washer-women by the river, I can see their washboards!

Galileo: Get out of the way. [*Looking through the lenses himself*] Aha!

SCENE II

> *No one's virtue is complete:*
> *Great Galileo liked to eat.*
> *You will not resent, we hope,*
> *The truth about his telescope.*

THE GREAT ARSENAL OF VENICE, overlooking the harbor full of ships. **Senators** and **Officials** on one side, **Galileo,** his daughter **Virginia,** and his friend **Sagredo,** on the other side. They are dressed in formal, festive clothes. **Virginia** is fourteen and charming. She carries a velvet cushion on which lies a brand-new telescope.

Behind **Galileo** are some **Artisans** from the Arsenal. There are onlookers, **Ludovico** among them.

Curator: [*Announcing*] Senators, Artisans of the Great Arsenal of Venice; Mr. Galileo Galilei, professor of mathematics at your University of Padua.

> [**Galileo** *steps forward and starts to speak.*]

Galileo: Members of the High Senate! Gentlemen: I have great pleasure, as director of this institute, in presenting for your approval and acceptance an entirely new instrument orginating from this our Great Arsenal of the Republic of Venice. As professor of mathematics at your University of Padua, your obedient servant has always counted it his privilege to offer you such discoveries and inventions as might prove lucrative to the manufacturers and merchants of our Venetian Republic. Thus, in all humility, I tender you this, my optical tube, or telescope, constructed, I assure you, on the most scientific and Christian principles, the product of seventeen years' patient research at your University of Padua.

> [**Galileo** *steps back. The* **Senators** *applaud.*]

Sagredo: [*Aside to* **Galileo**] Now you will be able to pay your bills.

Galileo: Yes. It will make money for them. But you realize that it is more than a money-making gadget? I turned it on the moon last night . . .

Curator: [*In his best chamber-of-commerce manner*] Gentlemen: Our Republic is to be congratulated not only because this new acquisition will be one more feather in the cap of Venetian culture—[*Polite applause*]—not only because our own Mr. Galilei has generously handed this fresh product of his teeming brain entirely over to you, allowing you to manufacture as many of these highly salable articles as you please—[*Considerable applause*]—but, Gentlemen of the Senate, has it occurred to you that—with the help of this remarkable new instrument—the battle fleet of the enemy will be visible to us a full two hours before we are visible to him? [*Tremendous applause.*]

Galileo: [*Aside to* **Sagredo**] We have been held

up three generations for lack of a thing like this. I want to go home.

Sagredo: What about the moon?

Galileo: Well, for one thing, it doesn't give off its own light.

Curator: [*Continuing his oration*] And now, Your Excellency, and Members of the Senate, Mr. Galilei entreats you to accept the instrument from the hands of his charming daughter Virginia.

[*Polite applause. He beckons to* **Virginia,** *who steps forward and presents the telescope to the* **Doge.**]

Curator: [*During this*] Mr. Galilei gives his invention entirely into your hands, Gentlemen, enjoining you to construct as many of these instruments as you may please.

[*More applause. The* **Senators** *gather round the telescope, examining it, and looking through it.*]

Galileo: [*Aside to* **Sagredo**] Do you know what the Milky Way is made of?

Sagredo: No.

Galileo: I do.

Curator: [*Interrupting*] Congratulations, Mr. Galilei. Your extra five hundred scudi a year are safe.

Galileo: Pardon? What? Of course, the *five hundred* scudi! Yes!

[*A prosperous man is standing beside the* **Curator.**]

Curator: Mr. Galilei, Mr. Matti of Florence.

Matti: You're opening new fields, Mr. Galilei. We could do with you at Florence.

Curator: Now, Mr. Matti, leave something to us poor Venetians.

Matti: It is a pity that a great republic has to seek an excuse to pay its great men their right and proper dues.

Curator: Even a great man has to have an incentive. [*He joins the* **Senators** *at the telescope.*]

Matti: I am an iron founder.

Galileo: Iron founder!

Mattie: With factories at Pisa and Florence. I wanted to talk to you about a machine you designed for a friend of mine in Padua.

Galileo: I'll put you onto someone to copy it for you, I am not going to have the time. How are things in Florence?

[*They wander away.*]

First Senator: [*Peering*] Extraordinary! They're having their lunch on that frigate. Lobsters! I'm hungry!

[*Laughter.*]

Second Senator: Oh, good heavens, look at her! I must tell my wife to stop bathing on the roof. When can I buy one of these things?

[*Laughter.* **Virginia** *has spotted* **Ludovico** *among the onlookers and drags him to* **Galileo.**]

Virginia: [*To* **Ludovico**] Did I do it nicely?

Ludovico: I thought so.

Virginia: Here's Ludovico to congratulate you, father.

Ludovico: [*Embarrassed*] Congratulations, sir.

Galileo: I improved it.

Ludovico: Yes, sir. I am beginning to understand science.

[**Galileo** *is surrounded.*]

Virginia: Isn't father a great man?

Ludovico: Yes.

Virginia: Isn't that new thing father made pretty?

Ludovico: Yes, a pretty red. Where I saw it first it was covered in green.

Virginia: What was?

Ludovico: Never mind. [*A short pause*] Have you ever been to Holland?

[*They go. All Venice is congratulating* **Galileo,** *who wants to go home.*]

SCENE III

January ten, sixteen ten:
Galileo Galilei abolishes heaven.

GALILEO'S STUDY AT PADUA. It is night. **Galileo** and **Sagredo** at a telescope.

Sagredo: [*Softly*] The edge of the crescent is jagged. All along the dark part, near the shiny crescent, bright particles of light keep coming up, one after the other, and growing larger and merging with the bright crescent.

Galileo: How do you explain those spots of light?

Sagredo: It can't be true . . .

Galileo: It *is* true: they are high mountains.

Sagredo: On a star?

Galileo: Yes. The shining particles are mountain peaks catching the first rays of the rising sun while the slopes of the mountains are still dark, and what you see is the sunlight moving down from the peaks into the valleys.

Sagredo: But this gives the lie to all the astronomy that's been taught for the last two thousand years.

Galileo: Yes. What you are seeing now has been seen by no other man besides myself.

Sagredo: But the moon can't be an earth with mountains and valleys like our own any more than the earth can be a star.

Galileo: The moon *is* an earth with mountains and valleys, and the earth *is* a star. As the moon appears to us, so we appear to the moon. From the moon, the earth looks something like a crescent, sometimes like a half globe, sometimes a full globe, and sometimes it is not visible at all.

Sagredo: Galileo, this is frightening.

[*An urgent knocking on the door.*]

Galileo: I've discovered something else, something even more astonishing.

[*More knocking.* **Galileo** *opens the door and the* **Curator** *comes in.*]

Curator: There it is—your "miraculous optical tube." Do you know that this invention he so picturesquely termed "the fruit of seventeen years' research" will be on sale tomorrow for two scudi apiece at every street corner in Venice? A shipload of them has just arrived from Holland.

Sagredo: Oh, dear!

[**Galileo** *turns his back and adjusts the telescope.*]

Curator: When I think of the poor gentlemen of the Senate who believed they were getting an invention they could monopolize for their own profit. . . . Why, when they took their first look through the glass, it was only by the merest chance that they didn't see a peddler, seven times enlarged, selling tubes exactly like it at the corner of the street.

Sagredo: Mr. Priuli, with the help of this instrument, Mr. Galilei has made discoveries that will revolutionize our concept of the universe.

Curator: Mr. Galilei provided the city with a first-rate water pump and the irrigation works he designed function splendidly. How was I to expect this?

Galileo: [*Still at the telescope*] Not so fast, Priuli. I may be on the track of a very large gadget. Certain of the stars appear to have regular movements. If there were a clock in the sky, it could be seen from anywhere. That might be useful for your shipowners.

Curator: I won't listen to you. I listened to you before, and as a reward for my friendship you have made me the laughingstock of the town. You can laugh—you got your money. But let me tell you this: you've destroyed my faith in a lot of things, Mr. Galilei. I'm disgusted with the world. That's all I have to say. [*He storms out.*]

Galileo: [*Embarrassed*] Businessmen bore me, they suffer so. Did you see the frightened look in his eyes when he caught sight of a world not created solely for the purpose of doing business?

Sagredo: Did you know that telescopes had been made in Holland?

Galileo: I'd heard about it. But the one I made for the Senators was twice as good as any Dutchman's. Besides, I needed the money. How can I work, with the tax collector on the doorstep? And my poor daughter will never acquire a husband unless she has a dowry, she's not too bright. And I like to buy books —all kinds of books. Why not? And what about my appetite? I don't think well unless I eat well. Can I help it if I get my best ideas over a good meal and a bottle of wine? They don't pay me as much as they pay the butcher's boy. If only I could have five years to do nothing but research! Come on. I am going to show you something else.

Sagredo: I don't know that I want to look again.

Galileo: This is one of the brighter nebulae of the Milky Way. What do you see?

Sagredo: But it's made up of stars—countless stars.

Galileo: Countless worlds.

Sagredo: [*Hesitating*] What about the theory that the earth revolves round the sun? Have you run across anything about that?

Galileo: No. But I noticed something on Tuesday that might prove a step towards even that. Where's Jupiter? There are four lesser stars near Jupiter. I happened on them on Monday but didn't take any particular note of their position. On Tuesday I looked again. I could have sworn they had moved. They have changed again. Tell me what you see.

Sagredo: I only see three.

Galileo: Where's the fourth? Let's get the charts and settle down to work.

[*They work and the lights dim. The lights go up again. It is near dawn.*]

Galileo: The only place the fourth can be is round at the back of the larger star where we cannot see it. This means there are small stars revolving around a big star. Where are the crystal shells now, that the stars are supposed to be fixed to?

Sagredo: Jupiter can't be attached to anything: there are other stars revolving round it.

Galileo: There is no support in the heavens. [**Sagredo** *laughs awkwardly*] Don't stand there looking at me as if it weren't true.

Sagredo: I suppose it is true. I'm afraid.

Galileo: Why?

Sagredo: What do you think is going to happen to you for saying that there is another sun around which other earths revolve? And that there are only stars and no difference between earth and heaven? Where is God then?

Galileo: What do you mean?

Sagredo: God? Where is God?

Galileo: [*Angrily*] Not there! Any more than He'd be here—if creatures from the moon came down to look for Him!

Sagredo: Then where is He?

Galileo: I'm not a theologian: I'm a mathematician.

Sagredo: You are a human being! [*Almost shouting*] Where is God in your system of the universe?

Galileo: Within ourselves. Or—nowhere.

Sagredo: Ten years ago a man was burned at the stake for saying that.

Galileo: Giordano Bruno was an idiot: he spoke too soon. He would never have been condemned if he could have backed up what he said with proof.

Sagredo: [*Incredulously*] Do you really believe proof will make any difference?

Galileo: I believe in the human race. The only people that can't be reasoned with are the dead. Human beings are intelligent.

Sagredo: Intelligent—or merely shrewd?

Galileo: I know they call a donkey a horse when they want to sell it, and a horse a donkey when they want to buy it. But is that the whole story? Aren't they susceptible to truth as well? [*He fishes a small pebble out of his pocket*] If anybody were to drop a stone—[*Drops the pebble*]—and tell them that it didn't fall, do you think they would keep quiet? The evidence of your own eyes is a very seductive thing. Sooner or later everybody must succumb to it.

Sagredo: Galileo, I am helpless when you talk.

[*A church bell has been ringing for some time, calling people to mass. Enter* **Virginia,** *muffled up for mass, carrying a candle, protected from the wind by a globe.*]

Virginia: Oh, father, you promised to go to bed tonight, and it's five o'clock again.

Galileo: Why are you up at this hour?

Virginia: I'm going to mass with Mrs. Sarti. Ludovico is going too. How was the night, father?

Galileo: Bright.

Virginia: What did you find through the tube?

Galileo: Only some little specks by the side of a star. I must draw attention to them somehow. I think I'll name them after the Prince of Florence. Why not call them the Medicean planets? By the way, we may move to Florence. I've written to His Highness, asking if he can use me as Court Mathematician.

Virginia: Oh, father, we'll be at the court!

Sagredo: [*Amazed*] Galileo!

Galileo: My dear Sagredo, I must have leisure. My only worry is that His Highness after all may not take me. I'm not accustomed to writing formal letters to great personages. Here, do you think this is the right sort of thing?

Sagredo: [*Reads*] "Whose sole desire is to reside in Your Highness' presence—the rising sun of our great age." Cosimo de' Medici is a boy of nine.

Galileo: The only way a man like me can land

a good job is by crawling on his stomach. Your father, my dear, is going to take his share of the pleasures of life in exchange for all his hard work, and about time too. I have no patience, Sagredo, with a man who doesn't use his brains to fill his belly. Run along to mass now.

[**Virginia** *goes.*]

Sagredo: Galileo, do not go to Florence.

Galileo: Why not?

Sagredo: The monks are in power there.

Galileo: Going to mass is a small price to pay for a full belly. And there are many famous scholars at the court of Florence.

Sagredo: Court monkeys.

Galileo: I shall enjoy taking them by the scruff of the neck and making them look through the telescope.

Sagredo: Galileo, you are traveling the road to disaster. You are suspicious and skeptical in science, but in politics you are as naïve as your daughter! How can people in power leave a man at large who tells the truth, even if it be the truth about the distant stars? Can you see the Pope scribbling a note in his diary: "Tenth of January, 1610, Heaven abolished"? A moment ago, when you were at the telescope, I saw you tied to the stake, and when you said you believed in proof, I smelt burning flesh!

Galileo: I am going to Florence.

Before the next scene, a curtain with the following legend on it is lowered:

By setting the name of Medici in the sky, I am bestowing immortality upon the stars. I commend myself to you as your most faithful and devoted servant, whose sole desire is to reside in Your Highness' presence, the rising sun of our great age.
—Galileo Galilei

SCENE IV

Galileo's house at Florence. Well-appointed. **Galileo** is demonstrating his telescope to **Prince Cosimo De' Medici,** a boy of nine, accompanied by his **Lord Chamberlain, Ladies** and **Gentle-** men of the court, and an assortment of university **Professors.** With **Galileo** are **Andrea** and **Federzoni,** the new assistant (an old man). **Mrs. Sarti** stands by. Before the scene opens, the voice of the **Philosopher** can be heard.

Voice of the Philosopher: Quaedam miracula universi. Orbes mystice canorae, arcus crystallini, circulatio corporum coelestium. Cyclorum epicyclorumque intoxicatio, integritas tabulae chordarum et architectura elata globorum coelestium.

Galileo: Shall we speak in everyday language? My colleague Mr. Federzoni does not understand Latin.

Philosopher: Is it necessary that he should?

Galileo: Yes.

Philosopher: Forgive me. I thought he was your mechanic.

Andrea: Mr. Federzoni is a mechanic and a scholar.

Philosopher: Thank you, young man. If Mr. Federzoni insists . . .

Galileo: I insist.

Philosopher: It will not be as clear, but it's your house. Your Highness . . . [*The* **Prince** *is ineffectually trying to establish contact with* **Andrea**] I was about to recall to Mr. Galilei some of the wonders of the universe as they are set down for us in the Divine Classics. [*The* **Ladies** *"ah"*] Remind him of the "mystically musical spheres, the crystal arches, the circulation of the heavenly bodies—"

Elderly Lady: Perfect poise!

Philosopher: "—the intoxication of the cycles and epicycles, the integrity of the tables of chords, and the enraptured architecture of the celestial globes."

Elderly Lady: What diction!

Philosopher: May I pose the question: Why should we go out of our way to look for things that can only strike a discord in the ineffable harmony?

[*The* **Ladies** *applaud.*]

Federzoni: Take a look through here—you'll be interested.

Andrea: Sit down here, please.

[*The* **Professors** *laugh.*]

Mathematician: Mr. Galilei, nobody doubts

that your brain child—or is it your adopted brain child?—is brilliantly contrived.

Galileo: Your Highness, one can see the four stars as large as life, you know.

[*The* **Prince** *looks to the* **Elderly Lady** *for guidance.*]

Mathematician: Ah. But has it occurred to you that an eyeglass through which one sees such phenomena might not be a too reliable eyeglass?

Galileo: How is that?

Mathematician: If one could be sure you would keep your temper, Mr. Galilei, I could suggest that what one sees in the eyeglass and what is in the heavens are two entirely different things.

Galileo: [*Quietly*] You are suggesting fraud?

Mathematician: No! How could I, in the presence of His Highness?

Elderly Lady: The gentlemen are just wondering if Your Highness' stars are really, really there!

[*Pause.*]

Young Lady: [*Trying to be helpful*] Can one see the claws on the Great Bear?

Galileo: And everything on Taurus the Bull.

Federzoni: Are you going to look through it or not?

Mathematician: With the greatest of pleasure.

[*Pause. Nobody goes near the telescope. All of a sudden the boy* **Andrea** *turns and marches pale and erect past them through the whole length of the room. The* **Guests** *follow with their eyes.*]

Mrs. Sarti: [*As he passes her*] What is the matter with you?

Andrea: [*Shocked*] They are wicked.

Philosopher: Your Highness, it is a delicate matter and I had no intention of bringing it up, but Mr. Galilei was about to demonstrate the impossible. His new stars would have broken the outer crystal sphere—which we know of on the authority of Aristotle. I am sorry.

Mathematician: The last word.

Federzoni: He had no telescope.

Mathematician: Quite.

Galileo: [*Keeping his temper*] "Truth is the daughter of Time, not of Authority." Gentlemen, the sum of our knowledge is pitiful. It has been

my singular good fortune to find a new instrument which brings a small patch of the universe a little bit closer. It is at your disposal.

Philosopher: Where is all this leading?

Galileo: Are we, as scholars, concerned with where the truth might lead us?

Philosopher: Mr. Galilei, the truth might lead us anywhere!

Galileo: I can only beg you to look through my eyeglass.

Mathematician: [*Wild*] If I understand Mr. Galilei correctly, he is asking us to discard the teachings of two thousand years.

Galileo: For two thousand years we have been looking at the sky and didn't see the four moons of Jupiter, and there they were all the time. Why defend shaken teachings? You should be doing the shaking. [*The* **Prince** *is sleepy*] Your Highness! My work in the Great Arsenal of Venice brought me in daily contact with sailors, carpenters, and so on. These men are unread. They depend on the evidence of their senses. But they taught me many new ways of doing things. The question is whether these gentlemen here want to be found out as fools by men who might not have had the advantages of a classical education but who are not afraid to use their eyes. I tell you that our dockyards are stirring with that same high curiosity which was the true glory of ancient Greece.

[*Pause.*]

Philosopher: I have no doubt Mr. Galilei's theories will arouse the enthusiasm of the dockyards.

Chamberlain: Your Highness, I find to my amazement that this highly informative discussion has exceeded the time we had allowed for it. May I remind Your Highness that the State Ball begins in three-quarters of an hour?

[*The* **Court** *bows low.*]

Elderly Lady: We would really have liked to look through your eyeglass, Mr. Galilei, wouldn't we, Your Highness?

[*The* **Prince** *bows politely and is led to the door.* **Galileo** *follows the* **Prince, Chamberlain,** *and* **Ladies** *toward the exit. The* **Professors** *remain at the telescope.*]

Galileo: [*Almost servile*] All anybody has to do is look through the telescope, Your Highness.

> [**Mrs. Sarti** *takes a plate with candies to the* **Prince** *as he is walking out.*]

Mrs. Sarti: A piece of homemade candy, Your Highness?

Elderly Lady: Not now. Thank you. It is too soon before His Highness' supper.

Philosopher: Wouldn't I like to take that thing to pieces.

Mathematician: Ingenious contraption. It must be quite difficult to keep clean. [*He rubs the lens with his handkerchief and looks at the handkerchief.*]

Federzoni: We did not paint the Medicean stars on the lens.

Elderly Lady: [*To the* **Prince,** *who has whispered something to her*] No, no, no, there is nothing the matter with your stars!

Chamberlain: [*Across the stage to* **Galileo**] His Highness will of course seek the opinion of the greatest living authority: Christopher Clavius, Chief Astronomer to the Papal College in Rome.

SCENE V

> *Things take indeed a wondrous turn*
> *When learned men do stoop to learn.*
> *Clavius, we are pleased to say,*
> *Upheld Galileo Galilei.*

A burst of laughter is heard and the curtains reveal A HALL IN THE COLLEGIUM ROMANUM. **High Churchmen, Monks,** *and* **Scholars** standing about talking and laughing. **Galileo** by himself in a corner.

Fat Prelate [*Shaking with laughter*] Hopeless! Hopeless! Hopeless! Will you tell me something people won't believe?

A Scholar: Yes, that you don't love your stomach!

Fat Prelate: They'd believe that. They only do not believe what's good for them. They doubt the devil, but fill them up with some fiddle-de-dee about the earth rolling like a marble in the gutter and they swallow it hook, line, and sinker. Sancta simplicitas!

> [*He laughs until the tears run down his cheeks. The others laugh with him. A group has formed whose members boisterously begin to pretend they are standing on a rolling globe.*]

A Monk: It's rolling fast, I'm dizzy. May I hold onto you, Professor? [*He sways dizzily and clings to one of the scholars for support.*]

The Scholar: Old Mother Earth's been at the bottle again. Whoa!

Monk: Hey! Hey! We're slipping off! Help!

Second Scholar: Look! There's Venus! Hold me, lads. Whee!

Second Monk: Don't, don't hurl us off onto the moon. There are nasty sharp mountain peaks on the moon, brethren!

Variously: Hold tight! Hold tight! Don't look down! Hold tight! It'll make you giddy!

Fat Prelate: And we cannot have giddy people in Holy Rome.

> [*They rock with laughter. An* **Infuriated Monk** *comes out from a large door at the rear holding a Bible in his hand and pointing out a page with his finger.*]

Infuriated Monk: What does the Bible say— "Sun, stand thou still on Gideon and thou, moon, in the valley of Ajalon." Can the sun come to a standstill if it doesn't ever move? Does the Bible lie?

Fat Prelate: How did Christopher Clavius, the greatest astronomer we have, get mixed up in an investigation of this kind?

Infuriated Monk: He's in there with his eye glued to that diabolical instrument.

Fat Prelate: [*To* **Galileo,** *who has been playing with his pebble and has dropped it*] Mr. Galilei, something dropped down.

Galileo: Monsignor, are you sure it didn't drop up?

Infuriated Monk: As astronomers we are aware that there are phenomena which are beyond us, but man can't expect to understand everything!

> [*Enter a very old* **Cardinal** *leaning on a* **Monk** *for support. Others move aside.*]

Old Cardinal: Aren't they out yet? Can't they reach a decision on that paltry matter? Christopher Clavius ought to know his astronomy after all these years. I am informed that Mr. Galilei transfers mankind from the center of the universe to somewhere on the outskirts. Mr. Galilei is therefore an enemy of mankind and must be dealt with as such. Is it conceivable that God would trust this most precious fruit of His labor to a minor, frolicking star? Would He have sent His Son to such a place? How can there be people with such twisted minds that they believe what they're told by the slave of a multiplication table?

Fat Prelate: [*Quietly to* **Cardinal**] The gentleman is over there.

Old Cardinal: So you are the man. You know my eyes are not what they were, but I can see you bear a striking resemblance to the man we burned. What was his name?

Monk: Your Eminence must avoid excitement the doctor said . . .

Old Cardinal: [*Disregarding him*] So you have degraded the earth despite the fact that you live by her and receive everything from her. I won't have it! I won't have it! I won't be a nobody on an inconsequential star briefly twirling hither and thither. I tread the earth, and the earth is firm beneath my feet, and there is no motion to the earth, and the earth is the center of all things, and I am the center of the earth, and the eye of the Creator is upon me. About me revolve, affixed to their crystal shells, the lesser lights of the stars and the great light of the sun, created to give light upon me that God might see me—Man, God's greatest effort, the center of creation. "In the image of God created He him." Immortal . . . [*His strength fails him and he catches for the* **Monk** *for support.*]

Monk: You mustn't overtax your strength, Your Eminence.

[*At this moment the door at the rear opens and* **Christopher Clavius** *enters followed by his* **Astronomers.** *He strides hastily across the hall, looking neither to right nor left. As he goes by we hear him say—*]

Clavius: He is right.

[*Deadly silence. All turn to* **Galileo.**]

Old Cardinal: What is it? Have they reached a decision?

[*No one speaks.*]

Monk: It is time that Your Eminence went home.

[*The hall is emptying fast. One little* **Monk** *who had entered with* **Clavius** *speaks to* **Galileo.**]

Little Monk: Mr. Galilei, I heard Father Clavius say: "Now it's for the theologians to set the heavens right again." You have won.

Before the next scene, a curtain with the following legend on it is lowered:

As these new astronomical charts enable us to determine longitudes at sea and so make it possible to reach the new continents by the shortest routes, we would beseech Your Excellency to aid us in reaching Mr. Galilei, mathematician to the Court of Florence, who is now in Rome . . .

—From a letter written by a member of the Genoa Chamber of Commerce and Navigation to the Papal Legation.

SCENE VI

When Galileo was in Rome
A Cardinal asked him to his home.
He wined and dined him as his guest
And only made one small request.

Cardinal Bellarmin's house in Rome. Music is heard and the chatter of many guests. **Two Secretaries** are at the rear of the stage at a desk. **Galileo,** his daughter **Virginia,** now twenty-one, and **Ludovico Marsili,** who has become her fiancé, are just arriving. A few **Guests,** standing near the entrance with masks in their hands, nudge each other and are suddenly silent. **Galileo** looks at them. They applaud him politely and bow.

Virginia: Oh, father! I'm so happy. I won't dance with anyone but you, Ludovico.

Galileo: [*To a* **Secretary**] I was to wait here for His Eminence.

First Secretary: His Eminence will be with you in a few minutes.

Virginia: Do I look proper?

Ludovico: You are showing some lace.

[**Galileo** *puts his arms around their shoulders.*]

Galileo: [*Quoting mischievously*]

Fret not, daughter, if perchance
You attract a wanton glance.
The eyes that catch a trembling lace
Will guess the heartbeat's quickened pace.
Lovely woman still may be
Careless with felicity.

Virginia: [*To* **Galileo**] Feel my heart.

Galileo: [*To* **Ludovico**] It's thumping.

Virginia: I hope I always say the right thing.

Ludovico: She's afraid she's going to let us down.

Virginia: Oh, I want to look beautiful.

Galileo: You'd better. If you don't they'll start saying all over again that the earth doesn't turn.

Ludovico: [*Laughing*] It *doesn't* turn, sir.

[**Galileo** *laughs.*]

Galileo: Go and enjoy yourselves. [*He speaks to one of the* **Secretaries**] A large fete?

First Secretary: Two hundred and fifty guests, Mr. Galilei. We have represented here this evening most of the great families of Italy, the Orsinis, the Villanis, the Nuccolis, the Soldanieris, the Canes, the Lecchis, the Estes, the Colombinis, the . . .

[**Virginia** *comes running back.*]

Virginia: Oh, father, I didn't tell you: you're famous.

Galileo: Why?

Virginia: The hairdresser in the Via Vittorio kept four other ladies waiting and took me first. [*Exit.*]

Galileo: [*At the stairway, leaning over the well*] Rome!

[*Enter* **Cardinal Bellarmin,** *wearing the mask of a lamb, and* **Cardinal Barberini,** *wearing the mask of a dove.*]

Secretaries: Their Eminences, Cardinals Bellarmin and Barberini.

[*The* **Cardinals** *lower their masks.*]

Galileo: [*To* **Bellarmin**] Your Eminence.

Bellarmin: Mr. Galilei, Cardinal Barberini.

Galileo: Your Eminence.

Barberini: So you are the father of that lovely child!

Bellarmin: Who is inordinately proud of being her father's daughter.

[*They laugh.*]

Barberini: [*Points his finger at* **Galileo**] "The sun riseth and setteth and returneth to its place," saith the Bible. What saith Galilei?

Galileo: Appearances are notoriously deceptive, Your Eminence. Once, when I was so high, I was standing on a ship that was pulling away from the shore and I shouted, "The shore is moving!" I know now that it was the ship which was moving.

Barberini: [*Laughs*] You can't catch that man. I tell you, Bellarmin, his moons around Jupiter are hard nuts to crack. Unfortunately for me I happened to glance at a few papers on astronomy once. It is harder to get rid of than the itch.

Bellarmin: Let's move with the times. If it makes navigation easier for sailors to use new charts based on a new hypothesis, let them have them. We only have to scotch doctrines that contradict Holy Writ.

[*He leans over the balustrade of the well and acknowledges various* **Guests.**]

Barberini: But Bellarmin, you haven't caught onto this fellow. The scriptures don't satisfy him. Copernicus does.

Galileo: Copernicus? "He that withholdeth corn, the people shall curse him." Book of Proverbs.

Barberini: "A prudent man concealeth knowledge." Also Book of Proverbs.

Galileo: "Where no oxen are, the crib is clean: but much increase is by the strength of the ox."

Barberini: "He that ruleth his spirit is better than he that taketh a city."

Galileo: "But a broken spirit drieth the bones." [*Pause*] "Doth not wisdom cry?"

Barberini: "Can one go upon hot coals and his feet not be burned?" Welcome to Rome, friend Galileo. You recall the legend of our city's origin? Two small boys found sustenance and refuge with a she-wolf and from that day we have paid the price for the she-wolf's milk. But the place is not bad. We have everything for your pleasure—from a scholarly dispute with Bellarmin to ladies of high degree. Look at that woman flaunting herself. No? He wants a weighty discussion! All right! [*To* **Galileo**] You people speak in terms of circles and ellipses and regular velocities—simple movements that the human mind can grasp—very convenient—but suppose Almighty God had taken it into His head to make the stars move like that—[*He describes an irregular motion with his fingers through the air*]—then where would you be?

Galileo: My good man—the Almighty would have endowed us with brains like that—[*Repeats the movement*]—so that we could grasp the movements—[*Repeats the movement*]—like that. I believe in the brain.

Barberini: I consider the brain inadequate. He doesn't answer. He is too polite to tell me he considers *my* brain inadequate. What is one to do with him? Butter wouldn't melt in his mouth. All he wants to do is to prove that God made a few boners in astronomy. God didn't study His astronomy hard enough before He composed Holy Writ. [*To the* **Secretaries**] Don't take anything down. This is a scientific discussion among friends.

Bellarmin: [*To* **Galileo**] Does it not appear more probable—even to you—that the Creator knows more about His work than the created?

Galileo: In his blindness man is liable to misread not only the sky but also the Bible.

Bellarmin: The interpretation of the Bible is a matter for the ministers of God. [**Galileo** *remains silent*] At last you are quiet. [*He gestures to the* **Secretaries.** *They start writing*] Tonight the Holy Office has decided that the theory according to which the earth goes around the sun is foolish, absurd, and a heresy. I am charged, Mr. Galilei, with cautioning you to abandon these teachings. [*To the* **First Secretary**] Would you repeat that?

First Secretary: [*Reading*] "His Eminence, Cardinal Bellarmin, to the aforesaid Galilei: 'The Holy Office has resolved that the theory according to which the earth goes around the sun is foolish, absurd, and a heresy. I am charged, Mr. Galilei, with cautioning you to abandon these teachings.'"

Galileo: [*Rocking on his base*] But the facts!

Barberini: [*Consoling*] Your findings have been ratified by the Papal Observatory, Galilei. That should be most flattering to you . . .

Bellarmin: [*Cutting in*] The Holy Office formulated the decree without going into details.

Galileo: [*To* **Barberini**] Do you realize, the future of all scientific research is—

Bellarmin: [*Cutting in*] Completely assured, Mr. Galilei. It is not given to man to know the truth: it is granted to him to seek after the truth. Science is the legitimate and beloved daughter of the Church. She must have confidence in the Church.

Galileo: [*Infuriated*] I would not try confidence by whistling her too often.

Barberini: [*Quickly*] Be careful what you're doing—you'll be throwing out the baby with the bath water, friend Galilei. [*Serious*] We need you more than you need us.

Bellarmin: Well, it is time we introduced our distinguished friend to our guests. The whole country talks of him!

Barberini: Let us replace our masks, Bellarmin. Poor Galilei hasn't got one. [*He laughs.*]

   [*They take* **Galileo** *out.*]

First Secretary: Did you get his last sentence?

Second Secretary: Yes. Do you have what he said about believing in the brain?

   [*Another cardinal—the* **Inquisitor**—*enters.*]

Inquisitor: Did the conference take place?

   [*The* **First Secretary** *hands him the papers and the* **Inquisitor** *dismisses the* **Secretaries.** *They go. The* **Inquisitor** *sits down and starts to read the transcription. Two or three* **Young Ladies** *skitter across the stage; they see the* **Inquisitor** *and curtsy as they go.*]

Young Girl: Who was that?

Her Friend: The Cardinal Inquisitor.

   [*They giggle and go. Enter* **Virginia.** *She curtsies as she goes. The* **Inquisitor** *stops her.*]

Inquisitor: Good evening, my child. Beautiful night. May I congratulate you on your betrothal? Your young man comes from a fine family. Are you staying with us here in Rome?

Virginia: Not now, Your Eminence. I must go home to prepare for the wedding.

Inquisitor: Ah. You are accompanying your father to Florence. That should please him. Science must be cold comfort in a home. Your youth and warmth will keep him down to earth. It is easy to get lost up there. [*He gestures to the sky.*]

Virginia: He doesn't talk to me about the stars, Your Eminence.

Inquisitor: No. [*He laughs*] They don't eat fish

in the fisherman's house. I can tell you something about astronomy. My child, it seems that God has blessed our modern astronomers with imaginations. It is quite alarming! Do you know that the earth—which we old fogies supposed to be so large—has shrunk to something no bigger than a walnut, and the new universe has grown so vast that prelates—and even cardinals—look like ants. Why, God Almighty might lose sight of a Pope! I wonder if I know your Father Confessor.

Virginia: Father Christopherus, from Saint Ursula's at Florence, Your Eminence.

Inquisitor: My dear child, your father will need you. Not so much now perhaps, but one of these days. You are pure, and there is strength in purity. Greatness is sometimes, indeed often, too heavy a burden for those to whom God has granted it. What man is so great that he has no place in a prayer? But I am keeping you, my dear. Your fiancé will be jealous of me, and I am afraid your father will never forgive me for holding forth on astronomy. Go to your dancing and remember me to Father Christopherus.

[**Virginia** *kisses his ring and runs off. The* **Inquisitor** *resumes his reading.*]

SCENE VII

Galileo, feeling grim,
A young monk came to visit him.
The monk was born of common folk.
It was of science that they spoke.

GARDEN OF THE FLORENTINE AMBASSADOR IN ROME. Distant hum of a great city. **Galileo** and the **Little Monk** of Scene V are talking.

Galileo: Let's hear it. That robe you're wearing gives you the right to say whatever you want to say. Let's hear it.

Little Monk: I have studied physics, Mr. Galilei.

Galileo: That might help us if it enabled you to admit that two and two are four.

Little Monk: Mr. Galilei, I have spent four sleepless nights trying to reconcile the decree that I have read with the moons of Jupiter that I have seen. This morning I decided to come to see you after I had said mass.

Galileo: To tell me that Jupiter has no moons?

Little Monk: No, I found out that I think the decree a wise decree. It has shocked me into realizing that free research has its dangers. I have had to decide to give up astronomy. However, I felt the impulse to confide in you some of the motives which have impelled even a passionate physicist to abandon his work.

Galileo: Your motives are familiar to me.

Little Monk: You mean, of course, the special powers invested in certain commissions of the Holy Office? But there is something else. I would like to talk to you about my family. I do not come from the great city. My parents are peasants in the Campagna, who know about the cultivation of the olive tree, and not much about anything else. Too often these days when I am trying to concentrate on tracking down the moons of Jupiter, I see my parents. I see them sitting by the fire with my sister, eating their curded cheese. I see the beams of the ceiling above them, which the smoke of centuries has blackened, and I can see the veins stand out on their toil-worn hands, and the little spoons in their hands. They scrape a living, and underlying the poverty there is a sort of order. There are routines. The routine of scrubbing the floors, the routine of the seasons in the olive orchard, the routine of paying taxes. The troubles that come to them are recurrent troubles. My father did not get his poor bent back all at once, but little by little, year by year, in the olive orchard; just as year after year, with unfailing regularity, childbirth has made my mother more and more sexless. They draw the strength they need to sweat with their loaded baskets up the stony paths, to bear children, even to eat, from the sight of the trees greening each year anew, from the reproachful face of the soil, which is never satisfied, and from the little church and Bible texts they hear there on Sunday. They have been told that

God relies upon them and that the pageant of the world has been written around them that they may be tested in the important or unimportant parts handed out to them. How could they take it, were I to tell them that they are on a lump of stone ceaselessly spinning in empty space, circling around a second-rate star? What, then, would be the use of their patience, their acceptance of misery? What comfort, then, the Holy Scriptures, which have mercifully explained their crucifixion? The Holy Scriptures would then be proved full of mistakes. No, I see them begin to look frightened. I see them slowly put their spoons down on the table. They would feel cheated. "There is no eye watching over us, after all," they would say. "We have to start out on our own, at our time of life. Nobody has planned a part for us beyond this wretched one on a worthless star. There is no meaning in our misery. Hunger is just not having eaten. It is no test of strength. Effort is just stooping and carrying. It is not a virtue." Can you understand that I read into the decree of the Holy Office a noble, motherly pity and a great goodness of the soul?

Galileo: [*Embarrassed*] Hm, well at least you have found out that it is not a question of the satellites of Jupiter, but of the peasants of the Campagna! And don't try to break me down by the halo of beauty that radiates from old age. How does a pearl develop in an oyster? A jagged grain of sand makes its way into the oyster's shell and makes its life unbearable. The oyster exudes slime to cover the grain of sand and the slime eventually hardens into a pearl. The oyster nearly dies in the process. To hell with the pearl, give me the healthy oyster! And virtues are not exclusive to misery. If your parents were prosperous and happy, they might develop the virtues of happiness and prosperity. Today the virtues of exhaustion are caused by the exhausted land. For that, my new water pumps could work more wonders than their ridiculous superhuman efforts. Be fruitful and multiply: for war will cut down the population, and our fields are barren! [*A pause*] Shall I lie to your people?

Little Monk: We must be silent from the highest of motives: the inward peace of less fortunate souls.

Galileo: My dear man, as a bonus for not meddling with your parents' peace, the authorities are tendering me, on a silver platter, persecution-free, my share of the fat sweated from your parents, who, as you know, were made in God's image. Should I condone this decree, my motives might not be disinterested: easy life, no persecution and so on.

Little Monk: Mr. Galilei, I am a priest.

Galileo: You are also a physicist. How can new machinery be evolved to domesticate the river water if we physicists are forbidden to study, discuss, and pool our findings about the greatest machinery of all, the machinery of the heavenly bodies? Can I reconcile my findings on the paths of falling bodies with the current belief in the tracks of witches on broomsticks? [*A pause*] I am sorry—I shouldn't have said that.

Little Monk: You don't think that the truth, if it is the truth, would make its way without us?

Galileo: No! No! No! As much of the truth gets through as we push through. You talk about the Campagna peasants as if they were the moss on their huts. Naturally, if they don't get a move on and learn to think for themselves, the most efficient of irrigation systems cannot help them. I can see their divine patience, but where is their divine fury?

Little Monk: [*Helpless*] They are old!

[**Galileo** *stands for a moment, beaten; he cannot meet the* **Little Monk***'s eyes. He takes a manuscript from the table and throws it violently on the ground.*]

Little Monk: What is that?

Galileo: Here is writ what draws the ocean when it ebbs and flows. Let it lie there. Thou shalt not read. [*The* **Little Monk** *has picked up the manuscript*] Already! An apple of the tree of knowledge, he can't wait, he wolfs it down. He will rot in hell for all eternity. Look at him, where are his manners? Sometimes I think I would let them imprison me in a place a thousand feet beneath the earth, where no light could reach me, if in exchange I could find out what stuff that is: "Light." The bad thing is that, when I find something, I have to boast about it like a lover or a drunkard or a traitor. That is a hopeless vice and leads to the abyss. I wonder how long I shall be content to discuss it with my dog!

Little Monk: [*Immersed in the manuscript*] I don't understand this sentence.

Galileo: I'll explain it to you, I'll explain it to you.

[*They are sitting on the floor.*]

SCENE VIII

Eight long years with tongue in cheek
Of what he knew he did not speak.
Then temptation grew too great
And Galileo challenged fate.

GALILEO'S HOUSE IN FLORENCE again. **Galileo** is supervising his assistants—**Andrea, Federzoni,** and the **Little Monk**—who are about to prepare an experiment. **Mrs. Sarti** and **Virginia** are at a long table sewing bridal linen. There is a new telescope, larger than the old one. At the moment it is covered with a cloth.

Andrea: [*Looking up a schedule*] Thursday. Afternoon. Floating bodies again. Ice, bowl of water, scales, and it says here an iron needle. Aristotle.

Virginia: Ludovico likes to entertain. We must take care to be neat. His mother notices every stitch. She doesn't approve of father's books.

Mrs. Sarti: That's all a thing of the past. He hasn't published a book for years.

Virginia: That's true. Oh, Sarti, it's fun sewing a trousseau.

Mrs. Sarti: Virginia, I want to talk to you. You are very young, and you have no mother, and your father is putting those pieces of ice in water, and marriage is too serious a business to go into blind. Now you should go to see a real astronomer from the university and have him cast your horoscope so you know where you stand. [**Virginia** *giggles*] What's the matter?

Virginia: I've been already.

Mrs. Sarti: Tell Sarti.

Virginia: I have to be careful for three months now because the sun is in Capricorn, but after that I get a favorable ascendant, and I can undertake a journey if I am careful of Uranus, as I'm a Scorpion.

Mrs. Sarti: What about Ludovico?

Virginia: He's a Leo, the astronomer said. Leos are sensual. [*Giggles.*]

[*There is a knock at the door, it opens. Enter the* **Rector of the University,** *the philosopher of Scene IV, bringing a book.*]

Rector: [*To* **Virginia**] This is about the burning issue of the moment. He may want to glance over it. My faculty would appreciate his comments. No, don't disturb him now, my dear. Every minute one takes of your father's time is stolen from Italy. [*He goes.*]

Virginia: Federzoni! The rector of the university brought this.

[**Federzoni** *takes it.*]

Galileo: What's it about?

Federzoni: [*Spelling*] D-e m-a-c-u-l-i-s i-n s-o-l-e.

Andrea: Oh, it's on the sun spots!

[**Andrea** *comes to one side, and the* **Little Monk** *the other, to look at the book.*]

Andrea: A new one!

[**Federzoni** *resentfully puts the book into their hands and continues with the preparation of the experiment.*]

Andrea: Listen to this dedication. [*Quotes*] "To the greatest living authority on physics, Galileo Galilei." I read Fabricius' paper the other day. Fabricius says the spots are clusters of planets between us and the sun.

Little Monk: Doubtful.

Galileo: [*Noncommittal*] Yes?

Andrea: Paris and Prague hold that they are vapors from the sun. Federzoni doubts that.

Federzoni: Me? You leave me out. I said "hm," that was all. And don't discuss new things before me. I can't read the material, it's in Latin. [*He drops the scales and stands trembling with fury*] Tell me, can I doubt anything?

[**Galileo** *walks over and picks up the scales silently. Pause.*]

Little Monk: There is happiness in doubting, I wonder why.

Andrea: Aren't we going to take this up?

Galileo: At the moment we are investigating floating bodies.

Andrea: Mother has baskets full of letters from all over Europe asking his opinion.

Federzoni: The question is whether you can afford to remain silent.

Galileo: I cannot afford to be smoked on a wood fire like a ham.

Andrea: [*Surprised*] Ah. You think the sun spots may have something to do with that again? [**Galileo** *does not answer*] Well, we stick to fiddling about with bits of ice in water. That can't hurt you.

Galileo: Correct. Our thesis!

Andrea: All things that are lighter than water float, and all things that are heavier sink.

Galileo: Aristotle says—

Little Monk: [*Reading out of a book, translating*] "A broad and flat disk of ice, although heavier than water, still floats, because it is unable to divide the water."

Galileo: Well. Now I push the ice below the surface. I take away the pressure of my hands. What happens?

[*Pause.*]

Little Monk: It rises to the surface.

Galileo: Correct. It seems to be able to divide the water as it's coming up, doesn't it?

Little Monk: Could it be lighter than water after all?

Galileo: Aha!

Andrea: Then all things that are lighter than water float, and all things that are heavier sink. Q.E.D.

Galileo: Not at all. Hand me that iron needle. Heavier than water? [*They all nod*] A piece of paper. [*He places the needle on a piece of paper and floats it on the surface of the water. Pause*] Do not be hasty with your conclusion. [*Pause*] What happens?

Federzoni: The paper has sunk, the needle is floating. [*They laugh.*]

Virginia: What's the matter?

Mrs. Sarti: Every time I hear them laugh it sends shivers down my spine.

[*There is a knocking at the outer door.*]

Mrs. Sarti: Who's that at the door?

[*Enter **Ludovico**. **Virginia** runs to him. They embrace. **Ludovico** is followed by a **Servant** with baggage.*]

Mrs. Sarti: Well!

Virginia: Oh! Why didn't you write that you were coming?

Ludovico: I decided on the spur of the moment. I was over inspecting our vineyards at Bucciole. I couldn't keep away.

Galileo: Who's that?

Little Monk: Miss Virginia's intended. What's the matter with your eyes?

Galileo: [*Blinking*] Oh, yes, it's Ludovico, so it is. Well! Sarti, get a jug of that Sicilian wine, the old kind. We celebrate.

[*Everybody sits down. **Mrs. Sarti** has left, followed by **Ludovico's** Servant.*]

Galileo: Well, Ludovico, old man. How are the horses?

Ludovico: The horses are fine.

Galileo: Fine.

Ludovico: But those vineyards need a firm hand. [*To **Virginia**] You look pale. Country life will suit you. Mother's planning on September.

Virginia: I suppose I oughtn't, but stay here, I've got something to show you.

Ludovico: What?

Virginia: Never mind. I won't be ten minutes. [*She runs out.*]

Ludovico: How's life these days, sir?

Galileo: Dull. How was the journey?

Ludovico: Dull. Before I forget, mother sends her congratulations on your admirable tact over the latest rumblings of science.

Galileo: Thank her from me.

Ludovico: Christopher Clavius had all Rome on its ears. He said he was afraid that the turning-around business might crop up again on account of these spots on the sun.

Andrea: Clavius is on the same track! [*To **Ludovico**] My mother's baskets are full of letters from all over Europe asking Mr. Galilei's opinion.

Galileo: I am engaged in investigating the habits of floating bodies. Any harm in that?

[*Mrs. Sarti re-enters, followed by the **Servant**. They bring wine and glasses on a tray.*]

Galileo: [*Hands out the wine*] What news from the Holy City, apart from the prospect of my sins?

Ludovico: The Holy Father is on his deathbed. Hadn't you heard?

Little Monk: My goodness! What about the succession?

Ludovico: All the talk is of Barberini.

Galileo: Barberini?

Andrea: Mr. Galilei knows Barberini.

Little Monk: Cardinal Barberini is a mathematician.

Federzoni: A scientist in the chair of Peter!
[*Pause.*]

Galileo: [*Cheering up enormously*] This means change. We might live to see the day, Federzoni, when we don't have to whisper that two and two are four. [*To* **Ludovico**] I like this wine. Don't you, Ludovico?

Ludovico: I like it.

Galileo: I know the hill where it is grown. The slope is steep and stony, the grape almost blue. I am fond of this wine.

Ludovico: Yes, sir.

Galileo: There are shadows in this wine. It is almost sweet but just stops short. . . . Andrea, clear that stuff away, ice, bowl, and needle. . . . I cherish the consolations of the flesh. I have no patience with cowards who call them weaknesses. I say there is a certain achievement in enjoying things.

[*The* **Pupils** *get up and go to the experiment table.*]

Little Monk: What are we to do?

Federzoni: He is starting on the sun.

[*They begin with clearing up.*]

Andrea: [*Singing in a low voice*]

The Bible proves the earth stands still,
The Pope, he swears with tears:
The earth stands still. To prove it so
He takes it by the ears.

Ludovico: What's the excitement?

Mrs. Sarti: You're not going to start those hellish goings on again, Mr. Galilei?

Andrea:

And gentlefolk, they say so too.
Each learned doctor proves
(If you grease his palm): The earth stands still.
And yet—and yet it moves.

Galileo: Barberini is in the ascendant, so your mother is uneasy, and you're sent to investigate me. Correct me if I am wrong, Ludovico. Clavius is right: these spots on the sun interest me.

Andrea: We might find out that the sun also revolves. How would you like that, Ludovico?

Galileo: Do you like my wine, Ludovico?

Ludovico: I told you I did, sir.

Galileo: You really like it?

Ludovico: I like it.

Galileo: Tell me, Ludovico, would you consider going so far as to accept a man's wine or his daughter without insisting that he drop his profession? I have no wish to intrude, but have the moons of Jupiter affected Virginia's bottom?

Mrs. Sarti: That isn't funny, it's just vulgar. I am going for Virginia.

Ludovico: [*Keeps her back*] Marriages in families such as mine are not arranged on a basis of sexual attraction alone.

Galileo: Did they keep you back from marrying my daughter for eight years because I was on probation?

Ludovico: My future wife must take her place in the family pew.

Galileo: You mean, if the daughter of a bad man sat in your family pew, your peasants might stop paying the rent?

Ludovico: In a sort of way.

Galileo: When I was your age, the only person I allowed to rap me on the knuckles was my girl.

Ludovico: My mother was assured that you had undertaken not to get mixed up in this turning-around business again, sir.

Galileo: We had a conservative Pope then.

Mrs. Sarti: Had! His Holiness is not dead yet!

Galileo: [*With relish*] Pretty nearly.

Mrs. Sarti: That man will weigh a chip of ice fifty times, but when it comes to something that's convenient, he believes it blindly. "Is His Holiness dead?" "Pretty nearly!"

Ludovico: You will find, sir, if His Holiness passes away, the new Pope, whoever he turns out to be, will respect the convictions held by the solid families of the country.

Galileo: [*To* **Andrea**] That remains to be seen.

Andrea, get out the screen. We'll throw the image of the sun on our screen to save our eyes.

Little Monk: I thought you'd been working at it. Do you know when I guessed it? When you didn't recognize Mr. Marsili.

Mrs. Sarti: If my son has to go to hell for sticking to you, that's my affair, but you have no right to trample on your daughter's happiness.

Ludovico: [*To his* **Servant**] Giuseppe, take my baggage back to the coach, will you?

Mrs. Sarti: This will kill her. [*She runs out, still clutching the jug.*]

Ludovico: [*Politely*] Mr. Galilei, if we Marsilis were to countenance teachings frowned on by the church, it would unsettle our peasants. Bear in mind: these poor people in their brute state get everything upside down. They are nothing but animals. They will never comprehend the finer points of astronomy. Why, two months ago a rumor went around, an apple had been found on a pear tree, and they left their work in the fields to discuss it.

Galileo: [*Interested*] Did they?

Ludovico: I have seen the day when my poor mother has had to have a dog whipped before their eyes to remind them to keep their place. Oh, you may have seen the waving corn from the window of your comfortable coach. You have, no doubt, nibbled our olives, and absentmindedly eaten our cheese, but you can have no idea how much responsibility that sort of thing entails.

Galileo: Young man, I do not eat my cheese absentmindedly. [*To* **Andrea**] Are we ready?

Andrea: Yes, sir.

Galileo: [*Leaves* **Ludovico** *and adjusts the mirror*] You would not confine your whippings to dogs to remind your peasants to keep their places, would you, Marsili?

Ludovico: [*After a pause*] Mr. Galilei, you have a wonderful brain, it's a pity.

Little Monk: [*Astonished*] He threatened you.

Galileo: Yes. And he threatened you too. We might unsettle his peasants. Your sister, Fulganzio, who works the lever of the olive press, might laugh out loud if she heard the sun is not a gilded coat of arms but a lever too. The earth turns because the sun turns it.

Andrea: That could interest his steward too and even his moneylender—and the seaport towns . . .

Federzoni: None of them speak Latin.

Galileo: I might write in plain language. The work we do is exacting. Who would go through the strain for less than the population at large!

Ludovico: I see you have made your decision. It was inevitable. You will always be a slave of your passions. Excuse me to Virginia. I think it's as well I don't see her now.

Galileo: The dowry is at your disposal at any time.

Ludovico: Good afternoon. [*He goes, followed by the* **Servant.**]

Andrea: Exit Ludovico. To hell with all Marsilis, Villanis, Orsinis, Canes, Nuccolis, Soldanieris . . .

Federzoni: . . . who ordered the earth stand still because their castles might be shaken loose if it revolves . . .

Little Monk: . . . and who only kiss the Pope's feet as long as he uses them to trample on the people. God made the physical world, God made the human brain. God will allow physics.

Andrea: They will try to stop us.

Galileo: Thus we enter the observation of these spots on the sun in which we are interested, at our own risk, not counting on protection from a problematical new Pope . . .

Andrea: . . . but with great likelihood of dispelling Fabricius' vapors, and the shadows of Paris and Prague, and of establishing the rotation of the sun . . .

Galileo: . . . and with *some* likelihood of establishing the rotation of the sun. My intention is not to prove that I was right but to find out *whether* I was right. "Abandon hope all ye who enter—an observation." Before assuming these phenomena are spots, which would suit us, let us first set about proving that they are not—fried fish. We crawl by inches. What we find today we will wipe from the blackboard tomorrow and reject it—unless it shows up again the day after tomorrow. And if we find anything which would suit us, that thing we will eye with particular distrust. In fact, we will approach this observing of the sun with the implacable determination to prove that the earth stands still, and only if hopelessly defeated in this pious undertaking can we allow ourselves to wonder if we may not have been right all the time: the earth revolves. Take the cloth off the telescope and turn it on the sun.

[*Quietly they start work. When the coruscating image of the sun is focused on the screen,* **Virginia** *enters hurriedly, her wedding dress on, her hair disheveled,* **Mrs. Sarti** *with her, carrying her wedding veil. The two women realize what has happened.* **Virginia** *faints.* **Andrea, Little Monk,** *and* **Galileo** *rush to her.* **Federzoni** *continues working.*]

SCENE IX

On April Fools' Day, thirty two,
Of science there was much ado.
People had learned from Galilei:
They used his teaching in their way.

Around the corner from the market place a **Ballad Singer** and his **Wife,** who is costumed to represent the earth in a skeleton globe made of thin bands of brass, are holding the attention of a sprinkling of representative citizens, some in masquerade, who were on their way to see the carnival procession. From the market place the noise of an impatient crowd.

Ballad Singer: [*Accompanied by his* **Wife** *on the guitar*]
When the Almighty made the universe
He made the earth and then he made the sun.
Then round the earth he bade the sun to turn—
That's in the Bible, Genesis, Chapter One.
And from that time all beings here below
Were in obedient circles meant to go:
  Around the pope the cardinals
  Around the cardinals the bishops
  Around the bishops the secretaries
  Around the secretaries the aldermen

Around the aldermen the craftsmen
Around the craftsmen the servants
Around the servants the dogs, the chickens, and the beggars.

[*A conspicuous reveller—henceforth called the* **Spinner**—*has slowly caught on and is exhibiting his idea of spinning around. He does not lose dignity, he faints with mock grace.*]

Ballad Singer:
Up stood the learned Galileo
Glanced briefly at the sun
And said: "Almighty God was wrong
In Genesis, Chapter One!"
  Now that was rash, my friends, it is no matter small:
  For heresy will spread today like foul diseases.
  Change Holy Writ, forsooth? What will be left at all?
  Why: each of us would say and do just what he pleases!

[*Three wretched* **Extras,** *employed by the Chamber of Commerce, enter. Two of them, in ragged costumes, moodily bear a litter with a mock throne. The third sits on the throne. He wears sacking, a false beard, a prop crown, he carries a prop orb and sceptre, and around his chest the inscription* **"The King of Hungary."** *The litter has a card with "No. 4" written on it. The litter bearers dump him down and listen to the* **Ballad Singer.**]

Ballad Singer:
Good people, what will come to pass
If Galileo's teachings spread?
No altar boy will serve the mass
No servant girl will make the bed.
  Now that is grave, my friends, it is no matter small:
  For independent spirit spreads like foul diseases!
  Yet life is sweet and man is weak and after all—
  How nice it is, for a little change, to do just as one pleases!

[*The* **Ballad Singer** *takes over the guitar. His* **Wife** *dances around him, illustrating the motion of the earth. A* **Cobbler's Boy** *with a pair of resplendent lacquered boots hung over his shoulder has been jumping up and down in mock excite-*

ment. *There are three more children, dressed as grownups, among the spectators, two together and a single one with mother. The* **Cobbler's Boy** *takes the three* **Children** *in hand, forms a chain and leads it, moving to the music, in and out among the spectators, "whipping" the chain so that the last child bumps into people. On the way past a* **Peasant Woman,** *he steals an egg from her basket. She gestures to him to return it. As he passes her again he quietly breaks the egg over her head. The* **King of Hungary** *ceremoniously hands his orb to one of his bearers, marches down with mock dignity, and chastises the* **Cobbler's Boy.** *The parents remove the three* **Children.** *The unseemliness subsides.]*

Ballad Singer:

The carpenters take wood and build
Their houses—not the church's pews.
And members of the cobbler's guild
Now boldly walk the streets—in shoes.
The tenant kicks the noble lord
Quite off the land he owned—like that!
The milk his wife once gave the priest
Now makes (at last!) her children fat.

Ts, ts, ts, ts, my friends, this is no matter
small:
For independent spirit spreads like foul
diseases.
People must keep their place, some down
and some on top!
(Though it is nice, for a little change, to
do just as one pleases!)

[The **Cobbler's Boy** *has put on the lacquered boots he was carrying. He struts off. The* **Ballad Singer** *takes over the guitar again. His* **Wife** *dances around him in increased tempo. A* **Monk** *has been standing near a* **Rich Couple,** *who are in subdued, costly clothes, without masks; shocked at the song, he now leaves. A* **Dwarf** *in the costume of an astronomer turns his telescope on the departing* **Monk,** *thus drawing attention to the* **Rich Couple.** *In imitation of the* **Cobbler's Boy,** *the* **Spinner** *forms a chain of grownups. They move to the music, in and out, and between the* **Rich Couple.** *The* **Spinner** *changes the gentleman's bonnet for the ragged hat of a beggar. The* **Gentleman** *decides to take this in good part, and a* **Girl** *is emboldened to take his dagger. The* **Gentleman** *is miffed, throws the*

beggar's hat back. The **Beggar** *discards the gentleman's bonnet and drops it on the ground. The* **King of Hungary** *has walked from his throne, taken an egg from the* **Peasant Woman,** *and paid for it. He now ceremoniously breaks it over the gentleman's head as he is bending down to pick up his bonnet. The* **Gentleman** *conducts the* **Lady** *away from the scene. The* **King of Hungary,** *about to resume his throne, finds one of the* **Children** *sitting on it. The* **Gentleman** *returns to retrieve his dagger. Merriment. The* **Ballad Singer** *wanders off. This is part of his routine. His* **Wife** *sings to the* **Spinner.]**

Wife:

Now speaking for myself I feel
That I could also do with a change.
You know, for me—[*Turning to a reveller*]—you have appeal
Maybe tonight we could arrange . . .

[The **Dwarf-Astronomer** *has been amusing the people by focusing his telescope on her legs. The* **Ballad Singer** *has returned.]*

Ballad Singer: No, no, no, no, no, stop,
Galileo, stop!
For independent spirit spreads like foul
diseases.
People must keep their place, some down
and some on top!
(Though it is nice, for a little change, to do
just as one pleases!)

[The **Spectators** *stand embarrassed. A* **Girl** *laughs loudly.]*

Ballad Singer and his Wife:

Good people who have trouble here below
In serving cruel lords and gentle Jesus
Who bids you turn the other cheek just so
 . . . [*With mimicry.*]
While they prepare to strike the second
blow:
Obedience will never cure your woe
So each of you wake up and do just as he
pleases!

[The **Ballad Singer** *and his* **Wife** *hurriedly start to try to sell pamphlets to the spectators.]*

Ballad Singer: Read all about the earth going around the sun, two centesimi only. As proved by the great Galileo. Two centesimi only. Written by a local scholar. Understandable to one and all. Buy one for your friends,

your children and your Aunty Rosa, two centesimi only. Abbreviated but complete. Fully
illustrated with pictures of the planets, including Venus, two centesimi only.

> [*During the speech of the* **Ballad Singer** *we hear
> the carnival procession approaching, followed by
> laughter. A* **Reveller** *rushes in.*]

Reveller: The procession!

> [*The litter bearers speedily joggle out the* **King
> of Hungary.** *The* **Spectators** *turn and look at
> the first float of the procession, which now makes
> its appearance. It bears a gigantic figure of* **Gali-
> leo,** *holding in one hand an open Bible with the
> pages crossed out. The other hand points to the
> Bible, and the head mechanically turns from side
> to side as if to say "No! No!"*]

A Loud Voice: Galileo, the Bible-killer!

> [*The laughter from the market place becomes up-
> roarious. The* **Monk** *comes flying from the mar-
> ket place followed by delighted* **Children.**]

SCENE X

The depths are hot, the heights are chill,
The streets are loud, the court is still.

Antechamber and staircase in the Medicean
palace in Florence. **Galileo,** with a book under
his arm, waits with his daughter **Virginia** to be
admitted to the presence of the **Prince.**

Virginia: They are a long time.

Galileo: Yes.

Virginia: Who is that funny-looking man? [*She
indicates the* **Informer,** *who has entered casually and
seated himself in the background, taking no apparent
notice of* **Galileo.**]

Galileo: I don't know.

Virginia: It's not the first time I have seen him
around. He gives me the creeps.

Galileo: Nonsense. We're in Florence, not
among robbers in the mountains of Corsica.

Virginia: Here comes the Rector.

> [*The* **Rector** *comes down the stairs.*]

Galileo: Gaffone is a bore. He attaches himself
to you.

> [*The* **Rector** *passes, scarcely nodding.*]

Galileo: My eyes are bad today. Did he ac-
knowledge us?

Virginia: Barely. [*Pause*] What's in your book?
Will they say it's heretical?

Galileo: You hang around church too much.
And getting up at dawn and scurrying to mass
is ruining your skin. You pray for me, don't
you?

> [*A* **Man** *comes down the stairs.*]

Virginia: Here's Mr. Matti. You designed a
machine for his iron foundries.

Matti: How were the squabs, Mr. Galilei? [*Low*]
My brother and I had a good laugh the other
day. He picked up a racy pamphlet against
the Bible somewhere. It quoted you.

Galileo: The squabs, Matti, were wonderful,
thank you again. Pamphlets I know nothing
about. The Bible and Homer are my favorite
reading.

Matti: No necessity to be cautious with me,
Mr. Galilei. I am on your side. I am not a man
who knows about the motions of the stars, but
you have championed the freedom to teach
new things. Take that mechanical cultivator
they have in Germany which you described
to me. I can tell you, it will never be used in
this country. The same circles that are ham-
pering you now will forbid the physicians at
Bologna to cut up corpses for research. Do
you know, they have such things as money
markets in Amsterdam and in London?
Schools for business, too. Regular papers with
news. Here we are not even free to make
money. I have a stake in your career. They
are against iron foundries because they say
the gathering of so many workers in one place
fosters immorality! If they ever try anything,
Mr. Galilei, remember you have friends in all
walks of life, including an iron founder. Good
luck to you. [*He goes.*]

Galileo: Good man, but need he be so affectionate in public? His voice carries. They will
always claim me as their spiritual leader, particularly in places where it doesn't help me
at all. I have written a book about the me-
chanics of the firmament, that is all. What
they do or don't do with it is not my concern.

Virginia: [*Loud*] If people only knew how you

disagreed with those goings-on all over the country last All Fools' day.

Galileo: Yes. Offer honey to a bear, and lose your arm if the beast is hungry.

Virginia: [*Low*] Did the Prince ask you to come here today?

Galileo: I sent word I was coming. He will want the book, he has paid for it. My health hasn't been any too good lately. I may accept Sagredo's invitation to stay with him in Padua for a few weeks.

Virginia: You couldn't manage without your books.

Galileo: Sagredo has an excellent library.

Virginia: We haven't had this month's salary yet—

Galileo: Yes. [*The* **Cardinal Inquisitor** *passes down the staircase. He bows deeply in answer to* **Galileo's** *bow*] What is he doing in Florence? If they try to do anything to me, the new Pope will meet them with an iron NO. And the Prince is my pupil, he would never have me extradited.

Virginia: Psst. The Lord Chamberlain. [*The* **Lord Chamberlain** *comes down the stairs.*]

Lord Chamberlain: His Highness had hoped to find time for you, Mr. Galilei. Unfortunately, he has to leave immediately to judge the parade at the Riding Academy. On what business did you wish to see His Highness?

Galileo: I wanted to present my book to His Highness.

Lord Chamberlain: How are your eyes today?

Galileo: So, so. With His Highness' permission, I am dedicating the book . . .

Lord Chamberlain: Your eyes are a matter of great concern to His Highness. Could it be that you have been looking too long and too often through your marvelous tube? [*He leaves without accepting the book.*]

Virginia: [*Greatly agitated*] Father, I am afraid.

Galileo: He didn't take the book, did he? [*Low and resolute*] Keep a straight face. We are not going home, but to the house of the lens-grinder. There is a coach and horses in his backyard. Keep your eyes to the front, don't look back at that man.

> [*They start. The* **Lord Chamberlain** *comes back.*]

Lord Chamberlain: Oh, Mr. Galilei, His Highness has just charged me to inform you that the Florentine court is no longer in a position to oppose the request of the Holy Inquisition to interrogate you in Rome.

SCENE XI

THE POPE

A CHAMBER IN THE VATICAN. The **Pope, Urban VIII**—formerly Cardinal Barberini—is giving audience to the **Cardinal Inquisitor.** The trampling and shuffling of many feet is heard throughout the scene from the adjoining corridors. During the scene the **Pope** is being robed for the conclave he is about to attend: at the beginning of the scene he is plainly Barberini, but as the scene proceeds he is more and more obscured by grandiose vestments.

Pope: No! No! No!

Inquisitor: [*Referring to the owners of the shuffling feet*] Doctors of all chairs from the universities, representatives of the special orders of the Church, representatives of the clergy as a whole, who have come believing with child-like faith in the word of God as set forth in the Scriptures, who have come to hear Your Holiness confirm their faith: and Your Holiness is really going to tell them that the Bible can no longer be regarded as the alphabet of truth?

Pope: I will not set myself up against the multiplication table. No!

Inquisitor: Ah, that is what these people say, that it is the multiplication table. Their cry is, "The figures compel us," but where do these figures come from? Plainly they come from doubt. These men doubt everything. Can society stand on doubt and not on faith? "Thou are my master, but I doubt whether it is for the best." "This is my neighbor's house and my neighbor's wife, but why shouldn't they belong to me?" After the plague, after the new war, after the unparalleled disaster of the Reformation, your dwindling flock look to their shepherd, and now the mathematicians turn their tubes on the sky and announce to the world that you have not the best advice about the heavens either—up to now your only uncontested sphere of influence. This Galilei started meddling in machines at an early age. Now that men in ships are venturing on the great oceans—I am not against that of course—they are putting their faith in a brass bowl they call a compass and not in Almighty God.

Pope: This man is the greatest physicist of our time. He is the light of Italy, and not just any muddlehead.

Inquisitor: Would we have had to arrest him otherwise? This bad man knows what he is doing, not writing his books in Latin, but in the jargon of the market place.

Pope: [*Occupied with the shuffling feet*] That was not in the best of taste. [*A pause*] These shuffling feet are making me nervous.

Inquisitor: May they be more telling than my words, Your Holiness. Shall all these go from you with doubt in their hearts?

Pope: This man has friends. What about Versailles? What about the Viennese court? They will call Holy Church a cesspool for defunct ideas. Keep your hands off him.

Inquisitor: In practice it will never get far. He is a man of the flesh. He would soften at once.

Pope: He has more enjoyment in him than any man I ever saw. He loves eating and drinking and thinking. To excess. He indulges in thinking-bouts! He cannot say no to an old wine or a new thought. [*Furious*] I do not want a condemnation of physical facts. I do not want to hear battle cries: Church, Church, Church! Reason, Reason, Reason! [*Pause*] These shuffling feet are intolerable. Has the whole world come to my door?

Inquisitor: Not the whole world, Your Holiness. A select gathering of the faithful.
[*Pause.*]

Pope: [*Exhausted*] It is clearly understood: he is not to be tortured. [*Pause*] At the very most, he may be shown the instruments.

Inquisitor: That will be adequate, Your Holiness. Mr. Galilei understands machinery.
[*The eyes of* **Barberini** *look helplessly at the* **Cardinal Inquisitor** *from under the completely assembled panoply of* **Pope Urban VIII.**]

SCENE XII

June twenty second, sixteen thirty three,
A momentous date for you and me.
Of all the days that was the one
An age of reason could have begun.

AGAIN THE GARDEN OF THE FLORENTINE AMBASSADOR at Rome, where **Galileo's** assistants wait the news of the trial. The **Little Monk** and **Federzoni** are attempting to concentrate on a game of chess. **Virginia** kneels in a corner, praying and counting her beads.

Little Monk: The Pope didn't even grant him an audience.

Federzoni: No more scientific discussions.

Andrea: The "Discorsi" will never be finished. The sum of his findings. They will kill him.

Federzoni: [*Stealing a glance at him*] Do you really think so?

Andrea: He will never recant.
[*Silence.*]

Little Monk: You know when you lie awake at night how your mind fastens on to something irrelevant. Last night I kept thinking: if only they would let him take his little stone in with him, the appeal-to-reason-pebble that he always carries in his pocket.

Federzoni: In the room *they'll* take him to, he won't have a pocket.

Andrea: But he will not recant.

Little Monk: How can they beat the truth out of a man who gave his sight in order to see?

Federzoni: Maybe they can't.
[*Silence.*]

Andrea: [*Speaking about* **Virginia**] She is praying that he will recant.

Federzoni: Leave her alone. She doesn't know whether she's on her head or on her heels since they got hold of her. They brought her Father Confessor from Florence.
[*The Informer of Scene X enters.*]

Informer: Mr. Galilei will be here soon. He may need a bed.

Federzoni: Have they let him out?

Informer: Mr. Galilei is expected to recant at

five o'clock. The big bell of Saint Marcus will be rung and the complete text of his recantation publicly announced.

Andrea: I don't believe it.

Informer: Mr. Galilei will be brought to the garden gate at the back of the house, to avoid the crowds collecting in the streets. [*He goes.*]

> [*Silence.*]

Andrea: The moon is an earth because the light of the moon is not her own. Jupiter is a fixed star, and four moons turn around Jupiter, therefore we are not shut in by crystal shells. The sun is the pivot of our world, therefore the earth is not the center. The earth moves, spinning about the sun. And he showed us. You can't make a man unsee what he has seen.

> [*Silence.*]

Federzoni: Five o'clock is one minute.

> [*Virginia prays louder.*]

Andrea: Listen all of you, they are murdering the truth.

> [*He stops up his ears with his fingers. The two other pupils do the same.* **Federzoni** *goes over to the* **Little Monk,** *and all of them stand absolutely still in cramped positions. Nothing happens. No bell sounds. After a silence, filled with the murmur of* **Virginia's** *prayers,* **Federzoni** *runs to the wall to look at the clock. He turns around, his expression changed. He shakes his head. They drop their hands.*]

Federzoni: No. No bell. It is three minutes after.

Little Monk: He hasn't.

Andrea: He held true. It is all right, it is all right.

Little Monk: He did not recant.

Federzoni: No.

> [*They embrace each other, they are delirious with joy.*]

Andrea: So force cannot accomplish everything. What has been seen can't be unseen. Man is constant in the face of death.

Federzoni: June 22, 1633: dawn of the age of reason. I wouldn't have wanted to go on living if he had recanted.

Little Monk: I didn't say anything, but I was in agony. O ye of little faith!

Andrea: I was sure.

Federzoni: It would have turned our morning to night.

Andrea: It would have been as if the mountain had turned to water.

Little Monk: [*Kneeling down, crying*] O God, I thank Thee.

Andrea: Beaten humanity can lift its head. A man has stood up and said No.

> [*At this moment the bell of Saint Marcus begins to toll. They stand like statues.* **Virginia** *stands up.*]

Virginia: The bell of Saint Marcus. He is not damned.

> [*From the street one hears the* **Town Crier** *reading* **Galileo's** *recantation.*]

Town Crier: I, Galileo Galilei, Teacher of Mathematics and Physics, do hereby publicly renounce my teaching that the earth moves. I forswear this teaching with a sincere heart and unfeigned faith and detest and curse this and all other errors and heresies repugnant to the Holy Scriptures.

> [*The lights dim; when they come up again the bell of Saint Marcus is petering out.* **Virginia** *has gone but the* **Scholars** *are still there waiting.*]

Andrea: [*Loud*] The mountain did turn to water.

> [**Galileo** *has entered quietly and unnoticed. He is changed, almost unrecognizable. He has heard* **Andrea.** *He waits some seconds by the door for somebody to greet him. Nobody does. They retreat from him. He goes slowly and, because of his bad sight, uncertainly, to the front of the stage, where he finds a chair and sits down.*]

Andrea: I can't look at him. Tell him to go away.

Federzoni: Steady.

Andrea: [*Hysterically*] He saved his big gut.

Federzoni: Get him a glass of water.

> [*The* **Little Monk** *fetches a glass of water for* **Andrea.** *Nobody acknowledges the presence of* **Galileo,** *who sits silently on his chair listening to the voice of the* **Town Crier,** *now in another street.*]

Andrea: I can walk. Just help me a bit.

> [*They help him to the door.*]

Andrea: [*In the door*] "Unhappy is the land that breeds no hero."

Galileo: No, Andrea: "Unhappy is the land that needs a hero."

Before the next scene, a curtain with the following legend on it is lowered:

YOU CAN PLAINLY SEE THAT IF A HORSE WERE TO FALL FROM A HEIGHT OF THREE OR FOUR FEET, IT COULD BREAK ITS BONES, WHEREAS A DOG WOULD NOT SUFFER INJURY. THE SAME APPLIES TO A CAT FROM A HEIGHT OF AS MUCH AS EIGHT OR TEN FEET, TO A GRASSHOPPER FROM THE TOP OF A TOWER, AND TO AN ANT FALLING DOWN FROM THE MOON. NATURE COULD NOT ALLOW A HORSE TO BECOME AS BIG AS TWENTY HORSES NOR A GIANT AS BIG AS TEN MEN, UNLESS SHE WERE TO CHANGE THE PROPORTIONS OF ALL ITS MEMBERS, PARTICULARLY THE BONES. THUS THE COMMON ASSUMPTION THAT GREAT AND SMALL STRUCTURES ARE EQUALLY TOUGH IS OBVIOUSLY WRONG.

—FROM THE "DISCORSI"

SCENE XIII

1633–1642
Galileo Galilei remains a prisoner
of the Inquisition until his death.

A COUNTRY HOUSE NEAR FLORENCE. A large room simply furnished. There is a huge table, a leather chair, a globe of the world on a stand, and a narrow bed. A portion of the adjoining anteroom is visible, and the front door, which opens into it. An **Official** of the Inquisition sits on guard in the anteroom. In the large room, **Galileo** is quietly experimenting with a bent wooden rail and a small ball of wood. He is still vigorous but almost blind. After a while there is a knocking at the outside door. The official opens it to a **Peasant** who brings a plucked goose. **Virginia** comes from the kitchen. She is past forty.

Peasant: [*Handing the goose to* **Virginia**] I was told to deliver this here.

Virginia: I didn't order a goose.

Peasant: I was told to say it's from someone who was passing through.

[**Virginia** *takes the goose, surprised. The* **Official** *takes it from her and examines it suspiciously. Then, reassured, he hands it back to her.*]

The **Peasant** *goes.* **Virginia** *brings the goose in to* **Galileo**.]

Virginia: Somebody who was passing through sent you something.

Galileo: What is it?

Virginia: Can't you see it?

Galileo: No. [*He walks over*] A goose. Any name?

Virginia: No.

Galileo: [*Weighing the goose*] Solid.

Virginia: [*Cautiously*] Will you eat the liver, if I have it cooked with a little apple?

Galileo: I had my dinner. Are you under orders to finish me off with food?

Virginia: It's not rich. And what is wrong with your eyes again? You should be able to see it.

Galileo: You were standing in the light.

Virginia: I was not. You haven't been writing again?

Galileo: [*Sneering*] What do you think?
[**Virginia** *takes the goose out into the anteroom and speaks to the* **Official**.]

Virginia: You had better ask Monsignor Carpula to send the doctor. Father couldn't see this goose across the room. Don't look at me like that. He has not been writing. He dictates everything to me, as you know.

Official: Yes?

Virginia: He abides by the rules. My father's repentance is sincere. I keep an eye on him. [*She hands him the goose*] Tell the cook to fry the liver with an apple and an onion. [*She goes back into the large room*] And you have no business to be doing that with those eyes of yours, father.

Galileo: You may read me some Horace.

Virginia: We should go on with your weekly letter to the Archbishop. Monsignor Carpula, to whom we owe so much, was all smiles the other day because the Archbishop had expressed his pleasure at your collaboration.

Galileo: Where were we?

Virginia: [*Sits down to take his dictation*] Paragraph four.

Galileo: Read what you have.

Virginia: "The position of the Church in the matter of the unrest at Genoa. I agree with Cardinal Spoletti in the matter of the unrest among the Venetian ropemakers . . ."

Galileo: Yes. [*Dictates*] I agree with Cardinal Spoletti in the matter of the unrest among the Venetian ropemakers: it is better to distribute good, nourishing food in the name of charity than to pay them more for their bell ropes. It being surely better to strengthen their faith than to encourage their acquisitiveness. St. Paul says: Charity never faileth.... How is that?

Virginia: It's beautiful, father.

Galileo: It couldn't be taken as irony?

Virginia: No. The Archbishop will like it. It's so practical.

Galileo: I trust your judgment. Read it over slowly.

Virginia: "The position of the Church in the matter of the unrest—"

> [*There is a knocking at the outside door.* **Virginia** *goes into the anteroom. The* **Official** *opens the door. It is* **Andrea**.]

Andrea: Good evening. I am sorry to call so late, I'm on my way to Holland. I was asked to look him up. Can I go in?

Virginia: I don't know whether he will see you. You never came.

Andrea: Ask him.

> [**Galileo** *recognizes the voice. He sits motionless.* **Virginia** *comes in to* **Galileo**.]

Galileo: Is that Andrea?

Virginia: Yes. [*Pause.*] I will send him away.

Galileo: Show him in.

> [**Virginia** *shows* **Andrea** *in.* **Virginia** *sits,* **Andrea** *remains standing.*]

Andrea: [*Cool*] Have you been keeping well, Mr. Galilei?

Galileo: Sit down. What are you doing these days? What are you working on? I heard it was something about hydraulics in Milan.

Andrea: As he knew I was passing through, Fabricius of Amsterdam asked me to visit you and inquire about your health.

> [*Pause.*]

Galileo: I am very well.

Andrea: [*Formally*] I am glad I can report you are in good health.

Galileo: Fabricius will be glad to hear it. And you might inform him that, on account of the depth of my repentance, I live in comparative comfort.

Andrea: Yes, we understand that the Church is more than pleased with you. Your complete acceptance has had its effect. Not one paper expounding a new thesis has made its appearance in Italy since your submission.

> [*Pause.*]

Galileo: Unfortunately there are countries not under the wing of the Church. Would you not say the erroneous, condemned theories are still taught—there?

Andrea: [*Relentless*] Things are almost at a standstill.

Galileo: Are they? [*Pause.*] Nothing from Descartes in Paris?

Andrea: Yes. On receiving the news of your recantation, he shelved his treatise on the nature of light.

Galileo: I sometimes worry about my assistants, whom I led into error. Have they benefited by my example?

Andrea: In order to work I have to go to Holland.

Galileo: Yes.

Andrea: Federzoni is grinding lenses again, back in some shop.

Galileo: He can't read the books.

Andrea: Fulganzio, our little monk, has abandoned research and is resting in peace in the Church.

Galileo: So. [*Pause*] My superiors are looking forward to my spiritual recovery. I am progressing as well as can be expected.

Virginia: You are doing well, father.

Galileo: Virginia, leave the room.

> [**Virginia** *rises uncertainly and goes out.*]

Virginia: [*To the* **Official**] He was his pupil, so now he is his enemy. Help me in the kitchen.

> [*She leaves the anteroom with the* **Official**.]

Andrea: May I go now, sir?

Galileo: I do not know why you came, Sarti. To unsettle me? I have to be prudent.

Andrea: I'll be on my way.

Galileo: As it is, I have relapses. I completed the "Discorsi."

Andrea: You completed what?

Galileo: My "Discorsi."

Andrea: How?

Galileo: I am allowed pen and paper. My superiors are intelligent men. They know the habits of a lifetime cannot be broken abruptly. But they protect me from any unpleasant consequences: they lock my pages away as I dictate them. And I should know better than to risk my comfort. I wrote the "Discorsi" out again during the night. The manuscript is in the globe. My vanity has up to now prevented me from destroying it. If you consider taking it, you will shoulder the entire risk. You will say it was pirated from the original in the hands of the Holy Office.

> [**Andrea,** *as in a trance, has gone to the globe. He lifts the upper half and gets the book. He turns the pages as if wanting to devour them. In the background the opening sentences of the "Discorsi" appear.*]

MY PURPOSE IS TO SET FORTH A VERY NEW SCIENCE DEALING WITH A VERY ANCIENT SUBJECT—MOTION. . . . AND I HAVE DISCOVERED BY EXPERIMENT SOME PROPERTIES OF IT WHICH ARE WORTH KNOWING. . . .

Galileo: I had to employ my time somehow.
> [*The text disappears.*]

Andrea: Two new sciences! This will be the foundation stone of a new physics.

Galileo: Yes. Put it under your coat.

Andrea: And we thought you had deserted. [*In a low voice*] Mr. Galilei, how can I begin to express my shame. Mine has been the loudest voice against you.

Galileo: That would seem to have been proper. I taught you science and I decried the truth.

Andrea: Did you? I think not. Everything is changed!

Galileo: What is changed?

Andrea: You shielded the truth from the oppressor. Now I see! In your dealings with the Inquisition you used the same superb common sense you brought to physics.

Galileo: Oh!

Andrea: We lost our heads. With the crowd at the street corners we said: "He will die, he will never surrender!" You came back: "I surrendered but I am alive." We cried: "Your hands are stained!" You say: "Better stained than empty."

Galileo: "Better stained than empty." It sounds realistic. Sounds like me.

Andrea: And I of all people should have known. I was twelve when you sold another man's telescope to the Venetian Senate, and saw you put it to immortal use. Your friends were baffled when you bowed to the Prince of Florence: science gained a wider audience. You always laughed at heroics. "People who suffer bore me," you said. "Misfortunes are due mainly to miscalculations." And: "If there are obstacles, the shortest line between two points may be the crooked line."

Galileo: It makes a picture.

Andrea: And when you stooped to recant in 1633, I should have understood that you were again about your business.

Galileo: My business being?

Andrea: Science. The study of the properties of motion, mother of the machines which will themselves change the ugly face of the earth.

Galileo: Aha!

Andrea: You gained time to write a book that only you could write. Had you burned at the stake in a blaze of glory they would have won.

Galileo: They have won. And there is no such thing as a scientific work that only one man can write.

Andrea: Then why did you recant, tell me that!

Galileo: I recanted because I was afraid of physical pain.

Andrea: No!

Galileo: They showed me the instruments.

Andrea: It was not a plan?

Galileo: It was not.
> [*Pause.*]

Andrea: But you have contributed. Science has only one commandment: contribution. And you have contributed more than any man for a hundred years.

Galileo: Have I? Then welcome to my gutter, dear colleague in science and brother in treason: I sold out, you are a buyer. The first sight of the book! His mouth watered and his scoldings were drowned. Blessed be our bargaining, whitewashing, death-fearing community!

Andrea: The fear of death is human.

Galileo: Even the Church will teach you that to be weak is not human. It is just evil.

Andrea: The Church, yes! But science is not concerned with our weaknesses.

Galileo: No? My dear Sarti, in spite of my present convictions, I may be able to give you a few pointers as to the concerns of your chosen profession. [*Enter* **Virginia** *with a platter*] In my spare time, I happen to have gone over this case. I have spare time. Even a man who sells wool, however good he is at buying wool cheap and selling it dear, must be concerned with the standing of the wool trade. The practice of science would seem to call for valor. She trades in knowledge, which is the product of doubt. And this new art of doubt has enchanted the public. The plight of the multitude is old as the rocks, and is believed to be basic as the rocks. But now they have learned to doubt. They snatched the telescopes out of our hands and had them trained on their tormentors: prince, official, public moralist. The mechanism of the heavens was clearer, the mechanism of their courts was still murky. The battle to measure the heavens is won by doubt; by credulity the Roman housewife's battle for milk will always be lost. Word is passed down that this is of no concern to the scientist, who is told he will only release such of his findings as do not disturb the peace, that is, the peace of mind of the well-to-do. Threats and bribes fill the air. Can the scientist hold out on the numbers? For what reason do you labor? I take it that the intent of science is to ease human existence. If you give way to coercion, science can be crippled, and your new machines may simply suggest new drudgeries. Should you, then, in time, discover all there is to be discovered, your progress must become a progress away from the bulk of humanity. The gulf might even grow so wide that the sound of your cheering at some new achievement would be echoed by a universal howl of horror. As a scientist I had an almost unique opportunity. In my day astronomy emerged into the market place. At that particular time, had one man put up a fight, it could have had wide repercussions. I have come to believe that I was never in real danger; for some years I was as strong as the authorities, and I surrendered my knowledge to the powers that be, to use it, no, not *use* it, *abuse* it, as it suits their ends. I have betrayed my profession. Any man who does

what I have done must not be tolerated in the ranks of science.

[**Virginia,** *who has stood motionless, puts the platter on the table.*]

Virginia: You are accepted in the ranks of the faithful, father.

Galileo: [*Sees her*] Correct. [*He goes over to the table*] I have to eat now.

Virginia: We lock up at eight.

Andrea: I am glad I came. [*He extends his hand.* **Galileo** *ignores it and goes over to his meal.*]

Galileo: [*Examining the plate; to* **Andrea**] Somebody who knows me sent me a goose. I still enjoy eating.

Andrea: And your opinion is now that the "new age" was an illusion?

Galileo: Well. This age of ours turned out to be a whore, spattered with blood. Maybe, new ages look like blood-spattered whores. Take care of yourself.

Andrea: Yes. [*Unable to go*] With reference to your evaluation of the author in question—I do not know the answer. But I cannot think that your savage analysis is the last word.

Galileo: Thank you, sir.

[**Official** *knocks at the door.*]

Virginia: [*Showing* **Andrea** *out*] I don't like visitors from the past, they excite him.

[*She lets him out. The* **Official** *closes the iron door.* **Virginia** *returns.*]

Galileo: [*Eating*] Did you try and think who sent the goose?

Virginia: Not Andrea.

Galileo: Maybe not. I gave Redhead his first lesson; when he held out his hand, I had to remind myself he is teaching now. How is the sky tonight?

Virginia: [*At the window*] Bright.

[**Galileo** *continues eating.*]

SCENE XIV

The great book o'er the border went
And, good folk, that was the end.
But we hope you'll keep in mind
You and I were left behind.

BEFORE A LITTLE ITALIAN CUSTOMS HOUSE early in the morning. **Andrea** sits upon one of his travelling trunks at the barrier and reads Galileo's book. The window of a small house is still lit, and a big grotesque shadow, like an old witch and her cauldron, falls upon the house wall beyond. Barefoot **Children** in rags see it and point to the little house.

Children: [*Singing*]

> One, two, three, four, five, six,
> Old Marina is a witch.
> At night, on a broomstick she sits
> And on the church steeple she spits.

Customs Officer: [*To* **Andrea**] Why are you making this journey?

Andrea: I am a scholar.

Customs Officer: [*To his* **Clerk**] Put down under "Reason for Leaving the Country": Scholar. [*He points to the baggage*] Books! Anything dangerous in these books?

Andrea: What is dangerous?

Customs Officer: Religion. Politics.

Andrea: These are nothing but mathematical formulas.

Customs Officer: What's that?

Andrea: Figures.

Customs Officer: Oh, figures. No harm in figures. Just wait a minute, sir, we will soon have your papers stamped. [*He exits with* **Clerk.**]

> [*Meanwhile, a little council of war among the* **Children** *has taken place.* **Andrea** *quietly watches. One of the* **Boys,** *pushed forward by the others, creeps up to the little house from which the shadow comes, and takes the jug of milk on the doorstep.*]

Andrea: [*Quietly*] What are you doing with that milk?

Boy: [*Stopping in mid-movement*] She is a witch.

> [*The other* **Children** *run away behind the customs house.* **One** *of them shouts* "Run, Paolo!"]

Andrea: Hmm! And because she is a witch she mustn't have milk. Is that the idea?

Boy: Yes.

Andrea: And how do you know she is a witch?

Boy: [*Points to shadow on house wall*] Look!

Andrea: Oh! I see.

Boy: And she rides on a broomstick at night—and she bewitches the coachman's horses. My cousin Luigi looked through the hole in the stable roof, that the snow storm made, and heard the horses coughing something terrible.

Andrea: Oh! How big was the hole in the stable roof?

Boy: Luigi didn't tell. Why?

Andrea: I was asking because maybe the horses got sick because it was cold in the stable. You had better ask Luigi how big that hole is.

Boy: You are not going to say Old Marina isn't a witch, because you can't.

Andrea: No, I can't say she isn't a witch. I haven't looked into it. A man can't know about a thing he hasn't looked into, or can he?

Boy: No! But THAT! [*He points to the shadow*] She is stirring hellbroth.

Andrea: Let's see. Do you want to take a look? I can lift you up.

Boy: You lift me to the window, mister! [*He takes a slingshot out of his pocket*] I can really bash her from there.

Andrea: Hadn't we better make sure she is a witch before we shoot? I'll hold that.

> [*The* **Boy** *puts the milk jug down and follows him reluctantly to the window.* **Andrea** *lifts the boy up so that he can look in.*]

Andrea: What do you see?

Boy: [*Slowly*] Just an old girl cooking porridge.

Andrea: Oh! Nothing to it then. Now look at her shadow, Paolo.

> [*The* **Boy** *looks over his shoulder and back and compares the reality and the shadow.*]

Boy: The big thing is a soup ladle.

Andrea: Ah! A ladle! You see, I would have taken it for a broomstick, but I haven't looked into the matter as you have, Paolo. Here is your sling.

Customs Officer: [*Returning with the* **Clerk** *and handing* **Andrea** *his papers*] All present and correct. Good luck, sir.

> [**Andrea** *goes, reading Galileo's book. The* **Clerk** *starts to bring his baggage after him. The barrier rises.* **Andrea** *passes through, still reading the book. The* **Boy** *kicks over the milk jug.*]

Boy: [*Shouting after* **Andrea**] She *is* a witch! She *is* a witch!

Andrea: You saw with your own eyes: think
it over!

> [*The* **Boy** *joins the others. They sing.*]

One, two, three, four, five, six,
Old Marina is a witch.
At night, on a broomstick she sits
And on the church steeple she spits.

> [*The* **Customs Officers** *laugh.* **Andrea** *goes.*]

> *May you now guard science' light,*
> *Kindle it and use it right,*
> *Lest it be a flame to fall*
> *Downward to consume us all.*

One should not be surprised to discover that the structural pattern of *Galileo* does not seem to fit any of his preconceptions regarding the nature of dramatic structure. Brecht himself claimed to be writing non-Aristotelian drama, and Brecht's success as a theorist, playwright, and director allowed him to test his own theories, both in writing and in the theatre, in a way that few theatrical innovators have enjoyed. Because Brecht wished his audience to think about the action portrayed before them, rather than to become emotionally involved with it, he deliberately attempted to create theatre in which empathy was negated. Brecht's word for this effect is *Verfremdung*; the English translation of this term became, rather unfortunately, "alienation." It was not Brecht's desire to alienate the members of his audience as much as to keep them at a distance; to prevent them from empathizing; to encourage thinking by discouraging emotional involvement. This idea is not as new as it sounds, for good comedy has generally depended on preventing empathy, and comedy can often be used to provoke thought. Brecht made frequent use of comic devices, but he bridged the gap between comedy and serious drama by mixing elements of both into ironic, thought-provoking plays. The further he got from pure comedy, the more Brecht found it necessary to use other devices to prevent empathy, and a whole new approach to the structuring of a play finally evolved. The essential elements of this structure can be traced in a number of dramatic forms which preceded Brecht's work, but in its present context at least, *Galileo* represents a markedly new way of putting the parts of a play together.

In the first place, *Galileo* does not appear to have a central action. Indeed, it has no plot in the ordinary sense with a beginning, middle, and end within the framework of the play. This does not mean that the play is lacking in unity, but Brecht is more interested in portraying the development of a historical force (scientific rationalism) than in telling a single story. The overt structural pattern of fourteen independent scenes is not the outgrowth, as in Shakespeare, of putting together the strands of a complex story, but rather of the need to show many aspects of social, economic, and historical forces at work. Any one scene in the play could almost stand as a playlet on its own; in many of Brecht's plays, the order of the scenes could

A Discussion of the Script

apparently be shifted around with very little negative effect. (Because Galileo's continuing efforts have a time relationship and thus form something of a "plot", reversal of the scenes would be confusing, but the story of Galileo, the man, is certainly not structured in any ordinary story form.) Each scene has one major idea to put across, and the point is made even before the scene starts by the bit of verse which precedes it. Suspense concerning the outcome of the scene is thereby eliminated—along with some of the empathy. These bits of verse must be made available to the audience, by means of projections, signboards, or other devices. The scenes fit together, not to build a climax, but to give a complete, over-all view of many aspects of the problem under consideration. One needs to take a close look, furthermore, at the structure of each of the separate scenes. There is variety, of course, but it is typical of Brecht to deliberately show some unusual or startling aspect of what is happening in the scene in order to make one stop and think about its significance. Galileo is told about a telescope, and immediately steals the idea to invent his own. Galileo is being formally honored for his "invention," and all he can talk about is getting back to his laboratory. Galileo is making his ultimate decision about whether or not to recant, but the audience only sees his assistants waiting for the news. Each time Galileo might appear to be a hero, some unpleasant aspect of his personality is brought up; each time he begins to appear a villain, the audience is reminded that his attitudes make good sense. Brecht's intent is to make his audience reconsider its preconceived attitudes, and thus avoid easy answers to complex questions. Brecht pointed out that everyone had seen apples fall, but Newton managed to take a new look at this phenomenon and discover the laws of motion.

This quick sketch of Brecht's structural ideas in their application to *Galileo* should not be interpreted as a total rejection of all previous concepts of what constitutes good theatre. Although the play has no clear central action, it is not completely without narrative; one is still concerned with "what happens next" to Galileo, but this is not the primary pattern of the play. Although empathy is discouraged, the audience is not totally indifferent to the characters; characterization is still a very important concept in Brechtian drama. Although unusual aspects of many of the scenes are chosen for primary emphasis, they often turn out to be master strokes of theatrical effectiveness; waiting for Galileo's return from the torture chamber turns out to be more effective than seeing him face the torturer; watching Cardinal Barberini being robed as the Pope is a theatrical metaphor that reveals more about what kind of thinking is going on within him than twenty pages of dialogue. (The more he becomes Pope, and thus a function of ritual, the less tolerant his reasoning becomes.) Although suspense may be eliminated by telling what will happen in a scene before it actually occurs, one can see in works as early as *Oedipus the King* that the resultant dramatic irony may be far more effective theatrically than actual suspense. Although the scenes may not build to a climax in the ordinary, structural sense, the impact and meaning of the scenes become more and more powerful as the play progresses, sustaining audience interest right through to the end. And, of course, it must be pointed out that emotion is never completely eliminated. Brecht probably never intended it to be, and the audience always becomes emotionally involved to some extent in Galileo's fate. One does not, however, become so completely involved as to lose his ability to think critically about the meaning of what is taking place.

Characterization in *Galileo* tends to follow a pattern comparable to the one observed in *Cyrano de Bergerac*—the central figure is fully and fascinatingly developed, but the other characters are primarily two-dimensional. What is of interest in the way Brecht handles these minor characters, however, is that the one or two aspects of their characters presented are frequently so interesting that a great deal more depth is suggested than is actually portrayed. Andrea, for example, is Galileo's eager pupil, and little more. Yet the struggle that goes on within him to understand Galileo's recanting adds tremendously to his interest as a human being. Cardinal Barberini is a prelate of the church, but his interest in science sets up a struggle within him that brings him startlingly to life on the stage. Many of the play's lesser characters also have this quality; Brecht finds one fascinating conflict in each to make him an interesting human being. Galileo, who is far more complex, is the living embodiment of Brecht's views on sociology and economics; for he is a great scientist who could make a wonderful contribution to society, but, at the same time, he has to pay his bills somehow. He is devoted to science, but he also likes to eat. His primary objective is the truth, but he quickly foreswears the truth when his life is in danger. Somehow none of this coincides with the generally accepted idea of what a hero should be like. Traditional views would lead one to classify characters as "good guys" or "bad guys," and a "good guy" should not allow paying his bills or filling his stomach to be too important nor, worst of all, should he surrender to the threat of torture. And yet, are not these the very contradictions which constitute a human being? Is not all of this really more "realistic" than romantic notions of a hero who is all good? Indeed, if Galileo had refused to recant, he might have been a "hero" temporarily, but he would never have written the principal work by which the world remembers him. Brecht deliberately establishes these contradictions, not just because they make his characters interesting, but because he understands that their maddening inconsistency gives a truer insight into humanity than would be achieved with more "consistent" characters. The great playwrights have always portrayed characters who were, in this sense, inconsistent, but Brecht goes much further than most in his deliberate contrasting of opposite qualities to gain maximum insight. It is an ironic technique, and fits well with the over-all irony of Brecht's situations, themes, and language.

Since *Galileo* is a play in translation, one must comment cautiously on its use of language. Brecht worked so closely with Laughton on preparing this translation, however, that it can be assumed to represent the playwright's wishes to an exceptional degree. Brecht is a poet of rare effectiveness; his plays, although not written in poetry, have a poetic quality in German which elevates them considerably above ordinary realistic dialogue. Even in translation his language is sparse, stripped of all but the absolute essentials. When spoken in the theatre, it is sharp, occasionally staccato, and must have a harsh, ironic quality. Yet, these seemingly disparate characteristics fit very well together to enhance the over-all effectiveness of the play. Even in English, Brecht's use of language is notably forceful; in German, it is widely regarded as outstanding.

The greatest impact of *Galileo* lies in the theme; like most plays that are strong thematically, the playwright's "point" cannot be stated simply. He explores issues rather than providing answers, and almost any statement must be coupled with "on the other hand . . ." Brecht is obviously concerned with the nature of truth and man's tendency to ignore it in favor of established dogma. The play is not really an attack upon the church as it has occasionally been pictured; some of the church's officials are ridiculous in their unwillingness to believe the evidence of their senses, but the church's side of the whole question is also clear: are scientists to be allowed to pursue the truth with *total* disregard for the sociological consequences? In the twentieth century, is not a major segment of society urging that scientists be forcibly prevented from pursuing atomic research too relentlessly, on the grounds that society may be destroyed? And is that not precisely the argument that the church leaders use in *Galileo?* The issue is not nearly so simple as it may at first appear. Galileo recants in an apparently cowardly fashion, and later calls himself a coward, but Andrea says, "I cannot think that your savage analysis is the last word." If one serves science to the exclusion of other human values, is that enough? The question is endlessly complicated, of course, and Brecht explores its ramifications in masterful fashion. Even more fundamental, perhaps, are the questions raised about an economic and social system in which these choices have to be made. Brecht has occasionally been attacked as a Communist propagandist, but one does not need to be a Communist to see certain flaws in the capitalist system. Economic necessities, Galileo suggests, should not be allowed to interfere with the work of a genius; however, in a free-enterprise system they are inescapable. The discoveries of science should not be devoted primarily to making war, but too often in today's world, they are. In a Utopian society, the pursuit of truth would hurt no one; if truth hurts in today's society, then society should be changed. Some of these ideas are vastly oversimplified, of course, but Brecht forces his audience to consider them. Brecht's acknowledged purpose in his structure, characterization, and language, is to force the audience to think, and the thematic ideas which he presents clearly merit attention.

To classify *Galileo* in terms of the traditional concepts of comedy and tragedy will prove to be impossible. Clearly, it is not a tragedy, as it does not conform in a number of ways to the established criteria. One might call it a serious drama, but would have difficulty in accounting for its many comic elements—chief among which is its basically comic technique of insisting that empathy be negated. Yet, to follow this lead and to classify the play as a comedy is also unsatisfactory, as so much of its plot line and its subject matter is by no means funny. The fact is that Brecht has, along with a number of other modern writers, deliberately broken down the old distinctions between comedy and tragedy, and has insisted that comedy and tragedy can be mixed together in the same work. Comedy and tragedy are really very close in the modern world, these writers point out: the predicament of modern man is potentially tragic, but it is so frustrating that one's only defense is to laugh at it. One laughs because it is his only alternative to losing his mind. Thus, the distinction between the serious and the comic has become a fine line indeed in modern life, and there is little point in maintaining a separation in modern art. Much of the absurdist theatre illustrates this point even more poignantly.

Brecht called the style in which he wrote his plays "epic" theatre, deriving the name from Aristotle. Other writers since Brecht have used elements of the epic style, but among the plays discussed in this book, the style is unique to *Galileo*. Manifestations of epic style in terms of structure, characterization, language, and theme have already been discussed; still to be considered, however, are some of the techniques by which this style is projected in the theatre. Brecht, as director of many of his own plays, worked out a number of theatrical devices which are usually associated with the epic style. The acting must be cool and detached; Brecht called for the actor to play his role in such a manner that he commented upon the character as he portrayed him. Again, this varies little from the traditional understanding of what constitutes much good comic acting; it is always apparent to an audience that the actor himself understands and enjoys the comedy of his role. In more serious drama, the acting becomes cool and dispassionate, generally in the presentational mode, tightly controlled and with a minimum of emotional histrionics. Settings for the epic drama are intended to illustrate a scene rather than represent it. *Galileo*, for example, has been performed on a series of platforms in front of projected maps and astronomical charts from the seventeenth century. The intent is not so much to provide an environment for the action, as a realistic approach might, but rather to be reasonably decorative while reminding the audience of the significance of what is going on. Lighting, Brecht felt, should provide full illumination and nothing more —he wanted no emotion-provoking, colorful effects, and, indeed, asked that the curtains be pulled up so that the lighting instruments might no longer be concealed from the audience. The idea was to remind them that they were in a theatre in order to prevent them from becoming emotionally involved in the action. Signboards, projections, and other devices were used to convey messages directly to the audience, and simultaneously break up any empathy that might be building. In plays which make use of music (as many of Brecht's do) the orchestra may be onstage in full view, and the singers often move downstage to deliver their songs directly to the audience. This, of course, is quite the opposite of the traditional musical comedy technique of trying to make the music and the acting blend imperceptibly, as though one were an outgrowth of the other. All of these factors working together constitute the epic style, a twentieth-century form markedly different from the pictorial realism which still dominates much of the modern theatre.

The job of the director, who oversees all phases of the production, has been discussed earlier at length. There has also been a discussion of acting, as well as of the six areas that make up technical production: sets, costumes, lights, properties, makeup, and sound. Coordinating all these diverse activities is the job of one person, who so far has been mentioned only in passing, the stage manager. During the early rehearsal period, when the director must maintain constant contact with each of his actors, and must make decisions regarding all of the technical areas, the stage manager may be little more than a director's assistant or a prompter. As the production moves into dress rehearsals and finally into performance, the director withdraws more and more from direct control. His control passes to the stage manager, who becomes responsible for the smooth running of every phase of the production. When plays enjoy a long run, the director normally leaves the company altogether, and the stage manager takes full charge. In amateur theatre, where plays often run only for a few nights, the director is usually present, but most directors find it expedient to remain in the front of the house and allow the stage manager to run the show uninterruptedly. The reason for this is obvious. Whatever else may happen, "the show must go on," and in any emergency there must be a clearly established power structure that can produce instant obedience. If the director and the stage manager are both backstage, no one quite knows who is really the boss—unless the director decides to remain backstage at all times, in which case he, in effect, becomes his own stage manager. If, during dress rehearsals, the director has been devoting his full attention to the over-all effect that the show is creating, then only the stage manager is fully aware of all the details that go into keeping it running smoothly. The stage manager sees that all actors are ready for entrances, that scene shifts proceed smoothly, that cues reach the lighting and sound people properly, that props are all in place, and that the theatre is locked up securely when everybody goes home. The job demands the utmost in organizational skill, combined with a real understanding of the demands of the script and a talent for getting along with people well enough to secure their instant and full cooperation.

A stage manager for a production of *Galileo* would have an especially difficult task because the

Stage Management

cast is large and there are many set changes. During the early stages of rehearsal, the stage manager is primarily an assistant to the director, attending all rehearsals, prompting as necessary (unless a separate prompter is used), and maintaining a complete record in his book of all the blocking and business that the director and actors work out. (In a long run production, the stage manager must have a complete record of what the director wants, since he later will be responsible for rehearsing understudies and cast replacements.) The stage manager will be the first to arrive at rehearsal and the last to leave, locking and unlocking the building, turning work lights on and off, setting up and striking rehearsal furniture and other props, and keeping track of the actors to see that everyone is present and ready for his entrance. The stage manager will act as the director's principal liaison man with the various technical areas, relaying routine messages to the costumer, the technical director, the prop manager, and the other people connected with the production who are not yet attending rehearsals. Throughout this period, the stage manager is preparing his prompt book, so that all the cues he will need to give and all the difficult spots in the show are clearly marked for instant comprehension. He knows that, particularly in dress rehearsals, he will have dozens of problems facing him at once, and he must have a firm grasp on all aspects of the show in order to deal with them.

The run-through and dress rehearsal period is one of transition for the stage manager from his relatively passive role of the early rehearsals to the active one of taking complete charge during performances. Let us turn to the duties of the stage manager during a performance of *Galileo*. Again, as during the rehearsal period, the stage manager is the first person to arrive at the theatre and the last to leave. He must unlock all areas of the theatre to which access is needed and see that all necessary equipment is checked and ready to go. Usually a stage manager will have a fairly long check list of specific items that must be verified before the play can begin. He must be sure that all cast members are present and getting into costumes and makeup, and if anyone is missing or incapacitated, he must make immediate plans to replace him. If the play is being done with a formalized set, the stage manager will have relatively few duties in that area; but if the play is *Galileo* and it is being done realistically, with all the sets called for in the script, the stage manager has a great deal of checking to do to insure that every set is properly positioned for the many shifts to come, and that any moving parts are working smoothly. For a show as complex as this he will need a shift-crew head who will report to him on these matters. The stage manager verifies that the various technical crew heads are present and that their equipment has been properly checked. He makes sure that calls are given throughout the backstage area, warning all personnel at thirty minutes, fifteen minutes, and five minutes before curtain time.

At the appointed hour, and assuming that everything is in order, the stage manager gives the call, "places for scene one." After verifying that all "beginners" (actors in the first scene) are in place and ready to go, he will check with the front of the house to see that the audience is, for the most part, in their seats rather than milling about the lobby or standing in long ticket lines. With everything in order, the stage manager gives direct cues to the lighting and sound technicians and to the person assigned to pull the curtain. With the frequent scene breaks in *Galileo*, the stage manager has to stay alert at all times, warning actors to get into their places for their next entrance, cueing lights and sound at the beginning and end of scenes, coordinating scene shifts with the scenery crew and the prop crew. Most directors expect the scene breaks to move like clockwork, with little or no delay from the time the lights come down on one scene until they go up on the next. Ten seconds spent sitting in total darkness can seem like a very long time to an audience, although they may seem to flash past to the harried stage manager. Every moment of such a scene shift has to be carefully plotted out, rehearsed, and timed. At intermission, there is a little more leisure, but for a show like *Galileo* intermission, at whatever point the director decides to take one, will probably be spent in storing away scenery and props no longer needed, and lining up those for the next several scenes. Starting the show again after an intermission will procede much like starting the show in the first place.

At the end of the performance, the stage manager has full charge of the curtain-call procedure, coordinating the lights and curtain and deciding how many calls should be taken. Once the curtain is finally down and the show is over, most stage managers have a fairly long check list of items that must be verified before the theatre can be locked up for the night. All props must be stored away and properly accounted for, all stage lights turned off and usually certain work lights left on; sets must be properly stored to insure that they do not get damaged before the next performance, and the entire backstage area must be locked up for the night. The stage manager reports to the director (if the latter is still with the company) on any unusual occurrences during the performance, and makes arrangements for the correction of any mistakes. He checks the dressing rooms to be sure that everyone is out and that no valuables have been left lying about, and, at last, he is free to leave the theatre. The stage manager's duties are so uniquely fitted to the needs of the immediate production that little more can be said here. Even when relating a discussion of stage management to a hypothetical production of *Galileo*, one cannot list specific, detailed duties without making so many assumptions about the production plan that any value in the exercise would be lost. The stage manager is ultimately responsible for everything that happens during a performance. The matter is as simple, and as difficult, as that.

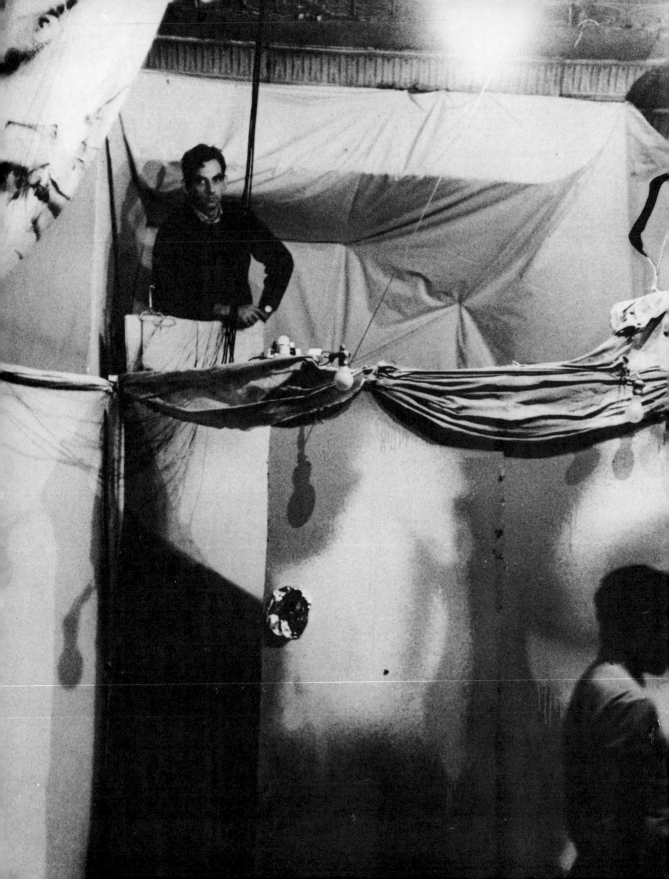

Claes Oldenburg was born in Stockholm in 1929. He came to the United States at an early age with his father, who was Swedish Consul General in New York and in Chicago. Oldenburg earned his bachelor of arts degree at Yale in 1950, and worked for two years as a reporter in Chicago. Abandoning journalism as a career, he studied at the Chicago Art Institute, after which he moved to New York. Oldenburg has achieved international prominence as a sculptor, outraging and delighting the art world with outsized renderings of hamburgers, plumbing fixtures, and other paraphernalia of the workaday world done in a wide array of substances. There is a distinct flavor of social and philosophical protest about these "pop culture" works which has lifted Oldenburg above the avant-garde coterie and marked him as an artist to be reckoned with in the last half of the twentieth-century.

Along with a number of other sculptors, painters, and musicians who feel the need to obliterate the traditional distinctions among the arts, Oldenburg has moved from success in sculpturing to an interest in the theatre. The theatrical works loosely known as "happenings," or (by one critic) "theatre of mixed means," have, in general, been the products of trained sculptors, painters and musicians rather than playwrights. In a sense, happenings may be regarded as the manipulation of theatrical elements in a manner appropriate to these other arts. Oldenburg's first theatrical presentation was *Snapshots from the City* in 1960, followed by *Fotodeath/Ironworks* (two presentations on a single bill) in February of 1961. Only the first part, *Fotodeath*, is reprinted here. Later works have included *Injun* (1962), *Washes* (performed in a swimming pool in 1965) and *Moviehouse* (performed, as the title implies, in the seating area of a motion picture theatre in 1965). He has published a book entitled *Store Days* (1967) which contains pictures and commentary on several of his presentations.

Page 546: Max Baker (the Operator) at the Reuben Gallery, February 1961, presentation of *Fotodeath*.

Page 549: Pat Oldenburg (Pat) in II, 1, Zone 4 of *Fotodeath*, 1961. Both photographs © 1971 by Fred W. McDarrah.

Fotodeath
by Claes
Oldenburg

Fotodeath

A Happening by
CLAES OLDENBURG

Lucas
Olga
Cliff, a wrestler
Judy
Carl, a photographer
Henry
Chippie } a family
Marilyn
Pat
Claire
Gloria
Edgar
two men

NOTES ON THE PERFORMANCE *Fotodeath*
(*Circus*)

The original title of the piece was *Circus* (referring to its structure, resembling the multiple simultaneous action of a circus). In two parts: *Ironworks* and *Fotodeath,* with an intermission feature: a set of slides, photos, and type, called *Pickpocket.*

Circus was given six times in the Reuben Gallery during February, 1961. The Reuben Gallery is a deep and wide store on Manhattan's East Third Street. The audience was seated as in a conventional theatre (and stood, when there were not enough chairs) facing a deep square stage. Over the stage were hung four strings of weak lightbulbs, producing when lit the sort of dingy light one remembers from circus tents.

In addition there were three individual lightbulbs over different areas of the stage, and a line of lights over a wall which marked the back of the stage, built across the store for the performance. There were thirty-four events in *Circus,* divided into seven sets. *Ironworks* was made up of four sets, *Fotodeath* of three sets. Excepting one set in *Ironworks,* there were five events in each set. Each event was assigned a zone on stage corresponding to a lightbulb or a

string of bulbs. Turning on of the light cued the entrance of the event. The sets were separated by periods of darkness, during which colored lightbulbs placed around the theatre blinked.

The effect (from the audience's point of view) when all events of a set were in action was one of overlapping, superimposition. The wall at the back of the stage area was about seven feet high, having two entrances, one at either side. The entrances were hung with strips of muslin. Muslin was bunched and draped along the top of the wall. The wall and muslin were sprayed red, yellow, and blue in abstract patterns, giving a foggy color effect.

Behind the wall, on a perch to the left, in view of the audience, sat the Operator (Max Baker), controlling lights and phonograph records and projecting the slide sequence during intermission. Above the wall, the store receded into darkness. Dressing rooms were behind the wall. Excepting the entrance of a man with a bag in *Ironworks* I.5, all the players entered from behind the wall. The floor of the stage was of tile, broken in spots and repaired with cement (the store had once been a restaurant and the stage area corresponded to the kitchen).

The left side of the stage, called "the masculine," was painted a flat black and dominated by blacks, greys, and neutrals. At the meeting of the left wall and the wall across the stage was a muslin screen on which a shadow effect was projected (*Fotodeath* I.2). In front of the screen was a large construction of wood and burlap, called the "chimney."

The right side of the stage, called "the feminine," was by contrast brightly colored in dominating pinks and reds. A pink form, made of muslin around a hoop resembling a windsock, jutted out of the wall and hung from the ceiling.

A black wooden settee stood on the left side against the wall and a hatrack and long mirror hung on the right. Other furniture and objects were brought on stage.

Exits of events were cued by a Timer in each set. His departure from the stage was followed by the turning off of the lights over the other events in a determined sequence. When the light over an event was extinguished, the players either went backstage or helped in the darkness to set up props for the next event.

A scrim was hung across the front of the stage and so lit that the actions of preparation for the performance were dimly seen by the entering audience. Music was played before and after the performance. When the piece was ready to begin, the scrim was taken down and slowly rolled on a long bamboo pole in a deliberate action functioning as an event in itself.

THE SCRIPT

I. FOTODEATH

1. *Pat's light*   Zone 1

A man, **Lucas,** enters from L. in a plain tight fastidious suit. He admires himself in many mirrors he takes from his pockets. He lies down with a tall mirror, posing himself in different ways, projecting himself upside down, etc.

drum record: Chavez, all way thru

2. *Scrim lights*   Zone 2

The scrim is illuminated in pink and purple from behind. A girl in a military cap saluting and taking various patriotic poses in a shadow dance. **Olga.**

3. *Light bank 3*   Zone 3

Cliff, a wrestler, enters from R. in black tights, nude to the waist, with a pink soft baglike object, a wrestler with which he wrestles fiercely.

Bugle sound

4. *Light bank 4   TIMER   Zone 4 L*

A woman dressed as a man in hat, shirt, tie, and baggy suit, **Judy,** enters from L., goes to dresser and undresses in front of mirror. She wears extremely feminine clothes underneath. She admires herself as a woman then redresses as a man. She leaves L. taking mirror with her.

5. *Henry's light*   Zone 4 R

A photographer, **Carl,** in a shiny black smock and a top hat brings out a camera and leads in a family of three to be photographed: **Henry, Chippie** and **Marilyn.** Sets them on a bench and then shows them several landscape samples. They disapprove. Finally he finds one they will accept. He hangs it behind them, gets under the fotocloth but the family collapses. The **photographer** sets them up again, gets under the cloth. Again they collapse, and so on.

When **Timer** leaves stage, the lights go out in the following sequence: 4—H—3—Pat's—Scrim, *but let scrim lights and record play a while at end.*
[*In blackout all leave stage or take new positions.*]

II. FOTODEATH

1. *Light bank 4*   Zone 4

A woman enters L., **Pat,** in long dragging plumage and wings, very colorful and bizarrely made up. She walks slowly and artificially, only interested in herself. She pulls herself up and down the ladder in R. center taking poses, sticking her leg out slowly, etc.

2. *Light bank 2*   Zone 2

Two girls in summer white costumes suggesting 1913 and a summer day on the ferry in the bay, **Claire** and **Judy** enter from R. One has a parasol. They walk slowly laughing and chatting to each other. There are bells on their ankles or under their skirts which jingle as they walk.

3. *Light bank 1*   *TIMER is Gloria*
Zone 1

A man in a coat and a woman in a coat with a happy birthday tiara. She carrying a piece of fresh ice and one arm in a black sling. Enter R. **Henry** and **Gloria.** She remains in the center, looking blankly. He knocks on door L. It opens showing a packed party in progress. Squeals and talk, etc. He retreats. He reconsiders. He knocks again. Again the view into the party. He does this again and again. Finally he enters without knocking. The woman then leaves the stage.

4. *Light bank 3*   Zone 3

Two men stumble in from L. **Lucas** and **Edgar.** They are drunk and make foul noises. One falls, the other picks him up. Then he in turn falls. They go back and forth then both fall and remain still. **Another man** enters from R. corner Zone 4 with a bag of black cans. He falls over the fallen men and the cans are thrown out on the floor. **A fourth man** enters with an empty bag and slowly picks up the cans. The other men lie still. The **picker** makes noises with the cans.

When **Timer** gets backstage, the lights are cut in the following sequence: 4—3—2—1 slowly so as to emphasize silhouettes. **Actors** stop when lights go out. Blackout.
[*All leave or take new positions.*]

III. FOTODEATH

1. *Strip lights*   Zone 1

Lights begin moving. After a while **Majorette** steps out from R. and saluting approximately at same rhythm moves by single steps back and forth across the stage. She does this throughout, always smiling. **Chippie.**

2. *Light band 2*　　　　　*Zone 2*

A man with a bandaged head and a white chair comes out from wall L. **Lucas.** He sits down gingerly but it hurts. He grimaces. He picks up the chair, moves it, tries sitting again. But it still hurts. He grimaces, etc. back and forth across stage.

3. *Light band 4*　　　　　*Zone 4 L*

A woman in a derby hat, mannish, dressed all in black with a patriotic band across bodice something like a Salvation Army woman. **Gloria.** Enters from R. She carries a black bag like a sample bag and a big can full of viscous liquid. She stops behind table center Zone 4, and takes out of the bag one by one, putting them on the table, numerous different objects of many colors but all marked clearly USA. It is as if she is demonstrating a product, but she has no expression on her face and says nothing. After piling up the objects, she pours from a huge can marked USA a viscous liquid which runs over the objects and on the floor. This she covers with a cloth marked USA. She remains standing over her work until blackout and forms a silhouette.

4. *Henry's light*　　　　　*Zone 4 R*

A man, **Cliff,** informally dressed, shirt open but wearing a jacket drags in as if dead a woman, **Olga,** dressed in sweater and skirt. He sits her in a chair by a table on which a meal is set. He props her up. He sits down to eat. She falls forward on the table and keeps doing this until the eater loses his patience. Each time he props her up. Finally he reverses the chair so that she will not fall into his food. But now she slides down on the floor. He ignores her and having finished his meal he wipes his mouth and leaves R.

5. *Light band 3*　　TIMER　　*Zone 3*

Two men bring out—from behind the audience, down the aisle—a topheavy, tied together, mass of boxes painted black. It is a big object which they manipulate with some difficulty into the center of action and leave there. **Carl** and **Edgar.** Then they exit, like movers. *Billboard march begins quietly*

When **Timers** come off, the lights go out in this sequence: 4—Henry's—3 —2—Strip

But very slowly, silhouetting first **Gloria** then object and finally on all alone the strip lights for a time. The music continues softly until strips off, then off abruptly.

[*Blackout and all leave stage.*]

Light band 3 on, over object.

House light

NOTES ON AND CHANGES IN THE EXISTING SCRIPT:

I.

1. Drum record was Carlos Chavez' "Concerto for Percussion."
2. The "scrim" referred to in script was the above mentioned screen of muslin at stage left.
3. The bugle sound was eliminated. Cliff wrestled with a white stuffed laundry bag.
4. There was no dresser. Judy hung her clothes on the hat-rack. Under the men's clothing she wore cotton stockings and an old fashioned baggy frilly yellow slip.
5. The landscape samples were fragments edged in black, ripped from a large photo-mural of the Battery (which appears whole in rehearsal photographs).

II.

1. The plumage was made of long tinted strips of muslin. The wings were eliminated. A sound effect record of cannonfire was played by the Operator.

III.

1. The "strip" lights were the above mentioned lights above the wall across the stage. They were wired to a knob, the turning of which lit one bulb then another in traveling effect such as in electric signs.
2. Lucas also wore an oversize G.I. raincoat.
3. The "viscous liquid" used was wheat paste.

A Discussion
of the Script

The more outspoken advocates of the avant-garde theatre insist that none of the traditional critical standards applies to a consideration of happenings and other mixed-media presentations. Many of the traditional values do apply, however, as long as it is understood at the outset that the intentions of the artists in question are notably different from those of more conservative artists, and that it is necessary to understand these intentions before one can adequately evaluate their works. In fact, happenings (and this handy title is used for a wide assortment of creative efforts) may be seen as a logical outgrowth of a series of events stretching back at least into the late decades of the nineteenth century, and by no means simply a bizarre contemporary aberration. The "theatre of the absurd" of Beckett, Ionesco, and Adamov represents one of a continuing series of efforts to counteract the naturalism which has held an icy grip on the theatre since Ibsen and Zola. In an attempt to express what is actually "real" behind the surface reality of the everyday theatre, absurdist theatre is inarticulate and full of ennui, acting as a metaphor of the life of modern man. From such an early work as *Ubu Roi* to Beckett's most recent static drama, there has been a continued diminution of plot and characterization to the point where, in several plays of the 1960s, plot has totally disappeared and characters are little more than ciphers. Happenings continue this trend by completely eliminating any semblance of plot, and by using actors simply as performers without calling upon them to submerge themselves in any characterization whatsoever. Language, as an artistic element, is largely eliminated by removing the literary dimension of performance; the audible aspects are hardly ever memorized lines with any suggestion of literary merit. Theme is still present in some happenings, but many purists would argue that, ideally, no thematic relationship should be evident among the separate compartments of the happening. When thematic impact does exist it is of minor significance.

At the same time, developments in the other arts, especially painting and sculpture, have tended generally toward greater freedom for the artist to express feelings and concepts totally outside of the traditional bounds of form and medium. Painting often consists of what may appear to be little more than disorganized smears of paint across a canvas, and sculpture sometimes involves abstract shapes or an assemblage of "found" objects, which, in their original environments, apparently exhibited no esthetic merit. Avant-garde music may sound to the uninitiated ear like a cacophonous blend of nonmusical sounds. The avant-garde artist, in each of the above cases, is trying to use the most basic elements of his medium, in a manner totally uninhibited by traditional concepts of form or structure. He includes especially the everyday elements which previous artists have failed to recognize as their proper concern. These artists feel that art has been unduly limited by historical standards and has failed to release the latent creativity of any but the most carefully trained precisionists. Each, then, has attempted to return to what he regards as really basic in his art and to find new ways to combine these basic elements that will expand the imagination and create new parameters for defining the art and the artist. This historical development has manifested itself in the theatre in the form of happenings and related events.

Fotodeath, then, may be described as an effort to use the elements of theatre in much the same manner that Oldenburg might use a variety of substances and textures in creating a piece of sculpture. The artist's imagination has allowed him to choose a wide variety of rather ordinary events and ideas and to bring them together in a performance situation with a structure totally unlike anything in the traditional theatre. Because the result is nonliterary, it is unusually difficult to evaluate it on the printed page; theatre, however, must be judged in performance rather than as literature, and hence it is important to discuss *Fotodeath* from this point of view. Clearly, plot in the traditional sense has been set aside. This does not mean, however, that the performance is without discernible structure, for the outline nature of the script makes it evident that a very careful structure is intended. The performance is divided into three parts (acts?) which have, respectively, five, four, and five parts. Within each act, however, the several parts occur simultaneously; hence a multi-focused performance is created that is more analogous to a three-ring circus or a track meet than to the traditional single-focus theatre. Oldenburg has designated a "timer" for each act on the understanding that, when the timer has completed his assigned task, the lights may be taken out to signal the end of the act. At any moment during the act a considerable number of events are taking place simultaneously, and the spectator is at liberty to focus his attention on any portion of the performance which may strike his fancy. He is bombarded with sensory impressions, both visual and audible, and from these he may select certain ones to receive his primary attention. Hence, every spectator sees something different during the performance—as he would at a circus or a track meet. Every spectator sees something different at a performance of *Oedipus the King* or *The Importance of Being Earnest* as well, since, even in the most controlled performance, the attention of the spectators centers on many different details, and their predispositions will inevitably lead them to "see" different concepts. *Fotodeath*, then, differs from these more traditional forms in degree rather than kind. The several events which occur simultaneously in any one act may be thought of as living, moving compartments in a giant collage—each of the parts may be interesting in its own way, and the over-all impact is subliminal or intuitive rather than ordered or logical.

Traditional concepts of characterization have also been eliminated in *Fotodeath*. One critic has described the acting in happenings as "nonmatrixed," meaning that characteristically the performer takes on no personality other than his own, but simply goes about his assigned task. Clearly, however, this is not altogether the case in *Fotodeath,* for one performer must be a wrestler, two others must appear drunk, still another must eat a meal with a cadaver, and so on. Characterization is eliminated in all but its most fundamental sense, but "acting" is not. The performer in *Fotodeath* must take on a set of characteristics other than his own and *then* carry out a set of assigned tasks. The fundamental ingredients of acting are there; if they are skillfully executed, they might be amusing, moving, poignant, or inspiring as the several artists involved may decide. Any evaluation of the script in terms of characterization, however, must be decidedly limited. The playwright (if the term still applies) has provided only the broadest outlines; any development of these concepts has been left to the performers. Allan Kaprow, a leading exponent of happenings, has suggested that the author of a happening is more like a basketball coach than a traditional playwright: he teaches his performers a series of carefully worked out movements and combinations, but the precise ways in which these elements are put together in any one performance are left to the performers. They exercise their own creative judgment as they respond to their audience, their environment, and the conditions under which they are performing. Again, the acting differs from the traditional theatre more in degree than in kind, for every director knows that actors vary their performances from night to night in accordance with their analysis of audience response and other performance-related factors; if they are skillful, the degree of variation is considerably less than that allowed in *Fotodeath.*

Theme is handled in *Fotodeath* in a manner somewhat more recognizable to the traditionalist. *Fotodeath* has no single over-all "meaning," but neither has any of the other plays in this volume. Traditional plays, however, manage to emphasize a few thematic concepts by the way they are organized throughout the whole work, whereas *Fotodeath* introduces thematic ideas in the same random manner in which other of its structural elements are employed; it remains for the spectator to focus on the ones that interest him and to find such overriding meanings as may predominate in the performance. Perhaps the broadest single thematic concept that underlies a very large segment of the theatre of happenings is a celebration of the mundane details of everyday life. As Richard Schechner has pointed out, the theatre of the absurd parodied the prevalence of *things* in modern life, whereas happenings accept this prevalence and celebrate it. Put a frame around the mundane, someone has said, and you see it in a new light. This is precisely what many happenings attempt to do. Just as Oldenburg in his sculpture has invited renewed attention to the infinite detail of the workaday world, so in his happening one is asked to think again about clothing, mirrors, eating meals, and so forth. In *Washes,* one of Oldenburg's best-known happenings, the artist began, by his own account, with the question, "What can I do with a swimming pool?" The answer to this question was a series of occurrences which, whatever else it accomplished, drew the attention of the spectators to the esssential nature of the pool and the multitude of possibilities it afforded. This return of attention to the nature of man's environment is not to be dismissed lightly in the twentieth-century. It is an essential aspect of the scientific age, and the more perceptive students of the age are finding that in chemistry, sociology, philosophy, or art it is necessary to re-examine the infinite detail of the physical world, to note with astonishment its properties, and then to reach new conclusions about its relationship to man. In many happenings, the theatre is responding to this trend. Of course, *Fotodeath* also makes use of other thematic matter. Oldenburg has said that it has "a great deal to do with darkness," that it has "a quality of desperation and misery," and that it deals with "events of the street and its inhabitants, beggars and cripples." One also perceives interesting commentary on the nature of death (as implied in the title) and on chauvinistic patriotism. Each of these themes, of course, is presented with only passing emphasis. The theatre traditionally employs broad thematic structures that finally narrow an audience member's attention to a relatively few values and leave him thinking about them when the performance has ended. In *Fotodeath,* one's attention is directed first to one theme and then to another, but he is never allowed to focus more than briefly on any one (just as he is not allowed to focus prolonged attention on one performer or structural segment of the performance).

Clearly, language is not a major factor in one's response to a happening. Indeed, one of the fundamental purposes usually espoused by advocates of happenings is to move beyond language to the direct communication of images, sublingual noises and gestures, or sometimes direct bodily contact between performer and audience. Some happenings, in fact, attempt to destroy the traditional division between performer and audience to the extent of turning audience members into performers and performers into an audience. All of these relationships go far beyond the kind of communication implied by language and strive for communication at a more visceral level. Although *Fotodeath* partakes of these concepts, it remains fairly conservative in their application. Of course audible stimuli of many sorts are clearly involved in the script; John Cage has called attention to the possibility that any sound, even the buzzing of a fly, may be regarded as music. Language in its classical sense, however, contributes little or nothing to this performance.

If plot, character, theme, and language are de-emphasized or used so little in *Fotodeath,* then on what terms can one evaluate it? Typically the avant-garde artist in music, theatre, or the visual arts will insist that a modern work can only be experienced; it cannot be evaluated. Nevertheless, the analysis offered above has elucidated some of the artist's purposes and has allowed comment upon the success with which Oldenburg carried them out in *Fotodeath.* It remains then to comment on the over-all value of the work. Boredom is still the cardinal sin in the theatre, and if a good production of *Fotodeath* would bore an audience, it would certainly fail this most pragmatic test. Even the most casual reading of the script, however, suggests that boredom is unlikely. A performance might annoy or frustrate, it might confuse or confound, but it would hardly bore. Too much happens, and what is happening is new, different, and hence interesting, at least on this level. Few theatre audiences today are attuned to illogicality, of course (as few of the general public are attuned to abstract expressionism in painting), and hence it is unlikely that a production of *Fotodeath* would be a great popular hit; but might it not awaken some members of the audience to a new awareness of the esthetic values in the mundane paraphernalia of their lives? Might it not, by breaking down old standards of rational characters and a plot with a beginning, middle, and end, free their minds for the acceptance of new and better theatrical concepts—perhaps concepts as yet undeveloped? Cannot one admire a performance for its own beauty and skill, without necessarily seeking out literary bases for this appreciation? *Fotodeath* and most avant-garde theatre are dedicated to some of these goals.

In every age, in every decade, there has been an element of the artistic world, and especially the theatre, that could be designated avant-garde. The naturalists were once avant-garde, and were widely deprecated for their attempts to lead the theatre in ways which seemed perverse and unreasonable. Now realism is the "establishment," and a continuing series of efforts is being made to replace it with something refreshing and different. The vast majority of these efforts, of course, are abortive—despite the wild claims of their adherents to have found the "new" theatre, they die as rapidly as they are born, and often become objects of ridicule. Such movements have usually included the efforts of some dedicated and sensitive artists, however; and the most refreshing insights of these avant-garde artists have a permanent, salutary impact upon the art of theatre. Happenings and other mixed-media, multifocus performances may not become the most important theatre form of the last third of the twentieth century, but they may well have a major impact on the future development of the theatre.

At the same time that dramatic forms have been undergoing close examination and repeated attack in recent years, the very form of the theatre itself has also been held up to scrutiny. Most of the discussion of theatrical production so far in these pages has been based upon the proscenium theatre. This viewpoint has been assumed because the great majority of theatres now in use in this country do follow this basic plan, and therefore students are likely to be more familiar with this form than with any other. In fact, however, the rather rigid nature of the proscenium theatre, and of the esthetic scheme which it forces upon the producer of plays, has for decades led critics and theoreticians to argue that some more fluid performing space was needed, and many producers of happenings prefer, in fact, to find an environment such as a swimming pool or Grand Central Station for their performances. A happening in a proscenium theatre would be almost as absurd as *The Little Foxes* in Grand Central Station. Actually, it is only since the rise of realism that the proscenium theatre has come into its own—they serve each other well. Fine drama was produced for many centuries, however, before anyone had thought of a proscenium. In fact, even after a proscenium opening became a common feature of theatrical design, its use was often confined to court masques, scenic extravaganzas, and everything except serious theatre. Gradually, from about the middle of the seventeenth-century to the middle of the nineteenth, the proscenium frame became more and more prominent in theatre design, but even during this period the area behind the proscenium was primarily intended for the scenery—the acting took place on a very large apron which allowed more immediate contact between the actor and the audience. Only in the nineteenth and twentieth centuries has the "traditional" proscenium theatre design become traditional, and many theorists today insist that it has been an abortive tradition which should be abandoned.

The fundamental question is not whether a theatre should contain a proscenium, but what the ideal relationship should be between the play and the audience. Proscenium adherents insist that esthetic distance must be maintained, that it is more realistically convincing for the actors to perform the play apparently oblivious of the presence of the audience, and for the audience to watch this play

Theatre Design

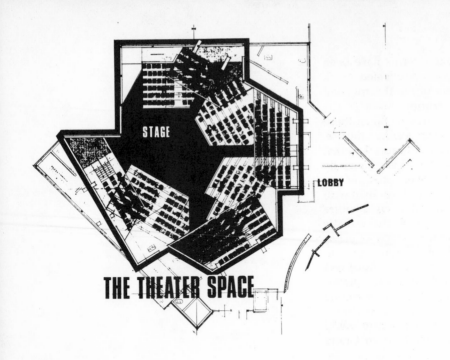

STAGE

LOBBY

THE THEATER SPACE

Opposite page (top): Architects' plan for the Performing Arts Center at the University of Toledo. *Left:* Model showing a portion of the eight sections of seats forming different angles to the stage which will not be bounded or defined in the formal sense; each production will in this way be shaped by its own needs. *Above:* A view from stage level. Photographs courtesy of the architects: Hardy Holzman Pfeiffer Associates.

as though one wall of a room had been removed and they were allowed to look through. If one grants this principle, then the mechanical advantages of the proscenium theatre for achieving it are obvious (assuming the theatre is properly designed): actors are maintained at a reasonable distance from the audience, large quantities of scenery are easily and quickly shifted, and audiences are comfortably arranged in a situation in which objective viewing is encouraged. Many, many styles other than realism are also possible in the proscenium theatre as has been noted, but whether they are *best served* by the proscenium theatre is not so clear. Opponents of the proscenium form insist that direct contact between the actor and the audience is a desirable thing, that it was always a fundamental fact of the theatre before the rise of the proscenium. The play should take place in the same room with the audience, they say, so that the audience may share in the experience. Many theatres

561

have been built with various experimental arrangements of audience and playing areas, but the fundamental fact that has related almost all of these experiments has been the placement of the playing area and the audience in the same room. In the so-called *arena* theatre, or *theatre-in-the-round,* the audience completely surrounds the playing space and scenery is almost totally eliminated. Every setting necessarily tends toward formalism, with perhaps only slight touches of other decorative styles. The arena theatre has gained many adherents in this country because it is relatively inexpensive both to build and to produce plays in. Many theorists feel, however, that it goes too far—that it combines the audience with the action so completely that the actor cannot achieve the stature and spiritual elevation which so many plays require. These theorists often favor some modification of what is known as the *thrust* stage, in which the audience surrounds the action on three sides. Admirers of the thrust stage point out that this is the essential form of the Greek theatre, Shakespeare's stage, and indeed, most theatres that achieved any distinction before the rise of the proscenium. It allows the actor to establish direct contact with the audience, but it also allows him to achieve a degree of separation by moving upstage, onto levels, or into whatever scenery is provided. Furthermore, it allows for a good deal of scenic background and thus the creation of a great many styles, although, admittedly, it is not as effective as the proscenium theatre for stark realism. Other variations of the actor-audience relationship have also been tried, including a stage which wraps completely around the audience and even forms in which the acting space is totally intermingled with the audience space. Each new experimental form has its fervid adherents.

It is not possible here to resolve so fundamental an argument in theatre esthetics, but certainly it is clear that the proscenium theatre is by no means the only arrangement in which plays can be produced. Probably the truth, as usual, lies somewhere between the extremes: some plays work better in the proscenium theatre, some work better in thrust, a few in arena or other forms. The theatre that each playwright had in mind when he wrote his script is likely to be the one in which it can be produced most effectively. Examine the plays in this volume: *The Little Foxes* was written for the proscenium theatre and would be most effective there; *Cynano de Bergerac* was also written for the proscenium—to produce it effectively elsewhere is very difficult; *J. B.* was written for a proscenium stage, but works at least as well on a thrust stage; *The Importance of Being Earnest* was written for proscenium, and works better there than elsewhere; *Twelfth Night, Tartuffe,* and *Oedipus the King* were all written for the thrust stage and could be produced most effectively there; *A View from the Bridge* and *Galileo* were written for proscenium, can be done effectively on a thrust stage, but perhaps work best in the proscenium; *Fotodeath* can be performed in almost any available space, but seems best for arena. Thus, of the ten plays listed, five seem definitely tied to the proscenium theatre, three would be better on a thrust stage, and one would work equally well on either stage; one seems to belong to the arena. Since this particular list of ten is heavily weighted in favor of modern drama (wherein proscenium theatre is the dominant influence), it is interesting that so even a balance results. Of course all of these plays *could* be produced in any of the theatrical forms. What were the factors that led to stating where and how *Fotodeath,* for example, could be produced? In the first place, its technical problems are almost nil. Plays with elaborate technical requirements, like *Cyrano de Bergerac,* are almost always products of proscenium theatre and need to be performed there. *Fotodeath,* on the other hand, requires only a playing space—a good many props are called for, but they could be used almost anywhere, and the few lighting effects are easily managed in almost any environment. If one returns, however, to the fundamental esthetic factors that influenced the artist as he prepared his script, one sees that he wanted an audience to become intimately involved with the experience. Whereas Brecht sought a marked degree of detachment, Oldenburg wanted an actor-audience relationship so intimate that it virtually destroys the distinction between the two. If one agrees, then, that the principal purpose of the play is to make the audience experience certain feelings (rather than just observe them), then the use of the thrust or arena stage will enhance this central purpose. In the case of *Fotodeath*, where no enhancing of the stature of the actor is needed and no single focus need be maintained, the advantages usually claimed for the thrust over the arena stage are negated, and the choice clearly goes to the arena. The argument, however, is based more on enhancing or effecting the central purposes of the script than on any detail of production convenience. Questions such as the ones raised here do not suggest easy solutions, and no doubt some directors would choose the proscenium theatre despite the above arguments. Ideally, each producing organization should have access to several theatres, one of each of the major types, and hence be able to choose the style in which each play will be done. The impracticality of this ideal, however, suggests that some hard decisions are going to have to be made over the next several years concerning the types of theatres to be built. New dramatic forms would seem to demand new theatres in which to present them. Ossification in the old forms has turned experimenters toward greater flexibility, including the possibility of constructing a building which is nothing more than a space in which any type of actor-audience relationship can be established. The issue is so fundamental that its resolution will influence the direction toward which the theatre will develop for the next century or more.

Conclusion: A Note on Dramatic Criticism

In a sense, all of what is written here has been about dramatic and theatrical criticism. Criticism at its best should be a penetrating and knowledgeable examination of all aspects of the work of art under consideration. The traditional formula for arriving at such a critical appraisal is to ask three questions: What is the artist trying to do? How well has he done it? Was it worth doing? The greater part of the present volume has dealt with the aims of various theatrical artists, and some criteria were established for making a responsible estimate of how well these aims were accomplished, and whether they were worth attempting. A thorough critique of a theatrical work of art would have to go into all aspects of the production—the writing, directing, acting, and the technical elements—and attempt to answer the above three questions as related to each of them. A critique of this kind might well attain book length in discussing any one production. Too often, it is assumed that the only alternative is a review, the type of essay often published in newspapers on the morning after a play opens, saying whether the reviewer enjoyed the production and why. Happily, however, it is possible for the responsible critic to be more than a reviewer and yet not have to go into every detail of the production. Assuming that the critic has some fundamental knowledge of the theatre, its history, traditions and potential, he can set aside less important features of the production and answer the fundamental question: how effectively has the production realized the values inherent in the script? In order to answer this question, he must first decide what these values are; the critic, like all the other artists of the theatre, begins with the script. In the case of *Fotodeath*, for example, the critic would have to decide what the playwright was trying to say or do with his script, and what its unusual and significant features are. He then looks at the production itself to determine how effectively these values are realized—understanding that many details involving lights, sound, set, makeup, even some of the acting and directing, will neither merit nor need special comment. His attention can focus on the special features of the production which seem to him to provide the key to its success or failure. He can become as searching in this analysis as space, time, or inclination will permit and feel that he has dealt with the fundamental elements in the production. He is thus, in a way, answering all three of the traditional questions at once.

Dramatic criticism, like all criticism of art, is complex and difficult. Rarely will two experts agree completely in their critical opinions, and yet, if the opinions are well founded, both may have validity. A thorough knowledge and understanding of the theatre is necessary for good theatrical criticism. Intelligence and sensitivity are also necessary, together with an unwillingness to be satisfied with glib, easy generalizations. The good critic is obligated to explain *why* he takes the position he does about a production, and to explain his reasons in terms that are solidly founded in theatrical good sense and an understanding of the script itself. Above all, the critic must have good theatrical taste, which, like "talent," is an almost undefinable quality possessed by relatively few individuals. It is often inborn, but also can be cultivated and developed through study, contemplation, and repeated exposure to theatrical art, both of good quality and of not-so-good. Whether one participates actively in the theatrical arts or confines himself to being a discriminating and sensitive member of the audience, well-developed critical faculties based upon knowledge, taste and the principles just discussed will bring him the theatre's wealth of beauty, stimulation, and enjoyment.

Glossary/Index

GLOSSARY/INDEX

Drama and Theatre Terms Only
Page numbers indicate the location of the fullest discussion of the term

Acting area, 230
> That portion of a stage visible to an audience.

Alexandrine verse, 397
> A verse scheme employing iambic hexameter and rhymed couplets.

Amplifier, 497
> A device for increasing the strength of an electrical signal.

Apron, 230
> That portion of the stage on the house side of the curtain line.

Arena theatre, 562
> A theatre form in which the audience completely surrounds the acting area.

Aside, 171
> A line delivered directly to the audience and presumably unheard by the other characters onstage.

Backstage, 231
> That portion of a stage concealed from the audience's sight.

Base, 449
> In makeup, the beginning layer which creates a foundation for further detail.

Battens, 231
> Pipes or wooden poles suspended in the flies parallel to the curtain line.

Beams, 354
> An opening in the auditorium ceiling through which spotlights may be directed to the stage.

Beginners, 544
> Those actors who appear at the beginning of a play or scene.

Blending and toning lights, 355
> Floodlight strips so arranged as to blend smoothly the primary light in adjacent areas.

Block, 178
> To outline movements for actors within a scene.

Border, 231
> A narrow cloth hung from a batten to conceal the audience's view into the flies.

Building for an entrance, 172
> Raising dramatic excitement and interest prior to the appearance on stage of a key character.

House, 230
    The seating area of a theatre.

Illusion of the first time, 69
    The illusion that a character in a performance is encountering the circumstances of the play for the first time.

Imagery, 445
    The use of evocative language to create unusually clear or trenchant impact.

Impressionism, 239
    That production style in which the play world is distorted through the vision of an omniscient viewer.

Inciting incident, 55, 61–62
    That single incident in a well-made play which gets the central action under way.

Inner approach, 68
    The actor's approach to his character whereby he first attempts to enter emotionally into the character's life and assumes that the outward physical details will follow.

Input, 496, 497
    A device for introducing variable electrical signals (representing the vibrations of sound) into an amplification system.

Legs, 232
    Tall, narrow draperies or flats used to mask an audience's view into the wings.

Melodrama, 51–52
    A play in which the plot is the principal force which holds an audience's interest (to the exclusion of other factors).

Method, 67
    The Americanized version of the Stanislavski acting system.

Mixer panel, 497
    A switching network in a sound amplification system.

Motivation, 72
    The believable circumstances which cause a character to behave as he does.

Naturalism, 237
    That production style which is as realistic as possible or practical.

Objective, 68
    What a character is attempting to accomplish at any given moment during a play.

Ode, 442
    A choral song in a Greek tragedy.

Offstage, 231
    That portion of a stage concealed from the audience's sight.

Up left, 231
That portion of the acting area located upstage and to the actors' left.

Up right, 231
That portion of the acting area located upstage and to the actors' right.

Upstage, 230
From a proscenium stage, the direction away from the audience.

Upstaging, 67
Moving into a position onstage which forces one's fellow actor to face upstage, thus losing the audience's attention.

Well-made play, 52ff
A play structure formula involving exposition, inciting incident, rising action, turning point, falling action, climax, and denouement.

Wing-and-drop set, 232
A set made up of several pairs of wings and a drop across the back.

Wings, 232
(1) Painted flats used in place of legs; or
(2) The offstage area on each side of the stage in which these flats are located.